SOME PROBLEMS OF
GREEK HISTORY

SOME PROBLEMS OF
GREEK HISTORY

═══

ARNOLD TOYNBEE

═══

'It is . . . often more useful to be refuted than to convince, and progress can only be made, it would seem,
by stating new theories with full conviction. . . . I . . .
am perfectly ready to scrap any opinions which the
argument may condemn. There is a great deal of scrap-
ping before us all, whatever our views may be.'

WALTER LEAF, *Homer and History*
(London, 1915, Macmillan), p. 9.

LONDON
OXFORD UNIVERSITY PRESS
NEW YORK   TORONTO
1969

Oxford University Press, Ely House, London W. 1

GLASGOW NEW YORK TORONTO MELBOURNE WELLINGTON
CAPE TOWN SALISBURY IBADAN NAIROBI LUSAKA ADDIS ABABA
BOMBAY CALCUTTA MADRAS KARACHI LAHORE DACCA
KUALA LUMPUR SINGAPORE HONG KONG TOKYO

PRINTED IN GREAT BRITAIN

PREFACE

THE problems discussed in this book have been in my mind since the years 1909–11, when I was reading for the Oxford School of Literae Humaniores. Since then, important work has been done by modern scholars on all these problems, especially on those that are the subjects of Parts I and III.

The field of Part I has also been illuminated by the progress of archaeological discovery. This has not only increased the amount of our first-hand information enormously; in adding to our knowledge, it has also changed our picture. The decipherment of the documents written on clay tablets in the Linear B script has been the most sensational single achievement in this field within these last sixty years, yet it is only one achievement among many. Exploration continues; the picture will continue to change with it; and therefore an account that has gone to press, as Part I of this book has, in 1968 can be no more than tentative and provisional. Opinions differ over the interpretation of the evidence that is already accessible, and all these differing opinions are likely to change as fresh archaeological material accumulates.

The scope of Part II is strictly limited to the subject described in its title. It is an inquiry into the northward spread of the Greek language in the course of the eighteen centuries that elapsed between *circa* 1200 B.C. and *circa* A.D. 600—i.e. between the respective opening dates of the irruptions into Greece of the North-West-Greek-speaking peoples and of the Slavs. This part is not, and is not intended to be, a comprehensive history of Macedon, Pelagonia, Paionia, and Epirus during these centuries. It is an attempt to make out the linguistic history of this region during that period, and the evidence on which my findings are based is the relevant linguistic and inscriptional evidence. A comprehensive history of this region, or of any one of its provinces, would have to take account of a wider range of literary evidence and of a vast mass of archaeological material of many different kinds. The inscriptional evidence for the northward spread of Greek has been increasing and is likely to continue to increase, but its increase is a trickle by comparison with the avalanche of new-found uninscribed masonry and potsherds.

For Part III as well as for Part II, in contrast to Part I, the rate of the accumulation of archaeological evidence is relatively slow and the volume of it is relatively small. On the other hand, opinions differ over the problems of the history of Sparta at least as widely and sharply as they differ over the problems of the history of Greece as a whole in the Mycenaean and the sub-Mycenaean ages.

As for Part IV, I hope my readers will take it in the spirit in which an Athenian audience took the satyr-play that an Attic playwright was expected to append to each of his trilogies. It is a *jeu d'esprit*, but it has a serious purpose, as we may guess that some Attic satyr-plays had.

My purpose here is to demonstrate the untenability of a deterministic interpretation of human history. The three lives that are in question in this Part are those of three men whose lives were prematurely cut short long before they had reached the age of three score years and ten, not to speak of the four score years which was an uncommon but not unknown life-span in the days of the author of the Ninetieth Psalm. All three were men whose actions had already produced a great effect on the course of human affairs within life-spans that were unusually short and that would have been considerably longer if two of them had not been shortened by assassination and the third by an illness that was lethal but that need not have been. In my *jeu d'esprit* I have assumed one of the prerogatives of a judge. I have issued an injunction restraining Atropos from making the premature play with her shears that she did make as a matter of historical fact. I have imaginarily rescinded three historical —and also historic—events, and this has given me an opening for imagining what alternative course mankind's history might have taken if any one of these three effective makers of history had lived out his life to its natural term. I have imagined that, if Philip's and Artaxerxes' lives had been prolonged, history would have taken one different course, and that, if these two men had died when they actually did die and Alexander's life had been prolonged, history would have taken another different course.

I have worked out these two imaginary alternative courses of history mainly for fun, but also, as I have already said, with the serious purpose of refuting determinism. Incidentally I am defending myself against a charge of being a determinist which has been brought against me by some critics under a misapprehension.

These critics have noticed that I believe (as in truth I do) that, in surveying the past, one can detect in it certain 'patterns' of regularities, uniformities, and recurrences. My critics have inferred that I believe that the future course of events can be predicted by extrapolating the past and applying it to the future—as an astronomer can predict correctly a future eclipse by making mathematical calculations on the basis of records of past eclipses. Actually, I do not believe that the astronomer's procedure is applicable to human affairs. I believe that a human being has a freedom to make choices that is partial yet is genuine so far as it goes; and I believe that this quantum of freedom is a joker in the pack of possible future developments in the realm of human affairs. Consequently I believe that, in this realm, the future is unpredictable, and

I do not believe that my disbelief in determinism is incompatible with my belief that 'patterns' can be detected in the shape of past events. I believe that these patterns are authentic, but I also believe that they were not inevitable, and, *a fortiori*, I believe that they are not bound to recur in a future that is at least partly determinable by present and future human acts of will. Here I have in mind such decisions as those that were taken by the assassins of Philip and Artaxerxes and by Alexander when he chose, once too often, to disregard the limitations on a human being's physical strength and health that are imposed by laws of nature which even an Alexander cannot defy persistently with impunity.

ACKNOWLEDGEMENT

I SHOULD like to express my gratitude to Mrs. Chester, who has seen the book through the press, and to Mrs. Bicknell, who made the index. During the last stages of the production of the book I was ill and out of action. They saved the situation by most kindly checking references and settling queries which the author himself would normally have dealt with.

CONTENTS

PART I

THE POST-MYCENAEAN VÖLKERWANDERUNG

PART II

THE HELLENIZATION OF THE
NORTHERN HINTERLAND OF
CONTINENTAL EUROPEAN GREECE

PART III

THE RISE AND DECLINE OF SPARTA

PART IV

THREE LIVES

PART I

THE POST-MYCENAEAN
VÖLKERWANDERUNG

1. *The Homeric Catalogue of the Contingents in Agamemnon's Expeditionary Force*[1]

THE Homeric Catalogue of the contingents in Agamemnon's host is one of the most baffling passages in the Homeric epic, but the reason why it is baffling is not peculiar to the Catalogue; it is a feature of the epic as a whole. The world described or implied in the epic is one that never existed in real life; it lived only in the imaginations of a series of post-Mycenaean Greek poets, culminating and concluding in the poet or poets who shaped part of their predecessors' common stock of matter into the *Iliad* and the *Odyssey*. The components of this imaginary world are historical. What is fictitious is the blending of authentic elements in the history of two different ages to make a composite picture that is not true to the life of either age. This blending was an artistic success because it was not deliberate.[2]

The post-Mycenaean Greek epic poets had derived their themes, and probably their art as well, from the Mycenaean World, and their intention was to preserve a true picture of that world as their setting for their lays. They were, however, sundered historically from the Mycenaean Age by the intervening post-Mycenaean Völkerwanderung. This had been a cataclysm that had changed the face of the Aegean basin.[3] The Mycenaean civilization had been obliterated; and the descendants of

---

[1] *Iliad*, II. 494–759.

[2] 'Homer weder im eigentlichen Sinne archaïsiert noch bewusst modernisiert' (V. Burr, Νεῶν Κατάλογος (Leipzig, 1944, Dieterich), p. 153).

[3] Lord William Taylour, *The Mycenaeans* (London, 1964, Thames and Hudson), pp. 173–4, notes that Mycenae, Tiryns, Midea, Pylos, Gla, Zagouries, Prosymna, Berbati, Korakou were all destroyed or abandoned at the end of Late Helladic III B, and that Egypt was invaded by sea-peoples from the west *circa* 1225 B.C. and from the east *circa* 1191 or 1186 B.C., and (ibid., p. 179) that there are no tablets dating from Late Helladic III C. L. R. Palmer, *Mycenaeans and Minoans: Aegean Prehistory in the Light of the Linear B Tablets* (London, 1961, Faber), p. 144, notes that the destruction of Pylos was part of a general catastrophe.

those Mycenaean Greek refugees who had carved out new homes for themselves along the west coast of Anatolia had preserved only fragmentary reminiscences of the lost world of their forefathers.[1] Evidently these reminiscences were inadequate materials for constructing a concrete and convincing picture of the vanished age with which the poets were concerned; and we may guess that, if they had possessed the means of constructing a picture of the Mycenaean Age that would have been one hundred per cent archaeologically correct, this might have been unacceptable to their listeners; for, though listeners and poets alike felt a nostalgia for the Mycenaean Age, the Post-Völkerwanderung World in which they themselves were now living was so different from its predecessor that, if they could have been translated into this dead world authentically, they would have found themselves strangers in it. However, the poets had not the means of resuscitating the Mycenaean World integrally; the most that they could do was to give partial glimpses of it in a picture that was pieced out with elements drawn from contemporary life; and this composite picture was probably the one that answered best to their listeners' requirements.

How much of the Catalogue is an authentic reminiscence of the Mycenaean World? There is a school of thought, represented in the past by T. W. Allen and today by Professor D. L. Page, which holds that so much of the Catalogue is authentic that we may take it as being, throughout, a faithful description of pre-Völkerwanderung Greece.[2] One dissents from eminent authorities at one's peril,[3] and probably most representatives of other schools will follow Professor Page over a large part of the way. For instance, we may guess that catalogues, as a literary genre in post-Mycenaean Greek literature, had their prototypes in Mycenaean administrative documents.[4] At any rate, the documents written in an archaic form of the Arcado-Cyprian Greek dialect, and conveyed in the Linear B script, which have been recovered at Knossos

---

[1] G. Jachmann, *Der homerische Schiffskatalog und die Ilias* (Köln and Opladen, 1958, Westdeutscher Verlag), goes almost to the length of denying that any reminiscences at all survived. He points out (pp. 13–14) that the human agents by whom Troy VII A was destroyed are shown, by archaeological evidence, to have been, not pre-Völkerwanderung Mycenaean Greeks, but Völkerwanderung Thracians. He maintains (pp. 96 and 97) that the role of overlord of an Achaean confederation, which is attributed to Agamemnon in *Iliad*, I. 78–80 and II. 100–8, is not a genuine reminiscence. Cp. Jachmann, p. 89.

[2] T. W. Allen, *The Homeric Catalogue of Ships* (Oxford, 1921, Clarendon Press); Burr, op. cit.; D. L. Page, *History and the Homeric Iliad* (Berkeley and Los Angeles, 1959, University of California Press), p. 120.

[3] Jachmann's dissent from Allen and Burr is unprofitably militant. Jachmann is usefully *impiger*, but he is needlessly *iracundus*, uncharitably *inexorabilis*, and excessively *acer*.

[4] Palmer, op. cit., p. 100, notes that the tablets 'reveal a meticulous and efficient bureaucracy'. See ibid., pp. 115 and 207, for the bureaucratic control over Phaistos by the government at Knossos in whatever may be the period in which the Linear B tablets found at Knossos were inscribed. Compare Taylour, op. cit., p. 135.

and at Pylos, are mostly catalogues of workers and materials. Page points out that forty-eight of the ninety-six place-names in the Catalogue whose sites have been identified prove to be sites on which there are material vestiges of the Mycenaean culture;[1] and he notes[2] that the Catalogue gives many of these places distinctive epithets. We can readily agree that this much in the Catalogue is authentic information dating from the Mycenaean Age.[3] When, however, Page goes on to contend[4] that the Catalogue as a whole is a Mycenaean-Age document that has been preserved by oral tradition, his contention runs into stumbling-blocks.[5] We may agree, again, that if there was a hegemon of the Mycenaean World named Agamemnon, and if he did take with him, overseas, an expeditionary force supplied by a number of principalities under his sovereignty or suzerainty, his secretariat must have recorded, as a matter of routine, a field-state of the contingents,[6] and must have made this record in Arcado-Cyprian Greek in the Linear B script on clay tablets. Yet, even if this record had been made, and if it had survived Agamemnon's stormy nostos and his assassination, it seems hardly credible that Agamemnon's refugee descendants could have carried this load of tablets with them on their flight to the west coast of Anatolia;[7] and it is even less credible that, if any of these fragile, friable, soluble tablets did arrive in Asia intact, and were then successfully preserved there for the next few centuries,[8] there would have been, in the ninth or eighth century B.C., any living Asian Greek who could decipher them. The unofficial catalogues that figure so prominently in post-Völkerwanderung Greek epic poetry may have been inspired by memories of pre-Völkerwanderung official catalogues, but it seems improbable that they were authentic replicas of these. If it is asked how forty-eight authentic entries in a written field-state which must have perished *circa* 1200 B.C. could have survived to find their way into an epic poem that did not take its definitive

---

[1] Page, op. cit., p. 120. The total number of place-names in the Catalogue is 164. Burr, op. cit., p. 111, reckons that there are sixty identified sites on which there are Mycenaean remains. Jachmann, op. cit., pp. 27–8, disputes the cogency of this point, on the ground that many of the cities of the Post-Völkerwanderung Hellenic World had been founded by squatters on ex-Mycenaean sites.

[2] Op. cit., p. 123.

[3] Jachmann, op. cit., pp. 142 and 195, concedes that the Catalogue is all of a piece. Indeed, he maintains that it is the only considerable passage of the *Iliad*, as we now have it, of which this can be said. He holds, however, on pp. 142 and 144, that the epithets and anecdotes with which both the Achaean Catalogue and the Trojan Catalogue are interlarded are sheer inventions of a 'poet' who was concerned to relieve the dullness of a string of names.

[4] In op. cit., pp. 122–3.

[5] Jachmann's comment, in op. cit., pp. 15–16 and 19, that the *Iliad* is poetry, not a versified chronicle, is pertinent and fundamental.

[6] This point is made by Burr, op. cit., p. 125, and by Walter Leaf, *Homer and History* (London, 1915, Macmillan), pp. 80–3.

[7] This is suggested, as a possibility, by Burr, op. cit., p. 127.

[8] This suggestion of Burr's is pardonably derided by Jachmann, op. cit., p. 16.

shape till four or five hundred years after that date, the answer may be that those points in the administrative document that would be of interest to the non-official public may have been given publicity contemporaneously by being transposed into oral poetry which was then preserved orally during the ensuing age. Points that would appeal both to contemporaries and to posterity would be the names and genealogies of war-lords and the names of the places from which their followers came.

In the Homeric Catalogue of Agamemnon's expeditionary force, there are some elements that are evidently Mycenaean; but it is also true that there are other elements in it that are no less evidently part and parcel of the Greek World of the Post-Völkerwanderung Age. In a number of points—and these important points—the author of the Catalogue is writing as a well-informed connoisseur of the Mycenaean World. He is aware that, at the time of the Trojan War, Thebes was in ruins, because it had been destroyed a few years before. He is therefore careful to write, not Θήβας, but Ὑποθήβας,[1] indicating the survival of an unwalled settlement below the now desolate citadel. He knows that, in the Mycenaean Age, the country that eventually became Boeotia was a pair of countries, one centring on Cadmean Thebes and the other on Minyan Orkhomenos; so he lists the contingents of these two territories separately.[2] He knows that the city of Mycenae,[3] not the city of Argos, was the seat of the hegemon of the Achaean Confederacy, Agamemnon, and of the Pelopids' predecessors the Perseids, though, in the Post-Völkerwanderung Age, Argos was important and Mycenae was insignificant. He knows that Pylos, which, in the Post-Völkerwanderung Age, was uninhabited,[4] had been the seat of Nestor, one of the most eminent of Agamemnon's allies.[5] He knows that Achilles, the most eminent ally of all, was the leader of a people called the Myrmidones,[6] who were not to be found anywhere on the post-Völkerwanderung map, and that there had been an important town—likewise no longer in existence—called Oikhalia in or near Nestor's principality or in what had since become the north-western tetrarchy of Thessaly, Histiaiotis, or in both these regions.[7] Oikhalia had been the city of a hero named Eurytos,[8] whose name

---

[1] *Iliad*, II. 505.

[2] In *Iliad*, II. 494–510 and 511–16.

[3] *Iliad*, II. 569. Cp. IV. 376; VII. 180; IX. 44; XI. 46; *Odyssey*, III. 304.

[4] Thucydides, Book IV, chap. 3.   [5] *Iliad*, II. 591–602.

[6] *Iliad*, II. 684. Cp. IX. 185; XVI. 155–220; *Odyssey*, III. 188; IV. 8.

[7] Jachmann, op. cit., p. 126 with n. 177, denies the authenticity of the Oikhalia in Messenia. He holds that the Dorion which is enumerated in the Catalogue, l. 594, among the places in Nestor's principality, and which is associated in this passage with Oikhalia, is a mistake, on the poet's part, for Dotion, which is the name of an authentic place in Thessaly, and that the Oikhalia of l. 596 is therefore fictitious. This hypercritical conjecture of Jachmann's is blown sky-high by the occurrence of the name Oikhalia on one of the Pylos tablets (see Part I, chap. 3, p. 26).

[8] *Iliad*, II. 596 and 730; *Odyssey*, IV. 224.

was commemorated in the Post-Völkerwanderung Age in the national
name of an Aetolian people, the Eurytanes. The poet knew that, before
the Völkerwanderung, the Ainianes were living, not in the Sperkheios
valley, but round Dodona.[1] He knew that, before the Völkerwanderung,
there was already a Greek-speaking population, included in Agamemnon's confederacy, on the islands off the south-west corner of Anatolia,[2]
in the region known in the poet's time as Doris, but that the future Ionia
and Aiolis had not been colonized by Greeks yet. He also knew that the
date at which the Trojan War was believed to have been waged was
earlier than the Völkerwanderung that had produced the different
Greek World of the poet's own age. He therefore took care not to mention
such names as Thessalians, Dorians, Messenians, Acarnanians, Ozolian
Locrians, Megara, Pharsalos, the Pelasgiotic Larisa, Krannon, Kierion,[3]
and the Phthiotic Thebes.[4] Pharsalos, Larisa, and Krannon were three
out of the four principal cities of post-Völkerwanderung Thessaly. (The
fourth of these, Pherai, does appear in the Catalogue, since it was also
prominent in Greek traditions of the Mycenaean Age.) Thebes was the
principal city in post-Völkerwanderung Phthiotic Akhaïa.

These features in the Catalogue, as far as they go, present pieces of
a picture that cannot be reconciled with the picture of the Aegean basin
as it had come to be in the Post-Völkerwanderung Age. But there are
other features in the Catalogue that indubitably belong to this later age
and that cannot be reconciled with the picture of the Mycenaean World
as it had been before the Völkerwanderung.

The author of the Catalogue (presumably imagining himself to be
standing at Aulis)[5] heads his list of contingents with those from central
Greece. He describes these in greater detail than any of the rest;[6] and
here he throws antiquarianism to the winds. The peoples in central Greece
whom he enumerates are the North-West-Greek-speaking peoples—
Boiotoi (meaning 'Pindus-people'), Phokeis, Lokroi—who took possession of this area during the Völkerwanderung.[7] Moreover, Thebes has
risen again from her ruins; for, though she is meticulously called, not
Θῆβαι, but Ὑποθῆβαι, she is described as being an ἐϋκτίμενον πτολίεθρον,
instead of being described as being the shanty-town that Ὑποθῆβαι must
have been at the time of the Trojan War. Attica, too, is assumed to be

---

[1] *Iliad*, II. 749–50.   [2] Ibid. 653–80.
[3] Burr, op. cit., p. 126.
[4] Burr, op. cit., p. 94.
[5] Aulis was the traditional assemblage-point of Agamemnon's armada, but, as Jachmann
points out (op. cit., p. 20), this tradition is not to be found anywhere in the *Iliad*. In the
Catalogue, Aulis is not given any special prominence (op. cit., pp. 22–4).
[6] Was he a Boeotian like Hesiod—a poet who was perhaps a contemporary of the author
of the Homeric Catalogue and who was likewise addicted to this genre of poetry?
[7] *Iliad*, II. 494–535. Cp. XIII. 685–700. Thucydides, Book I, chap. 12, notices that the
mention of the Boiotoi in the Catalogue is an anachronism.

already the unitary state, governed from the city of Athens,[1] that she had become by the seventh century B.C. The territory ascribed to her in the Catalogue appears to include even Eleusis, though it does not include Salamis.

The post-Völkerwanderung city of Argos, again, has reared up its head in the Catalogue over against Agamemnon's Mycenae.[2] Argos means 'cultivated land', and hence must originally have been the name, not of a city, but of a district: the cultivated plain in the basin of the River Inakhos.[3] Argeioi, as well as Akhaioi, is used in the epic as a collective name for the peoples included in Agamemnon's confederacy; and the word Argos itself is also used in this comprehensive sense.[4] This usage indicates that the plain of Argos was the home territory of the principality, exercising a hegemony over the rest of the Pelopid domain[5] and

---

[1] *Iliad*, II. 546–51. Cp. XIII. 689 and 685, where the Athenians seem to be identified with the ʼIáoves.

[2] *Iliad*, II. 559–68. Argos is a polis in IV. 52, and in XXI. 108 as well.

[3] Argos, in this original local meaning of the name, is Agamemnon's home according to *Iliad*, I. 30; II. 115; IV. 171; IX. 22; XIII. 379.

[4] e.g. in *Iliad*, VI. 456; VII. 363; XII. 70; XIII. 227; XIV. 70; XV. 372; XIX. 329; XXIV. 437; *Odyssey*, XXIV. 37.

[5] In *Iliad*, II. 107, Agamemnon's domain is described as being πολλῇσιν νήσοισι καὶ Ἄργεϊ παντί. Helen is called Ἀργείη in *Iliad*, II. 161 and in *Odyssey*, XVII. 118, presumably because 'Argos' could be used to mean the whole domain of the Pelopids, including Mene-laos' principality. In *Iliad*, XIX. 115, the domain of the pre-Pelopid Perseid king Sthenelos is called Ἄργος Ἀχαϊκόν. In *Iliad*, IX. 141 and 283, and *Odyssey*, III. 251, the Pelopids' domain is called Ἀχαϊκόν Ἄργος; in *Odyssey*, IV. 174, it is called simply Argos.

Seven places on the western flank of the Tainaron Peninsula are enumerated in *Iliad*, IX. 149–53, as being in Agamemnon's gift. Of these, only two can be located with certainty, namely Kardamyle, which still retains its Homeric name, and Pherai, which is presumably the Pharai of the Post-Völkerwanderung Age, whose site is occupied by the present-day city of Kalamáta. Locations for the other five cities in this list have been suggested, on the strength of a field study of Mycenaean remains round the shores of the Messenian Gulf, by R. Hope Simpson in *The Annual of the British School at Athens*, vol. 52 (1957), pp. 231–59, and vol. 61 (1966), pp. 113–31. In *Iliad*, IX. 153, it is noted that the seven cities are at the edge of the principality of Pylos: νέαται Πύλου; cp. νεάτη Πύλου in XI. 712. The meaning of νεάτη in this passage suggests that νέαται Πύλου ought to mean, not 'just outside' Pylos, but 'just inside' Pylos, and this district does, in fact, include Gerenia, which was Nestor's place of origin, to judge by his standing Homeric epithet Γερήνιος. Jachmann, op. cit., p. 53, points out that, in IX, Agamemnon cannot be asking Nestor to take to Achilles a message from Agamemnon offering to Achilles a piece of territory that belonged, not to Agamemnon, but to Nestor himself. Jachmann holds (op. cit., pp. 54–5) that the νέαται of *Iliad*, IX. 153, is an unintelligent piece of plagiarism from XI. 712. He also guesses (pp. 104–5) that these particular seven places have been selected, by the author of this passage in *Iliad*, IX, not because they were known to have belonged to Agamemnon, but because central and eastern Messenia was a blank space on the Homeric map. In reality it was not blank, and Agamem-non's assumption that the seven cities were at his disposal may have been disputable (see Part I, chap. 3, pp. 25–8).

These passages give us the area of Argos, in the sense, not just of the Argive plain, but of the Pelopids' domain of which the Argive plain was the nucleus. Argos, meaning the Pelopids' domain, extended, apparently, from Mycenae to Laconia and possibly also to south-eastern Messenia inclusive. The Ἴασον Ἄργος of *Odyssey*, XVIII. 246, and the Ἄργος of XXIV. 37, seem to mean the combined area of all the countries under Pelopid hegemony. The various

over the rest of Greece, whose seat was Mycenae and whose prince was Agamemnon himself. But in the Catalogue the lion's share of the Argive plain, almost up to the southern foot of the citadel of Mycenae, is assigned to Diomedes, with a seat in Argos city. The Akte of the Argolid is also assigned to Diomedes, and Agamemnon is fobbed off with Corinth and the northern seaboard of the Peloponnese along the Corinthian Gulf.[1] Yet, after the recital of this inadequate dominion, with no direct outlet on the Aegean except perhaps at Kenkhreai, we are told that Agamemnon's people were by far the most numerous and the best of all the contingents,[2] and that, besides mustering one hundred ships[3] (the largest single squadron of all) for his own contingent, he provided sixty more for the landlubber Arcadians.[4] The Catalogue's account of the partition of the north-western Peloponnese between the principalities of Agamemnon and Diomedes does not make sense[5]—and the reason why it fails to make sense is that, here, pre-Völkerwanderung Greece and post-Völkerwanderung Greece have come into head-on collision with each other.[6]

meanings of the word 'Argos' in the Homeric epic are set out by Walter Leaf, op. cit., pp. 194–6.   [1] *Iliad*, II. 569–80.
   [2] Ibid. 577–8 and 580.   [3] Ibid. 576.   [4] Ibid. 610–14.
   [5] The case against the partition of the Argolid in the Catalogue is put forcibly by Leaf, in op. cit. 'While Mykene was in strong hands, there was no room for Argos or Tiryns or any others' [as independent states] (p. 208). 'No monarch commanding such means as we know, on indisputable evidence, were at the command of the ruler of Mykene, could have maintained his own existence had he not held, in addition to the barren hillsides which surrounded his stronghold, the resources of the plain on which Argos flourished, and the harbours to which Tiryns held the approaches. . . . His kingdom would have been a mockery' (p. 209). 'The division which makes Argos a capital town while Mykene is still fortified, and the stronghold of a rival state, is impossible' (p. 235). Leaf points out (ibid., pp. 238–40) that the Aigialos, which the Catalogue assigns to Agamemnon, is no compensation for its denial to him of the Argive plain. Burr takes the same view (op. cit., p. 43). He points out (p. 88) that, elsewhere in the *Iliad*, Argos is Agamemnon's home (I. 30; II. 115; IV. 171; XIII. 379), besides being Diomedes' (VI. 224; XIV. 119), Eurystheus' (XIV. 114–24), Herakles' (ibid., and XV. 30), and Sisyphos' (VI. 152–3). Cp. Jachmann, op. cit., pp. 32 and 94.
   T. W. Allen suggests, in op. cit., p. 8, that the Pelopids' holdings at Mycenae, at Corinth, and along the north coast of the Peloponnese (*Iliad*, II. 569–80) were connected territorially with their holdings in Laconia and in south-eastern Messenia by the territory in Arcadia that was under their hegemony but was not under their direct rule. This suggestion is not convincing.
   According to Diomedes' own account of his ancestry in *Iliad*, XIV. 113–25, his father Tydeus had migrated from Pleuron and Kalydon to the court of Adrastos, the pre-Pelopid King of Argos (i.e. the country called Argos, not the post-Völkerwanderung city). Adrastos gave Tydeus his daughter in marriage and endowed him generously with property; but in this passage there is no mention of either Tydeus or Diomedes having succeeded to the rulership of Adrastos' principality. It is true, however, as is pointed out by Allen in op. cit., p. 66, that a principality with its capital at the city of Argos seems to appear, side by side with one with its capital at Mycenae, in *Iliad* IV. 372–81, and in *Odyssey*, XXI. 108, as well as in the Catalogue.
   [6] 'Argos tritt Mykenai ebenbürtig zur Seite. Dies weist auf die Zeit nach der dorischen Wanderung hin und ist eine Konzession an die Blütezeit des dorischen Argos' (Burr, op. cit., p. 44).

Argos, in the sense of the post-Völkerwanderung city of Argos, has been given the whole of the Argolid except the corner of it containing the city of Mycenae, which was known to have been the capital of a pre-Völkerwanderung Pelopid principality.

As for Arcadia, the Catalogue represents it as being already landlocked, though, down to the Völkerwanderung, and indeed throughout the Protogeometric and the Geometric Age of early Hellenic history (as is demonstrated by archaeological evidence), the Arcadians did possess a seaboard on the Aegean, from which they colonized Cyprus,[1] until they were eventually cut off from the sea by the extension of the hegemony of the post-Völkerwanderung city-state of Argos over the maritime Arcadian communities in Kynouria.

When we come to Lakedaimon, we find a similar anachronism. Sparta is enumerated among Lakedaimon's cities:[2] but Sparta, meaning 'the Sown Land', is the unwalled town, down in the vale of the Eurotas, which ruled Lakedaimon in the Post-Völkerwanderung Age. The Mycenaean-Age seat of government was probably at Therapne, on a bluff overhanging the Eurotas' eastern bank.

In the Catalogue of the contingents of the Trojan host, the author has forgotten that in the Pre-Völkerwanderung Age the Island of Rhodes and the Dodecanese were the only districts on the east side of the Aegean Sea that had yet been occupied by Greek-speaking colonists from Europe. One of the peoples enumerated among the Trojans' allies is the Pelasgoi of Larisa.[3] This was presumably a North-East-Greek-speaking people from Pelasgiotis that found asylum in Asia when, in the post-Mycenaean Völkerwanderung, Pelasgiotis was overrun by the Thessaloi. These Asian Pelasgians' city is called Larisa, like the chief city of Pelasgiotis, and Lethos, the name of their leaders' father, is the eponym of the Thessalian river Lethaios. The Asian Pelasgoi, like the Aioleis and the Asian Iones, will have been established in Asia by the poet's time, but surely not yet by the date of the Trojan War.

While the author of the Achaean Catalogue is correct in placing a Greek-speaking population in Rhodes and the Dodecanese in the Mycenaean Age,[4] the Rhodians and Dodecanesians whom he is describing are not those of the Pre-Völkerwanderung Age; they are the North-West-Greek-speakers who were deposited there in the Völkerwanderung.

---

[1] See Jachmann, op. cit., pp. 25–6.   [2] *Iliad*, II. 582. Cp. IV. 52.

[3] *Iliad*, II. 840–3. Cp. X. 429; XVII. 288–303. The Λάρισα ἐριβώλαξ of *Iliad*, II. 841, and XVII. 301, seems more likely to be the Larisa in the Troad than the Larisa Phrikonis in Aiolis. In the Catalogue it is enumerated immediately after Sestos and Abydos, and, though the leader of these Larisaeans, Lethos, is said in the other passage to have met his death 'far from Larisa' when he was killed at Troy, the word τῆλε may have been introduced here, as it has been in other passages of the *Iliad*, to create pathos rather than to measure geographical distance (see Jachmann, op. cit., pp. 170–2).

[4] *Iliad*, II. 653–80.

They are divided into three phylai (i.e. the Dorian phylai),[1] and their leaders (with the exception of Nireus of Syme) are descendants of Herakles.[2] The Heraklid genealogy and the three Dorian phylai were institutions of the post-Völkerwanderung Asian Doris which were transmitted, in the Post-Völkerwanderung Age, to the North-West-Greek-speaking conquerors of the Eastern Peloponnese.[3]

Again, while the poet, as has been noted above, correctly makes Achilles the leader of the extinct Myrmidones, he calls Achilles' followers alternatively by the names of two North-West-Greek-speaking peoples that had occupied the heart of Achilles' domain during the Völkerwanderung and were still in possession of it in the poet's day. He says[4] that, besides being called 'Myrmidones', they were called 'Hellenes' and 'Akhaioi'. In the Post-Völkerwanderung Age the Akhaioi were in occupation of south-eastern Phthia, while the Hellenes were living either round Anthela or round Delphi or round both—most probably in Malis.[5]

The domain ascribed in the Catalogue to Achilles[6] is by far the largest of the principalities under Agamemnon's hegemony. It is much larger than Agamemnon's own domain as described in the Catalogue. Achilles' domain includes, to begin with, the whole of the Πελασγικὸν Ἄργος;[7] and, if the meaning of the word 'argos' is 'cultivated land', this argos is likely to have embraced the whole of the Thessalian lowlands, and not just the post-Völkerwanderung Pelasgiotis. Achilles' domain also includes Phthia, i.e. the combined territory of the post-Völkerwanderung Phthiotic Akhaïa and the Thessalian tetrarchy Phthiotis, round Pharsalos. It includes, in particular, Halos and Alope, on the east coast and the south coast of what afterwards became the Phthiotic Akhaïa. It includes Trakhis; and, finally, it includes Hellas, which may be identical with Malis-cum-Trachide or with Phokis or with both.[8]

At the same time, nearly all parts of the vast area that figures here as Achilles' domain are also ascribed, in the immediately following entries in the Catalogue, to a number of other princes. The whole eastern half of the Phthiotic Akhaïa, except Halos, is ascribed to Protesilaos.[9] This prince's domain intervenes between Achilles' Halos and Achilles' Alope and makes Halos an isolated enclave. South-eastern Pelasgiotis (Iolkos, Pherai, Boibe) is ascribed to Admetos' son.[10] Olizon, Methone, and

---

[1] L. Pareti, *Storia di Sparta Arcaïca*, Parte I (Florence, 1920, Felice Le Monnier), p. 69.

[2] According to *Iliad*, XIV. 253 and XV. 28, Herakles had been driven by a storm to Cos on his way home after his sack of Ilion.

[3] See Part I, chap. 3, pp. 43–5.　　　[4] *Iliad*, II. 684.

[5] See Part I, chap. 3, pp. 35–6.　　　[6] *Iliad*, II. 680–5.

[7] Jachmann, op. cit., p. 185, n. 254, suggests that the Πελασγικὸν Ἄργος of line 681 is intended to cover, not Achilles' domain alone, but also the other eight principalities that are enumerated, in succession to his, as occupying parts of north-east Greece. This is contrary to the plain meaning of lines 181–5.

[8] See Part I, chap. 3, p. 36.　　　[9] *Iliad*, II. 693–710.　　　[10] Ibid. 711–15.

Meliboia in the future Magnesia, together with Thaumakia (? Dhomokó in western Phthiotic Akhaïa) are ascribed to Philoktetes,[1] though, according to later tradition, Philoktetes was neither a Magnete nor an Achaean but was a Malian.[2] Histiaiotis is ascribed to Podaleirios and Makhaon;[3] the future Thessaliotis, together with an enclave in Admetos' principality, to Eurypylos;[4] north-western Pelasgiotis and the future Perrhaibia to Peirithoos' son,[5] and Magnesia, including Mount Pelion, to Prothoos,[6] though Pelion, which has given Achilles' father Peleus his name, must originally have been included in the Peleidai's dominions, and though the whole of Magnesia has already been ascribed to Philoktetes. Moreover, Achilles' Hellas has been pre-empted by the Phokeis,[7] if his Hellas is Phokis and is not Malis-cum-Trachide.

When all these bites have been taken out of Achilles' domain, what is left of it? Nothing except Pharsalos, a piece of western Phthiotic Akhaïa, Halos, Alope, Trakhis, and the rest of the Sperkheios valley; and Trakhis and western Akhaïa are the most undesirable pieces of all.[8] This duplication of nearly the whole of Achilles' domain in other principalities is the biggest single discrepancy in the whole Catalogue, but it is a characteristic one.[9] Each of these two mutually incompatible political maps of north-eastern Greece in the Catalogue is also incompatible with the post-Völkerwanderung political map of the same area. Each of them,

---

[1] *Iliad*, II. 716–28.
[2] See Leaf, op. cit., pp. 127–8.
[3] *Iliad*, II. 729–33. Cp. IV. 200–2.
[4] Ibid. II. 734–7.
[5] Ibid. 738–47.
[6] Ibid. 756–9.
[7] Ibid. 517–26.

[8] In the *Iliad*, except for the Catalogue, the domain ascribed to Achilles is, in nearly all cases, Phthia, nothing more, but also nothing less. See, for example, I. 155 and 169; IX. 253 (the domain of Achilles' father Peleus), 363, 439, 479, 484 (ἐσχατίην Φθίης, Dolopia); XI. 766; XVI. 13; XIX. 299, 323, 330. In XVI. 494–6, a Myrmidon's home is located in Hellas, and in IX. 395 it is implied, though not expressly stated, that Hellas, as well as Phthia, is included in Peleus' domain. On the other hand, in IX. 678–80 it is implied that Hellas is not included in Peleus' domain, though Phthia is. According to IX. 447–8, Hellas was the principality of Amyntor Ormenides, and Amyntor's son Phoinix has to flee across Hellas to Phthia in order to find asylum from his father with Peleus (IX. 478–9). (According to X. 266, Amyntor's seat was Eleon, and Eleon was in Boeotia according to the Catalogue, II. 500. It seems to have lain east-north-east of Thebes.) The Phthioi, led by Philoktetes' lieutenant, though Protesilaos' protégé (*Iliad*, XV. 333–6), Medon, and by Protesilaos' lieutenant Podarkes, occur only in *Iliad*, XIII. 685–700, and this is a passage which is more akin to the Catalogue than it is to the rest of the *Iliad*. In *Odyssey*, XI (*Nekyia*), 494–6, Hellas, together with Phthia, is equated with the country of the Myrmidons and with the principality of Peleus. In *Iliad*, XIX. 329, and in *Odyssey*, XXIV. 37, Achilles is said to be going to die, and to have died, 'far from Argos', with the implication that Argos was his fatherland. It is not clear whether, in this passage, 'Argos' means the Pelasgian Argos (i.e. the Thessalian plain), which is included in Achilles' principality according to the Catalogue (*Iliad*, II. 681), or whether it means the country of the Argeioi in the sense of the total number of peoples under Agamemnon's hegemony. The principal river in Peleus' principality was the Sperkheios (*Iliad*, XXIII. 141–51; cp. XVI. 173–6); and this river's modern name is Elládha (see Part I, chap. 3, p. 36, footnote 2).

[9] Jachmann, op. cit., p. 22, cites B. Niese, *Der homerische Schiffskatalog* (Kiel, 1873), for the judgement that the north-east-Greece section of the Catalogue shows up the 'geographische Unwissenheit' of the Catalogue as a whole.

therefore, may represent a genuine pre-Völkerwanderung regime; but, if so, the two regimes must be of different dates; they cannot have been contemporaneous with each other. Nor, on the non-Peleid map, can Philoktetes' principality and Prothoos' principality have been contemporary with each other either.

This compositeness and self-contradictoriness of the Catalogue makes it extremely difficult for historians to use. Yet it is impossible to leave the Catalogue out of account if one is probing into the early history of Greece. In order to use it at all, we have to determine, if we can, the date of its composition, and, on this question, Jachmann shows acumen.

So far from seeing in the Catalogue the oldest component of the *Iliad*, Jachmann holds[1] that it is the latest addition of all. For instance,[2] Achilles' fifty ships in the Catalogue[3] are a replica of the fifty ships attributed to him in the *Iliad* in another context.[4] Similarly, Odysseus' twelve ships in the Catalogue[5] are a replica of the twelve with which he eventually set sail for home from Troy according to the *Odyssey*;[6] so the Catalogue is later in date than the *Odyssey* too.[7] Jachmann's derivation of these two figures in the Catalogue is convincing, because it accounts for the surprising smallness of the numbers of the ships here attributed to the two eminent heroes Odysseus and Achilles by comparison with the numbers with which some of the more obscure leaders are credited. Jachmann also presents evidence[8] that the Catalogue is younger, not only than the youngest stratum of the *Odyssey*, but than the *Telegony* as well. According to the Catalogue, Odysseus has subjects on the mainland, in Akarnania and in Elis.[9] Jachmann suggests that the author of the Catalogue has obtained this information from the *Odyssey* and from the *Telegony*, and this suggestion, too, is convincing.

As for the word Πανέλληνας,[10] this cannot be older than the date at which the name Ἕλληνες—originally borne only by a small North-West-Greek-speaking people that migrated from the interior of Epirus to central Greece during the post-Mycenaean Völkerwanderung[11]—had come, thanks to the growth of the prestige of the Delphi–Anthela amphictyony, to be used as a comprehensive name for all participants in the budding Hellenic civilization.[12] We may add that the warriors of north-east Arcadia—the remote corner lying under the shadow of Mount Kyllene—are likely to have been the last Arcadians to become ἄνερες ἀγχιμαχηταί,[13] i.e. to adopt the phalanx battle-order and tactics. The

---

[1] Op. cit., p. 38.   [2] Op. cit., p. 45.   [3] *Iliad*, II. 685.
[4] XVI. 168.   [5] *Iliad*, II. 637.   [6] *Odyssey*, IX. 159.
[7] Jachmann, op. cit., p. 34, n. 36.   [8] In op. cit., pp. 36–8.
[9] οἵ τ' ἤπειρον ἔχον ἠδ' ἀντιπέραι' ἐνέμοντο (*Iliad*, II. 635).
[10] *Iliad*, II. 530.   [11] See Part I, chap. 3, pp. 35–6.
[12] See Jachmann, op. cit., p. 109, and the present work, Part I, chap. 3, p. 50, with n. 2.
[13] *Iliad*, II. 604.

Spartans did not adopt these till half way through the seventh century B.C., and perhaps not till later.[1] The Tegeatan and Mantinean Arcadians are unlikely to have adopted phalanx tactics earlier than the Spartans, and the Arcadians of Pheneos, Stymphalos, and Orkhomenos are likely to have lagged behind their south-east-Arcadian fellow countrymen.

These pieces of evidence, taken together, suggest that the Homeric Catalogue must have been composed at some date in the latter part of the seventh century B.C.

[1] See Part III, chap. 3, section (ii), and Part III, chap. 3, Annex I.

2. Minyans and Cadmeans

THE legendary name of Minos, the sovereign of the seas, may preserve the historical name of an imperial people. For, in the Hellenic tradition, we seem to catch echoes of Μίνως in the plural number instead of the singular in the names Μνωῖται and Μινύαι.

The Μνωῖται (collectively called Μνοία, Μνωΐα, or Μνῴα) were the native serfs of the 'Dorian' conquerors of Crete; and in this term we may trace the degradation, in the latter-day Hellenic World, of a people who, in the *Odyssey*, are still remembered as the Ἐτεόκρητες μεγαλήτορες.[1] The affinity of the name Μινύαι with the name Μίνως is not so clear as the affinity with it of the name Μνωῖται is, but Μινύαι might be accounted for as a combination of the root of Μίνως with the place-name suffix -wa (Me-nu-wa is the name of a person on one of the Pylos Linear B tablets). L. R. Palmer (following Bossert) notes[2] that place-names ending in -wa are distributed over more or less the same area (in Anatolia, the Aegean, and continental European Greece) as the place-names ending in -assa; and Palmer points out that place-names 'of wholly un-Greek appearance', ending in -wa, appear frequently in the Linear B tablets from Pylos. Palmer holds that these terminations are Luvian, and that the Luvian language was current, before the Greek language, in Crete.[3] However, -wa is also a termination of place-names in Illyria.[4]

The Minyai were a people of the Pre-Hellenic Heroic Age who were located by Hellenic legend at three different points on the mainland of European Greece: along the southern part of the west coast of the Peloponnese at Pylos;[5] in the interior of central Greece, midway between

---

[1] *Odyssey*, XIX. 176.   [2] In *Mycenaeans and Minoans*, pp. 244–5.
[3] Ibid., p. 240.   [4] e.g. Butua, Pardua.

[5] In the Homeric epic, Pylos is not called 'Minyan' as Orkhomenos is, nor are the Pylians called 'Minyai' as are the Argonauts who sail from Iolkos. On the other hand, Neleus, the founder of the principality of Pylos, is said to have come from Iolkos and to have been the twin brother of the prince of Iolkos, Pelias; and we hear casually of a ποταμὸς Μιννήϊος in the Pylian territory (*Iliad*, XI. 722). In the fifth century B.C. the Greek inhabitants of one fragment of the *ci-devant* Pylian domain—the territory on the west coast of the Peloponnese, between Messenia and Elis, which is called first Paroreatis and afterwards Triphylia—are said to be Μινύαι by Herodotus (in Book IV, chap. 148). True, Herodotus brings his Minyai to the Paroreatis at a fairly recent date, as the last stage in a long migration which ultimately fetches them from Iolkos via Lemnos and Mount Taÿgetos. But this Herodotean saga (Book IV, chaps. 145–8) is a patchwork which is easily picked to pieces. The fact which remains is that the Paroreatai who were conquered by the Eleans in the fifth century B.C. laid claim to the Minyan name; and the simplest explanation of this claim is to suppose that they had inherited the name from their predecessors on the spot in the Pre-Völkerwanderung Age: that is to say, from the time when the Paroreatis was a part of the pre-Völkerwanderung principality of Pylos. The Pylians who survived in Paroreatis may have transferred the name

the Corinthian Gulf and the Euripos, at Orkhomenos;[1] and on the fringe of northern Greece, at the head of the Gulf of Volo, at Iolkos.[2]

The bare name of Minyai is not the only common property of these three legendary Minyan settlements. The common worship of a god of healing seems to be indicated by a comparison of the name of the Minyan hero Ἰάσων (i.e. 'the Healer') of Iolkos with the name Ἀσκάλαφος, which looks like a variant of Ἀσκλήπιος,[3] and which is given, in the Homeric Catalogue of the contingents contributed to Agamemnon's expeditionary force,[4] to one of the two kings of Minyan Orkhomenos.[5] Another link is the name Ἀμυθάων, which appears as a personal name in the genealogy of the Minyan rulers of Iolkos and as a place-name—Ἀμυθαονία[6]—in the Peloponnesian domain of the Minyans round Pylos; and, if we take the name Amythaon and the cult of a healing god as clues to the presence of Minyan settlers, we can perhaps espy, in two passages of the *Iliad*, the traces of a fourth Minyan settlement of which the Hellenic tradition has not preserved a record. For the Ἀμυδών on the banks of the Axios, from which the Paiones came,[7] is the name Ἀμυθάων applied in Paionia, as in the Peloponnese, to a place instead of a person and transliterated into its philologically correct equivalent in the Macedonian dialect of North-East Greek (in which the ordinary Greek θ is represented by δ);[8] and in another passage a Paeonian hero, Asteropaios,

Pylos to a site there (see Burr, Νεῶν Κατάλογος, pp. 63–4). The Minyai who, twice over, took refuge on Mount Taÿgetos (Herodotus, Book IV, chaps. 145 and 146) may be historical too. Though they are unlikely to have been sea-borne refugees from distant Lemnos, they may well have been refugees who had escaped on foot from the destruction of nearby Pylos and the extinction of the Pylian principality in the post-Mycenaean *Völkerwanderung*. The Linear B tablets from Pylos record the dispositions made for the defence of the principality against a final assault from the sea (Palmer, op. cit., pp. 18–19 and 132–43). It is likely enough that, when the defence was overwhelmed, survivors from the units stationed along the south coast may have escaped up into Taÿgetos, and that survivors from the units stationed along the west coast may have found shelter at its northern end, in Paroreatis (Triphylia), while the surviving Pylian ships may have sailed to Attica, as the Greek tradition declares that they did.

[1] The standing epithet of this Orkhomenos is Μινύειος or Μινυήϊος (e.g. in *Iliad*, II. 511).

[2] The heroes who sail from Iolkos under Jason's command on board the legendary ship Argo in quest of the Golden Fleece are called Μινύαι collectively.

[3] Ἀσκάλαφος is said to have been the name of a bird and, in the form ἀσκάλαβος or ἀσκαλαβώτης, the name of a lizard. Was Asklepios a lizard before he became a snake?

[4] *Iliad*, II. 512.

[5] Though a god of healing seems to be common to the Minyai of Orkhomenos and the Minyai of Iolkos, he may have been originally the god, not of the intrusive Minyai, but of the native North-East-Greek-speaking Phlegyai–Pelasgoi–Pelagones (see Part II, chap. 4, pp. 86–8), on whom the Minyai had imposed themselves. The healing god Asklepios' original seat was at Trikka in north-western Thessaly, i.e. in a North-East-Greek-speaking region that was never under Minyan rule. In the Homeric Catalogue the contingent from this sector of Thessaly is led by Asklepios' two sons Podaleirios and Makhaon, 'the pair of good physicians' (*Iliad*, II. 731–2).

[6] Stephanus of Byzantium, s.v., cited by M. P. Nilsson, *The Mycenaean Origin of Greek Mythology* (Cambridge, 1932, University Press), p. 141.   [7] According to *Iliad*, XVI. 288.

[8] Strabo (*Geographica*, Book VII, fragm. 20, C. 330) identifies the Homeric Ἀμυδών with

whose grandsire is the River Axios himself, is given Ἀκεσσαμενός ('the Healer')[1] for his great-grandsire on his grandmother's side.[2]

It would, indeed, be natural enough that a people which had picked out the head of the Gulf of Volo as one site for a settlement should plant a sister-settlement at the head of the Gulf of Salonica, and there is archaeological evidence that bearers of the Mycenaean culture were, in truth, active here. Out of twenty-five sites in the interior of Epirus, in Perrhaibia, and in Macedonia, in which Mycenaean artefacts have been discovered so far,[3] three are on or near the coast of Anthemous (the valley, running from east to west, that debouches into the Gulf of Salonica to the south of the city); three are on the west coast of Khalkidike; one is on the south coast of Khalkidike, at the head of the Gulf of Torone; one lies north-north-east of Salonica, on the route leading to the western end of the depression containing Lake Bolbe (Beşik Göl); and no less than eight are strung along the lower valley of the River Axios. Of these eight sites, two—Saratse[4] and Vardarophtsa (alias Axiokhórion)[5] —are of outstanding importance. Saratse 'produced Mycenaean pottery in relatively large quantity (Heurtley, *P.M.*,[6] p. 124), and it is inferred from this, and from similar evidence at Vardarophtsa, that there were actually Mycenaean coastal and riverside trading stations in Macedonia. The earliest Mycenaean pottery here appears to be L.H. III A 2.'[7] As for Vardarophtsa, 'this mound, on the bank of the Axios, may have been a secondary centre of manufacture and distribution for Mycenaean pottery (Heurtley, *P.M.*, p. 124). . . . The earliest Mycenaean sherds are L.H. III B.'[8] Either Vardarophtsa or Saratse may well be the Amydon of the *Iliad*.

Where was the centre of dispersion from which the Minyai radiated to these four widely scattered points in continental European Greece?

an historical fortress called Ἀβυδών which overlooked the lower valley of the Axios. Cp. fragm. 20a, 23, and 23d.

[1] According to the Macedonian authority Theagenes, cited by Steph. Byz., s.v. Ἀκεσσαμεναί, there was a city of this name in Macedon, which Akessamenos had founded. The cult of the god of healing will have been communicated to the Paiones by the Pelagones, who had become neighbours of the Paiones through migrating from north-eastern Thessaly to the Axios basin (see Part II, chap. 4, pp. 81–5 and 120–1). In Greek minds, the god came to be identified with the Paiones so intimately that the ethnikon 'Païan' became, for the Greeks, the epithet of Apollo in his capacity as the healer.

[2] *Iliad*, XXI. 140–3.

[3] See R. Hope Simpson, *A Gazetteer and Atlas of Mycenaean Sites* (London, 1965, Institute of Classical Studies, Bulletin Supplement No. 16), pp. 171–7, with Figure 2: 'Mycenaean Penetration in North Greece'.

[4] No. 17 in Hope Simpson's list of sites in northern Greece where Mycenaean artefacts have been found.

[5] No. 20 in Hope Simpson's list.

[6] i.e. W. A. Heurtley, *Prehistoric Macedonia* (Cambridge, 1939, University Press).

[7] Hope Simpson, *Gazetteer and Atlas*, p. 175.

[8] Ibid., pp. 175–6.

Three out of the four points lie on the coast; two of these—namely Iolkos and the hypothetical Minyan settlement at the mouth of the Axios —are ideal sites for commercial entrepôts between the Aegean Archipelago and its continental European hinterland; and the fourth Minyan settlement, Orkhomenos, which is the only one of the four that lies inland, is at the same time situated at the key-point of one of the portages between the Aegean Sea and the Corinthian Gulf. (The spur of Mount Akontios, on which the city of Orkhomenos stands, commands the passage across the River Kephisos for anybody travelling overland from the Aegean port of Larymna, on the Euripos, to the Corinthian-Gulf port of Kyrrha, at the head of the Bay of Krisa.) We may therefore conjecture that the Minyai were a maritime commercial people who came by sea to the three—or perhaps four—points on the Continent at which we find their settlements.

From what base of operations overseas did the Minyai come? If we take the resemblance between the names Μινύαι and Μίνωες as an indication that they came from Crete, we shall find independent legendary evidence of a Cretan origin for all four of the Minyan settlements. In the case of Iolkos, we may notice that the legendary name of Amythaon's father is Κρηθεύς. In the case of Orkhomenos, we may notice that the route from Orkhomenos to the head of the Crisaean Gulf passes, via the famous σχιστὴ ὁδός, through Delphi; and that, in the Homeric *Hymn to Apollo*, the historical Delphians are represented as being the descendants of a ship's company of Κρῆτες ἀπὸ Κνωσοῦ Μινωίου,[1] whose ship the god himself wafts to Krisa in order that these Cretans may settle at Delphi to preside over the Apollinean worship there. A connection between Crete and Pylos is suggested in the point, incidentally mentioned in the Hymn,[2] that this Cretan ship was originally bound on a commercial venture from Crete to Pylos, and was only diverted to Krisa from its intended destination by the supernatural intervention of the god. The Cretan origin of our hypothetical Minyan settlement at the head of the Gulf of Salonica is suggested by the Hellenic tradition which ascribes a Cretan origin to the Βοττιαῖοι; for these Bottiaeans were the people who were found in possession of the lowlands at the head of the Gulf by the Chalcidian Greek colonists who settled in the neighbourhood in the seventh century B.C. and by the Macedonian Greek conquerors who descended upon this same coast from the continental hinterland at about the same date.[3]

On this showing, the Minyai may be regarded as having been Minoan

---

[1] *Hymn to Apollo*, l. 393.
[2] *Hymn to Apollo*, ll. 397–9 and 469–70.
[3] See Aristotle, fragm. 485 Rose; Strabo, Book VI, chap. 3, § 2 (C. 279) and § 6 (C. 282); Book VII, frs. 11 and 11ª (C. 329); Plutarch, *Theseus*, chap. 16; *Quaestiones Graecae*, chap. 35.

pioneers who settled at these four points on the mainland of European Greece. But here a difficulty suggests itself. The results of Western archaeological research would appear to show that Pylos, Orkhomenos, Iolkos, and Amydon were all alike situated on the outermost fringe of the Minoan–Mycenaean World. The map of the distribution of the Mycenaean culture on the mainland, as it is revealed by the archaeological evidence up to date, seems now unlikely to be modified appreciably by future discoveries. We have therefore to ask ourselves why the Minoans should have chosen to plant their colonies so far afield, instead of planting them on those coasts of continental Greece that lay nearest to Crete.

Perhaps we may obtain an answer to this question by asking ourselves the corresponding question about the colonies which were planted upon continental Greek coasts, in the course of Hellenic history, by the Hellenic thalassocrats of Chalcis and Corinth. Why did the Chalcidians sail right out of the northern end of the Euripos, and then on past the dangerous coast of Magnesia, in order to plant their overseas Khalkidike, at last, ἐπὶ Θρᾴκης? And why did the Corinthians sail right out of their own gulf in order to plant their colonies on the coasts of Akarnania and Epirus? In these cases the answer is fairly clear. A colonizing Power can plant its colonies only on the territories of peoples who are so inferior to the intruders in culture that they are incapable of self-defence. But the immediate neighbours of the Chalcidians and the Corinthians were fellow Hellenes; and for one Hellenic community to attempt the subjugation of another was a superhumanly formidable undertaking for psychological as well as for material reasons. The inadvisability of making the attempt is illustrated by the history of the Spartan conquest of Messene and its sequel.[1] The Chalcidians and Corinthians showed their greater prudence by letting their Hellenic neighbours alone. In their voyages in search of new lands for Chalcidian and Corinthian ploughs, they did not put to shore till they had reached and passed the bounds of the Hellenic World as these bounds stood at the time. It is only at the outermost edge of the Hellenic World of the seventh century B.C. that the Chalcidian and Corinthian colonial areas begin.

[1] Medieval Western history gives an illustration in the shape of the policy and fortunes of the Teutonic Knights. So long as the Teutonic Knights confined their enterprise to the subjugation of the heathen Prussians and Lithuanians and Letts and Ests, right beyond the north-eastern pale of Western Christendom, the Order prospered. The trouble which was to end in disaster can be traced to the moment when the Teutonic Knights turned their arms against their own fellow Western Christians nearer home, in Pomerania. They ventured upon this fratricidal warfare because the Poles in the thirteenth century, like the English two centuries earlier, at the time of the Norman Conquest, were still only in the penumbra of the Western civilization. Yet, even so, the Poles were too little inferior in culture to the aggressive Teutonic Knights to submit tamely to a fate which was resisted desperately even by the heathen Prussians. The Poles fought for their existence with all the determination of the Messenians in their struggle against Sparta, and ultimately with a success which the Messenians never achieved.

On this analogy we may conjecture that the Cretan colonies at Pylos and Orkhomenos and Iolkos and Amydon were planted at the outer edge of the Minoan–Mycenaean World of the day at a time when the regions of continental European Greece that were less distant from Crete had already become the seat of a higher civilization—partly, perhaps, under the stimulus of Minoan cultural influences which had radiated out of Minoan Crete without any physical transfusion of blood from the island to the mainland, and possibly also partly as a result of earlier colonization which had proceeded not from Crete itself but from some of the other islands in the Aegean Archipelago which were cradles of other varieties of the Aegean civilization. For example, Perseus, who is the mythical founder of Mycenae, is brought by the legend to Argos from Seriphos;[1] and Kadmos, the eponym of the Καδμεῖοι who are the mythical occupants of Boeotian Thebes in the Pre-Hellenic Heroic Age, is brought by the legend to Thebes from Thera.[2] We may therefore perhaps picture our Minoan colonists from Crete as planting their colony of 'Minyan' Orkhomenos just beyond the radius of the 'Cadmean' colony which had been planted at Boeotian Thebes by earlier settlers from a sister Aegean island. Moreover, there are a number of correspondences between place-names and cult-names that survived into Hellenic times in the 'Cadmean' part of Boeotia on the one hand and on the other hand in a district along the west coast of the Gulf of Volo which in Hellenic times was called the Phthiotic Akhaïa.[3] These correspondences suggest that 'Cadmean' colonists from the Cyclades may have founded the Phthiotic Thebes on the west coast of the Gulf of Volo at the same time as the Boeotian Thebes in Central Greece, and that the 'Minyan'

[1] See Nilsson, op. cit., pp. 40–1. The legend, of course, makes Perseus come from Argos originally, so that he withdraws from Argos in infancy in order to return to his birthplace in his manhood. For our present purpose, we may regard Perseus as the mythical representative of some social movement which brought a higher culture to the Argolid from Seriphos. In the Hellenic Age the island of Seriphos was so unimportant and obscure that nobody would have thought of making the founder of Mycenae come from Seriphos unless his Seriphian origin was already an established feature of the legend. It was doubtless just because of this obscurity of Seriphos that Perseus was now said merely to have been brought up there and to have been born in Argos itself. In the Hellenic Age it would have seemed incredible that culture should ever have originated in Seriphos and spread thence to Argos at second hand. To us, with the knowledge of early Aegean culture which we have obtained through archaeological discoveries, a Seriphian origin of Mycenaean culture is not incredible at all, since it is quite in harmony with the archaeological evidence.

[2] Herodotus, Book IV, chap. 147.

[3] In both Cadmean Boeotia and Phthiotic Akhaïa there were places called Θῆβαι and Κορώνεια. In Cadmean Boeotia there was a cult of an Athena who was called 'Ιτωνία after a place named 'Ιτών in Phthiotic Akhaïa; and, conversely, in Phthiotic Akhaïa, at Halos, there was a cult of a Zeus who was called Λαφύστιος after a mountain named Λαφύστιον in Cadmean Boeotia. These correspondences seem too numerous to be accidental. If they do point to a Cadmean settlement in Thessaly, perhaps we may find an echo of this in Herodotus' statement that the ancestors of the Dorians of central Greece were driven out of the Thessalian district of Histiaiotis by Cadmeans (Herodotus, Book I, chap. 56).

colonists from Crete, who followed in the Cadmeans' wake, may have planted their Iolkos just beyond the Phthiotic Thebes in the one direction, as they planted their Orkhomenos just beyond the Boeotian Thebes in the other.

There is yet a third Thebes to be taken into account: the Asian Θήβη Ὑποπλακίη which lies at the southern foot of Mount Ida at the head of the Gulf of Edremid;[1] and, here again, we find a Minyan settlement in the offing, on the Island of Lemnos. Between the Asian and the Phthiotic Thebes there is no known connection beyond the bare identity of name. There seems to be no attempt to bring the two places into any historical relation with each other in the Hellenic tradition. On the other hand, the Minyai of Lemnos are presented in the *Iliad* as an off-shoot of the Minyai of Iolkos. The King of Lemnos at the time of the Siege of Troy is described as being a son of Jason, the Minyan hero from Iolkos who was the legendary leader of the Argonauts.[2] Perhaps, in spite of the legendary voyage of the Argonauts from Iolkos to Kolkhis and back, 'Jason' never really sailed farther from Iolkos than Lemnos, after all! Perhaps the Minyan principality on Lemnos and the Asian city of Thebes are the respective relics of two rival attempts, by the Minyan and the Cadmean settlers in the Gulf of Volo, to force their way up through the Dardanelles into the Black Sea—attempts which both alike failed because Troy was then still standing to bar the passage through the Straits against all interlopers.

[1] See W. Leaf, *Troy: A Study in Homeric Geography* (London, 1912, Macmillan), pp. 213–16.
[2] *Iliad*, VII. 468–9, and XXI. 41. See further Part II, chap. 7, pp. 118–19.

3. Who were the Achaeans? And who were the Dorians?

IN the Greece of the Hellenic Age—that is to say, the age subsequent to the post-Mycenaean Völkerwanderung—there were two peoples that bore the name 'Achaeans' (Ἀχαιοί). One of these two was then in occupation of the north coast of the Peloponnese between Elis on the west and Sikyon on the east (both exclusive). The other was in occupation of the Phthiotic Akhaïa, a satellite of Thessaly which divided with the Thessalian tetrarchy Phthiotis the region that is called Phthia in the Homeric Catalogue of the contingents of Agamemnon's expeditionary force[1] and in other passages of the *Iliad* and the *Odyssey*.[2] The Greek inscriptions that have been found in these two territories to which the name Akhaïa attached in the Hellenic Age show that, in this age, their inhabitants spoke the North-West-Greek dialect.[3] Since the post-Mycenaean Völkerwanderung, the area in which this dialect was spoken had come to extend diagonally across continental European Greece and the Aegean Sea from Epirus on the north-west as far south-eastwards as the south-west corner of Anatolia, together with the adjacent islands (Rhodes and the Dodecanese). We may guess that this dialect was carried that far south-eastwards by the people who took part in the post-Mycenaean Völkerwanderung, and that it was this people's mother-tongue.

The name 'Achaeans' also figures in Hittite and Egyptian official documents of the fourteenth and thirteenth centuries B.C. These documents do not enable us to locate the home of these Pre-Hellenic-Age Achaeans precisely; but the Hittite documents make it clear that these Achaeans were a considerable power—a power with which the Hittite Empire had to deal on a footing of equality—while both the Hittite and the Egyptian documents show that these same Achaeans made naval expeditions in the Levant. This contemporary non-Greek evidence about the pre-Völkerwanderung Achaeans is supplemented by the retrospective picture of the pre-Völkerwanderung Greek World that is

[1] *Iliad*, II. 683.   [2] See Part I, chap. i, pp. 9–11.
[3] See Leaf, *Homer and History*, p. 333; K. J. Beloch, *Griechische Geschichte*, 2nd ed., Erster Band, Erste Abteilung (Strassburg, 1912, Trübner), p. 88. Ibid., Zweite Abteilung (1913), pp. 89–90, Beloch notes that North-West Greek was the language of the Italiot Achaeans (who were presumably colonists of the Peloponnesian Achaeans) in the fifth century B.C., and that it was also the language of the Phthiotic Achaeans towards the close of the third century B.C. Beloch argues convincingly that, though this inscriptional evidence is late, the language of the inscriptions must have been the Phthiotic Achaeans' ancestral native language. They would not have learnt to speak North-West Greek from their former Thessalian overlords, who were North-East-Greek-speaking, nor from their recent Aetolian overlords, who did speak North-West Greek, but whose hegemony over the Phthiotic Akhaïa had been ephemeral.

given in the Homeric epic. Here the name 'Achaeans' is used, side by side with two other names, 'Danaans' and 'Argives', to describe collectively the peoples that were under the suzerainty of King Agamemnon of Mycenae and that contributed contingents to Agamemnon's expeditionary force.[1] According to the Catalogue, the states from which these contingents came covered the greater part of continental European Greece (including Thessaly, but excluding Epirus, Macedon, and Paionia). They also included Rhodes and the Dodecanese and part, at least, of Crete. This area is approximately conterminous with the area within which our archaeologists have found material relics of the pre-Hellenic civilization that has been labelled 'Mycenaean' because Mycenae seems to have been its most important site. We may guess that the Achaeans of the Homeric epic and those of the Hittite and Egyptian documents are one and the same people, and that the Mycenaean civilization was theirs.

Were these Pre-Hellenic-Age Mycenaean Achaeans the same people as the Hellenic-Age Achaeans in the northern Peloponnese and in south-eastern Thessaly? They bear the same name, but they seem to have spoken a different dialect of the Greek language. Whereas the Hellenic-Age Achaeans spoke North-West Greek, the people whose civilization was the Mycenaean civilization, and whom we have identified with the Achaeans of the Hittite and Egyptian records and of the Homeric epic, spoke an archaic form of the Arcado-Cyprian dialect. This has proved to be the language of the documents, written in the Cretan Linear B script, that have been found at Knossos and at Pylos.

Can this difference of dialect between the Post-Völkerwanderung-Age

---

[1] See Part I, chap. 1, p. 6, n. 5. In *Iliad*, IX. 141 and 283, XIX. 115, and *Odyssey*, III. 251, Ἄργος Ἀχαϊκόν appears to mean the domain of the rulers of Mycenae, both Perseid and Pelopid. In *Iliad*, XIX. 193 and XXIII. 236, and in *Odyssey*, I. 239 and XIV. 369, πάναχαιοί means the whole host of the peoples serving in Agamemnon's expeditionary force. The same generic meaning is to be found in the Ἀχαῖδες of *Iliad*, IX. 395, in the Ἀχαῖδα of *Iliad*, III. 75 and 258 and XI. 770; in the Ἀχαῖδος αἴης of *Odyssey*, XIII. 249; and in the Ἀχαῖδα γαῖαν of *Odyssey*, XXI. 107. As members of the confederacy of peoples under Pelopid hegemony, the Cephallenian nobles are called Ἀχαιοί in a number of passages in the *Odyssey*: e.g. I. 272, 286, 394; II. 7; XVI. 250; XVII. 413 and 415; XVIII. 301; XIX. 528 and 534; XX. 146 and 160; XXI. 344; XXIII. 357; XXIV. 141, 426, 438. Ἀχαῖδες is used similarly in XXI. 251 to mean Cephallenian ladies.

There is a parallel to this usage of the name 'Achaean', as a comprehensive label for the principalities of Mycenaean Greece, in the usage of the names 'Frank' and 'Latin' as comprehensive labels for the principalities of medieval Greece between its conquest by the Crusaders in and after the year A.D. 1204 and its subsequent conquest by the Ottoman Turks in the course of the fourteenth and fifteenth centuries. In the thirteenth, fourteenth, and fifteenth centuries of the Christian era, as in the fourteenth, thirteenth, and twelfth centuries B.C., the population of Greece was Greek-speaking; but in those medieval centuries the majority, though not all, of the rulers of Greece were 'Franks' or 'Latins'. These 'Franks' or 'Latins' were Romance-speaking Westerners of various nationalities: Burgundian, Champenois, Venetian, Genoese, Catalan, Florentine; but, in the course of time, the 'Franks' or 'Latins' lost ground to Greek reconquerors and to 'Osmanli conquerors of parts of Greece that had previously fallen under 'Frankish' ('Latin') rule.

Achaeans and the Pre-Völkerwanderung-Age Achaeans be accounted for? It can be, on the hypothesis that the pre-Völkerwanderung Achaeans who lived in the Mycenaean World and who gave their name to it were an aristocracy of North-West-Greek speakers, who had established their domination over an Arcado-Cyprian-Greek-speaking population in the Peloponnese and a North-East-Greek-speaking population in central Greece and Thessaly. The subject majority could have acquired the dominant minority's national name, while the dominant minority could have adopted the majority's civilization and dialect.[1]

In favour of this hypothesis, we can cite a suggestive, though inconclusive, piece of evidence. The personal names of some of the pre-Völkerwanderung Greek heroes are identical with the national names of some of the North-West-Greek-speaking peoples of the Post-Völkerwanderung Age. Among the members of the House of Atreus, for instance, Thyestes bears the name of one historical Upper Macedonian highland people, the Dyestai;[2] Orestes bears the name of another, the Orestai; Aigisthos' name is a synonym for the national name 'Thesprotian'.[3] Lynkos, the country of the Lynkestai, has given its name to Lynkeus. Athamas bears the name of the Athamanes in Pindus and the Odomantoi on the east bank of the lower Strymon. Amphilokhos bears the name of the Amphilokhoi of Amphilochian Argos. Epeios, the builder of the Trojan Horse, bears the name of the Epeioi, the masters of Elis. Thessalos, the father of the two leaders of the Dodecanesian contingent in Agamemnon's host, bears the name of the Thessaloi. Achilles (Achilleus), who has given his name to the River Akheloïos, may have derived it from a people that, in the Hellenic Age, was living somewhere on the shore of Lake Lykhnidos and perhaps also on the eastern shore of the Adriatic, and whose national name has been rationalized, for this reason, into 'Enkhelanes'[4] and 'Enkheleis'[5] ('Eel-men').[6]

---

[1] The 'Frankish' rulers of Greece took to speaking and writing the Greek language that was spoken by their subjects, though their mother-tongue was not another Greek dialect but was a completely different language. *The Chronicle of the Morea*, for instance, which is written in Greek in 'Constantinopolitan' verse, is thought to be the work of a feudal lawyer of French extraction.

[2] For the location of the Dyestai, see Strabo, *Geographica*, Book VII, chap. 7, § 8 (C. 326), as emended by Meineke. See further the present work, Part II, chap. 4, p. 80.

[3] Αἰγεσταῖοι· οἱ Θεσπρωτοί (Steph. Byz.).

[4] 'Enkhelanes' in Polybius, Book V, chap. 108, § 8. King Philip V of Macedon conquered, in 217 B.C., some places round the shores of Lake Lykhnidos, including Ἐγχελᾶνες. Polybius also mentioned the Enkheleai according to Stephanus of Byzantium, s.v. Ἄρπυια—but this, apparently, apropos of a myth, and not in connection with an historical event. According to Steph. Byz., s.v. Ἐγχελᾶνες, the Enkhelanes and the Enkheleai were explicitly identified with each other by Mnaseas in his *Periegeses*, Book III.

[5] 'Enkheleis' in Herodotus, Book V, chap. 61, and Book IX, chap. 43, and in Pseudo-Scylax, § 25; 'Enkheleoi' in pseudo-Scymnus, l. 436, and in Strabo, *Geographica*, Book VII, chap. 7, § 8 (C. 326); 'Encheleae' in Pliny, *Historia Naturalis*, Book III, chap. 21, § 139.

[6] None of these notices of the Enkheleis makes their exact location clear. Pseudo-Scylax

It will be noticed that the national names that are borne as personal names by princes in the Mycenaean World are the names of peoples whose homes were on the far side of the Mycenaean World's nearest North-West-Greek-speaking neighbours the Achaeans. In the time before the post-Mycenaean Völkerwanderung, these peoples must have been living still farther to the north than they were in the Post-Völkerwanderung Age. We may presume that Mycenaean princes of this more remote north-western origin were rarities, and that therefore the national names of the peoples from which they were descended were uncommon enough in the Mycenaean World to serve as distinctive personal names there.

The use of the name 'Achaeans' as a generic name for the peoples under Agamemnon's hegemony indicates that a majority of the leaders of these peoples were of Achaean descent. It is true that some of them were non-Achaean, e.g. the Minyai who ruled at Pylos, at Orkhomenos in central Greece, and at Iolkos, and the Kadmeioi who had ruled at Thebes in central Greece and perhaps also at the other Thebes in Phthia. The Pelopids themselves are said to have been of Asian origin, either from Paphlagonia[1] (the Hittite 'Pala') or from Lydia; and it was only in the generation immediately before Agamemnon's own that they had replaced the Perseids at Mycenae as the rulers of the Peloponnesian Argos. However, leaders of Achaean descent seem to have been in the majority; so, if all princes had been given their national name as their personal name, perhaps four out of every five of them would have been

appears to place them on the coast between the Bocche di Cattaro and Budua, Pseudo-Scymnus and Strabo appear to place them in the interior. Scymnus, in one of his erratic excursions from a familiar coast into an unfamiliar interior, puts the Enkheleis on the inland side of the (western) Brygoi (l. 436), who are, themselves, an inland people (l. 433). Hecataeus associates them with the Δέξαροι Χάονες (Steph. Byz. s.v. Δέξαροι). Strabo appears to identify the Enkheleoi with the Sesarethioi, and Hecataeus places Sesarethos in Taulantia (Steph. Byz., s.v. Σεσαρῆθος). For the Dexaroi and Sesarethioi, see further Part II, chap. 4, p. 80, n. 6, and chap. 6, p. 107, n. 7. Pomponius Mela, *Chorographia*, Book II, chap. 3, § 55, places the Encheleae between the Taulantii and the Phaeaces! This vagueness in the location of the Encheleis, taken together with the fact that, in the Post-Völkerwanderung Age of Greek history, their chief title to fame was that they had once been ruled by Kadmos and Harmonia, might lead one to suspect that they had perished in the post-Mycenaean Völkerwanderung and had lived on only in folk-memory. The Kadmos–Harmonia legend was associated with the Enkheleis already by Herodotus' time (Herodotus, Book V, chap. 61), and it has bedevilled the history and location of the Makednoi (Herodotus, Book I, chap. 56) and the Brygoi, besides the Enkheleis. Pseudo-Scylax's and Pseudo-Scymnus' locations of the Enkheleis at two widely separated points on the Illyrian coast may be nothing more than a tribute to the popularity of the Kadmos–Harmonia ('Law and Order') legend among Greek mariners (see, for example, Steph. Byz., s.v. Ἄρπυια and s.v. Βουθόη). However, Polybius' mention of the conquest of Enkhelanes on Lake Lykhnidos by Philip V in 217 B.C. shows that at least a remnant of this people was then still extant. The evidence, such as it is, for the location of the Encheleis is examined by J. M. F. May in *The Coinage of Damastion and the Lesser Coinages of the Illyro-Paeonian Region* (London, 1939, Oxford University Press), pp. 20–4.

[1] See Istros in *F.H.G.*, i. 426, and Diodorus, Book IV, chap. 74.

named 'Akhaios', and this name would have been useless in the Mycenaean World for a personal name's purpose, which is to provide a
monogram for identifying an individual.[1]

As Leaf sees it, the Achaean rulers of the Mycenaean World were 'new-
comers, interlopers'.[2] They were 'military adventurers'.[3] They 'were
descended from soldiers of fortune who had begun by occuping Pleuron
and Kalydon three generations back, and in the next had entered the
Peloponnesos'.[4] The Achaean conquest of Greece was 'the work of a
small number of determined men, perhaps only a few thousands all
told—the displacement of one ruling caste by another, involving little
destruction, not even much slaughter'.[5] Probably they 'were no more
than a small military caste, living in the castles from which they ruled
a subject population'.[6] 'The conquered country was annexed, not by
any occupation of the whole, but by the mere holding of strategic
points and lines of communication.'[7]

'They would be continually augmented by fresh arrivals from the
north, whence the pressure of migration still continued.'[8] Eventually, as
we know, this pressure from the Achaeans' kinsmen in the north-western
hinterland of the Mycenaean World became a threat to the Achaean
rulers of Mycenaean Greece, and the denouement was a mass-migration
of the Achaean rearguard (followed by its own non-Achaean rearguard)
which overwhelmed the Achaean advanceguard and, with it, the
Mycenaean civilization. By that time the Achaean rulers of the Mycenaean
World were on the defensive against their own backwoodsmen and were
fighting a losing battle to resist the backwoodsmen's mounting pressure.
Originally, however, the first concern of the Achaean adventurers in
the Mycenaean World seems to have been to eke out their insufficient
numbers by obtaining reinforcements.

The most desirable reinforcements were those that the Achaean
princes could gain at each other's expense; for such recruits would be
seasoned and experienced men of their own kind, not semi-barbarians
imported from the back of beyond.

The most welcome recruit of their own kind would be a promising,

---

[1] The national name 'Akhaios' does appear as a personal name in the fourth century B.C.
at Europos in eastern Lower Macedon. It was used in a collateral line of the House of Seleucus,
and, at this time and place, it will have been distinctive; for, in fourth-century-B.C. Macedon,
Achaeans—whether from the Phthiotic Akhaïa or from the Peloponnesian Akhaïa—will
have been rarities. Pict and Scot soldiers of fortune will likewise have been rare enough in
Late Roman Italy, and Alan settlers rare enough in Late Roman Gaul, for these national
names to be distinctive enough there to be used as personal names. Hence the aristocratic
names 'Pitti' and 'Scotti' in medieval Italy, and the Christian name 'Alan' and surname
'Allen' in present-day Britain—both derived, no doubt, from the French name 'Alain'.

[2] *Homer and History*, p. 225.   [3] Ibid., p. 251.
[4] Ibid., p. 257.   [5] Ibid., p. 52.   [6] Ibid., pp. 53–4.
[7] Ibid., p. 52.   [8] Ibid., p. 58; cp. p. 59.

even if not yet already distinguished, man who had had to leave his home principality because he had become an outlaw there.[1] The need to seek asylum sometimes proved to be the road to fortune. Among the outstanding warriors in Agamemnon's expeditionary force, the illustrious exiles were conspicuous. There was Patroklos, an exile from Opous, who had been given asylum in Phthia by Peleus.[2] There was Phoinix, an exile from Hellas, who had likewise been given asylum in Phthia by Peleus.[3] Epeigeus, an exile from Boudeion, had been given asylum by Peleus too.[4] Then there was Diomedes, whose father Tydeus of Pleuron and Kalydon had been given asylum in Argos by Adrastos.[5] There was Lykophron, an exile from Kythera, who had been given asylum at Salamis by Ajax.[6] There was Medon, an exile from Lokris, who had been given asylum at Phylake by Protesilaos and had taken service with Philoktetes.[7] In the post-war years, there was Theoklymenos of Argos, whom Telemachus took on board with him when he was sailing home to Ithaca from Pylos.[8]

An eligible outlaw was a windfall. But a far-sighted Achaean prince would not be content to depend, for reinforcements, solely on such human flotsam and jetsam. He would take the initiative in procuring reinforcements, and he would recruit, not isolated individuals in misfortune, but entire war-bands who might be attracted by an opportunity for bettering their position.

For instance, Menelaos told Telemachus that he had intended to offer to Odysseus a new home in Argos and to invite him to migrate thither from Ithaca with his family, property, and retainers. To give Odysseus vacant possession, Menelaos would have sacked one of the neighbouring cities that were under his rule.[9] This high-handed procedure would have been to Menelaos's advantage. He would have been replacing a community of sullen subjects by a band of congenial comrades whose loyalty to him would have been assured by their common interest in maintaining the Achaean dominant minority's privileged position *vis-à-vis* the non-Achaean subject majority in Menelaos' principality. The balance of numbers would thus have been altered in the minority's favour.

Agamemnon did actually offer to give to Achilles seven cities at—

---

[1] *Iliad*, XXIV. 480–2. See Leaf, *Homer and History*, pp. 252–5. Cp. p. 234.
[2] *Iliad*, XXIII. 84–92. [3] *Iliad*, IX. 437–84.
[4] *Iliad*, XVI. 570–6. [5] *Iliad*, XIV. 113–27.
[6] *Iliad*, XV. 430–2. [7] *Iliad*, II. 727–8; XIII. 694–7; XV. 333–6.
[8] *Odyssey*, XV. 223–86.
[9] καί κέ οἱ Ἄργεϊ νάσσα πόλιν καὶ δώματ' ἔτευξα,
ἐξ Ἰθάκης ἀγαγὼν σὺν κτήμασι καὶ τέκεϊ ᾧ
καὶ πᾶσιν λαοῖσι, μίαν πόλιν ἐξαλαπάξας
αἳ περιναιετάουσιν ἀνάσσονται δ' ἐμοὶ αὐτῷ.
Odyssey, IV. 174–7.

or possibly beyond—the south-western extremity of the Pelopids' domain.[1] He did not propose to evict their inhabitants. Achilles would find it profitable to retain them and to exploit them; for they were rich.[2] If Achilles had been willing to accept this compensation for the wrong that Agamemnon had done to him, Agamemnon would have gained a twofold advantage. He would have appeased his principal ally, and he would have notably reinforced the dominant Achaean minority in his own principality.

Nestor, or his father Neleus, had successfully negotiated a transaction of this kind at some date before the Achaean expedition to the Troad. In the Catalogue, Oikhalia, the city of Eurytos, appears twice over—first in, or next door to, the principality of Pylos,[3] and then in the future Histiaiotis.[4] Since Eurytos' son Iphitos appears in Messene in the *Odyssey*,[5] and since the place-name Ithome, with which Oikhalia is associated in the second mention of it in the Catalogue, is found only in Messene on the post-Völkerwanderung map of Greece, it might have been supposed that the Thessalian Oikhalia is a fiction or an error, if the presence of Eurytos in pre-Völkerwanderung Thessaly were not attested, as it is, by the survival of his people, the Eurytanes, in the Post-Völkerwanderung Age, as refugees in a mountain fastness in Aetolia. The historicity of the Oikhalia in Messene is vouched for by documentary evidence. In the Linear B document, setting out the disposition of the Pylian land-forces, the detachment from Ku-pa-ri-so is associated with the O-ka-rai:[6] i.e. in an alphabetic rendering, instead of a syllabic one, the men of Oikhalia are brigaded with the men of Kyparissia. This piece of evidence establishes the historicity of the Messenian Oikhalia beyond question; but the historicity of the Thessalian Oikhalia—and of the Thessalian Ithome too—need not be impugned on that account.[7] All our pieces of information can be reconciled with each other on the supposition that Eurytos' son Iphitos, if not Eurytos himself, had accepted an invitation from the prince of Pylos to transplant an apodasmos of the Eurytanes to Pylos' eastern march and to found a new Oikhalia there.

There are indications that, after the return from Troy, Nestor may also have planted a second apodasmos of the pre-Völkerwanderung population of north-western Thessaly in a location farther to the south-east than the pre-war new Oikhalia in Messene. According to the

---

[1] See Part I, chap. 1, p. 6, n. 5.　　　　　　　　[2] *Iliad*, IX. 149–57.

[3] *Iliad*, II. 594–6.　　　　　　　　　　　　　　[4] *Iliad*, II. 729–30.

[5] *Odyssey*, XXI. 13–16. Iphitos and Odysseus had met each other, before Odysseus had sailed for Troy, in Messene, in the house of Orsilokhos, i.e. at Pharai.

[6] See Palmer, op. cit., p. 87.

[7] However, we are not called upon to go bail for the historicity of all the five Oikhaliai in Strabo's list in *Geographica*, Book X, chap. 1, § 10 (C. 448). Stephanus, s.v. Οἰχαλία, reports Oikhaliai in Pelasgikon Argos, Euboea, Messene, Trakhis, Thessaly, and Arcadia.

Homeric Catalogue, the people of the Thessalian Oikhalia, together with those of Trikka and of the Thessalian Ithome, were under the command of the two sons of Asklepios, Podaleirios and Makhaon.[1] Since, in this passage, the Thessalian Oikhalia is described as being Eurytos' city, but its people are not under either Eurytos' or his son Iphitos' command, it looks as if the writer of the Catalogue is assuming that, before the expedition to Troy, Eurytos had died and Iphitos had migrated to Messene. After the Trojan War was over, Podaleirios and Makhaon (or their clans if the two men themselves had been war casualties) apparently followed suit to Iphitos, whose family had once been neighbours of the Asklepiadai in Thessaly. In the Post-Völkerwanderung Age, Podaleirios and Makhaon are associated with Gerenia[2] (the city on the western flank of the Tainaron Peninsula from which Nestor derived his epithet), with both Gerenia and Pharai,[3] and with Pharai alone,[4] while their father Asklepios had a temple at Abia.[5]

Since Kardamyle, whose location is known, lies to the south-east of Gerenia, while Abia lies between Gerenia and Pharai, the district in which we find the Asklepiadai installed after the Trojan War lies within the territory, containing the seven cities, that had been offered, during the war, by Agamemnon to Achilles. According to Pausanias,[6] Nestor took control of Messene, except for the Asklepiadai's domain. This is perhaps to be interpreted as meaning that Nestor imposed his suzerainty on Diokles, son of Orsilokhos, the prince with whom Nestor's son Peisistratos and Odysseus' son Telemachus spent the night at Pharai *en route* between Pylos and Lakedaimon, both coming and going.[7] We may guess that, simultaneously, Nestor planted the Asklepiadai immediately to the south-east of Diokles' domain,[8] to serve as a buffer between the Neleid and Pelopid dominions along the east shore of the Messenian Gulf.

When we piece these fragmentary scraps of information together, we catch a glimpse of a competition between the Neleidai and the Pelopidai for control over the territory of the seven cities together with Messene, i.e. the upper and lower basins of the River Pamisos—or, it might be more accurate to say, together with the rest of Messene, since the territory of the seven cities may have counted as being Messenian too. In this competition the Neleids appear to have been the eventual winners, and, if they were, they won by inducing congenial migrants from the north

---

[1] *Iliad*, II. 729–33.
[2] Pausanias, Book III, chap. 26, § 9; Book IV, chap. 3, § 9.
[3] Pausanias, Book IV, chap. 3, § 2.   [4] Ibid., chap. 30, § 3.
[5] Ibid., chap. 30, § 1.   [6] Ibid., chap. 3, § 1.
[7] *Odyssey*, III. 482–90 and XV. 185–8.
[8] For the Messenian principality of the Orsilokhos–Diokles dynasty, see Hope Simpson in *The Annual of the British School at Athens*, vol. 52 (1957), pp. 256–8.

to settle at key-points in the disputed area and to hold these points in
the Neleids' interest. Nestor persuaded Iphitos to found a new Oikhalia
in the upper basin of the Pamisos, and the Asklepiadai to establish themselves at Gerenia (once included in Nestor's own ancestral domain). The
Pelopidai failed to make good Agamemnon's claim to have the seven
cities in his gift, because Agamemnon failed to persuade Achilles to
accept this gift at Agamemnon's hands. As for Menelaos' dream of persuading Odysseus to settle in his domain, this had never even been
translated into a positive offer. In the Mycenaean World on the eve
of the Völkerwanderung, the weakness of the 'Ascendancy' was the
paucity of its man-power; and therefore a prince who was successful in
attracting new recruits would be apt to get the better of a rival whose
invitations were rebuffed.

If the Achaean princes of the Mycenaean World were, in truth, a small
number of adventurers from the Mycenaean World's North-West-Greek-
speaking hinterland, their descent on the Mycenaean World will have
been like the isolated drops of rain that precede and herald a thunder-
storm.[1] After them, the deluge. The sprinkling of barbarian North-West-
Greek-speaking adventurers could be absorbed and assimilated by the
Mycenaean society; but, when these forerunners' fellow clansmen eventually followed them *en masse*, the spate of this North-West-Greek Völkerwanderung manifestly overwhelmed the Mycenaean civilization and
obliterated it.

Archaeological and Homeric evidence enables us to locate approximately the area of the reservoir of North-West-Greek-speaking barbarian
peoples out of which the post-Mycenaean Völkerwanderung discharged
itself. The post-Völkerwanderung dialect-map of the Greek-speaking
World makes it possible for us to trace the course that the Völkerwanderung took and to distinguish the different streams into which it divided
on its way. The land and water routes leading from the reservoir to the
farthest points reached by the Völkerwanderung allow us, in some cases,
to guess the particular route by which a particular migrating people
made its way from its pre-Völkerwanderung to its post-Völkerwanderung
habitat. The landscape of the Greek World is mountainous and intractable, and, before the days of modern civil engineering, there was
only a small choice of routes along which a migrating people could
travel *en masse* with its women and children and flocks and herds. A
notable contribution to the study of the reservoir and the exits from it
has been made by Professor N. G. L. Hammond. His conclusions are
based on first-hand explorations of the topography.[2]

[1] See N. G. L. Hammond, 'Prehistoric Epirus and the Dorian Invasion', in *The Annual of
the British School at Athens*, vol. 32 (1934), pp. 131–79, on p. 171.

[2] See Hammond, ibid., pp. 131–79, and his *Epirus* (Oxford, 1967, Clarendon Press),
pp. 399–407.

As regards the location of the reservoir, Professor Hammond's conclusion is that

The Dorian[1] peoples were situated in an area outside Achaean suzerainty but close to the bounds of Achaean Greece (Achaean solely in the sense = Greece known to Homeric epic).[2] . . . The immediate centres of dispersion presuppose an earlier concentration in Epirus; only on this hypothesis can the Dorian invasion in the general sense and the geographical description of the wandering of the Dorians proper[3] be accepted as lying within the bounds of possibility.[4] . . . The archaeological evidence shows a homogeneous culture with local variations coinciding with the non-Achaean area. . . . The literary evidence and the archaeological evidence are mutually corroborative. . . . With the exception of the Enienes[5] . . . , Achaean Greece stopped east of Pindus, but occupation extended to the mouth of the east-west passes.[6]

In the Catalogue of the contingents in Agamemnon's expeditionary force, the Ainianes, in their pre-Völkerwanderung habitat round Dodona, are associated with the Perrhaiboi in their pre-Völkerwanderung habitat on the River Titaresios[7] (to be identified with one of the north-eastern tributaries of the upper Peneios). The two parts of this principality were connected by the Zygos (Métsovo) Pass. The Confederacy's only other foothold on the mainland of Greece, west of Pindus and north of the Peloponnese, is nuclear Aetolia—an isolated beach-head consisting of a chain of five coastal towns.[8] This is insulated from the Confederacy's domain in central Greece by a gap along the north shore of the Corinthian Gulf corresponding to the post-Völkerwanderung territory of the Western (Ozolian) Locrians. In the opposite direction, along the coast of the mainland to the north-west of nuclear Aetolia, the Confederacy has no foothold at all. Odysseus' principality is confined to the southern Ionian Islands from Zakynthos to Leukas (probably) inclusive. Odysseus is in friendly relations with one mainland people, the Thesprotoi,[9] but the Thesprotoi are not members of Agamemnon's Confederacy and the Taphioi are not only outside the Confederacy but are hostile to both the Thesprotoi and Odysseus' Kephallenes.[10] Even worse than the

---

[1] i.e. North-West-Greek-speaking.—A. J. T.

[2] Hammond, 'Prehistoric Epirus and the Dorian Invasion', p. 147.

[3] i.e. The North-West-Greek-speaking peoples who eventually called themselves Dorians.— A. J. T.   [4] Hammond, loc. cit., p. 155.

[5] The Homeric form of the ethnikon Ainianes.—A. J. T.

[6] Hammond, loc. cit. p. 149. The northern and north-western limits of the area within which Mycenaean sites and Mycenaean artefacts have been discovered stand out clearly in Hope Simpson, *Gazetteer and Atlas*, Figure 2: 'Mycenaean Penetration in Northern Greece', together with the general map in the pocket at the end of the book.

[7] *Iliad*, Book II. 748–55.

[8] *Iliad*, II. 638–44.

[9] *Odyssey*, XVI. 427. Cp. II. 328 (Ephyra).

[10] *Odyssey*, XVI. 426; cp. XV. 427–9. For details see Hammond, 'Prehistoric Epirus and the Dorian Invasion,' pp. 147–50.

Taphioi is the ogre King Ekhetos on the mainland.[1] It will be seen that
the area in north-western Greece that lies outside Agamemnon's Confederacy and beyond the bounds of the Mycenaean society and civilization covers post-Völkerwanderung Western Lokris, the whole interior
of post-Völkerwanderung Aetolia, the whole of Akarnania, and the
whole of Epirus except for a salient of Gouneus' principality which
projects into Epirus from the east, over the Zygos Pass, as far as Dodona
inclusive.[2] This is the area out of which the post-Mycenaean Völkerwanderung issued.

The post-Völkerwanderung dialect-map of the Greek-speaking World
displays a thrust of North-West-Greek-speaking peoples, echeloned
diagonally across the Greek-speaking World from the north-west corner
of European Greece to the islands and peninsulas of the south-west
corner of Anatolia, with an outpost, round the corner, in Pamphylia.
This thrust has pushed some of the Ionic-Greek-speakers and North-East-
Greek-speakers into the Aegean islands and on to the west coast of Anatolia, to the north-east of the North-West-Greek dialect's thrust. The only
Ionic-speakers now surviving on the mainland of European Greece are
those in Attica. The surviving North-East-Greek-speakers on the mainland have been split, by the thrust of the North-West-Greek-speakers,
into a fraction in Thessaly and a fraction in Boeotia; and, in both Boeotia
and south-western Thessaly, there has been a strong infusion of North-
West Greek into the local variety of the North-East-Greek dialect. The
speakers of the Greek dialect of the Pylos and Knossos Linear B tablets—
a dialect which, in the Pre-Völkerwanderung Age, was presumably
spoken all over the Peloponnese—is now confined, there, to Arcadia
and Triphylia, while other speakers of it have been pushed right off the
Peloponnese as far afield as Cyprus.

When we examine the area in which North-West Greek was spoken
in the Post-Völkerwanderung Age, we can distinguish several different
routes along which this dialect must have been carried to its post-
Völkerwanderung locations.

One route was evidently by sea. The Taphian pirates were seafarers;
and the expected invasion against which the principality of Pylos was
taking defensive measures *circa* 1200 B.C., on the evidence of the tablets,
was an invasion from the north by sea, not overland. On the dialect-map
of the Peloponnese in the Post-Völkerwanderung Age, the areas in the
Peloponnese in which North-West Greek has now come to be spoken
do not form one single continuous block. There is a northern North-West-
Greek-speaking area which includes Elis, the Peloponnesian Akhaïa, the
Argolid, the Corinthia, and the Megarid. There is also a southern

---

[1] *Odyssey*, XVIII. 85–7 and 115–16; XXI. 306–9.
[2] *Iliad*, II. 748–55.

North-West-Greek-speaking area consisting of Messenia and Laconia. The two areas are insulated from each other by a continuous belt of territory, stretching from the west coast to the east coast through Triphylia, Arcadia, and Kynouria, in which the Arcado-Cyprian dialect survived the Völkerwanderung. It is, of course, possible that the immigrants who brought the North-West-Greek dialect into the southern Peloponnese may have made their way thither overland from the northern Peloponnese either up the Alpheios valley from Elis or across Mount Parnon from the Argolid, but, if this had been their route, they might have been expected to occupy Triphylia and south-western Arcadia, or, alternatively, Kynouria, on their way. The survival of the Arcado-Cyprian dialect in these districts suggests that the invasion which carried the North-West-Greek dialect into Messenia and Laconia, and perhaps also into western Crete, was sea-borne, and that its starting-point was on the coast of Akarnania and Epirus.

There was a tradition that the North-West-Greek-speakers who had occupied the Argolid and the Corinthia in the post-Mycenaean Völkerwanderung had also come by sea all the way round the Peloponnese. The shrine of Temenos, the legendary leader of the North-West-Greek-speaking conquerors of the Argolid, was on the coast of the Argolic Gulf, between Lerna and Nauplia;[1] and his base of operations was said to have been here.[2] Similarly Aletes, the legendary leader of the North-West-Greek-speaking conquerors of the Corinthia, was said to have made his base of operations at Solygeia on the Corinthian shore of the Saronic Gulf.[3] Though not impossible, this roundabout route looks improbable. The overland route through the Peloponnesian Akhaïa seems more likely to have been the one that the North-West-Greek-speaking invaders of the Argolid and the Corinthia actually followed. The story that they came by sea to the Aegean coast of the Peloponnese may have been invented in the mistaken belief that the Akhaioi of the Peloponnesian Akhaïa were a surviving remnant of the pre-Völkerwanderung population of the Peloponnese, and that therefore the invaders could not have come in through this Achaean territory.

The most westerly of the North-West-Greek-speaking invaders' overland routes must have run from north-western Epirus through the Yannina basin and thence, southward, down the valley of the Louros (alias Viros, the Hellenic Oropos) River to the plain of Arta (Ambrakia), adjoining the north shore of the Gulf of Preveza (the Ambracian Gulf). This is the only practicable north-south route in all southern Epirus. There is no route down the course of the river of Arta (River Arakhthos)

[1] Strabo, *Geographica*, Book VIII, chap. 6, § 2 (C. 368); Pausanias, Book II, chap. 38, § 1.
[2] Pausanias, ibid.
[3] Thucydides, Book IV, chap. 42.

between the point where the Métsovo–Yannina road leaves this river and the point where the river debouches from the hills and swings round the citadel of Arta (Ambrakia) into the coastal plain. There is no route, either, down the course of the Akheloïos (the Aspropótamo) above Stratós. There is no route along the ridge of Pindus.[1] From Arta this westernmost overland invasion-route runs along the east shore of the Gulf of Preveza and thence through the easy pass from Limnaia (Karavassará), at the south-east corner of the Gulf, to Stratós on the Akheloïos, at the point where the Akheloïos debouches from the hills. 'The importance of this route of invasion from northern to southern Greece is as great as that via Thermopylae, the flanks of the Pindus Range stretching down to the coast in either case.'[2]

This was the route followed by the North-West-Greek-speaking conquerors of the northern Peloponnese. Like present-day wheeled traffic, the migrants will have crossed the Gulf of Corinth at its narrowest point, between Andirrhion and Rhion, and here the stream of migration was split by striking the northern mountain-ramparts of Arcadia. One branch of the stream here turned south-westward, through the lowlands of Elis and Pisatis, till it was brought to a stop by striking the lower course of the River Alpheios. The major branch turned eastwards, ran along the south coast of the Corinthian Gulf, and flooded over the Argolid, the Isthmus, and the Megarid. After reaching this section of the Aegean coast of the Peloponnese, the North-West-Greek-speaking invaders took to the sea and occupied the southern Sporades, the Asian Doris, Pamphylia, and eastern Crete, pushing the previous inhabitants of the Argolid ahead of them into Cyprus. The Dryopes ('Oakfolk'), whose ethnikon survived in the Post-Völkerwanderung Age in the territories of Asine and Hermione at the southern tip of the Argolic akte, were presumably one of the migrant peoples from the north-west that were carried along in this particular stream of the flood. The fraction of the Dryopes that settled in Styra and Karystos, in south-eastern Euboea, perhaps arrived there from the Argolid by sea. Pausanias notes[3] that the Asinaioi gloried in the name Dryopes, but that the Styreis were ashamed of it.

The easternmost overland migration route coincides with the westernmost one as far as a point about three-fifths of the way along the eastern shore of the Gulf of Preveza. Here, at the northern edge of the little plain of Amphilochian Argos, this second route branches off eastwards, plunges into the interior, and traverses successive ridges and rivers till, via Karpenísi, it crosses the watershed between the Akheloïos basin and

---

[1] See Hammond, 'Prehistoric Epirus and the Dorian Invasion', pp. 141 and 144.
[2] Ibid., p. 147.
[3] Pausanias, Book IV, chap. 34, § 11.

the Sperkheios basin and runs on down the level Sperkheios valley to the head of the Maliac Gulf of the Aegean Sea.

This is the most direct route from Epirus to central Greece, but Hammond, who walked it in twenty-five hours, concedes that it is 'certainly arduous'.[1] This judgement is confirmed by a glance at Hammond's Plate 32. The traveller by this route has to cross, one after the other, the rivers Patiópoulos (Inakhos), Aspropótamo (Akheloïos), Agraphiótiko, and Megdova (Kambylos); and, in the days before the building of the present bridges, this would have been a formidable migration-route even for relatively mobile pastoral peoples, such as the North-West-Greek-speaking peoples may have been at the time when they made their Völkerwanderung. The North-West-Greek-speaking peoples who established themselves in central Greece as a result of the Völkerwanderung may have made their crossing of Pindus, from Epirus, by this route; alternatively, they may have taken the physically easier option of crossing Pindus by the Zygos pass from the Yannina basin to the headwaters of the River Peneios. From there they would have travelled on south-eastwards over the west Thessalian plain and thence have reached the Sperkheios valley by the relatively easy route via Dhomokó (Thaumakoi) and Zeitoúni (Lamía).

Physiographical considerations tell in favour of this having been their route; and Thucydides says explicitly[2] that the Boiotoi came into the Kadmeioi's country (i.e. post-Völkerwanderung Boeotia) from Arne in south-western Thessaly. Linguistic considerations, however, tell against this. The North-West-Greek-speaking migrants who moved into central Greece occupied the whole of it, from Ainiania and the Phthiotic Akhaïa through Malis to Phokis and the two Lokrides inclusive, in strong enough force to be able to substitute their own dialect throughout this region for the North-East-Greek dialect that must previously have been spoken there, as it continued to be spoken on either side of this region, in Thessaly and in Boeotia. Only the Boiotoi, who were the advance-guard of the invaders, adopted the dialect of the conquered population, and even they were numerous enough to be able to infuse a strong dose of North-West Greek into the North-East Greek of the country that they had conquered. If this mass of North-West-Greek-speaking migrants had travelled from Epirus to central Greece via western Thessaly, they would surely have swamped the North-East-Greek dialect there *en route*; but, in fact, the North-East-Greek dialect survived there, as it did in Boeotia; and, though a dose of North-West Greek was also injected into the North-East Greek of south-western Thessaly (the tetrarchy of Thessaliotis), the dose here was not so strong as it was in Boeotia.

---

[1] Hammond, loc. cit., p. 143.   [2] In Book I, chap. 12.

These linguistic facts suggest that the west Thessalian plain was not, after all, on the route by which the North-West-Greek-speakers migrated into central Greece. On this account, Hammond holds[1] that the route from the east shore of the Gulf of Preveza to the head of the Sperkheios valley is likely to have been the one that this branch of the migrants took. His conclusion is that 'the spear-head of Doric peoples came through the Sperkheios valley, spreading laterally into south-west Thessaly and Boeotia to impose its speech in part upon earlier Aeolic[2] peoples'.[3]

Thucydides says[4] that the Boiotoi were driven out of south-western Thessaly by the Thessaloi. The implication is that the Thessaloi invaded Thessaly from the south-west, and this is borne out by the name Thessaliotis, which the south-western tetrarchy of Thessaly bore in the Post-Völkerwanderung Age. Herodotus says[5] that the Thessalians came to their post-Völkerwanderung North-East-Greek-speaking habitat from Thesprotia in south-western Epirus. If Thesprotia was in truth the Thessaloi's previous home, they must have migrated from there to Thessaliotis by the pass that crosses Pindus from Arta (Ambrakia) to Muzáki (near Gomphoi). This pass was of some importance in both the Second and the Third Romano-Macedonian War. Livy notes its arduousness.[6] Yet in 198 B.C. T. Quinctius Flamininus used this route successfully for provisioning his army in western Thessaly with grain that had been brought by sea to Ambrakia.[7]

The route from the north-west down the upper Peneios valley into western Thessaly could be reached from three directions: from the Yannina basin via the Zygos Pass; from north-western Epirus up the Aôos valley to this river's headwaters; and from the upper Haliakmon valley via Grevená. One or other of these routes must have been followed by the Histiaioi, whose name attaches to the north-westernmost tetrarchy of Thessaly, Histiaiotis, in the Post-Völkerwanderung Age, as well as to the north-western end of the island of Euboea. We have no information about the migration of the Histiaioi into the north-western quarter of Thessaly. They were not strong enough in numbers to be able to substitute North-West Greek for North-East Greek here. At the same time, they were strong enough to expel four splinters of the pre-Völkerwanderung population of Histiaiotis. They drove the Eurytanes and the

---

[1] Hammond, 'Prehistoric Epirus and the Dorian Invasion', p. 151 and p. 163, n. 4.

[2] i.e. North-East-Greek-speaking.—A. J. T.

[3] Hammond, ibid., p. 163.

[4] In Book I, chap. 12.

[5] In Book VII, chap. 176: Θεσσαλοὶ ἦλθον ἐκ Θεσπρωτῶν οἰκήσοντες γῆν τὴν Αἰολίδα τήνπερ νῦν ἐκτέαται.

[6] 'Iter est a Gomphis Ambraciam sicut impeditum ac difficile ita spatio perbrevi' (Book XXXII, chap. 15). 'Asperi ac prope invii soli cum ingenti difficultate parvis itineribus aegre ad Gomphos pervenit' [consul Romanus P. Licinius Crassus] (Book XLII, chap. 55).

[7] Livy, Book XXXII, chap. 15.

Makednoi to find refuge on the south side of the southern end of the Pindus Range: the Eurytanes in the eastern part of the Akheloïos basin and the Makednoi in the Doris at the headwaters of the River Kephisos.[1] The Histiaioi drove the Perrhaiboi eastwards from the eastern headwaters of the Peneios into the northern part of the basin of the Europos; and they started the Makednoi's fellow tribesmen the Makedones on a migration from Histiaiotis which was to lead them eventually, over the Pórtes Pass, into the Haliakmon basin.[2]

With the aid of the post-Völkerwanderung dialect-map and the route-map, which remained unchanged in Greece till the building of wheel-roads in our own time, we can follow the displacement of some of the North-West-Greek-speaking peoples from their pre-Völkerwanderung to their post-Völkerwanderung habitats.

The migrants in the vanguard of the Völkerwanderung must, like the isolated pre-Völkerwanderung adventurers, have been Achaeans. These Achaean migrants *en masse* must have been the ancestors of all the North-West-Greek-speaking peoples of the Post-Völkerwanderung Age from Rhodes on the south-east as far north-westward as the Peloponnesian Akhaïa and the Phthiotic Akhaïa inclusive. These two Achaean peoples who retained their national name must have been the hindmost of the Achaean migrants themselves. They must have been propelled from behind by a jostling crowd of kindred peoples with other national names.

The foremost of these non-Achaean North-West-Greek-speakers who were pressing upon the Achaeans from the rear may have been the Helloi (alias Hellopes, alias Hellenes). The Helloi make their first appearance in Achilles' famous prayer to the Pelasgian Zeus of Dodona. They are this remote god's uncouth interpreters.[3] After the post-Mycenaean Völkerwanderung, they eventually gave their name to the whole society of Greek-speaking peoples that had adopted the city-state way of life. The names 'Hellenes' and 'Hellas' must have won this comprehensive

---

[1] For the migration of the Makednoi from Histiaiotis via Pindus to the central Greek Doris, see Herodotus, Book I, chap. 56. It looks as if both the Eurytanes and the Makednoi must have reached their post-Völkerwanderung locations in central Greece from Histiaiotis via the Zygos Pass, the Yannina basin, the Louros valley, and the route from the eastern shore of the Gulf of Preveza into the interior.

[2] See Part II, chap. 7.

[3] *Iliad*, XVI, 233–5. This Homeric evidence is supported by Hesiod and by Aristotle. According to Strabo, Book VII, chap. 7, § 10 (C. 328), Φιλόχορος δέ φησι καὶ τὸν περὶ Δωδώνην τόπον, ὥσπερ τὴν Εὔβοιαν, Ἑλλοπίαν κληθῆναι· καὶ γὰρ Ἡσίοδον οὕτω λέγειν.

ἔστι τις Ἑλλοπίη, πολυλήϊος ἠδ᾽ εὐλείμων. . . .
ἐνθάδε Δωδώνη τις ἐπ᾽ ἐσχατίῃ πεπόλισται.

Ten verses of the passage, including these two lines, are quoted in a scholium on Sophocles' *Trachiniae*, l. 1169.

According to Aristotle, *Meteorologica*, I. 14 (352a), ὁ καλούμενος ἐπὶ Δευκαλίωνος ἐπικλυσμὸς . . . ἐγένετο περὶ τὴν Ἑλλάδα τὴν ἀρχαίαν· αὕτη δ᾽ ἐστὶν ἡ περὶ Δωδώνην· ᾤκουν γὰρ οἱ Σέλλοι ἐνταῦθα καὶ οἱ καλούμενοι τότε μὲν Γραιοί, νῦν δὲ Ἕλληνες.

connotation thanks to their previously having become the collective name for the twelve peoples in central and north-eastern Greece who were represented on the Delphi–Anthela amphictyony;[1] but, before the formation of the amphictyony, the two names must have had a narrower geographical range. Presumably they belonged originally to some people in the immediate neighbourhood of one or other or both of the two sanctuaries—one at Anthela and the other at Delphi—on which this amphictyony centred. Perhaps the original Hellenes of the Post-Völkerwanderung Age were one or both of two of the twelve amphictyonic peoples, namely the Phokeis and the Malieis, who, in this age, were each called, not by a national name, but by a locality. 'Phokeis' means simply 'inhabitants of Phokis'; 'Malieis' means 'inhabitants of the apple-growing country'. The Völkerwanderung could have uprooted the Helloi from their previous home in Epirus round Dodona, have swept them south-eastwards at the rearmost Achaeans' heels, and have deposited them either in the lower valley of the Sperkheios[2] or in the upper valley of the Kephisos.[3] If this region was the original post-Völkerwanderung Hellas, it could be identical with the Hellas that, in the Homeric Catalogue of the contingents in Agamemnon's host, is enumerated among the dominions of Achilles.[4] It could also be identical with the Hellas that is associated with 'the Middle Argos' in several passages of the *Odyssey*.[5] This 'Middle Argos' might be the Kephisos valley, together with the Cadmean part of the future Boeotia (the part round Thebes); for this is the principal stretch of lowland in central Greece, and it does lie between the Pelasgian Argos[6] and the Peloponnesian Argos.[7] If the post-Völkerwanderung Hellenes were the descendants of Helloi, evicted from Dodona, who had resettled themselves round Delphi, the same North-West-Greek-speaking people was successful, twice in its history, in exploiting an oracle.

[1] For these, see p. 51, n. 1.

[2] Leaf notes in *Homer and History*, p. 115, that the River Sperkheios' modern name is 'Elládha'. According to Thucydides, Book III, chap. 92, the Trakhinioi, whose territory extended from the south bank of the lower Sperkheios to the western end of the pass of Thermopylae, were a subdivision of the Malieis; and Trakhis was the district in which Anthela lay.

[3] Just across the water there was an Hellopia in the territory of the city-state Histiaia at the north-western end of Euboea (Herodotus, Book VIII, chap. 23; cp. Strabo, Book X, chap. 1, §§ 3–4. (C. 445–6)). Stephanus of Byzantium lists three more Hellopiai—one in Aetolia, one in Dolopia, and one in Boeotia in the territory of Thespiai.

[4] *Iliad*, II. 631–5. See also the present Part, chap. 1, pp. 9–11, with p. 10, n. 2.

[5] Ἀν' Ἑλλάδα καὶ μέσον Ἄργος (*Odyssey*, I. 344; IV. 726 and 816; XV. 80).

[6] *Iliad*, II. 681–5.

[7] See chap. 1, p. 6, n. 3. The Argos of *Iliad*, VI. 224, and XIV. 119, is the Peloponnesian Argos, not the central Greek Argos. In VI. 224, 'Ἄργεϊ μέσσῳ' means, not 'in the Middle Argos', but 'in the heart of [the Peloponnesian] Argos'. Leaf, in *Homer and History*, pp. 194–5, holds that the Argos which is associated with Hellas in the Odyssean formula is the Peloponnesian Argos likewise.

Others among these non-Achaean migrant Greeks were named after some of the adventurers of the Mycenaean Age, who have found a place among the Pre-Hellenic-Age Greek heroes. The Eurytanes will have been the followers of the Homeric Eurytos of Oikhalia.[1] The Ainianes will have been the followers of the Homeric Aeneas, notwithstanding the poets' transference of Aeneas to the Trojan side and their location of him among the foothills of the Anatolian Mount Ida, to serve there as the leader of the Dardanians.[2] Other non-Achaean North-West-Greek-speaking participants in the Völkerwanderung will have been the Histiaioi[3] and the Thessaloi, who imposed themselves and their names on the North-East-Greek-speaking population of Hellenic-Age Thessaly.

We can now reconstruct, tentatively, the pre-Völkerwanderung locations of the North-West-Greek-speaking migrant peoples in the re-servoirs in Epirus from which they poured out. In the stream that poured into central Greece, the foremost wave was the Boiotoi. Their name shows that, whatever the route may have been by which they reached the Minyan and Cadmean territories to which they now gave their own name, the Boiotoi must have come originally from somewhere in the Boion, i.e. in the Pindus Range. In central Greece in the Post-Völker-wanderung Age, the Boiotoi's immediate neighbours to the north-west are the Hellenes in Phokis, Trakhis, and Malis, and the Ainianes in the Sperkheios valley. The Hellenes and the Ainianes adjoined each other in the Pre-Völkerwanderung Age as well as in the Post-Völkerwanderung Age. The Homeric epic locates both these peoples round Dodona.[4] During the Völkerwanderung they must have kept together; and, if the route that they followed from the Yannina basin to central Greece was the one running from the east shore of the Gulf of Preveza to the head-waters of the Sperkheios, this must have been the section of the Pindus highlands in which the Boiotoi were living on the eve of the Völker-wanderung. The Hellenes and the Ainianes, migrating into central Greece by this route, must have pushed the Boiotoi, ahead of them, out of this part of Pindus into post-Völkerwanderung Boeotia. The backwoods

[1] *Iliad*, II. 730; *Odyssey*, VIII. 223–8.

[2] *Iliad*, II. 819–21. Conversely, Oïleus, the father of one of the two Ajaxes, must have been originally, not a Locrian, but an Ilian. Oïleus' son, like Ankhises' son, has changed sides in the course of the evolution of the epic. He has become an Achaean throughout, but he is a Locrian in the Catalogue, II. 527–35, and in XIII. 712, only.

[3] On this ethnic map of Post-Völkerwanderung-Age Greece, the Histiaioi have given their name to the north-westernmost of the four tetrarchies of Thessaly, and also to the city of Oreos, at the north-west end of the island of Euboea. Here they were next-door neighbours of the Phthiotic Achaeans. The names Akhaioi and Histiaioi reappear, in association with each other, as Ingaevones and Istaevones, in the Teutonic-speaking world beyond the northern frontiers of the Roman Empire in the Age of the Principate. For the phonetic correspondence between the names 'Ingaev-ones' and 'Akhai-woi', see B. F. C. Atkinson, *The Greek Language* (London, 1932, Faber), p. 14, n. 1.

[4] The Hellenes (Helloi) in *Iliad*, XVI. 233–5; the Ainianes in II. 749–50.

Akhaioi (as distinct from the Achaean rulers of the Mycenaean World) must have been living, on the eve of the Völkerwanderung, in Amphilokhia, Akarnania, the interior of Aetolia, and the country to the east of coastal Aetolia that eventually became the Western Lokris. The bulk of these backwoods Akhaioi must have migrated into the Peloponnese, and into the islands beyond, partly by sea and partly across the straits between Andirrhion and Rhion. The Akhaioi in Amphilokhia must have migrated eastwards, instead of southwards; and, like the Boiotoi, they must have been pushed in this direction by the migrating Hellenes and Ainianes; but, while the Boiotoi were pushed along the south shore of the Maliac Gulf into the Minyan and Cadmean country, this particular section of the Akhaioi was pushed along the Gulf's north shore into Phthia. As for the Thessaloi, if their pre-Völkerwanderung habitat was in Thesprotia, their route from there to Thessaliotis will have crossed the route of the Ainianes and Hellenes from the Yannina basin to central Greece.

It has been suggested above that *all* the North-West-Greek-speaking peoples of the Hellenic Age, from Pamphylia and Rhodes north-west-wards to the Peloponnesian and Phthiotic Achaeans inclusive, were descended from Achaeans who had poured out of the backwoods into the Mycenaean World in the Völkerwanderung. If these migrant peoples really were all Achaean backwoodsmen, we have to explain why only the two rearmost of them retained the name 'Achaean', while those of them who had settled to the east and south-east of the Peloponnesian Akhaïa, from Sikyon to Rhodes inclusive, were called, and called themselves, not 'Achaeans', but 'Dorians', in the Post-Völkerwanderung Age.[1]

The so-called 'Dorians' of this age were not differentiated from the two sets of contemporary Achaeans, and from the other North-West-Greek-speaking peoples to the west and north-west of these Achaeans, by any decisive difference in dialect. It is true that many of the modern treatises on the Greek dialects treat 'Doric' and 'North-West Greek' as if they were as distinct from each other as they both are from North-East Greek (Aeolic), Arcado-Cyprian, and Ionic. Of course, within the domains of each of the four dialects of Greek, each region,[2] and, within each region, each locality, had some distinctive dialectical peculiarities of its own. But, within the domain of the North-West-Greek dialect, there were not any regional peculiarities differentiating the so-called 'Doric-speaking' area as a whole from the remainder as a whole.[3]

---

[1] 'Si deve parlare di una migrazione achea in luogo di una dorica' (Pareti, op. cit., p. 204; cp. p. 75).

[2] See Pareti, ibid., p. 78.

[3] 'On the mainland . . . it [i.e. the name 'Dorian'] did not correspond to any definite national limits, so far as we can see. It included Spartans (with Messenians), Corinthians, and Argives, and, outside the Peloponnese, Megarians, all speaking dialects of the same

Modern philologists would never have thought of dividing the North-West-Greek dialect into two distinct dialects, one of them labelled 'Doric', if they had based their classification exclusively on the linguistic evidence, i.e. on the evidence of inscriptions and (secondarily) of literary texts.[1] Their listing of a 'Doric' dialect, distinct from North-West Greek, is derived, not from evidence, but from tradition.

In the Post-Völkerwanderung Age the Greeks gave themselves a genealogy which differentiated them into three groups : Dorians (Δωριεῖς), Aeolians (Αἰολεῖς), and Ionians plus Achaeans ("Ιωνες καὶ Ἀχαιοί). Modern philologists have followed this convention so far as to distinguish 'Doric' from North-West Greek. But they have tacitly rejected the rest of the conventional classification because it is too flagrantly at variance with the linguistic facts for them to be able to accept it. The conventional classification breaks up the speakers of the North-West-Greek dialect into no less than three groups, namely 'Dorians', Achaeans, and a remainder who are included conventionally among the Aeolians, in spite of the fact that their dialect was not 'Aeolic', i.e. was not North-East Greek. The speakers of the Arcado-Cyprian dialect are also included conventionally among the Aeolians. The Aeolians are, in fact, made into a hold-all for any Greek-speakers that are not 'Dorians', Achaeans, or Ionians. In rejecting these points in the traditional erroneous classification, our philologists have been right; but they have been inconsequent

---

family, but it excluded Eleans, Aetolians, and Phocians, and the inhabitants of the Peloponnesian Akhaïa, who also spoke kindred dialects. It included, too, the Doris on Mount Oeta, which spoke a wholly different Aeolic tongue.' (Leaf, *Homer and History*, p. 332 ; cp. Palmer, op. cit., p. 145.)

[1] There is, however, one piece of evidence, noted by Hammond, *Epirus*, p. 423, with n. 2, which indicates that two Peloponnesian sub-dialects of North-West Greek, both of which were traditionally called 'Doric', may have been more closely akin to each other than either of them was to the North-West Greek spoken by the Acarnanians. These two are the Corinthian, spoken by the Corinthians' colonists the Ambraciots, and the Messeno-Laconian, spoken by the refugee Messenians at Naupaktos. When the Athenian general Demosthenes was operating, during the first bout of the Atheno-Peloponnesian War of 431–404 B.C., in Amphilokhia against the Ambraciots with a mixed force of Athenian, Acarnanian, and Messenian troops, he wanted to take the enemy by surprise; so he placed in the van his Messenians, Δωρίδα . . . γλῶσσαν ἱέντας, to deceive the Ambraciots into thinking that the troops approaching them were some of their own, and this ruse was successful (Thucydides, Book III, chap. 112). Hammond points out that Demosthenes 'sent his Messenians ahead— not the Acarnanians, although they knew the terrain better', and he infers that 'the Acarnanians . . . probably spoke West Greek, certainly not Doric'.

This inference depends, however, on the assumption that Demosthenes had Acarnanians, as well as Messenians and Athenians, with him in that half of his force with which he was attacking the Ambraciots' camp. He had, however, divided his force and had sent the other half through the mountains of Amphilokhia (Thucydides, ibid.), and, since the Acarnanians did know the terrain better, it seems likely that Demosthenes had detailed them for making this march through more difficult country. If, in his own half of his force, he had only Athenians and Messenians, then he would naturally have used his North-West-Greek-speaking Messenians, not his Attic-speaking Athenians, to take in the North-West-Greek-speaking Ambraciots by talking to them in the Messenian form of North-West Greek.

in accepting the traditional distinction between 'Dorians' and other North-West-Greek-speakers. They ought to have rejected the traditional classification *in toto*, and to have based their own classification on the linguistic evidence exclusively.[1]

How did the erroneous traditional classification arise? Its origin is evident. It must have originated on the west coast of Anatolia and on the off-shore islands after the post-Mycenaean Völkerwanderung had deposited there a row of colonial Greek communities consisting of immigrants from continental European Greece. Most of these Greek settlements on the east side of the Aegean Sea were of mixed origin. Each was composed of a number of bands of migrants drawn from different parts of European Greece. Their compositeness is commemorated in the names Aiolis (*Αἰολίς*), meaning a variegated region, and Pamphyloi (*Πάμφυλοι*), meaning a people containing representatives of all races. The Asian Ionians, too, were a composite people. The diversity of their origins is noted by Herodotus[2] and by Pausanias.[3] However, after the migration had been completed, the eventual dialect-map of Asian Greece did not continue to reflect the compositeness of each of the Asian Greek communities. The dialect-map had become consolidated and simplified. Three dialects only survived in this Asian Greek colonial region, and each of these had come to be spoken in a compact area. The northernmost of these three dialect-areas was Aiolis, and the dialect that prevailed here was that of the pre-Völkerwanderung population of north-eastern and central European Greece. The middle dialect-area was Ionia, and the dialect that prevailed here was that of Attica, Euboea, and the Cyclades. The southernmost area was Doris, and the dialect that prevailed here was North-West Greek. There were some debatable border districts. Smyrna, for instance, was captured from Aiolis by the Ionians,[4] and Halikarnassos was captured from Doris by them. There were, however, three blocks and three only, and, on the whole, the boundaries between them were clear-cut.

The conventional classification of the Greek-speaking peoples as a whole, including those in Europe, was arrived at by applying to European Greece a classification that, in Asian Greece, was true to the local linguistic facts,[5] but that could not be applied, as it stood, in European

---

[1] Beloch, op. cit. (2nd ed.), Erster Band, Zweite Abteilung, pp. 88–9, rightly maintains that the distribution of the Greek dialects in the Post-Völkerwanderung Age is our only sound evidence for throwing light on the foregoing migrations, and that it is a mistake in method to contaminate the findings of the linguistic evidence with the picture given by Greek tradition and mythology. Cp. Palmer, op. cit., pp. 144–6; Pareti, op. cit., p. 66.

[2] Book I, chaps. 146–7.

[3] Book VII, chap. 2, § 1, to chap. 5, § 8.

[4] Herodotus, Book I, chaps. 149–50.

[5] 'The Dorians' name, like the Ionians' and the Aeolians', established itself on the coasts of Asia Minor ... and was transferred to the motherland from there' (Beloch, op. cit.,

Greece without forcing the facts to fit it. The one point in the conventional classification that was not derived from Asian Greek facts was the addition of Achaeans to Aeolians, Ionians, and Dorians. There were no Asian Greeks who called themselves Achaeans; on the other hand, all pre-Völkerwanderung Greeks were called Achaeans in Asian Greek epic poetry. Asian Greeks will therefore have felt that the Achaeans ought to find some place in the picture, and they found a place for them by coupling them with the Ionians. There was no linguistic warrant for this. The Hellenic-Age Achaeans in continental Greece did not speak Ionic; they spoke North-West Greek. The reason for associating the Achaeans with the Ionians in particular was because Achaeans and Ionians were both believed to be derived from the oldest stratum of Greek-speaking population in the Aegean World.

Why did it occur to anyone to try to classify the European Greek peoples on the pattern of the Asian Greek facts? The most probable reason is that, before the classification was devised, some of the European Greek peoples had already taken to calling themselves by one or other of the three Asian Greek national names. Why should they have taken to doing that?[1] Probably because they had been adopting an Asian Greek political institution—the city-state articulated into a number of components called phylai (φυλαί), meaning 'nations' in the sense in which the term 'nations' was used in medieval Western universities. A European Greek community that had adopted this Asian Greek institution will have come to think of itself as also being 'Dorian' or 'Ionian' or 'Aeolian', according to the local source in Asian Greece from which it had borrowed the institution of a city-state articulated into a number of phylai.

This institution eventually spread over the whole of the Hellenic World with the exception of northern continental European Greece, where the nation-state survived until the time of the Roman conquest. In the rest of the Hellenic World the city-state became the characteristic political institution, and indeed the master institution, of the Hellenic civilization. We may guess, however, that the eastern shore of the Aegean, which was colonized by Greek-speakers during the post-Mycenaean Völkerwanderung, was the region in which the Hellenic city-state had originated. The migrants from European Greece who settled here came, as has been noticed already, in a large number of small bands, each consisting of a splinter of some European Greek people that had been broken to pieces by the post-Mycenaean upheaval. These ship's-companies of would-be settlers were landing on a coast whose existing inhabitants were not only hostile—as they were bound to be towards foreign invaders—but were

Erster Band, Zweite Abteilung, p. 82; cp. Erste Abteilung, pp. 139–40). Leaf, *Homer and History*, pp. 330–1, and Pareti, op. cit., pp. 95, 102, 106, follow Beloch on this point.

[1] This question is raised by Leaf in *Homer and History*, p. 330.

also formidable. The invasion had become possible because the Hittite Empire, which had conquered and annexed western Anatolia in the fourteenth century B.C., had been losing its hold on this outlying part of its domain, even before the Empire itself was destroyed by the swarm of the post-Mycenaean Völkerwanderung that had poured into Anatolia out of Thrace. But the ex-subjects of the Hittite Empire in western Anatolia were at least the equals of the Greek invaders in degree of civilization; and their resistance to the Greek invasion from across the sea was reinforced by a counter-invasion overland from the interior of Anatolia. The Phrygian invaders from Thrace pushed their way south-westwards down the Maeander valley, displacing the pre-Völkerwanderung population of Anatolia *en route* and driving fragments of it, in front of them, towards the coast. Thus, at the time when the Greek migrants were making their lodgements along the west coast of Anatolia and on the off-shore islands, there was an intense pressure on this region from both sides.

In these circumstances the ship's-companies of Greek migrants could not have survived if each of them had tried to seize and colonize a patch of Asian countryside for and by itself. If they had acted independently of each other, they would have been wiped out, in detail, by the existing inhabitants or else by rival immigrants from the landward side. The immigrant Greek ship's-companies saved themselves by clubbing together in sufficient numbers, in each case, to be able to build and man a ring-wall enclosing a city-of-refuge or citadel (πόλις) within which they, and their flocks and herds, could find effective shelter in case of attack. The ship's-companies composing any one of the associations that were formed for this purpose will, more often than not, have been hetero-geneous. They will have come from a number of different parts of European Greece, and each of them will have brought with it its own local dialect. These national and linguistic differences will, however, have been transcended by the imperious overriding need to do what was necessary for the heterogeneous settlers' common self-preservation. This need will have led heterogeneous ship's-companies to unite with each other politically on colonial ground, and, in course of time, they will then have grown together into a single homogeneous community whose members had all taken to speaking some single one of the dialects of the Greek language that their ancestors had brought with them from Europe. However, in thus amalgamating with each other, the constituent 'nations' (φυλαί) will not have lost all memory of their original distinctive individualities. The memory of these will have been preserved in a colonial city-state's internal structure. The unified community will have continued to be organized as an association of phylai.[1]

---

[1] See *Iliad*, II. 362–3, and Dicaearchus of Messene, fr. 9 in C. Müller's *F.H.G.*, vol. ii

In Asian colonial Greece the need to establish city-states, each composed of a number of ship's-companies, will have arisen as soon as the
migrants had landed. But the same need will also have arisen, sooner or
later, in the Asian Greek migrants' European homeland; for in European
Greece, as in Anatolia, the Völkerwanderung had destroyed a more or
less orderly regime (in Europe, Agamemnon's hegemony) and had
replaced it by an anarchy in which every local community had to fend
for itself and could survive only by effective local self-help. In fact, the
conditions created in European Greece by the Mycenaean regime's
fall were similar to those created in Anatolia by the Hittite Empire's
fall. Consequently the political organization that had been worked out
by the Greek settlers on the west coast of Anatolia—an organization that
had, in fact, enabled these colonial Greek communities to survive—will
have been found apposite by European Greek communities that were
still having to struggle for their existence. Accordingly, some European
Greek communities will have borrowed the institution of a city-state,
articulated into phylai, from their Asian Greek daughter-communities,
and, in borrowing the institution, they will have taken over, with it, the
names with which it was associated in its Asian Greek place of origin.
When a European Greek community organized itself, on the Asian
Greek pattern, as a city-state articulated into phylai, it will have called
its own new artificial phylai by the names of the historic phylai in the
Asian city-states whose constitutions it was copying.[1] It will also have
come to think of itself as belonging to the particular Asian Greek people—
the Dorians or the Ionians, as the case might be—from which it had
borrowed its own new city-state constitution. Pre-Cleisthenic Athens, for
example, was organized as a city-state articulated into four phylai
bearing the names of four out of the six phylai of the Asian Ionian city-
states;[2] and, by this time, the Athenians were thinking of themselves

(Paris, 1878, Firmin-Didot), p. 238: φυλὴ δὲ καὶ φυλέται πρότερον ὠνομάσθησαν ἐκ τῆς εἰς
τὰς πόλεις καὶ τὰ καλούμενα ἔθνη συνόδου γενομένης· ἕκαστον γὰρ τῶν συνελθόντων φῦλον ἐλέγετο
εἶναι. K. Latte, 'Phyle', in Pauly-Wissowa, 39. Halbband (1947), col. 994, points out that
φυλή is a post-Homeric word. In the Homeric poems the form is always φῦλον. Phylai are
never found as independent political units (ibid.), and the state of which a phyle is a sub-
division is always a polis, never an ethnos (ibid., p. 996). The only exceptions to this rule
are the Pamphyloi who gave their name to Pamphylia and the ethnikon Dyman which occurs
in Western Lokris.

[1] Beloch, op. cit., Erster Band, Zweite Abteilung, pp. 98–9, maintains the traditional
view that the names of the Dorian and Ionian phylai came to Asia from Europe, not to
Europe from Asia.

[2] The names of the six Asian Ionian phylai were Geleontes, Hopletes, Argadeis, Aigikoreis,
Oinopes, Boreis. The first four of these six, but not the last two, were established in pre-
Cleisthenic Athens. The Geleontes were established in Teos and in the Samian colony
Perinthos. The Argadeis were established as a phyle on Delos and in the Milesian colony
Tomoi, and as a χιλιοστύς of the phyle Epheseis at Ephesus. The Aigikoreis were established
in the Milesian colonies Kyzikos and Istros and in the Samian colony Perinthos. The Boreis
were established as a phyle in Kyzikos and in Perinthos and as a χιλιοστύς of the phyle

as being Ionians, though, so far as we know, this name was indigenous, as a national name, only in the Cyclades[1] and in the Asian Ionia. Similarly, a number of Peloponnesian North-West-Greek-speaking communities—e.g. Argos, Sikyon, Corinth, Megara, Troizen, Kleonai, Phlious, Sparta—had each constituted itself into a city-state articulated into the three phylai—Dymanes (Westerners), Hylleis (Herakleidai), and Pamphyloi (All-comers)—that were indigenous in the Asian Doris;[2] and, in adopting the phylai of the Asian Doris, they had also adopted the name 'Doris-people' ($\Delta\omega\rho\iota\epsilon\hat{\iota}s$). According to Herodotus,[3] it was not until after the North-West-Greek-speaking migrants into the Peloponnese had arrived there that they came to be called 'Dorians'. At Sparta, we can perhaps catch a glimpse of the local adoption of the Asian Dorian phylai in the famous 'rhetra of Lycurgus'.[4] In this document the Spartans are recommended, among other things, to organize themselves into phylai and to institute a cult of Zeus Syllanios and Athana Syllania, who (if this is the correct spelling of their title)[5] look as if they were the patron divinities of the Dorian phyle named 'Hylleis'. The three Dorian phylai were certainly a going concern at Sparta halfway through the seventh century B.C., for they are named, as the units of the Spartan army, by Tyrtaios.[6]

The Asian Dorians were the Dorians from whom the North-West-

Epheseis at Ephesus. The Oinopes were established as a phyle in Kyzikos and Tomoi and as a $\chi\iota\lambda\iota\omega\sigma\tau\dot{\nu}s$ of the phyle Epheseis at Ephesus (Beloch, op. cit., Erster Band, Zweite Abteilung, pp. 97–100; cp. Erste Abteilung, pp. 128 and 133). The name of the traditional founder of Khios was Oinopion (ibid., p. 101).

[1] Homeric Hymn to the Delian Apollo, ll. 146–55.

[2] The three Dorian phylai were all established on Kos and on Kalymnos and on Melos and on Thera (Beloch, op. cit., Erster Band, Zweite Abteilung, p. 197; cp. Erste Abteilung, pp. 128 and 133), as well as in the continental European Greek cities mentioned above. In the Rhodian Peraia, the Hylleis occur in Tymnos, the Dymanes at Kedreai (Latte, in loc. cit., col. 996). In Crete, all three Dorian tribes are never found together in the same city-state. No Cretan city-state except Hierapytna has more than one of them (Latte, ibid., col. 997). In the Cretan city-states, one of the Dorian phylai is associated with phylai bearing other names (ibid.; see also R. F. Willetts, *Ancient Crete: A Social History* (London, 1965, Routledge and Kegan Paul), p. 34; eundem: *Aristocratic Society in Ancient Crete* (London, 1955, same publishers), p. 254, n. 1); C. Busolt and H. Swoboda, *Griechische Staatskunde*, 3rd ed., Zweite Hälfte (Munich, 1926, Beck), p. 745. One of these other names, $A\iota\sigma\chi\epsilon\hat{\iota}s$, occurs at Lato (Busolt and Swoboda in loc. cit.). Another, $A\iota\theta\alpha\lambda\epsilon\hat{\iota}s$, which occurs at Malla, Dreros, Gortyn, and Knossos, is found at Argos too (Latte, in loc. cit., col. 998). Argos added a fourth phyle, the $\Upsilon\rho\nu\dot{\eta}\theta\iota\omicron\iota$ (ibid.), and Epidauros replaced the Dymanes by Azantioi and Hymanates (ibid.).

[3] Book I, chap. 56.

[4] Text in Plutarch, *Lycurgus*, chap. 6, printed in the present work, Part III, on p. 269.

[5] If, however, the rhetra was an oracle from Delphi, it seems more likely that the manuscript readings 'Syllanios' and 'Syllania' are corruptions of 'Sellanios' and 'Sellania', and that Delphi was prompting the Spartans to institute a cult of two gods of the Hellenes, i.e. of the Delphic amphictyones. A. von Blumental, 'Zur "lykurgischen" Rhetra', in *Hermes*, 77. Band (1942), pp. 212–15, on p. 212, emends Plutarch's $\Sigma\upsilon\lambda\lambda$- to $\Sigma\kappa\upsilon\lambda\lambda$-, on the strength of Hesychius, $\Sigma\kappa\upsilon\lambda\lambda\alpha\nu\acute{\iota}s\cdot\ \dot{\eta}\ \pi\omicron\lambda\epsilon\mu\iota\kappa\dot{\eta}$.

[6] $\Sigma\tau\epsilon\acute{\iota}\chi\omega\mu\epsilon\nu\ \ldots\ \chi\omega\rho\grave{\iota}s\ \Pi\dot{\alpha}\mu\phi\upsilon\lambda\omicron\acute{\iota}\ \tau\epsilon\ \kappa\alpha\grave{\iota}\ \Upsilon\lambda\lambda\epsilon\hat{\iota}s\ \mathring{\eta}\delta\grave{\epsilon}\ \Delta\upsilon\mu\hat{\alpha}\nu\epsilon s$ (papyrus fragment 1, lines 11–12 = No. 1 (Diehl)). See further Part III, chap. 3, Annex II, p. 264.

Greek-speaking Peloponnesian communities, listed above, derived the three Dorian phylai, and, with them, the name 'Dorian' itself. There is a passage in the Homeric Catalogue of Agamemnon's host, describing the contingents from the Asian Doris, which shows that this was the Doris in which the three Dorian phylai originated, and that this was also the Doris that originally traced the lineage of its princes back to Herakles. According to the Catalogue, the Rhodians were organized in three settlements,[1] and each of these three settlements was the home of one of three phylai.[2] These three Rhodian phylai must be identical with the three Dorian phylai Dymanes, Hylleis, and Pamphyloi; and, in fact, in the Post-Völkerwanderung Age, we find one of the three, the Pamphyloi, occupying, by itself, a stretch of the south coast of Anatolia between Lycia and Cilicia, in a location that is just round the corner from the Asian Doris.

The earliest mention of 'Dorieis' in Greek literature is in the *Odyssey*,[3] and here they are named as one of the five peoples inhabiting the island of Crete. If it is assumed that the name 'Dorieis' came from north-western Greece, as well as the dialect of Greek that was eventually called 'Doric' and the migrants who carried this dialect southwards and south-eastwards, it is surprising that this name should be heard of first in Crete. This puzzle is solved if we suppose that these Cretan 'Dorieis' had come to Crete, not from Epirus, but from Rhodes and the Dode-canese. According to Staphylos,[4] the Cretan 'Dorieis' were located at the eastern end of the island, i.e. at the nearest point in Crete to the Anatolian Doris. Moreover, the founder and prince of the Mycenaean-Age Greek community on Rhodes, Tlepolemos, is a son of Herakles, and the two leaders of the contingent from the Dodecanese are grandsons of Herakles. The founder of Rhodes, Tlepolemos, is a refugee, as the Heraklid leaders of the Dorians were afterwards reputed to have been.

However, the Asian Doris was not the only district in the Hellenic World that bore the name 'Doris'. There was another Doris in central Greece, round the headwaters of the River Kephisos. There was a Deuriopos or Douriopos in northern Greece round the headwaters of the River Erigon.[5] There was a Dor on the coast of Palestine, just to the south-west of Mount Carmel. Besides these Post-Völkerwanderung-Age Dorides, whose exact locations are known, there had been, according to the Homeric Catalogue of the contingents of Agamemnon's host, a Dorion[6] somewhere in Nestor's principality in the south-western corner

---

[1] οἱ 'Ρόδον ἀμφενέμοντο διὰ τρίχα κοσμηθέντες, Λίνδον 'Ιηλυσόν τε καὶ ἀργινόεντα Κάμειρον (*Iliad*, II. 655–6).

[2] τριχθὰ δὲ ᾤκηθεν καταφυλαδόν (*Iliad*, II. 668).   [3] *Odyssey*, XIX. 177.

[4] Apud Strabonem, Book X, chap. 4, § 6 (C. 475).

[5] Strabo, *Geographica*, Book VIII, chap. 7, § 8 (C. 326); Livy, Book XXXIV, chap. 52.

[6] *Iliad*, II. 594.

of the Peloponnese. This Pylian Dorion was remembered as the place where the Muses had struck the Thracian bard Thamyras dumb.[1]

As far as the inflexions of the Greek language are concerned, the ethnic adjective 'Dorieis' might mean the inhabitants of any one of these different Dorides. The adjective 'Dorieis' is derived from the substantive 'Doris'; the substantive 'Doris' is not derived from the adjective 'Dorieis'.[2] Dorieis stands to Doris (and Aioleis to Aiolis) in the relation in which Malieis stands to Malis, Phokeis to Phokis, Khalkideis to Khalkis, Trakhinioi to Trakhis, Eleioi to Elis. There are, it is true, also cases in which a district-name terminating in '-is' is derived from a national or a personal name, instead of the derivation being the other way round. For instance, Lokris is derived from Lokroi, not vice versa; Orestis is derived from Orestai, Pisatis from Pisa, Seleukis from Seleukos. Even in a pair of names in which the district-name is the original from which the national name is derived, the district-name itself may be derived, in its turn, from some other word. For instance, Trakhis is derived from the descriptive adjective $\tau\rho\alpha\chi\acute{v}s$, and it means 'the rough country'; Malis is derived from the substantive $\mu\hat{a}\lambda o\nu$, and it means 'the apple-growing country', in contrast to the adjoining Trakhis, which was certainly no place for orchards. Byllis may be derived from $\phi\acute{v}\lambda\lambda o\nu$, like the Phyllis between Mount Pangaios and the River Angites,[3] if its initial beta is the Macedonian equivalent for the standard Greek phi, and in that case it would mean 'woodland' ('the leafy country'). Elis, however, seems to be a non-derivative word. In its proper North-West-Greek form $F\hat{a}\lambda\iota s$, it is the Greek equivalent of the Latin 'vallis', and means 'the vale'.

As for 'Doris', it may be a descriptive district-name derived from $\delta\hat{\omega}\rho o\nu$, meaning 'the hollow of the hand'. Both Douriopos and the central Greek Doris are hollows, and Palestinian Dor is another hollow. It nestles under the lee of Mount Carmel. 'The Hollows' would also be an appropriate descriptive name for the Asian Doris, with its fjords hollowed out between mountain-ranges overhanging them on both sides. If 'Doris' is, in truth, a descriptive name, this would account for the occurrence of the name in a number of different localities. The common feature of these localities, which will have earned them their identical name, will have been, as it was in the case of the districts called argos, meaning 'cultivated area', a similarity in their physical configuration; it will not have been a kinship between their respective inhabitants.[4] The inhabitants of each of the Dorides will have been called by the same derivative

---

[1] *Iliad*, II. 594–600.

[2] Both the national name 'Douriopes' (Strabo, *Geographica*, Book VIII, chap. 7, § 9 (C. 327)) and the district-name 'Douriopos' look as if they were derived from an original district-name 'Douris'. (See Beloch, op. cit., Erster Band, Zweite Abteilung, p. 46).

[3] See Herodotus, Book VII, chap. 113.

[4] This point is made by Pareti, op. cit., p. 5.

name 'Dorieis'; but their common name will not have signified that they had anything else in common beyond the single topographical fact that they were all 'dwellers in the hollow'; and any Greek community might be that, whatever the dialect of the Greek language that it happened to speak and whatever its national name.

The different sets of 'Doris-people' (Dorieis) seem, in fact, to have borne different national names. According to Herodotus,[1] the national name of the Doris-people of the Doris in central Greece was 'Makednoi'. The national name of the Post-Völkerwanderung-Age North-West-Greek-speaking Doris-people of the Asian Doris was presumably 'Akhaioi', as has been suggested above, since they were the vanguard of the North-West-Greek-speaking column of the post-Mycenaean Völkerwanderung; and, in this column, the foremost units seem to have been Achaeans. Similarly, the national name of the Aiolis-people (Aioleis) of the Asian Aiolis was presumably Pelasgoi, since a majority of their ancestors had probably come, in the course of the Völkerwanderung, from Thessaly, where, in the Hellenic Age, the North-East-Greek dialect spoken by the Asian Aiolis-people was still being spoken in the Thessalian tetrarchy named Pelasgiotis. The same North-East-Greek dialect must also have been the mother-tongue of the people that inhabited the central Greek Doris in the Hellenic Age, if Herodotus is right in saying[2] that they were a branch of a Greek-speaking people who had been driven out of Histiaiotis in the course of the Völkerwanderung. In the Hellenic Age the dialect of Histiaiotis was North-East Greek ('Aeolic') with a tincture of North-West Greek which the Histiaioi must have brought in with them. The national name 'Makednoi' ('Tallboys'), which Herodotus attributes to the Doris-people of the central Greek Doris, is evidently identical with the national name 'Makedones'. Presumably the Makednoi in Histiaiotis had been split in two by the impact of some invading people,[3] and, while one splinter had been driven south-eastwards into the Doris in central Greece, another had simultaneously been driven north-east-wards into the country to which it eventually gave the name 'Macedon'.

If it is true that the Doris-people of the central Greek Doris were a North-East-Greek-speaking ('Aeolic'-speaking) people, not a North-West-Greek-speaking ('Doric-speaking') people, this rules out any possibility of their having been the progenitors of those North-West-Greek-speaking

---

[1] Book I, chap. 56.   [2] In loc. cit.

[3] Herodotus, in loc. cit., says that the people who evicted the Makednoi from Histiaiotis were the Kadmeioi. (According to Herodotus in Book IV, chap. 147, Kadmos came from the Island of Thera to central Greece and founded Thebes there in the future Boeotia.) This seems unlikely (see Hammond, 'Prehistoric Epirus and the Dorian Invasion', pp. 174 and 179). Even if we were to credit Kadmos or his descendants with having also founded the Thebes in the Phthiotic Akhaïa, that would hardly bring the Kadmeioi within striking distance of Histiaiotis. The invaders of Histiaiotis who expelled the Makednoi from there are more likely to have been the Histiaioi, as has been suggested above (see pp. 34–5 and 37).

peoples in the Peloponnese who, in the course of the Post-Völkerwanderung Age, came to call themselves 'Doris-people'.[1] In any case, the
tiny central Greek Doris, which contained only four villages, could not
have produced the mass of migrants that, in the Völkerwanderung,
spread the North-West-Greek dialect south-eastwards from Sikyon to the
Asian Doris inclusive.[2] Moreover, the central Greek Doris cannot have
been the starting-point of the migration that spread the North-West-Greek
dialect over the whole of the Peloponnese except Arcadia. These North-
West-Greek-speaking migrants did not travel to the Peloponnese down
the Kephisos valley and then along the Isthmus of Corinth; for the
dialect of Boeotia continued to be North-East Greek, with only an infusion of North-West Greek, and the language of Attica continued to
be a variety of Ionic. The North-West-Greek-speaking invaders of the
northern Peloponnese must have travelled south-eastwards through south-
west Epirus, north-east Akarnania, and south-west Aetolia and have
crossed from central Greece into the Peloponnese at the point where the
Corinthian Gulf narrows at its mouth.[3]

On the evidence that we have now reviewed, it might seem clear
that the name 'Doris-people' (Dorieis), together with the names of the
three Dorian phylai and with the genealogy that traces the lineage of the
princes of the Dorians back to Herakles, came to the Peloponnese, not
from the Doris in central Greece, but from the Doris in Anatolia, and
that this was a migration of institutions and names that took place in
the Post-Völkerwanderung Age, not a migration of war-bands that took
place during the Völkerwanderung itself. Herodotus states,[4] as has already
been noted,[5] that the North-West-Greek-speaking immigrants into the
Peloponnese from the north did not come to be called 'Dorians' till
after they had settled in the Peloponnese. Yet, in spite of this evidence,
the Greek tradition, including Herodotus in the passage just cited,
associates the Herakleidai and their followers, not with the Doris in
Asia, but with the Doris in central Greece. The tradition agrees with the
Homeric Catalogue's notice of Tlepolemos in so far as it makes the
Herakleidai refugees. But it makes them find asylum, not in Rhodes, to
which the Catalogue brings Tlepolemos, but in the central Greek Doris;
it makes the original Dorians the inhabitants of this Doris, not of the
Asian one; and it makes the Dorians, under the leadership of the Herakleidai, descend on the Peloponnese from the central Greek Doris,
whereas the evidence indicates that the story of the conquest of part of
the Peloponnese by invaders from the central Greek Doris is fictitious.

[1] See Pareti, op. cit., pp. 75 and 92.
[2] See Leaf, *Homer and History*, p. 333.
[3] See Beloch, op. cit., Erste Abteilung, pp. 89–90; Pareti, op. cit., pp. 75–6; Hammond,
'Prehistoric Epirus and the Dorian Invasion', pp. 131–79; and the present chapter, pp. 31–2
and 38.   [4] In Book I, chap. 56.   [5] See p. 44.

What was the origin of this obviously untrue story?[1] Why was it invented, and why was it accepted, in the teeth of the evidence? Herodotus, for instance, accepts it unquestioningly, though he himself supplies part of the evidence that refutes it, when he informs his readers that the Dorians of the central Greek Doris had come there from Histiaiotis, and that their national name was 'Makednoi'. These two pieces of information tell us that the North-West-Greek-speaking 'Dorians' in the Peloponnese cannot have been the descendants of immigrants from the central Greek Doris, while, on the other hand, the Homeric Catalogue informs us that the Peloponnesian 'Dorians' did take their name, their three Dorian phylai, and the Heraklid descent of their princes from their fellow North-West-Greek-speakers in the Asian Doris.

What was the motive of the Peloponnesian 'Dorians' for wishing to associate themselves with the Doris in central Greece? Their motive was a political one. They wanted to obtain representation on the amphictyony that administered the sanctuary of Earth, Apollo, and Dionysos at Delphi and the sanctuary of Artemis at Anthela. The central Greek Doris, small and obscure though it was, did have representation on this amphictyony, simply because it happened to be one of the states that were near neighbours of the two shrines. When this particular amphictyony became important politically, representation on it also became important politically, and consequently those Greek states that had not been represented originally on the Delphi–Anthela amphictyony now sought to obtain representation on it on any grounds that the amphictyons could be persuaded to accept.[2]

[1] Refuted by Pareti in op. cit., pp. 66–75.

[2] The political explanation, here suggested, for the Peloponnesian 'Dorians' associating themselves with the central Greek Doris seems more likely to be right than the mythological explanation suggested by Beloch in op. cit., Zweite Abteilung, p. 82. 'Since there was a Doris in central Greece as well [as in Asia], at the foot of Mount Oeta, on which Herakles' pyre had burned, it was almost inevitable that these Dorians should have been made to migrate to the Peloponnese with the Herakleidae.'

Leaf, *Homer and History*, p. 333, follows Beloch in this point. On p. 332, however, he suggests that 'the Dorian name was . . . assumed by Sparta and her neighbours for political reasons, exactly as the Ionian was assumed by Athens'. Leaf does not indicate what political reasons he has in mind. Does he mean that (as has been suggested in the present chapter) the name 'Doris-people' was borrowed by the Peloponnesian North-West-Greek-speaking peoples from the North-West-Greek-speaking 'Doris-people' in Asia, together with the Asian Dorian institution of a city-state articulated into phylai? Or does he mean that they took the name 'Doris-people' in order to 'muscle in' on the representation on the Delphi–Anthela amphictyony that was a coveted possession of the central Greek 'Doris-people'? If this is Leaf's meaning, it is hard to see how the Spartans, Argives, and Corinthians could have brought off their *coup* of stealing votes from the central Greek 'Doris-people' just by assuming this people's name. Such a manœuvre would surely have been altogether too arbitrary and too barefaced. The Peloponnesian Dorians' claim to have a right to a share in the central Greek 'Doris-people's' votes must surely have been based on a pre-established identity of national names. The Peloponnesian 'Doris-people' must have come to be known by this name already. If so, they must have acquired the name by borrowing it from the Asian 'Doris-people'.

Originally the Delphi–Anthela amphictyony had been just one of a number of associations of the kind for the protection of local sanctuaries and for the maintenance of the cults there. The Kalaureia amphictyony, which lived to become one of the curiosities of Greek history, had probably outshone the Delphi–Anthela amphictyony originally. At any rate, the membership of the Kalaureia amphictyony included more of the leading states of the Hellenic World than the original membership of the Delphi–Anthela amphictyony included. The Delphi–Anthela amphictyony was comparatively obscure to begin with. The nucleus of its membership lay within the section of central and north-eastern European Greece that, in the Homeric Catalogue, is included in the principality of Achilles, and whose inhabitants are there called 'Hellenes', among other names.[1] This region lay on the fringe, not in the heart, of the domain of the new civilization that was arising out of the wreckage of the Mycenaean World. The primary focus of this new civilization was Asian Greece (Aiolis, Ionia, Doris); its secondary focus was the region round the Isthmus of Corinth, which was the location of those European Greek city-states (Corinth, Megara, Sikyon, Argos) that were the first to make their mark. The fortune of the Delphi–Anthela amphictyony was made by the rise of the sanctuary at Delphi to be 'the navel of the World' (i.e. of the Greek World). This made the amphictyony that administered this sanctuary something central to Greek life, instead of its remaining peripheral. It made this amphictyony something important, instead of its remaining obscure. The Delphi–Anthela amphictyony's rise in the world can be measured, as has been noticed already, by a change in the usage of the geographical name 'Hellas' and the corresponding national name 'Hellenes'. Originally this pair of names must have had a narrow local range that must have been confined to the neighbourhood of Anthela or of Delphi or of both. As a result of the rise of the Delphi–Anthela amphictyony, 'Hellas' came to mean the entire world of Greek-speaking city-state communities, and 'Hellenes' came to be the supra-national name for the totality of the participants in the civilization that, from now on, was known as the 'Hellenic'.[2]

One consequence of this was that the amphictyony's original membership became inadequate for sustaining the amphictyony's new role. The amphictyony had now come to be recognized as being the most authoritative international body in the Hellenic World; yet the membership of

---

[1] *Iliad*, II. 681–5.

[2] The word Πανέλληνας, used as a synonym for Ἀχαιούς, in *Iliad*, II. 530, clearly dates from the age in which the name 'Hellenes' had come to be generic, and this indicates that Zenodotus was right in stigmatizing this passage as an interpolation. According to Pareti, op. cit., p. 101, the earliest instances of the use of the name 'Hellenes' in the generic sense are in Arkhilokhos apud Strabonem, Book VIII, chap. 6, § 6 (C. 370), and in Hesiod's *Works and Days*, ll. 528 (Πανελλήνεσσι) and 654 (Ἑλλάδος).

the amphictyony did not include the most important Hellenic communities (taking the name 'Hellenic' now in its new and broader meaning). It was, however, in these states' interest, and in the amphictyony's interest too, that some means should be found for giving representation to these important outsiders. They could not afford to remain unrepresented on what had now become the most highly revered international association in the Hellenic World, and the amphictyony, on its side, could not make its authority effective if the leading states of Hellas (in the broader sense) were not represented on it. But how were these states to be brought in? The constitution of the amphictyony was sacrosanct. Its membership was confined to twelve central and north-eastern Greek peoples,[1] each of which had two votes (it was characteristic of this archaic and peripheral institution that the members were peoples, not city-states). The membership could not be altered overtly, but it might perhaps be manipulated, and the names of two of the original constituent peoples provided an opening for this. One of the amphictyonic peoples bore the name 'Dorieis'; another bore the name 'Iones'.

Can we identify the Ionic-Greek-speaking people who were the original Iones in the Delphi–Anthela amphictyony? The nearest Ionic-speakers who called themselves 'Iones' were the Cycladic Islanders, so far as we know, and these were too remote from Delphi and Anthela for it to seem probable that they were included among the amphictyony's original members. There was a group of Ionic-speaking communities—the city-states on the Island of Euboea—whose location was close to Anthela and who had a share in the Iones' votes on the amphictyony eventually. But Herodotus states expressly[2] that the Euboean Ionic-speakers called themselves, not 'Iones', but 'Abantes', and this is, in fact, the name by which the peoples of Euboea are called in the Homeric Catalogue.[3] The only other Ionic-speaking people located near enough to Anthela and Delphi to have possibly been an original member of the amphictyony is the Athenian people; and the Athenians did consider themselves to be members of the Ionian division of the Hellenic society; but, so far as we know, the Athenians never used the name 'Iones' as their national name,[4] any more than their Euboean neighbours did. Thus the identity of the original amphictyonic 'Iones' remains an unsolved puzzle.

On the other hand, the identity of the original amphictyonic 'Dorieis' is manifest. These were the inhabitants of the Doris in central Greece.

---

[1] The Phokeis, Dorieis, Lokroi, Boiotoi, Iones, Malieis, Akhaioi Phthiotai, Ainianes, Dolopes, Thessaloi, Magnetes, Perrhaiboi.

[2] Book I, chap. 146.

[3] *Iliad*, II. 536–45.

[4] In *Iliad*, XIII. 689 and 685, the Athenians do seem to be identified with the 'Iones'.

These central Greek 'Dorieis' possessed two amphictyonic votes; and
these votes could be shared with other communities bearing the name
'Dorieis' without any infringement of the letter of the amphictyony's
constitution.[1] When the amphictyony comes into the full light of history,
we find the Dorians' pair of votes being shared by the leading communities
that called themselves 'Dorieis', and the Ionians' pair of votes being
shared by the leading Ionic-speaking communities. How this was brought
about has not been recorded. Were the original Dorian and Ionian
members of the amphictyony bullied or cajoled or bribed into giving
part of their voting-rights away? Whatever the method may have been,
there is no doubt about the fact; and this explains why the Peloponnesian
'Dorians' forged for themselves a fictitious genealogy which represented
them as being an offshoot of the Dorians of central Greece. We have no
evidence for dating the invention of this story. Its perhaps earliest surviving occurrence is in a fragment of Hesiod.[2] At Sparta, at any rate,
it had already become a *fable convenue* by the middle decades of the
seventh century B.C., when Tyrtaios was writing his war-songs.[3]

Who, then, were the Achaeans? And who were the Dorians? Our
conclusion is that the Achaeans were the advance-guard of the peoples
whose mother-tongue was the North-West-Greek dialect. In the Mycenaean Age, Achaean adventurers became the rulers of a majority of the
Mycenaean World's leading principalities, and, in consequence, the
Mycenaean Greeks came to be known collectively by the national name
of their Achaean ruling caste, though all of them except their Achaean
rulers spoke non-North-West-Greek dialects of Greek, namely North-East
Greek ('Aeolic') or Arcado-Cyprian or Ionic. The mass of the Achaean
people, who had remained behind in the backwoods, beyond the north-
west frontier of the Mycenaean World, subsequently became the spear-
head of the post-Mycenaean Völkerwanderung. They carried themselves
and their North-West-Greek dialect diagonally across the Aegean basin
as far as Rhodes, and on, round the south-west corner of Anatolia, to
Pamphylia. Those of them who, beginning with the settlers in the Asian
Doris, eventually adopted the city-state way of life, dropped their
national name 'Achaeans' and took to calling themselves, instead, by
the names of the city-states whose citizens they had now become. In the
Hellenic Age the national name 'Achaeans' was retained only by the

---

[1] See Leaf, *Homer and History*, p. 333, and Pareti, op. cit., p. 89.

[2] πάντες δὲ τριχάϊκες καλέονται | οὕνεκα τρίσσην γαῖαν ἑκὰς πάτρης ἐδάσαντο (Hesiod,
fr. 191, in Rzach's second edition).

[3] Tyrtaios, *Eunomia*:

αὐτὸς γὰρ Κρονίων, καλλιστεφάνου πόσις ῞Ηρης,
Ζεὺς ῾Ηρακλείδαις τήνδε δέδωκε πόλιν·
οἷσιν ἅμα προλιπόντες ᾽Ερινεὸν ἠνεμόεντα
εὐρεῖαν Πέλοπος νῆσον ἀφικόμεθα.

two hindmost detachments of the Achaean people, which had come to rest in Phthiotic Akhaïa and in the Peloponnesian Akhaïa respectively.

As for the name 'Dorieis', it was borne by any Greeks, whatever their dialect, who happened to live in a district called 'Doris'; there were several of these 'Dorides'; and the reason for this plurality was that 'Doris' was a descriptive name for a district that had some particular topographical configuration. In the Post-Völkerwanderung Age the name 'Dorieis' spread from the North-West-Greek-speaking Achaean settlers in the Asian Doris to those among the North-West-Greek-speaking Achaean settlers in the Peloponnese who borrowed from their kinsmen in the Asian Doris the institution of the city-state articulated into the three Asian Dorian phylai. The Peloponnesian 'Dorians' also borrowed from the Asian Doris a genealogy that traced their princes' lineage back to Herakles. The Peloponnesian 'Dorians' were not an offshoot of the Dorians of the Doris in central Greece. The national name of these central Greek Dorians was 'Makednoi', and their mother-tongue was not North-West Greek but North-East Greek. The story that the ancestors of the Peloponnesian 'Dorians' had come from the central Greek Doris was an invention that had a political purpose. This purpose was to obtain for the Peloponnesian 'Dorians' a share in the central Greek Dorians' representation on the Delphi–Anthela amphictyony. The ancestors of the Peloponnesian 'Dorians' had in truth been immigrants who had come into the Peloponnese from the north-west; but they had not come from the central Greek Doris and their national name had been, not 'Dorians', but 'Achaeans'. As Leaf well puts it,[1]

When I speak . . . of the 'Dorian' invasion, I use the term to include, in the first place, that which brought into the Peloponnesos the new and rude tribes who afterwards, in Sparta, Corinth, and Argos, were called 'Dorians'; but it must also cover at least the Aetolians, who, at or about the same time, occupied Elis; and, in a more general sense, it may be taken to denote the whole great wave which overwhelmed the Achaian dominion, including even the Boeotian movement from Thessaly southwards. The 'Dorian' invasion is, in this use, no more than a shorthand term for the whole great Völkerwanderung from the north and north-west which transformed the face of Greece at the end of the twelfth and probably through the eleventh centuries.

[1] In *Homer and History*, p. 333.

PART II

THE HELLENIZATION OF THE NORTHERN HINTERLAND OF CONTINENTAL EUROPEAN GREECE

1. *The Question at Issue*

IN the course of the century A.D. 550–650 the linguistic map of continental European Greece, and of the rest of south-eastern Europe, south of the River Danube, was transformed by a Völkerwanderung from the north, as it had previously been transformed in the twelfth century B.C. On the earlier of the two occasions the incomers into Greece had been speakers of the North-West-Greek dialect, with Illyrian-speaking and Thracian-speaking peoples treading at their heels.[1] On the later occasion they were speakers of a Slavonic language. The Slav Völkerwanderung into south-eastern Europe, unlike its most recent predecessor, was confined to the mainland, since the Roman navy continued to command the sea. Even Euboea, which is virtually a part of the mainland, yields no more than nineteen Slavonic place-names,[2] so this time it suffered less than before, when the North-West-Greek-speaking migrants had taken to the sea and had succeeded in occupying both ends of Euboea as well as Rhodes and other islands at the south-east corner of the Aegean Sea. On the other hand, on the mainland itself, the Slav occupation was more nearly complete than the North-West-Greek occupation had been. Attica did escape occupation this time too;[3] but in the Peloponnese—which the Slavs, like their predecessors, invaded, not via the Isthmus of Corinth, but by crossing the narrow mouth of the Corinthian Gulf[4]—Arcadia, which had escaped occupation in the twelfth century B.C., was now overrun. For about a quarter of a millennium, ending in the reconquest of the Peloponnese by the East Roman

---

[1] See Part I, chaps. 1 and 3.
[2] M. Vasmer, *Die Slawen in Griechenland* (Berlin, 1941, De Gruyter), pp. 110–12.
[3] There are only eighteen Slavonic place-names in Attica (ibid., pp. 120–3).
[4] See Part I, chap. 3, pp. 31–2 and 38.

Government *circa* A.D. 847–50,[1] the Slavs held almost all of it except Patras, a few other coastal towns, and the Tainaron Peninsula, on which the Emperor Basil I (*imperabat* A.D. 867–86) found a Greek-speaking population that had escaped not only the Slav invasion but the forcible Christianization of the Roman Empire by Theodosius I. The Maniots were still worshipping the Olympian gods till Basil I saw to their conversion.[2] As late as the year A.D. 1204 the French invaders of the Peloponnese found that, after more than three centuries of East Roman rule, there were still two independent Slav peoples, the Ezeritai[3] and the Melingoi,[4] in the fastnesses of Mount Taÿgetos. The Melingoi were on the Messenian, the Ezeritai on the Laconian, side of the chain.[5]

In the age immediately before the Slav Völkerwanderung the linguistic map of south-eastern Europe had been very different. In the year A.D. 527, which was the date of the Emperor Justinian I's accession, almost the whole of this region was included in the domains of the Greek and Latin languages. The linguistic frontier between these coincided with the northern boundaries of the original Roman provinces of Macedonia (constituted in 148 B.C.) and Thrace (constituted in A.D. 46). Under the Principate it had been Roman policy to encourage the spread of the Latin language to the north of this line and the spread of the Greek language to the south of it. The line took off from the Adriatic coast just to the south of the mouth of the River Drilo (now called the Drin). It left the headwaters of the River Axios (Vardar) on the Latin-speaking side. Justinian himself was a Latin-speaker in virtue of having come from Tauresium on the upper Axios, just to the north of the northern boundary of Macedonia. East of the Axios basin, the line left on the Greek-speaking side not only the whole of the Strymon (Struma) and Hebros (Maritsa) basins, but a broad strip of territory on the north side of the Haemus (Balkan) Range. The line struck the shore of the Black Sea between the old Greek colonies Mesembria and Ankhialos.

Of course, the linguistic map of this date was not so simple and neat as the foregoing description of it might suggest. Among both the Latin-speakers and the Greek-speakers there may have been some (we cannot

[1] This is the approximate date according to J. B. Bury, *History of the East Roman Empire* (London, 1912, Macmillan), p. 373 and p. 379, n. 1. Our sole authority is Constantine Porphyrogennetos, *De Imperio Administrando*, chap. 50, pp. 220–1, Becker.

[2] Constantine, op. cit., cap. cit., p. 224.

[3] Their name suggests that their location may have included the present-day Limni, in the Vardhounokhoria, and may have extended eastwards into the coastal marshes in the lower basin of the River Eurotas.

[4] There is a modern village, in Epirus, on the route from Yannina to Suli, that still bears this name (see W. M. Leake, *Travels in Northern Greece* (London, 1835, Rodwell, 4 vols.), vol. i, p. 263; H. F. Tozer, *Researches in the Highlands of Turkey* (London, 1869, J. Murray, 2 vols.), vol. ii, p. 206.

[5] See A. Bon, *Le Péloponnèse byzantin jusqu'en 1204* (Paris, 1957, Presses Universitaires de France), p. 63, with n. 2.

guess how many) who were still bilingual—speaking some Illyrian or Thracian dialect as their mother-tongue, besides speaking one of the two oecumenical languages. For all that we know, Justinian may have spoken Dardanian as well as Latin. Within the Latin-speaking zone, Greek still survived in the Greek colonies along the shore of the Black Sea, from Mesembria northwards to the Danube Delta; and Latin, as well as Greek, was widely current in Thrace, as a result of Thrace's proximity to the Latin-speaking zone and of its service as a recruiting-ground for the Roman Imperial Army.

There was also at least one district, and perhaps a second as well, in which neither Greek nor Latin had become current, even as a second language. Albanian, which is one of the still-living Indo-European languages, must have been spoken in the sixth century of the Christian Era in what had been the western part of the original Roman province of Macedonia—the part on the Adriatic slope that had subsequently been erected into the separate province of Epirus Nova. Albanian may have been spoken also in the adjoining province of Praevalitana, the south-eastern extremity of the original Roman province of Dalmatia. In that case Albanian may have been the mother-tongue of the Emperor Dio-cletian. In A.D. 527 there may also still have been a second non-Greek-speaking and non-Latin-speaking area in Bessica, at the headwaters of the River Hebros. At any rate, the Bessoi, who had not been converted to Christianity till the fourth century, had had the Bible translated for them into their local Thracian dialect. For all that we know, Bessica may still have been a Thracian-speaking country when the Slavs descended upon it.[1] Thus there was still one certain and another possible enclave of non-Greek language on the Greek side of the linguistic frontier in south-eastern Europe between Greek and Latin. However, by the time of the Slav Völkerwanderung, the rest of south-eastern Europe, to the south of the linguistic frontier, was certainly Greek-speaking.

This linguistic situation at that date raises the question how and when the Greek language had replaced Thracian and Illyrian in the vast region between the eventual northern frontier of Greek and the line at which this linguistic frontier had stood in the early centuries of the last millennium B.C., after the post-Mycenaean Völkerwanderung had come to a standstill. We know for certain that, at this earlier date, Greek was the mother-tongue of the peoples of Thessaly, a portion of Aetolia, Akarnania, and the whole of European Greece to the south-east of these three Greek-speaking districts, besides the Aegean islands and the lodgements that had already been made by Greek settlers along the

---

[1] In the late sixth century there were still Bessian-speaking monks in the monastery at the foot of Mount Sinai (see P. Geyer, *Intinera Hierosolymitana* (Vienna, 1898, Tempsky), pp. 184 and 213).

west coast of Anatolia. The line within which it is certain that Greek was the local language at this date takes off from the western shore of the Aegean Sea at the mouth of the River Peneios, runs over the summit of Mount Olympus, and then inclines south-westwards along the Cambunian Range and southwards along the main ridge of Pindus, to reach the Ionian Sea circuitously at the south-east corner of the Gulf of Ambrakia (the Gulf of Preveza). The question at issue is whether, *circa* 1100 B.C. and thereafter, there were any peoples, to the north and north-west of this line, who spoke Greek as their mother-tongue. It is agreed that a great part of the area between this southerly line and the eventual linguistic frontier in south-east Europe between the Greek and Latin languages had been Illyrian-speaking and Thracian-speaking before it became Greek-speaking. The Illyrian and Thracian languages, like the Greek language, were members of the Indo-European family, but the differences between them and Greek were sharp. Greek is a member of the 'Centum' group, whereas Thracian certainly, and Illyrian probably, was a member of the 'Satem' group.[1] Between Greek-speakers and Thracian-speakers, and between Greek-speakers and Illyrian-speakers, interpreters were needed.[2] The question in dispute is whether from the outset (that is, from a date immediately after the end of the post-Mycenaean Völkerwanderung), the Makedones, Pelagones, Paiones, and Epirots were Greek-speaking, or whether they were originally Illyrian-speaking or Thracian-speaking and became Greek-speaking only by a process of acculturation, when the Greek language had won prestige and had therefore become attractive as a result of the Hellenic World's success in forging ahead of its northern neighbours in the arts of civilization. Beloch holds that the Paiones and Epirots, as well as the Makedones and Pelagones, were Greek-speakers from the outset. Some modern scholars have held that none of these four peoples were. Others, again, have held that some of them were but that others were not.

This controversial question is the subject of the present Part. It is an important question because the answer—or answers—that we give to it will affect our interpretation of the history of the Hellenic World—particularly from the fourth century B.C. onwards. A discussion of this question therefore seems worth while; but we can hardly hope to arrive at incontrovertible conclusions, because the evidence, literary and archaeological, is fragmentary, and some, at any rate, of the literary evidence is confused and self-contradictory.

---

[1] The criterion by which these two groups are distinguished from each other is their treatment of the two sets of guttural sounds in the 'Ursprache'.

[2] See Xenophon, *Anabasis*, Book VII, chap. 3, § 25 (as between Greeks and Thracians at the turn of the fifth and fourth centuries B.C.), and Polybius, Book XXVIII, chap. 8, § 9 (as between Macedonians and Illyrians in 170–169 B.C., a date at which the Macedonians were indisputably Greek-speaking, whether or not they had been so originally).

2. The Meanings of the Terms 'Barbarian' and 'Hellene' in Hellenic Usage

PART of the evidence that we have to consider is the application, in Greek literature, of the terms 'barbarians' and 'Hellenes' to one or other of the four peoples in question. We have therefore first to remind ourselves of the changes in the usage of these terms in the course of Hellenic history.

The word 'barbaros' seems to have had a purely linguistic meaning originally. It was an expressive word, coined to describe someone whose language sounded like gibberish to the ear of the Greek-speaker who was employing the term 'barbaros'. This linguistic connotation is made unmistakable in the compound epithet βαρβαρόφωνοι, which is applied to the Carians in the Homeric epic.[1] An emphatic and offensive Homeric synonym for βαρβαρόφωνοι is ἀγριόφωνοι, which is applied to the Sinties.[2] In course of time, however, the word 'barbaros' acquired a cultural connotation, in addition to, or even instead of and in contrast to, its original linguistic connotation. This development was a result of the word's having come to be thought of as being the correlative and antithesis of the word 'Hellene'.

We have already noticed the evolution of the meaning of the word 'Hellene' in Greek literary usage.[3] It was originally the name of a North-West-Greek-speaking people which, before the post-Mycenaean Völkerwanderung, lived round Dodona in the interior of Epirus but which was carried by the Völkerwanderung south-eastwards into Malis and into north-western Euboea. As a result of this people's having settled in Malis, it subsequently gave its name to the association of twelve peoples in central and north-eastern continental Greece that formed the Delphi-Anthela amphictyony. As a consequence of the success of the Delphic oracle, the rising Greek city-states to the south and south-east of this amphictyony's original area sought and obtained admission to membership. As a consequence of this, again, the Delphi-Anthela amphictyony came to be accepted as being the representative institution of the rising Greek city-state civilization, and the name 'Hellene' came to be used as a common name for all communities that were recognized as being participants in this civilization.

[1] *Iliad*, II. 867.
[2] *Odyssey*, VIII. 294. See Part II, chap. 7, Annex, pp. 133–4, for an attempt to make out who these Sinties were.
[3] See Part I, chap. 1, pp. 9–10, and chap. 3, pp. 35–6 and 50–1.

Thus the word 'Hellene' ceased to be the national name of a particular North-West-Greek-speaking people and became the oecumenical name for all participants in the new civilization that had arisen, in the course of the first half of the last millennium B.C., round the shores of the Aegean Sea and in southern continental European Greece. The principal distinctive feature of this new 'Hellenic' civilization was the city-state way of life—a way that had not been a feature of the foregoing Mycenaean civilization in the same region. Normally, a Hellenic community, in the new cultural connotation of the word 'Hellenic', would be a Greek-speaking one;[1] yet, as a test of Hellenism, the city-state way of life evidently counted for more than the Greek language. The Luvian-speaking city-states in Lycia and Caria seem always to have been accepted by the peoples of the Greek-speaking city-states as being members of the Hellenic society, and when, in 228 B.C., the Romans were allowed to compete at the Pythian festival[2] and were thereby tacitly recognized as being within the Hellenic fold, this remarkable concession to them was made, no doubt, partly in virtue of their city-state culture, in spite of the fact that the Romans, like the Lycians and the Carians, spoke a non-Greek language as their mother-tongue.

We can catch the word 'Hellenic' in the act of acquiring a cultural connotation, first in addition to, and then instead of, its original racial and linguistic connotation. Herodotus, writing perhaps in the third quarter of the fifth century B.C., puts into Athenian mouths, in 479 B.C., an asseveration that, for the Athenians, it would be unthinkable to become traitors to 'the Hellenic World, united, as it is, by community of race and language, or to this world's common shrines and rites or to its common way of life'.[3] In this Herodotean definition of what constitutes Hellenism, common race and language are still put first, though common culture is now added. On the other hand, Isocrates in his *Panegyricus*, which he published in 380 B.C., makes the point that the Athenians, through their advancement of the Hellenic culture, 'have given the name "Hellenes" a spiritual connotation instead of its former racial one. People who share in our Athenian culture are now felt to have a stronger title to the name "Hellenes" than people who share with us merely a common physical make-up.'[4]

[1] Thucydides, Book I, chap. 3, holds that the adoption of the name 'Hellenes' was a gradual process; that it was brought about by social intercourse (τῇ ὁμιλίᾳ); and that mutual intelligibility (ὅσοι ἀλλήλων συνίεσαν) was a limiting condition. N. G. L. Hammond, *Epirus* (Oxford, 1967, Clarendon Press), p. 420, maintains that the word συνίεσαν need not necessarily be understood in the linguistic sense.   [2] See Polybius, Book II, chap. 12.

[3] τὸ Ἑλληνικὸν ἐὸν ὅμαιμόν τε καὶ ὁμόγλωσσον, καὶ θεῶν ἱδρύματά τε κοινὰ καὶ θυσίαι, ἤθεά τε ὁμότροπα (Herodotus, Book VIII, chap. 144).

[4] τὸ τῶν Ἑλλήνων ὄνομα πεποιήκατε μηκέτι τοῦ γένους ἀλλὰ τῆς διανοίας δοκεῖν εἶναι, καὶ μᾶλλον Ἕλληνας καλεῖσθαι τοὺς τῆς παιδεύσεως τῆς ἡμετέρας ἢ τοὺς τῆς κοινῆς φύσεως μετέχοντας (Isocrates, *Panegyricus*, 50).

Thus, by the time of King Philip II of Macedon's reign (*regnabat* 359–336 B.C.), in which the question whether the Macedonians were or were not Hellenes first became a matter of acute controversy, the term 'Hellene' itself had become ambiguous—and, with it, the term 'barbarian', which, by this time, had long since come to be used as the antithesis of the term 'Hellene'. Even if Isocrates was in advance of his time in giving 'Hellenism' an exclusively cultural connotation, his definition of 'Hellenism' in the *Panegyricus* was 'the wave of the future'. According to this new definition, it was not only possible for non-Greek-speakers to be Hellenes in virtue of their having been initiated into the Athenian form of the Hellenic culture; it was also possible for Greek-speakers to be barbarians in the cultural sense of being strangers to the Hellenic city-state culture, or at any rate strangers to it in its advanced Athenian form.[1] This new conception of Hellenism is, no doubt, the ground on which Isocrates draws a distinction between Hellenes and Makedones; but it is significant that, in the same breath, he distinguishes the Makedones from the barbarians too.[2] The ambiguity that had overtaken this pair of correlative terms—'Hellenes' and 'barbarians'—makes it impossible for us to be sure of the sense in which the terms are being used, in the fifth century B.C. and thereafter, apropos of peoples beyond the Pale running from the mouth of the River Peneios to the Ambracian Gulf.

What, for instance, does Thucydides mean to imply when he stigmatizes, as being barbarians, the Thesprotoi in 432 B.C.,[3] the Amphilokhoi in 430 B.C.,[4] and the Khaones, Thesprotoi, Molossoi, Atintanes, Parauaioi, Orestai, and Makedones in 429 B.C.?[5] Does he mean that they were non-Greek-speaking? This is certainly the sense in which he speaks of the rural Amphilokhoi as being 'barbarians' in 430 B.C., for he is contrasting them with the people of the Amphilochian city of Argos, who, he tells us, had become Greek-speaking through having adopted settlers from the neighbouring Corinthian colony Ambrakia into their citizen-body.[6] Thucydides' unambiguously linguistic usage of the word 'barbarian' here, apropos of the rural Amphilokhoi, is presumptive evidence that, when he also calls other Epirot and Macedonian peoples 'barbarians', he means that they, too, were not Greek-speakers. We cannot be certain, however, that, in these other passages, Thucydides is not

---

[1] For instances in which Thucydides applies the term 'barbarians' to peoples that were probably Greek-speaking, see Hammond, *Epirus*, pp. 421–2.

[2] Isocrates, *Philippus*, 154 (113).

[3] Thucydides, Book I, chap. 48.

[4] Book II, chap. 68.   [5] Book II, chap. 81.

[6] Book II, chap. 68. Thucydides' words ἠλληνίσθησαν τὴν νῦν γλῶσσαν surely can only mean that the Argive Amphilokhoi had become Greek-speaking after having previously spoken some non-Greek language. Hammond, *Epirus*, pp. 421–3, interprets the passage to mean that they had adopted the Ambraciot (i.e. Corinthian) form of North-West Greek in place of a local Amphilochian form of it, but he concedes that the evidence is inconclusive.

using the word 'barbarian' in the non-linguistic sense which it had already acquired partially for Herodotus, and which it was to acquire completely for Isocrates. The Makedones, at any rate, were Greek-speaking,[1] and the Orestai, and perhaps the Parauaioi too, were Makedones, though they were politically autonomous in their relation to the Argead Kingdom of Macedon.

Our uncertainty is increased by our recognition of the pertinent fact that the Hellenic World never developed a science of philology in the modern sense. We therefore cannot be sure that, when a Greek writer makes a pronouncement about some people's mother-tongue, he has got his linguistic facts right. In the passage, cited above, in which Thucydides tells us that the rural Amphilokhoi were non-Greek-speakers, he is so circumstantial and so explicit that it is hard to believe that he is in error. Moreover, his description of the Aetolian Eurytanes as 'being reported to speak a language that is extremely difficult to understand'[2] seems to indicate that his informants had recognized the Eurytanes' language as being a dialect of Greek, though an outlandish one. But can we be sure that Greek-speaking observers who spoke one of the standard dialects of the Hellenic city-state world—Ionic, for instance, or Attic, or the Corinthian form of North-West Greek—invariably succeeded in recog nizing the Greekness of a Greek dialect which, from their point of view, was as outlandish as the Eurytanian dialect was, but which, to the ear of a professional philologist, if there had been such a person, would have proved to be Greek without a doubt if he had noted the sounds phonetically and had then studied them scientifically?

We can put this point in present-day terms by imagining someone whose mother-tongue is the High German κοινή created by Luther's translation of the Bible to be visiting some rural district in Luxembourg or in Alsace or in one of the forest cantons of Switzerland. Supposing that our imaginary visitor is not a trained philologist, is he likely to be aware that the, to him, unintelligible gibberish spoken by these country-folk is, in truth, a dialect of his own High German native language? This will be unlikely *a fortiori* if we make our visitor, not a High-German-speaker from, say, Frankfurt am Main, but a Low-German-speaker from Flanders or Holland.[3] Now let us imagine a North-West-Greek-speaking

---

[1] See Part II, chap. 3, pp. 64–79.

[2] Ἀγνωστότατοι γλῶσσαν (Thucydides, Book III, chap. 94). If the original 'Eurytos' city Oikhalia' lay in the future Histiaiotis (see Part I, chap. 3, pp. 34–5, 37, 47, and Part II, chap. 7, pp. 119 and 120), the Eurytanes, like the Makedones, were North-East-Greek-speaking refugees from the future Thessaly, and it was to be expected that, after centuries of seclusion, the dialect of both these displaced peoples would have become peculiar.

[3] After I had written this paragraph, I found that I had been anticipated, in suggesting this parallel, by P. Kretschmer, *Einleitung in die Geschichte der griechischen Sprache* (Göttingen, 1896, Vandenhoeck und Ruprecht), p. 285 ('Der Norddeutsche versteht auch nicht die Sprache des schwäbischen Bauern, die darum dennoch deutsch ist') and by F. Geyer,

Corinthian and an Attic-speaking Athenian visiting Eurytania. Can we be sure that they, and especially the Athenian, would have been the competent untutored philologists that Thucydides' informants evidently were? And can we be sure that, if they had visited Khaonia or Macedon or Pelagonia or Paionia, they could have detected unerringly whether the inhabitants were Greek-speakers or not?

The linguistic facts were evidently complicated in some cases. For instance, in 430 B.C. the Argive Amphilokhoi were Greek-speaking, while the rest of the Amphilokhoi were not. It seems probable, however, that all the Amphilokhoi alike had been Greek-speakers originally, considering that their national name is a Greek one and that at least four out of five recorded place-names in their country—Argos, Krenai, Metropolis, Idomene[1]—are Greek too. It looks as if the Amphilokhoi had been Greek-speakers who had become non-Greek-speaking (presumably through contact or fusion with non-Greek-speaking neighbours), while the Argive Amphilokhoi had become Greek-speaking once more (by contact and fusion with the Ambraciots, according to Thucydides). Again, we know from Thucydides[2] that the Makedones expanded, by conquest, over a wide area that had previously been occupied by non-Macedonian peoples, and that they evicted some of these but left others *in situ* as their subjects. In these historical circumstances the Makedones' original mother-tongue, whether this was Greek or was non-Greek, is likely to have spread only gradually among the Makedones' subjects, and these subjugated peoples' languages are likely to have had a counter-influence on the Makedones' ancestral language. No one will dispute that the whole of Macedonia, at least up to the widest limits of the former kingdom, had become Greek-speaking, and this long since, by A.D. 527. At the same time it seems probable that, from the beginning of the expansion of the Kingdom of Macedon in the seventh or sixth century B.C. until some time after this expansion had reached its final limits, the ancestral language of the Makedones was not the only language current in the territories under their rule, and it also seems probable that some of these non-Macedonian local languages left permanent traces on the Macedonians' ancestral language.

With these preliminary observations always in mind, let us now examine the evidence, such as it is, for determining what was the ancestral language of the Makedones, Pelagones, Paiones, and Epirots. When we have come to at least tentative conclusions in each case (and each of the

Makedonien bis zur Thronbesteigung Philipps II (Munich and Berlin, 1930, Oldenbourg), p. 35 ('Wie auch uns heute die holländische Sprache ein fremdes Idiom ist, und die Friesen und Oberbayern auf Grund ihrer Dialekte dem hochdeutsch sprechendem als fremdsprächig erscheinen können').

[1] The fifth known Amphilokhian place-name is Olpai, which is not transparently Greek, but is also not manifestly un-Greek. [2] Book II, chap. 99.

four cases must be considered independently of the others), let us then try to reconstruct, in the light of the geographical, archaeological, and literary evidence, the course of historical events through which these four peoples came to occupy the territories in which we find them in and after the sixth century B.C.

3. What was the Ancestral Language of the Makedones?

STRABO, writing during the reign of Augustus, reckons Macedonia as being part of 'what is undisputedly Hellas at the present day'.[1] This statement of Strabo's is unexceptionable, and it is evidence that Macedonia was a Greek-speaking country in Augustus' time—though, as has been noted,[2] there were some non-Greek-speaking countries, such as Lycia and Caria, which had nevertheless been felt by Greek-speaking Hellenes to belong to the Hellenic World in virtue of their having adopted the city-state way of life. Of course, no one disputes that Macedonia was Greek-speaking in Augustus' day; so Strabo's inclusion of Macedonia in contemporary Hellas is less informative than his exclusion from contemporary Hellas[3] of an adjacent country, Epirus, which was also Greek-speaking at that date. It looks as if Strabo had not thought out clearly what he meant by 'Hellas'. The northernmost districts of the traditional Hellas were Perrhaibia, the rest of Thessaly, Aetolia, and Akarnania; so the traditional Hellas had excluded Macedonia as well as Epirus. Thus Strabo's 'Hellas' is not the traditional one. On the other hand, if Strabo meant by 'Hellas' the Greek-speaking world of his day, he ought to have included in it not only Macedonia but also Epirus, Sicily, considerable tracts of western Anatolia, and some substantial enclaves in northern Syria, as a minimum, not to speak of Alexandria-on-Nile.

How far back in time the people of Macedonia had been Greek-speaking is a question that Strabo does not answer for us. We have evidence that they were already Greek-speaking 150 years and 200 years earlier than Augustus' time. In 167 B.C., L. Aemilius Paullus announced at Amphipolis the Roman Government's decisions for the settlement of continental European Greece in a public speech which he delivered in Latin. For the benefit of Paullus' audience, which was drawn from all parts of Greece, his speech was then translated into Greek.[4] This implies that, at that date, the Macedonians were Greek-speaking; for, in a concourse at Amphipolis, the majority of the participants must have been Macedonians, and the Macedonians were also the people who were most vitally affected. Polybius, in his account of the Battle of Kynoskephalai, which was fought in 197 B.C., says that when, in the first phase of the engagement, the Macedonians were getting the better of the Romans

---

[1] τῆς ἐν τῷ παρόντι Ἑλλάδος ἀναντιλέκτως οὔσης (Book VII, chap. 7, § 1 (C. 321); cp. chap. 7, § 4 (C. 323), and fragm. 13 of the same book).

[2] In Part II, chap. 2, p. 59.

[3] Book VII, chap. 7, § 1 (C. 321).

[4] Livy, Book XLV, chap. 29.

ἕτερος ἐφ᾽ ἑτέρῳ τῶν ἐκ τῆς ἐφεδρείας Μακεδόνων ἔθει πρὸς τὸν Φίλιππον, ἀναβοῶν· Βασιλεῦ, φεύγουσιν οἱ πολέμιοι· μὴ παρῇς τὸν καιρόν· οὐ μένουσιν ἡμᾶς οἱ βάρβαροι.[1] It would be difficult to believe that these Makedones who, in 197 B.C., were speaking of the Romans as 'barbarians', were saying this, not in Greek, but in a 'barbarian' language of their own. Livy, in a passage dealing with the year 200 B.C. which is presumably the translation of a lost passage of Polybius' work, puts into the mouths of Macedonian envoys, addressing the Aetolian public assembly, the statement that the Macedonians spoke the same language as the Aetolians and the Acarnanians.[2] Polybius, in a passage dealing with the year 211–210 B.C., puts into the mouth of an Acarnanian envoy, addressing the Spartan assembly, the words: 'Previously you were contending for honour and glory with the Achaeans and Macedonians, who are your kinsfolk, and their leader Philip; today a war is starting in which the enemy are aliens and in which the issue is slavery or freedom.'[3]

We know that the Kingdom of Macedon, within its northern frontiers as these ran in the reign of King Philip V (*regnabat* 220–179 B.C.), had been built up gradually, in the course of perhaps no fewer than four centuries, by a process of progressive conquest. The Argead dynasty and its successor the Antigonid dynasty had incorporated in the Kingdom a number of originally non-Macedonian territories, some of which may have been Greek-speaking; but others had certainly not been Greek-speaking before the Macedonian conquest, and the spread of the Greek language in these territories must have taken time. The ultimate question is whether the original Makedones were Greek-speakers from the beginning, or whether they, too, had, at some stage in their history, adopted the Greek language in place of some non-Greek ancestral language of theirs.

Some light is thrown on this question by the Macedonians' national name. 'Makedones' is a variant of 'Makednoi' (these two variations on the same root stand to each other in the same relation as 'Pelagones' and 'Pelignoi'). 'Makednoi' is a Greek word meaning 'tallboys', and Herodotus informs us[4] that 'Makednoi' was the national name of the people who, in the Post-Völkerwanderung Age, were in occupation of the Doris in central Greece and who, by Herodotus' time, were reputed to have been the progenitors of all the North-West-Greek-speaking communities in the Peloponnese and the Aegean from Sikyon, inclusive,

---

[1] Polybius, Book XVIII, chap. 22.

[2] 'Aetolos, Acarnanas, Macedonas, eiusdem linguae homines, leves ad tempus ortae causae diiungunt coniunguntque; cum alienigenis, cum barbaris, aeternum omnibus Graecis bellum est eritque' (Livy, Book XXXI, chap. 29).

[3] τότε μὲν γὰρ ὑπὲρ φιλοτιμίας καὶ δόξης ἐφιλοτιμεῖσθε πρὸς Ἀχαιοὺς καὶ Μακεδόνας ὁμοφύλους καὶ τὸν τούτων ἡγεμόνα Φίλιππον· νῦν δὲ περὶ δουλείας ἐνίσταται πόλεμος πρὸς ἀλλοφύλους ἀνθρώπους (Polybius, Book IX, chap. 37, § 7).   [4] Book I, chap. 56. Cp. Book VIII, chap. 43.

south-eastwards. Herodotus also tells us, in the same passage, that these Makednoi had migrated to the central Greek Doris from the Histiaiotis district in north-western Thessaly, from which they had been evicted (presumably in the course of the post-Mycenaean Völkerwanderung). Histiaiotis adjoins Macedon in the wider meaning of the name Macedon, which includes the Macedonian principalities in Upper Macedonia besides the kingdom of the Argead dynasty in Lower Macedonia. Moreover, the name of the Magnetes, who, in the Post-Völkerwanderung Age, occupied the mountains overhanging the Aegean coast of Thessaly, may be a third variation on the same root (Makedn-etes),[1] and there is some linguistic and anthropological evidence for an affinity between the Magnetes and the Makedones. The first B in the name of Lake Boibeïs (named after the goddess Phoibe), on the inland frontier of Thessalian Magnesia, shows that the Magnetes, like the Makedones, did not change the original Indo-European BH into PH (Φ), but either retained it[2] or replaced it, not by PH, as other Greek dialects did, but by B.[3] The Magnetes, as well as the Makedones, danced the Karpaia dance and celebrated the Hetairidia festival.[4]

These facts seem to prove conclusively that the original Makedones were a Greek-speaking people that had migrated to the Haliakmon Valley from Histiaiotis, at the time when the Makednoi had emigrated from Histiaiotis to the central Greek Doris and the Magnetes, perhaps, from Histiaiotis to the mountain fastness in eastern Thessaly to which they gave their name. But, even though these ethnika may indicate that the Makedones were a Greek-speaking people at the beginning of their history, as they undoubtedly were at the end of it, this does not prove that they spoke Greek persistently throughout the intervening time. This is evident when we recall the case of the Amphilokhoi, an Epirot people with a Greek name, all of whom, except the inhabitants of Argos Amphilokhikon, spoke a non-Greek language in 430 B.C., according to Thucydides' explicit testimony,[5] though by Augustus' time the Amphilokhoi, like the Makedones, were Greek-speakers undisputedly.

The evidence of geographical names is also inconclusive, as has been noted already apropos of the Greek place-names of the non-Greek-speaking Amphilokhoi.[6]

[1] Hesiod, fr. 5 (Rzach), makes Makednos and Magnes a pair of brothers.
[2] The Magnesian and Macedonian equivalent for the Indo-European BH may have been the sound that was represented, in these two variants of North-East Greek, by the Greek letter B, since in the Greek alphabet there was no letter or combination of letters that represented BH.
[3] See K. J. Beloch, *Griechische Geschichte*. 2nd ed., Erster Band, Erste Abteilung (Strassburg, 1912, Trübner), p. 88.
[4] O. Hoffmann, *Die Makedonen* (Göttingen, 1906, Vandenhoeck und Ruprecht), pp. 95 and 115.
[5] See Part II, chap. 2, p. 60, with n. 6.   [6] See Part II, chap. 2, p. 62.

For instance, those in the original Pieria, between the eastern spurs of Mount Olympus and the western shore of the Thermaic Gulf, were Greek for the most part, at any rate: e.g. the river-names Sys, Enipeus, Aison, and Leukos, and the place-names Leibethron and Petra. On the other hand the place-names (Phagres, Galepsos, Oisyme) were all non-Greek in the new Pieria, between the south-eastern foot of Mount Pangaios and the north shore of the Aegean Sea, where the Pieres had found asylum after they had been evicted from their original home by the Makedones. This geographical nomenclature tells us that either the Makedones or the Pieres were Greek-speakers, but it does not tell us which of the two peoples was the Greek-speaking one. Were the Greek geographical names in the original Pieria imposed by the Makedones? Or were they legacies to the Makedones from the Pieres? And were the non-Greek place-names in the new Pieria taken over by the Pieres from the previous inhabitants? Or were they introduced by the Pieres themselves? We are left in the dark.

The historical significance of the Greek place-names in the Amphaxitis —Ikhnai, Europos, Atalante, Gortynia, Eidomene—is similarly ambiguous. We know that the Amphaxitis was inhabited by Paiones before the Makedones conquered it.[1] On the strength of these place-names, Beloch[2] maintains that the Paiones were Greek-speaking. But how could he, or can we, be sure that these place-names were not imposed by Macedonian colonists? Again, when we are told that Pella was the name given by the Macedonian conquerors to a place previously called Bounomos,[3] we do not know whether Bounomos is in truth the Greek name that it is on the face of it, or whether it is a rationalization, in terms of the Greek language, of the Illyrian name Bouneima[4] which was to be found in Epirus and which Hoffmann associates[5] with Bounnos, the name of a place in Illyria[6] that was the word for 'hill' in fifth-century-B.C. Cyrenaica[7] and is also the word for 'mountain' in Modern Greek.

Nor do we know whether 'Pella' is a Greek or a non-Greek name. There is, however, one place, and this an important one, whose Macedonian name is certainly Greek, while its pre-Macedonian name is certainly Thraco-Phrygian. When the Argeadai conquered Edessa, overhanging the north-west corner of the plain of Emathia, from the Brygoi, they renamed it Aigai. This is a place-name that occurs in Euboea and

---

[1] See *Iliad*, II. 548–850; Thucydides, Book II, chap. 99.
[2] In op. cit., vol. cit., part. cit., p. 70.
[3] Steph. Byz., s.v. Βούνομος and s.v. Πέλλα.
[4] Steph. Byz., Βούνειμα· πόλις Ἠπείρου. See also eundem, s.v. Τραμπύα.
[5] In op. cit., p. 257.
[6] Steph. Byz., s.v. Βοῦννος.
[7] Herodotus, Book IV, chap. 199.

in other parts of Greece, with the meaning 'breakers',[1] and the river that flows through Aigai does break in waterfalls over a precipice at this city. Moreover, Aigai is a translation into Greek of the city's previous Thraco-Phrygian name Edessa. Stephanus of Byzantium tells us that Urfa in Mesopotamian Syria, which was renamed after the original Edessa in Macedon when the Macedonians conquered south-western Asia, was given this name because of the rushing of the waters there;[2] and we are told by Clement of Alexandria[3] that βέδυ (i.e. ϝέδυ) was the Phrygian word for 'water'.

The Greekness of the name 'Aigai' indicates that the Makedones were Greek-speaking at the time when the Argeadai conquered Edessa and made this place the capital of the Kingdom of Macedon. We may guess that this was the act of the first recorded king of the Argead line, Perdikkas I; and, as Alexander I, who came to the throne soon after the beginning of the fifth century B.C., was the sixth successor of Perdikkas I, in an unbroken succession from fathers to sons, according to Herodotus,[4] Perdikkas I must have reigned at some date in the middle decades of the seventh century B.C. Hoffmann has demonstrated that the names of Alexander I's six predecessors on the throne, as given by Herodotus,[5] are all Greek, as well as the names of all subsequent kings and other known members of the Argead house down to its extinction after the death of Alexander III.[6] The one possible exception is the name of Alexander I's sister Gygaia.[7]

Since there is no better evidence that the Argeads were of a different nationality from their Macedonian followers than there is for the Spartan Herakleidai having been of a different nationality from their 'Dorian' (i.e. North-West-Greek-speaking) followers, the Greekness of the names of the members of the Argead house is evidence that the Makedones had been Greek-speaking since at least as far back as Perdikkas I's time, *circa* 650 B.C. If their national name indicates convincingly that they had also been Greek-speaking originally, it is improbable that they were speaking a non-Greek language at any time between the date of their eviction from Histiaiotis, which probably occurred during the post-Mycenaean Völkerwanderung in the twelfth century B.C., and the date of the Argeads' conquest of Eordaia and the north-west corner of the Brygoi's country in Emathia, since, during the intervening centuries, the Makedones were presumably confined to the Haliakmon valley and had

---

[1] Cp. the name Αἰγαῖον Πέλαγος, the word αἰγιαλός, and the mythical personal name Αἰγεύς.

[2] Steph. Byz.: Ἔδεσσα· πόλις Συρίας, διὰ τὴν τῶν ὑδάτων ῥύμην οὕτω κληθεῖσα.

[3] *Stromata*, Book V, chap. 8, § 46.

[4] Book VIII, chap. 139.   [5] In loc. cit.

[6] See Hoffmann, op. cit., pp. 129–37. See also the present chapter, pp. 71–2.

[7] See Hoffmann, op. cit., pp. 217–18.

no non-Greek-speaking subjects—or masters—whose language they might have adopted.

Moreover, Hoffmann, in an examination of all known Macedonian personal names that is both exhaustive and scholarly,[1] demonstrates convincingly that all known Macedonian personal names are Greek. Names that look un-Greek at first sight turn out to be shortened forms, of the kind that is familiar in the Post-Alexandrine Age, of Greek names of the long-winded original Indo-European compound type consisting of a combination of two roots. An exception that proves the rule is Βυργῖνος Κραστῶνος, whose name is one of the forty decipherable names of King Perdikkas II's sureties in the Attic inscription[2] recording a treaty between Perdikkas and Athens. The Κραστῶν of this inscription is presumably Herodotus' Κρηστῶν;[3] and Herodotus notes[4] that, in his day, Κρηστῶν was inhabited by Pelasgoi who spoke a non-Greek language.[5] The other thirty-nine decipherable names of Macedonians in this inscription are all manifestly Greek.[6] So are the names of all Alexander III's ten somatophylakes;[7] and no known officer of Alexander III's has a name that is manifestly non-Greek.[8]

Nor are there any indubitably non-Greek names of Macedonians coming from the Upper Macedonian cantons,[9] though here, if anywhere in Macedonia, we might expect to find some non-Greek names, since Upper Macedonia marched with Epirus and Illyria. In 430 B.C. the king of the Orestai bore the Greek name Antiokhos,[10] and in 424 B.C. the king of Lynkestis bore the probably Greek name Arrhabaios, and his father the clearly Greek name Bromeros.[11] Alexander III's somatophylax Perdikkas was an Orestian,[12] and so was his somatophylax Krateros.[13] Polyperkhon son of Simmias came from Tymphaia,[14] and so did the four sons of Andromenes: Amyntas, Simmias, Polemon, and Attalos[15] (a name which Hoffmann interprets[16] as a short form for Atalophron). The Elimian name Derdas, too, can be interpreted in terms of Greek.[17] The Lyncestian king Arrhabaios' son-in-law Sirras[18] is identified by Hoffmann[19] as having

---

[1] See op. cit., pp. 116–231.   [2] *I.G.*, vol. i, No. 42, p. 27.
[3] Κρηστῶν? Κρηστών? Κρήστων?   [4] In Book I, chap. 57.
[5] See Part II, chap. 7, Annex, pp. 126–34, for a discussion of the question what this language was.   [6] Hoffmann, op. cit., p. 150.
[7] Ibid., pp. 178–9.   [8] Ibid., p. 201.   [9] Ibid., p. 167.
[10] Thucydides, Book II, chap. 80.
[11] Thucydides, Book IV, chap. 83.
[12] Arrian, *Anabasis*, Book VI, chap. 28, § 4; *Indica*, chap. 18, § 5.
[13] Arrian, *Indica*, chap. 18, § 5.
[14] Lycophron, l. 802; Diodorus, Book XVII, chap. 56, § 2.
[15] Arrian, *Indica*, chap. 18, § 6.
[16] In op. cit., p. 157.
[17] Hoffmann, op. cit., pp. 159–60.
[18] Strabo, *Geographica*, Book VII, chap. 6, § 8 (C. 326).
[19] In op. cit., pp. 160–3.

been, not an Elimian, but an Illyrian, and Hoffmann associates his name with that of the town Siris (the present-day Serrhés).[1]

Of the names of the Upper Macedonian cantons themselves, Orestis and Parauaia are transparently Greek,[2] and Lynkos, the country of the Lynkestai, may be the same word as the modern Greek λόγγος, meaning 'thicket' or 'forest'.[3] Whether the name of Mount Tymphe, which gave its name to Tymphaia, is or is not Greek, it would appear to be related to the name 'Tymphrestos', which is borne by a more southerly section of the main chain of Pindus above the headwaters of the River Sperkheios, in a country that was certainly Greek-speaking. Of the Upper Macedonian cantons, Elimiotis alone bears a name that has an un-Greek appearance.[4]

Hoffmann sums up his study of Macedonian personal names in his finding that 'the names of the genuine full-blooded Macedonians—above all, the names of the princes and nobles—are pure Greek both structurally and phonetically (ihrer Bildung und ihren Lauten nach)'.[5]

The Macedonian month-names[6] testify even more convincingly than the Macedonian personal names in favour of the conclusion that the Makedones were Greek-speakers. Hoffmann finds that only three month-names out of the twelve—namely Αὐδναῖος, Ξανδικός, and Γορπιαῖος—are not transparently Greek; and a less cautious scholar might have been tempted to derive Ξανδικός from ξάνθος and Γορπιαῖος from καρπός, leaving only the single name Αὐδναῖος unexplained in terms of the Greek language. Of the nine month-names that are certainly Greek, Hoffmann points out that six have counterparts in indisputably Greek-speaking communities. The Apellai festival, which gave its name to the Macedonian month Ἀπελλαῖος, was celebrated at a number of places in central Greece and in the Peloponnese, and the celebration of the Artemisia festival, which gave its name to the Macedonian month Ἀρτεμίσιος, was still more widely spread in the Greek-speaking World. The Dia festival,

---

[1] For Siris, see Herodotus, Book VIII, chap. 115, and Book V, chap. 15; Livy, Book XLV, chap. 4; Steph. Byz., s.v. Σίρρα.

[2] Orestis was also called Maketia according to Steph. Byz., s.v. Μακεδονία; The River Aôos, which gave Parauaia its name, means, in Greek, 'the river coming from the East'. But the original form of the name was Auas, according to N. G. L. Hammond, 'Prehistoric Epirus and the Dorian Invasion', in *The Annual of the British School at Athens*, vol. 22 (1934), p. 161, n. 4, or Aias, according to Hammond, *Epirus*, pp. 394, 447, 458.

[3] The pass between Lynkos and Eordaia was heavily wooded in 199 B.C. (see Livy, Book XXXI, chap. 29).

[4] The correct spelling in Greek appears to be Ἐλειμιωτίς or Ἐλειμεία. See A. J. B. Wace and M. S. Thompson, 'A Latin Inscription from Perrhaebia', in *The Annual of the British School at Athens*, vol. 17, pp. 193–204, on p. 197, n. 4. This is the spelling in an inscription found at Delphi (*Bulletin de Correspondance Hellénique*, 1897, p. 112) and in Thucydides, Book II, chap. 99, in a majority of the MSS. The spelling of the ethnikon in the Latin inscription found in Perrhaibia is 'Elemiotae'.

[5] Op. cit., p. 230.

[6] See ibid., pp. 100–11.

which gave its name to the Macedonian month Δῖος, was celebrated in Perrhaibia and in Aetolia. The Macedonian month-name Πάναμος occurs in a number of North-West-Greek-speaking and Ionic-speaking communities. The Macedonian month-name Δαίσιος occurs in the full form Θεοδαίσιος in a number of places in Crete and in the Anatolian Doris, as well as at Andros and at Mytilene. The Macedonian month-name Λώϊος occurs in the full form Ὁμολώϊος in several North-East-Greek-speaking communities (Thessaly, Boeotia, and Eresos on Lesbos), as well as in Aetolia and at Naupaktos. These correspondences, modified, in some cases, by variations, taken together with the fact that three of the nine Macedonian names of months that are transparently Greek—namely Περίτιος, Δύστρος, and Ὑπερβερεταῖος—seem to be peculiar to Macedon itself, point to the Macedonian month-names being indigenous and not being loans from abroad.

This evidence that the Makedones who progressively created the kingdom of Lower Macedon and the Upper Macedonian principalities were Greek-speakers from first to last is not merely impressive; it is also conclusive. Several considerations that have been held to invalidate it all prove, on examination, to be themselves invalid.

For instance, it has been pointed out that Isocrates, writing in 346 B.C., says of King Amyntas III of Macedon that 'he is the only Hellene who has taken it upon himself to rule over an alien race'.[1] Isocrates is here accepting, as historical, the Argeadai's claim to be descendants of the Temenidai of the Peloponnesian Argos. This claim had been accepted, as being valid, in the Hellenic World since the date—perhaps 496 B.C.[2]— at which, on the strength of it, Alexander I of Macedon had been admitted to compete at the Olympian festival after his title to count as a Hellene, which was a required condition for taking part in any of the athletic events, had been challenged by Alexander's prospective competitors.[3] This Argead pretension was, of course, fictitious. It was based solely on the apparent affinity of the names 'Argeadai' and 'Argos'. Alexander I had represented that 'Argeadas' was a synonym for 'Argeios'.[4] In truth, 'Argeadas' means 'a descendant of Argeas',[5] and the name of this eponymous ancestor of the Macedonian royal house may not even be derived from the same root as the word 'Argos'. It may be a derivative of the root ἀρχ-, meaning 'rule'. Alexander I was claiming that, whatever his Macedonian followers might be, he himself was a Peloponnesian

[1] μόνος . . . τῶν Ἑλλήνων οὐχ ὁμοφύλου γένους ἄρχειν ἀξιώσας (Isocrates, *Philippus*, 108 (104).
[2] See A. Dascalakis, *The Hellenism of the Ancient Macedonians* (Thessaloníki, 1965, Institute for Balkan Studies), p. 159.
[3] Herodotus, Book V, chap. 22. Cp. Book VIII, chap. 137.
[4] Herodotus, Book, V, chap. 22.
[5] For Argeas, see Steph. Byz., s.v. Ἀργέου νῆσος.

Argive Heraklid; and, in making this claim, he was taking a leaf out of King Kleomenes I of Sparta's book.

When, in 508 B.C., the priestess of Athena in the goddess's temple on the acropolis of Athens had told Kleomenes not to enter the temple because it was forbidden ground for 'Dorians', Kleomenes had answered: 'I am not a Dorian; I am an Achaean'.[1] The point that he had been making was that the two royal houses of Sparta claimed, like the royal house of Peloponnesian Argos, to be Herakleidai, who had 'returned' to the Peloponnese when their 'Dorian' followers had been entering the Peloponnese for the first time. Alexander I of Macedon, taking his cue from Kleomenes I of Sparta's quick-witted repartee to the Athenian priestess, had said, at Olympia: 'I am not a Macedonian; I am an Achaean'. Historically the Argeadai were, no doubt, as authentically Macedonian as the Peloponnesian 'Herakleidai' were authentically 'Dorian' in the sense of being of the same race as their North-West-Greek-speaking followers. Both these claims to a Heraklid ancestry were made and were accepted for the same reasons. Either claim was made in order to give a patent of Hellenic nobility to the ruling house of a people who, in the case of the 'Dorians', were looked upon as interlopers, and who, in the Macedonians' case, were looked upon as outsiders. Both claims were accepted because the Argead kings of Macedon, as well as the Temenid kings of Argos and the two royal houses of Sparta, had become important enough factors in Hellenic international affairs to make it politic for the Hellenic World to accept their pretensions to a particularly distinguished origin.

Corresponding claims were made, with the same success, by other dynasties. For instance, the royal house of Lynkestis retorted to the Argeads' claim to be Argive Temenids by claiming, for their part, to be Corinthian Bacchiads.[2] The Corinthian colonies, Apollonia and Epidamnos, on the Adriatic coast of southern Illyria will, no doubt, have traded with the interior as far east as Lynkestis, and this will have impressed the kings of Lynkestis with the splendour of the Corinthian form of the Hellenic civilization. The royal house of Molossia claimed, with the same motive, to be Aiakidai. Their effective credentials consisted in their political importance; and, no doubt, it was this that led Kleisthenes the despot of Sikyon (*dominabatur circa* 600–560 B.C.) to accept Alkon, king of the Molossians, as one of the suitors for his daughter Agariste.[3] At that date the Molossians may have been non-Greek-speaking (if Thucydides is to be understood as meaning that they were still non-Greek-speaking in 429 B.C.),[4] and there is no evidence that, in Alkon's

---

[1] Herodotus, Book V, chap. 72.
[2] Strabo, Book VII, chap. 7, § 17 (C. 326).
[3] Herodotus, Book VI, chap. 127. [4] See pp. 60–1.

day, the Molossian royal house had yet thought of claiming kinship with Achilles. In the latter part of the fifth century B.C., Teres, the founder of the Odrysian Empire, claimed descent from Tereus, the legendary Thracian king of Daulis. But this claim was rejected by Thucydides, at any rate.[1]

These fictitious genealogies of royal houses give us no authentic information about the nationality of these houses themselves or their subjects. In particular, the Argeads' claim to be Temenids does not prove that the non-Argead Makedones were not Greek-speaking. Nor, again, can the impressive evidence of the surviving Macedonian personal names be discounted by pointing out that some of them are also to be found in the Homeric epic or in other Greek literature that purports to give a record of the 'heroic' age before the post-Mycenaean Völkerwanderung. The Macedonian names Alexandros, Ptolemaios, and Menelaos, for instance, are also Homeric, and the Macedonian masculine name Kassandros is the counterpart of the Homeric feminine name Kassandra. But, as Hoffmann points out,[2] it is most improbable that the names Alexandros, Ptolemaios, and Kassandros, at any rate, were borrowed by the Makedones from Homer. The name Alexandros, which was made glorious by the Macedonian kings Alexandros I and III, is borne in the *Iliad* by a character who is not only a coward but is actually the villain of the piece. The name Alexandros must have been already a cherished one in the Argead house for it to survive, as it did survive, there after the Argeadai had become acquainted with the *Iliad*, in which this name is made notorious by its ill repute. Nor would Antipater have named his son Kassandros after a daughter of Priam whose legendary fate was so tragic, and whose name, in its epic context, was therefore so inauspicious. Kassandros, too, must have been an old-established Macedonian name. As for Ptolemaios, which was one of the most popular Macedonian names,[3] its epic associations are innocuous, but they are also undistinguished. In the *Iliad* the name appears once only,[4] and here it is borne by the father of Menelaos' charioteer. The Macedonian name Menelaos might conceivably have been taken from the Homeric epic. Yet the Homeric Menelaos is not one of the glamorous Achaean heroes. As Hoffmann points out,[5] no Macedonian, that we know of, was named Aias or Diomedes. We do not know of any Macedonian Agamemnon either, though this famous Homeric name was borne by a king of Kyme in Aiolis. Thus the appearance of a few Homeric names among the numerous known Macedonian personal names does not impugn the evidence, given

---

[1] See Thucydides, Book II, chap. 29, and S. Casson, *Macedonia, Thrace and Illyria* (London, 1926, Oxford University Press), pp. 108 and 163.
[2] In op. cit., pp. 119–20. [3] Hoffmann, op. cit., p. 173.
[4] In IV. 228. [5] In loc. cit.

by these names in the aggregate, that the Makedones were Greek-speakers.

The evidence that the Makedones were Greek-speakers has also been discounted on the strength of some passages in Greek literature in which someone, or some group of people, is reported to have spoken 'in Macedonian' (Μακεδονιστί). For instance, Alexander III, in the course of his fatal quarrel with Kleitos, is said to have shouted 'in Macedonian' (Μακεδονιστί) for his guard.[1] Eumenes is said to have been greeted, on one occasion, 'in Macedonian', by the Macedonian veterans in the Argyraspid corps.[2] When the Macedonians attacked Messene in 214–213 B.C., the defenders are said to have recognized that the assailants were Macedonians, not Lacedaemonians, by their accent as well as by their equipment.[3] Some of the Ptolemies who had preceded Cleopatra had even dropped speaking 'Macedonian'.[4] The crucial passage occurs in Q. Curtius Rufus' account of the trial of Philotas for high treason in a court which, in accordance with Macedonian custom in such cases, consisted of the entire Macedonian army.[5]

[Alexander] then turned his gaze on him [Philotas] and said: 'The Makedones are now going to pass judgement on you. I [therefore] put to you the question: are you going to speak in this forum in our ancestral tongue (*patrio sermone*)?' Philotas' reply was: 'Besides the Makedones, there are many people present who will, I believe, catch my meaning more easily if I speak in the same language in which you have just been speaking—and the reason why you spoke in it was, I think, in order to make sure that your speech should be understood by a wider audience.' The king then exclaimed: 'There! You see that Philotas has grown tired even of our ancestral language. He is the only Macedonian who disdains to learn it. However, he is free to speak in whatever way he pleases, so long as you remember that he has become alienated from our language, as well as from our standards of behaviour.'

These passages, and particularly the one last quoted, show that there was a difference between the language spoken by the Makedones and the contemporary standard form of Greek. What did this unquestionable difference amount to? Was Macedonian, like Illyrian and Thraco-Phrygian, a different language from Greek, as some authorities have held? Or was it a non-standard Greek dialect? There is nothing either in the word Μακεδονιστί[6] or in the context of these passages that rules

---

[1] Plutarch, *Alexander*, chap. 51.

[2] ἀσπασάμενοι Μακεδονιστὶ τῇ φωνῇ (Plutarch, *Eumenes*, chap. 14).

[3] ἐκ τῶν ὅπλων καὶ τῆς φωνῆς Μακεδόνας γινώσκουσιν ὄντας (Pausanias, Book IV, chap. 29, § 4).

[4] τῶν πρὸ αὐτῆς βασιλέων οὐδὲ τὴν Αἰγυπτίαν ἀνασχομένων παραλαβεῖν διάλεκτον, ἐνίων δὲ καὶ τὸ μακεδονίζειν ἐκλιπόντων (Plutarch, *Marcus Antonius*, chap. 27).

[5] Q. Curtius Rufus, Book VI, chap. 9, §§ 34–6.

[6] If the word Μακεδονιστί were to be held to imply a non-Greek language, it would follow that the words Ἰαστί, Δωριστί, Ἀττικιστί carry the same implication, *quod est absurdum*.

out the second of these two alternative possibilities, and the dates to which the passages refer suggest that the second alternative is the truth.

The references are all to the age in which the Makedones had already emerged from their original isolation and had made their entry into the great world of the Hellenic city-states. This stage of Macedonian history began with the reign of King Arkhelaos I (*regnabat circa* 413–399 B.C.), who invited distinguished Hellenic intellectuals to his court; and the process was completed by the successive military and political achievements of Kings Philip II and Alexander III. Whether the Macedonians' ancestral language was a non-Greek language or was a dialect of Greek, their leaders, at any rate, would have had to speak, in addition to Macedonian, one of the contemporary standard forms of Greek in order to do their business in the Greek-speaking world in which the Kingdom of Macedon was now operating.

This need to speak two languages, or at any rate to speak two dialects of the same Greek language, was not peculiar to the Makedones in this age. It was an age in which Greek-speaking communities were coming into increasingly intimate relations with each other; and, to provide for this intensified intercourse between Greeks whose ancestral dialects differed from each other, several standard forms of Greek had been taking shape. The earliest of these Greek κοιναί was the Ionic. It had captured Halikarnassos from the North-West-Greek dialect by Herodotus' day and had captured Smyrna from the North-East-Greek dialect long before that.[1] The Attic dialect and the Corinthian variety of the North-West-Greek dialect won their way to becoming κοιναί rather later than Ionic, but with more lasting success. Attic, which eventually superseded all other dialects of Greek, had started on this career in 478 B.C., when the Confederation of Delos had been founded under Athens' presidency. King Philip II of Macedon adopted Attic as the diplomatic and administrative language of his kingdom.

When a standard form of a language has established itself side by side with a dialect of the same language, the standard form tends to gain ground at the dialect's expense. The upper strata of society, which have effectively entered the wider world which is served by the standard form of the language as its *lingua franca*, tend to speak the standard language among themselves, as well as in their intercourse with foreigners, though they change over, spontaneously and perhaps almost unconsciously, to their ancestral dialect when they are doing business with the uncultivated lower classes of their fellow countrymen. As time goes on, the speakers of dialects come to be expected at least to understand the standard language, if not to speak it themselves, till eventually they, too, drop their distinctive dialect and become, in their turn, speakers of the

[1] See Part I, chap. 3, p. 40.

standard language. On the other hand, speakers of the standard language will not be expected to speak any dialect (except, perhaps, their own ancestral one when speaking to their clansmen); and, therefore, in a mixed company, the standard language will be used. This was coming to be the situation in the Hellenic World from the later decades of the fifth century onwards, and, in the light of it, all the passages cited above are explicable on the hypothesis that the language spoken by the Makedones was a non-standard dialect of Greek.

At the drinking-party which ended in Alexander III's murdering Kleitos, the company, as we are explicitly informed, included non-Macedonian Greeks as well as Macedonians, so everyone will have been talking standard Attic till Alexander broke into the Macedonian dialect in shouting for his Macedonian guard. At the trial of Philotas by the Macedonian army, a crowd of civilian camp followers[1] was present, besides the Macedonian troops. Though, according to Macedonian customary law, the Macedonians alone were empowered to pass judgement, Alexander in making his indictment, and Philotas in making his defence, felt the need to appeal as well to the non-Macedonians in their audience; for, though these had no say in the trial, they represented Hellenic public opinion, and this, though it was an imponderable political force, was too potent a one to be ignored even by Alexander. This is why first Alexander and then Philotas preferred to speak in standard Greek instead of speaking in the Macedonian dialect, which the non-Macedonians in the audience might have found it difficult to follow. The Macedonian troops had to put up with being addressed in standard Greek. It was part of their education to be addressed in it by their officers—except, perhaps, for actual military words of command such as 'pike-points up' (ἄγχαρμον, from ἀνὰ χάρμαν).[2]

The other passages are explicable on the same lines. The Argyraspides greeted their non-Macedonian Greek commander Eumenes in the Macedonian dialect in a moment of emotional enthusiasm for him which made them feel as if he were one of themselves. The Macedonian troops attacking Messene were talking to each other. The Ptolemies naturally took to talking the Attic κοινή exclusively in cosmopolitan Alexandria, after they had left their native Eordaia for ever and had also ceased to live in camp with their Macedonian soldiery.

One reason why the Macedonian language has been held to be non-Greek is because there are some un-Greek-looking words among the surviving specimens from a collection of 'glosses' made by a Macedonian named Amerias. However, it does not follow from Amerias' Macedonian nationality that all the 'glosses' in his collection were culled from the

---

[1] 'Turba lixarum calonumque' (Q. Curtius Rufus, Book VI, chap. 28, § 5).
[2] Hoffmann, op. cit., p. 88.

Macedonian dialect.¹ There are, as we should expect, non-Greek as well as Greek elements in the Macedonian vocabulary.² But none of the non-Greek Macedonian 'glosses' can be identified as being Illyrian or Thraco-Phrygian,³ and such a big majority of the Macedonian 'glosses' can be interpreted as being Greek 'that the over-all Greekness of the Macedonian vocabulary cannot be wiped out by the non-Greek residue'.⁴ It is significant that 'there is not a single non-Greek word [in Macedonian] in the fields of public administration, military affairs, and law'.⁵ Indeed the very fact that Macedonian 'glosses' were noted and collected by Greek-speaking grammarians is evidence that Macedonian was a dialect of Greek; for a 'gloss' is a word or phrase that is unintelligible, unless explained, to a speaker of any one of the standard forms of Greek, and, from the Greek-speaking grammarian's point of view, a non-Greek language would consist entirely of 'glosses' except for standard Greek loan-words in it.

It has been contended by some authorities that, if the Makedones did speak Greek, they must have learned it from the Greek colonies that had been planted on the coasts of Pieria and the Chalcidic Peninsula. It is true that the earliest of these colonies were probably already established by the time when the Argeadai, descending from Aigai, added to the Kingdom of Macedon the Emathian lowlands in the maritime Greek colonies' immediate hinterland. It is also true that the economic, technological, and cultural influence of the Chalcidian colonies, in particular, penetrated, through and beyond both Lower and Upper Macedon, into the interior of south-eastern Europe. For instance, there was strong Chalcidian influence on both the artistic style and the workmanship of the earlier issues of the coinage of Damastion.⁶ 'Damastion was at all times much more in touch with trade approaching from the east or south-east than from the west.'⁷ However, this Chalcidian cultural influence did not extend to the field of language. Not only the Chalcidian colonists ἐπὶ Θρᾴκης but the Eretrian and Andrian and Parian colonists there, as well, were Ionic-speaking. The only other Greek dialect that was re-presented among these colonies was the North-West-Greek dialect of the Corinthian colony Poteidaia. But 'the Macedonian glosses prove that neither Athens nor the Ionic-speaking cities can have conveyed the Greek language to the Makedones; for the Macedonian glosses bear the unmistakable stamp of the Thessalian dialect'.⁸

---

¹ This point is made by Hoffmann, op. cit., pp. 2–3 and 11.
² Ibid., p. 35.   ³ Ibid., p. 36.   ⁴ Ibid., p. 111.   ⁵ Ibid., p. 112.
⁶ See J. M. F. May, *The Coinage of Damastion and the Lesser Coinages of the Illyro-Paeonian Region* (London, 1939, O.U.P.), pp. vii, 17–19, and 38. 'The dominant feature of the earliest issues of Damastion is their marked Chalcidian style. This and the series of deliberate imitations of Chalcidian types show the connexion between Damastion and the League to have been close' (p. 38).   ⁷ Ibid., p. 20.   ⁸ Hoffmann, op. cit., p. 114.

For instance, Macedonian Greek shares with Thessalian Greek the excision of the final vowels of prepositions in compound words—a tendency that is common to all varieties of North-East Greek but that is carried farthest in Thessalian.[1] Macedonian Greek also agrees with Thessalian Greek in changing ω into ου,[2] α into ο[3] (e.g. in Macedonian Ὀδομάντοι, as compared with North-West-Greek Ἀθαμᾶνες), and δια- into διε- (e.g. in Σέλευκος, as compared with Locrian Ζάλευκος),[4] and in coining place-names from personal names in an adjectival form (e.g. Ἀλεξάνδρεια from Ἀλέξανδρος) corresponding to the Thessalian adjectival patronymika.[5] Macedonian personal names 'display a dialect-colouring and appear to be related the most closely to Thessalian names'.[6]

Did the Makedones borrow their Thessalian Greek from their Thessalian neighbours? Or did they bring it with them from Thessaly? The second of these two alternatives seems to be the truth, in view of the fact that the Macedonian variety of the Thessalian dialect has some features that are peculiar to it. The most striking of these—a feature which the Macedonian dialect shares with the Magnesian alone, so far as we know[7]—is that the original Indo-European BH, DH, GH have not been changed, as they have in all other Greek dialects, into PH (Φ), TH (Θ), KH (X). In the Greek alphabet the Macedonian equivalents are written B, Δ, Γ—letters which may stand here, as usual, for the sounds B, D, G but, alternatively, may stand for the original Indo-European sounds, for which the Greek alphabet provides no special signs.[8] Another peculiarity of the Macedonian dialect is the changing of αἰθ- into ἀδ- (e.g. ἀδῆ for αἰθήρ).[9]

Hoffmann holds[10] that these two are the only features that are peculiar to Macedonian Greek. Perhaps we may venture to add a third peculiarity —the changing of B into V— which occurs in a few Macedonian proper names and which anticipates a change that has become universal in Modern Greek. By the time of the Third Romano-Macedonian War (*gerebatur* 171–168 B.C.), Bolou Stena had become Volou Stena (Volustana in Latin)[11] and Bottiaioi had become Vettioi (Vettii in Latin),[12] while the Macedonian city facing Berrhoia across the lower Haliakmon is called alternatively Balla and Vallae.[13]

To sum up, it seems to be fairly well established by the evidence, such

[1] Hoffman, op. cit., pp. 99–100, 114, and 246.　　　[2] Ibid., pp. 114 and 244.
[3] Ibid., p. 241.　　　[4] Ibid., pp. 174–5 and 241.
[5] Ibid., p. 255.　　　[6] Ibid., p. 230. Cp. p. 255.
[7] See above, p. 66.

[8] See ibid. and, for expert discussions, Hoffmann, op. cit., pp. 22 and 232–41; Kretschmer, op. cit., pp. 111 and 288.

[9] Hoffmann, op. cit., pp. 22, 37, 244.　　　[10] Ibid., p. 23.
[11] Livy, Book XLIV, chap. 2.　　　[12] Livy, Book XLV, chap. 30.

[13] Βάλλα (Steph. Byz., s.v., citing Theagenes); Vallaei (Pliny, *Historia Naturalis*, Book IV, chap. 10 (17), § 34).

as it is, that the Makedones were Greek-speakers from first to last; and that, when Thucydides calls the Orestai and the Makedones of Lower Macedon 'barbarians' apropos of events in the year 429 B.C.,[1] he is using the term in the cultural, not the linguistic, sense. The most authoritative dissenter is Kretschmer.[2] Yet Kretschmer concedes[3] that, if the Makedones had migrated from Histiaiotis, not northwards, but southwards (as their kinsmen and homonyms the Makednoi did when they found an asylum in the central Greek Doris), the Makedones would have become as Hellenic as the Dorians, Thessalians, and Boeotians.

[1] Thucydides, Book II, chap. 81, cited on p. 60.
[2] In op. cit., pp. 283–8.
[3] Ibid., p. 288.

4. What was the Ancestral Language of the Pelagones?

OUR earliest contemporary evidence relating to the Pelagones is the coinage of a place—perhaps a city-state—named Pelagia (the ethnikon on the coins is spelled [Π]ελαγιτα[ων] or Πελαγιτέων or Πελαγίτας).¹ This coinage started *circa* 360–350 B.C.² and continued long enough for the Pelagian artificers to see, and imitate, the Alexander-Ammon coins of Lysimachus.³ Since Pelagia's coinage is all that we know about her, we cannot locate her exactly. Correspondences between some of her coin-types and some of those of the fourth-century-B.C. Kingdom of Paionia suggest that Pelagia was a neighbour of this kingdom's, and we know that fourth-century-B.C. Paionia straddled the upper Axios basin, though this probably without including Skoupoi or the Axios' headwaters. Pelagia's coinage belongs to a group of coinages that were dependent on the coinage of a place named Damastion, which 'is by far the most important and prolific'.⁴

Strabo⁵ locates 'the silver-mines at Damastion' in the neighbourhood of the Epirot peoples' Illyrian neighbours the Bylliones, Taulantioi, Parthinoi, and Brygoi, and adds (if Meineke's emendation of the text⁶ is adopted)⁷ that these mines were the centre of the dominion of the Dyestai. Strabo then mentions the Enkheleoi, whom he appears to identify (the text is corrupt here too) with the Sesarethioi—a name which might be a variant of the well-known ethnikon 'Dassaretioi'⁸—and he says that these are adjoined by the Lynkestai and by Deuriopos and by the Tripolitis (or Tripolis) district of Pelagonia⁹ and by the Eordoi and Elimeia and Eratyra. These geographical indications of Strabo's—especially the mention of the Enkheleoi, who seem to have lived on the shores of Lake Okhrida¹⁰—point to a location for Damastion somewhere

---

¹ May, op. cit., pp. 170–1. ² Ibid., p. 172.
³ Ibid., pp. viii, 170, and 182–3. ⁴ Ibid., p. v.
⁵ Book VII, chap. 7, § 8 (C. 326).

⁶ πλησίον δέ που τὰ ἀργυρεῖα τὰ ἐν Δαμαστίῳ—περὶ ἃ Δυέσται [Meineke's emendation for the manuscripts' περισάδνές τε] συνεστήσαντο τὴν δυναστείαν—καὶ 'Εγχέλειοι οὓς [Gaebler's emendation for the manuscripts' 'Εγχελέους] καὶ Σεσαρηθίους καλοῦσι.

⁷ It is rejected by Hammond, *Epirus*, p. 467, n. 2.

⁸ Hammond, in *Epirus*, p. 467, identifies the Dassaretioi with Hecataeus' Δεξάροι (Steph. Byz., Δεξάροι· ἔθνος Χαόνων, 'Εγχελέαις προσεχεῖς. 'Εκαταῖος Εὐρώπῃ). The Dassaretioi might be identical with both the Dexaroi and the Sesarethioi. However, the word Sesarethioi is presumably the ethnikon of the place-name Sesarethos, and Sesarethos is said by Stephanus, s.v., citing Hecataeus, to be a πόλις Ταυλαντίων (see Part I, chap. 3, p. 22, n. 6).

⁹ In a later passage—Book VII, chap. 7, § 9 (C. 327)—Strabo confuses this Pelagonian Tripolis with the Perrhaebian Tripolis—perhaps because of the affinity between the names of the Pelagonian city Bylazora and the Perrhaebian city Azoros.

¹⁰ See Part I, chap. 3, p. 22, n. 4.

near the watershed between the basins of the Axios and the Drin. Since 'Damastion was at all times much more in touch with trade approaching from the east or south-east than from the west'[1] (the strong Chalcidian influence on the earlier Damastine issues is replaced by strong Paeonian influence later),[2] and since southern Serbia is the area in which the finds of Damastine coins are the most numerous,[3] Damastion—and, with it, Pelagia and the other places whose coinages were dependent on Damastion's—seems likely to have lain on the Axios-basin side of the continental divide. Since Strabo informs us that Damastion was not included in either Lynkestis or Deuriopos or the Tripolitis district of Pelagonia, it looks as if it must have lain on or near one of the two western headwaters of the Axios (the rivers that are now called the Treska and the Tetovo Vardar) which adjoin the basin of the Vardar's Črna tributary on the north-north-west. Since, in the eighteen-thirties, silver was being mined at the south-western end of the Shar (Skardos) Range,[4] which overhangs the Tetovo Vardar on the north-west, and since Damastion's mint dominated the other mints in the group, we shall perhaps not go far wrong if we locate Damastion in the neighbourhood of the present-day Tetovo, *alias* Kalkandalen, and locate Pelagia in the Treska valley.

The name Pelagia is evidently a variant of the names Pelagones and Pelagonia, and we meet with the name Pelagonia in the third century B.C. Pelagonia must originally have been the name, not of a city, but of a country, i.e. the country of the Pelagones, and this appears to be the sense in which the name is used by Polybius, in calling Pissaion a πόλισμα Πελαγονίας,[5] and by Livy (following Polybius, no doubt) in his reference to the 'angustiae quae ad Pelagoniam sunt'[6] or 'fauces ad Pelagoniam'[7] or 'fauces Pelagoniae'[8] apropos of the Romano-Macedonian hostilities in 199 B.C. We may perhaps identify these narrows with the gorge through which the Vardar makes its way just south-south-east of its confluence with the Pčinja (Egrisu) beyond the southern end of the plain of Skoplje.[9]

[1] May, op. cit., p. 20, cited already on p. 77.
[2] Ibid., p. vii.   [3] Ibid., pp. 7 and 10–11.
[4] Ibid., p. 29, citing A. Grisebach, *Reise durch Rumelien und nach Brussa 1839*, 2 vols., vol. ii (Göttingen, 1841, Vandenhoeck und Ruprecht), pp. 282 sqq.
[5] Polybius, Book V, chap. 108, § 1.
[6] Livy, Book XXXI, chap. 28.
[7] Ibid., chap. 33.   [8] Ibid., chap. 34.
[9] There are four gorges on the course of the River Vardar. The highest of these is the one below the confluence of the Vardar with the Pčinja, just to the south-east of the two villages Taor (Tauresium) and Bader (Bederiana) at the southern edge of the Skoplje plain (Tozer, op. cit., vol. i, pp. 371–2). In 1865, when Tozer travelled from Skoplje to Thessaloníki, the road ran through a pass which avoided this gorge. Tozer's barometrical observations recorded a fall of 290 feet, in this gorge, between the respective altitudes of Skoplje and Veles (Bylazora, Köprülü). Philip V had been in possession of this northernmost of the Vardar gorges since his conquest—or reconquest—of Bylazora in 218–217 B.C. (see Polybius, Book V, chap. 97, §§ 1–2). The second Vardar gorge is just below Veles (Tozer, op. cit., vol. i, p. 374; Casson, op. cit., p. 19). Tozer's road ran through this gorge (op. cit., vol. i, p. 375). The

Stoboi, at the confluence of the Erigon (Črna) with the Axios (Vardar), lay in Pelagonia according to Ptolemy.[1] The country on both sides of the Vardar, from Veles (Bylazora) to Negotin, seems a likely location for Strabo's Tripolitis (or Tripolis) district of Pelagonia, and we may perhaps guess that the three cities whose territories constituted this tripolis were Bylazora (Veles), Stoboi, and Antigoneia (which was at or near Negotin). At any rate, these three cities lay in Pelagonia, whether they were or were not the members of the Pelagonian tripolis; and Deuriopos was their immediate neighbour to the south-west; for Perseis, which King Philip V of Macedon founded in 183 B.C., was not far from Stoboi, was near the River Erigon (Črna), and was in Deuriopos.[2]

Deuriopos, as well as the Tripolitis district of Pelagonia, must have been a part of Pelagonia,[3] though Strabo distinguishes the Deuriopes from the Pelagones in his list of the peoples (Lynkestai, Brygoi, Deuriopes, Pelagones) through whose territories the Erigòn flows on its way to join the Axios. What clinches the proof that Deuriopos was part of Pelagonia is the fact that there was a piece of Pelagonia to the south of Deuriopos, besides the piece to the north-east of it. The name Pelagonia turns up— as the name of a city now, not of a country—in Livy's account of the Romans' disposal of Macedon in the peace-settlement of 167 B.C.[4] Pelagonia here figures as the capital of Macedonia Quarta—one of the four cantons into which the Romans now partitioned the former domain of the liquidated Kingdom of Macedon. This city Pelagonia seems to be

third gorge (Demir Kapu) is below Negotin (Tozer, op. cit., vol. i, pp. 379–81; Casson, op. cit., loc. cit.). Tozer's road ran through the Demir Kapu, and Tozer gives a graphic description of the gorge, with its rapids between precipitous limestone cliffs. This must be Livy's 'quae ad Antigoneam fauces sunt—Stena vocant Graeci' (Book XXXII, chap. 5), which Perseus held for his father Philip V in 198 B.C. A fourth gorge (the Čingane gorge), just below Ghevgheli, is mentioned by Casson, loc. cit. Tozer does not mention this one. From Gradiska onwards, Tozer's road to Thessaloníki veered away from the Vardar, south-south-eastwards. All four passes are noted by J. Kromayer, *Antike Schlachtfelde in Griechenland*, Zweiter Band (Berlin, 1907, Weidmann), p. 28, n. 1.

Our location of the 'fauces ad Pelagoniam' will depend on our interpretation of Livy's usage of 'ad' followed by the name of a country (e.g. 'ad Pelagoniam' here, and 'ad Lyncum in Book XXXI, chap. 33). If, in these contexts, 'ad' means, not 'at' or 'in', but 'up against' or 'on the edge of', then we shall identify the fauces 'ad Pelagoniam' of 199 B.C. with the fauces 'ad Antigoneam' of 198 B.C. It would, indeed, seem probable that the force posted with a view to meeting an invasion by the Dardani would have been stationed at the same point on each occasion. On the other hand, a position at the Negotin defile would have covered Lower Macedon only, and would have left the whole of Pelagonia, up to Bylazora inclusive, at the invaders' mercy.

[1] Ptolemy, *Geographia*, Book III, chap. 12, § 31.

[2] 'Oppidum in Deuriopo condere instituit—Paeoniae ea regio est—prope Erigonum flumen, qui ex Illyrico per Paeoniam fluens in Axium amnem editur, haud procul Stobis (Livy, Book XXXIX, chap. 53).

[3] Livy says that Styberra was in Pelagonia (Book XXXI, chap. 39); Strabo says that Stybara (*sic*) was in Deuriopos (*Geographica*, Book VII, chap. 7, § 9 (C. 327)). See also Geyer, op. cit., pp. 14 and 22.

[4] Livy, Book XLV, chaps. 29–30.

identical with the city (on or near the site of the present-day Monastir, *alias* Bitolj) which had previously been called Herakleia, and which continued to be called Herakleia (by Caesar, for instance, in his account of his operations in 48 B.C., and in all the itineraries of the roads of the Roman Empire).[1] The Romans would hardly have re-named this Herakleia 'Pelagonia' if Herakleia had not lain inside the country called Pelagonia. There is no evidence that it lay outside it; for, in the extant references to this Herakleia in Greek and Latin literature, it is in no case said to be a Lyncestian city.[2]

Herakleia is not mentioned by Livy in his account of the campaign of 199 B.C. in the Second Romano-Macedonian War;[3] and this is strange, for Herakleia was the key-point in the plain of Monastir. It was one of the stations on the road—the Via Egnatia—which was subsequently built by the Romans from Epidamnos (Dyrrhachium) and Apollonia on the Adriatic coast to Thessalonike on the Aegean coast, and thence to the Dardanelles. In the campaign of 199 B.C. the Roman proconsul P. Sulpicius Galba followed the route of the future Via Egnatia[4] as far as the north-east corner of Lake Ostrovo (Lake Begorritis), where he turned southward through Eordaia instead of marching on eastwards towards Edessa. It is true that Galba did not travel direct; he marched and countermarched for a considerable time on the plain of Monastir and on the smaller plain of Prilep, to the north of it, before eventually heading for the pass leading into Eordaia from Lynkestis. All the same, it is difficult to see how he could have avoided Herakleia at some stage of his operations (unless this city was so heavily fortified and so strongly garrisoned that Galba gave it a wide berth). In 199 B.C. Herakleia must

---

[1] 'Domitius . . . Heracliam [Senticam MSS.], quae est subiecta Candaviae, iter fecerat' (Caesar, *B.C.*, Book III, chap. 79).

[2] This important point is made by Richard Kiepert on sheet 2, col. 2 (section *Macedonia*) of his notes on Map XVI (*Graecia cum Macedonia et Epiro, anno 270 a. Chr. n.*) of his *Formae Orbis Antiqui* (Berlin, 1908, Reimer). [3] Book XXXI, chaps. 33–40.

[4] This has been demonstrated conclusively by Leake (see pp. 84–5) and it is also the opinion of Kromayer, op. cit., p. 13, and of F. W. Walbank, *Philip V of Macedon* (Cambridge, 1940, University Press), p. 142. The Via Egnatia climbed the valley of the River Genusus (Škumbi), ran just to the north of the northern end of Lake Okhrida, and crossed the Adriatic–Aegean watershed into the plain of Monastir. On his return to the coast at the close of his campaign, Galba crossed the watershed from the upper Haliakmon basin into the Apsus (Semeni) valley, and descended this valley to the Adriatic shore. This is certain, because the city of Celetrum, which capitulated to him when he threatened, *en route*, to attack it, can be identified with the present-day Kastoria by Livy's description of its site (Book XXXI, chap. 40).

Hammond, *Epirus*, p. 616, holds that Galba took the Semeni–Devol route both coming and going. This seems improbable *a priori*, since he would have exhausted the supplies of grain along his outward route during the first stage of his campaign, and would therefore take a route back along which he would find the supplies still intact. Moreover, if Galba had taken the Semeni–Devol route on his outward march, this would have brought him into Orestis (the upper basin of the Haliakmon), whereas his outward route actually brought him into Lyncus (Livy, Book XXXI, chap. 33), which is in the basin of the Erigon.

have been in existence. Its name indicates that it was founded by an
Argead king of Macedon, and this can have been only Philip II.[1]
Herakleia's location, which is established by the itineraries, was at or near
the present Monastir; Monastir is identical with the city of Pelagonia
(ὁ Πελαγονίας is the bishop of Monastir's title in Greek); and Livy's
account of the peace-settlement of 167 B.C. implies that the Pelagonia
which was then made the capital of Macedonia Quarta was an already
existing city, not a new foundation. Pelagonia can only have been
Herakleia; and, if its name had not been Herakleia before the Romans
called it Pelagonia, the name Herakleia, with its Argead associations,
would surely never have been given to Pelagonia under the Roman
regime.

The Upper Macedonian principality Lynkestis must have been approximately conterminous with the present-day Greek province of
Florina, and the border between Lynkestis and Pelagonia will have
coincided with the present frontier between Greece and Yugoslavia in
the sector between Lake Prespa and the Nidže Mountains. Lynkestis
cannot have been a large or populous canton in Alexander III's time;
for, in Alexander's expeditionary force, the contingents of pikemen from
Lynkestis and Orestis were brigaded together to form one of the six
taxeis of the phalanx, whereas Elimiotis and Tymphaia provided one whole
taxis each.[2] If Macedonian, as distinct from Paeonian, Pelagonia was
eventually attached to Lynkestis, as it appears to have been by 199 B.C.,
this administrative change must have been made at some date later than
that at which the cantonal contingents for Alexander's phalanx were
fixed. Indeed, the date must have been still recent enough in 167 B.C.
for the consciousness of Pelagonian nationality to have been still alive
in this territory at that date.

The evidence that Macedonian Pelagonia was included in Lynkestis
in 199 B.C. is to be found in Livy's account of that year. According to
Livy, Galba, after traversing Dassaretia, 'ad Lyncum stativa posuit'—
that is to say, on the edge of, or just inside, Lynkestis—a position from
which Galba sent foraging parties back into Dassaretia.[3] Galba did not
enter Pelagonia till after his victory over King Philip V at Ottolobos.[4]
We know the position both of Galba's first camp 'ad Lyncum . . . prope
flumen Bevum' and of his second camp at Ottolobos, thanks to W. M.
Leake's having discerned[5] that both places appear in the itineraries as
stations on the Via Egnatia. The 'stativa ad Lyncum' are the station

---

[1] As Steph. Byz. says, s.v. Ἡράκλεια, apropos of his Herakleia No. 23 (Μακεδονίας),
which may be identical with his No. 17 (Πισσαϊκή), since he locates Πίσαιον in Pelagonia. See
also Geyer, op. cit., p. 14.

[2] Diodorus, Book XVII, chap. 57, § 3.

[3] Book XXXI, chap. 33.   [4] Ibid., chap. 39.

[5] Op. cit., pp. 310–14.

'Castra', forty-two Roman miles to the east of Lychnidus according to the Antonine Itinerary, *alias* the station 'Parembole' of the Jerusalem Itinerary, forty-four miles east of Lychnidus. Ottolobos is the Station 'Nicia' or 'Nicea' (i.e. 'Nikaia', meaning 'site of victory'), which the Antonine Itinerary locates thirty-four miles east of Lychnidus on an alternative route to the one passing through 'Castra', and which the Peutinger Table places sixteen miles east of some station, intermediate between 'Nicaea' and Lychnidus, which, in this itinerary, has dropped out. These indications enable us to locate Galba's 'stativa ad Lyncum' inside the Erigon basin just to the east of its western watershed, on the headwaters of the Šemnica (Bevus) tributary of the River Črna (Erigon). Ottolobos-Nicaea, which was about eight Roman miles[1] from Galba's first camp, will have lain to the north-east of it, on or near the River Šemnica, down-stream. These two positions are both in Macedonian Pelagonia; so Macedonian Pelagonia must have been incorporated in Lynkestis by 199 B.C.

Perhaps we have now ascertained approximately the extent of the territory that was inhabited by the nation called Pelagones in and after the fourth century B.C. They occupied the whole of the basin of the Erigon (Črna) affluent of the Axios (Vardar),[2] except for the southern-most bay of the plain of Monastir, to the south of the present-day Graeco-Yugoslav frontier, which was the territory of the Macedonian canton Lynkestis. The Pelagones also perhaps bestrode the Axios from a point above Bylazora (Veles) as far down-stream as Antigoneia (near the present-day Negotin). In addition, they occupied at least one of the western headwaters of the Axios, and perhaps both of them, right up to the natural frontier constituted by the Skardos (Shar) Range, if the Damastini were Pelagones as well as the Pelagitai. This territory was a compact one; for there is a practicable passage between the northern headwaters of the Erigon and the western headwaters of the Axios.

Compact though Pelagonia was in terms of topography, it was not a political unity during the eighty years' period which began with the accession of Philip II of Macedon in 359 B.C. and ended with the Gallic Völkerwanderung of 280 B.C. During this period the one undoubtedly Pelagonian community that was independent was Pelagia. Her independence is attested by her coinage. On the same evidence, Damastion, Daparria, the Tenestini, and Sarnoa were independent too; but we do not know whether any of these other coining communities were Pelagones. The rest of Pelagonia—and this will have been by far the greater part— seems to have been partitioned between the Kingdom of Macedon and the Kingdom of Paionia. The Paeonian crown seems to have obtained—

[1] Livy, Book XXXI, chap. 36.
[2] See Geyer, op. cit., p. 14.

or retained—the lion's share of the Pelagonian spoils. The Kingdom of
Paionia seems to have annexed all Pelagonia up to the southern frontier
of Deuriopos. On the other hand, Philip II secured for Macedon the
south-western corner of Pelagonia, which contained the route from
Lynkestis over the continental divide and round the north end of Lake
Okhrida (Lykhnidos) to the Adriatic ports Epidamnos and Apollonia.[1]
Herakleia must have been founded in order to cover this route against
the risk of a flank attack from the direction of the Kingdom of Paionia.
The name, like the name of the older Herakleia Sintikē (founded to
cover the silver mines on Mount Dysoros), indicates that it was founded
by an Argead, since the name asserts the Argeads' claim to be Herakleidai.

The Macedonian and Paeonian portions of Pelagonia were reunited
eventually when Macedon annexed the Kingdom of Paionia outright
and abolished the Paeonian monarchy. Philip seems to have made the
Paeonian crown submit to Macedonian suzerainty. The Kingdom of
Paionia seems then to have recovered its independence during the wars
of Alexander III's succession; to have been forced once again to submit
to Macedonian suzerainty by Lysimachus not many years before his fall;
to have recovered its independence for the second and last time after
280 B.C.; and to have been annexed to, and incorporated in, the Kingdom
of Macedon definitively at some date during the reign of Antigonos
Gonatas (*regnabat* 274–239 B.C.). Though Paionia may have profited
from the Gallic invasion politically, it looks as if she suffered from it
economically more severely than Macedon did. The coinages of the
independent communities—Damastion, Pelagia, and the rest—had been
deteriorating in style and workmanship for some time before the onset
of the Gallic Völkerwanderung, and this disaster may have given the
independent Pelagonian communities their *coup de grâce*.

What was the Pelagones' ancestral language? To judge by their
national name, it must have been Greek; for 'pelagos' is a Greek word—
though, in this application of it, it can hardly bear its usual meaning,
which is 'sea'.[2] Whatever the name 'Pelagones' may signify, its root

---

[1] This is one of six practicable routes across the Pindus Range and its northern prolonga-
tion the Skardos (Shar) Range. North of the Monastir–Okhrida route, the next is the gap,
north of Skoplje, which leads from the upper Vardar basin to the plain of Kosovo and to the
upper Morava basin. South of the Monastir–Okhrida route, there is the gap that leads, from
the north-west corner of the Haliakmon basin, to the headwaters of the River Devol. The next
to the south is the Métsovo Pass, linking the headwaters of the Peneios, the Arakhthos (Arta
River), and the Aôos with each other and with the Haliakmon basin. The next is the Portes
Pass leading from the plain of western Thessaly to the Ambracian Gulf (the Gulf of Preveza).
This Pórtes Pass must not be confused with the Portes Pass across the Cambunian Range,
between the Peneios basin and the Haliakmon basin. The sixth and last trans-Pindus route
runs from the eastern shore of the Gulf of Preveza (the Ambracian Gulf) to the headwaters
of the River Sperkheios. See Hammond, 'Prehistoric Epirus and the Dorian Invasion',
pp. 141–3, with the map on p. 142.

[2] Unless, at the time when the name 'pelagos-people' was coined, this people was living

'Pelag-' is clearly also the root of the name 'Pelasgoi',[1] and the same root may also reappear in the name 'Phlegyai'.[2] The Pelasgoi were the pre-Völkerwanderung inhabitants of the eastern half of the plain of Thessaly who had survived the conquest of their country by the Thessaloi and had given their name to one of the tetrarchies into which Thessaly had been divided by the conquerors. The Phlegyai, unlike the Pelasgoi and the Pelagones, did not survive under their own name in the Post-Völkerwanderung Age. They may, however, have survived in fact. They were remembered as having been the pre-Minyan occupants of the central Greek city Orkhomenos. In the Post-Völkerwanderung Age, the language spoken in Boeotia, like that spoken in Thessaly, was the North-East dialect of Greek with an infusion of the North-West-Greek dialect which had evidently been contributed by the invading Boiotoi and Thessaloi. In Thessaly the preponderant North-East-Greek element in the local language must have been contributed by the subjugated but not submerged Pelasgoi;[3] in Boeotia it may have been contributed by the Phlegyai.

If we accept the suggestion that the names 'Pelagones', 'Pelasgoi', and 'Phlegyai' are variants of one and the same ethnikon, does it follow that the peoples who bore these kindred names were all members of one and the same nation? This seems to follow in the case of the Makedones–Makednoi; for, in this case, the meaning of the name—it means 'tall'—is descriptive of the people themselves. 'Pelagos', on the other hand, refers, not to the people, but to their habitat; and the inhabitants of different regions that all qualified for being called 'pelagos' (whatever 'pelagos' may mean)[4] would not necessarily be akin to each other on

in Pelasgiotis on the marge of a freshwater inland sea which subsequently shrank into the two lakes, Nessonis and Boibeïs.

[1] See Eduard Meyer, *Forschungen zur alten Geschichte*, vol. i (Halle, 1892, Niemeyer), p. 32, n. 4. Beloch, op. cit., Erster Band, Zweite Abteilung, p. 55, notes that $\Pi\epsilon\lambda\alpha\gamma\delta\varsigma$ stands to a presumed original $\Pi\epsilon\lambda\alpha\gamma$-$\sigma\kappa\delta\varsigma$ as $\mu\acute{\iota}\sigma\gamma\omega$ stands to an original $\mu\acute{\iota}\gamma$-$\sigma\kappa\omega$. However, the adjectival suffix -sk-, which is so common in the Teutonic, Slavonic, and Thracian languages, seems to be foreign to Greek, and it therefore seems probable that $\Pi\epsilon\lambda\alpha\gamma\delta\varsigma$ is a contraction, not of $\Pi\epsilon\lambda\alpha\gamma$-$\sigma\kappa\delta\varsigma$, but of $\Pi\epsilon\lambda\alpha\gamma$-$\acute{\iota}\sigma\kappa o\varsigma$—-$\acute{\iota}\sigma\kappa o\varsigma$ being a Greek diminutive termination that appears in, for example, $\mathcal{A}\nu\delta\rho$-$\acute{\iota}\sigma\kappa o\varsigma$, $\beta\alpha\sigma\iota\lambda$-$\acute{\iota}\sigma\kappa o\varsigma$, $\lambda\upsilon\kappa$-$\acute{\iota}\sigma\kappa o\varsigma$, $K\upsilon\nu$-$\acute{\iota}\sigma\kappa\alpha$.

[2] The name 'Phlegyai' has the same -wa termination as the name 'Minyai' (for this, see Part I, chap. 2, p. 13). The root 'Phleg-' may correspond to the 'Pelag-' in the names 'Pelagones' and 'Pelasgoi'. There is, indeed, a passage in the *Iliad* (XIII. 298–302) which pictures the gods Ares and Phobos going on the warpath, from Thrace, against the Ephyroi and the Phlegyai. Strabo, Book IX, chap. 5, § 21 (C. 442), says that the Phlegyai here in question lived at Gyrton, a city at the confluence of the Europos with the Peneios. If Strabo has any warrant for this statement, these Phlegyai were living in Pelasgiotis and will have been, in fact, Pelasgoi. A mythical ruler of the Dotian plain—the bay of the plain of Pelasgiotis, between Ossa and Pelion—was Phlegyas the father of Koronis.

[3] 'Certo i Pelasgioti della Tessaglia dei tempi storici erano Greci, e il loro nome e spiegabilissimo colla lingua ellenica' (L. Pareti, *Storia di Sparta Arcaïca*, Parte I (Florence, 1920, Le Monnier), p. 4). Cp. Meyer, op. cit., pp. 29, 47, 112.

[4] On terra firma, 'pelagos' may mean 'a sea of trees'. There was an oak-forest called 'the

account of all being 'pelagos-people', any more than the various 'doris-people' were necessarily each other's kinsmen.[1] This is true, yet the two cases are not entirely parallel; for the Makednoi of the central Greek Doris and the post-Völkerwanderung inhabitants of the Anatolian Doris had, originally at any rate, spoken different dialects of Greek. The Anatolian Dorians spoke North-West Greek, whereas the Makednoi had come from North-East-Greek-speaking Histiaiotis. On the other hand, Pelasgiotis the home of the Pelasgoi and Boeotia the home of the Phlegyai were both North-East-Greek-speaking countries; and they were two remnants of an original North-East-Greek-speaking area which must have stretched, without a break, from Mount Olympus southwards to the Boeotian shore of the Corinthian Gulf till the North-West-Greek-speaking invaders in the post-Mycenaean Völkerwanderung cut the North-East-Greek-speaking area in two by pushing their way down to the shores of the Maliac Gulf.[2] We may infer that the Pelasgoi and the Phlegyai, at any rate, not only bore the same name but were actually two fragments of one and the same people. If they were, then the Pelagones will have been a third fragment of this people and their original language will have been North-East Greek, as the language of their southern neighbours, the Makedones, had been and had continued to be.

The place-names in Pelagonia-on-Axios are not Greek, except for Antigoneia, which must have been founded after the Kingdom of Paionia, including Pelagonian Paionia, had been annexed to Macedon. 'Bylazora' is certainly an un-Greek name,[3] and 'Stoboi' can be interpreted as being Greek only by giving it the improbable meaning 'abusive language'. On the other hand, the place-name 'Damastion' is Greek,[4] all the known place-names in Deuriopos and in Macedonian Pelagonia (i.e. the Herakleia district) are manifestly Greek, and so are the very few Pelagonian personal names that have survived.

In a previous part,[5] we have identified the name 'Deuriopos' (or 'Douriopos') itself with the name 'Doris'. The suffix -op- is a common Greek formation. 'Erigon' means, in Greek, 'very angular', and this name aptly describes the River Erigon's course. Strabo has recorded the names of three of the Deuriopes' cities (all their cities, he tells us, lay on the Erigon). The three names are Stybara, Alalkomenai, and

Pelagos' in Arcadia, between Mantinea and Tegea (Pausanias, *Graeciae Descriptio*, Book VIII, chap. 11, § 1).

[1] This point has been made in Part I, chap. 3, on pp. 46–7.

[2] See Pareti, op. cit., pp. 55–8.

[3] See further Part II, chap. 5, p. 99.

[4] Δᾱμάστιον is a compound of the two Greek words Δᾶ ('Earth') and μάστος ('breast') according to H. Krahe, *Die alten balkanillyrischen geographischen Namen* (Heidelberg, 1925, Winter), p. 1. If Krahe's etymology is right, this was a felicitous name for a mining-town.

[5] Part I, chap. 3, p. 45.

Bryanion.[1] Livy mentions Stuberra (*sic*)[2] and Bruanium (*sic*), and adds Pluinna.[3] 'Stybara' means 'stronghold' in Greek. 'Alalkomenai' means 'protectresses' and the Homeric epithet Ἀλαλκομενηὶς Ἀθήνη[4] shows who these 'protectresses' were. They were counterparts of the Attic Athena Promakhos and Athena Polias, and they were the patronesses, not only of the Alalkomenai in Deuriopos, but of a city with the same Greek name in Boeotia between Haliartos and Koroneia[5]—that is to say, in a district of central Greece that, according to tradition, had been the home of the Phlegyai. It is from this Phlegyan Alalkomenai, no doubt, that Athena's Homeric epithet 'Alalkomenêis' is derived; for she had a temple there.[6] The third of Strabo's Deuriopan place-names, Bryanion, may be derived from the same root βρυ- ('swell', 'burst') as the Modern Greek word βρύσις, meaning a water-spring.[7] The fourth known Deuriopan place-name, Pluinna, which has been preserved by Livy, looks like a garbled form of the place-name Pelinna or Pelinnaion in Histiaiotis.

Most informative, perhaps, of all is the place-name 'Ottolobos' ('Eight Hills') in Macedonian Pelagonia.[8] It has the Macedonian B for PH; and, if the name was given to the natural feature by the Pelagones, the name is evidence that the Pelagones not only spoke Greek but spoke the Macedonian variety of Thessalian North-East Greek. There was another Ottolobos—a southward spur of Mount Olympus—on the border between Pieria and Perrhaibia.[9] In independent Pelagonia the name 'Damastion', as well as the name 'Pelagia', is manifestly Greek, but not the names Daparria, Sarnoates, and Tenestini.

Four Pelagonian personal names are known for certain. A Pelagonian named Menelaos, son of Arrhabaios, gave Timotheos aid against the Chalcidians in 363/2 B.C.[10] and is mentioned in an Ilian decree of 360/59 B.C.[11] The name Menelaos was popular among Macedonians.[12] The name Arrhabaios was borne, in the reign of King Perdikkas II of Macedon, by the contemporary king of Lynkestis, which was Pelagonia's immediate neighbour to the south; and it is possible that one of Alexander's officers,

---

[1] Ἐπὶ τῷ Ἐριγῶνι πᾶσαι αἱ τῶν Δευριόπων πόλεις ᾤκηντο, ὧν τὸ Βρυάνιον καὶ Ἀλαλκομεναὶ καὶ Στυβαρά (Strabo, *Geographica*, Book VII, chap. 7, § 9 (C. 327)). See also Steph. Byz. s.v. Ἀλαλκομεναί.

[2] This variant form 'Stuberra' might have been contracted from an original 'Stubaria' if the Pelagones' ancestral language was North-East Greek. In both the Lesbian and the Thessalian varieties of this dialect, an i following a consonant is dropped and, in compensation, the consonant is doubled. E.g. ἀργύριοι becomes ἀργύρροι (Kretschmer, op. cit., p. 278).

[3] Livy, Book XXXI, chap. 39.   [4] *Iliad*, IV. 8.

[5] See Pausanias, *Graeciae Descriptio*, Book IX, chap. 3, § 4; chap. 33, §§ 5–6; chap. 34, § 1.

[6] Pausanias, locc. citt.

[7] There was a Bryanion in Thesprotia (Steph. Byz., s.v. Βρυάνιον).

[8] Livy, Book XXXI, chap. 30.   [9] Livy, Book XLIV, chap. 3.

[10] Dittenberger, *Sylloge*, third ed., vol. i, pp. 238–9, No. 174.

[11] *Sylloge*, third ed., vol. i, pp. 262–3, No. 188.

[12] See Hoffmann, op. cit., pp. 138, 176, 201.

who was named Amyntas son of Arrhabaios, was a Lyncestian too.[1] A third certain Pelagonian personal name is that of Ἀγάθων Βούτα [Δε]υριόπιος Μακεδών who was proxenos of Oropos at some date in the third century B.C.;[2] and this Agathon's father Boutas gives us a fourth. We also know the name of a fifth and sixth Pelagonian if Arrian is right in saying, as he does say in one passage,[3] that Alexander's somatophylax Peithon son of Krateuas came from the Alalkomenai in Deuriopos. In another passage,[4] however, Arrian says that Peithon came from Eordaia, and this metropolitan province seems a more probable provenance for a high-ranking officer. Of these four certainly Pelagonian personal names and two possibly Pelagonian personal names, five are Greek, and the sixth, Boutas, may be Greek too. Two of the later series of Damastine coins bear the Greek personal names Herakleidas and Kephisophon,[5] and a later issue than these bears the name Kakiôn[6] (a bad name, but good Greek). May guesses[7] that Herakleidas and Kephisophon were representatives of the Dyestai, whose dominions centred on Damastion, if Meineke's emendation of Strabo is right.[8] One very late and degenerate Damastine issue bears the name Sokratidas,[9] and Damastine-type coins bear the names Simon and Nikarkhos.[10]

These Greek place-names and personal names are strong presumptive evidence that the Pelagones were Greek-speaking in the fourth, third, and second centuries B.C. The Greekness of all but one of the personal names—and, above all, the transparent Greekness of the names on the coinages of the independent communities—is impressive. Yet, impressive though this evidence is, it is inconclusive, as we can infer from the case of the Amphilokhoi, who, on the explicit and precise testimony of Thucydides, were non-Greek-speaking in 430 B.C., though the place-names in their territory, as well as their national name, were Greek.[11] If Polybius, say, had thought of giving us the corresponding information about the language spoken by the Pelagones in his time, we might have learnt, for all that we know, that the Pelagones, like the Amphilokhoi, had lost their ancestral Greek language. Indeed, there was one branch— a far-wandering branch—of the Pelagones that certainly did change its language no less than three times in the course of its history.

Though Paelignia (Pelignia) in central Italy is a long way from Pelagonia in the heart of the Balkan Peninsula, there can be no doubt that the two ethnika are identical. 'Pĕlignoi' (as the name is usually spelled in Greek)[12] stands to 'Pelagones' exactly as 'Makednoi' stands

---

[1] Hoffmann, op. cit., pp. 165 and 192. [2] *I.G.*, vol. vii, No. 356[2].
[3] *Indica*, chap. 18, § 5. [4] *Anabasis*, Book VI, chap. 28, § 4.
[5] See May, op. cit., pp. 82–95.
[6] Ibid., pp. 148–9. [7] Ibid., p. 109. [8] See p. 80, n. 9.
[9] See May, op. cit., pp. 139–43. [10] Ibid., pp. 189–91. [11] See Part II, chap. 2, p. 60.
[12] P.–W., 36. Halbband, 1. Drittel, col. 2227.

to 'Makedones'. If the Pelagones were Greek-speaking originally, the Pelignoi must have been too. Yet, at the earliest date at which local inscriptions begin to give us contemporary information about the Pelignoi, they were Oscan-speaking, were soon to become Latin-speaking, and had previously been Illyrian-speaking on the evidence of their personal names. According to Conway[1] the name Lucceius—i.e. the name of a fourth-century-B.C. Derronaean king of the Kingdom of Paionia—was a frequently occurring gens-name in Pelignia two centuries or so later;[2] and the Pelignian names Ammaus, Accavus, Accaus, Annaus have the same suffix as the name of the fourth-century king of Paionia, Patraos the father of King Audoleon. Names in -avus and -aus were common in Illyria and Venetia.[3] This Pelignian nomenclature bears out Festus' statement 'Paeligni ex Illyrico orti'.[4]

The Pelignian people must have been an offshoot of the Pelagones that had pushed its way so far north-westward into Illyricum that it had not only taken to speaking Illyrian instead of its ancestral Greek but had been caught up in the wave of Illyrian migrants—Calabri, Peucetii, Iapyges, and others—who had crossed the Adriatic from continental south-eastern Europe into peninsular Italy in the wake of the preceding Osco-Umbrian wave and the still earlier Latin-Faliscan wave.[5] The Pelagones who stayed in the Axios basin, next-door to the Greek-speaking Makedones, may, of course, have retained their own ancestral Greek language when their offshoot, the Pelignoi, abandoned it. The question of the nationality of the Axios-basin Pelagones partly turns on their relation to the Axios-basin Paiones. The nationality of the Paiones is the subject of the next chapter. Before proceeding to discuss it, it will be convenient to look at our information about the Pelagones' relation to them, though we shall not be able to assess the significance of this information till we have examined our information about the Paiones' nationality.

[1] R. S. Conway, *The Italic Dialects* (Cambridge, 1897, University Press, 2 vols.), vol. i, p. 250.

[2] It was also a gens-name, though a less frequently occurring one, among the Marrucini (ibid., p. 257), and the Vestini (ibid., p. 264), whose territories lay between Pelignia and the Adriatic.   [3] Kretschmer, op. cit., p. 246.   [4] Festus, p. 222 M, 248 L.

[5] A perhaps once Greek-speaking people that may have become Illyrian-speaking without migrating so far afield as the Pelignoi are the Penestai who, in the second century B.C., inhabited the upper valley of the River Drin, immediately to the north of Lake Lykhnidos. The same ethnikon was borne, in the Post-Völkerwanderung Age, by the Thessaloi's peasant subjects who were said to be descended from the population that had inhabited Thessaly before the Thessaloi had conquered the country. In the Pre-Völkerwanderung Age, were the Penestai the North-East-Greek-speaking occupants of the south-western portion of Thessaly that became the Thessalian tetrarchy Thessaliotis? If they were, it is conceivable that one section of them, being unwilling to submit to the Thessaloi, may have migrated northwards, like their neighbours and kinsmen the Makedones and Pelagones, and may have come to rest again eventually in the valley of the River Drin. For the Penestai in Illyria, see Livy, Book XLIII, chaps. 18, 19, 20, 21, and 23; Book XLIV, chap. 11.

In considering the relation between the Pelagones and the Paiones, we have to distinguish between language and politics. Politically the greater part of Pelagonia was united with Derronaean Paionia under Derronaean rule[1] from *circa* 359 B.C. The original home of the Derronaioi was perhaps the valley of the Strumnica (?Astraios), a right-bank tributary of the middle Struma (Strymon).[2] After having suffered a political and economic reverse when King Alexander I of Macedon, profiting from the Persian Empire's disaster in 479 B.C., suppressed the coinages, and subjugated at least some of the territories, of the communities in the middle and lower Strymon basin that had been issuing coinages down to that date,[3] the Derronaioi seem to have repaired their fortunes in the fourth century B.C. by annexing the greater part of Pelagonia.[4] The Derronaean Kingdom of Paionia thus included a Pelagonian portion as well as a Paeonian portion from the start, and this union seems to have been maintained when, in the third century B.C.— at some date, perhaps, during Antigonos Gonatas' reign[5]—the Kingdom of Paionia was annexed definitively to the Kingdom of Macedon. As a result of this enduring political union, the Pelagones and the Derronaean Paiones will have influenced each other reciprocally. If Astibos, the capital of the kingdom, was the present-day Stiplje on the Bregalnica tributary of the Vardar (Axios),[6] it will have lain only just on the

---

[1] King Lykkeios of Paionia (see p. 91) calls himself 'Derronaios' on one of his issues of coins (May, op. cit., p. 32, n. 1).

[2] The Derronaioi's coinage, dating from the period before 479 B.C., bear their name in the variant forms Δερρῶνες, Δερρονικόν, Δερρο. The ethnikon Δερρωναῖος is inscribed on the obverse of one of the issues of King Lykkeios (May, op. cit., p. 32, n. 1), who was on the throne of the Kingdom of Paionia about halfway through the fourth century B.C. The ethnikon may survive in the present-day name Doiran, which is borne by a lake and a village between Lake Butkova and the River Vardar, and which appears in the Peutinger Table in the form Tauriana.

These Paeonian Derronaioi seem to be a different people from the Dersaioi, whom Herodotus, Book VII, chap. 110, and also Steph. Byz., s.v. Δεραῖοι, call Thracians, and who are located by Herodotus between the Sapaioi and the Edonoi, i.e. somewhere in the trackless highlands between the Nestos gorge and the Angites basin.

[3] See May, op. cit., p. 32.

[4] Strabo, Book VII, fragm. 4, is describing the boundaries of this fourth-century-B.C. Paeonian Kingdom, consisting of Derronaia together with the greater part of Pelagonia. He is not describing the boundaries of the total area occupied by Paeonian peoples. 'Paionia', he says in this passage, 'lies to the east of these peoples [the reference is to a lost passage] and to the west of the Thracian mountains, while it is the Macedonians' northern neighbour. It contains the approaches, through Gortynion and Stoboi, to the [gorge on the south] through which the River Axios flows and thereby makes Macedon difficult to invade from Paionia, as the Peneios, flowing through Tempe, fortifies Macedon against Hellas. Paionia is the southern neighbour of the Autariatai, Dardanioi, and Ardiaioi. It extends as far as the Strymon.' Cp. fragm. 36.

[5] See p. 86.

[6] The Paeonian portion of the Derronaean Kingdom of Paionia-Pelagonia will, no doubt, have included the lower (i.e. the south-western) part of the Bregalnica basin, as well as the Strumnica Valley, which may have been the Derronaioi's homeland; but the upper part of the Bregalnica basin may have been held, not by the Derronaioi, but by the Maidoi. The

Paeonian side of the border between the Paeonian and the Pelagonian part of the kingdom. On this site the capital will, no doubt, have served as a cultural melting-pot. This political involvement of a majority of the Pelagones with a Paeonian people makes the determination of both the Pelagones' and the Paiones' nationality difficult.

For instance, when Livy, in a passage already quoted,[1] says that Deuriopos is a district of Paionia and that the River Erigon flows through Paionia on its way from Illyricum to join the Axios, is he using the term 'Paionia' in the ethnic, or merely in the political, sense? And is Strabo speaking in ethnic, or merely in political, terms when he says that 'the Paiones were called Pelagones'?[2] It is true that, from some date *circa* 359 B.C. onwards, there were people who were Paiones politically but were Pelagones ethnically, but this political fact throws no light on the identity of either the Paiones' or the Pelagones' ancestral language. Again, when Pliny says[3] that Paeonia and Pelagonia protect the northern part of Macedonia from the Triballi, is he drawing an ethnic distinction between two countries that were not separate from each other politically? And what were the relations between the Paiones and the Pelagones before the foundation of the Derronaean kingdom in the Axios basin? The association of the Paiones and the Pelagones with each other here is anticipated in a passage of the *Iliad*[4] in which Asteropaios, the leader of the Paiones, is made a son of Πηλεγών, and Πηλεγών is made a son of the River Axios, while Asteropaios' own name seems to mean 'a Paeonian from the River Astraios'.

Maidoi were the eastern neighbours of the Thounatai division of the Dardanoi (Strabo, *Geographica*, Book VII, chap. 5, § 7 (C. 316)); the Thounatai must have held the north-eastern headwaters of the Vardar; and, when, in 181 B.C., King Philip V of Macedon marched from Stoboi to climb one of the high peaks of the Haemus Range (probably one of those in the Rilo massif), he traversed Maedica before reaching an uninhabited zone between Maedica and the Haemus (Livy, Book XL, chaps. 21–2).

[1] On p. 82, n. 2.
[2] Strabo, *Geographica*, Book VII, fragms. 38 and 39 (C. 331).
[3] Pliny, *Historia Naturalis*, Book IV, chap. 10, § 37.
[4] XXI. 140–60.

5. What was the Ancestral Language of the Paiones?

I N our quest for the Paiones' nationality, it may be helpful to begin by ascertaining their earliest known habitat.

The passage of the *Iliad* that has just been cited is our earliest reference to the Paiones in Greek literature. It seems to indicate that, at the time at which it was composed, there were Paiones and Pelagones who were neighbours of each other in the Axios valley. Thucydides, in his account[1] of the progressive expansion of the Argead Kingdom of Lower Macedon, says that the Argeadai acquired, in Paionia, a narrow strip along the River Axios extending to Pella and the sea. This agrees with the statement, in the Homeric Catalogue of the Trojan forces, that the Paeonian contingent came 'from Amydon on the Axios',[2] if we have been right in identifying with each other the place-name 'Amydon' and the personal name 'Amythaon', and in seeing in Amydon a Minyan settlement at the head of the Thermaic Gulf, in a position corresponding to that of Iolkos at the head of the Gulf of Volo.[3] These Paiones along the Axios, whom the Argeadai evicted or subjugated, will have straddled the section of the river's course below Negotin, while the Pelagones who were the Axian Paiones' neighbours will have straddled the section extending from Negotin to Veles, where we find them still in possession in 199 B.C. If the mouth of the Axios was the first point, and perhaps the only point, at which any of the Paiones ever reached the north shore of the Aegean Sea, we should expect these Axian Paiones to have been, as they were, the first representatives of that nation to come within the ken of the Greeks. But it does not follow from this that the lower valley of the Axios was the Paiones' earliest or principal habitat. If the Axios above Negotin was already Pelagonian, the Paiones could have reached the Axios below Negotin by the easy east-west route, now traversed by a railway, along the depression between the Belašica (Kerkine) Range on the north and the Kruša (Dysoros) Range on the south. They had no need to make their way over the forest-clad Belašica Range, as the Odrysian war-lord Sitalkes did when, after descending the Struma and mounting the Strumnica, he invaded the ex-Paeonian district of Macedon, along the lower Axios, in 429 B.C.[4]

It looks as if the majority of the Paeonian peoples were to be found,

[1] Book II, chap. 99.
[2] ἐξ Ἀμυδῶνος, ἀπ' Ἀξίου (*Iliad*, II. 849; cp. XVI. 287–9).
[3] See Part I, chap. 2, pp. 14–15.
[4] See Thucydides, Book II, chap. 98.

not in the Axios basin, but in the Strymon basin. Indeed, Herodotus, apropos of Megabazos' operations *circa* 511 B.C., puts into Paeonian mouths the statement that 'the location of Paionia is on the River Strymon'.[1]

The Paiones do not seem ever to have occupied the whole of the Strymon valley. They were cut off from the coast here by the Thracian Bisaltai and Thracian Edonoi, who occupied respectively the western and the eastern side of the lowest reach of the Strymon valley; and, though the middle course of the Strymon must once have been occupied by the Paiones who had reached Lake Kerkinitis and Mount Pangaios and the lower valley of the Axios,[2] by the second century B.C., at any rate, this middle section of the Strymon valley, above the gorge through which the river squeezes its way between the eastern end of the Kerkine Range and the western end of the Orbelos,[3] was in the hands of another Thracian people, the Maidoi, who also held the upper valley of the Nestos (Mesta), and perhaps the upper valley of the Bregalnica as well. However, the headwaters of the Strymon were held by the Agrianes—a Paeonian people according to all our authorities—at the time of Megabazos' campaign *circa* 511 B.C.,[4] at the time of Sitalkes' campaign in 429 B.C.,[5] and at the time of Alexander's campaign in 335 B.C.;[6] and both they and their neighbours and kinsmen the Dentheletai seem to have held their ground in this region continuously until they were swamped, at last, by the Slav Völkerwanderung in the sixth and seventh centuries of the Christian Era.

The other Paeonian peoples, besides the Agrianes, that are named by Herodotus in connection with Megabazos' campaign are, on the one hand, the Siropaiones, the Paioplai, and their neighbours as far as Lake Prasias, all of whom were deported by Megabazos to Phrygia,[7] and on the other hand the Paiones in the neighbourhood of Mount Pangaios, the Doberes, the Odomantoi, and the Paeonian lake-dwellers in Lake Prasias, whom Megabazos failed to conquer. The Paiones had expected Megabazos to follow the coast-road, so they had concentrated their forces in that quarter. Megabazos outmanœuvred them by procuring guides who led him by an inland route and so enabled him to take the Paiones in the rear and to occupy the Siropaiones' and Paioplai's towns while their fighting-men were still absent, holding the approaches from the coast.[8] This inland route cannot have been the one between Mounts

---

[1] εἴη δὲ ἡ Παιονίη ἐπὶ τῷ Στρυμόνι ποταμῷ πεπολισμένη (Herodotus, Book V, chap. 13).
[2] See Strabo, *Geographica*, Book VII, fragm. 36.
[3] For this gorge, see Casson, op. cit., p. 7.
[4] Herodotus, Book V, chap. 16; cp. Strabo, *Geographica*, Book VII, fragms. 36 and 37.
[5] Thucydides, Book II, chap. 96.   [6] Arrian, Book I, chap. 5, §§ 1–4.
[7] Herodotus, Book V, chaps. 15 and 98.
[8] This manœuvre was repeated by the Persians twice, and each time successfully, when they

Pangaios and Orbelos, in the basin of the Strymon's left-bank tributary the Angites; for this route would have taken Megabazos through the country of the Pangaian Paiones and the Doberes and the Odomantoi, and these were among the Paeonian peoples that escaped Megabazos' attentions. His route must therefore have been the one that runs, considerably farther inland, through Nevrokop, in the upper valley of the Nestos, to Melnik in the Strymon basin, approximately opposite the Strymon's confluence with the Strumnica. Megabazos' guides must have been good; for they must have shown him a way of circumventing the impassable gorge through which the Nestos flows between Buk and Okcilar.[1]

On the assumption that Megabazos did take the Nevrokop–Melnik route to the Strymon valley, and allowing for the possibility that Herodotus' Lake Prasias may be either the present-day Lake Takhyno or the present-day Lake Butkova,[2] we can locate, at least approximately, not only the Agrianes, but most of the other Paeonian peoples whom Herodotus mentions in his narrative. The location of the Siropaiones is certain. Their town was Siris, the present-day Serrhés. The Odomantoi must have

were invading Greece in 480 B.C. They circumvented a Greek holding-force first at Tempe and then at Thermopylae.

   [1] See Casson, op. cit., pp. 9, 22, and 26.

   [2] We should have expected Lake Butkova to be Lake Kerkinitis, since it is evident, from Thucydides' description of Sitalkes' itinerary, that the Belašica Range, which overhangs Lake Butkova immediately to the north of the lake, is Thucydides' Mount Kerkine; and this mountain must have given Lake Kerkinitis its name. However, Arrian's account (Book I, chap. 11, § 3) of the place where Alexander III assembled his fleet at the outset of his expedition against the Persian Empire makes it certain that Arrian's Lake Kerkinitis is Lake Takhyno, through which the River Strymon flows immediately to the north of Amphipolis (see Thucydides, Book IV, chap. 108, § 1). Herodotus' Lake Prasias must therefore be Lake Butkova—unless 'Prasias' and 'Kerkinitis' are alternative names for the same lake, which then can only be Lake Takhyno, on the evidence of the passage in Arrian's *Alexandri Anabasis*. The two names could well be synonymous—the name 'Prasias' being descriptive of the lake's colour, and the name 'Kerkinitis' indicating its location. Geyer, op. cit., pp. 4–5, in an able discussion of the problem, rules out the identification of Lake Prasias with Lake Kerkinitis as being inadmissible; yet none of our authorities mentions both names, which would be the only conclusive proof that they did refer to two different lakes; and Herodotus' account of Megabazos' march (Book V, chap. 15), and also his description of the route from Lake Prasias to Macedon, would allow of our identifying his Lake Prasias with either Lake Butkova or Lake Takhyno. If we identify Lake Prasias with Lake Takhyno, the 'very short' (σύντομος κάρτα) road from Lake Prasias to Macedon over Mount Dysoros (Herodotus, Book V, chap. 17) will be the present-day road from Serrhés to Thessaloníki over the hill country (Krestonike) between the Kruša Range to the north-west and the Beşik Range to the south-east. Lake Takhyno seems to fit better than Lake Butkova does with Herodotus' location of the Paioplai in Book VII, chap. 13, and with Ptolemy's location in Bisaltike of Euporia (*Geographia*, Book III, chap. 12, § 32)—the city founded by King Alexander I of Macedon (Steph. Byz., s.v. Εὐπορία) at the mines near Lake Prasias (Herodotus, Book V, chap. 17). The south-west shore of Lake Takhyno is in Bisaltike, whereas Lake Butkova is in Sintike. Whichever identification one favours, one cannot bring Megabazos to the Strymon valley by any other route than the northern one through Nevrokop and Melnik, since this route alone is compatible with Herodotus' account of the course of events.

been the Siropaiones' immediate neighbours to the south-east, for, by 168 B.C., Siris had passed into the Odomantoi's hands.[1] In the opposite direction, Odomantike must have extended as far south-eastwards as the Pangaean mining-district, since the Odomantoi were one of the peoples that had a share in the mining industry there.[2] The Doberes, whom Herodotus seems to associate with Mount Pangaios in two passages,[3] will have lived at the place called Domerus on the Roman road between Amphipolis and Philippi. The Paioplai seem to be located by Herodotus between the Siropaiones and Lake Prasias.[4] The deportation of the Paioplai by Megabazos will have created a vacuum here as well as at Siris. It is true that some of the Paeonian deportees seized the opportunity of the outbreak of the Ionian Revolt in 499 B.C. to make their way back home, and, according to Herodotus,[5] there were Paioplai once again in the interior in 480 B.C. However, not all the Paeonian deportees in Phrygia ventured to decamp,[6] so, as a result of the deportations, the Odomantoi, who had escaped, may have extended their territory at the expense of the Paioplai as well as the Siropaiones.

It seems clear that, before the establishment of the Derronaean Kingdom of Paionia in the upper Axios basin at some date *circa* 359 B.C., the Strymon basin was the Paiones' principal habitat, and this geographical fact has a bearing on the question of the Paiones' ancestral language. The Paiones' original habitat was much farther away than Pelagonia was, and very much farther away than the original nucleus of Macedon was, from the unquestionably Greek-speaking region to the south of Mount Olympus.

Beloch, who is convinced that the Paiones' ancestral language was Greek, cites, as evidence for this, the place-name Paionidai, which is found in both Attica and Argos.[7] One could add the Aetolian place-name Paianion,[8] the Attic place-name Paiania, the Arcadian place-name Paion,[9] and the district called Dentheliatis[10] round the headwaters of the River Nedon in the borderland between Messenia and Laconia. These names are evidence that bands of Paiones had once reached southern continental European Greece, presumably during the post-Mycenaean Völkerwanderung, and had made permanent lodgements there, but they are not evidence that the Paiones were a Greek-speaking people, though

[1] Livy, Book XLV, chap. 4.
[2] Herodotus, Book VII, chap. 112. Cp. Strabo, *Geographica*, Book VII, fragm. 36.
[3] Book V, chap. 16, and Book VII, chap. 113.
[4] Book V, chap. 15. Cp. Book VII, chap. 113.
[5] Book VII, chap. 130.
[6] Herodotus, Book V, chap. 98.
[7] Beloch, op. cit., Erster Band, Zweite Abteilung, p. 55.
[8] Polybius, Book IV, chap. 63, §§ 3 and 11.
[9] Herodotus, Book VI, chap. 127.
[10] Or Δελθάνιοι (Steph. Byz., s.v.).

no doubt these Paeonian enclaves in a Greek-speaking milieu did become
Greek-speakers in the course of time, even if the ancestral language that
they had brought with them had been non-Greek. If Beloch's argument
were cogent (it is not), then the presence of the name 'Phrygia' on the
border between Boeotia and Attica and on Mount Oeta[1] would prove
that the Phrygians were Greek-speaking, the traditions about Thracian
settlements in Central Greece would prove that the Thracians were
Greek-speaking,[2] and the occurrence of the place-name Sermaize at two
places in France would prove that the Sarmatae were French-speaking.
Bands of Thracians, Phrygians (i.e. Brygoi, the western fraction of the
Phrygian people), and Paiones may have been carried along with the
Völkerwanderung of North-West-Greek-speaking peoples into southern
Greece and the Aegean. The correspondence between the name 'Hylleis',
which was borne by one of the three phylai of the Anatolian Doris, and
the name of an Illyrian people, the Hylloi, in north-western Dalmatia,[3]
indicates that at least one band of Illyrians was involved. But, if the
wave of migrants did include these Paeonian, Illyrian, Phrygian, and
Thracian components, this does not prove that they had originally
spoken Greek as their mother-tongue.

The evidence on which we have to determine, if a decision proves
possible, what the Paiones' ancestral language was is the evidence of
geographical names, ethnika, and personal names; and in each of these
three fields we find Greek names and non-Greek names side by side.

Among the geographical names, for instance, 'Prasias' and 'Dysoros'
are transparently Greek, and, if Lake Prasias were the present-day Lake
Butkova and Mount Dysoros were the present-day Kruša Range, these
two names would tell strongly in favour of Greek being the Paiones'
ancestral language. If, however, Lake Prasias is the present-day Lake
Takhyno and Mount Dysoros is the heights between the south-east end
of the Kruša Range and the north-west end of the Beşik Range, Greek
geographical names in that coastward region will tell us nothing

---

[1] Thucydides, Book II, chap. 22; Steph. Byz., s.v. Φρυγία. The place on Oeta was ἡ Φρυγία;
the place on the Attica–Boeotia border was τὰ Φρύγια.

[2] A useful conspectus of these traditions is given by Casson, op. cit., pp. 102–5. No doubt
the traditions are partly legendary, but Casson (op. cit., p. 105, n. 2) justly criticizes Beloch
for writing them off as being wholly fictitious.

[3] These Hylloi are mentioned by Pliny, *Historia Naturalis*, Book III, chap. 21 (25), § 139,
together with the Mentores, Himani, Encheleae, Bulini, and Peucetii, as fractions of the
Liburnian people whose names were no longer in use in Pliny's own day. But Ptolemy,
Geographia, Book II, chap. 16, § 5, mentions the Hyllaioi and the Boulimeis and locates
them along the coast of Illyria, immediately to the south-east of the Iapodes, as if they were
still extant; and Pseudo-Scylax, too, writing about halfway through the fourth century B.C.,
speaks (§ 23) of the Boulinoi and the Hylloi as if they were still in existence in his day.
According to him, the χερσόνησος Ὑλλική (i.e. north-western Dalmatia) is as big as the
Peloponnese. Pseudo-Scylax's notice of the Hylloi has been copied by Pseudo-Scymnus,
lines 404–9.

about the Paiones' nationality, since these names could have been given to these natural features by the colonial Greeks in the adjacent Andrian and Chalcidian colonies.[1] 'Astibos', the name of the capital of the fourth-century-B.C. kingdom of Paionia, can be interpreted in Greek terms as a variant of the word ἀστιβής and as meaning 'a place on which it is tabu to set foot'. The place-name Astraion, from which the Homeric personal name Asteropaios[2] seems to have been formed, might be akin to the personal names Astraios and Astraia, which figure in Greek mythology. On the other hand Domerus on the Amphipolis–Philippi road and its homonym Doberos[3] on Sitalkes' route between Mount Kerkine and Eidomene *in* the Macedonian Amphaxitis look un-Greek; and so does a set of names ending in -azoros or -azora: Azoros in the Perrhaebian Tripolis; Gazoros in Edonike;[4] Hypsizorus, a mountain on or near the Pallene Peninsula;[5] Bylazora on the upper Axios. Some of these names have a distinctly Slavonic flavour: 'Astraios' calls to mind 'Ostrov' and Ostrva;[6] 'Doberos' calls to mind 'Dobro';[7] -azor- calls to mind both 'izvor'[8] and 'gora';[9] the 'Byl-' in Bylazora calls to mind the Slavonic word for 'white'. These assonances would not be surprising if the 'azor' geographical names were Illyrian or Thracian, since the Illyrian-speakers and Thracian-speakers and Slavonic-speakers are likely to have been each other's next-door neighbours at some stage in the differentiation and diffusion of the Indo-European languages. It is also conceivable that the Paiones may actually have been a Slavonic-speaking people that had been caught up in the Thracian and Illyrian Völker-wanderung into south-eastern Europe some 1,700 or 1,800 years before the massive Völkerwanderung of the Slavs in the sixth and seventh centuries of the Christian Era.

---

[1] In that case the native name for Mount Dysôros might be Mount Bertiskos, which Ptolemy locates in this neighbourhood (*Geographia*, Book III, chap. 12, § 16)—though Strabo (Book VII, fragm. 10) places Mount Bertiskos to the west of Mount Skardos (Shar), far away from the Strymon valley.

[2] *Iliad*, XXI. 140–60.   [3] Thucydides, Book II, chaps. 98 and 100.

[4] Steph. Byz., s.v.; Ptolemy, Book III, chap. 13, § 31.

[5] Pliny, *Historia Naturalis*, Book IV, chap. 10 (17), § 36. Hypsizorus, which is the reading in the MSS., has been emended to Hypsizonus by Detlefsen. This makes the name an all-Greek compound, instead of a half-Greek one, and this name might well be purely Greek, since the region in which Pliny seems to locate Mount Hypsizorus had been colonized by the Greek city-states Eretria, Corinth, and Chalcis. On the other hand, it is also conceivable that the local Greek colonists Graecized the first component of an already existing place-name that had been wholly non-Greek in its authentic form.

[6] Bulgarian 'ostrov' and Serbo-Croat 'ostrvce' mean 'island'; Bulgarian 'ostr' means 'sharp' and Croat 'ostrva' means 'pole'; and there may have been other Paeonian lake-dwellers, living in houses built on piles, besides those in Lake Prasias.

[7] 'Dobro' means good in both Bulgarian and Serbo-Croat. In present-day Greece, there is more than one village that still bears the Slavonic name 'Dobrena'.

[8] 'Izvor' means 'water-spring' in both Bulgarian and Serbo-Croat.

[9] 'Gora' means 'mountain' in both Bulgarian and Serbo-Croat.

Among the Paeonian ethnika, the name 'Paiones' itself could pass for Greek on the analogy of 'Pelagones', 'Makedones', 'Aones', 'Myrmidones'; but there are also many names of non-Greek-speaking peoples that likewise end in -ŏnes in the Greek versions of them: for instance, the Illyrian ethnika Bylliones, Skirtones, Mentores; the Thracian ethnika Mygdones, Bistones, Kikones; the Anatolian (perhaps Phrygian) ethnika Mêïones and Lykaones (we must reserve judgement on the Epirot ethnikon Khaones till we come to discuss what the Epirots' ancestral language was).

The ethnikon 'Agrianes', on the other hand, is not linguistically ambiguous; it is pure Greek. Peoples whose ethnika end in -ânes, in contrast to those whose ethnika end in -ŏnes, seem to be Greek-speakers in most cases,[1] and the eponym of the Agrianes, Agrios, figures in Hesiod's *Theogony*[2] as a son of Circe by Odysseus. Though the Agrianes were the most remote of the Paeonian peoples from the main body of the Greek-speaking World, we are bound to conclude from their name that, like the Amphilokhoi and the Pelignoi, they had been Greek-speakers originally, whatever their language may have been in 429 B.C., which is the earliest date at which we have any surviving notice of them.[3] If the Agrianes, like the Pelignoi, were originally Greek-speaking, they are likely to have been Pelagones; and, if they had migrated to their eventual home at the headwaters of the Strymon from the plain of Monastir, that would have been a shorter and easier journey[4] than the Pelignoi's migration across the Adriatic to the central Italian highlands.

The Agrianes' Paeonian neighbours the Dentheletai have an un-Greek-sounding name. Their territory lay on the right bank of the Strymon;[5] and this accounts for there being no mention of them in Thucydides' narrative of Sitalkes' expedition in 429 B.C., since the Strymon was the western frontier of Sitalkes' dominions.[6] The Laiaioi Paiones, who, like the Agrianes, were Sitalkes' subjects, must therefore have lived on the left bank of the Strymon, and this down-stream from the Agrianes, since Sitalkes traversed the Agrianes' territory before traversing theirs. If 'Laiaioi' means 'left-bankers', it is not a Greek word but a Paeonian one from the same root as the Latin 'laevus'. The Salesioi[7] sound like kinsmen of the Sallentini across the water.

The name of the Odomantoi, who were the south-easternmost of the

---

[1] See the list of ethnika ending in -anes in Hammond, 'Prehistoric Epirus and the Dorian Invasion', p. 156. Hammond points out that this form of ethnikon is characteristic of north-west Greece.

[2] l. 1013.

[3] See Thucydides, Book II, chap. 96.

[4] A Roman road was eventually built from Herakleia (Monastir) through Stoboi to Pautalia.

[5] Pliny, *Historia Naturalis*, Book IV, chap. 11, § 40.

[6] Thucydides, loc. cit.

[7] Σαλήσιοι· μοῖρα Παιόνων (Steph. Byz.).

Paeonian peoples except for the Doberes, corresponds to the name of the Athamanes[1] at the headwaters of the River Akheloïos, when we have allowed for the general North-East-Greek change of A into O and for the specifically Macedonian D in place of TH. If the coins from the lower Strymon region that bear the name 'Tyntenoi'[2] are authentic, they give us a second correspondence between an ethnikon in the lower Strymon basin and one in Epirus, where we find the Atintanes in between the Parauaioi and the Khaones. If the Odomantoi-Athamanes and the Tyntenoi-Atintanes were, in truth, each a fractured Paeonian people whose original unity is attested, in either case, by the survival of an identical name, we can account for this by supposing that, in the course of the post-Mycenaean Völkerwanderung, both these Paeonian peoples were split, by impacts from the rear, somewhere in the basin of the River Morava, with the result that their eastern splinters were driven down the Strymon valley, while their western splinters were pushed away to the Adriatic side of the continental divide.

As for the Paioplai, the suffix -pl- which appears in their name has Illyrian parallels in the Liburnian place-name Ortopla and in another Illyrian place-name, Oplus, for which there is inscriptional evidence.[3]

When we examine the surviving Paeonian personal names, we find some that are transparently Greek, others that look non-Greek, and others again that are evidently Illyrian.

Both the earliest and the latest of the kings of Paionia whose names we know bore Greek names. The occupant of the throne of Paionia in 359 B.C., when Philip II came to the throne in Macedon, was named Agis.[4] The king who temporarily re-established the independence of Paionia after Lysimachus' fall in 280 B.C. was named Dropion, son of Leon,[5] and these two names are both Greek.[6] So is the name of Ariston, the commander of the Paeonian cavalry in Alexander III's expeditionary force; and there is no evidence that Ariston was a Macedonian and not a Paeonian. On the other hand, the Paeonian king Lykkeios' name is certainly un-Greek, and is convicted of being Illyrian by its frequent occurrence in Pelignia.[7] King Audoleon's name[8] has Illyrian parallels

---

[1] Ἀθαμανία· χώρα Ἰλλυρίας, οἱ δὲ Θεσσαλίας (Steph. Byz., s.v.).

[2] See Casson, op. cit., p. 192.   [3] Kretschmer, op. cit., pp. 246–8.

[4] Diodorus, Book XVI, chap. 4, § 2.

[5] See Pausanias, Book X, chap. 13, § 1 (at Delphi there was a bronze head of a Paeonian bull bison dedicated by Dropion son of Leon); Dittenberger, *Sylloge*, 2nd ed., vol. i, p. 335, No. 208 (Δρωπίωνα Λέοντος βασιλέα Παιόνων καὶ κτίστην, τὸ κοινὸν τῶν Παιόνων ἀνέθηκε, at a date that was probably later than the Gallic invasion in 280 B.C.).

[6] See Hoffmann, op. cit., p. 183, for the name Drop-.

[7] See Part II, chap. 4, p. 91 and p. 92, n. 2.

[8] ὁ Παιόνων β[ασ]ιλεὺς [Α]ὐδω[λέω]ν and τὸμ βασιλεί[α] Αὐδωλέοντα Πατράου Παίονα in a decree passed by the Athenian demos in 286/5 B.C. (*Sylloge*, 2nd ed., vol. ii, pp. 316–18, No. 195).

in the names Audata, borne by Philip II of Macedon's Illyrian wife;[1] Audasius and Autus, which appear at Verona on inscriptions; and Autoscuttus, found on an inscription in Noricum; and there are further parallels in the Illyrian ethnikon 'Autariatai' and in the name of the Macedonian month Audnaios, the one, out of the twelve, that cannot be interpreted as being Greek.[2] The name of Audoleon's father, Patraos, is also convicted of being Illyrian by its termination.[3]

This co-existence of Greek and Illyrian names meets us in the case of the Agrianes too. While this Paeonian people's ethnikon is Greek, their king in 335 B.C. bore the un-Greek name Langaros,[4] and this un-Greek name is proved to be Illyrian by its evident identity with the name Longarus, which was borne by the father of Bato, the king of the Dardani, in 200 B.C.[5] The Dardani were certainly Illyrians;[6] and Bato was a common name in the Illyrian countries Dalmatia and Pannonia. Strabo mentions a Bato who was the leader of a people, the Daisitiatai,[7] in the great Illyrian insurrection against Rome in A.D. 6–9. The other principal insurgent leader was another Bato, whose people were the Pannonian Breuci.

The Agrianian King Langaros' name indicates that the Agrianes had become Illyrian-speaking by his time, while the Greek names of some of the members of the Derronaean royal house do not impugn the evidence given by the Illyrian names of other members of the Derronaean royal family. By this date the Derronaioi were united politically with the Greek-speaking Pelagones, and this association would account for their adopting Greek names in some cases.

When we travel back in time, we find that the evidence of earlier Paeonian personal names is similarly ambiguous. The name of Polles, who was king of the Odomantoi in 422 B.C.,[8] might be identical with the Greek name Pollis.[9] However, this would not prove that the Odomantoi were Greek-speakers; for Pittakos, the king of the Edonoi, who was assassinated in 424 B.C., also bore a Greek name, and so did his wife Brauro, who was one of his assassins. Yet the Edonoi were certainly Thracians, not Greeks, and King Pittakos' other assassins, the sons of Goaxis, had a father whose name was Thracian as well as his nationality.[10] Three out of four personal names inscribed on Derronaean coins of the period ending in 479 B.C. are Greek, namely Dokimos, Euergetes, and

---

[1] Satyrus in Müller, *F.H.G.*, vol. iii, p. 161, Satyrus, fragm. 5.
[2] See Kretschmer, op. cit., p. 247.   [3] See Part II, chap. 4, p. 91.
[4] Arrian, Book I, chap. 5, §§ 1–5.   [5] Livy, Book XXXI, chap. 28.
[6] See Strabo, *Geographica*, Book VII, chap. 5, § 6 (C. 315); Appian, *Illyrica*, chap. 2.
[7] Strabo, Book VII, chap. 5, § 3 (C. 314).
[8] Thucydides, Book V, chap. 6.
[9] Borne by a Spartiate naval officer who is heard of in 390 B.C. (Xenophon, *Hellenica*, Book IV, chap. 8, § 11) and again in 376 B.C. (ibid., Book V, chap. 4, §§ 60–1).
[10] See Thucydides, Book IV, chap. 107.

Ekg[onos], and the fourth name, of which the first syllable was Khe-, may have been Greek too. On the other hand the two Paiones, Pigres and Mantyes (with variant readings Mastyes and Masties), who are said by Herodotus[1] to have induced Darius to send Megabazos' expeditionary force to the Strymon basin *circa* 511 B.C., bore names that are not Greek, whatever they may be.

On the whole, the evidence seems to point to the Paiones' ancestral language having been not Greek but Illyrian or possibly Slavonic. However, in this case, so much of the evidence is ambiguous that we cannot feel so sure of our conclusion as we are perhaps justified in feeling in the clearer cases of the Pelagones and the Makedones.[2]

[1] Book V, chap. 12.
[2] Geyer, op. cit., pp. 22–4, has given a verdict of *non liquet*.

6. What was the Ancestral Language of the Epirots?

STRABO excludes Epirus[1] from the Hellas of his own day as emphatically as he includes Macedon in it.[2] He brackets the Epirot peoples with the Thracians in an enumeration of barbarian peoples who are still trespassing on Hellas' flanks, and, in particular, he names the Thesprotoi, Kassopaioi, Amphilokhoi, Molottoi, and Athamanes as Epirot peoples who are barbarian trespassers on the interior of Akarnania and Aetolia.[3] This distinction between Epirus and Macedon, which Strabo draws so sharply, must have become academic, long since, by his time. By that date, the whole of Epirus, as well as the part (and it was the major part) of the Roman province of Macedonia that had formerly been included in the Kingdom of Macedon, must have been Greek-speaking, even if there were pockets of territory in both provinces in which, side by side with Greek, some pre-Greek language or languages might still be current. Strabo's distinction, if it had any justification, will have been justified, not by the contemporary situation, but by memories of the respective histories of the two countries. The Makedones (if the argument of a previous chapter of this Part is convincing) had been Greek-speakers from the start, though, in the course of their expansion, they had annexed a number of non-Greek-speaking peoples whom they had only gradually been assimilating. By contrast, the Epirots, we may guess, had been an originally non-Greek-speaking people who, like the non-Greek-speaking peoples subjugated by the Makedones, had become Greek-speaking in course of time. On this point, Strabo's testimony, which would not count for much by itself, is supported by the more authoritative testimony of Polybius and Thucydides.

In an earlier chapter of this Part,[4] it has been noted already that, apropos of events in 432, 430, and 429 B.C., Thucydides calls the Khaones, Thesprotoi, Molossoi, and Atintanes barbarians, and also brackets with them the Macedonian Parauaioi, Orestai, and Makedones of Lower Macedon.[5] It has also been noted that Thucydides states, in so many words, that, in 430 B.C., the only Amphilokhoi who were Greek-speaking

---

[1] For the history of the name 'Epirus', see G. N. Cross, *Epirus* (Cambridge, 1932, University Press), pp. 1–19; P. R. Franke, *Alt-Epirus und das Königtum der Molosser* (Kallmünz-Opf., 1955, Lassleben), pp. 3–54; Hammond, *Epirus*, pp. 460–2, 476, 506, 537, 559–61.

[2] For Strabo's inclusion of Macedon in Hellas, see *Geographica*, Book VII, chap. 7, § 1 (C. 321), and fragm. 9, cited already in the present Part, chap. 3, p. 64, n. 1.

[3] Book VII, chap. 7, § 1 (C. 321).

[4] Chap. 2., p. 60.

[5] Thucydides, Book I, chap. 48, and Book II, chaps. 68 and 81.

were the citizens of the Amphilochian Argos, and that these had become
Greek-speaking as a result of their having adopted into their citizen-body
a detachment of settlers from the neighbouring Corinthian colony Ambrakia.[1] Thucydides' statements about the linguistic situation in Amphilokhia in 430 B.C. are very precise, and they are borne out by a quip that
was made by King Philip V of Macedon in 198/7 B.C. and that has been
recorded by Polybius.[2] In the abortive peace-talk at Nikaia on the
Maliac Gulf in that winter, one of the Aetolian delegates, Alexander
Isios, had demanded that Philip should evacuate all his holdings in
Hellas. Philip retorted by asking Alexander: 'What do you mean by the
"Hellas" that you are requiring me to evacuate? What boundaries do you
give to it? Why, a majority of the Aetolians themselves are not Hellenes.
The Agraoi, the Apodotoi, and the Amphilokhoi too, are not Hellas.
Well, are you proposing to cede these territories to me?'[3]

Philip had a ready wit and a sarcastic tongue. He was making a telling
repartee to an opponent's offensive harangue; he was not expecting that
the point that he was making would be taken as a basis for negotiation.
By this date, one of the three Upper Aetolian peoples, here named by
Philip, the Apodotoi, had been associated with nuclear Aetolia for nearly
a quarter of a millennium at least,[4] and all three peoples must now have
been Greek-speaking. Yet, though Philip's quip was not serious diplomacy,
it may have been good history. As far as the Amphilokhoi, at any rate,
were concerned, Philip's statement agreed with what Thucydides had
written apropos of the situation in Amphilokhia in 430 B.C.; and this
agreement is remarkable, considering that the passage in Thucydides'
work was certainly not in King Philip's mind when he was speaking, and
was not, apparently, in Polybius' mind either when he was recording
what Philip had said. All the three peoples whom Philip singled out, on
this occasion, as being non-Hellenic are also suspect on evidence that is
independent of Philip's allegation. Thucydides says expressly that in
430 B.C. the Amphilokhoi, except for those of Argos, were non-Greek-
speaking. The name Salynthios, borne by the king of the Agraioi in
426–424 B.C.,[5] is identified by Kretschmer[6] as being Illyrian on the
strength of its affinity with the Illyrian place-name 'Salluntum' and the
Calabrian ethnikon 'Sallentini'. The Apodôtoi are one of three peoples
in post-Völkerwanderung western and central Greece—the other two

---

[1] Thucydides, Book II, chap. 68, cited in chap. 2 on p. 60.
[2] Polybius, Book XVIII, chap. 5, §§ 7–9.
[3] ποίας δὲ κελεύετέ με, φησίν, ἐκχωρεῖν Ἑλλάδος καὶ πῶς ἀφορίζετε ταύτην; αὐτῶν γὰρ
Αἰτωλῶν οὐκ εἰσὶν Ἕλληνες οἱ πλείους· τὸ γὰρ τῶν Ἀγραῶν ἔθνος, καὶ τὸ τῶν Ἀποδωτῶν, ἔτι δὲ τῶν
Ἀμφιλόχων, οὐκ ἐστὶν Ἑλλάς. ἢ τούτων μὲν παραχωρεῖτέ μοι;
[4] The Apodotoi had been an Aetolian people in 426 B.C. (Thucydides, Book III, chap. 94).
[5] Thucydides, Book III, chaps. 111 and 114; Book IV, chap. 77.
[6] In op. cit., p. 258.

being the Thesprôtoi and the Boiôtoi—whose ethnika have the un-Greek termination -ôtoi.[1]

It is significant that Philip V should have put his finger on just these three Upper Aetolian peoples as being non-Hellenes. He could not, of course, deny the Hellenicity of nuclear Aetolia, i.e. the country round the two cities Pleuron and Kalydon. The original Aetolia had been part of the civilized world since the Mycenaean Age. It figures in the Homeric epic. But Philip might have stigmatized as being barbarians all the Upper Aetolian peoples who had come to be associated politically with nuclear Aetolia in the course of time. In 426 B.C., at any rate, all the Upper Aetolian peoples had been equally wild.[2] Yet Philip discriminated among them in picking out the three whom he declined to accept as being Hellenes. He did not include the Eurytanes in his black list, though in 426 B.C. the Eurytanes had had the reputation of being raw-meat-eaters.[3] This, too, is significant, since Thucydides appears[4] to concede that the Eurytanes were Greek-speakers, though their dialect was barely intelligible to speakers of the standard forms of Greek. The Eurytanes, must, indeed, have been Greek-speakers originally; for their name, taken together with their location in and after the fifth century B.C., shows them to have been refugees from the Oikhalia in Histiaiotis, which had had Eurytos for its king at some date in the Pre-Völkerwanderung Age.[5]

We may infer that, even as late as 198/7 B.C., it was remembered that the three Aetolian peoples whom Philip V stigmatized at that date had once been non-Greek-speaking, whereas the rest of the Aetolians had not. If these three peoples had been non-Greek-speaking, the Epirot peoples to the north-west of them are likely to have been non-Greek-speaking too down to some still more recent date. If these inferences are justified, they indicate that, after the post-Mycenaean Völkerwanderung, the linguistic frontier, in this quarter, between Greek-speakers and non-Greek-speakers ran through Upper Aetolia; and this is where we might have expected it to run, considering the lie of the land.

Two geographical names that have successively attached to this region are eloquent. One is 'Aperantia', the name of an Aetolian canton, in between Agraia and Amphilokhia, astride the confluences of the River Aspropótamo (Akhelôïos) with its pair of right-bank tributaries the Agraphiótiko and the Megdova. 'Aperantia' means 'the Impenetrable' or 'the Impassable'. The second eloquent geographical name in this region is the one from which the River Agraphiótiko's name is derived. 'The Ágrapha' means 'the Unregistered', i.e. a district which the

---

[1] Kretschmer, op. cit., p. 257. Since 'Boi-ôtoi' means 'Boion-people' (i.e. 'Pindus-people'), we may guess that the roots of the other two ethnika ending in -ôtoi also have geographical meanings.

[2] See Thucydides, Book III, chaps. 96–8.

[3] Thucydides, Book III, chap. 94. [4] Ibid. [5] *Iliad*, II. 730.

Constantinopolitan fiscal authorities had never entered in their books, because they knew that, even if they did succeed in assessing this district, they would be unable to collect the tax. The Ágrapha district is about fifty English miles long from south-east to north-west, and about thirty-five broad.[1] It borders on Aperantia to the south and on the Thessalian plain to the north-east, and it corresponds approximately to the Dolopia of the Hellenic Age. Leake observes[2] that, 'to judge from the names of places, and from the absence of every language but the Greek, Ágrafa had preserved itself before the Turkish conquest from admixture with Bulgarians [i.e. Eastern Slavs] and Wallachians [i.e. Vlachs] in a greater degree than most other parts of Greece. Fifteen years ago[3] it still enjoyed the self-government which it obtained by capitulation with Mahomet II when he had conquered Albania.' It will be seen that Aperantia and the Ágrapha, together, constitute a formidable barrier to communications. The barrier was not strong enough to prevent the post-Mycenaean Völkerwanderung from sweeping over it, from the north-west, into central Greece.[4] It seems, however, to have been strong enough, after the migrations had come to a standstill, to form a linguistic water-shed between a predominantly Greek-speaking area to the south-east of it and a predominantly non-Greek-speaking area to the north-west of it. Of the three 'non-Hellenic' Aetolian peoples named by Philip, two, namely the Amphilokhoi and the Agraioi, were located immediately to the west-north-west of this physical barrier; only the Apodotoi occupied an enclave on the south-eastern side of it.[5]

The non-Greek language that, in the Post-Völkerwanderung Age, was originally prevalent to the north-west of Aperantia can only have been Illyrian; and, indeed, this is indicated by some of the Epirot place-names and ethnika and personal names of which a record has survived. For instance, the description of a Chaonian as being a Peukestos,[6] and the mention of another subdivision of the Khaones named the Dexaroi,[7] are

---

[1] Leake, op. cit., vol. iv (1835), p. 269. See the whole section, entitled 'Ágrafa, its Topography, Population, and Produce', in this volume of Leake's book, pp. 266–74. The journal, of which this volume consists, was written in 1809–10, and the passage containing the account of the Ágrapha is dated 25 November 1809. [2] Ibid., pp. 266–7.

[3] i.e. in A.D. 1820? Or in A.D. 1795? [4] See Part I, chap. 3, pp. 31–5.

[5] In the first phase of the Post-Völkerwanderung Age, there will have been another enclave of Illyrian-speakers much farther to the south-east, if there was a place called *Graia* in Euboea, in the territory of Eretria (Steph. Byz., s.v. Γραία), and if, on the coast of the mainland, facing Eretria, Graia (named in *Iliad*, II. 497) was a synonym for Oropos or was the name of a place in Oropos' territory (Steph. Byz., s.v. Τάναγρα and s.v. Ὠρωπός). The name Oropos, borne by the town in Boeotia, is also borne by a river in Kassopia, the present-day Louros (*alias* Viros). If the Graioi in Eretrian territory and in Oropia were Illyrian-speaking immigrants, no doubt they will soon have taken to speaking the language of the Greek-speaking populations in whose midst they had established themselves.

[6] *I.G.*, vol. ix, fasc. 1, No. 484³, as punctuated by the editor.

[7] Steph. Byz., Δεξάροι· ἔθνος Χαόνων, Ἐγχελέαις προσεχεῖς. Ἑκαταῖος Εὐρώπῃ. Cp. Pseudo-Scylax, § 27: ἐν μεσογαίᾳ Ἀτιντᾶνες ὑπὲρ τῆς Ὠρικίας καὶ Δεξαρίας μεχρὶ Δωδωνίας.

evidence that the Khaones had been Illyrian-speakers originally, since the name 'Peukestos' is identical with that of the Apulian Peuketioi, while the name 'Dexaroi' looks like a variant of the name 'Dassaretioi',[1] which was borne by an Illyrian people whose territory extended from the shores of Lake Okhrida (Lykhnidos) south-south-westwards to the upper valley of the River Uzúmi, which joins the Devol to form the Semeni (Apsos). Above all, the most prominent mountain in Epirus, Mount Tomaros or Tmaros, which overhangs the Yannina basin, bears the same name as the most prominent mountain in southern Illyria, the Mount Tomaros that divides the Uzúmi valley from the Devol (Eordaïkos) valley. There are Epirot personal names that tell the same tale. The name of Salynthios, who was king of the Agraioi in 425/4 B.C., has been noticed already.[2] The names of Tharyps, who was king of the Molossoi in 429 B.C., and his guardian Sabylinthos, also look un-Greek, and so does the name of Photys, one of the two principal public officers of Khaonia for that year. The un-Greek look of these names strikes the eye by contrast with the manifest Greekness of the names of Antiokhos king of Orestis and Perdikkas II king of Macedon, which appear in Thucydides' narrative in the same context.[3]

If the evidence does indicate that the post-Mycenaean Völkerwanderung carried the Illyrian language into Epirus and north-western Aetolia, this is what we should expect. We know that, in the Mycenaean Age, the Yannina basin, which was the heart of Epirus and was also the seat of the oracle at Dodona, was inhabited by a North-West-Greek-speaking people, the Helloi-Hellopes-Hellenes, who were carried by the Völkerwanderung from Dodona to the head of the Maliac Gulf, and who, by a freak of fortune, subsequently gave their name to the whole of the city-state Greek world and its civilization.[4] Before the Völkerwanderung, Epirus must have been the reservoir of North-West-Greek-speaking man-power—Helloi, Akhaioi, and other peoples speaking the same Greek dialect—whose advance-guard had established the Achaean ascendancy over the Mycenaean World and whose rearguard eventually descended, *en masse*, upon southern Greece and the Aegean, overthrew its Achaean kinsmen's regime there, and extinguished the Mycenaean civilization itself.[5] This deluge of North-West-Greek-speaking population, pouring out of Epirus over the Mycenaean World, must have left the reservoir in Epirus empty; and the space vacated by the North-West-Greek-speaking migrants will then have been filled by

---

[1] See Hammond, *Epirus*, p. 467.   [2] See p. 105.

[3] Book II, chap. 81. Thucydides could not foresee that these two rustic personal names were going, one day, to become world-famous.

[4] See Part I, chap. 1, pp. 9–10; chap. 3, pp. 35–6 and 50; Part II, chap. 2, pp. 58–9.

[5] See Hammond, 'Prehistoric Epirus and the Dorian Invasion', pp. 148–9, and the present work, Part I, chap. 3, pp. 29–38.

Illyrian-speaking peoples treading on their heels. We can infer this by analogy with what happened as a result of the East Germans' Völkerwanderung from the north European plain into the Roman Empire in the fifth and sixth centuries of the Christian Era. On that occasion the territory vacated by Teutonic-speaking peoples was occupied by Slavonic-speaking peoples up to the line of the River Elbe and the Böhmer Wald. We may also note that, in the fourteenth-century-A.D. Albanian Völkerwanderung, which followed the same lines as the post-Mycenaean Völkerwanderung, the Chams, who were the advance-guard of the Albanian migrants, penetrated farthest south-eastward in south-western Epirus. In this quarter, the Chams nearly reached the Gulf of Arta (the Ambracian Gulf).

If the Epirots, and some of the Upper Aetolian peoples as well, were an Illyrian rearguard of a Völkerwanderung in which the advance-guard consisted of North-West-Greek-speakers, this would account for Thucydides' description of them as being barbarians in 432–429 B.C.,[1] for Philip V's refusal in 198/7 B.C. to recognize them as being Hellenes, and finally for Strabo's refusal to include Epirus even in the Hellas of his own day. But, if we accept this conclusion, we have then to account for the fact that our authorities distinguish Epirus not only from Hellas but from Illyria too.

Pliny, for instance, notes that 'the Taulantii and the Pyraei are correctly called Illyrians',[2] with the implication that, when one is approaching so near to Epirus as this, one will be expecting to meet with non-Illyrian peoples here. He then notes that 'Nymphaeum [a famous mineral-oil well in the lower valley of the River Aôos] has barbarian neighbours, the Amantes and Buliones',[3] and that Epirus begins after Oricum, with the implication that, where Epirus begins, the barbarians end. There can be no doubt about the Amantes and the Buliones being Illyrians. The ethnika of both these peoples are found, farther north-west, in what was unquestionably Illyrian country. Sirmium in Pannonia, on the River Save, is described by Pliny as being 'civitas Sirmiensium et Amantinorum'.[4] The north-western homonyms of the Buliones are mentioned, under the name Boulinoi, by both Pseudo-Scylax[5] and Pseudo-Scymnus[6] as being the north-western neighbours of the Dalmatian

---

[1] Pseudo-Scymnus, likewise, calls the Khaones and Thesprotoi barbarians (ll. 443–4), mentions μιγάδες βάρβαροι in the interior of Epirus round Dodona (ll. 450–1), and says that the people in the hinterland of the Amphilochian Argos are barbarian too (l. 457). It looks as if Pseudo-Scymnus is simply copying Thucydides here.

[2] 'Proprieque dicti Illyrii et Taulantii et Pyraei' (*Historia Naturalis*, Book III, chap. 22, § 114). According to Pomponius Mela, *Chorographia*, Book II, chap. 3, § 56, however, the Taulantii and the Pyraei are *not* included among the peoples 'quos proprie Illyrios vocant'.

[3] 'Nymphaeum accolunt barbari Amantes et Buliones' (Pliny, *Historia Naturalis*, Book III, chap. 23, § 145).

[4] Book III, chap. 25, § 148.   [5] § 23.   [6] ll. 403–4.

Hylloi, and Ptolemy too mentions them, likewise in association with the Hylloi, under the name Boulimeis.[1] At the same time, Pseudo-Scylax, like Pliny, insists on the difference between the Illyrians and the Epirots. At two points in his periplûs,[2] he notes that the Illyrians extend from Liburnia exclusive as far as Khaonia exclusive.

If the Epirots' ancestral language was Illyrian, as it seems to have been, why do Pliny and Pseudo-Scylax distinguish the Epirots from the Illyrians? Pseudo-Scylax's discrimination between Epirots and Illyrians is particularly noteworthy, since he was writing not later than 338–335 B.C.[3] and he refers to no event or situation that is later than 380 B.C. in his sections on Illyria, Italy, and Asia Minor.[4] Thus Pseudo-Scylax's source for his section on Illyria may have been published only half a century after the date at which Thucydides had been calling the Epirots 'barbarians'. Why was it that, by 338–335 B.C., and perhaps even by 380 B.C., Greek observers had begun to draw a distinction between Epirots and Illyrians? It must have been because the Hellenization of Epirus, of which we can discern the beginnings even in Thucydides' narrative of the events of 429 B.C., had been making perceptible progress since then. The Hellenization of Epirus was not merely linguistic; it was cultural too. The beginnings of linguistic Hellenization are indicated by the Greek name—Nikanor—of one of the two principal public officers of Khaonia for the year 429 B.C. The beginnings of cultural Hellenization are indicated by the constitutional development that had taken place in both Khaonia and Thesprotia by that date. Both these Epirot cantons had, by then, already adopted the republican form of government. The earliest so far known Greek inscriptions in Epirus are two that were set up at Dodona by the Molossian public authorities in 370–368 B.C.[5] 'To

---

[1] *Geographia*, Book II, chap. 16, § 5.

[2] § 23 (μετὰ δὲ Λιβυρνούς εἰσιν ᾿Ιλλύριοι ἔθνος) and § 29 (μετὰ δὲ ᾿Ιλλυρίους Χάονες).

[3] Hammond, *Epirus*, p. 511, on the authority of C. Müller, *Geographi Graeci Minores*, vol. i, pp. xliv–xlix.

[4] Hammond, ibid.

[5] The texts of these two inscriptions are printed by Hammond in *Epirus*, pp. 525–6. On pp. 527–31 he prints the text of a third, dated by him tentatively as being earlier than 343 B.C., with a restoration of the missing parts. Hammond holds (*Epirus*, p. 423) that these inscriptions are evidence that the Molossian and Thesprotian communities mentioned in them 'certainly spoke Greek before the time of Thucydides'.

The three inscriptions are all written in North-West Greek, and a majority of the names of the Molossian officers of state, named in the inscriptions, are Greek, as well as a majority of the names of the communities (clans, not city-states, with only one exception) of which these officials were members. Out of ten clan-names, listed by Hammond on p. 531, six are Greek or have been Graecized, namely Arktanes, Triphylai, Omphales, Ethnestai, Tripolitai, Amymnoi; the other four look non-Greek, namely Genoaioi, Peiales, Kelaithoi, Onopernoi. Of the four non-Greek clan-names, the first two are Molossian, and the third and fourth Thesprotian. There are eighteen personal names in the two inscriptions taken together. All the persons, except one, who are named in the second inscription are identical with persons named in the first. Out of these eighteen persons named, eleven have Greek or Graecized names, namely King Neoptolemos (his appearance in the two inscriptions as

Thucydides the Epirots are barbarians, but in the third century they are everywhere recognized as Greeks.'[1]

The influences that were now Hellenizing Epirus will have come from three quarters: from the south-west, from the north-east, and from within. The influence from within may have been not the least effective of the three.

The discovery at Dodona of Greek inscriptions dating from 370–368 B.C. supports Kretschmer's suggestion[2] that, in (post-Völkerwanderung) Epirus, there was a Greek stratum of population underlying an Illyrian one, and this seems probable if it is true that the population of Epirus had been a Greek-speaking one in the Pre-Völkerwanderung Age. However ruthlessly conducted a conquest may have been, and however great may have been the conquerors' numerical strength, a conquered people is seldom entirely exterminated or evicted. Herodotus[3] calls Thesprotia part of $\tau\hat{\eta}s$ $\nu\hat{\nu}\nu$ $\mathrm{E}\lambda\lambda\dot{\alpha}\delta\delta s$; and in the Thesprotia of Thucydides' day there may have been a Greek-speaking peasantry surviving here and there[4] under an Illyrian-speaking stratum's ascendancy—as, in the same region at Suli, down to its fall in A.D. 1803, the dominant Albanian-speaking element was living on the product of a subject Greek-speaking peasantry's labour.[5]

In the Kassopia district[6] of post-Völkerwanderung Thesprotia (Kassopia is the modern Chamouria) there was one transparently Greek place-name, Pandosia, which must have been a survival from the Pre-Völkerwanderung Age,[7] since it was of old enough standing in Kassopia

---

sole king dates them within the years 370–368 B.C.), Neoptolemos' father Alketas, Philista (on whom Molossian citizenship is being conferred in the first inscription), Philista's husband Antimakhos, the clerk Amphikorios, and the damiorgoi Androkadas, Eustratos, Amynandros, Deinon, Agelaos, Damoitas. Three persons have non-Greek names, namely Laphyrgas, Sabon, Datyios (if Datyios is a person and not a month). Four have names that might be Greek or non-Greek, namely Eidymmas the prostatas Molossôn, Thoinos, Kartomos, and Phinto (on whom Molossian citizenship is being conferred in the second inscription).

Both the recipients of Molossian citizenship, Philista and Phinto, come from a place called Arronon—a non-Greek place-name.

The two inscriptions give the impression that in 370–368 B.C. the population of the Molossian state, which then included some Thesprotian as well as Molossian clans, was partly Greek-speaking and partly Illyrian-speaking, and that Greek was gaining ground at the expense of Illyrian. Evidently Greek personal names were popular, and apparently the government and people were literate in Greek exclusively.

[1] Cross, *Epirus*, p. 3.   [2] In op. cit., p. 255.   [3] Book II, chap. 56.

[4] Cross, op. cit., p. 2, n. 1, holds that the Thesprotoi and Molossoi were Greek-speaking, but that the Khaones were Illyrian-speaking.

[5] See Leake, op. cit., vol. i, p. 227.

[6] For Kassopia, see Strabo, Book VII, chap. 7, § 5 (C. 324).

[7] According to [Pseudo-?] Demosthenes, *De Halonneso*, chap. 32, the three cities of Kassopia—Pandosia, Boukheta, and Elateia (or Elatria)—were Elean colonies. There is no other record of Elean colonizing activity, but considerable evidence for the authenticity of these three alleged Elean colonies is presented by Hammond, *Epirus*, pp. 427, 432–5, 481–2, 498–9.

to have been carried across the Straits of Otranto into Apulia and into the 'toe' of Italy by Illyrian-speaking pursuers of Italy's Oscan-speaking invaders. The original Pandosia in Thesprotia seems to have stood on the River Akheron, somewhere above its confluence with the Kokytos.[1] In the 'toe' of Italy, too, there was an Akheron as well as a Pandosia,[2] and the territory of the eighth-century-B.C. Greek colony, Sybaris, in which the Italian Pandosia and Akheron lay, had previously been held by the Khones, whose name tells us that they were an offshoot of the Khaones in Epirus. Horace's ode 'O fons Bandusiae', which has made the name 'Pandosia' famous,[3] reveals the word's origin. The Epirot city was named after a spring;[4] and, for a spring in this part of the world, the name 'All-bountiful' is felicitous. In a thirsty land, all life may be the gift of a spring of water.

Even if, in post-Völkerwanderung Epirus, the Greek language was submerged for a time, the Greeks' memory of Epirus' Greek past was not extinguished. The oracle at Dodona retained its prestige in the post-Völkerwanderung Greek-speaking world; and, after the oracle's former ministrants the Hellenes themselves had migrated to Malis to find a greater destiny there, their name still clung to the Yannina basin,[5] as is attested by Hesiod's lines

ἔστι τις Ἑλλοπίη πολυλήϊος ἠδ' εὐλείμων . . .
ἔνθα δὲ Δωδώνη τις ἐπ' ἐσχατίῃ πεπόλισται.[6]

Moreover, Illyrian Epirus, like Thracian Pieria, was incorporated by the post-Völkerwanderung Greeks in their fairyland before they annexed it to the workaday world in which they fought and traded and eventually planted colonies. The authentic Epirot rivers Acheron and Kokytos were translated to the Greek Hades; an authentic Epirot people, the Atintanes, gave the Greeks their name for a mythical race of giants, the Titanes (titans);[7] and Khaos, the authentic Epirot land from which the Khaones

---

[1] See Thucydides, Book I, chap. 47, and the description of the landscape in Leake, op. cit., vol. iv, pp. 55–6. Hammond, *Epirus*, p. 478, locates Pandosia at or near Gourana (Trikastron), on the Akheron just up-stream from its gorge.

[2] Beloch, op. cit., 2nd ed., Erster Band, Zweite Abteilung, p. 38.

[3] Horace, *Carmina*, Book III, carmen 13.

[4] 'A little beyond Glyký, to the left of the entrance of the klisúra leading to Suli, a large body of water issues from the foot of the rocks' (Leake, op. cit., p. 56).

[5] The Graioi who, according to Aristotle (see Part I, chap. 3, p. 35, n. 3), were identical with the Selloi, may, in truth, have been Illyrian-speaking successors of the Greek-speaking Helloi. The Graioi may have taken Dodona and its oracle from the Selloi in the course of the post-Mycenaean Völkerwanderung. However, Herodotus, Book IV, chap. 33, calls the Dodonaioi the north-westernmost of the Hellenes in the wider meaning of the name 'Hellenes' that had become prevalent by Herodotus' time. The implication is that in the fifth century B.C. the Dodonaioi were still Greek-speaking. Cp. Herodotus, Book II, chap. 52.

[6] Hesiod, quoted, via Philochorus, by Strabo, *Geographica*, Book VII, chap. 7, § 6 (C. 328). See the present work, Part I, chap. 3, p. 35, n. 3.

[7] According to A. Thumb, *Handbuch der griechischen Dialekte*, Erster Teil, 2nd ed., edited

derived their name, supplied the Greeks with their name for the primeval chaos out of which the Universe had taken shape.

Thus the Hellenization of Epirus was, in part, the resuscitation of an indigenous Hellenism that had been there, all the time, beneath the surface; but, at the same time, it was also partly the effect of Greek influences that were playing upon Epirus from outside.

One of these influences from abroad was that of Corinth and the Corinthian colonies along the Acarnanian and Epirot coasts: Leukas, Anaktorion, Corcyra, Apollonia, Epidamnos. These colonies had been founded in the course of the eighth and seventh centuries B.C., most of them by Corinth alone, but at least one of them, Epidamnos, by Corinth and Corcyra jointly.[1] Corinth and her colonies opened up trade with the interior of Epirus; their traders carried their ancestral language with them; and this, which was the North-West dialect of Greek, was also the ancestral language of the Epirots' southern neighbours the Greek-speaking Aetolians and the Acarnanians. The Corinthian variety of North-West Greek was the matrix of the North-West-Greek koinê, and this koinê was eventually adopted as the official language of Epirus, as well as of Akarnania and of Aetolia. In Epirus this form of Greek also gradually became the language of everyday life; and, in consequence, the linguistic frontier between Greek and Illyrian moved back again north-westwards from the east-south-eastern border of Agraia to the north-western extremities of Khaonia and Atintania. Thus, in Epirus, the paramount linguistic and cultural influence from abroad was the Corinthians'; but another Greek-speaking people, the Makedones, who were expanding, not by sea, but overland, had simultaneously been making an impact on Epirus from the north-west. 'The prestige and power of the Thettaloi and the Makedones were so great that some of the Epirot peoples— particularly those that were the Thettaloi's and the Makedones' immediate neighbours—became parts of Thessaly or of Macedon, some voluntarily, some unwillingly. The Athamanes, Aithikes and Talares became parts of Thessaly; the Orestai and Pelagones and Elimiotai became parts of Macedon.'[2]

---

by E. Kiechers (Heidelberg, 1932, Winter), p. 312, the name Ἀ-τιντ-ᾶνες means 'raw-meat-eaters'. It is true that Hesychius interprets the gloss τιντόν as meaning ἐφθόν. It is also true that Thucydides says that the Eurytanes, who were less remote from the civilized world than the Atintanes were, were reputed to be raw-meat-eaters in 426 B.C. (see p. 106). However, before accepting Kiechers' interpretation of the name 'Atintanes' in terms of Greek, we should have to satisfy ourselves that it was not an Illyrian name but was a Greek one (as its termination -ânes perhaps suggests that it may have been).

[1] Thucydides, Book I, chap. 24.

[2] διὰ γὰρ τὴν ἐπιφάνειάν τε καὶ τὴν ἐπικράτειαν τῶν Θετταλῶν καὶ τῶν Μακεδόνων, οἱ πλησιάζοντες αὐτοῖς μάλιστα τῶν Ἠπειρωτῶν, οἱ μὲν ἑκόντες, οἱ δ' ἄκοντες, μέρη καθίσταντο Θετταλῶν ἢ Μακεδόνων, καθάπερ Ἀθαμᾶνες καὶ Αἴθικες καὶ Τάλαρες Θετταλῶν, Ὀρέσται δὲ καὶ Πελαγόνες καὶ Ἐλιμιῶται Μακεδόνων (Strabo, *Geographica*, Book IX, chap. 5, § 11 (C. 434)).

While the Argead Kingdom of Lower Macedon expanded eastwards across the Emathian plain and beyond,[1] the Makedones of the Upper Macedonian principalities were expanding south-eastwards. 'Routes are not difficult.'[2] The Makedones' political expansion in this direction was eventually brought to a halt by the rising power of Molossia, whose economic base in Hellopia (the Yannina basin) made Molossia strong enough to enable her to establish a political union of the Epirot peoples under her hegemony. This, however, did not prevent the spread of Macedonian linguistic and cultural influence from going farther. According to Strabo,[3]

The region that includes Lynkos, Pelagonia, Orestias, and Elimeia used to be called 'Upper Makedon'. Later it[4] acquired the name 'Free Makedon' as well. Some authorities extend the name 'Makedon' to cover the whole country as far as Corcyra. Their argument is that they [i.e. the inhabitants of the whole of this region] have a uniform culture, exemplified in their way of cutting their hair and in their dialect and in the style of the cloak that they wear. Some of these people are also bilingual.[5]

By 'bilingual', Strabo must mean 'speaking some non-Greek language as well as Greek'; he cannot mean 'speaking two different dialects of Greek'; for he has just said that these peoples all speak the same dialect. The non-Greek language that some of them spoke besides Greek must have been Illyrian. What Strabo is telling us is that, from the upper basin of the River Haliakmon south-westwards towards the coast of Epirus, the Illyrian language had been encroached upon, but had not been put entirely out of currency, by the Macedonian variety of the North-East dialect of Greek.

As an instance of a linguistic peculiarity that the Molossoi and Thesprotoi shared with the Makedones, Strabo mentions[6] that they call old women πελίας and old men πελίους (i.e. instead of πολίας and πολίους, which is the normal Greek for 'grey-headed'). Two place-names, 'Baiake' in Khaonia[7] and 'Byllis', the Buliones' city on the River Aôos, just beyond the north-western extremity of Epirus, are spelled with the

---

[1] See the present Part, chap. 8.

[2] Hammond, 'Prehistoric Epirus and the Dorian Invasion', p. 146.

[3] *Geographica*, Book VII, chap. 7, § 8 (C. 326–7).

[4] Actually, Orestis only. Orestis had capitulated to the Roman proconsul Galba in 199 B.C. (Livy, Book XXXI, chap. 40), and it had been given the status of an autonomous protectorate, independent of the Kingdom of Macedon, in the peace-settlement of 196 B.C. (Livy, Book XXXIII, chap. 34).—A. J. T.

[5] καὶ δὴ καὶ τὰ περὶ Λύγκον καὶ Πελαγονίαν καὶ Ὀρεστιάδα καὶ Ἐλίμειαν "τὴν ἄνω Μακεδονίαν" ἐκάλουν, οἱ δ᾽ ὕστερον καὶ "ἐλεύθερον". ἔνιοι δὲ τὴν σύμπασαν μεχρὶ Κερκύρας "Μακεδονίαν" προσαγορεύουσιν, αἰτιολογοῦντες ἅμα ὅτι καὶ κουρᾷ καὶ διαλέκτῳ καὶ χλαμύδι καὶ ἄλλοις τοιούτοις χρῶνται παραπλησίως· ἔνιοι δὲ καὶ δίγλωττοί εἰσι.

[6] In Book VII, fragms. 1 and 2.

[7] See Steph. Byz., s.v. Βαιάκη, citing Hecataeus.

distinctively Macedonian B in place of the normal Greek PH. 'Baiake' means 'the city of the Phaiakes' (the Phaiekes of the *Odyssey*). 'Byllis' looks like a rationalization, in terms of Macedonian Greek, of the ethnikon of the Buliones-Bulinoi. In the Macedonian dialect of North-East Greek, 'Byllis' is the equivalent of 'Phyllis', meaning 'Leafy'—a place-name that, in the normal Greek form 'Phyllis', was borne by a district of Edonike whose bounds were Mount Pangaios, the River Strymon, and the Strymon's tributary the Angites.[1] It will be noted that the Macedonian dialect is the only Greek dialect in which the ethnikon of the Buliones could have been given this particular Greek meaning.

Some of the Greek personal names assumed by Epirots are also likely to have been of Macedonian origin. For instance, the name 'Nikanor', borne by one of the two principal public officers of Khaonia in 429 B.C.,[2] was a popular name among the Makedones, though it was not a Macedonian name exclusively. The name 'Alexander', borne by King Philip II of Macedon's brother-in-law and son-in-law the King of Molossia, must surely have been given to him because, in the Argead house, this was a family name[3] (and, thanks to Alexander I, already an illustrious one). No doubt, this Molossian Alexander's father Neoptolemos was named after the legendary son of Achilles, as an assertion of the Molossian royal house's claim to be Aiakidai.[4] But, as has been noted already,[5] no one would have borrowed the name 'Alexander' from legend, considering that, in the Homeric epic, the bearer of the name 'Alexander' plays such an unheroic and invidious part. Indeed, anyone who was already familiar with the epic would have hesitated to borrow the name even from some other source, unless, in the quarter from which he was borrowing it, the name had such old-established auspicious associations that these would outweigh the slur that had been cast on this name by Homer.

These two Macedonian Greek names borne by Epirots are good evidence of Macedonian Greek linguistic influence in Epirus, because they date from early stages in the Hellenization of Epirus. By 198/7 B.C., when King Philip V of Macedon was stigmatizing as non-Hellenes three Aetolian peoples, two of whom—the Agraioi and the Amphilokhoi—were ex-Epirot peoples, Greek must already have become the language not only of these three peoples but of all their Epirot neighbours as well. All the Epirot personal names that are mentioned in the surviving parts of Polybius' and Livy's histories are Greek, and it would be difficult to identify any of these later Greek names of Epirots as being distinctively Macedonian. Nor is there anything distinctively Macedonian about the

[1] Herodotus, Book VII, chap. 113.
[2] Thucydides, Book II, chap. 81.
[3] See Hoffmann, op. cit., pp. 119 and 133.
[4] See ibid.
[5] In Part II, chap. 2, p. 73.

name Kleophanes the son of Agapetos that is borne by the Χάων Πευκεστός who is known to us from a surviving inscription,[1] or the name Leomakhos that, on another inscription,[2] is borne by an Atintan.

How far afield westwards did the influence of Macedonian Greek extend? And how far eastward and for how long did the Illyrian language continue to hold its ground?

The two Illyrian rulers Kleitos son of Bardyles, who was perhaps the king of the Dassaretioi,[3] and Glaukias, the king of the Taulantioi, who went to war with Alexander III of Macedon in 335 B.C.,[4] both bore names that are known to have been borne by Makedones.[5] Whether this Illyrian Kleitos was given his Macedonian Greek name by his Illyrian-named father Bardyles,[6] or whether he assumed the name himself, the intention must have been to assert that the bearer was no longer a barbarian; and the significance of Kleitos' Taulantian ally Glaukias' name will have been the same. Thus the prestige that Macedon had acquired during the reign of King Philip II had carried Macedonian cultural influence north-westwards, beyond the bounds of Epirus, into southern Illyria.

On the other hand, Hecataeus, who was writing at the turn of the sixth and fifth centuries B.C., is reported to have called the Orestai a Molossian people.[7] By the time when Thucydides was writing, the Lynkestai, Elimiotai, and also 'other peoples farther away in the interior', were not only Makedones in nationality but were under the suzerainty of the kingdom of Lower Macedon, though they enjoyed a local autonomy.[8] In view of Hecataeus' description of the Orestai as being a Molossian people, it may be significant that Thucydides does not include their name in his list of Upper Macedonian peoples. However, in 429 B.C. the king of the Orestai bore the Macedonian Greek name Antiokhos.[9]

---

[1] *I.G.*, vol. ix, fasc. 1, No. 484³, cited already on p. 107, with n. 6.

[2] Dittenberger, *Sylloge*, 1st ed., No. 324, cited by Beloch, op. cit., Erster Band, Zweite Abteilung, p. 41.

[3] Evidently Kleitos was the more powerful of the two allies; it was he who took the initiative on this occasion (Arrian, Book I; chap. 5, § 1). It is also evident, from the sequel, that Kleitos' country was nearer to the western frontier of Macedon than Taulantia was (ibid., chap. 5, § 4–chap. 6 inclusive). Kleitos had seized the Macedonian frontier fortress Pelion on the upper reaches of the Eordaïkos (Devol) River. All this points to Dassaretia's having been Kleitos' country.

[4] Arrian, Book I, chap. 5, § 1. For Glaukias, see also Plutarch, *Pyrrhus*, chaps. 3–4 et alibi.

[5] For the name 'Kleitos', see Hoffmann, op. cit., pp. 153 and 158; for the name 'Glaukias', see ibid., p. 182.

[6] Kretschmer, op. cit., p. 265, notes that the Illyrian personal name 'Bardyles' (Arrian, loc. cit.) or 'Bardylis' (Diodorus, Book XVI, chap. 4, § 3), or 'Bardyllis' (Plutarch, *Pyrrhus*, chap. 9) is related to the word 'bardulos', meaning 'grey', in the 'Messapian' (i.e. Calabrian) language.

[7] Steph. Byz., 'Ορέσται· Μολοσσικὸν ἔθνος. Ἑκαταῖος Εὐρώπη.

[8] Thucydides, Book II, chap. 99.

[9] Thucydides, Book II, chap. 81.

On the other hand, at the same date, the king of the Parauaioi, under whose command Antiokhos had placed a contingent of one thousand Orestai, bore the un-Greek-looking name 'Oroidos'.[1] Theopompus, who was a contemporary of Philip II of Macedon, gave a list of fourteen Epirot peoples.[2] Strabo names eleven.[3] The eleven peoples called 'Epirot' by Strabo include the Parauaioi, the Orestai, and the Tymphaioi,[4] though Philip II appears to have annexed the Parauaioi and Tymphaioi to the Kingdom of Lower Macedon *circa* 343 B.C.,[5] and though the Tymphaioi and Orestai are known to have contributed contingents to the phalanx in Alexander III's expeditionary force,[6] which makes it certain that, whether they were Makedones or were Epirots in nationality, their countries had been annexed to the Kingdom of Lower Macedon by Philip II. Parauaia, Tymphaia, and Orestis were all still included in Macedon down to 294 B.C., when Tymphaia and Parauaia were annexed to the Kingdom of Epirus by Pyrrhus.[7] The known personal names of Orestai and Tymphaioi seem all to be clearly Greek,[8] with the important possible exception of the name Ὀρόντης or Ὀρώντης, which was borne by the father of Alexander III's Orestian somatophylax Perdikkas.[9] It will be seen that, while the ancestral language of the Elimiotai and the Lynkestai was unquestionably Macedonian Greek, there is some uncertainty about the ancestral language of the Orestai, the Parauaioi, and perhaps the Tymphaioi too.

[1] Thucydides, ibid.

[2] Strabo, *Geographica*, Book VII, chap. 7, § 5 (C. 323).

[3] Hammond, *Epirus*, pp. 461, 468–9, and 538, holds that Strabo, in calling these eleven peoples 'Epirot', is following, not Theopompus' list, but Hecataeus' *Europa* via Ephorus.

[4] See Hammond, *Epirus*, p. 538.

[5] See Hammond, ibid., pp. 529, 534, 538.

[6] See Part II, chap. 4, p. 84.

[7] τήν τε Τυμφαίαν καὶ τὴν Παραυαίαν τῆς Μακεδονίας (Plutarch, *Pyrrhus*, chap. 6).

[8] Hoffmann, op. cit., pp. 153–7.

[9] Ibid., p. 153.

7. The Dispersion of North-East-Greek-Speaking Peoples from Thessaly

IN the post-Mycenaean Völkerwanderung the reservoir out of which the deluge burst was Epirus and its northern hinterland; the axis of the main thrust was from north-west to south-east, in a diagonal line across the Peloponnese to Crete and the Anatolian Doris. The migrating peoples were North-West-Greek-speakers, with Illyrian-speaking peoples pushing them forward from the rear and probably mingling with them to some extent. This major cataclysm, however, was not the whole story. The impact of the main thrust generated secondary thrusts with other starting-points. For instance, Peloponnesians speaking the dialect of Greek that survived in Arcadia, and that had probably been spoken throughout the Peloponnese before the North-West-Greek-speaking invaders broke in, now invaded and colonized Cyprus, and Ionic-Greek-speakers, pushed out of some of the easterly parts of central Greece, now invaded and colonized the Cyclades and the Anatolian Ionia. The third of these secondary movements that were set in motion by the North-West-Greek Völkerwanderung was a migration of North-East-Greek-speaking peoples out of Thessaly under the impact of the North-West-Greek-speaking Histiaioi and Thessaloi. This movement from Thessaly was a centrifugal one. It scattered North-East-Greek-speaking refugees in all directions—some of them across the sea to Crete and Aiolis and the Troad, and others overland both into southern Greece and into the interior of south-eastern Europe.[1] The northward thrust overland turned out in the end to be the most important of all those of which Thessaly was the common starting-point; for this thrust was the prelude to the eventual rise of the Kingdom of Macedon.

This dispersion of population out of Thessaly seems to have begun already before the impact of the North-West-Greek Völkerwanderung increased the North-East-Greek movement's scale and impetus. The *Iliad*[2] represents Euneos, son of Ieson (Jason) of Iolkos, as reigning on the island of Lemnos at the time when Agamemnon's expeditionary force was encamped on the Asian shore of the Hellespont. Jason was a Minyan, but his home town, Iolkos, was the port of south-eastern Pelasgiotis and, in the Homeric Catalogue of the contingents contributed to Agamemnon's expeditionary force, Iolkos is included in the dominions of the ruler of

[1] See H. T. Wade-Gery, 'The Dorians', in *The Cambridge Ancient History*, vol. ii (1924), p. 528.
[2] *Iliad*, VII. 467–75; XXI. 40–1.

this part of Pelasgiotis, Eumelos of Pherai.[1] In another passage of the Catalogue there is an indication that King Eurytos of Oikhalia, a city that lay somewhere in the north-western sector of the Thessalian plain, had migrated voluntarily, with some of his people, to the plain of Steny-klaros in Messene, and had founded a new Oikhalia there.[2] At a later point in the Catalogue[3] there is a plainer reference to the eviction of a wild people from the highlands of Pelion to the headwaters of the River Peneios, at the south-eastern end of the future Macedonian canton Tymphaia.

In this passage of the *Iliad*, the evicted people are referred to allusively as the 'shaggy wild beasts' (φῆρας λαχνήεντας). We know from other sources that these were the Centaurs, and that Peirithoos' people, who evicted them, and whose home, according to this passage in the *Iliad*, was in north-western Pelasgiotis and in the future Perrhaibia, were the Lapithai. The Centaurs did not, of course, come out of Pelion; they came out of fairyland. Their name belongs to the common stock of Indo-European mythology, and its Greek form, 'Kentauros', has a Sanskrit counterpart in the form 'Gandharva'.[4] However, in the story of the war between the Centaurs and the Lapithai, the name of the legendary monsters looks as if it were doing duty for the lost name of an historical tribe of wild highlanders; for, though the Centaurs are legendary, the Lapithai are not.

The historicity of the Lapithai is attested by the survival of their name both near home, at Lapathous, a highland fastness between Mount

---

[1] *Iliad*, II. 711–15. For the Pelasgoi on Lemnos, see the present Part, chap. 7, Annex, pp. 126–34.

[2] *Iliad*, II. 595–6, discussed in Part I, chap. 3, on pp. 26–8.

[3] ll. 743–4.

[4] The Gandharvas, as represented in Indian sculpture of the Gupta Age (the fourth and fifth centuries of the Christian Era), were not *Mischwesen* but were boisterous trolls in human form, and we may guess that this was also the form in which the author of the Homeric Catalogue and his audience pictured to themselves 'the shaggy wild beasts' on Mount Pelion (see J. C. Lawson, *Modern Greek Folklore and Ancient Greek Religion*, 2nd ed., (New Hyde Park, N.Y., 1964, University Books), pp. 235–9). The classical Greek picture of a Centaur was, of course, a *Mischwesen* that was part man and part horse; but neither the horse-part nor the man-part of the classical centaur was shaggy. Moreover, the notion of a composite creature of this kind must have been formed by someone who was seeing, for the first time, a man riding on horseback. (We know that when the peoples of Middle America first set eyes on Cortés' six cavalrymen, they thought that horse and rider were a single animal, one and indivisible.) Horsemen are not likely to have been seen in Thessaly before the seventh century B.C., considering that the Cimmerians were the first riders (as contrasted with charioteers) whom the Greeks encountered; and the Cimmerian cavalry did not make their appearance in Western Anatolia and on the Black Sea steppe before the closing years of the eighth century B.C. So far from the classical centaur's being the Thessalian lowlander's picture of the Pelian highlander, he will have been the Pelian highlander's picture of his hated lowlander overlord when he met him mounted, Cimmerian-fashion, for the first time. The Thessalian plain is an ideal terrain for Centaurs of the classical format; the crags of Pelion are an impossible terrain for them.

Olympus and the Tempe defile,[1] and, also, far afield, at Lapethos, a city on the north coast of Cyprus.[2] Lapathous was 'in the news' for one moment when, in 169 B.C., Q. Marcius Philippus was turning King Perseus' westward-facing position in the Tempe defile by transporting a Roman army, elephants and all, from the Perrhaebian Tripolis to Pieria over Mount Olympus' gigantic southern outworks. (Xerxes, too, may have passed close by Lapathous, travelling in the opposite direction to Philippus', when, in 480 B.C., Xerxes outflanked an eastward-facing Greek force, holding Tempe, by following an inland route into Thessaly from Pieria; but Herodotus does not tell us which of the three alternative possible routes[3] it was that Xerxes chose; and Lapathous does not figure in Herodotus' narrative.) The subjects, if not the rulers, of the Lapith principality in north-western Pelasgiotis will have been Pelasgoi, like the subjects of the Minyan rulers of Iolkos; and, in these Lapith Pelasgoi, we may have put our finger on the ancestors of the Pelagones who, at the turn of the third and second century B.C., were in occupation of the basin of the Erigon tributary of the River Axios.[4]

Inhabitants of the Thessalian plain who were being evicted from their homes by invaders from the west had a choice of three avenues of escape. They could take to the sea, as Jason's Argonauts had taken to it, at Iolkos, and could sail in search of new homes overseas in Crete or on the west coast of Anatolia or anywhere else round the shores of the Levant where they might succeed in establishing a beachhead. This was the choice made by the Pelasgian settlers in the Troad and on the island of Lesbos and in continental Aiolis—and perhaps also the choice made by the Pelasgoi who are enumerated in the *Odyssey*[5] among the peoples of Crete—unless these Cretan Pelasgoi had come from Thessaly to Crete, not as refugees, fleeing from North-West-Greek-speaking invaders, but as participants in the Achaean conquest of the island two centuries or two and a half centuries earlier.[6] Alternatively, Thessalian refugees could flee southwards overland and dive for shelter into the natural fastnesses at the southern end of the Pindus Range and in its south-eastward ramifications. This was the choice made by the section of the Eurytanes that had not migrated from Histiaiotis to Messene before being overtaken by the North-West-Greek *Völkerwanderung*. It was also the choice made by one section of the Eurytanes' neighbours in Histiaiotis, the Makednoi-

---

[1] See Livy, Book XLIV, chaps. 2 and 6. See also Steph. Byz., s.v. Λαπίθη.

[2] See Steph. Byz., s.v. Λαπῆθος.

[3] The Lapathous route to the south of Mount Olympus, the Petra route to the north of it, and the Volustana route through the Cambunian range.

[4] See chap. 4 of the present Part, pp. 82–5.   [5] *Odyssey*, XIX. 177.

[6] The length of the time-interval depends on the date of the Achaean conquest of Crete. Did this take place at the beginning of the Late Minoan II Period or at the beginning of the Late Minoan III Period? At the time of writing, this question was part of the subject of an acrimonious controversy.

Makedones. The Makednoi trekked through the mountains southwards and south-eastwards till they found an asylum in the central Greek Doris.[1] Both sections of the Makednoi-Makedones escaped from Thessaly overland. However, the two turned their backs on each other and trekked in opposite directions. While the Makednoi moved south-eastwards to the headwaters of the River Kephisos in central Greece, the Makedones turned eastwards and then northwards. We may guess that it is likely to have been the Makedones, pushed from behind by the Histiaioi, who drove the Lapithai-Pelasgoi (i.e. the Pelagones) out of north-western Pelasgiotis and out of Perrhaibia (except for the remnant that survived at Lapathous).[2] In any case the Pelagones, followed by the Makedones, escaped by the third avenue that was open to refugees from Thessaly. They crossed the watershed between the Peneios basin and the Haliakmon basin over the Volustana (Pórtes) Pass.

This is the route by which, some nine centuries or so later, the Romans tried and failed to invade Macedon from Thessaly in 170 B.C., after King Perseus of Macedon, marching from north to south, had successfully invaded Thessaly by this route at the beginning of the Third Romano-Macedonian War in 171 B.C.[3] The Pórtes Pass is aptly described by Colonel Leake as being 'the natural gate between Macedonia and Perrhaebia', in virtue of its 'being the most direct and easy passage across the Cambunian ridge'.[4] 'The road from the castle [of Servia, on the north side] to the Pórtes is wide and level, and occupies the whole of a natural opening in the mountain.'[5] Leake, travelling on horseback, took only five hours to traverse the pass from Servia to Livádhi—and this in mid-winter, on 7 December 1806.[6] Leake's experience of the Pórtes Pass is of historical interest because, at the date when he traversed it so easily, it was still virtually in the state of nature in which it had been since the beginning of history, and in which it was to remain until the construction of the present road for wheeled traffic.[7] Servia, Leake notes, 'is now the most important station of the dervént agá's troops on the . . . post road from Lárisa and Tríkkala to Bitólia [Monastir, Pelagonia, Herakleia], the first post on which from hence is Kaliári [in Eordaia] and the second Filúrina [Flórina].'[8] For the refugee Pelagones and Makedones in the twelfth century B.C., the Pórtes Pass led to new homes in the Haliakmon basin, in compensation for the ancestral homes

[1] See Part I, chap. 3, p. 47.

[2] Step. Byz., Λαπιθαῖον· ὄνομα ὄρους τῆς Λακωνικῆς, indicates that some Lapithai found asylum as far away from home as the eastern shelf of Mount Taΰgetos. Bölte, in P.–W., Zweite Reihe, 3. Band, A2, col. 1331, locates this Lapithaion near Anóyia.

[3] Livy, Book XLII, chap. 53.　　[4] Op. cit., vol. iii, p. 332.　　[5] Ibid.　　[6] Ibid., p. 334.

[7] I travelled by this road, not through, but round, the Pórtes Pass on wheels on 26 July 1965. Unfortunately, wheels abandon the historic direct routes that feet and hooves used to take, in order to find ways round that have less steep gradients.

[8] Leake, ibid., p. 332.

in the Peneios basin from which they were being evicted. There is, of course, no record of their passage through the pass or of their subsequent occupation of the Haliakmon valley; but these unrecorded events in their history can be inferred from the locations of these two peoples at the earliest dates at which we have a record of them. For the Makedones this date is the turn of the sixth and fifth centuries B.C.; for the Pelagones it is the turn of the third and second centuries B.C.

We may guess that, after both peoples had evacuated Thessaly, trekking northwards, the Pelagones continued to move on northwards gradually under pressure from the Makedones, who were following at their heels. Strabo notes[1] that 'Pelagonia is said to have been called Orestias previously'. It seems unlikely that there were ever two cantons, both called 'Orestias' or 'Orestis', in Upper Macedon and the adjoining region; and 'Orestias' would have been an inappropriate name for the Pelagonia of the third and second centuries B.C., since the most striking physical features of this historical Pelagonia are, not mountains, but the plains of Monastir and Prilep. If Strabo's statement has any historical basis, it can only mean that the Pelagones had once occupied the well-known Orestis, round the headwaters of the Haliakmon. If this is an historical fact, then the Pelagones must subsequently have been pushed out of Orestis north-eastwards, into the region in which we eventually find them; and, since a king bearing the Macedonian name Antiokhos was reigning in Orestis in 429 B.C.,[2] the Pelagones must have been evicted from Orestis by that date, and this by the Makedones. One piece of evidence that the Makedones remained in contact with the Pelagones after both peoples had ceased to be each other's neighbours in northern Thessaly is the adoption by the Argeadai, into their own genealogy, of two mythical heroes, Koronos and his father Kaineus, who, in the Homeric Catalogue,[3] figure as the father and grandfather of Leonteus, Polypoites' colleague in the leadership of the contingent from north-western Pelasgiotis. The Lapith Koronos seems to have usurped the role, given by Herodotus[4] to Perdikkas I, of being the founder of the Argead kingdom; and both he and Kaineus became familiar and important enough mythical figures in Macedon for their names to become popular there. In being used in Macedon as names for ordinary mortals, the forms of both names were rationalized to convey laudatory meanings. Kaineus became 'Koinos' ('the Impartial Judge'); Koronos became 'Karanos', or Macedonicè 'Korannos', ('the Chief').[5]

[1] *Geographica*, Book VII, fragm. 38.
[2] See Thucydides, Book II, chap. 81. See also the present Part, chap. 6, p. 108.
[3] *Iliad*, II. 705–6. For Kaineus, see also I. 264.
[4] Herodotus, Book V, chap. 22, and Book VIII, chaps. 137–9.
[5] For this adoption of a Lapith genealogy by the Argeadai, see Hoffmann, op. cit., pp. 122–7 and 258.

Though the eventual destinations of the North-East-Greek-speaking colonists and refugees who issued out of Thessaly were so far afield from their common starting-point and were dispersed in so many different directions, their common origin is attested by the fact that a number of geographical names that are found in Thessaly are also found in one or more of the widely scattered regions, outside Thessaly,[1] in which, in the Post-Völkerwanderung Age, the North-East dialect of Greek was spoken, or with which the ethnika Pelasgoi, Pelagones, Makedones were associated. The recurrence of some single Thessalian geographical name in some country outside Thessaly would not be significant evidence for any historical connection between that country and Thessaly. Most of the Thessalian geographical names in question are also to be found in other parts of Greece; some of them occur frequently; and, in these circumstances, a single correspondence might be a mere coincidence. When, however, a bunch of Thessalian geographical names recurs elsewhere, the likelihood of this being a mere coincidence is evidently much slighter, and, in such cases, it seems more probable that the bunch had been carried from Thessaly by migrants to the country where the bunch recurs.[2] The names that recur in bunches and that are therefore likely to have been exports are not all Greek words. The North-East-Greek-speaking occupants of Thessaly and central Greece were not the earliest inhabitants; and, though, after taking possession, they renamed some geographical features of the occupied country in their own Greek language, they also adopted some of the geographical names that were already current there.

These points are illustrated by the case of the city-name Larisa. This cannot be interpreted as Greek.[3] It may be Luvian, if Palmer is right in holding that geographical names found with the suffixes -ss- and -nth- or -nd- are Luvian coinages.[4] However, all but one of Stephanus of Byzantium's twelve Larisai and Strabo's fourteen Larisai[5] were located in lands that had become Greek-speaking, and the one exception, which was the Larisa in Syria, really proves the rule, since it was evidently given its name by some of the Thessalian settlers who were planted in Syria by the Seleucidae. Three of Stephanus' Larisai, including the famous Larisa in north-western Pelasgiotis, were in Thessaly, and one, Larisa

---

[1] See the list in Pareti, op. cit., p. 5.

[2] However, Pareti, who recognizes the set of correspondences between place-names in Pelasgiotis and in the territory of the Cretan city Gortyn (op. cit., p. 4), disbelieves (ibid., p. 4, n. 1) in the historicity of a Pelasgian settlement in Crete.

[3] The root 'Lar-' also cannot be identical with the Latin—and perhaps originally Etruscan —word 'lar' meaning 'god'; for the R in the Latin 'lar' represents an earlier S, which survives in the opening line—'enos, lases, iuvate'—of the Arval Brethren's incantation.

[4] See L. R. Palmer, *Mycenaeans and Minoans* (London, 1961, Faber), pp. 229–50.

[5] See Strabo, *Geographica*, Book IX, chap. 5, § 19 (C. 440). See also Book XIII, chap. 3, § 2 (C. 620).

Kremaste,[1] was near Thessaly in the adjoining Phthiotic Akhaïa; but another of them—and this the second most famous—was one of the two citadels of the city of Argos in the Peloponnese, which was never occupied by North-East-Greek-speakers, so far as we know. Evidently the occurrence, outside Thessaly, of the name Larisa, by itself, is no proof of any historical connection between any of the non-Thessalian Larisai and the famous Larisa-on-Peneios. On the other hand, if a non-Thessalian Larisa is found in company with some other city-name or river-name that also occurs in Thessaly, then it is much more likely that this bunch of names is of Thessalian provenance.

The Thessalian geographical names in question, besides the city-name Larisa, are another city-name, Gyrton, borne in Thessaly by a city to the north of Larisa-on-Peneios, in the angle above the Peneios' confluence with its left-wing tributary the River Europos, and the names of this River Europos itself and of a higher left-bank tributary of the Peneios, the River Lethaios, which runs through Trikka (Tríkkala).

In Crete, the presence of Pelasgoi is recorded in the *Odyssey*;[2] in the Cretan Mesará we find a city called Gortyn standing on the bank of a river called Lethaios; and, though we do not find a Cretan river named Europos, we do find a mythical queen of Crete named Europa who had been conveyed to Crete from overseas. A Cretan Larisa is reported by both Strabo and Stephanus.[3] In the territory of Gortyn there was a place called Boibe.[4]

The conjunction here, in Crete, of six geographical names that are found in Thessaly makes it seem probable that, in Crete, there was a settlement of immigrants from north-western Pelasgiotis.

In the region between Edessa (Aigai), the earliest capital of the Kingdom of Lower Macedon, and the west bank of the River Axios below the Demir Kapu gorge, we find one city called Gortynia on the Axios[5] and two cities called Europos, one on the Axios, below Gortynia,[6] and the other in Almopia, on the upper course of the River Loudias. East of the River Axios, and north-north-east of Thessalonike, we find a city named Lete, which calls to mind the Thessalian and Cretan river-name Lethaios. These places with Thessalian names lay in districts—Almopia, Bottiaia, ex-Paeonian Amphaxitis, and Mygdonia—which had been conquered from their previous occupants and been annexed to the Kingdom of Lower Macedon by the Argeadai. We know that the Bottiaioi, at

---

[1] Called 'Pelasgia' (Strabo, loc. cit.).
[2] XIX. 177, cited on p. 120, with n. 5.
[3] Steph. Byz., s.v. Λάρισσα. Cp. eundem, s.v. Γόρτυν· ἐκαλεῖτο δὲ καὶ Λάρισσα· πρότερον γὰρ ἐκαλεῖτο Ἑλλωτις· οὕτω γὰρ παρὰ Κρησὶν Εὐρώπη.
[4] Steph. Byz., s.v. Βοίβη.
[5] Thucydides, Book II, chap. 100.
[6] Thucydides, ibid.

any rate, had been evicted; for, beyond the eastern bounds of the original Bottiaia, there was in 479 B.C. a settlement, in a new Bottike at Olynthos,[1] of Bottiaioi who are explicitly stated to have been refugees from country that the Makedones had conquered. It seems probable that the Argeadai had reinforced their hold on their eastward conquests by planting colonies of their own Macedonian people in places from which they had evicted the previous inhabitants. If the two Europoi and Gortynia and Lete were Macedonian colonial foundations, the choice of this bunch of Thessalian place-names does suggest that the Makedones had not forgotten their own Thessalian origin. The Thessalian names may have continued to be used by the Makedones in their first settlements to the north of the Pórtes Pass in the Haliakmon valley.

In the Homeric Catalogue of the Trojans and their allies there is a contingent of Pelasgoi whose city is called Larisa and whose two leaders are the sons of a Pelasgian called Lethos.[2] These cannot be the Pelasgoi of the Larisa-on-Peneios in Thessaly; for, though this famous Larisa is not mentioned in the catalogue of Agamemnon's forces, the Thessalian section of this catalogue covers the whole of Thessaly without a gap, and this twice over.[3] The Homeric Larisa was presumably in or near the Troad; the conjunction here of the names 'Pelasgoi', 'Larisa', and 'Lethos' indicates that this Troadic Larisa was, like the Cretan Gortyn, a settlement of migrants from north-western Pelasgiotis; and we may identify it with the Larisa in the neighbourhood of Cape Lekton (Baba Burnu)[4] that is mentioned by Thucydides[5] and by Xenophon,[6] and is also enumerated by Strabo.[7] This Pelasgian settlement may have extended along the south coast of the Troad as far east as Antandros, since Herodotus calls Antandros 'Pelasgis'.[8]

The name of Larisa Phrikonis in Aiolis[9] is less informative, since the name is not associated here with any of the other Thessalian geographical names on our list, and this single Thessalian geographical name, by itself, would not have warranted the conjecture that the Asian Greek cities in Aiolis were Thessalian colonies. The reason why we know that these Aioleis had come from Thessaly or from Boeotia or from both is because we know that their dialect was North-East Greek.

Similarly, the occurrence in Deuriopos of the place-name Alalkomenai,

[1] Herodotus, Book VIII, chap. 127.
[2] *Iliad*, II. 840–3. See also the present work, Part I, chap. 1, p. 8.
[3] See Part I, chap 1, pp. 9–11.
[4] See Part I, chap. 1, p. 8, n. 3.
[5] Thucydides, Book VIII, chap. 101.
[6] Xenophon, *Hellenica*, Book III, chap. 1, § 16.
[7] Strabo, *Geographica*, Book IV, chap. 5, § 19 (C. 440); Book XIII, chap. 3, § 2 (C. 620).
[8] Herodotus, Book VII, chap. 42.
[9] See Herodotus, Book I, chap. 149; Strabo, *Geographica*, Book IX, chap. 5, § 19 (C. 440); eundem, Book XIII, chap. 3, § 2 (C. 620).

which is also found in the Phlegyan part of Boeotia,[1] is not enough in itself, nor perhaps even taken in conjunction with the affinity between the ethnika 'Phlegyai' and 'Pelagones', to prove that the Pelagones were migrants from the North-East-Greek-speaking region in north-eastern and central Greece. All that the name 'Alalkomenai' does indicate, taken in conjunction with the name of the neighbouring Deuriopan city 'Stybara', is that the Deuriopes were a Greek-speaking people.

One of the four Macedonian cities on the lower Axios that are named by Thucydides[2] is Eidomene. We have no record of any place of this name in Thessaly,[3] but we can infer the existence of a place-name Eidomene in Crete from the personal name Idomeneus, which is borne by the leader of the Cretan contingent in Agamemnon's host.[4] Considering that there are six geographical names of recognizably Thessalian provenance in Crete and three of recognizably Thessalian provenance in Macedon, it seems legitimate to infer that the affinity between the Macedonian place-name 'Eidomene' and the Cretan personal name 'Idomeneus' is not fortuitous, and that these two names are connected with each other historically through a Thessalian missing link.

PART II, CHAPTER 7, ANNEX

Herodotus' Non-Greek-Speaking Pelasgoi

IN chapter 4 of this Part it has been argued that 'Pelasgoi', 'Pelagones', and 'Phlegyai' are variant forms of one and the same ethnikon. In chapter 7 it has been argued that the Pelasgoi-Pelagones-Phlegyai, together with the Makednoi-Makedones and the Lapithai, were speakers of the North-East dialect of the Greek language, which came, in the Post-Völkerwanderung Age, to be known as 'Aeolic' because it was spoken in Aiolis, the Asian territory that had been colonized by North-East-Greek-speaking refugees who had been evicted from their previous homes in continental European Greece by North-West-Greek-speaking intruders. This account of the Pelasgoi is in direct contradiction with Herodotus' account of them. Herodotus holds that the Pelasgoi were

[1] See the present Part, chap. 4, pp. 88–9.
[2] Thucydides, Book II, chap. 100.
[3] Unless Eidomene was a synonym for the Ἀστέριον Τιτάνοιό τε λευκὰ κάρηνα of the Homeric Catalogue (*Iliad*, II. 735; see Leake, op. cit., vol. iv, p. 323, for the conspicuousness of Mount Vlokhó).
[4] *Iliad*, II. 645.

a non-Greek-speaking people. The contrary view presented in the present work cannot stand against Herodotus' view unless it can be demonstrated that his view is erroneous and unless it can also be shown how Herodotus arrived at this misconception, if it is one.

Herodotus asserts[1] that the Ionian race (γένος), of which the Athenians were members, was a Pelasgian people (ἔθνος). He then goes on[2] to say:

I am unable to identify, for certain, the language that the Pelasgoi spoke. Perhaps, however, it is legitimate to make an inference from [the language spoken by] the Pelasgoi who still survive. There are surviving Pelasgoi who live, above [i.e. up-country in relation to] some Tyrsenoi, in the city of Kreston. (These Pelasgoi were once neighbours of the so-called 'Dorians', and at that time they were living in the country now called Thessaliotis.) There are other Pelasgoi who have settled at Plakia and Skylake on the Hellespont. (These were once co-inhabitants [of Attica] with the Athenians.)[3] There are also a number of small Pelasgian communities (πολίσματα) that have taken to calling themselves by another name. If it is legitimate to make an inference from these cases, we can only infer that the Pelasgoi were speakers of a non-Greek (βάρβαρον) language.

It follows that, if all Pelasgoi were [originally] non-Greek-speaking, the Athenian people (ἔθνος), being Pelasgian, must have changed their language in the act of becoming Hellenes. Neither the inhabitants of Kreston nor those of Plakia speak the same language as the populations by whom they are surrounded. They do, however, speak an identical language as between themselves, and this is proof that they have [each] preserved the idiom that they brought with them when they migrated to their respective present habitats.

[By contrast,] the Hellenes have continued—it seems obvious to me—to speak the same language ever since this language [i.e. Greek] came into existence. However, at the time when they split off from the Pelasgoi, the Hellenes were still weak. They were a tiny community at the start, but they have grown into a multitude of peoples (πλῆθος τῶν ἐθνεῶν) through the accession of numerous peoples—Pelasgians above all—who had previously been non-Greek-speaking aliens. In my opinion, for what it is worth, the Pelasgian people [has had the same fate as the Hellenes' other originally non-Greek-speaking recruits]. The Pelasgoi, too, were non-Greek-speaking; they, too, nowhere came to anything much.

In this passage, Herodotus not only declares that all surviving Pelasgoi known to him are non-Greek-speaking. On the strength of this observation of his, he constructs a theory that all the peoples who were Greek-speakers in his day had originally been Pelasgian non-Greek-speakers, with the one signal exception of the 'Dorians'. In constructing this theory, Herodotus has ignored the fact that the non-Greek-speaking Pelasgoi whom he cites were not the only communities that bore the

[1] In Book I, chap. 56.   [2] In Book I, chap. 57.
[3] Herodotus repeats this statement in Book II, chap. 51.—A.J.T.

name 'Pelasgoi' in his own day, and that there was at least one conspicuous contemporary community of Pelasgoi that was Greek-speaking. The inhabitants of the Thessalian tetrarchy known as Pelasgiotis in Herodotus' own day were North-East-Greek-speakers. Herodotus could, and should, have inferred that these Greek-speaking inhabitants of Pelasgiotis must be Pelasgoi. If they were not, the North-West-Greek-speaking Thessaloi, who had conquered Pelasgiotis in the course of the post-Mycenaean Völkerwanderung, would not have given this tetrarchy that label.

How, then, did Herodotus come to fall into the manifest error of holding that the Pelasgoi's original language was non-Greek? The first point to notice is that Herodotus' non-Greek-speaking Pelasgoi at Plakia and Skylake on the Hellespont were, according to Herodotus' own testimony,[1] refugees from the island of Lemnos, from which they had been evicted by Miltiades II, the Athenian despot of the Thracian Chersonese (the Gallipoli Peninsula). The second point to notice is that Herodotus is singular in calling the pre-Athenian inhabitants of Lemnos and Imbros simply 'Pelasgoi'. All other authorities call them either 'Tyrsenoi-Pelasgoi' or else just 'Tyrsenoi'.

For instance, Herodotus' fellow countryman Dionysius (a contemporary of Augustus) informs us, in his work on the early history of Rome,[2] that his (fabulous) story of a Pelasgian migration from Thessaly via the Adriatic Sea to Etruria, where, according to him, most of these migrant Pelasgoi were subsequently supplanted by the Tyrsenoi,[3] appeared, almost word for word, in the work of Myrsilos of Lesbos, except that Myrsilos told it, not of the Pelasgoi, but of the Tyrsenoi. Dionysius also informs us[4] that, according to Myrsilos, the Tyrsenoi took the name 'Pelargoi'[5] in the course of their migration, whereas, according to Hellanikos of Lesbos, it was the Pelasgoi who took the name Tyrsenoi after they had settled in Italy. It will be seen that these two Lesbian writers agree in holding that the Pelasgoi and the Tyrsenoi were the same people, though they give mutually contradictory accounts of the way in which the double name arose. The two peoples are also identified with each other by two Athenian writers who, like Hellanikos, were

[1] Herodotus, Book VI, chaps. 136–40.
[2] ʿΡωμαϊκὴ Ἀρχαιολογία, Book I, chap. 23.
[3] See ibid., Book I, chaps. 17–26.
[4] Ibid., chap. 28.
[5] 'Pelargoi' is the Greek for 'storks', and the roving Pelasgoi were supposed to have been called 'Pelargoi' in allusion to this migratory bird (Strabo, *Geographica*, Book IX, chap. 1, § 18, (C. 397)). The 'Pelargikon teikhos' of the acropolis at Athens (Herodotus, Book V, chap. 64; Thucydides, Book II, chap. 17; Aristophanes, *Birds*, l. 832) was said by Hecataeus (Herodotus, Book VI, chap. 137) to have been built by the Pelasgoi, and it may have been in this connection that their national name was equated with the word 'Pelargoi'. (See Meyer, *Forschungen zur alten Geschichte*, vol. 1, pp. 8–9).

writing in the fifth century B.C. Sophocles uses the double name 'Tyrsenoi-Pelasgoi' in a passage in his *Inachus* which Dionysius quotes;[1] and Thucydides likewise identifies the Pelasgoi with the Tyrsenoi.[2]

Herodotus, however, in contrast to his Lesbian and Athenian contemporaries, expressly distinguishes the ex-Lemnian Pelasgoi from the Tyrsenoi in a passage that has been quoted above.[3] He here defines the habitat of the Pelasgoi of Kreston as being 'above' (i.e. up-country in relation to) the habitat of some adjoining Tyrsenoi; and, since he says that the Krestonian Pelasgians' non-Greek language was different from the languages of any of their neighbours, he implies that the languages of these Pelasgoi and these Tyrsenoi, at any rate, were not the same. On this point, Herodotus is implicitly contradicted by Thucydides, who identifies the Athonian non-Greek-speaking Pelasgoi with the Tyrsenoi who had formerly inhabited Lemnos. At the same time, Thucydides and Herodotus agree in one point. They both inform us that, in their time, Krestonians and Tyrsenoi were living next door to each other. Herodotus identifies the inhabitants of Kreston with the Pelasgoi, and gives them Tyrsenoi for their neighbours. Thucydides identifies the Athonian Pelasgoi with the Tyrsenoi, and gives them Krestonians for their neighbours.

We can put our finger on the place on the map where the pair of names Tyrsenoi and Pelasgoi was applied to one and the same people. The Lesbian and Athenian writers' 'Tyrsenoi-Pelasgoi' were the pre-Athenian inhabitants of the two north-Aegean islands Lemnos and Imbros; and both the Lesbians and the Athenians had first-hand knowledge on this point. A Lesbian naval squadron had been mobilized by Otanes, the governor of the Persian Empire's north-west-frontier province, for the conquest of the Pelasgoi of Lemnos and Imbros[4] soon after Darius' abortive expedition against the nomads on the western bay of the Eurasian Steppe. The date of this Persian conquest of the two islands must have been *circa* 511 B.C. They had been conquered again, at some date before 493 B.C.,[5] by the Athenian despot of the Thracian Chersonese,

---

[1] Dionysius, Book I, chap. 25.

[2] In Book IV, chap. 109, where he is enumerating the components of the variegated population of the Athos Peninsula, Thucydides says that the numerically predominant element was Πελασγικόν, τῶν καὶ Λῆμνόν ποτε καὶ Ἀθήνας Τυρσηνῶν οἰκησάντων, together with fragments of three Thracian peoples, the Bisaltai, the Krestonaioi, and the Edonoi.

[3] Book I, chap. 57.

[4] Herodotus, Book V, chap. 26.

[5] Herodotus records Otanes' and Miltiades' conquests of Lemnos and Imbros in two different contexts, without telling us which of the two events was the earlier. Meyer, op. cit., pp. 14–16, and G. De Sanctis, *Atthis* (Turin, 1912, Bocca), p. 298, hold that Miltiades' conquest must have been the earlier of the two. Herodotus mentions that Lykaretos, the brother of Maiandrios of Samos, whom Otanes installed as the Persian Empire's vassal despot of the conquered islands, treated the inhabitants harshly on the grounds that they had failed to fulfil their military obligation to serve in Darius' expedition against the nomads in the

Miltiades II, and this time the inhabitants had been evicted[1] and the vacant islands had been presented by their Athenian conqueror to his mother-country.[2] The Lesbian and Athenian writers must have known what they were about when they identified the Pelasgoi and the Tyrsenoi with each other. On the islands of Lemnos and Imbros, at any rate, the two names must have denoted a single people; and this local identity between Pelasgoi and Tyrsenoi presents us with a puzzle; for Dionysius

western bay of the Eurasian Steppe and that they had made piratical attacks on Darius' expeditionary force when it was on its return journey. De Sanctis argues that the islanders would not have been subject to Persian military service at the time of Darius' expedition unless they had been conquered already, by that time, by the Persian Empire's vassal despot of the Thracian Chersonese, Miltiades. He also argues that, if Miltiades had conquered the islands during the Ionian Revolt, the first act of the Persian authorities after the suppression of the revolt would have been to reinstate the pre-Athenian population which Miltiades had evicted, whereas we know that the descendants of the evicted pre-Athenian Lemnians and Imbrians were still living, in Herodotus' day, as expatriated refugees. Neither of these arguments is convincing. Lemnos and Imbros could have submitted to Persian suzerainty, at some date earlier than that of Darius' expedition, on their own account, and not in consequence of having been conquered, at this time, by the Persian Empire's vassal Miltiades; and, if the Persians did retake the islands when Miltiades fled to Athens in 493 B.C., they may well have refrained from reinstating the former inhabitants who had been evicted by Miltiades, considering that these people's previous record had been an unsatisfactory one from the Persian point of view.

There are three decisive arguments in favour of dating Miltiades' conquest of the islands later than Otanes' conquest of them, and for conjecturing that Miltiades' conquest was a hostile act against the Persian Empire which Miltiades had committed during the Ionian Revolt. In the first place, Herodotus says that Otanes conquered the islands from the Pelasgoi; so, at the time of this conquest, the Pelasgian population had not yet been evicted and supplanted by Athenian colonists. In the second place, Miltiades must have compromised himself with the Persians, or he would not have had to flee from his principality when the Ionian Revolt collapsed; and his seizure of the two islands is the only recorded act of his, before his flight to Athens, that might have made him obnoxious to the Persian authorities. (Miltiades' proposal to cut the bridge of boats across the Danube, when Darius and his expeditionary force were on the far side of it, had not been carried out, and, if this had been held against him by the Persians, he would have had to flee from the Chersonese, not in 493 B.C., but in 511 B.C.) In the third place, Miltiades, at his trial at Athens after his fiasco at Paros, claimed credit for having presented Lemnos and Imbros to Athens after he had conquered them (Herodotus, Book VI, chap. 136). This plea would hardly have been made by Miltiades and have been taken into consideration by the Athenians if, at the time of the trial, *circa* 489 B.C. or later, the islands had been under Persian rule for twenty-two years or more.

Thus it seems probable that Miltiades conquered the islands at some date between 499 and 493 B.C. and presented them to Athens when he returned there, in the latter year, as a refugee. We do not know whether Athens succeeded in taking effective possession of Lemnos and Imbros before the defeat of Xerxes' expedition against European Greece. Certainly these islands were not under effective Athenian rule in the years 480 and 479 B.C., when Attica itself was under Persian military occupation. Antidoros of Lemnos, who, according to Herodotus, Book VIII, chap. 11, was the only man serving in Xerxes' fleet who deserted to the Greeks at the Battle of Artemision, was a Greek, to judge by his name, and was therefore presumably an Athenian colonist. The Athenians rewarded him by giving him a piece of land on Salamis. This suggests that they were not in possession of Lemnos at the time and were also not expecting to obtain, or recover, possession of it.

[1] Herodotus, Book VI, chaps. 137–40.
[2] Herodotus, Book VI, chaps. 136 and 140.

is evidently also right in contending, as he does,[1] that, all the same, the
Tyrsenoi and the Pelasgoi were really two different peoples.

On this question the linguistic evidence tells decisively in favour of
Dionysius' view. The inscriptional evidence attests that, both in Etruria
and on Lemnos, before the Athenian occupation of Lemnos, closely related dialects of one and the same non-Indo-European language were
spoken; and this inscriptional evidence is confirmed by the testimony of
fifth-century-B.C. historians. Thucydides informs us[2] that in 424 B.C. the
'barbarian' (i.e. non-Greek) inhabitants of the Athos Peninsula were
bilingual; i.e. they had native non-Greek languages of their own, besides
speaking Greek, which by this time had already become the lingua
franca of the whole Aegean basin. Thucydides enumerates four bilingual
barbarian elements in the Peninsula's population, a Pelasgian-Tyrsenian
element, a Bisaltian, a Krestonian, and an Edonian. The Pelasgian-
Tyrsenian element in the population of the Athos Peninsula is said by
Thucydides to have lived in Lemnos and Athens once upon a time. They
will have been descended from some of the former Pelasgian-Tyrsenian
inhabitants of Lemnos and Imbros whom Miltiades had evicted; so
their non-Greek native language will have been the language of the inscriptions found on Lemnos at Kaminia. Herodotus informs us[3] that the
Pelasgoi who survived in his day at Kreston in the eastern marches of
the Kingdom of Macedon and at Plakia and Skylake on the Hellespont
spoke one and the same non-Greek language that was not spoken by any
of the neighbours of either of these two Pelasgian communities. Herodotus here says that the Hellespontine Pelasgoi were descendants of
those who had once lived in Attica according to Athenian tradition
(i.e. were descendants of the Pelasgoi who had been evicted by Miltiades
II from Lemnos and Imbros);[4] and the geographical locations of the
Krestonian and Athonian Pelasgoi indicate that these, too, were refugees
from Lemnos and Imbros, though Herodotus[5] brings the Krestonian
Pelasgoi to Kreston, not from Lemnos, but from Thessaly.

How had the Lemnian and Imbrian Pelasgoi come to speak a language
that was known to Herodotus to be non-Greek and that is known to us,

---

[1] In Book I, chaps. 28–9.
[2] Thucydides, Book IV, chap. 109, cited already on p. 129, n. 2.
[3] Herodotus, Book I, chap. 57, quoted already in full, on p. 127.
[4] See Herodotus, Book II, chap. 51, and Book VI, chaps. 136–9. The Athenian story that
the pre-Athenian inhabitants of Lemnos and Imbros were the descendants of non-Greek
trespassers on Attic soil from Samothrace looks as if it had been invented to justify the
Athenian Miltiades' brutal act of evicting them from the two islands. However, the Tetrapolis on the east coast of Attica, where the trespassers are located in the Athenian story, is
recorded to have been also called 'Hyttenia' (Androtion, cited by Stephanus of Byzantium,
s.v. 'Tetrapolis'); and 'Hyttenia' would be synonymous with 'Tetrapolis' if it were derived
from the word 'huth', which means 'four' in Etruscan.
[5] In Book I, chap. 57.

on the evidence of the Kaminia inscriptions, to be non-Indo-European?
The ethnikon 'Pelasgoi' tells us that these Pelasgoi, like the Pelasgoi of
Pelasgiotis, must have originally been North-East-Greek-speakers. It is,
indeed, probable that Pelasgiotis was the Lemnian and Imbrian Pelasgoi's original home.[1] The ancestors of the non-Greek-speaking Pelasgoi
of Herodotus' day in Macedon and on the Hellespont, who were refugees
from Lemnos and Imbros, must have spoken North-East Greek before
they took to speaking the language of the Kaminia inscriptions. This
language is almost identical with the Etruscan language of the numerous
Etruscan inscriptions in Italy. The affinity is so close that Lemnian and
Etruscan can properly be described as being two dialects of one and the
same language. The Greek name for the Etruscans is 'Tyrsenoi', and,
as has been noted above, all our authorities except Herodotus call the
pre-Athenian Lemnians and Imbrians and their refugee descendants not
simply 'Pelasgoi' but 'Tyrsenoi-Pelasgoi' or 'Tyrsenoi'. Here, surely,
we have the key to the Lemnian and Imbrian Pelasgoi's change of
language. After settling on these islands from Pelasgiotis, they must have
been conquered subsequently by Tyrsenian invaders and have been
assimilated by these to the extent of losing their native Greek language
and adopting the alien language of their non-Greek-speaking Tyrsenian
conquerors. The double name 'Tyrsenoi-Pelasgoi', which was applied
to the pre-Athenian non-Greek-speaking population of Lemnos and
Imbros by fifth-century-B.C. Lesbian and Athenian observers, indicates
that the local Pelasgoi had been assimilated by their Tyrsenian conquerors without having been completely exterminated by them.

The Lemnian Pelasgoi's national name survived; yet there are indications that the Tyrsenian conquest of the Lemnian Pelasgoi may have
been accompanied by atrocities that were startling enough to make a
permanent mark on the Hellenic World's folk-memory. Herodotus notes[2]
that, in his time, 'Lemnian deeds' were proverbial in the Greek World
as a synonym for atrocities; and their atrociousness was illustrated by at
least two traditional stories. There was an Athenian story, recounted by
Herodotus,[3] that a Greek-speaking community on Lemnos had once
been massacred—women included—by their non-Greek fellow-islanders.[4]
There was another story that the women of Lesbos had once massacred
all the men on the island but one—the King Thoas whose life was saved
surreptitiously by his daughter Hypsipyle.[5] If these stories were echoes of
authentic historical events, they perhaps indicate that the Tyrsenian
conquerors of Lemnos massacred the men and forcibly married the

---

[1] See Part II, chap. 7, p. 118.   [2] Herodotus, Book VI, chap. 138.   [3] Ibid.

[4] As usual, Herodotus here labels these atrocious non-Greek Lemnians 'Pelasgoi' instead
of 'Tyrsenoi'. Actually the Lemnian Pelasgoi will have been the Lemnian Tyrsenoi's victims.

[5] The Greek tradition dated this massacre before the arrival of the Argonauts, since it
made Euneos Jason's son by Hypsipyle.

women of the conquered Pelasgian Greek population of the island, and that the Pelasgian women then avenged their murdered men by massacring their unwanted Tyrsenian husbands. If these stories of 'Lemnian deeds' are, in truth, memories of atrocities accompanying the Tyrsenian conquest, the legendary form in which these memories survived suggests that the conquest must have taken place at a date before accurate records were kept—a date which, in the Hellenic World, would be some time before the middle of the eighth century B.C. at the latest.

A memory of atrocities committed by the Tyrsenian conquerors of Lemnos against Lemnian Greeks might also partly account for the harshness of the treatment that was inflicted on the Tyrsenoi-Pelasgoi of Lemnos and Imbros when these were conquered, in their turn, by the Greek despot of the Thracian Chersonese, Miltiades II. In the fifth century B.C. their descendants still spoke the non-Greek language of the Kaminia inscriptions and still bore the double name Tyrsenoi-Pelasgoi or one or other name of the two; but they survived only as refugees. Some were to be found in the no-man's-land of the Athos Peninsula; others in the eastern marches of the Kingdom of Macedon; others on the shores of the Hellespont. We may guess that the Hellespontine Pelasgoi were refugees who had been given asylum by the Persian Imperial Government at some date before the shores of the Hellespont had come under Athenian control. The Pelasgoi and Tyrsenoi in the eastern marches of Macedon may have been planted there by King Alexander I when, after the failure of Xerxes' attempt to conquer European Greece, Alexander was extending his dominions eastward in the wake of an ebbing Persian tide.[1]

Can we locate the Tyrsenoi, 'above' whom Kreston, with its Pelasgian inhabitants, was situated according to Herodotus?[2] We may find a clue in two passages of the Homeric epic[3] which give an entirely different picture of Lemnos from the glimpse of the island in another passage of the *Iliad*[4] that has been cited already.[5] In these two passages, Lemnos is represented as being inhabited, not by descendants of the Argonauts, but by people called 'Sinties' who are worshippers of Hephaistos, and, in the passage in the *Odyssey*, these 'Sinties' are called ἀγριόφωνοι, with the implication not only that their language was non-Greek but also that it grated on Greek ears. This epithet would fit the Etruscan-like language of the Kaminia inscriptions. May we conclude that these two passages give us a picture of Lemnos after the Tyrsenian conquest, in contrast to the passage[6] in the *Iliad* which gives us a picture of a pre-Tyrsenian Greek Lemnos?

[1] See p. 134 and Part II, chap. 8, p. 149.
[2] Book I, chap. 57.
[3] *Iliad*, I. 594, and *Odyssey*, VIII. 294.
[4] *Iliad*, VII. 467–75.
[5] In Part II, chap. 7, on p. 118.
[6] *Iliad*, VII. 467–75.

If, as Philochorus conjectured,[1] the word 'Sinties' is derived, like the Homeric adjective σίντης,[2] from the Greek verb σίνω, it will have been, not a true ethnikon, but a Greek term of abuse, signifying 'buccaneers'. Whatever the derivation of the name may be, it reappears, in the form 'Sintoi', on the European mainland in the Strymon valley, on the right bank of the river immediately to the north-east of Krestonia. The Strymonian Sintoi were synoecized in the Macedonian city named Herakleia Sintike. Were these Strymonian Sintoi a party of Tyrsenian refugees from Lemnos to whom the Macedonian crown had given a new home in this recently acquired Macedonian territory? The Macedonians, being Greek-speaking, might have known the Lemnian Tyrsenoi by the opprobrious Greek name for them.

The Strymonian Sintoi and the Lemnian Sinties must have been two detachments of the same people, and one of these was presumably an offshoot of the other. It seems to be commonly assumed that the Sintoi-Sinties were a Thracian people who had conquered Lemnos; Strabo takes them to have been Thracians,[3] and certainly they may have been. Herodotus informs us[4] that the island of Samothrace had been conquered by Thracians from previous Pelasgian occupants who were of the same stock as the Pelasgoi of Lemnos and Imbros. There may have been a Thracian conquest of Lemnos and Imbros too. However, there is no tradition of this, and the non-Indo-European language of the Kaminia inscriptions is, not Thracian (which, like Greek, was an Indo-European language), but Etruscoid. It is just as likely that the Strymonian Sintoi were refugee survivors of the Lemnian Sinties. We do know that the Tyrsenoi-Pelasgoi were expelled from Lemnos by Miltiades II; and King Alexander I of Macedon may well have given them a new home on the frontiers of his newly acquired eastern marches.[5] If the Sintoi were non-Thracians in nationality, this will have been a recommendation from the Macedonian point of view, since the Thracians were one of the two peoples (the Paiones were the other) against whom the newly established frontier had to be held. We know that it was the Argeads' policy to confirm their hold on conquered territory by planting on them refugees from elsewhere. We have a record of one case in which King Alexander I's father Amyntas I offered an asylum to a refugee, and of two cases in which an asylum was given to refugees by Alexander I himself.[6]

---

[1] Philochorus, fragm. 6 = schol. *Iliad*, I. 584.
[2] *Iliad*, XI. 481; XVI. 353; XX. 165.
[3] *Geographica*, Book VII, fragms. 45 (46) and 45a.
[4] Book II, chap. 51.
[5] See p. 133 and Part II, chap. 8, p. 149.
[6] See ibid., pp. 137–8.

8. *The Expansion of the Argead Kingdom of Lower Macedon*

IN Macedonian history there are three separate and distinct movements that must not be confused with each other. The first of thes eis the migration of the Makedones from the Peneios basin to the Haliakmon basin. If, as seems probable, this was one of the secondary effects of the North-West-Greek Völkerwanderung, it must have taken place in the twelfth century B.C. or not much later. The second movement is the gradual expansion of the Makedones, after their arrival in the Haliakmon basin, up-stream, towards the Haliakmon's source, and then south-westward, across the main chain of Pindus, into the interior of Epirus. We do not know when this second movement began nor how long it took. We only have Thucydides' testimony that, by the year 429 B.C., Lynkestis, as well as Elimiotis, and also other districts farther away in the interior, had been occupied by a population that was Macedonian in nationality,[1] and that, in the same year, the throne of Orestis was held by a king who bore the Macedonian Greek name 'Antiokhos'.[2] The third movement in Macedonian history was the foundation and subsequent expansion of the Argead Kingdom of Lower Macedon. The direction of the Argead Kingdom's expansion was the opposite to that of the expansion of the Upper Macedonian principalities. The Argead Kingdom expanded eastward. As far as we can reckon from Herodotus' statement[3] that King Amyntas I, who was on the throne of Lower Macedon at the time of Megabazos' campaign in the Strymon valley *circa* 511 B.C., was the sixth successor of the founder of the dynasty, King Perdikkas I, in a succession that had passed, each time, from father to son, we may tentatively date the foundation of the Argead Kingdom in the middle decades of the seventh century B.C.[4] It will be seen that the time-interval between the arrival of the Makedones in the Haliakmon basin and the foundation of the Kingdom of Lower Macedon may have been as long as 500 years.

Though our dating of the foundation of the Kingdom of Lower Macedon is only an approximate one, it may nevertheless give us a clue to at least one of the reasons why the expansion of the Argead Kingdom started at about this time. The middle decades of the seventh century B.C. were about a generation later than the beginning of the colonization of the north coast of the Aegean Sea, from Mount Olympus to the Helles-pont, by the rising Hellenic city-states in the south. These maritime

[1] Thucydides, Book II, chap. 99.   [2] Book II, chap. 81.
[3] In Book VIII, chap. 139.   [4] See the present Part, chap. 3, p. 68.

south Greek colonies must soon have begun to open up trade with their hinterland; their trade would be a carrier for their culture; and this Hellenic civilization, which was now blossoming, would have a stimulating effect on peoples whose civilization was relatively backward. The Makedones in the lower Haliakmon valley will have been played upon by this Hellenic cultural radiation and will have been stimulated by it.

This however, cannot be the whole explanation of the Argead Kingdom's rise; for the influence of the Hellenic civilization on the other native communities within range of the colonial Greek city-states ἐπὶ Θρᾴκης will have been equally stimulating for them; and the influence of the two Greek colonies that had been planted on the northern stretch of the coast of Pieria, Pydna and Methone,[1] which were the nearest south Greek settlements to nuclear Lower Macedon, will not have been so potent as the influence of the more massive Greek settlements on the two peninsulas Pallene and Sithonia and on the island of Thasos. Moreover, the native peoples that were within the closest range of these densest south Greek settlements—the Thracian Bisaltai and Edonoi and refugee Pieres and the Paeonian Derronaioi and Odomantoi and Doberes—had the important additional advantage of possessing gold and silver mines in their home territories;[2] and, though the lion's share of this asset may have been appropriated by the distant but redoubtable Satrai,[3] whose home was in the inaccessible mountains round the headwaters of the River Hebros (Marica),[4] the local peoples had sufficient supplies of metal to enable them, before the close of the sixth century B.C., to strike coinages in the contemporary Hellenic style.

The Argead Kingdom did not strike any coinage that we know of till 479 B.C., when King Alexander I annexed Bisaltike, in which the mines near Lake Prasias lay.[5] The second of the two principal mining districts ἐπὶ Θρᾴκης did not come into Macedonian hands till 358 B.C., when King Philip II of Macedon annexed Krenides and founded Philippi there. It is significant that, when Alexander I suppressed the Thracian and Paeonian peoples' coinages and issued coins in his own name, he adopted the suppressed coinages' types.[6] These facts show that the rise of the Argead Kingdom in and after the seventh century B.C. cannot

---

[1] Pseudo-Scylax notes that both these are Greek cities (§ 67).

[2] According to Casson, op. cit., the mines, *pace Herodoti*, Book VII, chap. 112, were not *on* Mount Pangaios itself, but were in two neighbouring localities: Daton-Krenides (the future Philippi) and the mountains near the beginning of the road from Lake Prasias to Macedon (see the present chapter, p. 149). These latter mines were in the territory of the Bisaltai; Daton was in the territory of the Edonoi.

[3] See Herodotus, Book VII, chap. 112.

[4] Herodotus, Book VII, chap. 111.

[5] Herodotus, Book V, chap. 17. See the present Part, chap. 5, p. 96, n. 2.

[6] Casson, op. cit., p. 178.

be accounted for solely as being an effect of the stimulus from the neighbouring south Greek colonies; for this stimulus was producing the same
effect in a greater degree upon the non-Macedonian peoples in the lower
Strymon basin during the first two centuries after the foundation of the
earliest of these colonies.

Nor can the Argead Kingdom's eventual victory in its competition
with these more precocious native peoples to the east of Macedon be
accounted for by the linguistic fact that the Makedones were Greek-
speakers. There was no special virtue—or magic—in that; and there is
no reason to suppose that the Thracians and Paiones were any less highly
gifted by nature than the Makedones and the rest of the Greeks were.
The reason why, in the end, the Makedones succeeded in profiting more
than their neighbours profited from the common stimulus of Hellenism
must be sought in the ability, the policy, and the persistence of successive
Argead kings. The expansion of the Argead Kingdom was deliberately
planned, and these plans were progressively carried out.

The earliest of the Argead kings about whose personality and achievements we have any substantial information is Alexander I, who came to
the throne soon after the opening of the fifth century B.C. and reigned,
on the evidence of his coinage, until some date in the four hundred and
fifties. Alexander I's ability and success are not in question. But his father
Amyntas, who cuts a poor figure in Herodotus' narrative,[1] may have
been unduly depreciated by Herodotus for the artistic purpose of using
him as a foil for his spirited son. From another passage in Herodotus'
work,[2] we know that, when the despot of Athens, Hippias, was ejected
from Athens in 511 B.C., Amyntas I offered him Anthemous, a district to
the south-east of the site of the future city of Thessalonike, at the head of
the Thermaic Gulf, on the north-western approaches to the three-
pronged Chalcidic Peninsula. This notice gives us two significant pieces
of information: first that, by 511 B.C., the Argead Kingdom had already
expanded beyond the head of the Thermaic Gulf from a starting-point
that must have lain somewhere in the lower valley of the Haliakmon; and,
second, that, by this date, the Argead Government had already adopted
a policy, which it continued to pursue in later reigns, for securing its
hold on Thracian or Paeonian territories that it had annexed.

Besides planting colonies of Makedones in conquered territories, the
Argeadai also offered new homes there to refugees from elsewhere who,
like Hippias, had lost their own homes. For the Argeads' purpose, such
refugees would make the next best colonists to the Makedones themselves. Their loyalty to the Argead crown would be assured by their
gratitude to it for having behaved as a friend in need, by their retreat
having been cut off through their eviction from their ancestral homes,

[1] See Book V, chaps. 17–21.   [2] Book V, chap. 94.

and, above all, by the hostility of the subjugated and evicted native populations, who would resent being supplanted by imported foreign protégés of the Argead crown's as hotly as they resented being supplanted by Macedonian colonists. Though Hippias did not accept the offer of asylum in Argead territory, other refugees did. When, in 468/7 B.C., Peloponnesian Argos reconquered and destroyed Mycenae,[1] which had been maintaining its independence of Argos since Argos' disastrous defeat by Sparta at Sepeia *circa* 494 B.C., more than half the surviving Mycenaeans were given asylum in Macedon by King Amyntas I's successor King Alexander I.[2] When, in 445 B.C., the revolt of the Euboean states against Athens was suppressed by Pericles, and the people of Histiaia capitulated on the condition that they should evacuate their city, they were given a new home in Macedon by Alexander's successor Perdikkas II.[3] When, in 432 B.C., the colonial Chalcidians had revolted against Athens, Perdikkas persuaded them to evacuate their cities on the Sithonian Peninsula and to synoecize themselves at Olynthos, where they would be less at the mercy of Athenian sea-power. To mitigate the hardship for them, Perdikkas give them, for the duration of the war, the use of Macedonian territory in Mygdonia, round Lake Bolbe (Beşik Göl).[4]

At an earlier point in the present Part[5] it is suggested that the same policy may account for the location of the Pelasgoi who, in Herodotus' day, were in occupation of the city of Kreston;[6] for the location of the Tyrsenoi who were the neighbours of these Pelasgoi less far up-country;[7] and for the location of the Sintoi who gave their name to the Macedonian city Herakleia Sintike, on the right (west) bank of the River Strymon at the northern end of the plain through which the Strymon runs in its lower course. These communities may all have been Tyrseno-Pelasgian refugees from the islands Lemnos and Imbros, who had been given asylum by King Alexander I in the eastern marches of Macedon after they had been evicted from their islands, probably *circa* 499–493 B.C.,[8] by the Athenian despot of the Thracian Chersonese, Miltiades II. Krestonia and Sintike will have required settlers on whom the Macedonian crown could depend, since the Thracians in the hinterland of Krestonia, who

[1] Diodorus, Book XI, chap. 65. Diodorus says that the Argives were seizing the opportunity given to them by Sparta's prostration as a result of the earthquake of *circa* 466 or 464 B.C.; but Diodorus' own dating of the destruction of Mycenae in 468/7 B.C. is hardly reconcilable with this. The Argives' opportunity may have been Sparta's preoccupation with the Arcadian insurrection of 469 B.C.

[2] Pausanias, Book VII, chap. 25, § 6.

[3] Theopompus apud Strabonem, Book X, chap. 1, § 3 (C. 445).

[4] Thucydides, Book I, chap. 58.

[5] In Part II, chap. 7, Annex, on p. 134.

[6] Herodotus, Book I, chap. 57. [7] Herodotus, ibid.

[8] See Part II, chap. 7, Annex, pp. 129–30.

were presumably the Maidoi along the middle course of the Strymon, were exceptionally barbarous,[1] while the Strymonian Paiones, whom the Sintian settlement split in two,[2] will have been still more hostile.

It is evident that both the eastward expansion of the Argead Kingdom and the Argeads' policy of consolidating their conquests by giving asylum on conquered territory to foreign refugees date from before Alexander I's accession to the Argead throne. If Alexander's father and immediate predecessor Amyntas I was not the originator of the policies of expansion and colonization, the credit will be due to one or more of his predecessors.[3] Everything that we know about the history of the Argead Kingdom indicates that it had the good fortune to throw up a succession of strong and able leaders. In the course of the two centuries ending in the extinction of the Argead House after the death of Alexander III, the only time when the dynasty failed conspicuously was the period of forty years between King Arkhelaos' death in 399 B.C. and King Philip II's accession in 359 B.C. 'In Macedon there was an encounter between two different cultures. The more highly organized of the two, which was the Greek one, represented by the kings and the nobility, conquered the country step by step and became the basis of the Macedonian state.'[4]

A short but masterly account of the expansion of the Argead Kingdom down to the year 429 B.C. has been given by Thucydides[5] apropos of the invasion of Macedon in that year by the Odrysian war-lord Sitalkes.

The Macedonian nation includes the Lynkestai and Elimiotai and other peoples in the interior (ἐπάνωθεν), who are the Makedones' allies and subjects, but have royal houses of their own. The present maritime Macedon is a creation of Perdikkas [II]'s and his ancestors', who, by origin, are Temenidai from [the Peloponnesian] Argos. This dynasty acquired by force of arms the country that they brought under their rule. They evicted from Pieria the Pieres, who afterwards established themselves, east of Strymon, at the foot of Mount Pangaios, at Phagres and other places (to this day the seaboard at the foot of Pangaios is called the Pieric Gulf). From Bottiaia they [the Argeadai] evicted the people called Bottiaioi, who now live next door to the [colonial] Chalcidians. In Paionia they acquired a narrow strip along the River Axios, stretching from inland as far as Pella and the sea-coast. Beyond the Axios, up to the Strymon, they hold the country called Mygdonia, from which they expelled the Edones. They also evicted from the country now called Eordaia

---

[1] See Herodotus, Book V, chap. 5. [2] See also pp. 95 and 134.

[3] Aristotle, *Athenaiôn Politeia*, chap. 15, § 2, has recorded that the Athenian despot Hippias' father Peisistratos established himself at Rhaikelos, on the Thermaic Gulf, after his second expulsion from Athens perhaps *circa* 556 B.C.; Rhaikelos is called 'a city of Macedonia' by Stephanus of Byzantium. Aristotle does not say that Pesistratos went to Rhaikelos on an invitation from the Macedonian crown, but it seems improbable that, at this date, a south Greek refugee could have settled at any point on the Thermaic Gulf without the reigning Argead's good will.

[4] Hoffmann, op. cit., p. 112. Cp. Dascalakis, op. cit., pp. 10–11.

[5] In Book II, chap. 99.

the Eordoi. Most of the Eordoi were exterminated, but a small remnant of them has found a new home at Physka. From Almopia they evicted the Almopes. These Makedones [i.e. the lowlanders] also made themselves masters of the other countries that they hold down to this day, namely Anthemous and Grestonia and Bisaltia and the extensive territory that is inhabited by the Makedones themselves. The whole of this dominion is called Macedon.

In this passage, Thucydides has given us a catalogue of the conquests by which the Argead Kingdom had acquired the frontiers of the year 429 B.C.,[1] but the order in which he recites these conquests is manifestly not the chronological order in which they were made. For instance, Bisaltike, which must have been the last, being the most easterly, of the lands that had been conquered by the Argeadai by 429 B.C., is only the last but one in Thucydides' list, while the last of all is 'the territory inhabited by the Makedones themselves', which, *ex hypothesi*, must already have been under the rule of the Argeadai before they started out on their career of conquest. The location of the starting-point of the Argeadai's conquests, and the chronological order of the conquests themselves, are two points on which Thucydides has left us in the dark. Since both points are historically important, it is fortunate that we can get some light on them from the physical structure of the region.

After migrating, in the course of the post-Mycenaean Völkerwanderung, out of the Peneios basin into the Haliakmon basin, the Makedones will have found themselves in the lowest section but one of the Haliakmon valley—the section between the present-day towns Servia, on the south-east side of the river, and Kožani, on the north-west side. In this new location their retreat by the way they had come will have been cut off by the influx into the Peneios basin of the Perrhaiboi followed by the Thessaloi. The Makedones will also have been unable to follow the Haliakmon farther down-stream. 'There is no passage along the river, as both banks are here bordered by impracticable precipices';[2] and, though there are practicable tracks between the Haliakmon valley and the maritime lowlands over the mountains on both sides of the Haliakmon gorge, both tracks are difficult, particularly the one above the right (i.e. the south-eastern) bank of the river.[3] On 5 December 1806 Colonel Leake, travelling on horseback, in the reverse direction, over the left-bank track, took five hours and a quarter in all, spread over two days, to ride from Vérria (Berrhoia) to the plain of Buja, the first piece of level country above the gorge on the north-western side of the river.[4]

[1] The one name that is conspicuously absent from Thucydides' list is that of the Brygoi.
[2] Leake, op. cit., vol. iii, p. 297.   [3] Ibid.
[4] Ibid., pp. 295–7. Leake's first-hand account of the difficulty of the passage through the mountainous country overhanging the Haliakmon gorge is confirmed by reports of later travellers cited by J. Kromayer, op. cit., 2. Band, p. 14, n. 3. 'Von Elevtherochori . . . führt nach Veria . . . ein Saumweg über den Rücken des Kalkgebirges (Doxa-Berg), und beträgt die Seehöhe des Sattels 1269 m, nach Djuma . . .' (Col. Anton Tuma, *Griechenland, Make-*

By contrast, the route up-stream is relatively open and easy, and this is the route that will have been followed by those of the Makedones who eventually occupied Western Elimeia and the Upper Macedonian cantons Orestis, Tymphaia, and Parauaia. The branch of the Makedones that eventually created the Kingdom of Lower Macedon will have been the one that, in the first phase of Macedonian history to the north of the Pórtes Pass, had been the least adventurous. It will have been the branch that stayed in the section of the Haliakmon valley on which the Pórtes Pass debouches—that is to say, the section between the gorge on the north-east and the Haliakmon's southward elbow on the south-west. This section of the Haliakmon valley was probably included in Elimeia;[1] so, if the Argeadai started from here, they will have originally been members or subjects of the Elimeian royal family.

For someone who finds himself in this lowest section but one of the Haliakmon valley, there is a fourth possible exit from it besides the Pórtes Pass and the route up-stream and the mountain track down-stream to Vérria. This is the route northward through the Kayalar ('Crags') basin (Eordaia). The strategic importance of Eordaia will have become apparent to anyone who, after traversing the Pórtes Pass and crossing the Haliakmon between Servia and Kožani, has travelled on from Kožani northwards.[2] An effective master of this little canton is the potential

donien und Süd-Albanien, oder die südliche Balkan-Halbinsel, militärgeographisch, statistisch und kriegshistorisch dargestellt* (Hannover, 1888, Helwing), p. 146). Looking out of a railway-carriage window to the left when approaching Verria from Thessaloníki, 'ein wenig südlich von Karaferia [Verria] sieht man deutlich an der Bergwand den tiefen Spalt, dem der Indje Karassu, die Bistritza [Haliakmon], entströmt, ähnlich wie der Saccaria bei Vezierhan. Auch hier ist die Schlucht so eng, dass neben dem Wasser kein Raum für die Strasse bleibt, welche daher die seitlichen Höhen hinaufsteigen muss' (Baron W. L. C. von der Goltz, *Ein Ausflug nach Makedonien* (Berlin, 1894, Decker), p. 79). Kromayer also cites A. Boué, *Recueil d'itinéraires dans la Turquie d'Europe* (Vienna, 1854, 2 vols), vol. ii, p. 85. This volume has not been accessible for me, but, in an earlier and more detailed work, Boué notes that, below the stretch of open country to the north of Servia, 'pour gagner le golfe de Salonique, l'Indge-Karasou [Haliakmon] se jette dans les gorges dirigeés du S.-O. au N.-E., qui existent au S. de Velvendos et se prolongent vers Egri-Boudschak' (A. Boué, *La Turquie d'Europe* (Paris, 1840, Bertrand, 4 vols.), vol. i, p. 189. See further Kromayer, op. cit., vol. cit., p. 25, n. 3, *ad fin*.

[1] See Hammond, 'Prehistoric Epirus and the Dorian Invasion', p. 146. The evidence that Hammond cites is a Latin inscription found, in a ruined church on the road between Elassóna and Servia, by A. J. B. Wace and M. S. Thompson (see the *Annual of the British School at Athens*, vol. 17, pp. 193–204). This inscription records a boundary award between the city-state Azoros in the Perrhaebian Tripolis and the Elemiotae (*sic*). The award was made in A.D. 101 by Verginius Publianus, a special arbitrator appointed by the Emperor Trajan, but it is stated, in the inscription, to have been based on a previous award made by Amyntas [?III], father of Philip [?II], which had been found inscribed on a stele in the market-place at Doliche. 'Since the territory of Doliche lay to the south of the Cambunian hills that separate the upper basin of the Sarantoporos from the Haliacmon valley by Serfije [Servia], the district round the latter town and Velventos was probably part of Elemiotis in antiquity' (p. 201). There are a facsimile and a text of the inscription on pp. 194–5; there is a sketch-map of the district on p. 200.

[2] I myself travelled through Eordaia, going south, on 4 September 1921, and, going north, on 6 September 1921 and 26 July 1965.

master of all the rest of Greater Macedon, both Upper and Lower. Eordaia, walled in, as it is, by high mountains on the east, west, and north, is like the keep of a castle; but this is a keep that has no less than five sally-ports. From Kožani, at the southern end of Eordaia, an aggressor can invade both the Peneios basin (via the Pórtes Pass) and the upper Haliakmon basin (via the kleisoura of Šatišta)[1] with ease, and can reach Vérria (Berrhoia), overhanging the coastal plain, with rather greater difficulty; but the most important of Eordaia's five sally-ports are the two at its north-east and north-west corners, and the key-point in the canton is the point, near the north-east corner of Lake Ostrovo (Lake Begorritis), where the road running up Eordaia from south to north makes its junction with the road running west and east across the canton's northern end, between Lake Ostrovo and the Nidže Range. This west-east road is the Roman Via Egnatia. Through the north-western exit from Eordaia the Via Egnatia led, via Lynkestis and Macedonian Pelagonia and the continental divide, to the shore of the Adriatic. Through the north-east exit this historic road led eastward, via the Telovo Valley[2] and the city of Edessa (Aigai)—for Alexander I to the River Strymon and for Alexander III to the River Beas in the distant Panjab.

From the Haliakmon valley the entry into Eordaia is physically easy for a peaceful traveller; but it can be made militarily difficult for an invader if the owners of Eordaia offer a determined resistance. The resistance offered by the Eordoi to the Makedones must have been stubborn if, as Thucydides records, the conquest was not achieved until the Eordoi had been almost exterminated. We may guess that Eordaia was the Argeadai's earliest acquisition,[3] and that it was the founder of the Argead Kingdom, King Perdikkas I, who, starting from eastern Elimeia, acquired both Eordaia and the city of Edessa, the north-eastern sally-port of Eordaia, which was the Argeadai's first capital and continued to be the burial-place of the kings of their line.

The Argeadai could not have acquired Edessa till they had made themselves masters of Eordaia; for this was the only route by which they could reach Edessa from the Haliakmon valley above the gorge so long as the country between the crest of Mount Bermion, Eordaia's eastern rampart, and the coast was held by the Thraco-Phrygian people named the Brygoi;[4] and the Brygoi were still in possession of their ancestral territory between Mount Bermion, the lower Haliakmon River, and the River Loudias in 492 B.C., when Macedon was occupied by the Persian general Mardonios.[5] We do not know the date of the foundation of the

[1] See Leake, op. cit., vol. 1, pp. 311–13.   [2] See Geyer, op. cit., p. 1.
[3] Geyer, too, thinks so. See op. cit., pp. 25, 38, 39.
[4] See Strabo, Book VII, fragm. 25.   [5] See Herodotus, Book VI, chap. 45.

Macedonian city of Berrhoia (i.e. in standard Greek, Pheraia), nor who the Thessalian-named Macedonian Beras (Pheres) was who gave his name to it. Berrhoia overhangs the maritime plain from a spur of the southern end of Mount Bermion, as Edessa overhangs it from another spur at the northern end of the same range; but, for the Argeadai and their Macedonian followers, there can have been no passage between Berrhoia and Edessa on the seaward side of Mount Bermion so long as the lowland Brygoi—and these were a majority of the Brygoi—continued to maintain their independence.

Physka, where Thucydides records that a remnant of refugee Eordoi had survived, was in Mygdonia,[1] and here these Eordian refugees, who must have escaped by the north-eastern exit from Eordaia via Edessa, will have been overtaken already, by Thucydides' time, by the continuing progress of the Argead Kingdom's expansion. Another, and perhaps larger, band of Eordian refugees escaped by the north-western exit, trekked along the route of the future Via Egnatia to the Adriatic side of the continental divide, and found asylum here. The location of the western refugee Eordoi is indicated by the name Eordaïkos, which is borne by the tributary, now called Devol, of the Apsos, now called Semeni, River in Arrian's account of Alexander III's operations in southern Illyria in 335 B.C.[2] Ptolemy names two of these western refugee Eordoi's towns.[3] One of them, Dibolia, the modern Selásforo,[4] stood on the north side of the upper Devol River; the second, Skampis, will have been the station of that name on the Via Egnatia which, to judge by the mileages given in the Antonine and Jerusalem itineraries and in the Peutinger Table, was at or near the present-day Elbasan on the River Škumbi (Genusus).

These westward-migrating Eordoi were followed by westward-migrating Brygoi; for, though the main body of the Brygoi lived to the east of Mount Bermion and held their own there till 492 B.C., Edessa, on the brow of the northernmost cliff of Mount Bermion, must have been a Brygan town before the Argeadai conquered it; for 'Edessa' is a Thraco-Phrygian word ($Ƒέδεσσα$, meaning 'Watertown'),[5] while the irrigated land at the foot of the falls over which the river of Edessa tumbles to the

---

[1] Ptolemy, *Geographia*, Book III, chap. 33. Cp. Steph. Byz.; *'Εορδαίαι· δύο χῶραι Μυγδονίας*. Stephanus notes that there was a third Eordaia in Thrace. Stephanus cites Theagenes for Physka.

[2] Arrian, Book I, chap. 5, § 5—chap. 6, § 11. The gorge on this river, at Tzangon, described by Arrian, was traversed by Leake on 9 September 1805 (see op. cit., vol. i, p. 335).

[3] *Geographia*, Book III, chap. 23.

[4] For the identity of the medieval Deavolis with Selásforo, see Leake, op. cit., vol. i, pp. 339–40.

[5] See Part II, chap. 3, p. 68. The Argeadai renamed Edessa 'Aigai' (the Greek for 'Breakers' or 'Falls'). The town's modern name Vódena is a reversion to its Thraco-Phrygian name; for Vódena, like $Ƒέδεσσα$, means 'Watertown'.

maritime plain was called 'the Gardens of Midas'[1]—and 'Midas' is a Phrygian royal name or title. Brygan refugees from this north-western corner of the Brygan country must have been the ancestors of the Brygoi who gave their name to the station called Brucida, between Castra (Parembole) and Lykhnidos on the Via Egnatia, in the intramontane basin of Lake Prespa, just to the east of the road's transit to the Adriatic slope.[2] These must be the Brygoi whom Strabo associated,[3] perhaps not quite accurately, with the Lynkestai, Deuriopes, and Pelagones, as being one of the peoples from whose territories the River Erigon receives tributaries on its way from its source in the Illyrian mountains to its confluence with the Axios.

'When [the Argeadai] had made themselves masters of the country round "the Gardens of Midas", they used it as their base of operations for the progressive conquest of the rest of Macedon.'[4] Now that they were astride the main east-west route between the Adriatic and the Aegean, the Makedones were free to advance along it from Edessa in either direction, and they did move in both directions.

The lie of the land tells us that the Macedonian principality of Lynkestis must have been founded by Makedones who reached the Florina bay of the Črna (Erigon) basin from Eordaia. Lynkestis must therefore have been founded, after the Argeadai had conquered Eordaia, by Macedonian migrants from the Argead dominions, following the refugee Eordoi and Brygoi up along the first stage of the course of their westward trek.[5] Lynkestis, however, unlike Eordaia, did not come, or at any rate

---

[1] Μίδεω τοῦ Γορδίεω κῆποι (Herodotus, Book VIII, chap. 138).

[2] Brucida is named in the Jerusalem itinerary. Steph. Byz. records both Brygias and Brygion as being 'a city of Macedonia', Brykai as being 'a people in Thrace', and (under 'Bryx') Brygai as being 'a Macedonian people near the Illyrians'. Strabo, Book 7, § 8 (C. 326), mentions Brygoi in his list of Illyrian peoples who are intermingled (ἀναμέμικται) with the Epirot peoples. In this context he associates the Brygoi with the Bylliones, Taulantioi, and Parthinoi, and this is perhaps the evidence on which Krahe, op. cit., p. 6, states that there were splinters of Thracian peoples, interspersed among the Illyrians, as far to the west as the shore of the Adriatic. Pseudo-Scymnus mentions Βρύγοι βάρβαροι as living in the interior of southern Illyria (l. 433), but this without relating their habitat to any precise point on the coastline. Moreover, he locates the Enkheleioi farther inland than these Brygoi (l. 437), and, since the only inland Enkheleioi (and, indeed, the only Enkheleioi at all) whose approximate location we know are those that gave their name to a place on the shores of Lake Lykhnidos (Okhrida) called Enkhelanes, which is mentioned by Polybius, Book V, chap. 108, § 8, Pseudo-Scymnus' Brygoi would be a different community from those at the Jerusalem Itinerary's Brucida—supposing that we were to take Pseudo-Scymnus's locations of inland peoples as being precise. We cannot, however, take Pseudo-Scymnus so seriously as that. In l. 438 he suddenly transports his Enkheleioi from the far interior to the coast by making them next-door neighbours of Apollonia. For the location of the Enkheleioi, see Part I, chap. 3, p. 22, footnotes 4, 5, 6.

[3] *Geographica*, Book VII, chap. 7, § 8 (C. 327).

[4] ἐνθεῦτεν δὲ ὁρμώμενοι, ὡς ταύτην εἶχον, κατεστρέφοντο καὶ τὴν ἄλλην Μακεδονίην (Herodotus, Book VIII, chap. 138).

[5] See Geyer, op. cit., p. 38.

did not remain, under the Argeadai's direct rule. It became an autonomous Macedonian principality, under the Argeadai's suzerainty, like
the Macedonian principalities in the valley of the Haliakmon and,
beyond Pindus, in the upper valleys of the Aôos and the Peneios.
Though Lynkestis was the nearest to Edessa of all the Upper Macedonian
principalities and was also linked with it by a trans-continental route,
the pass between the Kayalar basin and the Črna basin was difficult,
so long as its forest fleece survived, to traverse in the teeth of military
opposition, as Brasidas found in 423 B.C.[1] and Galba in 199 B.C.[2] This
natural obstruction enabled the princes of Lynkestis to maintain their
autonomy *vis-à-vis* the Argeadai, and, indeed, to assert it by inventing
for themselves a rival heroic genealogy. Their choice of a Bacchiad ancestry suggests that, by the time when they chose this, their country was
already in commercial relations with Corinth and her colonies along the
Adriatic coast.[3] It was not till the reign of King Philip II (*regnabat* 359–
336 B.C.) that the Argead crown succeeded in bringing Lynkestis and the
other Upper Macedonian principalities under its direct rule.

The territories that the Argeadai added to their own kingdom, as a
result of the conquests that they made from their base of operations at
Edessa, lay, not to the north-west of Edessa, but to the east and south of
it. 'The Gardens of Midas' at the foot of the Edessan waterfalls lie in the
extreme north-west corner of a plain across which four rivers—the
Haliakmon (Vistrica, Vistritza), the Loudias (Moglenica), the Axios
(Vardar), and the Ekheidoros (Gallikó)—flow after issuing from the
mountains on their way to the sea. This plain is called 'Emathia' in the
Iliad,[4] but this name is not mentioned either by Herodotus or by Thucydides. It is a descriptive name, meaning 'the Sandy Land'; it is not
a term of political geography.

In order to understand the 'geopolitics' of the Argead Kingdom's
expansion, we have to put out of our minds the present configuration
of the Emathian plain and to try to reconstruct the topography as it was
at the successive dates with which we are dealing.[5] We can do this only
approximately; for contemporary information is scanty and casual, and
the topography has been changing all the time, ever since the mountains
surrounding the Emathian plain were first ruckled up. Ever since then,
the four rivers issuing from these mountains have been constantly de-
positing alluvium on the last stage of their courses, and this deposited

---

[1] See Thucydides, Book IV, chaps. 127–8.
[2] See Livy, Book XXXI, chap. 39.
[3] See Part II, chap. 3, p. 72.   [4] *Iliad*, XIV. 226.
[5] See Casson, op. cit., pp. 14–16, with the three sketch-maps on p. 15, in which Casson
gives tentative pictures of the distribution of land and water in this region at three dates,
ranging from the end of the fifth century B.C. to the first century of the Christian Era. See
also Geyer, op. cit., pp. 6–8.

alluvium has been constantly pushing the coastline forward. Today the coastline, between the western corner of the plain, below the north-western extremity of the Pierian Range, and the plain's south-eastern corner at Thessaloníki, is convex, and the alluvium has now spread near enough to Cape Kara Burnu (Aineion), at the north-west corner of the Chalcidic Peninsula, to be threatening to obstruct the channel for ship-ping between Thessaloníki and the open sea.[1] At the time of the foundation of the Argead Kingdom the shores of the Thermaic Gulf will have run far to the north-west of the present shore-line. The marshes of Yenice (Yanitza), through which the Loudias (Moglenica) passes, and from which it now emerges again before reaching the sea, probably extended then farther north-west then they do today, and were connected with the sea by a bay of open water. The greater part of the present-day Campania of Thessaloníki was either submerged or waterlogged, and the Emathian plain was confined to two narrow strips of dry land, one run-ning from 'the Gardens of Midas' southward, along the eastern foot of Mount Bermion, to the point on the Haliakmon where this river emerges from the Vérria gorge, and the other strip running from 'the Gardens' eastward through Pella to the mouth of the Axios, which was then probably due east of Pella.

Today the distance from Pella to the nearest point on the coast is about twenty miles. When Herodotus was writing, in the third quarter of the fifth century B.C., and when Thucydides was writing, round about the turn of the fifth and fourth centuries B.C., Pella was on the coast.[2] When Pseudo-Scylax was writing, perhaps more than half a century later than Thucydides, ships could still reach Pella by sailing up the River Loudias.[3] Demetrius Poliorketes built ships at Pella in 289 B.C.[4] As late as 169 B.C. the sea was still near enough to Pella for treasure stored at Pella to be thrown into the sea from there.[5] However, in 169 B.C. Paullus found Pella bordered, no longer by the sea, but by im-passable marshes. The citadel of Pella stood in the marshes on an artificial mound, and between this and the city there ran a 'river' which may have been either the Loudias or a ship-canal.[6]

Thus the Argeadai, after they had installed themselves in Edessa, had to choose which of two different directions they should follow in their next advance. Should their first move forward from Edessa into the Emathian

---

[1] When on 6 August 1865 Tozer was sailing from Thessaloníki to the skala of Ekateríni, he 'passed, some way from the land, through the stream of the Vardar, whose pale and turbid water is distinguished by a clear line of demarcation from the deep blue sea into which it runs' (Tozer, op. cit., vol. ii, p. 4).

[2] Herodotus, Book VII, chap. 123; Thucydides, Book II, chap. 99, § 4.

[3] Pseudo-Scylax, § 67.   [4] Plutarch, *Demetrius*, chap. 43.

[5] Livy, Book XLIV, chap. 10.

[6] See ibid., chap. 46.

plain be southwards, to the west of the marshes and the gulf? Or should it be eastwards, to the north of them?

The southward direction was the less attractive of the two. Immediately to the south of 'the Gardens of Midas' the Macedonian aggressors would encounter the main body of the Brygoi, who commanded the strip of plain between Bermion and the sea from their fastnesses in the eastern recesses of Bermion. If the Argeadai were to succeed in subduing the Brygoi, they would find themselves, at the next stage southward, in Pieria; and this would be, for practical purposes, a cul-de-sac; for the three difficult passes—those via Petra, Lapathous, and Tempe—that lead out of Pieria all lead, like the Pórtes Pass, into Thessaly; and at this date the Argeadai had no prospect of being able to make any conquests in that quarter. It was not till King Arkhelaos' day, towards the close of the fifth century B.C., that the Argead Kingdom became powerful enough to be able to interfere effectively in the affairs of a Thessaly which, by that date, had come to be fatally divided against itself.

The prizes to be won by a successful advance along the eastward route were more alluring. In this direction the narrow strip of plain between the mountains and the coast broadened out northwards beyond Pella. From a point, due east of Pella, on the present course of the Axios—the point, that is, at which the Axios probably entered the sea in the sixth and fifth centuries B.C.—the plain expands inland and becomes about twenty-four miles deep before it ends at the southern exit of the Ghevgheli defile—the farthest down-stream of the four defiles through which the Axios works its way between Pelagonia and Lower Macedon.[1] 'The downlands just west of the Axios and between the Axios and Echeidoros and again between the Echeidoros and Salonika are by far the most fertile parts of Central Macedonia.'[2] This fertile country on the far side of the Emathian plain was the Argeadai's objective in their advance beyond Edessa, and it beckoned them eastward instead of southward. After this desirable region had been acquired by Macedon, it attracted her capital away from Edessa to Pella.

The possession of Edessa, and of 'the Gardens of Midas' below Edessa, probably carried with it the possession of the rest of the course of the Telovo River eastward to its confluence with the Loudias. The country west of the Loudias was γῆ Μακεδονίς in 480 B.C. according to Herodotus;[3] and this presumably means territory that was already Macedonian before the Argeadai conquered Bottiaia; for, in the same passage, Herodotus

[1] See Part II, chap. 4, p. 81, n. 9.
[2] Casson, op. cit., p. 80. Cp. p. 57. 'These . . . downlands are more thickly sown with ancient sites than any other parts' (ibid., p. 80). 'The Mygdonian lowlands are particularly fertile, and during the years 1916–1918 the British Army was able, by sowing large areas, to provide almost enough grain for its own purposes' (ibid., p. 57).
[3] Book VII, chap. 127.

makes the River Loudias Bottiaia's western boundary. In advancing eastward, the Argeadai must first have conquered and annexed Almopia in
the upper valley of the Loudias. Though small, Almopia is fertile;[1] and,
even if it had not been worth having in itself, the Argeadai would have
had to master it before advancing farther eastward. They could not have
ventured to leave an independent Almopia to threaten their left flank.
In the plain, the next country beyond the Loudias was Bottiaia. After the
Argeadai had conquered not only Bottiaia but the narrow strip of
Paeonian territory along the lower Axios,[2] Macedonian Bottiaia extended
eastward to the Axios, which was its boundary with Mygdonia.[3] Even
so, Bottiaia had a short seaboard, with room on it for no more than two
cities, Pella and Ikhnai.[4] Mygdonia, to the east of the Axios, was the
country that the Argeadai had coveted. It contained the fertile arable
land. Mygdonia was bounded on the north-east by the hill-country of
Krestonia; on the south, however, Mygdonia included the narrow but
long and fertile basin of Lake Bolbe, between the Crestonian highlands
and the mountain range, running east and west, which divides the Bolbe
basin from the Chalcidic Peninsula.[5] This southern strip of Mygdonia
extended eastwards, beyond the Bolbe basin, through the Arethousa
defile to the western shore of the Gulf of Argilos (now called the Gulf
of Réndina, or of Orfaná). By the year 511 B.C. the Argeadai had conquered not only Bottiaia and Mygdonia but also Anthemous, to the
south of Mygdonia, at the head of the Thermaic Gulf; for, in that year,
King Amyntas I offered Anthemous to Hippias.[6]

In building up so extensive a kingdom from such small beginnings,
the Argeadai were indebted chiefly to their own ability, foresight, and
persistence, but they also owed a good deal to Fortune. On at least
three occasions, other people 'worked for the King of Macedon' undesignedly but efficaciously. In each of these three cases, King Alexander I
was the fortunate beneficiary.

Alexander was helped undesignedly by the south Greek allies when—
fighting, not for the liberation of Macedon, but in self-defence—they
enabled Macedon to liberate herself, and incidentally to carry her
eastern frontier forward to the west bank of the lower Strymon, by
winning their decisive victory over the Persian Empire in 480–479 B.C.
Alexander had been compelled to submit to the Persian Empire in 492 B.C.,
when his kingdom had been occupied by Mardonios. In 480–479 B.C. he
had been compelled to fight on the Persian side. To be liberated by

---

[1] Geyer, op. cit., p. 10.   [2] Thucydides, Book II, chap. 99.
[3] Herodotus, Book VII, chap. 123.
[4] Herodotus, ibid. According to Strabo, Book VII, frag. 20, Abydon was destroyed by the
Argeadai. According to Strabo, Book VII, fragm. 22, Bottaïke also contained the city of
Aloros, which Herodotus does not mention.
[5] For this range, see Leake, op. cit., vol. iii, p. 162.   [6] See p. 137 above.

Xerxes' victorious opponents was something more than Alexander could have hoped for before the war's astonishing denouement.[1]

Before that, the Persian Emperor Darius had worked for Alexander twice.

When Megabazos, on Darius' instructions, deported the Siropaiones and Paioplai to Phrygia,[2] the Paiones' hold on the lower Strymon valley must have been permanently weakened, even though some of the deportees managed to make their way back home in 499 B.C. This will have facilitated the expansion of the Argead Kingdom up to the right (west) bank of the Strymon as far up-stream as the Rupel gorge out of which the Strymon debouches, between the Kerkine and Orbelos ranges, into the plain through which it runs on its lower course. We know that it was Alexander I who annexed Bisaltike, the Thracian kingdom between the west bank of the Strymon, along the river's lowest reach, and the north-eastern bounds of Mygdonia and Krestonia. It was Alexander I who founded a Macedonian city, which he named 'Euporia',[3] near the Bisaltian mines, which he had now appropriated. We do not know whether the annexation to Macedon of Krestonia and Sintike was Alexander I's work, and, if it was, whether these two other territories between Mygdonia and the Strymon were annexed by him at the same time as Bisaltike. These two other districts seem likely in any case to have been annexed to Macedon simultaneously with each other, if there is any substance in the conjecture that the Tyrsenoi and Pelasgoi in Krestonia, and the Sinties to the north-east of them round Lake Butkova, were, all alike, refugees from Lemnos and Imbros.[4]

Whatever the nationality of the Sinties between Lake Butkova and the right bank of the Strymon may have been, they were certainly not Paiones. They were a wedge of alien nationality that insulated from each other the Odomantoi Paiones along the left bank of the lower Strymon and the Derronaioi Paiones in the valleys of the Strumnica

[1] Alexander I was not, of course, the only beneficiary from Xerxes' disaster. While Alexander regained his independence and gained the Strymon frontier, the colonial Chalcidians gained the refugee Bottiaioi's city Olynthos. After the campaign of 480 B.C., Xerxes' general Artabazos, suspecting the Olynthian Bottiaioi of intending to revolt, besieged and captured Olynthos, massacred the inhabitants, and placed the city in the safe-keeping (so he thought) of a Chalcidian, Kritoboulos of Torone. In consequence, Olynthos became a permanent possession of the Chalcidians when, in 479 B.C., the Persians evacuated their conquests in Europe (Herodotus, Book VIII, chap. 127). The possession of Olynthos, which carried with it an hegemony over the remnant of the refugee Bottiaioi, strengthened the Chalcidians so much that, in the second decade of the fourth century B.C., they nearly succeeded in breaking up the Argead Kingdom and reigning in its stead. The party that 'worked for the King of Macedon' on this occasion by frustrating the Chalcidians was Sparta.

[2] See Part II, chap. 5, pp. 95–7.

[3] For Euporia, see Steph. Byz., s.v., and Ptolemy, *Geographia*, Book II, chap. 32. See also the present Part, chap. 5, p. 96, n. 2.

[4] See pp. 133, 134, 138.

right-bank tributary of the Strymon and the Bregalnica left-bank tributary of the Axios. This wedge must have been inserted here deliberately either by Alexander I or by one of his successors. But the opening for inserting it will have been prepared for the Argead Kingdom, unintentionally, by Darius I's general Megabazos when he deported the Siropaiones and Paioplai *circa* 511 B.C. Before these deportations the south-eastern Paiones must have occupied the whole of the lower Strymon plain to the east of Bisaltike and must have been immediate neighbours of their north-western kinsmen the Derronaioi. Without Megabazos' previous intervention, the Macedonian wedge in Sintike might not have been driven between the two fractions of the Paiones so easily.

The second occasion on which Darius I worked undesignedly for the King of Macedon was when his general Mardonios occupied Macedon in 492 B.C. Alexander I submitted,[1] but the independent Brygoi, to the south of Edessa, had the audacity to make a night attack on Mardonios' camp, in which Mardonios himself was wounded. Mardonios retorted by subjugating the Brygoi; and, in these hostilities, the Persians suffered heavy casualties.[2] After the Brygoi's resistance had been overcome, Mardonios seems to have made Skydra,[3] a Brygan city in the plain, into the administrative capital of a new Persian province, which was to include Macedon and other existing and future Persian acquisitions to the west of the Strymon.

For this purpose, Skydra was a good choice. Its site, which has been ascertained through the evidence of inscriptions there,[4] commanded the southward road leading, between Mount Bermion and the Loudias marshes, to Berrhoia and thence, via Ballai and Agassai, into Pieria, with its three alternative passes leading on into Thessaly. In the three latest of the six surviving official lists of the lands of the Persian Empire,[5] the new dahyāuš 'Skudra' figures side by side with the older transmarine province.[6] The Persian plan was grandiose, but the achievement was short-lived. After thirteen years, Persian and Macedonian fortunes were reversed as a result of the south Greeks' victory over Xerxes in 480–479 B.C. Instead of the Kingdom of Macedon's being merged in a

---

[1] Herodotus, Book VI, chap. 44.

[2] Herodotus, Book VI, chap. 65.

[3] For the location of Skydra, see Ptolemy, *Geographia*, Book II, chap. 36. See also Strabo, Book VII, chap. 7, § 9 (C. 327) (Κύδραι δὲ Βρύγων); Pliny, *Historia Naturalis*, Book IV, chap. 10, § 34; Steph. Byz., s.v. Σκύδρα, citing Theagenes.

[4] Geyer, op. cit., p. 10.

[5] Darius' inscription *e* at Susa; Darius' tomb-inscription at Naqš-i-Rustam; Xerxes' inscription *h* at Persepolis.

[6] This older transmarine province, which included the country between the Dardanelles, the lower Danube, and the lower Strymon, is called 'Those who are beyond the sea' ('Tyaiy para draya') in DS*e*, 'The Saka beyond the Sea' ('Saka tyaiy para draya') in DN*a*, and 'those who live beyond the Sea' (Tyaiy para draya dārayatiy') in XP*h*.

Persian province centred on the territory of the Brygoi, the Persian ascendancy evaporated and the territory of the Brygoi was incorporated in the liberated Kingdom of Macedon. In crushing the Brygoi in 492 B.C., as in deporting the Siropaiones and the Paioplai in 511 B.C., the Persian Empire had been preparing the ground for the Kingdom of Macedon to occupy.

At what stage did the Argeadai annex Pieria? Was this a sequel to their annexation of the Brygan country that lay between Pieria and Edessa? The Argeadai had an open road to Pieria after Skydra had fallen into their hands. On the other hand, so long as the Brygoi retained their independence, they screened Pieria from Macedonian attack via the coastal plain. The asylum eventually found by the refugee Pieres, after the Macedonian conquest and annexation of the original Pieria, lay to the east of the lower Strymon, between Mount Pangaios and the sea; and this location may indicate that the Pieres were not evicted until after Alexander I had advanced Macedon's eastern frontier to the right bank of the lower Strymon—that is to say, not till after 479 B.C. However, Herodotus mentions the refugee Pieres as being already *in situ* in 480 B.C., and as being one of three peoples that were participants at that date in the mining industry in the Pangaios district.[1] If this is correct, the eviction of the Pieres from Pieria must have been earlier than that, and it must have taken place at a date at which the Brygoi were still independent of Macedon. If so, the Argeadai must have invaded and conquered Pieria by the difficult, but not impracticable, track that led from the Haliakmon valley along the west flank of the Pierian Range, overhanging the right bank of the Haliakmon where the river traverses the Vérria gorge. This would have been a remarkable military feat. It would also have been a delicate political enterprise, if this section of the Haliakmon Valley lay, not in the Argeadai's home territory, but in the autonomous kingdom of Elimeia.[2]

---

[1] Herodotus, Book VII, chap. 112.
[2] See p. 141, n. 1.

PART III

THE RISE AND DECLINE OF SPARTA

1. *Our Sources of Information*

SPARTA played a part of first-class importance in the history of the Hellenic World from at least as early as midway through the eighth century B.C. until 371 B.C., the date of her disaster at Leuktra; and, though the territorial losses that followed this disaster cut away the ground from under the social and military organization on which Sparta's power had been based since *circa* 600 B.C., this crippling blow did not break the Spartans' spirit and did not move them to withdraw from the international arena. Lakedaimon was the only continental European Greek state that refused in 338 B.C. to join Philip II of Macedon's Confederation of Corinth; she rose in arms against Alexander III in 332 B.C.; she joined with Athens in 266 B.C. in contesting Antigonos Gonatas' hegemony over continental European Greece; and, after Antigonos had defeated the allies, Sparta still did not withdraw from the arena, as Athens withdrew, once for all, from that time onwards.[1] In 227 B.C. Sparta reaugmented her military man-power at the price of a drastic social revolution and proceeded to fight for the hegemony over continental European Greece against the combined forces of Macedon and the Achaean Confederation. This temerity brought on Sparta, in 222 B.C., a defeat that was comparable to her disaster in 371 B.C.; and this time, for the first time in Sparta's history, the City of Sparta itself was occupied by a victorious enemy army. Yet, even after this, Sparta still stayed in the arena and dared, in 195 B.C., to defy Rome, who had just overthrown Macedon. Sparta was now put out of action at last through being deprived of all her remaining dependent perioecic city-states, and perhaps of part of her own remaining Spartiate territory as well. Considering the importance of Sparta's record over this period of not less than 550 years, it is remarkable that the surviving information about her domestic history should be, as it is, scantier and more enigmatic than our

[1] This refusal of Sparta's to submit to Philip, Alexander, and their successors is noted by Plutarch in *Instituta Laconica*, § 42.

information about the contemporary history of other Hellenic states of relatively minor importance—not to speak of the relative abundance of our information about the contemporary history of Athens.

Our ignorance about Sparta is partly due to the deliberate policy of the Spartans themselves. By the year 418 B.C. they were making a point of not divulging either the strength of their forces in the field[1] or the number of their casualties.[2] Already, in 424 B.C., the prisoners captured on Sphakteria by the Athenians had been secretive under interrogation;[3] and, after the Lacedaemonian disaster at Leuktra, Epameinondas ascertained the number of Lacedaemonian dead only by insisting that the Lacedaemonians should not bury them till their allies had buried theirs. Even so, it is doubtful whether he succeeded in discovering how many of the Lacedaemonian dead were Spartiatai and how many of them were perioikoi.[4]

We do not know what public records the Lacedaemonian Government kept. Presumably there was a list of the names of the annually elected five ephors (or at least of one member of the board, if only one of the five served as the eponym for the year), since the date of the institution of the office; and there is no reason to doubt the correctness of the date arrived at by the Alexandrian scholars Eratosthenes and Apollodorus, which seems to be 755/4 B.C.[5] W. G. Forrest[6] is perhaps unduly sceptical in holding that the earlier entries in this list were fictitious. The only other Spartan public records about which there is no doubt[7] are the oracles obtained from Delphi, and perhaps filed at Sparta, by the Pythioi, who were officers of the kings of the two royal houses; and some of the oracles produced from the royal archives may have been spurious. There were rhetrai; but the meaning of this word is in dispute. It has been divergently interpreted as meaning an oracle from Delphi or a law passed by the public assembly of Spartiate peers (οἱ ὅμοιοι) or, again, a bill approved by Delphi before being presented to the Spartan public assembly. In any case, 'one of the so-called rhetrai' prohibited the committing of Spartan laws to writing, according to Plutarch.[8]

---

[1] Thucydides, Book V, chap. 68, § 2.

[2] Ibid., chap. 74, § 3.

[3] Thucydides, Book IV, chap. 40.

[4] See Pausanias, *Graeciae Descriptio*, Book IX, chap. 13, 11. οὕτω δὲ, Pausanias concludes, Λακεδαιμόνιοί τε ἔθαπτον τοὺς ἑαυτῶν, καὶ ἤδη Σπαρτιάτας ἐξελήλεγκτο εἶναι τοὺς κειμένους. This is, of course, a *non sequitur*.

[5] i.e. Olympiad 6, year 2, not Ol. 5, year 3 or year 4, which is the date given in the MSS. of Eusebius' and Jerome's chronicles. See Eduard Meyer, *Forschungen zur alten Geschichte* (Halle, 1892, Niemeyer), 1. Band, p. 247, with n. 1.

[6] W. G. Forrest, *A History of Sparta, 950–192 B.C.* (London, 1968, Hutchinson), p. 20.

[7] See V. Ehrenberg, *Neugründer des Staates* (Munich, 1925, Beck), pp. 11–12.

[8] Plutarch, *Lycurgus*, chap. 13.

There appear to be only two Laconian inscriptions for which a date earlier than the second century B.C. is claimed: the ὄϝα Ἀρκαλὸν inscription[1] and Damonon's record of his victories in chariot races and horse races.[2] The date attributed to the ὄϝα inscription on the strength of the style of the lettering is early fifth century or late sixth century B.C. This is, of course, possible, but the inscription is no longer extant, and its solitariness brings it under some suspicion. There are no early inscriptions recording the names of public officers or the acts of the gerousia or of the assembly.[3]

There also appears to be only one known Spartan writer on the subject of Spartan history and institutions whose date is earlier than the second century B.C. This is King Pausanias. After he had gone into exile in 395 B.C., he is said to have published a political pamphlet which dealt with the alleged legislation of Lycurgus and was based on oracles. The passage of Strabo's *Geographica* containing this information[4] is in tatters, and the lacunae in it can be filled by conjectures that make the pamphlet either friendly to Lycurgus or hostile to him.[5] Whichever way King Pausanias' bias may have inclined, the circumstances in which he was writing make it probable that his bias will have been strong and his approach have been polemical. If the text of his pamphlet had survived, it would have been a tricky source for the history of Sparta.

King Pausanias' pamphlet was a rare breach of the Spartans' habitual deliberate reticence about public affairs throughout the five and a half centuries, ending in 195 B.C., during which Lakedaimon was a power in the Hellenic World. The Spartans held their peace and the stones of Sparta did not cry out. The dates of Sparta's victory over Argos *circa* 544 B.C.[6] and of her victory over Athens in 404 B.C. are two peaks in the curve of Sparta's power; yet, at either of these dates, a visitor to Sparta would have found the city less impressive than it was when the antiquary Pausanias visited it in the second century of the Christian Era—a time at which Sparta was only one among the innumerable minor provincial towns of the Roman Empire. Thucydides has warned future archaeologists not to base estimates of the power of the Lacedaemonian

---

[1] *C.I.G.*, vol. i, No. 15; *S.G.D.*, i (iii) 2, No. 4412; *I.G.*, vol. v, fasc. 1, p. 151, No. 722. See A. J. Beattie, 'An Early Laconian Lex Sacra', in the *Classical Quarterly*, vol. xlv (1951), pp. 46–58. See also the present work, Part III, p. 262, n. 3. A. H. M. Jones, *Sparta* (Oxford, 1967, Blackwell), p. 165, holds that the earliest extant Spartan inscriptions date from after the beginning, in 31 B.C., of the Age of the Principate.

[2] Text in F. Solmsen, *Inscriptiones Graecae ad Inlustrandas Dialectos Selectae* (Leipzig, 1930, Teubner), pp. 34–6.

[3] K. M. T. Chrimes, *Ancient Sparta: A Re-examination of the Evidence* (Manchester, 1949, University Press), pp. 85 and 206.

[4] Book VIII, chap. 5, § 5 (C. 366).

[5] See the pro-Lycurgan reconstruction of the text in Meyer, op. cit., pp. 233–4.

[6] For the date, see H. T. Wade-Gery, 'A Note on the Origin of the Spartan Gymnopaidiai', in the *Classical Quarterly*, vol. xliii (1949), pp. 79–88, on p. 79.

state at its zenith on the material remains of the city as it stood at that date; and this warning has been borne out by the findings of archaeological exploration at Sparta in the present century.[1]

Thucydides wrote[2] shortly before or after the year 400 B.C.:

If Sparta were to cease to be inhabited, and if the temples and the foundations of the city's lay-out were to survive, I think that posterity at a distant future date would find it quite incredible that Sparta's power really corresponded to its reputation. Nevertheless, the truth is that Sparta possesses two-fifths of the Peloponnese and exercises a hegemony over the whole of it, not to speak of her numerous allies farther afield. All the same, the city would appear comparatively insignificant, because it has not been unified physically and does not go in for costly temples and public works, but is just a congeries of villages in the Hellenic World's antique style. On the other hand, if Athens were to meet with the same fate, the city's material remains would suggest an estimate of the state's power which would be twice as great as the reality.

What positive evidence, then, do we possess for Sparta's history and institutions during the centuries of the Lacedaemonian state's political power in the Hellenic World? While Sparta's political power during this age is not reflected in the remains of contemporary buildings, her artistic prowess, during a century and a half ending *circa* 550 B.C., is reflected in the quality of her contemporary painted pottery and metallic figurines.[3] We have fragments of the poetry of two seventh-century-B.C. poets, Alkman and Tyrtaios,[4] who wrote in and for Sparta, whether or not they themselves were Spartan-born. We have the constitutional rhetra and its rider (if this document is genuine and if the rider is really a subsequent addition to the original text); and this document embodies some, though not all, of the measures of the constitutional reform that was carried out, probably, towards the close of the seventh century B.C. Finally, we have the works of a series of non-Lacedaemonian Greek historians, political scientists, sociologists, and antiquaries which begins with Herodotus, who was writing, probably, during the third quarter of the fifth century B.C., and ends with Pausanias (the antiquary, not the king), who was writing in the second century of the Christian Era.

[1] Forrest, in *A History*, p. 15, points out that, so far, there has been much more archaeological exploration of the prehistoric and Mycenaean stages of the history of Laconia and Messenia than of the Hellenic stage. Until this stage has been explored with comparable thoroughness, archaeology will continue to be of little help to us in supplementing our unsatisfactory literary evidence for the history and institutions of Sparta.

[2] In Book I, chap. 4.

[3] See G. L. Huxley, *Early Sparta* (London, 1962, Faber), pp. 62–4; Guy Dickins, 'The Growth of Spartan Policy', in the *Journal of Hellenic Studies*, vol. xxxii (1912), pp. 1–42, on pp. 11–12.

[4] L. Pareti, *Storia di Sparta Arcaïca*, Parte I (Florence, 1920, Le Monnier), pp. 207 and 223, points out that Tyrtaios is our only genuine authority for the history of the First Spartano-Messenian War. Cp. Jones, op. cit., p. 2.

Herodotus and Thucydides, who is the other fifth-century-B.C. non-Spartan Greek student of Lacedaemonian affairs whose work has survived,[1] describe Sparta as she was, in so far as they knew the facts. On the other hand, in appraising our later non-Spartan Greek literary information about Sparta, from the early fourth century B.C. onwards, we have always to allow for the possibility that the findings of observation and study may have been coloured to some extent either by political partiality or by ideological preconceptions.

Political partiality is apparent in at least one of Xenophon's works, the *Lakedaimonión Politeia*,[2] and this is, indeed, only to be expected, considering that Xenophon had been banished from his own fatherland, Athens, had been given military employment by the Lacedaemonian Government, and had served these foreign employers of his so satisfactorily that they had endowed him with a small estate at Skillous in Triphylia. Xenophon's partiality for Sparta is natural but unfortunate, because he was probably better informed about Sparta than any foreigner had been since the foreign poets, musicians, architects, and practitioners of the visual arts who had visited Sparta, and had worked there, in the seventh and sixth centuries B.C. Xenophon's information about Sparta is relatively copious, and, in spite of his prejudice in Sparta's favour, it is utilizable, since the partiality with which it is coloured is not difficult to detect and discount.

After the defeat of Athens by Sparta and her allies in the war of 431–404 B.C., some eminent Athenians who were then reacting against Athenian democracy eulogized Sparta's institutions and êthos as a foil for their condemnation of their own country's regime and ideology; and this Attic use of Sparta as ammunition for propaganda spread wide and

---

[1] Chrimes, in *Ancient Sparta*, p. 206, points out that we have no literary evidence for Spartan history between the sixth-century-B.C. poets and these fifth-century-B.C. historians.

[2] In the present book, the *Lakedaimonión Politeia* is taken as being a genuine work of Xenophon's, and it is drawn upon extensively; for, if it is genuine, then obviously it is authoritative. This pamphlet has, however, been condemned, as being spurious, by at least two modern scholars: Chrimes, in *The Respublica Lacedaemoniorum Ascribed to Xenophon* (Manchester, 1948, University Press), and F. R. Wüst, 'Laconica', I, 'Zur pseudo-xenophontischen Λακεδαιμονίων Πολιτεία, in *Klio*, 37. Band (1959), pp. 53–60. Wüst has put his finger on a number of details in the account, in the *Lak. Pol.*, of Spartan institutions and practices which, so Wüst argues, are incorrect apropos of Sparta in Agesilaos' reign, but are correct apropos of her in Kleomenes III's reign. Many of Wüst's points are slight in themselves, but the cumulative effect is telling. All the same, they do not amount to a conclusive proof that the *Lak. Pol.* was written, not in the first decade of the fourth century B.C., but at some date between 227 B.C. (the year of Kleomenes III's revolution) and 222 B.C. (the year of his fall).

Of course, there are stumbling-blocks in the *Lak. Pol.* even for scholars—and these are still in a majority—who accept it as being a genuine work of Xenophon's. The notorious crux is the discrepancy in tone between the critical chapter 14 of the pamphlet and the laudatory chapters 1–13 and 15.

lasted long.[1] It was ironical that Sparta should have been idealized by foreigners at the very moment when both her man-power and her citizens' moral stamina were proving inadequate for meeting the challenge with which Sparta had just been confronted by a sudden great increase in her political power and her wealth. This axe-grinding picture of Sparta was not true to life. Kritias and Plato were not so much interested in giving an accurate account of what Sparta really was and had been as they were in creating an imaginary Spartan model for Athens to copy. Their portrayals of Sparta were political and social propaganda, not history; but they came to be mistaken for genuine history owing to the dearth of authentic records, and this infusion of propaganda eventually coloured the conventional picture of Spartan history and institutions to an extent that must be considerable, though it is hard to gauge.[2] The latest, but perhaps not the least effective, of these foreign writers on Sparta who had an ideological and political axe to grind was Sphairos of Borysthenes, the Stoic mentor of King Kleomenes III (*regnabat* 237–222 B.C.).[3]

In contrast to this roseate haze in which Sparta was enveloped by non-Spartan Greek philosophers in the course of the fourth and third centuries B.C., the details of certain Spartan practices and institutions are illuminated by contemporary inscriptions which begin at last, at Sparta, in the second century B.C., after Sparta's final loss of power, and which are numerous throughout the quarter of a millennium of the Age of the Principate. Documentary inscriptions are the antithesis of ideology and propaganda. Can they serve as an antidote to it? They could if the period covered by the inscriptions were the period to which the ideology and the propaganda relate: i.e. the centuries, ending in the year 195 B.C., during which Lakedaimon was a power in the Hellenic World. Unfortunately, the two periods are mutually exclusive, and attempts, such as Miss K. M. T. Chrimes's,[4] to use post-200-B.C. inscriptional data as evidence for the 'Lycurgan' agoge are as hazardous as they are tempting.

In truth, we have no means of telling how much of the 'Lycurgan' agoge survived the series of violent changes at Sparta during the

[1] See F. Ollier, *Le Mirage spartiate: étude sur l'idéalisation de Sparte dans l'antiquité grecque de l'origine jusqu'aux Cyniques* (Paris, 1st ed. 1933, Boccard; 2nd ed. 1943, Les Belles Lettres). See also Forrest, *A History*, pp. 16–17.

[2] It has been over-emphasized, in the present writer's judgement, by E. Kessler, *Plutarchs Leben des Lykurgos* (Berlin, 1910, Weidmann).

[3] See Plutarch, *Cleomenes*, chap. 2, and F. Ollier, 'Le Philosophe stoïcien Sphairos et l'œuvre réformatrice des rois de Sparte Agis IV et Cléomène III', in *La Revue des études grecques*, vol. 49 (1936), pp. 536–70.

[4] Chrimes, *Ancient Sparta*, pp. 52, 85, 116–17, 137, 205, and, indeed, *passim*. Miss Chrimes concentrates on trying to reconstruct the 'Lycurgan' system of education for boys and epheboi.

half-century beginning in the year 227 B.C., in which King Kleomenes III revolutionized the constitution and diluted the citizen body constituted by holders of kleroi in Spartiate territory. Antigonos Doson seems to have reversed some of Kleomenes' acts when he occupied Sparta in 222 B.C.[1] The dual monarchy, which Kleomenes had abolished in 227 B.C., was restored, but this only momentarily, in 219–218 B.C. Sparta was then ruled by two despots in succession, Makhanidas and Nabis, of whom Nabis, at any rate, made some revolutionary social changes. In 192 B.C. Sparta was chevied into the Achaean Confederation; in 188 B.C. the Achaeans abrogated, at Sparta, the 'Lycurgan' constitution and agoge.[2] These were eventually restored by the Romans[3]—presumably in 146 B.C., when they dissolved the Achaean Confederation. From then onwards the Spartan state was under direct Roman suzerainty, and the inscriptions show that at Sparta, as in some other historic Greek city-states, there was an enthusiasm, in the Age of the Principate, for re-establishing ancient national institutions.[4] It is well known, however, that the would-be archaist is often an innovator *malgré lui*, for there are likely to be lacunae in his information about his country's past institutions, and his zeal may tempt him to use his imagination for filling these gaps in. Considering what the cumulative effect of all these distorting and disintegrating factors may have been, it seems rash to try to use inscriptional data from the Age of the Principate as materials for reconstructing the original 'Lycurgan' regime that had been established probably before 600 B.C.[5] This would be as rash as it would be to try to use the buildings and monuments that Pausanias saw and described in the second century of the Christian Era, and those that Western archaeologists have excavated in the twentieth century, as evidence for reconstructing the lay-out of the Sparta of Thucydides' day.

Another difficulty that confronts the student of Spartan history and institutions is the trickiness—perhaps, in part, deliberate—of the

---

[1] Plutarch, *Cleomenes*, chap. 30: καὶ νόμους καὶ πολιτείαν ἀποδούς. Pausanias, Book II, chap. 9, §§ 2–3, agrees that Λακεδαιμονίοις μὲν οὖν ἀπέδωκεν Ἀντίγονος καὶ Ἀχαιοὶ πολιτείαν τὴν πάτριον. He goes on to say: Λακεδαιμόνιοι δὲ ἄσμενοι Κλεομένους ἀπαλλαγέντες βασιλεύεσθαι μὲν οὐκέτι ἠξίωσαν, τὰ δὲ λοιπὰ καὶ ἐς τόδε διαμένει σφίσιν ἐκείνης τῆς πολιτείας. Here the word ἐκείνης is ambiguous. It might mean the πάτριος πολιτεία minus the monarchy, or it might mean Kleomenes' revolutionary constitution minus Kleomenes himself and the monarchy. See also Pausanias, Book VIII, chap. 27, § 16.

[2] 'Lycurgi leges moresque [imperatum ut] abrogarent' (Livy, Book XXXVIII, chap. 34; cp. Book XXXIX, chaps. 33 and 37). ἀνεῖλε γὰρ καὶ διέφθειρε τὴν Λυκούργειον ἀγωγήν, ἀναγκάσας τοὺς παῖδας αὐτῶν καὶ τοὺς ἐφήβους τὴν Ἀχαϊκὴν ἀντὶ τῆς πατρίου παιδείαν μεταβαλεῖν (Plutarch, *Philopoemen*, chap. 16). See also Polybius, Book XXII, chaps. 3, 7, 10, 11, 12; Book XXIII, chap. 4.

[3] Plutarch, *Philopoemen*, chap. 16; Pausanias, Book VIII, chap. 51, § 3.

[4] See P. Roussel, *Sparte* (Paris, 1939 and 1960, Boccard), pp. 152–4.

[5] At the same time, Miss Chrimes is justified in saying (*Ancient Sparta*, p. 205) that our cognizance of these inscriptions makes us better informed about Sparta than the fourth-century-B.C. students of Spartan institutions were.

Lacedaemonian official terminology and the slipshodness of non-Lacedaemonian Greek historians in their use of Lacedaemonian official terms.[1]

For instance, the Spartan state was invariably called οἱ Λακεδαιμόνιοι officially, by Spartans and non-Spartans alike.[2] We do not know at which stage in Sparta's history this usage was introduced;[3] it was well established by the fifth century B.C., and it lasted till Sparta's dominions were reduced, in 195 B.C., to the city-state territory (ἡ πολιτικὴ χώρα)[4] of Sparta herself. The Spartiatai are officially Lakedaimonioi in the assembly[5] and, above all, in the field.[6] The Spartan state is styled οἱ Λακεδαιμόνιοι in the text of a treaty;[7] and ἐς Λακεδαίμονα means 'to Sparta' in official contexts, e.g. the sending of dispatches[8] and of ambassadors,[9] and the convening of the representatives of the Peloponnesian League.[10] On the other hand, when the reference is to the City of Sparta in the physical sense—for instance, apropos of the earthquake of 466 or 464 B.C.—the topographical name Sparta, not the official title Lakedaimon, is employed.[11]

This usage is unparalleled in contemporary Hellenic practice,[12] and it is strange for two reasons. In the first place the politeuma—i.e. the politically effective citizen-body—within the Lakedaimonioi consisted exclusively of Spartiatai who were members of syssitia; and, in calling themselves 'Lakedaimonioi', these Spartan 'homoioi' were arrogating to themselves the right to act politically in the name of a community in which they were in a minority. The Spartiatai, homoioi and hypomeiones together, were outnumbered by the perioikoi and the emancipated helots (neodamodeis)—leaving out of account the unemancipated majority of the helots, who counted politically as being slaves and therefore, according to general Hellenic custom, as being politically null. It would have been logical for the Athenians, if they had chosen, to have styled themselves οἱ Ἀττικοί officially, since every freeborn native inhabitant of Attica was an Athenian citizen. The Spartiates' practice of styling themselves Λακεδαιμόνιοι officially flew in the face of the facts, and it was all the stranger because, in the second place, Sparta, not Lakedaimon, was,

---

[1] Forrest puts his finger on this point in *A History*, pp. 131–2.
[2] See Bölte in P.–W., Zweite Reihe, 3. Band, A2, cols. 1273–4.
[3] On this point, see, further, the present Part, chap. 2, section (ii) (a), below.
[4] Polybius, Book VI, chap. 45, § 3.
[5] e.g. Thucydides, Book I, chaps. 86–7.
[6] e.g. Herodotus, Book IX, chap. 28.
[7] Thucydides, Book V, chap. 18.
[8] Thucydides, Book IV, chap. 108; Xenophon, *Hellenica*, Book I, chap. i, § 23.
[9] Thucydides, Book I, chap. 72; Herodotus, Book IX, chap. 6.
[10] Thucydides, Book I, chap. 66.
[11] Thucydides, Book I, chap. 128.
[12] Ehrenberg, *Neugründer des Staates*, p. 108.

after all, the word that, in Spartan hearts, carried the emotional charge.[1] The point is illustrated in the peroration of a speech made in the Spartan assembly by the ephor Sthenelaïdas in 432 B.C., as reported—or plausibly composed—by Thucydides:[2] ψηφίζεσθε οὖν, ὦ Λακεδαιμόνιοι, ἀξίως τῆς Σπάρτης τὸν πόλεμον ('Lacedaemonians, vote for war and thereby show yourselves to be worthy sons of Sparta').

By thus equating themselves with the Lakedaimonioi, the Spartiatai eclipsed the non-Spartiate, mainly perioecic, majority of their fellow Lacedaemonians. A passage in which Pausanias equates the Lakedaimonioi with the Spartiatai, forgetting the existence of the perioecic Lacedaemonians, has been quoted already.[3] Herodotus, in his account of the campaign of Plataia in 479 B.C., records[4] that, in the Lacedaemonian contingent of the Greek ally forces, Spartiatai and perioikoi were represented in equal numbers, and he does not forget the perioecic Lacedaemonians in describing the ally order of battle.[5] At this point he states that each Spartiate hoplite was accompanied by seven helots, and each perioecic hoplite by one light-armed soldier, who was presumably a perioikos himself. When, therefore, Herodotus tells us that, after the battle, the Lacedaemonians buried their dead in three separate graves,[6] we expect the three to be for Spartiatai, helots, and perioikoi respectively. However, Herodotus assigns two graves out of the three to two different categories of Spartiatai,[7] and the third to the helots. Herodotus has forgotten the perioikoi, as Pausanias forgot them six centuries later.

Thucydides, too, seems to have forgotten the perioikoi in his description of the Lacedaemonian order of battle at Mantinea in 418 B.C.;[8] and Plutarch, or his source, seems to have anticipated Pausanias' mistake of equating Spartiatai and Lakedaimonioi in telling the story[9] of how Agesilaos contrived an ocular demonstration of his point that, though the Spartiatai were outnumbered by their allies, they alone were full-time professional soldiers. In Plutarch's version of this story, when the representatives, in Agesilaos' army, of all the civilian trades had successively stepped out of the ranks, only the Lacedaemonians were left. Plutarch must mean 'only the Spartans'; for the perioecic Lacedaemonian

---

[1] Similarly, 'British subjects' who are 'citizens of the United Kingdom' feel themselves to be English, Scottish, or Welsh (in Ulster, Protestant or Catholic), as the case may be.

[2] Book I, chap. 86.   [3] On p. 153, n. 4.

[4] In Book IX, chaps. 10 and 11.

[5] Ibid., chaps. 28 and 29.

[6] Ibid., chap. 85.

[7] For our present purpose, it makes no difference whether the special category of Spartiatai, who are alleged by Herodotus to have been buried separately from 'the rest of the Spartiatai', were priests (ἱρέες), which is the reading of the MSS., or were epheboi (ἱρένες), which is Valckenaer's emendation (see W. den Boer, *Laconian Studies* (Amsterdam, 1954, North Holland Publishing Co.), pp. 288–98.

[8] Book V, chap. 68. See further the present Part, chap. 5, Annex III.

[9] Plutarch, *Agesilaus*, chap. 26; *Apophthegmata Laconica*, Agesilaos, 72.

hoplites, like the non-Lacedaemonian hoplites in the army, were, in contrast to the Spartiatai, men who had to make their living as farmers,
artisans, or traders, and who could train and serve as soldiers in their
spare time only.

Besides writing 'Lakedaimonioi' where they meant 'Spartiatai' exclusively, non-Spartans were apt to write 'Spartiatai' where they meant
'homoioi' exclusively.[1] A clear case of this latter mistake is to be found
in Xenophon's report of a scene in the agora at Sparta.[2] Another possible
example of the same error is Thucydides' use of the word 'Spartiatai' in
recounting the surrender of the Lacedaemonian garrison on Sphakteria.[3]
Thucydides may be meaning 'homoioi', since Spartiatai who were not
homoioi could not be members of syssitia and were therefore presumably
ineligible for military service.[4]

In dealing with the new organization of the Lacedaemonian army that
was probably introduced at some date between 479 B.C. and 424 B.C.,[5]
both Thucydides, in his account of the Lacedaemonian order of battle
at Mantinea in 418 B.C.,[6] and Xenophon, in describing the same organization,[7] seem to have failed to appreciate the distinction between the terms
'lokhos', 'politike mora', and 'mora'. A mora seems to have been a
brigade of two lokhoi, one of which was entirely manned by perioikoi
while the companion-lokhos was manned by Spartiatai supplemented by
a contingent of perioikoi. A 'politike mora' seems to have been this
mainly or partly Spartiate lokhos if and when it was serving apart from
its all-perioecic companion-lokhos. These distinctions were tricky, but
a failure to appreciate them could make havoc of the true facts and
figures, as these two cases show.

One Spartan age-class term, 'eiren', is interpreted in incompatible
senses in one and the same passage of Plutarch's *Lycurgus*.[8] In this passage,
Plutarch states that the oldest class of παῖδες were called μελλείρενες; that
youths who were starting their second year since passing out of the
παῖδες-class were called εἰρένες; and that an εἰρήν was a young man who
had turned twenty. This account leaves a gap of one year between
melleirenes and eirenes and implies that youths were still called παῖδες
when they were nineteen. The true account seems to be that given by

---

[1] 'The term "Spartiatai" has a technical usage different from the popular one. In its
more accurate sense, it must denote a class of Spartan citizens with higher privileges than the
rest' (Chrimes, *Ancient Sparta*, p. 354; cp. p. 425, n. 1). It is correct that there were two
grades of Spartan citizens, and that these are sometimes confused with each other, as in the
instances cited in this paragraph. But it seems paradoxical to suggest that the use of 'Spartiatai' to mean 'homoioi' is more accurate than its use to mean 'homoioi and hypomeiones
together'.

[2] *Hellenica*, Book III, chap. 3, § 6.
[3] Book IV, chap. 38, § 3.
[4] See chap. 4, section (ii) of this Part.
[5] See chap. 5, section (iv).
[6] Book V, chap. 68.
[7] *Lak. Pol.*, chap. ii, § 4.
[8] Chap. 17.

the scholiast on Herodotus, Book IX, chap. 85, who makes the melleiren year the boy's thirteenth year, and makes the eiren-age run from the fourteenth to the twentieth year inclusive—i.e. makes it terminate, instead of starting, at the youth's twentieth birthday. This account makes sense, since, at his twentieth birthday, a Spartiate became liable to military service, and this would surely have made it impossible for him to serve as the permanent leader of a gang of boys at home. Moreover, the supervision exercised by the eiren gang-leader's elders over his conduct of his leadership[1] suggests that the eiren himself was not an adult. The Spartan age-groups below the minimum age for military service are discussed further at a later point in this Part.[2] All that needs to be noted in the present context is that there was no unanimity among non-Spartan observers of Spartan institutions over such a simple question of fact as the year-class or year-classes which the term 'eiren' denoted.

[1] Plutarch, *Lycurgus*, chap. 18.   [2] In chap. 4, section (iii).

2. Sparta's Conquest of Laconia and Messenia

(i) The Spartan Conquests and the Post-Mycenaean Völkerwanderung

SPARTA seems to have conquered Laconia and Messenia in the course of the eighth century B.C. This is the date indicated by our evidence as far as this goes. Yet some Greek authorities, followed by some modern scholars,[1] have confused this eighth-century-B.C. episode in the history of the southern two-fifths of the Peloponnese with the Völkerwanderung of North-West-Greek-speaking barbarians into Laconia round about the year 1200 B.C. The kleroi, and other holdings of land, which the Spartan homoioi had in their hands by the sixth century B.C., were sometimes alleged to have been distributed to their ancestors at the time of the Völkerwanderung.[2] The genealogies of the two Spartan royal houses, the Agiadai and the Eurypontidai, were extended backwards, by the insertion of fictitious names, both after and before those of the eponyms Agis and Eurypon, in order to make both houses into descendants of Herakles after currency had been given to the legend that the North-West-Greek-speaking migrants in the twelfth century B.C. had had Heraklids among their leaders.[3] Even the three categories of inhabitants of Sparta's post-eighth-century-B.C. domain—Spartiatai, helots, and perioikoi—are said to have originated at the time either of the Völkerwanderung or of its immediate sequel, though it is manifest that they were products of the political synoecism of Sparta and of the Spartan conquests by which this was followed.[4] The Spartiatai have been identified with the descendants of the post-Mycenaean North-West-Greek-speaking immigrants into Laconia,[5] the helots with the

[1] e.g. T. Lenschau, 'Die Entstehung des spartanischen Staates', in *Klio*, 30. Band (1937), pp. 269–89, on p. 278.

[2] See H. Berve, *Sparta* (Leipzig, 1937, Bibliographisches Institut), p. 20; Roussel, op. cit., pp. 31–2; Th. Meier, *Das Wesen der spartanischen Staatsordnung* (Aalen, 1962, Scientia Verlag: *Klio*, Beiheft 42), p. 36; V. Ehrenberg, 'Spartiaten und Lakedaimonier', in *Hermes*, 59. Band (1924), pp. 23–72, on p. 43; eundem, *Neugründer des Staates*, p. 40.

[3] E. Cavaignac, *Sparte* (Paris, 1948, Fayard), p. 10, maintains that the two Spartan royal houses were descended from the leaders of two war-bands of the Völkerwanderung Age. K. J. Neumann, 'Die Entstehung des spartanischen Staates', in *Die Historische Zeitschrift*, 96. Band (Neue Folge, 60. Band) (1906), pp. 1–80, on p. 8, cites Plato, *Laws*, Book III, 684 E, for the view that, at Sparta, the distribution of the land had been made at the time of the Völkerwanderung.

[4] The chronological gap between the post-Mycenaean Völkerwanderung and the synoecism of Sparta is noted by C. Busolt and H. Swoboda, *Griechische Staatskunde*, 3rd ed., Zweite Hälfte (Munich, 1926, Beck), 'Der Staat der Lakedaimonier', pp. 633–737, on pp. 644 and 647.

[6] 'The fully enfranchised Spartan peer must be a descendant of the original conquerors of Laconia' (H. Michell, *Sparta* (Cambridge, 1952, University Press), p. 36; cp. pp. 35 and 42).

descendants of the pre-Völkerwanderung inhabitants of the country,[1] the perioikoi sometimes with the immigrants[2] and sometimes with the natives.[3] Actually, there is no evidence that there was any difference in language or nationality between these three political categories within the Lacedaemonian state that the Spartan conquests brought into existence.[4] It is probable that the Laconians and Messenians in all three categories were of mixed origin.[5]

The Spartan conquests in the eighth century B.C. did not begin till a date that was about 400 years later than the date of the Völkerwanderung. The history of eighth-century-B.C. Laconia and Messenia is obscure; the history of the preceding four centuries is a blank.[6] Indeed, some modern scholars have held that the Völkerwanderung is legendary, not historical. This degree of scepticism is unwarranted; for the Greek tradition that the Mycenaean Age was followed by a Völkerwanderung is borne out by the dialect-map of the Greek World in the last millen-

[1] This seems to have been the view of Theopompus apud Athenaeum, Book VI, 272 a. See also Meier, op. cit., p. 33; Michell, op. cit., p. 10. Jones, *Sparta*, p. 11, thinks it unlikely that all non-Spartan Laconians were of pre-Völkerwanderung origin.

[2] Isocrates, *Panathenaïcus*, 177. This is Pareti's view. See op. cit., p. 206.

[3] Neumann in loc. cit., p. 52. F. Kiechle, *Lakonien und Sparta* (Munich, 1963, Beck), p. 112, n. 2, notes that the Skiritai, who were politically perioikoi, were Arcadians in nationality.

[4] In the fifth century B.C. the helots, including those in Messenia, spoke the same dialect as their Spartiate masters (Thucydides, Book IV, chap. 3, § 3; Book III, chap. 112, § 4). It is possible that the helots acquired this dialect from the Spartiatai after the conquest, but this seems improbable (see Berve, op. cit., p. 25), considering the helots' overwhelming superiority in numbers. If one party did borrow the common dialect from the other, the borrowers are more likely to have been the Spartiatai. Pareti, op. cit., pp. 138–9, maintains, in spite of Thucydides' express statement, that the Messenian helots spoke a pre-North-West-Greek dialect, though he concedes that the Laconian helots did not. Cp. ibid., p. 223, where Pareti makes the River Pamisos the linguistic frontier. Kiechle, *Lakonien und Sparta*, p. 103; Ehrenberg, 'Spartiaten und Lakedaimonier', p. 53; B. Niese, 'Neue Beiträge zur Geschichte und Landeskunde Lakedaimons: die lakedaimonischen Periöken', in *Nachrichten von der Königlichen Gesellschaft der Wissenschaften zu Göttingen*: philologisch-historische Klasse (1906), pp. 101–42, on pp. 106 and 136; idem, 'Zur Verfassungsgeschichte Lakedaimons', in *Die historische Zeitschrift*, 62. Band (Neue Folge, 26. Band) (1889), pp. 58–84, on p. 76, hold that there was no difference between the helots' and the Spartiates' dialect. Miss Chrimes holds (*Ancient Sparta*, pp. 252 and 277–9; cp. Roussel, op. cit., pp. 20–1, 32–3) that both Laconia and Messenia were already North-West-Greek-speaking before the Spartan conquest.

[5] Kiechle, *Lakonien und Sparta*, p. 96, conjectures that the Spartans admitted some of the pre-Völkerwanderung Greek inhabitants of Laconia into their body politic. See also Ehrenberg, 'Spartiaten und Lakedaimonier', pp. 51 and 57; D. Lotze, Μεταξὺ Ἐλευθέρων καὶ Δούλων (Berlin, 1959, Akademie-Verlag), holds (p. 72) that the helots were of mixed origin, and he cites (p. 72) Pausanias, Book IV, chap. 3, § 6, for a tradition that the pre-Völkerwanderung inhabitants of Messenia had come to terms with the North-West-Greek-speaking invaders. Cp. Strabo, *Geographica*, Book VIII, chap. 4, § 7 (C. 361).

[6] As Forrest points out in *A History*, p. 25, archaeology shows that all settlements in Laconia except Amyklai were destroyed *circa* 1200 B.C. Hardly any Late Helladic III C pottery has been found in Laconia, and there is a hiatus of about 200 years between Laconian Late Helladic III B pottery and Laconian Proto-Geometric. Hellenic Sparta is a new town; no Mycenaean remains have been found there.

nium B.C.,[1] in so far as this map can be reconstructed from the evidence of inscriptions and literature. The dialect-map reveals a thrust of North-West-Greek-speakers across the Greek-speaking World from north-west to south-east, and it shows this thrust splitting the speakers of other Greek dialects into mutually isolated groups, sundered from each other by the entering wedge of North-West-Greek-speakers. This retrospective evidence from the subsequent dialect-map is good as far as it goes, but it does not go very far; and it is the only trustworthy evidence that we have for the Völkerwanderung itself and for its sequel during the next 400 years.

To confuse the eighth-century-B.C. Spartan conquests with the Völker-wanderung of *circa* 1200 B.C. is therefore an unwarranted and egregious chronological and historical error. It is as if one were to confuse the conquests made in the fourteenth century of the Christian Era by the city-state of Milan at the expense of neighbouring north-Italian city-states with the Lombard migration into Italy in A.D. 568; and the Heraklid genealogy of the two Spartan royal houses is as fictitious[2] as the genealogy of the Visconti would be if we were to fabricate for them an ancestry that would make them lineal descendants, in an unbroken line, of the Lombard war-lord Alboin. We readily recognize that, in the history of Italy, the events of the sixth century of the Christian Era and the events of the fourteenth century have no direct connection with each other; *inter enim iectast vitai pausa*. Similarly, in the history of Greece, there is no direct connection between the events of the twelfth century B.C. and those of the eighth century B.C.[3]

Such evidence as we have for the sequel to the post-Mycenaean Völkerwanderung indicates that the North-West-Greek-speakers were not the only immigrants from the north who established themselves, at the time of the Völkerwanderung, in Laconia and Messenia. The evidence also indicates that, though the North-West-Greek dialect eventually became predominant in both regions, the dialect previously spoken there was not supplanted everywhere completely. This, in turn, indicates that the previous population was not completely exterminated or evicted. There must have been some fusion between natives and immigrants; and this is, of course, what we should expect *a priori*.

[1] See W. Norvin, 'Zur Geschichte der spartanischen Eunomia', in *Classica et Mediaevalia*, ii (Copenhagen, 1939, Gyldendal), pp. 247–93, on p. 249, and the present work, Part I, chap. 3, p. 20.

[2] See Pareti, *Storia di Sparta Arcaïca*, p. 72.

[3] Grote, with his usual acumen, perceived that 'the institutions of Sparta were not Dorian but peculiar to herself' (*A History of Greece*, Part II, chap. 6 (Everyman's Library edition, vol. iii, pp. 112–86, on p. 116). See also, to the same effect, Niese, 'Zur Verfassungsgeschichte Lakedaimons', p. 80; Neumann, loc. cit., pp. 1–80, on pp. 11 and 64, citing Thucydides, Book III, chap. 18, § 1; C. Jannet, *Les Institutions sociales et le droit civil à Sparte*, 2nd ed. (Paris, 1880, Pedone-Lauriel), pp. 15–16.

For instance, inscriptions testify that the Poseidon of Cape Tainaron continued to be called, Arcadian-wise, Pohoidan, and did not come to be called, North-West-Greek-wise, Poteidan. This, again, is what we should expect, since the Tainaron peninsula (the Mani) is a natural fastness in which, on other occasions too, antique practices have survived after they have been abandoned in other parts of the Greek World. Down to a late date in the ninth century of the Christian Era, the Olympian pantheon was still being worshipped in the Mani, some five centuries after the Roman Emperor Theodosius I had suppressed pre-Christian religion elsewhere.[1] The festival in Poseidon's honour was called Pohoidaia at Thouria and at Helos,[2] and the form Ποθοιδᾶνος (genitive) occurs on an inscription found at a point between the sites of Amyklai and Vaphio.[3] Tzakonia—a natural fastness between the Parnon Range and the east coast of the southern Peloponnese—is today the only part of Greece in which a dialect of Greek not derived from the Attic koinê is still being spoken today. The Tzakonian dialect is descended from North-West Greek; and Herodotus informs us[4] that the inhabitants of Kynouria (i.e. Tzakonia) had survived the North-West-Greek invasion of the Peloponnese without being displaced, but had afterwards gradually come to speak North-West Greek, instead of their native dialect, as a result of their having become subject to the North-west-Greek-speaking Argives.[5]

One other community of pre-North-West-Greek-speaking Peloponnesian Greeks, a fragment of the Minyai,[6] had survived by taking refuge in yet another Laconian natural fastness: the 'shelf' on the Laconian side of the ridge of the Taÿgetos Range which, in the last millennium B.C., was known as Therai,[7] meaning 'the hunting grounds'. Taÿgetos rises from the plain of 'Hollow Lakedaimon' in two storeys: first a wall of cliffs, split by deep precipitous ravines which have given 'Hollow Lakedaimon' its second Homeric epithet, κητώεσσα; behind the cliffs, a 'shelf', with the present-day village of Anavrýti on it, overhanging the plain from Xerokámboi to Mistrá; and finally, set back from the 'shelf' and rising high above it, the chain of peaks now called Pendedháktylon, Pausanias' Taleton and Euoras.[8]

[1] See Part II, chap. 1, p. 55.
[2] Kiechle, *Lakonien und Sparta*, p. 14.
[3] Ibid., pp. 14 and 102–3.
[4] In Book VIII, chap. 73.
[5] ἐκδεδωρίευνται δὲ ὑπό τε Ἀργείων ἀρχόμενοι καὶ τοῦ χρόνου, ἐόντες Ὀρνεῆται καὶ περίοικοι (Herodotus, ibid.).
[6] These Laconian Minyai seem likely to have been refugees from Pylos (see Part I, chap. 2, p. 13, n. 5). They certainly were not refugees from Lemnos, as Herodotus alleges (Book IV, chaps. 145–9; cp. Book VIII, chap. 73).
[7] See Pausanias, Book III, chap. 20, § 5.
[8] Pausanias, ibid.

On the same 'shelf' in Pausanias' day there was a shrine called the Lapithaion whose name indicates that North-East-Greek-speaking refugees from north-western Pelasgiotis had also found refuge there.[1] North-East-Greek-speaking Eurytanes from Histiaiotis had already established themselves on the Stenyklaros plain in Messenia before the North-West-Greek-speakers' Völkerwanderung.[2] In south-eastern Messenia in Pausanias' day there was a tomb of Makhaon at Gerenia and a temple of Makhaon's sons at Pharai, and these monuments were cited as evidence that the Asklepiadai of Trikka in Histiaiotis, as well as the Eurytanes of the same Thessalian tetrarchy, had settled in Messenia.[3]

The reigning dynasty on the Stenyklaros plain in north-eastern Messenia at the time of the outbreak of the First Spartano-Messenian War bore the name Aipytidai. The tomb of this dynasty's eponym, Aipytos, is mentioned in the Homeric Catalogue of the contingents of Agamemnon's expeditionary force as being located in Arcadia, at the foot of Mount Kyllene.[4] The conventional version of Messenian history makes Aipytos a Heraklid by making him the grandson, by an Arcadian mother, of Kresphontes, the legendary Heraklid recipient of Messenia.[5] Evidently the Messenian Aipytidai were of pre-Völkerwanderung Peloponnesian origin, even if their subjects included North-West-Greek-speaking immigrants into Messenia, as well as pre-North-West-Greek natives.[6] Like Aipytos, Temenos, the allegedly Heraklid conqueror of the Argolid, also appears in Arcadia, at Stymphalos[7] and at Psophis,[8] as a local hero. If the Messenian Aipytidai and the Argive Temenidai were in truth of local pre-Völkerwanderung origin, one or both of the two Spartan royal houses, the Agiadai and the Eurypontidai, may also have been of local non-immigrant origin for all that we know. When the Agiad Spartan King Kleomenes I declared 'I am not a Dorian; I am an Achaean',[9] he was referring to his claim to be a Heraklid. It is possible that he may in truth, without knowing it, have been descended from some native Laconian royal house.

In the field of religion, shrines and cults dating from before the North-West-Greek-speakers' arrival continued, in the last millennium B.C., to

---

[1] See Pausanias, Book III, chap. 20, § 7, and the present work, Part II, chap. 7, p. 121, n. 2.
[2] See Part I, chap. 3, pp. 26–7, and Part II, chap. 7, p. 119.
[3] See Pausanias, Book IV, chap. 3, § 2. Kiechle, *Lakonien und Sparta*, pp. 15–20, 23, 37–9, finds traces of Aeolic (i.e North-East-Greek) elements in Laconian Greek. For Eurytanian and Asklepiad settlements in Messenia, see also the present work, Part I, chap. 3, p. 27.
[4] *Iliad*, II. 603–4.   [5] Pausanias, Book IV, chap. 3, §§ 6–8.
[6] If this was the situation in Messenia before the Spartan conquest, it would be comparable to the situation in Scotland from the tenth century of the Christian Era onwards, when a dynasty of Celtic-speaking origin was ruling over a mixed population of English-speakers in the Lothians and Celtic-speakers in the rest of the kingdom.
[7] Pausanias, Book VIII, chap. 22, § 2.
[8] Pausanias, ibid., chap. 24, § 10.   [9] Herodotus, Book V, chap. 72.

play leading parts in the life of Laconia and Messenia.[1] The temple of Pohoidan at Tainaron has been mentioned already.[2] In Sparta itself, the cult of Artemis Orthia appears to be of Mycenaean-Age origin, and the Dioskouroi are the pre-Greek Tyndaridai (the sons of the Tyrsenian high god Tin) in Greek dress. Pausanias notes that Artemis Issoria, alias Limnaia, at Sparta, was, in truth, not Artemis; she was the Cretan Britomartis.[3] At Amyklai the tomb of Hyakinthos survived below the base of the statue of Apollo; the annual festival continued to be called the Hyakinthia; and offerings were made at Hyakinthos' tomb before the sacrifice in Apollo's honour.[4] On Therapne there was a shrine of Menelaos,[5] which is still extant.

In our ignorance of the history of Laconia and Messenia during the four hundred years immediately preceding the eighth century B.C., it is manifestly hazardous to try to establish links between Sparta, as we find her in and after that century, and the Völkerwanderung of *circa* 1200 B.C. The only elements in Spartan life, in and after the eighth century B.C., that look as if they might be a legacy from the North-West-Greek-speaking immigrants are some of the primitive-looking institutions that were systematized and frozen in the 'Lycurgan' agoge.[6] This, is, however, merely an unverifiable guess.

The irrelevance of the post-Mycenaean Völkerwanderung to the history of the long-subsequent rise of the city-state Sparta has been clarified by Niese:[7]

We see clearly that the peculiar political structure of Laconia is not the product of the intrusion of a foreign people in a mythical antiquity, and is not the product of any action whatsoever from outside. It has been developed from inside, i.e. from Sparta, and it is the product of a definite Spartan policy. The origin of helots and perioikoi is to be found, not in a Dorian Völkerwanderung about which we are completely in the dark; it is to be found in the formation of the Spartan body politic and the Spartan constitution.

(ii) *The Stages of the Spartan Conquests*

(a) *The Names 'Sparta' and 'Lakedaimon'*

It has been noted already[8] that, in the fifth century B.C., it was the established usage, both at Sparta itself and in the rest of the Hellenic World, to style the Spartan state οἱ Λακεδαιμόνιοι officially. We do not

---

[1] See Berve, op. cit., p. 29; Roussel, op. cit., pp. 21 and 76–7; Ehrenberg, 'Spartiaten und Lakedaimonier', p. 52.

[2] On p. 166. [3] Pausanias, Book III, chap. 14, § 2.

[4] Pausanias, ibid., chap. 19, § 3. Cp. chap. 1, § 3, and chap. 16, § 2.

[5] Pausanias, ibid., chap. 19, § 9. [6] See the present Part, chap. 4, section (iii).

[7] In 'Neue Beiträge zur Geschichte und Landeskunde Lakedaimons', p. 136. Cp. eundem, 'Zur Verfassungsgeschichte Lakedaimons', pp. 76 and 77. [8] On p. 159.

know at what stage in the territorial expansion of the Spartan state this usage was introduced. Nor do we know whether Lakedaimon, in this official usage, originally stood for a region or for a particular place, within a region, that was, or once had been, the region's seat of government. In the fifth century B.C. the name 'Lakedaimon' was certainly used officially as the equivalent of Sparta in contexts in which Sparta the political entity, not Sparta the physical locality, was in question.[1] We do not know what 'Lakedaimon' means. We do not even know whether the word is Greek or pre-Greek. But its two epithets in the Homeric epic, 'hollow' (κοίλη) and 'scarred with ravines' (if this is the meaning of κητώεσσα), indicate that it was originally the name of a country,[2] namely, the relatively small[3] but fertile basin, enclosed on all sides by ravine-scarred mountains and hills, through which the River Eurotas flows in the middle section of its course.

The appropriateness of the two epithets to this landscape is borne in on an observer who climbs to the crown of Therapne or to the summit of Mistrá. Looking from either of these two commanding heights, the observer might have expected to see, spread out before him, between the parallel ranges of Taÿgetos and Parnon, the whole course of the Eurotas from its sources in south-western Arcadia to its debouchure into the Laconian Gulf. What the observer actually sees is a plain enclosed by mountains or hills in every quarter. He sees the Eurotas issuing from a barrier of hills on the north-north-west and disappearing into a barrier of hills on the south-south-east after a short transit of the intervening plain. He does not catch even a glimpse of the sea. His south-south-eastern horizon is bounded by the hill-country through which the Eurotas has to force a passage in order to make its way from 'hollow Lakedaimon' into the coastal swamp (helos). This hill-girt basin is aptly called 'hollow' and is no less aptly said to be 'scarred with ravines'; for, when the observer, sitting on the parapet at the summit of Mistrá, turns his gaze from the south-south-east to the west, he finds himself facing a series of ravines that break up the cliff-wall of the 'shelf' which rises between the plain of 'hollow Lakedaimon' and the crest of the Taÿgetos Range. This is surely the landscape that is described as κοίλην Λακεδαίμονα κητώεσσαν in the opening line[4] of the description, in the Homeric Catalogue of the contingents of Agamemnon's host, of the principality ruled by Agamemnon's brother Menelaos.

---

[1] See p. 159.

[2] See Pareti, *Storia di Sparta Arcaïca*, Parte I, p. 155, n. 2; Cavaignac, op. cit., p. 9.

[3] Relatively small compared both to the total area of Laconia (even exclusive of Kynouria) and to the area of the plain of Argos, the Peloponnesian state that anticipated Sparta in attempting to make itself the paramount power in the Peloponnese as a whole. Forrest, *A History*, p. 13, reckons that the Vale of Sparta is about twenty miles long and seven miles wide. [4] *Iliad*, II. 581.

'Hollow ravine-scarred Lakedaimon' will have been the name of Menelaos' territory; but the territory must have had a seat of government, and, in the Mycenaean Age, this will have been a castle, not a city serving as the civic centre of a city-state, which was subsequently the structure of the Spartan state and was in fact the normal structure of a polity in the post-Völkerwanderung Hellenic World at the earliest date at which this World comes into our ken. We do not know where Menelaos' seat of government was. It may have been at Therapne, where the vestiges of a Mycenaean-Age settlement have been found.[1] Alternatively it may have been at Amyklai. On the other hand, Sparta, to judge by the apparent meaning of its name, seems unlikely to have been the original seat of government; for 'Sparta' appears to mean 'sown land'[2] or open agricultural country, and this name must originally have denoted the fields attaching to a settlement that was not, itself, cultivated because it was inhabited. Therapne, which overhangs the site of Hellenic Sparta from above the opposite bank of the River Eurotas,[3] seems the most likely settlement to have had its fields originally on that piece of the plain of 'hollow Lakedaimon' on which the city of Sparta eventually came to stand.

If Therapne was the seat of government of the principality of Lakedaimon in the Mycenaean Age, the Spartans may have taken to styling themselves 'Lakedaimonioi' as soon as Therapne came into their possession. We do not know at what stage in Sparta's history Therapne fell into her hands. At first sight it might seem impossible for an unwalled cluster of four villages, such as the City of Sparta—in the physical sense—was, to maintain itself at all if it did not hold such a commanding position at such close quarters. Yet Sparta, like another low-lying city, Florence, had a commanding position of her own in virtue of being the point of convergence for roads entering her river-basin from the north-east, north, and north-west, and Florence managed to live—and not only to live but to expand—while Fiesole—which was as close to Florence as Therapne was to Sparta, and which, like Therapne, crowns a commanding height —continued to be an independent state. Florence did not annex Fiesole till *circa* A.D. 1125, and this was more than 1,300 years later than the probable foundation-date of Florence at the foot of Fiesole, as a station on the Roman road—the second Via Flaminia—which, in 187 B.C., was carried across the Appennines to link Arretium (Arezzo) with Bologna. This historical parallel makes it conceivable that Sparta did not annex

[1] See Pareti, *Storia di Sparta Arcaïca*, Parte I, pp. 135 and 155; Bölte in P.-W., Zweite Reihe [R–Z], Dritter Band, A2 (1929), col. 1329.
[2] This interpretation of the word seems likelier than Bölte's interpretation—'esparto grass'—in loc. cit., col. 1273.
[3] See Polybius' vivid and accurate description of the topography of Sparta town and Therapne in Book V, chaps. 18–24, especially chap. 22.

Therapne until after she had acquired possession of the whole of 'hollow Lakedaimon', and of much of the adjoining hill-country as well, by conquering the city-states Amyklai, Pharis, and Geronthrai.

All that we can say is that the Spartans seem likely to have begun to style themselves Lakedaimonioi as soon as they had incorporated Amyklai and Pharis, as well as Therapne, in the territory of the Spartan city-state—the πολιτικὴ χώρα, as this was called by the Spartans, to distinguish it from the aggregate area of the territories of Sparta's perioecic city-states, of which there were reputed to be a hundred in the remainder of Laconia and in Messenia by the time when the Spartan conquests had been completed and been confirmed.

(b) *The Synoecism of Sparta*

The City of Sparta consisted of four settlements—Pitane, Limnai, Kynosoura, Messoa—which were close enough to each other to be included within one and the same city-wall[1] when the Lacedaemonian Government tardily and reluctantly decided that Lakedaimon was no longer a powerful enough state to be able to afford to leave unfortified the city that was its political nucleus.[2] We know that the tombs of the Agiadai were in the Krotanoi quarter of Pitane,[3] and that those of the Eurypontidai were at the far end, from the agora, of the street called Aphetaïs, just inside the city-wall,[4] i.e. in a location that seems to have lain in Limnai. We may reasonably infer that the Agiadai had originally been the royal house of the Pitanatai, and the Eurypontidai the royal house of the Limnatai. We may also infer that these two communities united with each other voluntarily on terms of equality. Only this would account for the continued co-existence of the two royal houses as joint dynasties, on an equal footing, of the Spartan state as a whole.[5] If the synoecism had been brought about by the subjection of one community to another, the weaker community's royal house would presumably have been eliminated. The Spartan city-state was unique in the Hellenic World in

---

[1] For the topography of Sparta City, see Bölte in P.–W., Zweite Reihe [R–Z], Dritter Band. A2 (1929), cols. 1362–5; Pareti, *Storia di Sparta Arcaïca*, Parte I, pp. 183 and 187.

[2] According to Bölte in loc. cit., col. 1356, Sparta City was fortified for the first time—and, even then, only partially—in 317 B.C. (in 318 B.C. according to Jones, *Sparta*, p. 150) to meet the threat in that year from Cassander (Justin, Book XIV, chap. 5, § 6; Livy, Book XXXIV, chap. 38, § 2). See also Forrest, *A History*, p. 141. Sparta still lacked a complete ring-wall when she was attacked by Flamininus in 195 B.C. The first complete ring-wall was built by Nabis after that date (Pausanias, Book VII, chap. 8, § 5; Livy, Book XXXIX, chap. 37). Nabis' wall was pulled down in 188 B.C. by the Achaeans (Livy, Book XXXVIII, chap. 34, § 4; XXXIX, 36, 4; 37, 1; Pausanias, Book VII, chap. 8, § 5). It was rebuilt *circa* 183 B.C. (Pausanias, Book VII, chap. 9, § 5). It was still standing in Pausanias' own day (Book III, chap. 12, § 8; 15, 3; 16, 4).

[3] Pausanias, Book III, chap. 14, § 2.

[4] Pausanias, Book III, chap. 12, § 8.

[5] See Michell, op. cit., pp. 103–4; Norvin, loc. cit., pp. 247–93, on p. 262.

preserving the royal houses of two of its constituent communities. We do not know whether Messoa was already associated with Pitane, and Kynosoura with Limnai,[1] before the synoecism of the Agiad community and the Eurypontid community with each other, or whether these two settlements were subsequent additions to an original pair.

We also do not know the date of the foundation of the Spartan city-state through this union between the Agiadai and the Eurypontidai. The date must be later than the beginning of the ninth century B.C.; for the earliest of the Geometric-Age remains on the site cannot be dated earlier than that,[2] and there do not appear to be any remains there dating from the foregoing Sub-Mycenaean and Mycenaean Ages.[3] The synoecism must also have preceded the conquest of the Aigytis (alias Aigys), which is the first Spartan enterprise that is recorded to have been a joint operation of the two royal houses.[4] This achievement is attributed to the Agiad king Agesilaos and the Eurypontid king Kharilaos. The Aigytis is the south-western fringe of Arcadia, astride the watershed between the Eurotas basin and the Alpheios basin. Sparta's conquest of the Aigytis presupposes that she had previously conquered the city-state Pellana, whose territory bestrides the upper valley of the Eurotas. Even if we assume that Agesilaos and Kharilaos are historical personalities, not fictitious ciphers, we can only guess at their dates. The earliest pair of Spartan kings whom we can date approximately from independent evidence are the Agiad Polydoros and the Eurypontid Theopompos.[5] These two kings were reigning during and after the First Spartano-Messenian War; this war can be dated *circa* 740–720 B.C. on the evidence of the dates at which Messenian and Lacedaemonian names respectively cease to appear and begin to appear in the lists of victors at the Olympic festival, if we may assume that these lists are authentic right back to the earliest entries;[6] and the dates of Theopompos' and Polydoros' predecessors have to be guessed at by dead reckoning—assigning an arbitrary average number of years to a generation. In the genealogy of the Agiads (in which there are fewer variants than there are in the Eurypontids'

---

[1] For the pairing of Kynosoura with Limnai and of Messoa with Pitane, see Pausanias, Book III, chap. 16, § 9. Forrest, *A History*, p. 28, notes that the Agiadai ranked as the senior of the two royal houses. He suggests that Pitane and Messoa may have been founded earlier than Kynosoura and Limnai.

[2] See Roussel, op. cit., p. 18; Forrest, *A History*, p. 25.

[3] See Pareti, *Storia di Sparta Arcaïca*, Parte I, pp. 135–6 and 182. The Protogeometric pottery found at Sparta is of the same style as that found at Amyklai (Kiechle, *Lakonien und Sparta*, pp. 55 and 58–9). At Amyklai, some Mycenaean sherds have been found, though in smaller quantities than the Protogeometric (Kiechle, op. cit., p. 49; Pareti, op. cit., p. 136). In Berve's view (op. cit., p. 14), Sparta was not yet in existence in the Mycenaean Age.

[4] Pausanias, Book III, chap. 2, § 5.   [5] See Jones, *Sparta*, p. 3.

[6] See chap. 2, section (ii) (e), p. 180, with n. 4. Forrest, *A History*, p. 20, accepts the Olympic victor lists as being substantially authentic. He dates the First Spartano-Messenian War *circa* 735–715 B.C.

genealogy),[1] Polydoros is the great-grandson of Arkhelaos, the joint conqueror, with his Eurypontid colleague Kharilaos, of the Aigytis. The date of Arkhelaos and Kharilaos would then be round about the opening of the eighth century B.C., and the foregoing synoecism, produced by the union of the two houses, might have taken place towards the close of the ninth century B.C. Achievements ascribed to earlier representatives of each dynasty, acting independently of each other, are not worthy of credence. Indeed, we have no guarantee of the historicity of the kings to whom these achievements are attributed.[2]

We do not know the ethnic origins of any of the first four constituent communities of the Spartan body politic.[3] The fact that, in the fifth century B.C., the Spartiatai spoke the same North-West-Greek dialect as the rest of the population of Laconia and Messenia indicates that at least a considerable portion of the original Spartiate citizen-body must have been descended from the North-West-Greek-speaking migrants who had settled in Laconia in the post-Mycenaean Völkerwanderung. This is what we should expect; for Sparta lay in the northern corner of the plain of hollow Lakedaimon, and the agricultural productivity of this plain, together with the treasure that had accumulated in the local Mycenaean-Age seat of government, wherever this may have been located, will have been the two principal magnets in Laconia by which the invaders will have been attracted. There is therefore likely to have been a concentration of North-West-Greek-speaking migrants in hollow Lakedaimon, as there is said to have been in the productive plain of Stenyklaros in the interior of Messenia.[4] Before the beginning of the Spartan conquests,

[1] Jones, *Sparta*, pp. 3 and 170, notes that Herodotus' and Pausanias' versions of the Eurypontids' genealogy disagree, and that the names of the Eurypontid kings before Theopompos are really unknown.

[2] For instance, Agis I, the eponym of the Agiadai, is alleged (Pausanias, Book III, chap. 2, § 1) to have taken part in the synoecism of Patrai, at the north-western extremity of the Peloponnese; yet the Aigytis, which is only the second stop on the long road from Sparta to Patrai, is not claimed to have been conquered by Sparta till the reign of King Arkhelaos, who is reckoned to have been Agis I's great-great-great-grandson. In the Eurypontid house the son of the eponym is alleged to have made war on Kynouria and to have consequently fallen foul of Argos (Pausanias, Book III, chap. 7, § 2; cp. chap. 2, § 2). It is inconceivable that, before the synoecism of Sparta, one of the future constituent communities of the Spartan city-state can have challenged Argos single-handed. It is hardly more credible that the Eurypontid king Nikandros—who, if historical, will have reigned before the outbreak of the first Spartano-Messenian War—should have invaded the Argeia itself in alliance with the Asinaioi (Pausanias, Book III, chap. 7, § 4), though Forrest accepts this story as being historical fact (*A History*, p. 36). As late as 669 B.C. the Argives inflicted a crushing defeat at Hysiai on a Lacedaemonian invading army, and this at a date by which Sparta's territory included Messenia, as well as the whole of Laconia to the west of the Parnon Range. See urther p. 184, n. 3.

[3] See Norvin, loc. cit., pp. 247–93, on p. 258. A. Momigliano, 'Sparta e Lacedemone: una ipotesi sull'origine della diarchia spartana', in *Atene e Roma*, nuova serie, anno xiii (1932), pp. 3–11, holds that the Agiadai had originally reigned at Therapne. This is unconvincing.

[4] See Pausanias, Book IV, chap. 3, §§ 6–7.

the greater part of these North-West-Greek-speaking inhabitants of hollow Lakedaimon were, of course, citizens of non-Spartan city-states that will have been synoecized at about the same time as Sparta—at the time, that is to say, at which the institution of city-states was being propagated from the Asian to the European part of the Hellenic World.[1]

The later political map of Spartan Laconia tells us that Sparta did not incorporate her first conquests—if Pellana and the Aigytis were, in truth, her first[2]—in her own city-state territory. Sparta imposed on these conquered communities the status of perioikoi, i.e. autonomous, though subordinate, states under her suzerainty.[3] In the next stage of her expansion, however, Sparta did, apparently, incorporate in her body politic one community of non-North-West-Greek origin, the Minyai on the 'shelf' of Mount Taÿgetos,[4] and, with their aid, she then succeeded in conquering Amyklai and Pharis, which, between them, had possessed the greater part of hollow Lakedaimon, together with Geronthrai in the western foothills of the Parnon Range.

(c) *The Incorporation of the Taÿgetan Minyai in the Spartan Body Politic and the Conquest and Incorporation of Amyklai*

The conquest and incorporation of Amyklai in the Spartan body politic was perhaps the most decisive single event in the history of Sparta's expansion.[5] It brought into Sparta's possession the previously non-Spartan major part of hollow Lakedaimon; and this opened the way for Sparta eventually to become first the equal and then the superior of Argos in military and political power.

Unfortunately our sources for this crucial episode in Sparta's history are fragmentary and dubious. We have to piece the story together from a tale told by Herodotus[6] and from some casual notices in Pausanias' guide-book. Herodotus' story is vitiated by ill-conceived attempts at rationalization. He is trying to derive all the Minyai of whom he knows, wherever located, from the Minyai who, according to him, had been evicted from Lemnos by Pelasgoi (i.e. by Tyrsenoi).[7] Herodotus also identifies the Theras who was the eponym of the district called Therai on the 'shelf' of Taÿgetus with the Theras who was the eponym of the Aegean island called Thera (now called Santoríni). There is, however, no reason to suppose that all Minyai came from Lemnos; it is more

[1] See Part I, chap. 3, pp. 41–5.
[2] Forrest holds that they were (*A History*, p. 31).
[3] For the status of Sparta's perioecic communities, see further section (ii), Annex II.
[4] For these, see Kiechle, *Lakonien und Sparta*, pp. 24–9.
[5] See ibid., p. 151.
[6] In Book IV, chaps. 145–9.
[7] Herodotus, Book IV, chap. 145. See also Part II, chapter 7, Annex, pp. 128–32. The Lemnian Pelasgoi seem really to have been identical with the Lemnian Minyai who were conquered by the Tyrsenoi.

likely that they all came originally from Minoan Crete ;[1] nor is there any necessary, or even probable, ethnic or historical connection between different places called 'Thera' or 'Therai' ; for, in Greek, this is a common noun meaning 'a hunting-ground' or 'hunting-grounds', while, in the Luvian or pre-Luvian language of western Anatolia, 'teira' appears to mean 'city'.[2] As for the passages in Pausanias' work, they offer us information which is not forthcoming in any other of our surviving sources, but which, for just this reason, we are unable to verify.

According to Herodotus' story, a band of Minyai that had taken refuge on Taÿgetos asked the Lacedaemonians (i.e. the Spartans), at some stage in Sparta's history which Herodotus does not date, to incorporate them in the Lacedaemonian body politic and to give them a share in the government and in the land.[3] The Lacedaemonians adopted them, gave them a share in their land, and distributed them among the Spartan phylai.[4] There was then extensive intermarriage between the new and the old citizens. Afterwards they fell out with each other, and the Minyai migrated—the majority to Triphylia, where the local population claimed (probably correctly) in Herodotus' day to be Minyai. (The Peloponnesian Minyai were probably all descended from survivors of Nestor's pre-Völker-wanderung principality.) A minority of the Laconian Minyai, however, went, according to Herodotus, overseas under a leader named Theras, the guardian of the children of Aristodamos, the legendary Heraklid who had obtained Laconia as his share of the North-West-Greek-speaking invaders' conquests in the Peloponnese. Theras took his Minyai to the Aegean island called Kalliste, which, from that time on, was called Thera in Theras' honour. However, when Theras, with his Minyai, left Sparta, his descendants, Herodotus tells us, stayed on there. Aigeus, the eponym of the Aigeidai, who were a big phyle[5] at Sparta in Herodotus' day, was Theras' grandson.

Since we know from Pausanias[6] that the 'shelf' of Taÿgetos, overhanging hollow Lakedaimon, was called Therai, and since we know from Herodotus that the Minyai who were incorporated in the Spartan body politic came from Taÿgetos, it seems evident that Herodotus' Theras is the eponym of this Minyan community's highland home. Moreover, since we know from Herodotus that the Aigeidai, whose eponym Aigeus was reputed to be Theras' grandson, were an important family at Sparta

---

[1] See Part I, chap. 2.
[2] e.g. Teira, Thyateira, Hadrianotherai.
[3] δέεσθαί τε οἰκέειν ἅμα τούτοισι, μοῖράν τε τιμέων μετέχοντες καὶ τῆς γῆς ἀπολαχόντες (Herodotus, Book IV, chap. 145).
[4] δεξάμενοι δὲ τοὺς Μινύας, γῆς τε μετέδοσαν καὶ ἐς φυλὰς διεδάσαντο (ibid.).
[5] Here Herodotus is probably using the word 'phyle', not in the technical sense, but in the general meaning of 'clan' or 'family'.
[6] Book III, chap. 20, § 5, cited already on p. 166.

in Herodotus' own day, and since we know from Pausanias[1] that, in Pausanias' day, there was an herôon in honour of Aigeus at Sparta, it is evident that, whatever the cause and the outcome of the Laconian Minyai's quarrel with the rest of the Spartans may have been, some of them, at least, must have remained members of the Spartan citizen-body. In any case it is certain that the Arcadian-speaking Triphylians, and probable that the North-West-Greek-speaking inhabitants of the island of Thera, were not of Laconian origin.

A fragment of Aristotle[2] informs us why the Spartans agreed to incorporate the Taÿgetan Minyai in their body politic on an equal footing with themselves. Timomakhos, the leader in the final victorious Spartan assault on Amyklai, was an Aigeid—that is to say, a member of the paramount family in the ex-Taÿgetan Minyan community that had now become part of the Spartan citizen-body. The Spartans had needed this reinforcement to overcome Amyklai's resistance. Thereafter, Timomakhos' bronze breastplate was displayed every year at Amyklai during the celebration of the Hyakinthia.

Amyklai is said to have resisted Sparta longer and more stubbornly than either Pharis or Geronthrai,[3] but, after Amyklai had been conquered or had been betrayed or had capitulated on terms, she appears to have been given more favourable treatment than the other two conquered city-states.[4]

The people of Pharis and Geronthrai are said to have surrendered their cities to the Spartans on condition of being allowed to emigrate under a safe-conduct. We may guess that they moved to the eastern side of the Parnon Range and found asylum there under the protection of the Argives, who will have been extending their dominion down the coast of Kynouria in competition with the Spartans' extension of their dominion down the Eurotas valley. Pharis ceased to be inhabited.[5] Geronthrai perhaps became a Spartan colony and probably acquired the status of a perioecic city-state.[6] According to Pausanias, Amyklai had eventually been taken by assault by the Spartans; a trophy com-

---

[1] Book III, chap. 15, § 8.

[2] Fr. 532 (Rose) in the scholion to Pindar, *Isthm.*, Ode 6 (7), line 18: εἰσὶν Αἰγεῖδαι φρατρία Θηβαίων, ἀφ' ἧς ἧκόν τινες εἰς Σπάρτην Λακεδαιμονίοις βοηθήσοντες, ἐν τῷ πρὸς Ἀμυκλαεῖς πολέμῳ, ἡγεμόνι χρησάμενοι Τιμομάχῳ, ὃς πρῶτος μὲν πάντα τὰ πρὸς πόλεμον διέταξε Λακεδαιμονίοις.

[3] Pausanias, Book III, chap. 2, § 6.

[4] See Pareti, *Storia di Sparta Arcaïca*, Parte I, p. 187.

[5] Pausanias, Book III, chap. 20, § 3.

[6] See Pausanias, ibid., chap. 2, § 6; chap. 22, § 6. In chap. 2, § 6, Pausanias says that, when the Lacedaemonians conquered Geronthrai, they evicted the inhabitants and planted colonists of their own there. In chap. 22, § 6, he dates this in the reign of the Agiad king of Sparta, Teleklos. Geronthrai was one of the Eleutherolaconian city-states in Pausanias' day (ibid., chap. 22, § 6), and this makes it probable, though not certain, that it had become a perioecic city-state before 195 B.C.

memorating this victory was on view in Pausanias' day;[1] and the conquest of Amyklai was one of the victories commemorated by the temple, at Sparta, of Zeus Tropaios.[2] On the other hand, according to Strabo,[3] Amyklai was betrayed to the conquerors by a traitor named Philonomos.[4] In any case, Amyklai, unlike Pharis, had continued, down to Pausanias' day, to be an inhabited place on the scale of a village.[5]

We know that, in 390 B.C., the inhabitants of Amyklai were Spartiatai and that Amyklai was one of the five obai of which the Spartiate citizen-body was constituted[6] before the creation of a sixth oba by King Kleomenes III in or after the year 227 B.C.[7] We do not know whether any of the Spartiate Amyklaioi of the age following the Spartan conquest of Amyklai were descendants of the previous inhabitants who had been given Spartan citizenship at the time of the conquest,[8] or whether Amyklai, like Geronthrai, had been completely cleared of its former inhabitants and had been given an entirely new population of Spartan settlers—with the difference that, at Amyklai, these were allowed to retain their Spartan citizenship, owing to the nearness of Amyklai to Sparta, while the Spartan settlers in the relatively distant Geronthrai were organized politically as an autonomous community with perioecic, instead of Spartiate, status. Since the representative of the Aigeidai had played the leading part in the conquest of Amyklai, and since the Aigeidai seem thereafter to have presided over the Hyakinthia festival at Amyklai, it seems probable that, whether some or all of the pre-conquest inhabitants of Amyklai were evicted and were dispossessed of their lands, the Taÿgetan Minyai who had just been given Spartan citizenship will have been given this as members of a new oba, located at Amyklai, and will have been endowed with land, not at the expense of the members of the four previously existing Spartan obai, but at the expense of the conquered Amyklaioi.

At the same time, we have one clue which suggests that some, at any rate, of these conquered Amyklaioi—perhaps the traitor Philonomos'

---

[1] Ibid., chap. 2, § 6.   [2] Ibid., chap 12, § 9.

[3] *Geographica*, Book VIII, chap. 5, § 4 (C. 364) and § 5 (C. 365).

[4] According to Strabo, in loc. cit., Amyklai was betrayed to Eurysthenes and Prokles, the fictitious Heraklid progenitors of the Spartan Agiadai and Eurypontidai; but it is, of course, incredible that a record of any particular incidents in the post-Mycenaean Völkerwanderung should have been preserved.   [5] Pausanias, Book III, chap. 19, § 6.

[6] Forrest, *A History*, p. 32, holds that the incorporation of Amyklai in the Spartiate body politic dated from the immediate sequel to the Spartan conquest.

[7] See chap. 3, Annex II.

[8] This is Kiechle's opinion (*Lakonien und Sparta*, pp. 106 and 133); Berve's (op. cit., p. 15); Roussel's (op. cit., p. 20); Neumann's (loc. cit., p. 54); and Norvin's (loc. cit., p. 252). Norvin takes the survival of the shrine at Amyklai as being evidence that the incorporation of Amyklai in the Spartan state had been effected by agreement. Cp. Niese, 'Zur Verfassungsgeschichte Lakedaimons', p. 79, n. 6; Lenschau, 'Die Entstehung des spartanischen Staates', p. 280.

faction, if Philonomos is an historical character—were also taken into the Spartan citizen-body on this occasion. Aristotle records a tradition that 'in the time of the earlier kings [of Sparta], the Spartans did enfranchise aliens, with the result that Sparta did not suffer from any dearth of man-power at that stage, in spite of her engaging in long-protracted wars'.[1] This report is vague; it might refer solely to the enfranchisement of the Minyai; but it reads like a reminiscence of enfranchisements on a larger scale than that; and, whether or not some of the pre-conquest Amyklaioi were given Spartan citizenship, it is certain that no conquered community was given it at any of the stages of Sparta's territorial expansion subsequent to the conquest of Amyklai, Pharis, and Geronthrai.

(d) *The Conquest of the Lower Part of the Eurotas Basin*

The scanty information that has come down to us about the Spartan conquest of the lower part of the Eurotas basin has been coloured and vitiated by the mistaken explanation of the Lacedaemonian political term 'helots' (εἵλωτες) as having originally been the ethnikon of the geographical name 'Helos'.[2] 'Helos' means 'marsh'; there was a marsh in the coastal plain through which the River Eurotas runs after forcing its way through the hills that enclose, on the south-south-east, the plain of hollow Lakedaimon; and, on the eastern edge of this marsh, there was a place named Helos which is mentioned by Damonon[3] in connection with a festival held there in the fifth century B.C.; by Thucydides[4] in connection with Athenian naval operations in 424/3 B.C.; and by Xenophon[5] in connection with the Theban invasion of Laconia in 370 B.C. Ruins that were alleged to be those of Helos were pointed out in Pausanias' day.[6] Helos was said to have been conquered and destroyed by the Spartans during the reign of the Agiad king Alkamenes,[7] who was the son of Teleklos the reputed conqueror of Amyklai, Pharis, and Geronthrai, and was the father of Polydoros, the Agiad king whose reign was partly contemporaneous with the First Spartano-Messenian War. Geopolitical considerations suggest that the lower basin of the Eurotas must have been annexed by Sparta after her conquest of those three city-states

---

[1] λέγουσι δ' ὡς ἐπὶ μὲν τῶν προτέρων βασιλέων μετεδίδοσαν τῆς πολιτείας, ὥστ' οὐ γίνεσθαι τότε ὀλιγανθρωπίαν, πολεμούντων πολὺν χρόνον (Aristotle, *Politics*, Book II, chap. 6 (9), § 12 (1270a).
[2] See the present chapter, Annex II.
[3] For Damonon's inscription, see p. 154.
[4] Book IV, chap. 54, § 4.
[5] Xenophon, *Hellenica*, Book VI, chap. 5, § 32.
[6] Pausanias, Book III, chap. 22, § 3.
[7] Pausanias, Book III, chap. 2, § 7.

in the middle part of the Eurotas basin and before she made the assault on the Aipytid kingdom in the Stenyklaros plain that precipitated the First Spartano-Messenian War.[1]

It also seems likely that, as Pausanias states,[2] Helos, at the time when attacked by Sparta, was under an Argive protectorate, and that Sparta therefore had to fight and defeat Argos in order to gain possession of Helos. This, however, would suggest that Sparta may not have annexed Helos till after the end of the First Spartano-Messenian War, since we have no credible information that Sparta ever ventured to challenge Argos before that. Evidently there was no genuine record of the date of the Spartan conquest of Helos; for Strabo[3] dates it in the reign of the Agiads' eponym Agis I.

In any case, Sparta must have secured a frontage, containing a port, on the coast of the Laconian Gulf before the foundation, towards the close of the eighth century B.C., of a Spartan colony overseas, at Tarentum. Sparta's port cannot have lain anywhere along the marsh-coast; it can have lain only at Gythion,[4] which was Sparta's naval base during and after the Decelean War (413–404 B.C.); Sparta can hardly have annexed Gythion without simultaneously persuading or compelling the little poverty-stricken communities on the Tainaron Peninsula to accept the status of perioikoi; and she must have converted into perioikoi not only the Tainaron communities but the larger and wealthier city-states of south-eastern Messenia too before trying conclusions with the Aipytid kingdom on the plain of Stenyklaros.

The perioecic status given to the local communities on the Tainaron Peninsula and in south-eastern Messenia was the status that had been given already to the Aigytis and to Geronthrai. It was a status of local autonomy under Spartan suzerainty and control. By contrast, the lower basin of the Eurotas was annexed outright to the territory of the city-state of Sparta itself; and there was a fateful innovation here in the treatment of the local population. It was not evicted, as it had been at Geronthrai and at Pharis, and it was not given the Spartan citizenship, as it may have been given this at Amyklai. The conquered population of the lower basin of the Eurotas was given the status of 'prisoners of war' or 'captives' (heilotes). These 'captives' were virtually enslaved. They were allowed, on sufferance, to continue to cultivate their ancestral land; but they and their production were at the Spartan state's disposal. It had empowered itself to exploit the helots in any way that it might choose for the benefit either of the Spartan community as a whole or of some section of it.

---

[1] See Kiechle, *Lakonien und Sparta*, p. 254.
[2] Pausanias, Book III, chap. 2, § 7.
[3] *Geographica*, Book VIII, chap. 5, § 4 (C. 365).
[4] See further, pp. 191–3.

(e) *The First and Second Spartano-Messenian Wars*

Sparta had been in immediate territorial contact with the Aipytid kingdom on the plain of Stenyklaros ever since her subjugation of the Aigytis. However, the Aigytis and Stenyklaros were separated from each other by mountains. So, too, were hollow Lakedaimon and south-eastern Messenia; but the incorporation of the Taÿgetan Minyai in the Spartan body politic gave Sparta access to south-eastern Messenia across the Taÿgetos Range;[1] this access made it possible for Sparta to compete with the Aipytid kingdom for the political control over south-eastern Messenia;[2] and this competition may have been one of the causes of the death (if the story is historical) of the Spartan king Teleklos, the con- queror of Amyklai, in a Spartano-Messenian brawl at the temple of Artemis at Limnai, in the Dentheliatis, on the Messenian side of the pass.[3]

On the evidence of the nationalities of the victors at the Olympic festival, it looks as if the date of the First Spartano-Messenian War was *circa* 740–720 B.C.[4] This war ended in a Spartan victory; and we know that, in the peace-settlement, Sparta annexed the Stenyklaros plain, which had been the heart of the Aipytid kingdom, to the territory of the Spartan city-state and reduced the inhabitants, as she had already reduced those of the lower basin of the Eurotas, to the status of 'captives' (heilotes). On the other hand Sparta is said[5] to have given an appanage

[1] According to Forrest, *A History*, p. 14, the Langádha Pass across the Taÿgetos Range was probably not used in the Hellenic Age, but the pass a little farther to the south, leading from Anavrýti to Giannitsa (i.e. leading, like the Langádha Pass, into the Dentheliatis), may have been used. The much more southerly route from Gythion to Kardamyle was much easier, and this would explain why Augustus gave Kardamyle to Sparta (see the present work, p. 411) as a port in lieu of Gythion. The route round the northern end of Taÿgetos from the upper valley of the Eurotas to the upper valley of the Pamisos via the upper valley of the Alpheios was the easiest of all (Forrest, op. cit., p. 14). Forrest guesses that this was the Spartans' invasion-route in the First Spartano-Messenian War (p. 37). But surely, if the Spartans had trespassed on Arcadian territory to that extent and for that length of time, many Arcadian communities would have intervened in this war on the Messenian side. Moreover, the 'incident' that, according to tradition, precipitated the First Spartano-Messenian War— a clash between Spartans and Messenians in which the Spartan King Teleklos was killed— is located at the temple of Artemis Limnatis in the Dentheliatis, and this, together with the tradition that Pharai was a Spartan colony (Forrest, op. cit., p. 37), suggests that the Spartans pushed their way into Messenia at Messenia's south-eastern corner.

[2] For alleged activities of the Spartan king Teleklos in the south-eastern corner of Messenia, see Strabo, *Geographica*, Book VIII, chap. 4, § 4 (C. 360).

[3] See Pausanias, Book III, chap. 2, § 6; Book IV, chap. 4, § 2. Jones, *Sparta*, p. 11, rejects Pausanias' chronology, according to which the First Spartano-Messenian War followed close on the heels of the Spartan conquest of Amyklai.

[4] See J. Kroymann, *Sparta und Messenien* (Berlin, 1937, Weidmann), pp. 13–17. Den Boer, op. cit., p. 71, dates the end of the First Spartano-Messenian War *circa* 720–710 B.C. H. T. Wade-Gery, 'The Rhianos-Hypothesis', in *Ancient Society and Institutions* (Oxford, 1966, Blackwell), pp. 289–302, on p. 296, dates the First War *circa* 735–715 B.C. Forrest's dating is the same as Wade-Gery's (see p. 172, n. 6).

[5] Pausanias, Book IV, chap. 14, § 3.

in a district in Messenia called the Hyameia (location unknown) to the refugee descendants of Androkles, a pro-Spartan Aipytid who had lost his life in a civil war in Messenia, between pro-Spartan and anti-Spartan factions, before the outbreak of the First Spartano-Messenian War.[1] The Spartans also now gave asylum in their newly conquered Messenian territory to refugees from Nauplia and from the Dryopian city-state of Asine in the Argolid who had been evicted from their homes by the Argives.[2] The Spartans gave new homes to these refugees at the two corners of the southern tip of Messenia. They settled the Nauplians at Methone,[3] the present-day Modhon, and the Asinaeans at a new Asine,[4] on the site occupied by the present-day Koron. We do not know whether, in the First Spartano-Messenian War, the Spartans had already con- quered the whole of Messenia, as far west as the west coast and as far north as the mouth of the River Neda. It seems probable that they had; for the Second War is represented in our sources as having been a war between the Spartans and their Messenian subjects who had revolted against their rule. There is no suggestion in the sources that this, too, was a war of conquest, such as were the First Spartano-Messenian War and the subsequent series of Spartano-Tegeatan wars, in which the Spartans attempted, but failed, to conquer the territory of Tegea.

If we are to take literally Tyrtaios' statement that the First Spartano- Messenian War had been fought by the grandfathers of the Spartans who were now fighting the Second War,[5] the Second War would have started *circa* 690 B.C. It is possible, however, that, by 'fathers of our fathers', Tyrtaios means vaguely 'ancestors'; and, if he is using the phrase in this imprecise sense, the interval between the two wars may have been longer than the length of a single generation. The Second War may have been fought in the middle decades of the seventh century;[6] and the result of Sparta's eventual victory in this war will have been to restore to her, or, perhaps less probably, to give to her for the first

---

[1] Ibid., chap. 5, §§ 6–7.

[2] According to Huxley, op. cit., p. 21, archaeological evidence indicates that the Asine in the Argolid was abandoned *circa* 700 B.C.

[3] See Strabo, Book VIII, chap. 6, § 11 (C. 373); Pausanias, Book IV, chap. 24, § 4; chap. 35, §§ 1–2.

[4] See Herodotus, Book VIII, chap. 73; Strabo, loc. cit.; Pausanias, Book IV, chap. 34, §§ 9–12.

[5] Tyrtaios, frs. 3, 4 (Bergk–Hiller–Crusius) = 4 (5) (Diehl), 5, 1. 6: πατέρων ἡμετέρων πατέρες. Pausanias, Book III, follows Tyrtaios in dating the outbreak of the Second War in the reigns of Polydoros' grandson Alexandros (chap. 3, § 4) and Theopompos' grandson Zeuxidamos (chap. 7, § 6).

[6] Kroymann, *Sparta und Messenien*, p. xix; Forrest, *A History*, p. 58. Wade-Gery dates 'the Second War' (i.e. the first Messenian revolt) *circa* 660–650 B.C. in *Ancient Society and Institutions*, p. 289, and *circa* 650 B.C. at latest, ibid., p. 296. Jones, *Sparta*, p. 3, notes that Pausanias' datings of the two wars are 743–724 and 685–668 B.C., but points out, on p. 4, that all recorded dates are based on generation-counts in which the average length of a generation is over- estimated.

time, the dominion over the whole of Messenia up to the southern frontier of Triphylia and the south-western frontier of Arcadia.

(f) *Sparta's Unsuccessful Wars with Tegea*

In the course of the first half of the sixth century B.C. the Spartans made at least two attempts to conquer the Tegeatis, as they had already conquered the Eurotas basin and Messenia. These attempts failed;[1] and, at some date about half-way through the century, Sparta deliberately abandoned the policy of progressive conquest that she had been pursuing, by then, for more than two hundred years. She did not renounce her ambition to go on increasing her power and widening the range of its effectiveness; but, with the one big exception of her policy towards Argos, Sparta worked, from now onwards, to expand by negotiating alliances with other states on liberal terms on the basis of common interests, instead of trying to make further annexations by force. Sparta first came to terms with Tegea,[2] and then with the moderate oligarchic regimes that, in some cases with Spartan help, were now replacing the previous revolutionary despotic regimes in the Isthmian states.[3] This sudden change, which marked a turning-point in Sparta's foreign policy,[4] may have been the work of the ephor Khilon (*fungebatur* (?)556/5 B.C.).[5] Khilon is said to have been the author of the famous precept μηδὲν ἄγαν.[6]

(g) *Sparta's Successful Establishment of her Military Superiority over Argos*

Tegea's success in foiling Sparta's attempt to conquer her had been a remarkable feat, considering the greatness of the disparity between the resources of the two belligerents. We may guess that, in this successful resistance to Spartan aggression, Tegea had received support and aid from Argos.[7] At any rate, it was manifestly in Argos' interest to save

---

[1] Herodotus, Book I, chap. 66. Wade-Gery, in *Ancient Society and Institutions*, p. 297, dates the first Spartano-Tegeatan War 575–550 and the second 555–545 B.C. Jones, *Sparta*, pp. 1–2, notes that the first of the Spartano-Tegeatan wars recorded by Herodotus was earlier than the reigns of Leon and Agesikles, who were the respective grandfathers of Kleomenes I and Damaratos. See also D. M. Leahy, 'The Spartan Defeat at Orchomenos', in *The Phoenix*, vol. xii (1958), pp. 141–65.

[2] The price of Sparta's renunciation of her ambition to conquer Tegea may have been the cession to her, by Tegea, of some districts along the southern fringe of Tegea's territory, the Oiatis and the Karyatis. See also p. 234, n. 1, and p. 285. A list of despots deposed by Sparta is given by Plutarch, *De Herodoti Malignitate* (*Moralia*, 859 c–d). See Jones, *Sparta*, pp. 45–6.

[3] See also p. 234, n. 1, and p. 285. A list of despots deposed by Sparta is given by Plutarch, *De Herodoti Malignitate* (*Moralia*, 859 c–d). See Jones, *Sparta*, pp. 45–6.

[4] Roussel, op. cit., p. 82; Forrest, *A History*, pp. 75–6.

[5] See p. 187, with n. 1.

[6] Aristotle, *Rhetoric*, 1389b.

[7] According to Diodorus, Book VII, fragm. 13, § 2, King Meltas of Argos, Pheidon's grandson, had supported the Arcadians against Sparta and had helped them to recover some lost territory. See A. Andrewes, 'Ephorus I and the Kings of Argos', in the *Classical Quarterly*, vol. xlv (1951), pp. 39–45.

Tegea from being conquered by Sparta, since, if the Tegeatis were to fall into Spartan hands, a Spartan force, operating from there, could threaten to cut the overland communications between Argos' home territory and the chain of Cynurian city-states, between the Parnon Range and the east coast of the Peloponnese, over which Argos had established her suzerainty all the way down to Cape Malea and beyond, across the water, to the island of Kythera.[1] At the present day, both the road from Sparta to Argos and the railway from Kalamata (Pharai) to Argos run through the plain of Tegea, and this is, and always has been, the natural route, dictated by the permanent features of the physiography of the Peloponnese.

The reversal in the relations between Tegea and Sparta from belligerency to alliance was therefore almost as great a blow for Argos as if, instead of being forced by Sparta into an alliance with her, Tegea had been conquered by Sparta and had been annexed to Sparta's dominions. Sparta was now no longer hindered by the presence of a hostile Tegea on the left flank of her line of march from attacking Argos at her weakest point. This was the Thyreatis, at the northern end of Argos' straggling perioecic domain in Kynouria. At some date shortly after the mid point of the sixth century B.C.,[2] Argos' defeat by the Spartans at Thyrea lost, for Argos, not only the Thyreatis itself, but all Argos' dependencies to the south of that. Sparta appears to have annexed the Thyreatis to her own territory and to have made it part of her public domain.[3] The rest

[1] Herodotus, Book I, chap. 82.

[2] Wade-Gery, 'A Note on the Origin of the Spartan Gymnopaidiai', pp. 79–81, on p. 79, dates Sparta's conquest of the Thyreatis, Kynouria, and Kythera from Argos *circa* 544 B.C. Herodotus, Book I, chaps. 81–3, dates it in the year in which Cyrus conquered the Lydian Empire. According to Herodotus, Croesus called for help from the Spartans and his other allies after he had been defeated by the Persians in the field and had been besieged by them on the citadel of Sardis. The message reached Sparta after her victory over Argos; the Spartans at once fitted out an expeditionary force; but, before this force had time to set sail, the news came that Sardis had already fallen. The Persian conquest of the Lydian Empire is dated 547 B.C. by modern scholars in the light of surviving Babylonian historical records. So, if the defeat of Argos and the overthrow of Lydia did both occur in the same campaigning season, as Herodotus says that they did, the date of the defeat of Argos will have been, not *circa* 544 B.C., but 547 B.C. However, Herodotus' exact synchronization of these two historic events may have been an exercise of poetic licence for the sake of the dramatic effect. We have it from Herodotus himself, Book I, chaps. 56 and 68–9, that the achievement of Sparta's that had won for her an international prestige and had consequently moved Croesus to contract an alliance with Sparta on the eve of his war with Cyrus had been, not Sparta's decisive victory over Argos, but the previous successful outcome, for Sparta, of her wars with Tegea. Sparta had turned this military success to account in a diplomatic *coup* by which Argos had been isolated. But, so long as Argos' own dominions in the Peloponnese remained intact, Sparta could not afford to take the risk of embarking on overseas adventures. Sparta's preoccupation with Argos seems likely to have been one of the reasons why she did not come to Croesus' help in 547 B.C. For all that we know, the victory over Argos that relieved Sparta of this preoccupation may have been won, not in the same year as Cyrus' victory over Croesus, but several years later.

[3] In 424 B.C. both Thyrea town and its skala were inhabited by Aeginetan refugees whom

of the Cynurian city-states, from Anthana to Kythera inclusive, now became perioecic dependencies of Sparta.

These gains at Argos' expense completed Sparta's acquisition of the two-fifths of the Peloponnese that were in her possession at the time of the Atheno-Peloponnesian War.[1] There was no question of Sparta's being able to conquer Argos itself; when Sparta had failed to annex Tegea, she could not hope to annex Argos. Nor was there any question of Argos' following Tegea's example by coming to terms with Sparta and entering into an alliance with her. On the other hand, from now onwards, Argos was insulated and encircled. Sparta's north-east frontier, along the northern boundary of the Thyreatis, now ran within a few miles of the southern entry, via the Myli (Lerna) Pass, into the Argive plain; and Sparta also now succeeded in drawing into her Peloponnesian alliance the independent city-states on the Argolic akte: Epidauros, Troizen, and Hermione. Argos' political influence was thus confined to her own home territory, the Argeia.

These political fruits of Sparta's victory over Argos *circa* 544 B.C. were certainly notable enough to justify the commemoration of this victory at an old-established and important annual festival, the Gymnopaidiai.[2] Sparta's first attempt,[3] *circa* 669/8 B.C.[4] to achieve what she eventually

the Spartans had planted there (Thucydides, Book IV, chaps. 56 and 57). In 431 B.C., which was the date at which the Aeginetans had been given this territory (Thucydides, Book II, chap. 27), it must have been at the Spartan Government's disposal. We may infer that, when Sparta had conquered Kynouria from Argos *circa* 544 B.C., she had not given to Thyrea the perioecic status which she had given to the rest of the Cynurian city-states. The previous population of the Thyreatis may either have been evicted by the Spartans or else have emigrated voluntarily to the Argeia.

[1] See p. 155.

[2] Sosibius apud Athenaeum, Book XV, 678 b-c. The Gymnopaidiai Festival itself had been founded in 668 B.C. according to Wade-Gery, in the *Classical Quarterly*, vol. xlviii (1949), p. 80, or in 669 or 665 B.C. according to Andrewes, ibid., p. 77. Wade-Gery interprets 'gymnopaidiai' as meaning 'unarmed dances' (ibid., p. 79).

[3] According to the conventional version of the history of Sparta's expansion, Sparta's attack on Argos *circa* 669 B.C. was not the first but the third. The alleged attack on Argos' domain in Kynouria by the Eurypontidai, single-handed, in the generation of the son of the house's eponym, is manifestly fictitious (see p.173, n. 2). Almost equally incredible is the alleged Spartan invasion of the Argeia itself, in co-operation with the anti-Argive Argolic city-state Asine, in the reign of King Nikandros, i.e. at some date before the outbreak of the First Spartano-Messenian War (Pausanias, Book III, chap. 7, § 4). The first undoubtedly authentic Spartan invasion of the Argeia was King Kleomenes I's in 494 B.C., and this invasion was made feasible thanks only to Sparta's command of the sea-power of the Aeginetans, who had become members of Sparta's Peloponnesian alliance by this date. After having failed to invade the Argive plain overland from the Thyreatis, Kleomenes put his army on board an Aeginetan and Sicyonian flotilla and made a successful landing at the south-east corner of the Argive plain, somewhere between Nauplia and Tiryns (see Herodotus, Book VI, chaps. 76–83 and 92). The story of the Spartan invasion of the Argeia, in co-operation with the Asinaioi, before the First Spartano-Messenian War, looks as if it had been invented to account for the subsequent eviction of the Asinaioi by the Argives and for the grant by the Spartans of a new home in Messenia to the Asinaean refugees (see p. 181, n. 4).

[*Notes 3 and 4 continued opposite.*]

achieved, at Argos' expense, *circa* 544 B.C. had brought upon her a crushing defeat at Argive hands. This Spartan disaster at Hysiai, on the road from Sparta to Argos via Tegea, had been followed by the great Messenian revolt that had been suppressed eventually only after the long-drawn-out 'Second Spartano-Messenian War'. It is not surprising that Sparta should have waited for more than a hundred years before venturing to challenge Argos again; and it was only at this long-deferred second attempt that Sparta established her superiority over her.[1]

(h) *The Residual Weaknesses in Sparta's Position after her Triumph over Argos circa 544 B.C.*

Sparta had achieved relative security for her possession of two-fifths of the Peloponnese now that she had annexed Argos' former dominion in Kynouria, from Kythera to the Thyreatis inclusive, and had isolated and encircled Argos by drawing into her own Peloponnesian alliance all other still independent states in the Peloponnese except the secluded and unimportant Achaean city-states along the south coast of the Corinthian Gulf. Yet, even now, Sparta's security was not complete. Achilles had had one vulnerable heel; Sparta had three vulnerable points in the structure of her body politic. On the morning after Sparta's triumph over Argos *circa* 544 B.C., two of these three Spartan weaknesses were obvious to every Spartan and to all the world as well. Sparta's third weakness is said to have been hinted at by the contemporary Spartan statesman Khilon, though even this wise man cannot have foreseen the future extent of the weakness on which he put his finger.

Sparta's first weakness was the irreconcilable hostility of her helots.

These two events can be explained more simply. The eviction of the Asinaioi by the Argives does not necessarily imply that the Argives were making a reprisal for some offence that the Asinaioi had previously committed against them. The eviction seems at least as likely to have been an unprovoked act of aggression, like the eviction of the people of Pharis and Geronthrai by the Spartans. At this stage of Hellenic history—and, indeed, at almost all stages of it—the more powerful city-states sought, as a matter of course, to expand their dominions at the expense of weaker neighbours. As for the Spartans' provision of a new home in Messenia for the evicted Asinaioi, this, again, does not necessarily imply that the Spartans were paying the Asinaioi for services previously rendered. By her recent conquest of Messenia, Sparta had doubled the size of her dominions and had thereby saddled herself with the problem of how she was to hold down a large unreconciled subject population. One obvious expedient was to plant in Messenia garrisons of homeless refugees—victims of the aggressive expansion of other powers. Such garrisons could be relied upon to be loyal to Sparta, not so much out of gratitude as because they had no other home now to return to and because they could not hope to hold their own in their new home unless they co-operated with the Spartans to hold down the subjugated Messenian population. This Spartan policy of planting garrisons of refugees in conquered territories was also followed by the Macedonian Argeadai (see Part II, chap. 8, pp. 137–8).

4 See Pausanias, Book II, chap. 24, § 7.

1 See Roussel, op. cit., pp. 24–5.

She had now insulated the helots, by the double curtain of her perioikoi and her independent Peloponnesian allies, from Argos or any other power, hostile to Sparta, that might have wished to foment further helot revolts by coming, overland, to the aid of helot insurgents.[1] The helots were thus temporarily impotent, but their determination to recover their freedom was unabated; and, if any now unforeseen opportunity for a fresh insurrection were to offer itself, they would be certain to take it.[2]

Sparta's second weakness was the irreconcilable hostility of Argos. Like the helots, Argos was temporarily impotent; but her determination to recover her former position of primacy in the Peloponnese was un-

---

[1] It is significant that in the treaty, concluded *circa* 550 B.C. between Sparta and Tegea, implementing Sparta's decision to desist from trying to conquer Tegea and Tegea's decision to become Sparta's ally, there was a clause stipulating that 'the Tegeatans shall expel Messenian refugees' (ἐκβαλεῖν Μεσσηνίους καὶ μὴ χρηστοὺς ποιεῖν) (Plutarch, *Moralia (Aet. Graec.*, 292 B), citing Aristotle). There was also a clause stipulating that the treaty should be inscribed on a stele, common to both parties, that was to be set up 'on the River Alpheios' (Plutarch in loc. cit.). The site designated was presumably on the frontier between Sparta's territory and south-western Arcadia, and this choice of site implies that south-western Arcadia was under Tegea's control at this time. The nearest place in Arcadia to the point where the Alpheios passed out of Lacedaemonian into Arcadian territory was Oresthasion (alias Orestheion). For the location of Oresthasion, see E. Meyer, s.v., in P.–W., 35. Halbband, cols. 1014–16. A band of one hundred Oresthasians had assisted the Phigaleians in retaking Phigaleia after Phigaleia had been captured by the Lacedaemonians (Pausanias, Book VIII, chap. 39, §§ 3–5, and chap. 41, § 1). The Phigaleians had fallen foul of Sparta—presumably because they had been giving aid to Messenian insurgents. Hira, the mountain fastness just inside Messenia in which the Messenian hero Aristomenes had held out, is next door to Phigaleia, and Aristomenes is said to have had a Phigaleian brother-in-law (Wade-Gery, 'The Rhianos-Hypothesis', pp. 196 and 292–4). 'It was the Hira War [see the next footnote] which involved the Spartans in Arkadia, with Phigalea first and then with Oresthasion (or Orestheion) and Tegea; and that is why in her treaty with Tegea in *ca.* 550 Sparta insisted on the clause about Messenian refugees' (Wade-Gery, ibid., p. 296).

Tegea was not the first Arcadian state that had given aid to Messenian insurgents. Phigaleia appears to have helped Aristomenes during the Hira War. King Aristokrates of Orkhomenos may have intervened, on the Messenian insurgents' side, in 'the Second Spartano-Messenian War', i.e. the first Messenian revolt (Leahy in loc. cit., p. 162). Leahy conjectures (ibid., pp. 162–3) that, at the time of the first Messenian revolt, south-western Arcadia may have been under Orkhomenos' hegemony, but will have passed out of Orkhomenos' control into Tegea's by the time of the Spartano-Tegeatan wars. If this guess hits the mark, we may go on to guess that Orkhomenos had forfeited her hegemony over south-western Arcadia as a result of her failure to prevent the Spartans from resubjugating Messenia at the time of the first Messenian revolt.

[2] By 544 B.C. there had probably been at least two serious Messenian revolts already. 'Epameinondas claimed in 369 that the Thebans had "founded Messene after an interval of 230 years"' (Wade-Gery, 'The Rhianos-Hypothesis', p. 295, following Pseudo-Plutarch, *Moralia*, 194 B, and Aelian, *Varia Historia*, Book XIII, chap. 42). Wade-Gery suggests (ibid., p. 297) that the event *circa* 600 B.C. with which Epameinondas was equating the eclipse of Messenia was the fall of Hira, and that the Messenian revolt led by Aristomenes was one towards the close of the seventh century B.C., and was not either the preceding 'Second Spartano-Messenian War', with which Aristomenes has been traditionally associated, or the revolt in 490 B.C. which is attested by Plato, *Laws*, Book III, 698 D-E, and is accepted as being authentic by Forrest, *A History*, p. 92, and with which Aristomenes has been associated by some modern scholars. See also L. Pearson, 'The Pseudo-History of Messenia and its Authors', in *Historia*, 11. Band (1962), pp. 397–426.

abated; and she, too, would be certain to seize any now unforeseen opportunity of combating Sparta's supremacy. She could no longer hope to find allies against Sparta in the Peloponnese, but perhaps one day she might find them farther afield.

Sparta's third weakness was indicated by Khilon when he said (if this saying, attributed to him,[1] is authentic) that he wished that the island of Kythera had sunk below the surface of the sea. This saying, whether authentic or not, must have been apropos of Sparta's acquisition of Kythera from Argos as a result of the Spartan victory at Thyrea. Since Kythera had not foundered and was not going to founder, the annexation of the island was, for Sparta, a lesser evil than it would have been to leave in hostile Argive hands this possible base of operations for fomenting and aiding a revolt of Sparta's helots in the lower part of the Eurotas basin. On the other hand, Sparta's acquisition of an island committed her to having to defend her possession of it against potentially hostile sea-powers; and, though the inclusion of the Isthmian maritime city-states in Sparta's Peloponnesian alliance insured Sparta against all risks of naval attack from that quarter, nothing could insure her against naval attack from farther afield. While, under the technological conditions of the time, overland movement was slow and laborious, movement by sea was relatively swift and easy. By *circa* 544 B.C. the Greeks, Phoenicians, and Etruscans had planted trading posts and colonies all round the shores of the Mediterranean and the Black Sea. A naval attack on Kythera, and also on vulnerable points along the coasts of Sparta's possessions on the mainland of the Peloponnese, could be delivered suddenly from any point in the Mediterranean basin.

Though Xerxes did not act on Damaratos' alleged advice to him to use his naval power to occupy Kythera,[2] Khilon's forebodings were borne out in the first bout of the Atheno-Peloponnesian War. The Athenian navy occupied Kythera in 424 B.C.[3] Meanwhile, in 425 B.C., the Athenians had achieved an even more effective stroke by occupying and fortifying the deserted site of Pylos, on the west coast of Messenia. Their success at Pylos had been twofold. They had captured the survivors of the garrison that the Spartans had posted on the adjoining island of Sphakteria; and they had secured a permanent base of operations for inciting the helots to revolt and for giving support to those who did seize this opportunity.[4]

One of the factors that made the Athenian occupation of Pylos possible in the first instance and effective in the event was that not only

[1] By the exiled Spartan king Damaratos in a conversation with the Emperor Xerxes in 480 B.C., according to Herodotus, Book VII, chap. 235.

[2] Herodotus, loc. cit.

[3] Thucydides, Book IV, chaps. 53–5.

[4] Ibid., chap. 41.

Pylos itself but a large tract of adjoining Spartan territory was un-inhabited at this date.[1] This is an astonishing fact on two accounts.

In the first place, the west coast of Messenia, like the rest of the west coast of the Peloponnese, up to its north-western corner, is one of the most fertile strips of country in all European Greece. It is a continuous garden today, and in the Mycenaean Age it had provided the agricul-tural basis for Nestor's Minyan principality—the next most important state in the Peloponnese of that age after the dominions of the house of Pelops itself. If this west coast of Messenia was still under cultivation at the time of the First and Second Spartano-Messenian wars, why did the Spartans let it go out of cultivation when they had first acquired, and then reacquired, this valuable piece of territory? And, if, as seems less likely, this coast had been uninhabited and uncultivated since the over-throw of Nestor's principality in the post-Mycenaean Völkerwanderung *circa* 1200 B.C., why did not the Spartans put it under cultivation at the time when, after their eventual victory in the Second Spartano-Messenian War, they were increasing Sparta's hoplite man-power[2] by endowing Spartiatai with allotments of land (κλῆροι) cultivated by helot labour?

The second reason why it is astonishing that the Spartans should have left the west coast of Messenia uninhabited is the military point that was made patent by the Athenian *coups* at Pylos and Sphakteria in 425 B.C. The Spartans must have been aware of this potential military danger when they garrisoned the south-western tip of Messenia by planting there two refugee communities from the Argeia: Asinaean refugees at New Asine, and Nauplian refugees at Methone.[3] It is also possible, though not certain, that, at some date, the Spartans had established a perioecic city-state at Aulon, at the northern end of the west coast of Messenia.[4] But it is evident that they had never closed the gap along the coast between Methone and Aulon by planting permanent garrisons there too. We may infer that, in spite of Khilon's alleged warning apropos of Kythera, the Spartan Government had never, before 425 B.C., considered seriously the possibility that Sparta's dominions in western Messenia might be attacked from the sea.

---

[1] ἐρῆμον [ὂν τὸ χωρίον] αὐτό τε καὶ ἐπὶ πολὺ τῆς χώρας (Thucydides, Book IV, chap. 3, § 2; cp. [Plato], *Alcibiades*, 1, 122 D).

[2] For this dating (which is, of course, disputable) of the Spartans' adoption of phalanx-tactics, see chap. 3, Annex I. [3] See p. 181, nn. 2, 3, and 4.

[4] See Xenophon, *Hellenica*, Book III, chap. 3, § 8. In this passage the Aulonitai are mentioned, so Aulon must have been a village or town; and the Aulonitai are distinguished from the helots, which makes it probable that the Aulonitai were perioikoi.

The Boundaries of the Territory of the City-State of Sparta

THE two-fifths of the Peloponnese which were in the possession of the Lacedaemonian state from the date of the annexation of the Thyreatis *circa* 544 B.C. down to the date of the loss of Messenia in 370 B.C. was made up of two areas which differed from each other in political status. On the one hand there was the territory of the city-state of Sparta (ἡ πολιτικὴ χώρα).[1] This territory had two categories of inhabitants: the Spartiatai, who were concentrated at two points—in the cluster of four settlements that constituted the City of Sparta in the physical sense and at the neighbouring town or village of Amyklai—and the helots, who inhabited the greater part of the countryside, though not the original nucleus of this, which had belonged to Sparta before she had reduced to the status of helots the population of the additional territory that she had subsequently acquired by conquest. The rest of the aggregate territory of the Lacedaemonian state was made up of the local territories of the autonomous perioecic cities, of which there were reckoned, in round numbers, to be as many as a hundred. The perioikoi, as well as the Spartiatai, were officially Lakedaimonioi, though, on the territory of the Spartan city-state, the perioikoi were juridically aliens (ξένοι), and we may presume that, conversely, the Spartiatai were aliens in perioecic territory. The helots were not Lakedaimonioi;[2] for, though they, too, were inhabitants of Lakonike, and of the Spartan section of it, they counted juridically as slaves, and, as such, they were incapable of possessing any political status.

The boundaries of Sparta's city-state territory are less uncertain in Messenia than they are in Laconia to the east of the Taÿgetos Range.

In Messenia, the Stenyklaros plain, i.e. the upper basin of the Pamisos River, was certainly Spartan territory, and its native peasants were helots. It also appears, in default of any evidence to the contrary, that the country to the south-west of the Stenyklaros plain and of Mount Ithome, as far as the west coast of Messenia between Aulon and Methone, both exclusive, was also Spartan territory; and, in so far as this region was inhabited and was utilized for any economic purpose besides hunting— for instance, for pasture[3]—the permanent inhabitants will have been helots here too. In the western half of Messenia, New Asine, Methone, and possibly Aulon are the only perioecic city-states of which we have any

---

[1] Polybius, Book VI, chap. 45, § 3.
[2] See Busolt and Swoboda, op. cit., p. 653, n. 1, and p. 663.
[3] See ibid., p. 639.

knowledge.[1] Niese conjectures that there was a continuous chain of perioecic city-states along the northern border of the Stenyklaros plain, linking Aulon with the Aigytis,[2] but this guess is not supported by any evidence. South-eastern Messenia, including, probably, the whole of the Makaria plain, i.e. the lower basin of the Pamisos, was covered by the territories of perioecic cities.[3] The Makaria plain may have been shared by Thouria with her neighbour Aithaia, whose existence is known to us solely from a single passage in Thucydides' history.[4] We do not know whether the territory of Aithaia marched with the territory of New Asine, or whether the Spartan territory in western Messenia touched the coast between Aithaia and Asine as well as between Methone and Aulon.

To the east of the Taÿgetos Range, the bounds of the Spartan city-state territory are still more difficult to identify. Its approximately western and approximately eastern bounds coincided more or less with the Taÿgetos Range and the Parnon Range respectively; but the correspondence with these natural barriers was not at all exact. The Dentheliatis, through which the route between Sparta and Pharai (Kalamata) runs, west of the passes, must, in this period, have been Spartan territory, and this was a big salient which made an equally big dent in the perioecic territory in south-eastern Messenia. An inscription[5] records that the western frontier of the Spartan city-state territory, as demarcated in A.D. 78, ran parallel to the crest of the Taÿgetos Range, but to the west of it;[6] but we have no means of knowing whether this was a confirmation of a previous line or whether it was an innovation. On the Parnon side, the territory of the perioecic city-state Geronthrai must have been a salient of perioecic territory protruding into the Spartan territory in the middle section of the Eurotas basin.

In the upper basin of the Eurotas, Pellana and Sellasia were perioecic city-states,[7] and the boundary between their territories and Sparta's must have cut across the Eurotas basin in a more or less east-and-west direction. The northern boundary of the Spartan territory was presumably

---

[1] For New Asine and Methone, see p. 181, with nn. 2, 3, and 4. For Aulon, see p. 188, with n. 4. The Lacedaemonians used New Asine as a naval station during the war of 431–404 B.C. (see Thucydides, Book IV, chap. 13, § 1 (425 B.C.); Book VI, chap. 93, § 3 (415 B.C.)).

[2] See Niese, 'Neue Beiträge zur Geschichte und Landeskunde Lakedaimons: die lakedaimonischen Perioken', pp. 101–42, on p. 122.

[3] See Forrest, *A History*, p. 37.

[4] Book I, chap. 101.

[5] *I.G.*, vol. v, fasc. 1, pp. 282–4, No. 1431.

[6] For details, see Chrimes, *Ancient Sparta*, pp. 60–7. See also the present work, Part III, chap. 6.

[7] In 405/4 B.C., when the Athenians were proposing peace-terms to the Spartan authorities, their envoys were allowed to come as far as Sellasia, which was non-Spartan territory; but they were not allowed to come on from Sellasia to Sparta till they had made an offer which the Spartan authorities regarded as providing a satisfactory starting-point for negotiations. See Xenophon, *Hellenica*, Book II, chap. 2, §§ 13 and 19.

demarcated by the 'Kharakoma' ('palisade') which the traveller from Sparta to Pellana crossed just before arriving at the latter city.[1] We may guess that the boundary marked out by the 'Kharakoma' was the same as the boundary described in the rhetra presented to the gerousia by the ephor Lysander in the reign of King Agis IV.[2] The proposed redistribution of the Spartan territory into 4,500 new allotments (κλῆροι) was to start from this line; and the line was to follow the torrent (that discharges into the River Eurotas) at Pellana and was to extend to the Taÿgetos range (on the west) and to Malea (?i.e. the Parnon Range, which terminates in Cape Malea, on the east), passing (on the eastern side of the Eurotas) via Sellasia.[3] This interpretation of the rhetra's obscure formula is, of course, conjectural and disputable; but, since it was provided in the rhetra that the re-allotment of the Spartan territory was to start from this line, and since no other boundaries are mentioned, we may perhaps infer that the unspecified boundaries were all natural features—namely the Taÿgetos Range, the Parnon Range, and the coast of the Laconian Gulf —and that the boundary which is described is described because it is an artificial one, cutting, as it did, across the upper part of the Eurotas basin.[4] The 'outside territory' that was to be divided into 15,000 lots[5] would then be the two blocks of perioecic territory that were still under Sparta's rule, i.e. southern Kynouria east of Parnon and the Tainaron Peninsula in which the Taÿgetos Range juts out into the sea.

A difficult question is that of the extent of the Spartan territory's frontage on the coast of the Laconian Gulf. Helos must have lain in Spartan, not in perioecic, territory; for, though the interpretation of the term 'heilotes' as being the ethnikon of Helos is incorrect,[6] this false etymology would not have been thought of if the population of the Helos district had not been helots;[7] and, if they were helots, the district must have lain within Spartan territory. Helos is not one of the Eleutherolaconian city-states in Pausanias' list of these;[8] and a place that was not either one of the surviving free Laconian states or one of the formerly free Laconian states that Augustus had given back to Sparta is unlikely to have been a perioecic city-state before 195 B.C., since all the perioecic states still attaching to Sparta at that date seem to have been detached from her then.

---

[1] Pausanias, Book III, chap. 21, § 2.

[2] Plutarch, *Agis*, chap. 8.

[3] τὴν μὲν [γῆν] ἀπὸ τοῦ κατὰ Πελλήνην χαράδρου πρὸς τὸ Ταΰγετον καὶ Μαλέαν καὶ Σελλασίαν κλήρους γενέσθαι τετρακισχιλίους πεντακοσίους (Plutarch, ibid.).

[4] See J. Kromayer, 'Studien über Wehrkraft und Wehrverfassung der griechischen Staaten', in *Klio*, 3. Band (1903), pp. 47–67 and 173–212, on p. 175, n. 1.

[5] Plutarch, *Agis*, chap. 8.

[6] See pp. 178 and 196–7.

[7] This point is made by Neumann in loc. cit., p. 54.

[8] In Book III, chap. 21, § 7. See the present work, Part III, chap. 6, p. 411.

We cannot, however, be sure that all the territory detached from Sparta in 195 B.C. was perioecic and that none of it was Spartan. The disputable case is that of Gythion,[1] which heads Pausanias' list of Eleutherolaconian cities, but which had been Sparta's naval base, before that, since at least the time of the Decelean War (413–404 B.C.).[2] As early as 370 B.C. Gythion was a town and a fortified one—fortified, in fact, well enough to withstand, successfully, a three days' assault by the Thebans and their allies.[3] In 195 B.C., Gythion's defences were still formidable.[4] The facts that Gythion was a town, that it was strongly fortified, that it was detached from Sparta in 195 B.C.,[5] and that it was an Eleutherolaconian city-state in Pausanias' day have led some scholars to infer that, before its cession by Sparta in 195 B.C., Gythion had been a perioecic city-state. This seems improbable for several reasons.

In the first place, if Gythion had been perioecic territory, not Spartan territory, Sparta, after her conquest of the lower basin of the Eurotas, would still have had no coastline of her own on the Laconian Gulf except, perhaps, a short strip of marshy alluvial coast, round the mouth of the Eurotas, which could not have offered her a practicable port. The harbours on the coasts of the Malea peninsula were not at Sparta's disposal till after she had conquered Kynouria from Argos; it seems that she did not achieve this till *circa* 544 B.C.;[6] and anyway, by comparison with Gythion, these harbours were relatively distant from Sparta. Down to the time when Sparta conquered the lower basin of the Eurotas, she had been a land-locked state. She must have valued her acquisition of a seaboard—the more so since the date (perhaps about, or shortly after, 750 B.C.) at which she expanded her dominions to the coast of the Laconian Gulf was the very time at which some of the other Greek city-states were beginning to plant colonies far and wide round the shores of the Mediterranean. Before the close of the eighth century B.C., Sparta herself took a direct part in this Greek colonizing movement by founding Tarentum. By then, Sparta must surely have established a port of her own[7] on Spartan territory; Gythion is the nearest Laconian port to Sparta city; and it seems unlikely that Sparta would have been content to use a port located in alien territory, even though the alien state in which the port lay had been reduced to perioecic status. Though, in Pausanias' day, Gythion was an Eleutherolaconian city-state, both Krokeai, on the road to Gythion from Sparta, and Aigiai, just off this road and only three or

[1] See p. 179.
[2] Xenophon, *Hellenica*, Book I, chap. 4, § 11.
[3] Ibid., Book VI, chap. 5, § 32.
[4] See Livy, Book XXXIV, chap. 29. The point is noted by Jones, *Sparta*, p. 159.
[5] Livy, Book XXXIV, chap. 35, § 10.
[6] See pp. 183–4.
[7] See Pareti, *Storia di Sparta Arcaïca*, Parte I, p. 170.

four miles away from Gythion, were then still Spartan, not Eleuthero-laconian, territory;[1] and it seems unlikely that Sparta would have annexed the hinterland of Gythion, up to so short a distance from Gythion itself, without annexing Gythion as well.

It is true that, if Gythion lay in Spartan, not in perioecic, territory, it presents an exception to the rule that, on Spartan territory, there should be no towns except the two—Sparta itself and Amyklai—in which the Spartiatai were concentrated.[2] But this exception was inevitable if Sparta was to have a commercial port and a naval base and dockyard on Spartan soil. It is also true that all other Laconian towns, known to have been liberated from Sparta in 195 B.C., were perioecic as far as we can tell; but, if Gythion was not perioecic but was Spartan, it was natural that it should be the exception to the rule on this point also. In detaching territories from Sparta in 195 B.C., T. Quinctius Flamininus' primary purpose was not to liberate Sparta's perioikoi; it was to insulate Sparta herself from the sea and to reduce her naval power to vanishing point.[3] This objective would not have been achieved if Sparta had not been deprived of Gythion, which, whatever its status, was her principal port. This consideration, which was Flamininus' principal motive for liberating Gythion, was reinforced by the consideration that Gythion had capitulated to Flamininus, instead of waiting to be taken by assault.[4]

Thus it seems probable that Gythion was included in the city-state territory of Sparta herself from *circa* 750 B.C. to 195 B.C. continuously.

We have still to look for the boundary, within Spartan territory, between the nucleus of it, which must have been cultivated by free labour, and those extensions of it that were cultivated by helots. In the nuclear territory of Sparta the conditions of ownership and of cultivation will have been no different from those in the territory of any other Hellenic city-state. The soil will have been private property, in freeholds of unequal sizes. The typical Spartan in this territory will have been a peasant who cultivated his own land. There will also have been owners of larger estates who cultivated these with hired free labour; and there will have been landless Spartiatai who earned their living by serving as

---

[1] Pausanias, Book III, chap. 21, §§ 4–6.

[2] Bölte, in P.–W., Zweite Reihe [R–Z], Dritter Band, A 2 (1929), col. 1336, notes that Pausanias found no cities in Spartan territory beyond the village of Amyklai. The helots were not concentrated in villages. The same point is made by Niese in 'Neue Beiträge zur Geschichte und Landeskunde Lakedaimons', pp. 127–9, and in 'Zur Verfassungsgeschichte Lakedaimons', p. 74; by Ehrenberg in 'Spartiaten und Lakedaimonier', pp. 23–72, on p. 50; by Pareti, *Storia di Sparta Arcaïca*, Parte I, p. 200; by Berve, *Sparta*, p. 23; by Roussel, *Sparte*, pp. 53–4. Wade-Gery, *Essays in Greek History* (Oxford, 1958, Blackwell), p. 78, n. 1, interprets τὰ χωρία of Xenophon, *Hellenica*, Book III, chap. 3, § 5, as meaning the country-estates of the homoioi. Cp. τὰς οἰκίας of Book V, chap. 5, § 30, which are the homoioi's country houses.

[3] See Livy, Book XXXIV, chap. 35, § 5.

[4] Livy, Book XXXIV, chap. 29; chap. 35, § 10.

labourers on the larger estates. There is no reason to suppose that, in this metropolitan area, freehold tenure and free labour were ever replaced by allotments (κλῆροι) cultivated by helots. The land that was distributed in allotments at the reform of the Spartan constitution towards the end of the seventh century B.C. will have been exclusively land that had come into the Spartan state's possession by right of conquest. There is no record of there having been, on this occasion, a revolutionary transfer of the ownership of land that was private property; and there is no record, either, of helots ever having been deported from their ancestral lands after these had been expropriated by the Spartan state and had subsequently been distributed to Spartiatai in allotments; and some helots would have had to be deported if helot labour had been conscripted for cultivating the private estates of Spartans in Sparta's nuclear territory.[1] After the 'Lycurgan' reform there were still Spartiate 'hypomeiones' to continue to serve as hired labourers, even after a large part, perhaps a majority, of the Spartiate citizen-body had been converted into 'homoioi' through being endowed with kleroi.

Where, then, did the dividing line run between non-helot and helot Spartan territory? All Spartan territory in Messenia was undoubtedly helot country. The question is where the dividing line between these two categories of Spartan land ran in the Eurotas basin. We can only guess at the answer to this question; and our guess will depend on our previous guess about the terms on which Amyklai was incorporated in the Spartan body politic. If all the Amyklaioi were enfranchised, and if they were allowed to retain as much of their land as they were not required to cede to the Taÿgetan Minyai, then the whole of the previously non-Spartan part of the plain of hollow Lakedaimon, right down to its south-south-eastern end, will have been added to the freehold section of Sparta's city-state territory, and the helot section will have been confined, in Laconia, to the lower part of the Eurotas basin. On the other hand, the dividing line between non-helot and helot Spartan land will have cut across the plain of hollow Lakedaimon if some, at least, of the Amyklaioi were not exterminated or evicted and were not enfranchised either, but were left on the land with the status of helots.

We have no means of ascertaining which of these two alternative possibilities is the truth. We have, however, one indirect indication that the helot portion of the Spartan territory in Laconia began at no great distance to the south-south-east of Sparta city. In 466 or 464 B.C.,[2] when the news of the earthquake that hit Sparta in either the one or the other of

---

[1] See U. Kahrstedt, 'Die spartanische Agrarwirtschaft', in *Hermes*, 54. Band (1919), pp. 279–94, on p. 288.

[2] The dating of the earthquake depends partly on the dating of the accession of King Arkhidamos (see p. 346, n. 4).

these two years came to the helots' ears, they started to march on the city; but King Arkhidamos had forestalled the helots' intended attack by making the homoioi fall in, in battle order, as soon as the earthquake shocks had ceased. According to the story, the king's prompt action just, but only just, anticipated the embattled helots' arrival on the scene. If this story is authentic history, we can perhaps infer from it that the south-south-eastern end of the former territory of Amyklai in hollow Lakedaimon was helot land, not freehold; for the helots could not have reached Sparta so quickly from anywhere farther away than that.[1]

PART III, CHAPTER 2, ANNEX II

The Origin and Status of the Helots

THERE are at least four different and mutually irreconcilable accounts of the date and the circumstances in which helotage originated. This indicates that all four accounts are guesses, and that there was no authentic record.[2] Moreover, two out of the four accounts are based on the mistaken interpretation of the word εἵλωτες as being an ethnikon meaning 'inhabitants of Helos', a place in the south-east corner of the coastal plain of the Eurotas basin.[3]

According to Ephorus' account,[4] the people of Helos had been reduced to helotage by the Spartan King Agis I, the eponym of the Agiad house. This account is obviously untrue; for, even if Agis I was an historical personage (and we cannot be sure that he is not a legendary figure), his range of action will have been limited to a few square miles at the north-north-west corner of hollow Lakedaimon, and in his time Helos will have been screened from Spartan interference by the then still independent territories of Amyklai, Pharis, and Geronthrai. According to the second account, the helots had been reduced to helotage by Sŏŏs, the fictitious father of Eurypon, the eponym of the Eurypontid house.[5] According to the third account, Helos was captured and destroyed by the Agiad king Alkamenes[6] in the generation between that of Alkamenes' father

---

[1] Plutarch, *Cimon*, chap. 16. See also Lotze, Μεταξὺ Ἐλευθέρων καὶ Δούλων, p. 73.
[2] See Norvin in *Classica et Mediaevalia*, iii, p. 55.
[3] See, for example, Hellanicus, fr. 188 (Jacoby); Theopompus, fr. 13 (15) (Jacoby) apud Athenaeum, Book VI, 272 a: τὸ τῶν Εἱλώτων ἔθνος· οἱ μὲν ἐκ Μεσσήνης ὄντες, οἱ δὲ Ἑλεᾶται κατοικοῦντες πρότερον τὸ καλούμενον Ἕλος; Ephorus apud Strabonem, *Geographica*, Book VIII, chap. 5, § 4 (C. 365) (Jacoby, Zweiter Teil A, p. 73, No. 117 (18)).
[4] Strabo, *Geographica*, Book VIII, chap. 5, § 4 (C. 365).
[5] Plutarch, *Lycurgus*, chap. 2.
[6] Pausanias, Book III, chap. 2, § 7.

Teleklos, who had conquered Amyklai, Pharis, and Geronthrai, and that of Alkamenes' son Polydoros, who was reigning at the time of the First Spartano-Messenian War. Alkamenes' reign may well be the true date of Sparta's annexation of Helos and the rest of the coastal plain of the Eurotas basin; but this does not give us the date and origin of helotage, if we are right in holding that the word εἵλωτες is not the ethnikon of Helos. According to the fourth account,[1] the helots were descended from Spartiatai who had been reduced to this status as a penalty for their having refused to take part in the First Spartano-Messenian War.

The etymology of the word εἵλωτες, whatever the right interpretation of the word's meaning may be, will determine our view of the origin of the institution. If it were in truth an ethnikon, it would be parallel to the terms 'Mnoïtai' and 'Penestai',[2] which were used respectively to designate the slave or semi-slave peasantry in Crete and in Thessaly in the Post-Völkerwanderung Age. Presumably these ethnic names are those of the peoples who were in occupation of Crete and of Thessaliotis at the time of the post-Mycenaean Völkerwanderung; and, on this analogy, the 'heilotes' would be the population of Helos in the Laconian coastal plain, and the term would have originated at the date, perhaps shortly after 750 B.C., at which the coastal plain was conquered and annexed by Sparta.[3]

However, the interpretation of εἵλωτες as being the ethnikon of ῾Ελος is not the right one, as is revealed in Stephanus of Byzantium's entry *sub voce* ῾Ελος: πόλις Λακωνική . . . οἱ πολῖται Εἵλωτες λέγονται καὶ Εἱλῶται καὶ ῾Ελεᾶται, καὶ ἡ χώρα Εἱλωτεία. Εἵλωτες, which Stephanus puts first, is evidently the correct form of the word. Stephanus' variant Εἱλῶται is evidently an attempt to make an ethnikon out of what is, in truth, the perfect participle passive of a verb.[4] ῾Ελεᾶται, and not either Εἵλωτες or Εἱλῶται, is one of the true ethnika of ῾Ελος. The other is ῾Ελεῖοι, which is used by Strabo in a passage already cited.[5] The word εἱλωτεία, cited by Stephanus, does not mean, as he alleges, 'the country inhabited by the people of Helos'. Heleia is the correct name for that.[6] 'Heloteia' means 'the helot community' or 'the status of helotage'.

---

[1] Antiochus, cited by Strabo, *Geographica*, Book VI, chap. 3, § 2 (C. 278).

[2] 'Penestai' looks like an ethnikon of the same type as 'Orestai'. Besides the semi-slave Thessalian Penestai, there was a people of this name in southern Illyria. These Illyrian Penestai are mentioned by Livy only, according to H. Krahe, *Die alten balkanillyrischen geographischen Namen* (Heidelberg, 1925, Winter), p. 32.

[3] This is Pausanias' account in Book III, chap. 20, § 6.

[4] Εἱλῶται is, however, the form used by Herodotus in Book VI, chaps, 58 and 75, and in Book IX, chap. 28. On the other hand, in Book VII, chap. 229, he uses the form εἵλως. He varies his declension according to the case.

[5] Strabo, *Geographica*, Book VIII, chap. 5, § 4 (C. 365).

[6] τὴν ῾Ελείαν, ἥτις ἐστὶν ὡς πρὸς μέρος θεωρουμένη πλείστη καὶ καλλίστη χώρα τῆς Λακωνικῆς (Polybius, Book V, chap. 19).

The right interpretation of εἵλωτες is surely Boisacq's interpretation of the word as being a perfect passive participle of the verb ἑλεῖν-ἁλίσκεσθαι.[1] On this interpretation the helots were 'captives', 'prisoners of war', or 'dediticii' (the corresponding Roman technical term).[2] They will, of course, have had a local habitation, but their name will not have derived from that, and their status will not have depended on ·it.[3] The helots were the descendants of the population of local communities, originally foreign to Sparta and independent of her, which had been annexed to the city-state territory of Sparta by Spartan acts of conquest.[4] Their name, commemorating this act of conquest, as it does, proves that they were not the descendants of originally free Spartans who had been reduced to a penal status on account of some political or military misdemeanour of theirs or who had lost their liberty, like the Attic 'hektemoroi', as a result of economic adversity.[5] As a defeated enemy population that had surrendered to Sparta unconditionally, the helots were at Sparta's disposal, to do what she chose with their lives and their property. The Spartan

---

[1] This interpretation of Boisacq's is endorsed by Forrest, *A History*, p. 31; by J. Oehler, s.v. 'Heloten', in P.-W., 15. Halbband (1912), cols. 203–6, in col. 203; by Busolt and Swoboda, op. cit., p. 667, n. 1; and by Lotze, *Μεταξὺ Ἐλευθέρων καὶ Δούλων*, p. 36. This interpretation is supported by the *Etymologicum Magnum*: εἵλωτες· παρὰ Λακεδαιμονίοις οἱ νόθοι οἱ ἐξ αἰχμαλώτων δοῦλοι γινόμενοι. Cp. Hellanikos' interpretation χειρωθέντες in Harpocration, s.v. εἱλωτεύειν, and Theopompus apud Athenaeum, Book VI, 272 a: καταδεδουλωμένοι.

[2] See Ehrenberg, 'Spartiaten und Lakedaimonier', pp. 23–72, on pp. 39–40. Cp. Lotze, *Μεταξὺ Ἐλευθέρων καὶ Δούλων*, pp. 69 and 75.

[3] For instance, there is no record of there having been any difference in status between the helots in Laconia and those in Messenia (Kahrstedt, 'Die spartanische Agrarwirtschaft', pp. 285 and 290).

[4] Thus the origin of the Spartan helots will have been the same as that of the subject peasantry in Crete and Thessaly. In all three cases the status will have originated in a conquest, though this at two widely different dates. The Spartan conquests which created the Laconian and Messenian helots will have been made in the eighth century B.C., whereas the Penestai will have been conquered by the Thessaloi, and the Mnoïtai by the North-West-Greek-speaking immigrants into Crete, in the post-Mycenaean Völkerwanderung, i.e. at least 500 years earlier than the date of the Spartan conquests. Lotze, in *Μεταξὺ Ἐλευθέρων καὶ Δούλων*, p. 76, points out that, in the Hellenic world, conquest did not invariably result in the enslavement of the conquered peasantry. In post-Völkerwanderung Boeotia, for instance, there is no trace of an enslaved rural population. Lotze also holds that Pollux, Book III, chap. 83, is mistaken in classing as semi-slaves the Argive Gymnetes and the Sicyonian korynephoroi. Lotze thinks that these, and also the Epidaurian konipodes, were depressed classes of freemen (ibid., pp. 53–5 and 79). 'It is surely no accident that the localities in which there was [rural] slavery were the fertile plains of Laconia, Messenia, and Thessaly' (ibid., p. 76).

[5] This is Kahrstedt's thesis in 'Die spartanische Agrarwirtschaft'. Kahrstedt explicitly equates the status of the Laconian helots with that of the Athenian hektemoroi before these recovered their freedom through Solon's measures on their behalf (loc. cit., p. 292). At the same time, Kahrstedt rightly derives the word εἵλωτες from the verb ἑλεῖν (ibid., p. 293); and this compels him to conjecture (p. 292) that the Laconian helots were not reduced to helotage until after the Spartan conquest of Messenia, and that these ex-Spartiatai were then given the status and the name that had already been imposed on Sparta's Messenian 'dediticii'. Lotze, *Μεταξὺ Ἐλευθέρων καὶ Δούλων*, p. 69, points out that there is no evidence in our sources in favour of Kahrstedt's view.

state perpetuated its original freedom of action *vis-à-vis* the helots by making a formal declaration of war on them every year.¹

Can the status of the Spartan helots be defined more precisely?

Pollux² cites, as being 'something between freemen and slaves' (μεταξὺ δὲ ἐλευθέρων καὶ δούλων), 'the Lacedaemonians' helots and the Thessalians' Penestai and the Cretans' klarotai and Mnoïtai and the Mariandynians' "gift-bringers" (δωροφόροι) and the Argives' gymnetes³ and the Sicyonians' "fleece-wearers" '.⁴

Lotze points out that the Spartan helots are classified as being slaves outright in some other contexts. Popularly, they are called οἰκέται;⁵ officially, e.g. in the texts of treaties, they are called δοῦλοι.⁶

If the helots were slaves, whose slaves were they? Pausanias⁷ calls them 'slaves of the Spartan state' (Λακεδαιμονίων δοῦλοι τοῦ κοινοῦ). Strabo⁸ says that 'the status in which the Lakedaemonians held them was of the nature of state slavery' (τρόπον γάρ τινα δημοσίους δούλους εἶχον οἱ Λακεδαιμόνιοι τούτους). The helots must, indeed, have been state slaves at the start, for the acts of war through which they had lost their political independence and their personal freedom had been collective acts of the Spartan state, not individual acts of Spartan private citizens. Lotze proposes⁹ the term 'collective slavery' to describe their status; for he points out¹⁰ that the helots, as we find them in the accounts of Spartan institutions dating from the fifth century B.C. and after, were, by that time, neither wholly state property nor wholly private property.¹¹

¹ This was one of the first acts of the ephors of the year, after taking office, according to Aristotle cited by Plutarch, *Lycurgus*, chap. 27.

² In loc. cit. (Book III, chap. 83). In the context, Μαριανδύνων δωροφόροι ought to mean 'the Mariandynians' tributaries', but Pollux's source must have meant 'those of the Mariandynians who are tributary [to the Herakleiotai]'.

³ Does this mean 'men who went into battle without armour'?—A. J. T.

⁴ Lotze, Μεταξὺ Ἐλευθέρων καὶ Δούλων, p. 54, identifies Pollux's Sicyonian 'Korynephoroi' with Theopompus' 'Katonakophoroi' (Theopompus apud Athenaeum, Book VI, 271 d; Jacoby, Zweite Teil B, p. 573, No. 176 (195)).

⁵ e.g. in Xenophon, *Lak. Pol.*, chap. 7, § 5; Isocrates, *Panathenaïcus* § 178; Myron apud Athenaeum, Book XIV, 657 c–d (Jacoby, Zweiter Teil B, p. 510, No. 2 (1)).

⁶ Thucydides, Book IV, chap. 118, § 7; Book V, chap. 23, § 3 : ἦν δὲ ἡ δουλεία ἐπαναστῆται.

⁷ Book III, chap. 20, § 6.

⁸ *Geographica*, Book VIII, chap. 5, § 4 (C. 365).

⁹ Μεταξὺ Ἐλευθέρων καὶ Δούλων, pp. 77 and 79.   ¹⁰ Ibid., pp. 40 and 42.

[¹¹ In contrast to the position in the Spartan state, where, after the constitutional reform towards the end of the seventh century B.C., the property-rights over the helots were partly in the Spartan state's hands and partly in the individual Spartiate kleros-holder's hands, the state rural peasant slaves and the private rural peasant slaves were two distinct categories in Crete. Athenaeus, Book VI, 263 e–f, cites Sosicrates to the effect that τὴν μὲν κοινὴν δουλείαν οἱ Κρῆτες καλοῦσι Μνοΐαν, τὴν δ' ἰδίαν ἀφαμιώτας, τοὺς δὲ ὑπηκόους περιοίκους. Hesychius identifies the Cretan perioikoi with the aphamiotai (ἀφαμιῶται). οἰκέται ἀγροῖκοι, περίο.κοι). Athenaeus, in loc. cit., identifies the Cretan aphamiotai with the Cretan klerotai, and defines them as being a native rural population that had been conquered in war. He contrasts them with the Cretans' urban slaves, who had been purchased (χρυσωνήτους). Lotze, op. cit. pp. 38–9, holds that the Spartans, unlike the Cretans had no purchased slaves, since the

At some date before the fifth century B.C.[1] the land that the helots inhabited and cultivated had been parcelled out into allotments (κλῆροι) assigned to Spartiatai; the helots on each of these allotments were now paying their contribution to the Spartiate kleros-holder; and their obligations to him were not limited to this economic servitude; at least one helot, attached to the kleros, had to accompany the Spartiate kleros-holder on campaign.[2] However, the Spartan state had retained some important rights over the helots, and it had also placed limits on the rights over them that it had granted to the Spartiate kleros-holders. As Lotze puts it,[3] 'It is true that the individual Spartiate was the helots' immediate master, but his rights of dominion over them stemmed from the dominion over them that was possessed by the κοινωνία τῶν πολιτῶν [i.e. the Spartan body politic]. To this extent, the individual Spartiate's rights of ownership over the helots were of the same derivative kind as his rights over his land-allotment [i.e. kleros].'

The most potent right over the helots that the Spartan state kept in its own hands was the right to put any helot to death at any moment. The most atrocious case of this that is on record is one that is vouched for by Thucydides. During the Archidamian War, in the year 424 B.C., the Spartan Government

made a proclamation to the helots. They announced that helots who considered that they had performed particularly distinguished war-service for Sparta were to present themselves for review. The Government's professed intention was to emancipate [those of them whom they found deserving]; the real object was to apply a test. The Government's way of thinking was that any helot who was forward in staking his claim to emancipation would [presumably] be a man of spirit and accordingly would be one of the most likely to revolt. The Government picked out as many as about 2,000 of these helot volunteers. The picked men crowned themselves with garlands and made the round of the temples to celebrate their supposed emancipation. Not long afterwards the Government made away with them, without anyone getting to know how each of the Government's victims was done to death.[4]

This disgustingly treacherous and atrocious act of state may have been exceptional; and no doubt the Spartans will have condoned it to

Spartan currency had no purchasing power outside Sparta's own dominions. Busolt and Swoboda, op. cit., p. 667, n. 1, hold that the Spartans did have ordinary slaves, as well as helots. They cite Phylarchus apud Athenaeum, Book VI, 271 f, for a list of various categories of freedmen at Sparta.

[1] For a discussion of the date and the circumstances, see the present Part, chap. 3, section (ii), pp. 221–34.

[2] Herodotus, Book VII, chap. 229: Book IX, chap. 28; Thucydides, Book IV, chap. 8, § 9. The presence of helots in the Spartan contingent of a Lacedaemonian army in the field required the taking of security measures (Xenophon, *Lak. Pol.*, chap. 12, §§ 2 and 4).

[3] In Μεταξὺ Ἐλευθέρων καὶ Δούλων, p. 42. Cp. p. 41.

[4] Thucydides, Book IV, chap. 80, §§ 2–3.

themselves on the ground that the Athenians' seizure of Pylos, Sparta's loss of prestige through the surrender of the garrison of Sphakteria, and the desertion of a number of helots who were able to make their way to the Athenian beach-head was a combination of reverses for Sparta that had placed in jeopardy the supremacy of the 'homoioi' within Sparta's Peloponnesian dominions and that therefore called for drastic preventive counter-action. However, according to Myron of Priene,[1] it was the Spartan Government's regular practice to put to death any helots of outstanding physique; and the Spartiate 'secret patrol' (κρυπτεία) killed, as a matter of routine, any helot that it caught out and about at night.[2] Lotze points out[3] that this practice implies that helots were subject to a curfew; but helots could be put to death by the Spartan Government even if they had not infringed any regulation. If the Spartan authorities decided that it was not in the public interest that a helot should remain alive, this was enough.

Moreover, short of putting to death any helots who were judged to be potentially dangerous characters, the Spartan Government, according to Myron,[4] took measures for keeping the whole helot population cowed, and the Spartiate kleros-holders were constrained to serve as the Government's agents for this purpose. According to Myron, the helots were given a gratuitous beating once a year to remind them that they were slaves; and a Spartiate 'homoios' would be punished by the Government if they convicted him of having been remiss in cowing the helots on his kleros.

There seem to have been helots—for instance, one of King Kleomenes I's gaolers[5]—who were servants of the Spartan state, not of some individual Spartiate kleros-holder. Certainly the Spartan state also retained the right to enlist helot volunteers for hoplite service,[6] and to emancipate these, or alternatively to make away with them, according to its judgement of their performance and their temper.[7] Some, though not all, helot hoplite volunteers who were emancipated and were allowed to live were styled 'neodamodeis', meaning 'persons with a status approximating to that of members of the Spartan damos'.[8] This term was a long-

[1] In Athenaeus, Book XIV, 657 d.

[2] Plutarch, *Lycurgus*, chap. 27. In Plato, *Laws*, Book I, 633 B–C, the Spartan interlocutor mentions the physical hardships endured by the members of the Krypteia, but is silent about the atrocities committed by them.

[3] In Μεταξὺ Ἐλευθέρων καὶ Δούλων, p. 44.

[4] In Athenaeus, Book XIV, 657 c–d.

[5] Herodotus, Book VI, chap. 75 (see Lotze, Μεταξὺ Ἐλευθέρων καὶ Δούλων, pp. 34, 35, 36).

[6] Thucydides, Book IV, chap. 80, §§ 1–3; Xenophon, *Hellenica*, Book VI, chap. 5, §§ 28–9.

[7] Thucydides, Book IV, chap. 80, §§ 2–3, quoted above.

[8] Pollux, Book III, chap. 83, says that 'neodamodeis' was the Lacedaemonians' term for emancipated helots. Actually the neodamodeis must have been one particular category of these. According to Athenaeus, Book VI, 261 f, πολλάκις ... ἠλευθέρωσαν Λακεδαιμόνιοι δούλους, καὶ οὓς μὲν ἀφέτας ἐκάλεσαν, οὓς δὲ ἀδεσπότους, οὓς δὲ ἐρυκτῆρας, δεσποσιοναύτας

winded euphemism, for the damos consisted of the homoioi, and the status of the neodamodeis did not truly approximate to theirs.[1] Like the perioikoi, the neodamodeis were freemen, and they may have counted politically as Lakedaimonioi; but, like the Spartiate hypomeiones and the perioikoi, they were without a vote in the Spartiate assembly; only homoioi were entitled to that; and, unlike the hypomeiones and perioikoi, the neodamodeis were homeless within Sparta's dominions; for an emancipated helot could not and would not go back to live on his former Spartiate master's kleros.[2] After the conclusion of peace in 421 B.C. had brought the first bout of the Atheno-Peloponnesian War to a close, the surviving neodamodeis and Brasideioi (i.e. the volunteer helot hoplites whom Brasidas had enlisted in 424 B.C. for his expedition in the north) were parked, just outside Lacedaemonian territory, at Lepreon,[3] an ex-perioecic dependency of Elis' which had seceded from Elis and had been placed under a Spartan protectorate.[4] This was shabby treatment; yet apparently the neodamodeis 'were consistently loyal'.[5]

It will be seen that the Spartan state's concern for security against the helots remained paramount over the rights over the helots that the state had granted to Spartiate kleros-holders. This was logical and

---

δ' ἄλλους, οὓς εἰς τοὺς στόλους κατέτασσον, ἄλλους δὲ νεοδαμώδεις. Non-neodamodeis hoplite helot volunteers are mentioned by Thucydides, Book VII, chap. 19, § 3, and chap. 58, § 3.

[1] See Ehrenberg, s.v. 'Neodamodeis', in P.–W., 16. Band (1935), cols. 2396–2401, in col. 2399.

[2] R. F. Willetts, 'The Neodamodeis', in *Classical Philology*, vol. xlix (Jan.–Oct. 1954), pp. 27–32, guesses that the neodamodeis were not, in truth, homeless in Laconia, but had kleroi of their own there. He suggests that they were ex-helots who had inherited the kleroi on which they had formerly been serfs. They had inherited them because the previous homoian Spartiate holders of these kleroi had left neither male heirs nor female heirs (ἐπίκληροι) of their own. He points out that, in the Cretan city-state Gortyn, 'serfs could, in default of heirs, inherit estates', according to the laws recorded in the famous inscription (p. 30). This is Willetts's conjectural answer to the question what became of kleroi that were left without homoian Spartiate heirs. The answer surely is that vacant kleroi will have been assigned to hypomeiones Spartiatai. As candidates for receiving them, these will surely have had priority over any of the helots attached to the kleroi in question. Moreover, the only recorded domicile of neodamodeis who were not on active service is Lepreon, which lay not inside but outside Sparta's dominions (see the reference in n. 3). Thus Willetts's guess that the neodamodeis were kleros-holders seems, on the whole, improbable. He may, however, be right in thinking (p. 28) that the neodamodeis financed themselves; for, as is noted at a later point in this annex, we know that helots could, and in some cases did, accumulate property, though this not in the form of real estate. Willetts is certainly correct in pointing out (p. 27) that, though the earliest date at which the existence of neodamodeis is mentioned is 421 B.C., this category of emancipated helots may have been instituted earlier than that, for all we know.

[3] Thucydides, Book V, chap. 34. The two categories are distinguished from each other in Book V, chap. 67, too.

[4] Thucydides, Book V, chap. 31. Ehrenberg, in P.–W., loc. cit., cols. 2397–8, gives a calendar of notices of neodamodeis in our sources. The earliest mention of them is in 421 B.C. (Thucydides, Book V, chap. 34, § 1). The latest mention of them is in 370/369 B.C. (Xenophon, *Hellenica*, Book VI, chap. 5, § 24). See also Busolt and Swoboda, op. cit., p. 668, n. 1.

[5] Jones, *Sparta*, p. 9.

inevitable, considering that 'security was the overriding consideration that determined the greater part of Lacedaemonian policy towards the helots'.[1]

Besides retaining these powers over the helots in its own hands, the Spartan state had imposed restrictions on the powers over the helots that it had granted to the individual Spartiate kleros-holders. 'The helots had been conquered by force of arms and had been condemned to be slaves, but this on certain stipulated terms. The [individual Spartiate] possessor of helots was not authorized either to emancipate them or to sell them beyond the frontiers.'[2]

Moreover, the Spartiate kleros-holder was debarred from exacting from the helots on his allotment more than a permanently fixed maximum amount of their produce as their contribution (ἀποφορά) to the kleros-holder's income.[3] Presumably this maximum had been fixed by the state at the time, probably towards the end of the seventh century B.C.,[4] at which the kleroi had been distributed.[5] The sanction for this limitation of the helots' economic liability was not a law. Helots could not be protected by law because, as slaves, they were not legal persons.[6] The sanction was a religious one,[7] and it seems to have been effective; for a non-affluent Spartiate kleros-holder was in a constant state of anxiety for fear that his income from his kleros might not cover his contribution to his syssition; and his dread of losing his membership of his syssition and therefore ceasing to be an 'homoios' and sinking to the status of an 'hypomeion' became a dominant factor in Spartan life which eventually decided Sparta's destiny.[8]

According to Myron, the helots, in consideration of their contribution, were given security of tenure on their land.[9] Plutarch notes[10] that the

---

[1] ἀεὶ γὰρ τὰ πολλὰ Λακεδαιμονίοις πρὸς τοὺς εἵλωτας τῆς φυλακῆς πέρι μάλιστα καθειστήκει (Thucydides, Book IV, chap. 80, § 3).

[2] κατὰ κράτος ἁλῶναι πολέμῳ καὶ κριθῆναι δούλους ἐπὶ τακτοῖς τισιν, ὥστε τὸν ἔχοντα μήτε ἐλευθεροῦν ἐξεῖναι μήτε πωλεῖν ἔξω τῶν ὅρων τούτους (Strabo, *Geographica*, Book VIII, chap. 5, § 4 (C. 365)).

[3] Plutarch, *Lycurgus*, chap. 24; *Inst. Lac.*, § 40; Myron in Athenaeus, Book XIV, 657 d. The amount for each kind of produce is given by Plutarch, *Lycurgus*, chap. 8. The figures are puzzling. They are rejected by Jones, *Sparta*, p. 9, and attempts to make sense of them have been inconclusive. See, for example, Kahrstedt, 'Die spartanische Agrarwirtschaft', pp. 279–94.

[4] See the present Part, chap. 3, Annex I.

[5] We do not know how the helots' apophora had been disposed of before that; but we do know, from Tyrtaios, fr. 6 (Bergk–Hiller–Crusius) = 6. 7 (1) (Diehl), that, between the First and the Second Spartano-Messenian War the Messenian helots paid, not a fixed amount, but one-half of their annual product.

[6] Lotze, *Μεταξὺ 'Ελευθέρων καὶ Δούλων*, p. 31.

[7] ἐπάρατον δ' ἦν πλείονός τινα μισθῶσαι (Plutarch, *Inst. Lac.*, 41).

[8] See further, pp. 305–10.

[9] καὶ, παραδόντες αὐτοῖς τὴν χώραν, ἔταξαν μοῖραν ἣν αὐτοῖς ἀνοίσουσιν ἀεί (Myron in loc. cit.). Cp. Plutarch, *Apophthegmata Laconica*, Alexandridas [Anaxandridas], 3 : πυνθανομένου δέ τινος διὰ τί τοῖς εἵλωσι τοὺς ἀγροὺς ἐγχειρίζουσι, καὶ οὐκ αὐτοὶ ἐπιμελοῦνται, ὅτι, ἔφη, οὐ τούτων ἐπιμελούμενοι, ἀλλ' ἑαυτῶν, αὐτοὺς ἐκτησάμεθα.

[10] In loc. cit.

limitation of the amount of the Spartan helots' contribution to their
Spartiate masters' income enabled them to make profits, and he states
that this was deliberate Spartan policy. In 223/2 B.C., 6,000 helots were
able to purchase their freedom by paying five Attic minas each[1]—not
to their respective Spartiate masters, but to the Spartan Government.
This emancipation of 6,000 helots in 223/2 B.C., like the previous emancipation of 6,000 of them in 370/369 B.C.,[2] was forced upon Kleomenes III
by military necessity in a supreme military crisis. Neither Agis IV nor
Kleomenes III had shown concern for improving the helots' position.[3]
Nabis seems to have been the first Spartan statesman who emancipated
helots on a large scale as a matter of deliberate policy.[4] Even Nabis did
not emancipate all the remaining helots. There were still some helots in
rural Laconia in 195 B.C., at the time of the invasion of Laconia by the
Romans and their Greek allies.[5] In 188 B.C., when Sparta was occupied
by the Achaeans, the helots liberated by Kleomenes and Nabis were given
the choice between going into exile by a fixed date or being sold into
slavery.[6] Yet Strabo mentions that helotage survived in Spartan territory
until the time of the Roman Empire.[7] We do not know when helotage
was finally extinguished; but we may credit Nabis with having reduced
the number of helots to a figure at which helotage ceased to be a serious
social and political problem for the Spartan state.[8] Helotage was not
one of the classic Spartan institutions that the Spartan archaists tried
to revive in the Age of the Principate.[9]

---

[1] Plutarch, *Cleomenes*, chap. 23.

[2] Xenophon, *Hellenica*, Book VI, chap. 5, § 29.

[3] Neumann, loc. cit., pp. 76–7; W. H. Porter, 'The Antecedents of the Spartan Revolution
of 243 B.C.', in *Hermathena*, No. xlix (1935), pp. 1–15, on p. 14.

[4] See Polybius, Book XVI, chap. 13, § 1; Livy, Book XXXIV, chaps. 31, 32, and 36;
Book XXXVIII, chap. 34. Livy, Book XXXIV, chap. 31, leaves it uncertain whether or not
the emancipated helots were among the beneficiaries of Nabis' land distribution. However,
it is recorded that emancipated helots, besides some of Nabis' mercenaries, were endowed
with the wives and property of exiled Spartiatai (see Polybius, Book XIII, chap. 6, § 2;
Book XVI, chap. 13, § 1; Livy, Book XXXIV, chap. 35, § 7, and chap. 36, § 5).

[5] Livy, Book XXXIV, chap. 27.

[6] 'Uti quae servitia tyranni liberassent (ea magna multitudo erat) ante diem certam
abirent; qui ibi mansissent, eos prehendendi, vendendi, abducendi Achaeis ius esset' (Livy,
Book XXXVIII, chap. 34).

[7] τὴν εἰλωτείαν τὴν συμμείνασαν μέχρι τῆς Ῥωμαίων ἐπικρατείας (Book VIII, chap. 5, § 4
(C. 365)).   [8] See Meier in loc. cit., p. 34.

[9] Roussel, *Sparte*, p. 152.

The Origin and Status of the Perioikoi

IN the Hellenic world the helots and the Spartiate homoioi were two peculiar institutions, and their respective peculiarities were complementary to each other. The homoioi could not have been kept permanently mobilized at Sparta and Amyklai as full-time professional hoplites if they had not been endowed with an income from kleroi cultivated by helots; and the helots would not have been kept in a state of slavery which was not the common lot of the Greek peasantry[1] if there had not been homoioi for them to support. In contrast to the helot majority and the Spartiate minority of the population of the city-state territory of Sparta, the Lacedaemonian perioikoi led the normal life of Hellenes. They were citizens of city-states[2] that were autonomous;[3] they were freemen; and they had to earn their living by their own work, and to do their military training in their spare time. In the Lacedaemonian perioecic city-states, there were no helots,[4] no kleroi,[5] and therefore no full-time professional hoplites.

[1] See Niese, 'Zur Verfassungsgeschichte Lakedaimons', p. 78. Even the other enslaved rural populations were not treated so badly as the helots were. According to Plato, *Laws*, 776 C, the helots were treated worse than the Penestai and the Mariandynoi. Lotze, in *Μεταξὺ Ἐλευθέρων καὶ Δούλων*, p. 25, notes that we have no record of any insurrections of Cretan rural slaves. Cp. Neumann, 'Die Entstehung des spartanischen Staates', p. 71.

[2] See Busolt and Swoboda, op. cit., pp. 637 and 663; Ehrenberg, 'Spartiaten und Lakedaimonier', p. 51; Pareti, *Storia di Sparta Arcaïca*, Parte I, p. 200; Niese, 'Die lakedaimonischen Periöken', p. 102. Isocrates, *Panathenaïcus*, 270, says that the Spartans have divided up the perioikoi into the largest possible number of the smallest possible communities, and that, though the perioecic communities rank nominally as city-states (poleis), they are lower-powered (τὴν δὲ δύναμιν ἔχοντας ἐλάττω) than the Attic demes. It may well be true that, in organizing their perioecic dependencies, the Spartans did 'divide in order to rule', and that the smallest perioecic city-states were inferior to the largest Attic demes in physical calibre (if that is what Isocrates means here by δύναμιν). On the other hand, we may guess that the perioecic poleis had considerably larger powers of self-government than the Attic demes, and that they were true poleis in this pertinent sense.

[3] See Forrest, *A History*, p. 30. The two perioecic states Kythera and Skandeia (Pausanias, Book III, chap. 23, § 1), on the island of Kythera, were under the authority of a Spartiate annual public officer, the Kytherodikes, and a Spartiate garrison was kept on the island (Thucydides, Book IV, chap. 53); but this exercise of direct control over Kythera was probably something exceptional. The strategic importance of the island was exceptionally great.

[4] There is no evidence that any of the Lacedaemonian perioecic states had helots (Ehrenberg, 'Spartiaten und Lakedaimonier', pp. 40–1 and p. 50; Cavaignac, op. cit., p. 35), and there is no likelihood of this either, considering that none of these states except those in south-eastern Messenia had good enough agricultural land to be able to maintain an economically unproductive class of professional soldiers corresponding to the Spartan homoioi. At Plataea in 479 B.C., οἱ τῶν λοιπῶν Λακεδαιμονίων καὶ Ἑλλήνων ψιλοί, one for each hoplite, are contrasted by Herodotus, Book IX, chaps. 28 and 29, with the Spartiates' ψιλοὶ τῶν

[Notes 4 and 5 continued opposite.

Like most Hellenic communities, the Lacedaemonian perioecic communities made their living mainly by agriculture, though any industry and trade that was carried on in Laconia from *circa* 550 B.C. onwards was in perioecic hands.[1] The Lacedaemonian perioecic city-states were numerous,[2] their average area was small, and the average quality of their soil was poor; but in all these points they were typical Hellenic city-states; and, like the rest of the small-scale majority of the city-states of the Hellenic World, they had a strong sense of civic pride. Though, in Spartan official parlance, the perioikoi, as well as the Spartiatai, were Lakedaimonioi,[3] Nikokles of Akriai, who, as a Greek-speaking freeman, had been entitled to compete at Olympia and had won five victories, in all, at two Olympic festivals, was commemorated, not as a Lakedaimonios, but as an Akriatas.[4] Conversely, the perioikoi were juridically aliens (ξένοι) at Sparta.[5]

Nor were the Lacedaemonian perioecic city-states peculiar in being autonomous without being sovereign. While many Hellenic states that were on the same small scale were sovereign states, there were many others that, like the Lacedaemonian perioecic states, were dependent politically on some bigger and more powerful neighbour.[6] In the Peloponnese, Argos and Elis, as well as Sparta, had their perioecic dependencies; and Athens, too, had at least four, namely Oinoê, Eleutherai, Plataiai, and Oropos. There was no clear-cut distinction between a perioecic dependency and an ally. In fact, from *circa* 550 B.C. onwards,

Εἰλωτέων, seven for each hoplite. Nevertheless, the perioikoi are credited with possessing helots by Grote, Part II, chap. 6, vol. iii, p. 144 and p. 146, n. 2, in the Everyman's Library edition; Chrimes, *Ancient Sparta*, p. 285; Roussel, op. cit., p. 58; Lotze, *Μεταξὺ Ἐλευθέρων καὶ Δούλων*, p. 34; Fr. Hampl, 'Die lakedämonischen Perioken', in *Hermes*, 72. Band (1937), pp. 1–49, on pp. 35–9; Berve, op. cit., pp. 23, 26, 27, 53.

5 There is no evidence that the perioecic states' territories were ever divided into kleroi before King Agis IV's projected γῆς ἀναδασμός was carried out by King Kleomenes III (see Plutarch, *Agis*, chap. 8; *Cleomenes*, chap. 11). Nevertheless, the perioikoi are credited with possessing kleroi by Roussel, op. cit., p. 58; Michell, op. cit., p. 69; Cavaignac, op. cit., p. 35.

---

1 See the references to the evidence in Michell, op. cit., p. 73, n. 2.
2 Herodotus, Book VII, chap. 234. The conventional number was one hundred (Strabo, Book VIII, chap. 4, § 11 (C. 362)). Stephanus has included eighty perioecic city-states of Sparta's in his gazetteer (Michell, op. cit., p. 74). According to Busolt and Swoboda, op. cit., pp. 637–8, thirty of these eighty states were in Messenia. See Niese's gazetteer in 'Neue Beiträge zur Geschichte und Landeskunde Lakedaimons' and Bölte's gazetteer in P.–W., Zweite Reihe [R–Z], Dritter Band, A 2 (1929), s.v. 'Sparta', cols. 1316–1321.
3 See Busolt and Swoboda, op. cit., p. 653, n. 1, and p. 663; Huxley, op. cit., p. 25; Roussel, op. cit., pp. 32–3; Michell, op. cit., p. 64; Ehrenberg, 'Der Damos im archaïschen Sparta', in *Hermes*, 68. Band (1933), pp. 288–305, on p. 302; Pareti, *Storia di Sparta Arcaïca*, Parte I, p. 201.   4 Pausanias, Book III, chap. 22, § 5.
5 This seems to be implied in Plutarch, *Cleomenes*, chap. 10; *Aratus*, chap. 38. On the other hand, they are included, with the Spartiatai, under the term πολῖται by Xenophon, *Hellenica*, Book IV, chap. 4, § 19; Book V, chap. 3, § 25, and chap. 4, § 41; Book VII, chap. 4, §§ 21 and 27.   6 See Niese, 'Zur Verfassungsgeschichte Lakedaimons', p. 78.

Sparta might have been said to have two circles of allies: a Lacedaemonian inner circle, consisting of her perioecic states, and an outer circle, consisting of her non-Lacedaemonian Peloponnesian partners.

The perioikoi were, of course, tied to Sparta by tighter constitutional bonds. The two Spartan royal houses had crown estates in some, at least, of the perioecic city-states.[1] Presumably they had acquired these at the time when these states had submitted to Spartan suzerainty; and this suzerainty may have been symbolized in the assignment of these $\tau\epsilon\mu\acute{\epsilon}\nu\eta$ to the sovereigns of the suzerain power. This token of dependence was not an irksome one for the perioecic states; and there is no evidence that any tribute, either in kind or in money, was ever exacted from them. Jones notes[2] that the perioecic states were 'almost consistently loyal to Sparta'.

The most serious infringement of the perioecic cities' sovereignty and of their citizens' personal rights was the power, taken by the Spartan ephors, to put any perioikos to death without trial.[3] The perioikoi's most arduous obligation to Sparta was to serve in the Lacedaemonian army. This obligation was shared by Sparta's non-Lacedaemonian allies; but, at any rate by the year 432 B.C., these had a constitutional right, implemented by the provision of constitutional machinery, to consult with the Spartans about issues of war and peace, so that, if and when the Peloponnesian alliance went to war, Sparta's allies would at least have had a voice in deciding for war, though they had to wage the war, when declared, under Spartan leadership. By contrast, Sparta's perioikoi had to go to war at Sparta's bidding without having any voice in the foregoing political decisions.

In the Lacedaemonian army the contingents of the perioecic states seem to have served originally in separate hoplite formations from the Spartiate hoplite phalanx. As a result of the reorganization of the Lacedaemonian army which seems to have been carried out at some date before 425 B.C., the perioikoi seem to have been required to supplement the Spartan formations, besides continuing to provide their own formations.[4] We may guess, however, that, even after this, the incidence of military service on the perioikoi was not so heavy as it was on the Spartiatai. One of the unintended and unexpected but marked and continuous effects of the reform of Spartan institutions towards the close of the seventh century B.C. was to produce a gradual decline in the numbers of the Spartiate homoioi.[5] The perioecic communities were not

[1] Xenophon, *Lak. Pol.*, chap. 15, § 3.
[2] Jones, *Sparta*, p. 8.
[3] Isocrates, *Panathenaïcus*, 271.
[4] These points in the history of the Lacedaemonian military organization are discussed in chap. 5, sections (i) (a), (ii), (iii).
[5] See chap. 4.

exposed to the play of these peculiarly Spartan economic and social forces.

Sparta's perioecic city-states seem to have had diverse origins.[1] At least two, Geronthrai[2] and Pharai,[3] may have been Spartan colonies. Three others—New Asine, Methone, and Thyrea—are said to have been settlements of refugees from abroad—Asinaeans, Nauplians,[4] and Aeginetans[5] respectively—to whom Sparta had given asylum and perioecic status in order that they might serve her as garrisons of strategic points in conquered territory. We do not know that this short list of perioecic city-states that were colonies is complete,[6] but, since these are the only examples of this category that are known to us,[7] we may guess that the great majority of Sparta's perioecic dependencies will have been already existing city-states which had accepted Spartan suzerainty in lieu of either a previous independence or a previous dependence on the Aipytid Messenian kingdom or on Argos.[8]

The geographical distribution of Sparta's perioecic city-states since *circa* 544 B.C. is instructive. They fall into four groups: first, the five known colonial perioecic states, together with Aulon (if Aulon was a perioecic state);[9] second, a group between Sparta City and Arcadia; third, a group (the largest of the four) which extended north-north-westwards continuously from the tip of the Tainaron peninsula into south-eastern Messenia up to the line of the lower Pamisos at least, and perhaps to the west of it as well. The fourth group included the two states, Kythera and Skandeia, on the island of Kythera, while, on the mainland, it covered the eastern seaboard of the Peloponnese as far north as the southern boundary of the Thyreatis.[10] This fourth group occupied all the

---

[1] See Ehrenberg, 'Spartiaten und Lakedaimonier', pp. 51 and 55. 'Die Zeugnisse zeigen, wie sich in der Perioikie Eroberung, autonomer Anschluss und Kolonisation vereinigen' (p. 55). Cp. Forrest, *A History*, pp. 33–4.

[2] See p. 176.   [3] See Forrest, *A History*, p. 37.

[4] See p. 181, with nn. 2, 3, and 4.

[5] See p. 183, n. 3.

[6] According to Theopompus, cited by Strabo, *Geographica*, Book VIII, chap. 6, § 11 (C. 373), the planting of colonies of refugees was a regular Spartan policy, οἱ γὰρ Λακεδαιμόνιοι, φησὶν ὁ Θεόπομπος, πολλὴν κατακτησάμενοι τῆς ἀλλοτρίας, εἰς ταύτην κατῴκιζον οὓς ἂν ὑποδέξαιντο τῶν φευγόντων ἐπ᾽ αὐτο[υς· καὶ οἱ] ἐκ Ναυπλίας ἐκεῖσε ἀνεχώρησαν.

[7] Cornelius Nepos, *Conon*, chap. 9, §1, may be right in calling Pharis a Lacedaemonian colony, According to Busolt and Swoboda, op. cit., p. 638, n. 1, the names of seven perioecic states that were colonies are known, and six of these lay to the west of Taÿgetos.

[8] Isocrates, *Panathenaïcus*, 178, holds that Sparta's perioikoi were descendants of the Spartan demos, who had been deprived of their original political status by a domineering minority at Sparta. This theory of the origin of the perioikoi assumes that Sparta had possessed the whole of Laconia since the post-Mycenaean Völkerwanderung, i.e. it confuses with the Völkerwanderung the Spartan city-state's conquests in the eighth century B.C. Berve, *Sparta*, p. 21, seems to take Isocrates' view.

[9] See p. 188.

[10] The Thyreatis, after its cession to Sparta by Argos, may have been annexed to Sparta's own χώρα πολιτική till the refugee Aeginetans were planted there (see p. 183, n. 3).

territory, except for the Thyreatis, that Sparta had acquired from Argos *circa* 544 B.C.

It is perhaps no accident that the five known colonial perioecic states were all planted in strategically important but exposed positions. New Asine and Methone, and Aulon too, were bound, whenever the Messenian helots revolted, to be cut off, so long as the revolt lasted, from Sparta —cut off, that is, from the home base of the Spartiate wing of the Lacedaemonian army, on whose support the survival of these outlying perioecic garrisons ultimately depended. Geronthrai was Sparta's frontier fortress over against the Argive dominion in Kynouria during the two centuries, ending *circa* 544 B.C., between Sparta's conquest of Amyklai, Pharis, and Geronthrai and her conquest of Kynouria. After Sparta's frontier in this quarter had been moved forward to the northern boundary of the Thyreatis, on the threshold of the Argeia itself, the role perhaps once performed by a Spartan colony at Geronthrai was eventually taken over by the refugee Aeginetan community which the Spartans established at Thyrea in 431 B.C.[1] Geronthrai and Thyrea each commanded, respectively, one of the two principal lines of communication between the Eurotas basin and the east coast of the Peloponnese.

The group of Sparta's perioecic states that lay between Sparta and Arcadia commanded the route leading north-westwards from Sparta over the watershed between the Eurotas basin and the Alpheios basin and the route leading northwards from Sparta to Tegea. The north-westward route was bestridden by the territory of Pellana; by the Aigytis (said to have been the earliest joint conquest made by the two Spartan royal houses);[2] and by the Maleatis. The northward route, which ran up the valley of the Oinous (Kelephina) tributary of the Eurotas, was bestridden by the territory of Sellasia and by the cantons Oiatis and Karyatis, which may have been acquired by Sparta from Tegea in the Spartano-Tegeatan wars in the first half of the sixth century B.C.[3] The Oiatis was certainly included in a larger district called the Skiritis;[4] but the Skiritis may not also have comprised either the Karyatis, which lay to the east of Oion, or the Aigytis and the Maleatis, which lay to the west of Oion. Xenophon[5] appears to distinguish the Skiritis from both the Karyatis and the Maleatis. On the other hand, Thucydides informs us that the Skiritis had a common frontier with Parrhasia,[6] and this seems to imply that the Skiritis did include both the Aigytis[7] and the Maleatis. Moreover, the

---

[1] Thucydides, Book II, chap. 27. Cp. Book IV, chaps. 56 and 57.
[2] See p. 172.   [3] See pp. 182, n. 2.
[4] Xenophon, *Hellenica*, Book VI, chap. 5, §§ 24 and 25.
[5] In loc. cit.
[6] Thucydides, Book V, chap. 33, 1.
[7] There is inscriptional evidence that the Skiritis included the Aigytis if [. . . τὰ]ν Σκιρῖ [τιν . . .] . . . ἐν αἷ κ[αὶ ἁ Αἰγῦτι]ς χώρα is the correct restoration of Dittenberger, *Sylloge*,

Skiritis must have been a territory of some size; for it contributed a whole lokhos to the Lacedaemonian army.[1] It is true that this was a lokhos, not of hoplites, but of light-armed troops; it could therefore have been raised from a smaller and poorer area than would have been needed for raising a hoplite force of the same numerical strength. However, the whole of this Lacedaemonian perioecic borderland between Laconia and Arcadia was exceptionally rocky and barren, even for Greece. 'Skiritis' means 'land of limestone' (skiros); and Mount Skiros, from which the Skiritis presumably derived its name, seems to have stood some distance to the west of Oion, in the neighbourhood of Oresthasion. On balance, it seems probable that the Skiritis comprised the whole of the strip of ex-Arcadian perioecic territory from the Maleatis and Aigytis to the Karyatis inclusive.

The locations of the third and the fourth group of Sparta's perioecic states are clear.

Sparta's grant of perioecic status to the communities in these particular four areas must have been deliberate policy. Can we discern the motive in each case? The motive for founding the garrison colonies and for giving perioecic status to the Skiritis is evident. The motive in these cases was strategic. What about the other two groups? Was the motive strategic there too?

Geronthrai and Thyrea, in succession, shielded Sparta's city-state territory against Argos; and this must have been Sparta's intention in colonizing them. The Skiritis, backed by the territories of Sellasia and Pellana, shielded Sparta's city-state territory against Arcadia. It has been suggested that the geographical lay-out of the Lacedaemonian perioecic territories as a whole had been designed by Sparta to insulate the helot-inhabited portion of Sparta's city-state territory from direct contact with the territories of independent foreign powers.

This thesis is refuted by the administrative map of Sparta's dominions, and this at all stages of Sparta's territorial expansion. For nearly 200 years, running from the date of Sparta's acquisition of the lower basin of the Eurotas to the date of her acquisition of Kynouria, her helot-inhabited territory in the Helos coastal plain must have marched with Argive territory, since it marched with the territories of Akriai, Zarax, Glympeis, and Marion, and these, during those 200 years, remained under Argive suzerainty. The garrison at Geronthrai could not shield this politically vulnerable southern extension of Spartan territory in Laconia. It has also been noted[2] that we have no evidence of there having been

3rd ed., vol. ii, No. 665 (p. 33). However, in a later passage of the same inscription, on pp. 235–6, we find [. . . τὰν Σκιρ]ῖτιν καὶ τὰν Αἰγῦτιν.

[1] See chap. 5, Annex III, p. 398, n. 2.
[2] On p. 190.

a continuous chain of Lacedaemonian perioecic territories between the northern border of the helot-inhabited Spartan territory in the Stenyklaros plain and the adjoining part of Arcadia. In the third place, the administrative map shows that the largest of the four groups of Lacedaemonian perioecic communities—namely the group that comprised both the Tainaron peninsula and south-eastern Messenia—did not touch the land frontiers of Sparta's dominions at any point. At every point except where the Thouriatis marched with the Aigytis, the third group of perioecic states was, itself, insulated from the outer world by Spartan territory, and for the most part by Spartan territory that was helot-inhabited. These geographical facts indicate that Sparta's motive in giving perioecic status to the communities to which she did give it cannot have been a concern to insulate her helot-inhabited territories. Some other motive or motives have therefore to be looked for.

Sparta's motive for refraining from annexing the Tainaron peninsula and Kynouria—and, indeed, the Skiritis too—to her own city-state territory may have been a lack of any economic incentive. In all these three areas the land was too poor to excite covetousness and so invite conquest. The population of these regions could hardly support itself; it could not have produced a surplus for providing contributions to the upkeep of Spartiate kleros-holders; so the Spartiatai will not have been under any temptation to annex these areas and to carve them up into allotments. The Spartans will have left the existing inhabitants of these areas undisturbed for the same reason that the Maniot descendants of Sparta's Taenarian perioikoi and the Tzakonian descendants of her Cynurian perioikoi were likewise left undisturbed, in later ages, by the Slavs and by the 'Osmanlis. The word 'Limera' ('famished'), which was the distinguishing epithet of the Cynurian Epidauros, proclaims that an attempt to exploit Kynouria economically would be unrewarding.

I can testify to the economic unattractiveness of Kynouria and the Tainaron peninsula from first-hand experience. In the course of the ten days 20–29 April 1912 I walked from Sparta, via Yeráki (Geronthrai) to Neapolis (Boiai) on the Malea peninsula, and thence, via Monemvasía, Epidauros Limera, the Zarax fjord, Helos, and Gythion to the tip of the Tainaron peninsula; but on my way back northwards from Cape Matapan (Cape Tainaron) I collapsed, and I had to finish my journey home to the British Archaeological School at Athens by mule, boat, and train. Between the iron bridge over the lower Eurotas and Gythion, I had contracted dysentery by drinking from a treacherously limpid stream. The 'red water' (κόκκινο νερό) of the cisterns in the Mani, and the Mani's cruel limestone-shingle paths, finished the contaminated stream's work. Maniot water is red because, in the whole of the Mani, there is only one spring, and the cistern-water is coloured by the red soil in the interstices between the knife-edged limestone reefs. The Mani deserves the name 'Skiritis' still better than the district by which this forbidding name was actually borne. Like Athens in the generation of Perikles, the Mani in every age has been 'Hellados Hellas' in its own way. If Athens was the quintessence of Hellenic artistic and intellectual creative genius, the Mani was, and is, the quintessence of the physical harshness of southern Greece.

Does the economic uninvitingness of the Mani, Tzakonia, and the Skiritis account for Sparta's willingness to spare the second, third, and fourth groups of her perioecic communities from being annexed to her own city-state territory and from being divided up into kleroi for Spartiate homoioi? No, not entirely; for, in addition to the Mani, the third group of perioecic states included Pharai (Kalamata), Thouria, and Aithaia, and the territories of these three perioecic states contained agricultural land, in the Makaria plain in the lower basin of the River Pamisos,[1] that was as fertile as any other land anywhere in European Greece. Sparta fought a twenty-years-long war to conquer and annex the adjoining Stenyklaros plain in the upper Pamisos basin; and, when the subjugated population of the Stenyklaros plain rose in revolt, she fought a second, and perhaps even more arduous, war to reconquer this temporarily lost territory. Why, then, had she not also annexed the equally desirable Makarian plain? The explanation must be that, here, greed was kept in check by policy.

When Sparta made her first moves in Messenia, the strongest of the Messenian states was the Aipytid kingdom in the upper basin of the River Pamisos. If Sparta had attempted to annex and expropriate the lower basin of the Pamisos while this Aipytid kingdom was still standing, she would have thrown the south-east Messenians into the Aipytids' arms and have driven all Messenians to make common cause against Spartan aggression. Sparta could hope to acquire Messenia only if she could succeed in keeping it divided politically; and, since the Aipytid kingdom was bound to be Sparta's most formidable Messenian adversary, it was obvious policy for Sparta to persuade Pharai, Thouria, and Aithaia to accept the status of Lacedaemonian perioikoi in consideration of a guarantee that, on this condition, she would leave them in possession of their fertile fields.[2]

In this case, political prudence must have prevailed over economic greed; and we may guess that, in the case of Kynouria, the absence of economic incentive was not the only reason why Sparta left the poverty-stricken city-states in this district autonomous. Here, too, there are some patches of fertile territory—for instance, the plain of Leukai and the

---

[1] See Pausanias, Book IV, chap. 34, § 1.
[2] See Chrimes, *Ancient Sparta*, pp. 298–300.

densely populated district round Nymphaion.[1] Here, too, however, political considerations must have played a part in restraining Spartan covetousness. Though, *circa* 544 B.C., Sparta had at last succeeded in acquiring Kynouria from Argos, the defeated power was still in being and was still Kynouria's next-door neighbour. In these circumstances it was not enough for Sparta to have demonstrated, as she had, that she was now more than a match for Argos in the field. If her newly acquired hold over Kynouria was to be secure, Sparta must also make the Cynurians feel that they were not the worse off politically as a result of their having been transferred from Argive to Spartan suzerainty. Their association with Argos had been a long-standing one, and it had gone deeper than the political level. They had not only been under Argive suzerainty. They had been influenced by Argive culture. They had taken to speaking the Argive variety of the North-West Greek dialect,[2] and, down to the antiquarian Pausanias' day, their religious institutions continued to be perceptibly different from those of Laconia to the west of Mount Parnon.[3]

---

[1] See Pausanias, Book III, chap. 23, § 2.
[2] Herodotus, Book VIII, chap. 73.
[3] Sam Wide, *Lakonische Kulte* (Leipzig, 1893, Teubner), p. 224, n. 1.

3. Sparta's Constitutional Development

(i) The Aigeidai's Failure to Win Royal Status and the Abortive Attempt at Reform after the First Spartano-Messenian War

NON-LACEDAEMONIAN Greek students of Spartan affairs in and after the fifth century B.C. sought to account for the origin of the political constitution, and the peculiar social system with which the constitution was bound up, which were in force at Sparta at that time and which remained in force there until they were overthrown in 227 B.C. by King Kleomenes III. There was fairly general agreement that the dual monarchy was the oldest of all Spartan institutions and that the rest had all been established by some single legislator or pair of legislators at one and the same moment. Beyond these two points, opinions differed widely—as they still do.

Hellanikos ascribed the establishment of the fifth-century-B.C. Spartan constitution and way of life (ἀγωγή) to Kings Eurysthenes and Prokles,[1] the fictitious Heraklid forebears of the eponyms of the two Spartan royal houses. A more widely held view was that the regime had been inaugurated by a later legislator who, if given a name, was called 'Lycurgus'. Believers in the 'Lycurgan' origin of Sparta's institutions mostly also held that, in the age before 'Lycurgus', Sparta had been in a state of unusually acute domestic disturbance for an unusually long time, in contrast to the unusual degree of domestic stability that she had been enjoying since she had adopted 'Lycurgus's' reforms. The Lacedaemonians 'had been the worst-governed of all the Hellenes, almost, before they had become law-abiding' [thanks to 'Lycurgus'].[2]

Lakedaimon [i.e. the city-state of Sparta], after its foundation by its present North-West-Greek-speaking inhabitants, began by going through a longer bout of domestic disorders than any other state of which we know; but she was also the earliest to become law-abiding and she has never fallen under the rule of a despot. For a little more than four centuries, reckoning back from the end of the present war [i.e. from the year 404 B.C.], the Lacedaemonians have been living under their present constitution.[3]

In this passage, Thucydides dates towards the close of the ninth

[1] See p. 180, with n. 3.

[2] κακονομώτατοι ἦσαν σχεδὸν πάντων Ἑλλήνων . . . μετέβαλον δὲ ὧδε ἐς εὐνομίην (Herodotus, Book I, chap. 65).

[3] ἡ γὰρ Λακεδαίμων μετὰ τὴν κτίσιν τῶν νῦν ἐνοικούντων Δωριῶν ἐπὶ πλεῖστον ὧν ἴσμεν χρόνον στασιάσασα ὅμως ἐκ παλαιτάτου καὶ ηὐνομήθη καὶ ἀεὶ ἀτυράννευτος ἦν· ἔτη γάρ ἐστι μάλιστα τετρακόσια καὶ ὀλίγῳ πλείω ἐς τὴν τελευτὴν τοῦδε τοῦ πολέμου ἀφ' οὗ Λακεδαιμόνιοι τῇ αὐτῇ πολιτείᾳ χρῶνται (Thucydides, Book I, chap. 18, § 1.)

century B.C. the establishment of the Spartan constitution that was in force in his own day. Later Greek chronologists dated its establishment soon after the beginning of the same century. They were no better informed than Thucydides was. They were simply equating 'Lycurgus's' generation with a particular generation of the Spartan kings of one or other or both of the two royal houses, and were making a dead reckoning backwards—allowing an arbitrary number of years for each generation—from the earliest generation of Spartan kings that could be dated with approximate certainty. Aristotle, on the other hand, dated 'Lycurgus' in the generation of the foundation of the Olympic festival, the traditional date of which was 776 B.C. Aristotle adopted this date on the strength of the occurrence of the name 'Lykourgos'—apparently in association with the name 'Iphitos'—on a discus preserved at Olympia. This discus bore an inscription in which these two statesmen (or superhuman heroes or gods) proclaimed the international truce that was to last for the duration of the festival.[1] In the second century of the Christian Era, Pausanias saw at Olympia a discus which was alleged to be Iphitos'.[2]

This lack of consensus among our Greek sources is reflected in corresponding differences of opinion among modern scholars. It can, perhaps, be agreed that Herodotus and Thucydides are correct in stating that Sparta went through a prolonged bout of domestic political disorders before she attained stability on lines that were peculiar to her. It may also be guessed—though there will be no agreement about this—that Sparta's antecedent domestic disorders had been due to two events in her history that were connected with each other. The first of these events was the incorporation of the Taÿgetan Minyai, led by the Aigeid house, in the Spartan body politic; the second event was Sparta's conquest, thanks to this reinforcement, of Amyklai, Pharis, and Geronthrai—a crucial success which was followed by the conquest of the lower basin of the Eurotas and by the subsequent conquest of Messenia.

Sparta's expansion of her dominions over the southern two-fifths of the Peloponnese to the west of the Parnon range was evidently rapid. The whole process, from the capture of Amyklai down to the end of the First Spartano-Messenian War, seems to have been completed within a span of only about forty years (*circa* 760/755–720/715 B.C.).[3] These military triumphs had put the Spartan state in possession of wide additional territories, together with these territories' subjugated and enslaved inhabitants (now εἵλωτες). The coastal plain of the Eurotas basin was productive agricultural land in so far as it was not waterlogged; on the Stenyklaros plain in north-eastern Messenia, the soil was at least as good,

---

[1] Plutarch, *Lycurgus*, chap. 1. See also the present work, pp. 221–2, 278, and 279.
[2] Pausanias, Book V, chap. 20, § 1.
[3] This chronology, which is Pausanias', is rejected by Jones, *Sparta*, p. 11 (see p. 180, n.3).

and the productive area was larger. The helot peasantry of these rich agricultural districts that were now Spartan public property had been condemned to surrender one-half of their annual produce to the Spartan body politic.[1] The Greek equivalent of this imprecise abstract modern Western term is 'the Lacedaemonians'; and the concrete plural number raises the questions: Who exactly were 'the Lacedaemonians' who were now entitled, by right of conquest, to receive the helots' contributions? And in what shares was this permanent revenue from the spoils of war to be distributed between different sections or categories of the Spartiate citizen-body?

Were the enfranchised Minyai who had descended from the 'shelf' of Taÿgetos and had been installed in Amyklai to be on a footing of equality with the members of the four previously existing Spartan obai, located at Sparta itself? Were the Aigeidai, who were the leading clan among the Minyai, to be on a footing of equality with the Agiadai and the Eurypontidai, who were the established pair of Spartan royal houses, and who were reigning on a footing of equality with each other? Apart from the question of the relative status of these different local divisions of the Spartan citizen-body, how were the spoils of conquest to be apportioned between different social classes? In the Hellenic World as a whole, the eighth century B.C. was an age in which the social cleavage between the aristocracy and the demos was sharply marked; and the aristocratic minority enjoyed valuable political and economic privileges. We have no evidence that eighth-century-B.C. Sparta was, in this point, an exception to the general Hellenic rule.[2] Social cleavages and local divisions would, no doubt, in any case have set up tensions in Sparta, as they did in many other Hellenic states, in this phase of Hellenic history. But we may guess that, at Sparta, the tension was heightened and the dissension was exacerbated by the magnitude of the prize which the successful wars of conquest had tossed into the domestic Spartan arena to be competed for by the Spartan citizen-body's contending factions.[3] 'If there was direct allotment it will have been to a comparatively small number of the already privileged; one thinks rather of a disorganized scramble.'[4]

In the Spartan wars of conquest in the eighth century B.C. the Aigeidai —and, under their leadership, the rest of the Taÿgetan Minyai, too, no

[1] Tyrtaios, fr. 6 (Bergk–Hiller–Crusius) = 6.7(1) (Diehl), cited on p. 202, in n. 5.

[2] Busolt and Swoboda, op. cit., p. 662, and Jones, *Sparta*, p. 170, hold that there was an hereditary aristocracy at Sparta. Cp. Forrest, *A History*, pp. 29 and 63. Ehrenberg, however, holds that Sparta never went through the stage of living under an aristocratic regime ('Spartiaten und Lakedaimonier', p. 59; *Neugründer des Staates*, p. 22).

[3] See Pausanias, Book IV, chap. 18, § 3, and Dickins, loc. cit., p. 10. Behind both the 'Partheniai's' conspiracy and the 'Lycurgan' reform 'lay the same issues, status and land, and these issues were created by the stresses put on the Spartan economy and Spartan society by the annexation of Messenia' (Forrest, *A History*, p. 62).

[4] Ibid., p. 38.

doubt—played a major part, according to our scanty surviving records. It has been noted already that the Aigeid Timomakhos is said to have been in command of the Spartan army at the taking of Amyklai.[1] Another Aigeid, Euryleon, in the fifth generation from the eponym of the Aigeid house, is said to have commanded the centre of the Spartan army in the opening battle in the second campaign of the First Spartano-Messenian War, with the Agiad King Polydoros commanding the left wing and the Eurypontid King Theopompos commanding the right.[2] If this information is authentic,[3] it indicates that, at this date, the Aigeidai were on a par with the Agiadai and the Eurypontidai, at least *de facto*. This conclusion is supported by a story told by Herodotus. After recounting the incorporation of the Taÿgetan Minyai in the Spartan body politic and their intermarriage with the original Spartan citizen-body,[4] Herodotus goes on to relate that, 'not long after that, the Minyai were quick to make themselves objectionable. They asked for a share in the kingship and made other indefensible moves.'[5] Herodotus proceeds to tell how the Spartans arrested and imprisoned the obstreperous Minyai and decided to put them to death; but the Minyan prisoners were rescued by their high-born Spartiate wives. They then retreated to their former home on the Taÿgetos 'shelf', and then emigrated from Laconia under a safe-conduct from the Spartan Government which was negotiated for them by 'Theras', a personification of their home on the shelf and the reputed ancestor of the eponym of the Aigeidai. According to Herodotus, a few of the Minyan émigrés went with Theras to the island of Thera; the majority went to Triphylia.[6]

It has been suggested already, in another context, that 'Theras' and his plantation of a Lacedaemonian colony on the island of Thera are a rationalizer's fabrications.[7] On the other hand, we need not reject Herodotus' statements that the Minyai fell foul of the rest of the Spartans and that the quarrel was settled, without civil war, by an agreement under which some of the Minyai—though not all of them, nor all of their leading family, the Aigeidai—emigrated from Laconia to a destination overseas. This part of Herodotus' story is identical with the story that, at

---

[1] See p. 176, with n. 2.

[2] Pausanias, Book IV, chap. 7, § 8.

[3] W. G. Forrest, 'The Dating of the Lycurgan Reforms in Sparta', in *The Phoenix*, vol. xvii (1963), p. 167, points out that Theopompos and Polydoros cannot have been in joint command at so early a date as *circa* 730 B.C. Euryleon, however, might have been joint commander with Theopompos as early as that date, or with both Theopompos and Polydoros towards the end of the war.

[4] See pp. 174–6.

[5] χρόνου δὲ οὐ πολλοῦ διεξελθόντος, αὐτίκα οἱ Μινύαι ἐξύβρισαν, τῆς τε βασιληίης μεταιτέοντες καὶ ἄλλα ποιεῦντες οὐχ ὅσια (Herodotus, Book IV, chap. 145).

[6] Herodotus, Book IV, chaps. 146–9.

[7] See pp. 174–5.

Sparta, after the end of the First Spartano-Messenian War, a faction called the 'Partheniai'[1] or the 'epeunaktai'[2] conspired to make a revolution on the occasion of the Hyakinthia festival.[3] The conspiracy is said to have been detected and frustrated; but, as in Herodotus' version of the story, there was no bloodshed, and the crisis was resolved by an agreement that the foiled conspirators should emigrate. According to this version of the story the émigrés settled at Tarentum, a Spartan colony whose traditional foundation-date is *circa* 708–706 B.C.[4]

Evidently the only authentic information about this incident was that the name of the Spartan settlers at Tarentum was 'Partheniai' and that they were the sons of fathers called 'epeunaktai'.

'Partheniai' was interpreted as meaning 'children of virgins'; but virgins do not have children in real life; and this word looks as if it were the Illyrian ethnikon 'Parthinoi',[5] mistakenly interpreted as if it were a derivative of the Greek common noun 'parthenos'.[6] Detachments of several Illyrian peoples—e.g. the Khaones-Khônes, the Iapodes-Iapyges, the Galabrioi-Kalabroi, the Pelagones-Pelignoi—had crossed the Adriatic from continental south-eastern Europe and had gained a foothold in peninsular Italy. A detachment of the Parthinoi, from the hinterland of Epidamnos (Dyrrhakhion), may have been the previous population of the territory, on the heel of Italy, in which Tarentum was planted by Spartan colonists, and the colonists may have been nicknamed 'Parthinoi' at Sparta, as New Englanders might have been nicknamed 'Mohawks' in England.

The meaning of the word 'epeunaktai' seems to be 'men who had been granted the right of marrying women of high social status'. Theopompus[7] guesses that they were helots; Ephorus and (perhaps following him) Aristotle[8] guess that they were Spartiatai of the highest category.

[1] Antiochus in Strabo, *Geographica*, Book VI, chap. 3, § 2 (C. 278–9); Ephorus in Strabo Book VI, chap. 3, § 3 (C. 279–84); Aristotle, *Politics*, Book V, chap. 6, § 1 (1306b); Justin, Book III, chap. 4; Book XX, chap. 1, § 5.

[2] Theopompus, apud Athenaeum, Book VI, 271 c–d; Diodorus, Book VIII, fragm. 21. In this passage, Diodorus mentions the Partheniai as well as the epeunaktai, and seems to distinguish them from each other.

[3] Strabo, Book VI, chap. 3, § 2 (C. 278–9).

[4] Kiechle, *Lakonien und Sparta*, p. 183, interprets the foundation of Tarentum as being evidence of contemporary unrest at Sparta. He also finds evidence that Tarentum held aloof from Sparta during the first century of Tarentine history (pp. 182–3). This is what we should have expected if the colonists were Spartans who had been disappointed of receiving what they considered to have been their due after the First Spartano-Messenian War. 'If the colony failed, the Partheniai were to be given land in Messenia, according to Ephorus' (Forrest, *A History*, p. 61). The 'Lycurgan' reforms at Sparta after the Second War, which did give satisfaction to Spartiate commoners who had not emigrated, will have made Sparta more congenial to the Tarentines—at any rate, until the 'Lycurgan' regime began to produce its probably unintended effect of militarizing Spartan life.

[5] See Krahe, op. cit., pp. 31–2 and 43–4. Cp. Forrest, *A History*, p. 61.

[6] See Pareti, *Storia di Sparta Arcaïca*, Parte I, p. 225.

[7] In loc. cit.

[8] In locc. citt.

According to Ephorus,[1] they were Spartiatai of the younger age-classes in the Spartan army in Messenia who, unlike their elders, had not taken a vow to stay in Messenia, without ever returning to Sparta, till Messenia had been conquered. It is not credible that, in the eighth century B.C., any Spartiatai should have made this vow and have kept it for twenty years on end. In the Hellenic world of that age, it would not have been economically practicable to keep a national militia mobilized for longer at a time than a single short campaigning season. The incredibility of Ephorus' version of the story, and its incompatibility with Theopompus' version of it, are evidence that both versions are mere guesses. A more convincing guess would be that the 'epeunaktai' are identical with the Minyai who, according to Herodotus, had married 'Spartan wives who were the daughters of the most eminent of the Spartiatai'.[2] If it is true that the intended revolution had been planned to take place at Amyklai during the Hyakinthia, we may guess, further, that the Aigeidai were moving spirits in the plot, since the Aigeidai had the prerogative of presiding at the Hyakinthia festival.[3]

After the failure of the conspiracy of the 'epeunaktai' and the emigration of the 'Partheniai' to Tarentum, the Aigeidai continued to be a great clan at Sparta.[4] The failure of the conspiracy, however, was fatal for the Aigeidai's ambition (if this had been their ambition) to become a third Spartan royal house. So long as the monarchy survived at Sparta, the Agiadai and Eurypontidai continued to be the only two Spartan royal families.

If it is true that the Aigeidai had been making a bid to win parity with the Agiadai and the Eurypontidai, it is possible that they had lost the first round of this political struggle already before the First Spartano-Messenian War had started. If the dating, in 755/4 B.C., of the inauguration of the board of ephors at Sparta[5] is an authentic record and has not been arrived at merely by making a dead reckoning backwards from some less insecurely dated later event,[6] and if it is also true, as King Kleo-

[1] Apud Strabonem, ibid. Cp. Polybius, Book VI, chap. 49, § 2, and Book XII, chap. 6b, §§ 9–10.

[2] ἀσταί τε καὶ τῶν πρώτων Σπαρτιητέων θυγατέρες (Herodotus, Book IV, chap. 146).

[3] See Wide, op. cit., p. 89.

[4] φυλὴ μεγάλη ἐν Σπάρτῃ (Herodotus, Book IV, chap. 149).

[5] See p. 153.

[6] E. von Stern, 'Zur Entstehung und ursprünglichen Bedeutung des Ephorats in Sparta', in *Berliner Stüdien für klassische Philologie und Archäologie*, 15. Band, 2. Heft, pp. 1–62 (Berlin, 1894, Calvary), pp. 8–9; Pareti, 'Le tribù personali e le tribù locali a Sparta', in *Rendiconti della Reale Accademia dei Lincei*, Classe di Scienze Morali, Storiche, e Filologiche, serie quinta, vol. xix (1910), pp. 457–73, on p. 469, n. 1; Meyer, *Forschungen zur alten Geschichte*, p. 247; Ehrenberg, *Neugründer des Staates*, p. 47; and Kiechle, *Lakonien und Sparta*, p. 256, hold that this dating is authentic. Dickins, loc. cit., pp. 12–13, and Forrest, *A History*, p. 20, hold that it is not based on a genuine record, but is fictitious. Norvin, in *Classica et Mediaevalia*, vol. iii, fasc. 1, p. 105, holds that the dating in the reign of King Theopompos (Plutarch, *Lycurgus*,

menes III declared in 227 B.C., that the ephors had been created originally by the kings to serve as their deputies,[1] the date suggests that this new public office at Sparta had been instituted in order to cope with the sudden increase in the amount of public business that must have been one of the consequences of Sparta's conquest and annexation of Amyklai, Pharis, and Geronthrai. If this was the way in which provision was actually made for the administration of a greatly expanded Spartan territory, we can see that it was not the only possible way that could have been followed. Alternatively, Sparta, after the incorporation of Amyklai in her body politic, might have followed the precedent that had been set on the occasion of the Spartan city-state's original synoecism. On that occasion, two hitherto independent communities had been united politically under the joint kingship of their respective royal houses.[2] The union of Amyklai with the two pairs of settlements constituting nuclear Sparta could have been provided for by placing Amyklai on a par with each of the two pairs, and by giving the Aigeidai royal status, on a par with the Agiadai and the Eurypontidai, as representatives of the Minyan Spartan conquerors of, and settlers in, Amyklai, and of the native Amyclaeans, if some, at least, of these had been taken into the Spartan citizenbody. If this was the Aigeidai's plan for reorganizing the administration

chap. 7) is merely a chronological inference. If it is, it is an incorrect inference; for it is almost certain that Theopompos was not yet reigning in 755/4 B.C. (Meyer, op. cit., p. 248). Stern, op. cit., p. 10, holds that the creation of the ephorate was attributed to Theopompos merely because he was the earliest king of whom there was any authentic record. The dating 755/4 B.C. is, however, supported by the fact that there were ephors at Tarentum (see Pareti, op. cit., p. 225); for Tarentum was founded from Sparta *circa* 708–706 B.C.

The institution of the ephorate is attributed to Theopompos by Plato, *Laws*, Book III, 692 A (a τρίτος σωτήρ); by Aristotle, *Politics*, Book V, chap. 11 (9), § 1 (1313a); and by Plutarch, *Lycurgus*, chap. 7. It is attributed to 'Lycurgus' by Herodotus, Book I, chap. 65; Xenophon, *Lak. Pol.*, chap. 8, § 3; Isocrates, *Panathenaïcus*, 152; Plato, *Ep.* VIII, 354 B; Satyrus apud Diogenem Laertium, Book I, chap. 68; and also by Ephorus, according to Kiechle, *Messenische Studien* (Kallmünz, Opf., 1959, Lassleben), p. 23, n. 17. Diogenes Laertius himself, in loc. cit., attributes the creation of the ephors to Khilon.

Niese, 'Zur Verfassungsgeschichte Lakedaimons', p. 66, holds that the diversity of the accounts of the ephorate's age and origin is an indication that there was no genuine record. Cp. Stern, op. cit., pp. 16 and 46. It was, of course, common practice to attribute to 'Lycurgus' the creation of any Spartan institution whose origin was unknown. (See G. Dum, *Entstehung und Entwicklung des spartanischen Ephorats, bis zur Beseitigung desselben durch König Kleomenes III* (Innsbruck, 1878, Wegner), p. 32; Berve, op. cit., p. 33). If we equate the 'Lycurgan' reform with the reform that was carried out after the Second Spartano-Messenian War, the ephorate will have been a pre-'Lycurgan' institution.

[1] Plutarch, *Cleomenes*, chap. 10, endorsed by Meyer, *Forschungen zur alten Geschichte*, p. 250, n. 1; by Chrimes, *Ancient Sparta*, p. 408; and by Jones, *Sparta*, pp. 174–5, but not by Jones, 'The Lycurgan Rhetra', in *Ancient Society and Institutions: Studies Presented to Victor Ehrenberg* (Oxford, 1966, Blackwell), pp. 165–75, on p. 174, n. 40. Stern, op. cit., p. 56, holds that the ephorate was created by the anonymous author or authors of the 'Lycurgan' constitution. He (or they) did not give the task of overseeing, on behalf of the damos, the observance of the monthly exchange of oaths between the ephors and the kings (see p. 241) to an already existing board of public officers, hitherto appointed by the kings.

[2] See pp. 171–2.

of the Spartan city-state after its first important enlargement, this plan will have been countered effectively by the establishment of a board of five ephors ('overseers'), responsible to the existing two royal houses, to help these two houses to administer the original four settlements together with Amyklai.[1] Under this arrangement, Amyklai counted as only one in five, not one in three, of the settlements (obai) of which the Spartan citizen-body was now composed,[2] and the Aigeidai were effectively prevented from attaining the royal status to which they aspired. This first reverse that the Aigeidai had suffered will have been confirmed when, at their second bid, the 'epeunaktai' were foiled and the 'Partheniai' emigrated.

The internal tension in the Spartan body politic over the division of the political and economic spoils of conquest in the eighth century B.C. must have been formidable; for there are indications that the discontent was not confined to the Aigeidai and their Minyan followers. The issue between new citizens and old citizens seems to have been complicated by an issue between aristocrats and commoners—or, in economic terms, landowners and the landless—which cut across the issue, on lines of locality, between the different communities of which the Spartan state was composed. There are indications that the commoners' cause, without distinction of locality, was championed by the Agiad King Polydoros, who reigned during and after the First Spartano-Messenian War.

Polydoros was remembered at Sparta as having been a friend of the Spartan damos[3] (in the peculiar, yet, within its limits, genuine, Spartan meaning of that word). At Sparta in the second century of the Christian Era, there was an eikon (?bust ?portrait) of Polydoros not far from the big statue of the Spartan damos.[4] At this date, the Spartan public officers were still using a seal with a likeness of Polydoros on it;[5] and presumably the ephors were the principal users of this seal down to 227 B.C., when the

---

[1] Though Stern does not believe that the ephorate was a creation of the crown's, he does believe that its original function was administrative, not judicial (op. cit., pp. 25–7 and 33).

[2] It seems unlikely to have been an accidental coincidence that the number of the ephors was the same as the number of the obai. It seems more probable that, when the board of ephors was instituted, the number of the members was fixed at five in order to provide one 'overseer' for each of the five obai as the deputy of the pair of kings. The association of the five ephors with the five obai is accepted by Huxley, op. cit., p. 39, and by Neumann, loc. cit., pp. 43–4, among other scholars. Miss Chrimes, *Ancient Sparta*, p. vi, asserts, vehemently but unconvincingly, that 'there were never at any time five Spartan tribes, or five villages, which could account for the number of the ephors', and, p. 319, 'there is no satisfactory evidence either that there were five local divisions at Sparta in the pre-Hellenistic period, or that there were ever five main army divisions, or that in Sparta local administrative divisions at any time formed the basis either of the military units or of political representation'. Cp. eandem, ibid., pp. 163, 164, 313, 392, and Norvin in *Classica et Mediaevalia*, vol. iii, fasc. 1, p. 62. An authoritative voice on the same side as Norvin's and Miss Chrimes' is Ehrenberg's in P.–W., 14. Halbband (1937), cols. 1693–1704, s.v. obai, in col. 1702.

[3] Pausanias, Book III, chap. 3, § 2.

[4] Ibid., chap. 11, § 10.   [5] Ibid.

ephorate was broken by Polydoros' kinsman, King Kleomenes III. There was also a house—now state property—called 'the Booneta' ('Purchased with oxen') which was believed to have been bought by the Spartan state from Polydoros' widow.[1]

The reason why Polydoros had become the hero of the Spartan damos was remembered. Polydoros had stood for the distribution to Spartan citizens, in allotments (kleroi), of conquered Messenian land, and he had suffered for this policy by being assassinated. It was told of him that, when asked what was his objective in attacking Messenia, he had replied that it was 'the unallotted land'.[2] He was credited with having been the true distributor of either 3,000 or 4,500 out of the 9,000 allotments that were usually credited to 'Lycurgus'.[3] It was also remembered that Polydoros had been assassinated by an aristocrat named Polemarkhos;[4] and, since Polemarkhos' tomb survived at Sparta to be seen there by Pausanias,[5] it looks as if Polemarkhos' party and policy had prevailed over Polydoros' in the short run,[6] though the distribution of conquered Messenian territory in allotments, which Polydoros had tried, but had probably failed, to carry out, was achieved subsequently—perhaps in the latter part of the seventh century B.C.—in the so-called 'Lycurgan' settlement. Meanwhile, the dissension at Sparta between 'have-nots' and 'haves' continued. The poet Terpander, who visited Sparta *circa* 676–673 B.C., is said to have been invited in the hope that he might be able to mend the breach.[7]

(ii) *The so-called 'Lycurgan' Reform after the Second Spartano-Messenian War*

We have no authentic record of the date at which the so-called 'Lycurgan' regime was instituted. The date that won general acceptance from the fourth century B.C. onwards was an early date in the ninth century B.C. Aristotle dated 'Lycurgus' more than a hundred years later than that, on the strength of the name's appearing on an inscription on a discus at

---

[1] Ibid.

[2] ἐπὶ τὴν ἀκλήρωτον τῆς χώρας βαδίζει (Plutarch, *Apophthegmata Laconica*, Polydoros, 2).

[3] Plutarch, *Lycurgus*, chap. 8. The date of the so-called 'Lycurgan' settlement was probably later than the end of the Second Spartano-Messenian War; i.e., so far from being before Polydoros' time, it was perhaps nearly a hundred years after it (see chap. 3, section (ii)). The conventional chronology dated 'Lycurgus' and all his reputed acts earlier than Polydoros' reign, because no vacant room could be found for inserting 'Lycurgus' into Spartan history at any date later than the ninth century B.C. (see chap. 3, Annex V).

[4] Pausanias, Book III, chap. 3, § 3.

[5] Ibid.

[6] Kiechle, *Messenische Studien*, pp. 63–4, holds that, after the First Spartano-Messenian War, the Spartan royal houses and aristocracy succeeded in monopolizing the conquered lands.

[7] Kiechle, *Lakonien und Sparta*, pp. 200–1.

Olympia.[1] Neither of these datings can be taken seriously.[2] Both of them are attempts to solve the problem of finding a place for 'Lycurgus' within the framework of Spartan history. There was no room for an historical Lycurgus within the period for which there was even a hazy knowledge of the genuine course of events, and this historical or semi-historical period extended backwards in time perhaps as far as the reigns of Poly-doros[3] and Theopompos. Accordingly, 'Lycurgus' had to be dated earlier than that if he was to be accepted as being a genuine historical human personality.

The only trustworthy kind of evidence for dating the inauguration of the 'Lycurgan' regime is internal evidence, and, fortunately, this is forthcoming. The key-point in the 'Lycurgan' reform was its practical recognition of the capital importance of the hoplite phalanx.[4] Under this constitution, as we find it in operation in and after the fifth century B.C., the Spartiate hoplites were endowed with allotments (kleroi) and pos-sessed, collectively, the ultimate sovereign power in the Spartan state. What we know of the history of the development of the hoplite equipment and the hoplite phalanx in the Hellenic World in general and at Sparta in particular indicates that, at Sparta, the hoplite phalanx is unlikely to have won the political powers, granted, in the 'Lycurgan' constitution ('rider' and all), to the Spartiate damos, before the close of the Second Spartano-Messenian War.[5] If this conclusion is correct, the 'Lycurgan' constitution cannot be dated earlier than, at the earliest, the mid point of the seventh century B.C.

All that we know, not by internal evidence, but by contemporary testimony, is that the so-called 'Lycurgan' regime was already long since in force at Sparta by the time, about half-way through the fifth century B.C., when Herodotus was writing his history, in which we have the earliest still extant notices of Spartan affairs by a contemporary non-Spartan Greek student of them. However, there is one extant piece of retrospective literary evidence that tallies with our evidence about the date of the institution of the hoplite phalanx in indicating that there was a resurgence of domestic dissension at Sparta after the Second Spartano-Messenian War. In a passage of his *Politics*,[6] Aristotle gives illustrations

[1] See p. 214 and chap. 3, Annex V, pp. 278 and 279.
[2] Notwithstanding N. G. L. Hammond's able defence of the ninth-century dating in 'The Lycurgean Reform at Sparta', in the *Journal of Hellenic Studies*, vol. lxx (1950), pp. 42–64.
[3] 'Except for Polydoros' colleague Theopompos—and Theopompos' memory was kept alive almost exclusively through Tyrtaios—Polydoros himself seems to be the first figure in early Spartan history whose lineaments are, at least to some extent, discernible' (Jacoby, *F.G.H.*, Dritter Teil: Kommentar zu NR 217–607 (1955), pp. 660–1, No. 596 Anonymi (15)).
[4] See Jones, *Sparta*, p. 32.
[5] Norvin, 'Zur Geschichte der spartanischen Eunomia', in *Classica et Mediaevalia*, vol. iii, fasc. 1 (1940), pp. 47–115, on p. 104. See also the present work, Part III, chap. 3, Annex 1.
[6] Aristotle, *Politics*, Book V, chap. 6 (7), §§ 1–2 (1306b–1307a).

of various political situations which lead to dissension (στάσις) in states living under aristocratic regimes. One of his illustrations, cited already,[1] is the case of the 'Partheniai' at Sparta after the First Spartano-Messenian War; another is the situation at Sparta after the Second Spartano-Messenian War. Another situation in which stasis arises under an aristocratic regime is

when the difference in wealth between the rich and the poor is too extreme. This situation is particularly apt to be produced by wars. This, too, happened in Lakedaimon at the time of the [second] war with the Messenians. The evidence for this is to be found in Tyrtaios' poem *Eunomia*. There were Spartans who were so hard pressed [economically] by the war that they demanded that the country should be carved up into allotments (ἠξίουν ἀναδαστὸν ποιεῖν τὴν χώραν).

This was a renewal of the demand that had been made already after the First Spartano-Messenian War. On that occasion the conspiracy of the 'epeunaktai' had been foiled, and King Polydoros appears to have paid with his life (as King Agis IV was to pay in 240 B.C.) for having attempted to carve into kleroi, for the benefit of landless Spartiatai, some part, at least, of the lands that the Spartan state had, by then, already acquired by conquest. The demand was now the same, but the situation was not.

Since the defeat of Polydoros and of the 'epeunaktai' by the vested interest of the Spartan aristocracy, Sparta had suffered her crushing defeat by Argos at Hysiai in 669 B.C.; this had been followed by a general revolt of the Messenian helots; and the eventual suppression of this revolt had cost Sparta a second war with the Messenians which had been at least as arduous for Sparta as the original war of conquest. The conquered Messenian territory had been recovered in the end. But the lesson, for Sparta, of the Second Spartano-Messenian War, following on the Spartan disaster at Hysiai, had been clear. In an age in which phalanx-tactics were replacing long-range fighting in open order, Sparta could not hope to retain her hold—just re-established with such difficulty—over two-fifths of the Peloponnese unless she now adopted phalanx-tactics whole-heartedly; and she could not do this if she did not give the means and the leisure, for arming and training as hoplite phalangites, to the majority of the Spartiate citizen-body that had been compelled by poverty to fight as relatively ineffective light-armed skirmishers hitherto.

Sparta had the means for endowing her poorer citizens with the necessary land-allotments on a large scale. She was now once again in possession of all the lands in the Stenyklaros plain, as well as in the lower basin of the Eurotas, that had become the Spartan state's property by conquest. If it is true that, hitherto, the aristocracy had monopolized the

[1] On pp. 216–17.

income from these public lands for itself, and had succeeded in retaining this monopoly in the domestic crisis at Sparta after the First Spartano-Messenian War, it must now have become evident—and this even to the Spartan aristocrats—that the aristocrats could no longer hope to continue to retain their monopoly under the new conditions.[1] They must now share the conquered public lands with their commoner fellow citizens in order to enable Sparta to equip herself with a hoplite phalanx by making hoplites out of at least a majority of her former light-armed citizen soldiers. The alternative to this economic sacrifice on the aristocrats' part would not be the continuance of their monopoly; it would be the renewed loss—and, this time, perhaps the irretrievable loss—of these conquered lands for Sparta, and, with it, the loss of even an equal share per head in these lands for the Spartan aristocrats themselves. When the Spartan aristocrats took this point and acted on it, they opened the way for bringing to an end the chronic domestic dissension to which the aristocrats' obstinate selfishness had been condemning Sparta since the close of the First Spartano-Messenian War. The Spartiate commoners, on their side, wanted, above all, a fair share for themselves in the lands that they had helped to conquer. They will hardly have hesitated to undertake full-time hoplite service as the *quid pro quo* for the distribution to them of the coveted kleroi.[2] No one at Sparta will have

---

[1] 'As Andrewes has shown, the new order marked a victory for the *demos* over a presumably unwilling establishment; it was imposed from beneath not from above, it was liberating not restrictive' (Forrest, 'The Dating of the Lycurgan Reforms in Sparta', pp. 157–79, on p. 179).

[2] A. M. Snodgrass, 'The Hoplite Reform and History', in the *Journal of Hellenic Studies*, vol. lxxxv (1965), pp. 110–22, on p. 115, suggests that 'it remains difficult to see in the hoplite class a driving force for military or political innovation, let alone revolution'. On p. 121 Snodgrass holds, on the strength of our literary information about the date and circumstances of the adoption of the hoplite phalanx in the Etruscan city-states and at Rome, that, in Greece too, 'the adoption of hoplite tactics took place, for purely military reasons, at the behest of the heads of state, who could apply compulsion to a possibly reluctant body of men'. Snodgrass's conclusion is (ibid., p. 122) that 'hoplites . . . were an instrument before they became a force'.

This may well have been true in general. As soon as the hoplite phalanx tactics had proved themselves, in action, to have become a *sine qua non* for winning battles, a competition will have set in, among rival states, to put the maximum number of hoplites into the line; and this will have led to the compulsory enrolment, in the register of hoplites, of citizens whose means did not extend, or extended only with a painful effort, to procuring for themselves the full hoplite equipment. This certainly happened at Rome, as Classes II–V were added successively to Class I. Hoplites in these depressed classes are, no doubt, likely to have been reluctant, as Snodgrass suggests.

It looks, however, as if Sparta had been a special and peculiar case. In ordinary Hellenic city-states, including Sparta's perioecic dependencies, the hoplite had to equip himself out of such means as he already possessed. Sparta was exceptional in possessing a large fund of public land, cultivated by helots, which could be carved up into kleroi large enough to support full-time professional hoplites on the product of helot labour. The distribution of this public land had long been demanded by the hitherto landless majority of the Spartiate citizen-body. It would seem therefore that, at Sparta at any rate, if not elsewhere, landless men who could become hoplites if they were endowed with kleroi had been a force before

foreseen, at the time, the rigour of the demands on the Spartiate hoplites that were going to be entailed by the invidious task of permanently holding the helots down.

The adoption of the 'Lycurgan' reforms will have been the consequence of this agreement between aristocrats and commoners. The probable dates of the Battle of Hysiai and of the Second Spartano-Messenian War coincide with the probable dates of the adoption of phalanx-tactics in the Hellenic World in general and at Sparta in particular. These dates, in combination, indicate that the 'Lycurgan' regime must have been instituted in Sparta at a date after the mid point of the seventh century B.C.[1]

To adopt this date is to reject the unanimous opinion of Robert Wade-Gery, Theodore Wade-Gery, and W. G. Forrest,[2] and one dissents from this consensus at one's peril. Forrest takes Aristotle, in the passage quoted above,[3] to mean by 'the war' the First Spartano-Messenian War, not the Second.[4] He dates the 'Lycurgan' reform about half-way through the first half of the seventh century B.C.—perhaps in the year 676/5 B.C., which was the inaugural year of the Spartan Karneia festival.[5] Forrest's trains of reasoning are acute. Yet they cannot stand against the objective evidence, presented by Snodgrass since Forrest's article was published,[6]

they became an instrument. They had been a force already at the time of the domestic upheaval at Sparta that had followed the First Spartano-Messenian War; but at that stage they had been an ineffective force because the hoplite phalanx had not yet been recognized to be a military necessity. In the fresh bout of domestic unrest that followed the Second Spartano-Messenian War, these men's descendants became an effective force because the hoplite phalanx had come, in the meantime, to be recognized to be a necessary instrument for the maintenance of Sparta's hold on her exceptionally extensive conquered territories.

[1] See Niese, 'Zur Verfassungsgeschichte Lakedaimons', p. 81. A date as late as the close of the seventh century B.C. is suggested to the reader's mind by Herodotus' way of recording the sequence of events in Spartan history (Book I, chaps. 65–6). After describing 'Lycurgus's' reforms, death, and apotheosis, Herodotus goes on to say that Sparta 'immediately shot up and flourished' (ἀνά τε ἔδραμον αὐτίκα καὶ εὐθηνήθησαν), and that this tempted her to make her unsuccessful attempts (in the course of the first half of the sixth century B.C.) to conquer the Tegeatis. The natural inference from this passage is that Herodotus is dating the institution of the 'Lycurgan' regime immediately before the Spartan attack on Tegea, i.e. is dating it towards the close of the seventh century B.C. Actually Herodotus, in this same passage, dates 'Lycurgus' far earlier (see Chrimes, *Ancient Sparta*, p. 319). He dates him in the next generation after Agis, the eponym of the Agiad royal house. It looks, however, as if Herodotus had no information about any events in Spartan history between the 'Lycurgan' reforms and the attack on Tegea; and, in truth, there would not have been any intervening events if the historical date of the 'Lycurgan' reforms was post 650 B.C.

[2] See Forrest, 'The Dating of the Lycurgan Reforms in Sparta', pp. 157–79, introductory note.

[3] On page 223.

[4] Forrest in 'The Dating of the Lycurgan Reforms', p. 171.

[5] Ibid., p. 172. Jones, *Sparta*, p. 33, suggests that the Karneia may have been inaugurated as a festival of reconciliation. In 'The Lycurgan Rhetra', in *Ancient Society and Institutions*, pp. 165–75, on p. 172, Jones definitely associates the inauguration of the Karneia with the inauguration of the 'Lycurgan' constitution.

[6] Forrest's presentation of his view in *A History of Sparta* is discussed in a supplementary note to the present Part of the present book, on pp. 413–17.

that the phalanx-tactics did not come into general use in the Hellenic World earlier than about the middle of the seventh century B.C.[1]

Forrest accepts Andrewes's thesis[2] that the Spartan constitution embodied in the 'Lycurgan' rhetra was 'the first hoplite constitution of Greek history'.[3] Writing before the publication of Snodgrass's work, Andrewes, like Forrest, believed that the hoplite army was introduced at Sparta at the beginning of the seventh century B.C.[4] Nevertheless, Andrewes, unlike Forrest, dates the 'Lycurgan' constitution after the Second Spartano-Messenian War, not before it,[5] and this dating has now been confirmed by Snodgrass's findings in regard to the date at which phalanx-tactics came into use. On the strength of this new light on the question of the date of Sparta's 'Lycurgan' constitution, it seems necessary to date it, at the earliest, about twenty-five to thirty-five years later than Forrest's dating, i.e. *circa* 650–640 B.C. instead of *circa* 675 B.C. Herodotus' sketch of the rise of Sparta suggests[6] a date as late as *circa* 600 B.C. This dating of the introduction of the 'Lycurgan' regime at Sparta would tally with the evidence, presented by Wade-Gery,[7] that there was a second serious Messenian revolt in the closing years of the seventh century B.C. If the Spartan aristocrats had been reluctant to take to heart the lesson of the first revolt ('the Second Spartano-Messenian War'), the outbreak of a second revolt only thirty or forty years later will have left them no choice. The second revolt will have been at least as formidable as the first had been, if Wade-Gery is right in identifying it with the revolt led by the Messenian hero Aristomenes. The cumulative effect on Spartan minds will have been potent enough to reconcile the Spartan aristocrats, at last, to the drastic reforms that the 'Lycurgan' constitution embodied.

Andrewes makes the point[8] that, 'before *circa* 600 B.C., Sparta was not governed on the Lycurgan system or anything that resembled it'. 'Everything goes to show that the period round 600 B.C. was a period of important change, and the overwhelming probability is that the classical Spartan system was set up in this period.'[9]

The 'Lycurgan' regime remained in force till the year 227 B.C., when King Kleomenes III made the first breach in it by breaking the power of the ephorate—a revolution which he defended as being a restoration of the 'Lycurgan' regime in its pristine form. Between 227 B.C. and 146 B.C. there was a series of further revolutionary changes which had

[1] See chap. 3, Annex I.
[2] In A. Andrewes, *The Greek Tyrants* (London, 1956, Hutchinson), chap. 6, 'The Spartan Alternative to Tyranny'.
[3] Andrewes, ibid., p. 75.   [4] Andrewes, ibid., p. 74.   [5] Andrewes, ibid., p. 75.
[6] See p. 225, n. 1.   [7] See p. 186, n. 1.
[8] In 'Eunomia', in the *Classical Quarterly*, vol. xxxi (1937), pp. 89–102, on p. 100.
[9] Ibid., p. 101.

the cumulative effect of dismantling the 'Lycurgan' regime almost completely. In 146 B.C. the dissolution of the Achaean Confederation by Rome released Sparta from the membership in the Confederation that had been imposed upon her since 192 B.C. Sparta now became directly dependent on Rome; the Romans did not hinder her from trying to re-establish the 'Lycurgan' regime; and thereafter, in the Age of the Principate, archaism became a craze at Sparta as in other historic Greek states.[1] Unlike Kleomenes III, the Spartan archaists of this age had no political axe to grind, since Sparta now no longer had any political power; they were archaists bona fide; but sincerity was no guarantee of success in reinstating a regime which, by the generation of Augustus, had been in ruins for two hundred years.

In the 'Lycurgan' regime as we find it during the quarter of a millennium ending in 227 B.C., we can distinguish three elements: a political constitution,[2] a social system,[3] and a military organization.[4] The constitution—or, at least, that part of it which provided for a revision of the constitutional relations between the kings, the gerousia, the damos, and the helots—must have been established by a single act of state at a particular moment. On the other hand, the increase in the power of the ephorate, after the prerogative of appointing the ephors had been transferred from the kings to the damos,[5] seems to have been a gradual progress, and the evolution of the social system, too, must have been the work of time.[6] There are elements in it which look like antique customs that might have become obsolete if the Spartan public authorities had not taken partial control over them in order to make them serve the 'Lycurgan' political constitution's purposes. There are other elements that look like effects—perhaps unexpected and unintended effects—of the pressure of the 'Lycurgan' constitution on the private behaviour of the 'homoioi', constituting the damos, whom the constitution had called into existence. As for the military organization, it was grounded on both the constitution and the social system and was also required by them as a necessary instrument for preserving them against attempts, on the helots' part, to overthrow them by force. The military organization, like the social system, underwent changes during the period during which the political constitution remained in force. The changes in the military organization,

---

[1] See p. 158.   [2] Dealt with in the present chapter.
[3] Dealt with in chap. 4.   [4] Dealt with in chap. 5.
[5] This transfer must have taken place at some date or other, if the ephorate had been created in 755/4 B.C. and if the ephors had originally been the kings' deputies (see pp. 218–20). The most likely occasion for the transfer will have been the inauguration of the 'Lycurgan' constitution. Whether the prerogative of appointing the ephors was transferred from the crown to the damos, or whether the ephorate, elected by the damos, was a new creation, the conferment of this prerogative on the damos was a crucial event in Sparta's constitutional history, and it is astonishing that we have no record of how and when it was brought about.
[6] Roussel, op. cit., p. 40; Niese, 'Zur Verfassungsgeschichte Lakedaimons', p. 83.

and the eventual overthrow of the constitution itself in 227 B.C., were responses to a problem that was becoming, all the time, more and more difficult for Sparta to solve. This was the problem of meeting constantly growing political and military demands with a gradually diminishing quantity of man-power in the ranks of the Spartiate 'homoioi'.

Our contemporary sources of information about the 'Lycurgan' regime are all non-Spartan, with the one outstanding exception of the enigmatic 'rhetra'[1] which purports to be the charter in which the 'Lycurgan' constitution was embodied. The meaning of almost every syllable of this 'rhetra' is in dispute, and, in the text as we have it, there is no mention of two innovations that were both of capital importance. One of these was the creation of a damos of whole-time professional hoplites through the provision for their maintenance from allotments (kleroi), cultivated by helots, which were carved out of the land that had come into the Spartan state's possession by conquest. The other crucial innovation on which the 'rhetra' is silent is the transference to the damos, from the kings, of the prerogative of appointing the annual board of ephors.[2]

Some of our non-Spartan Greek authorities on Sparta have been preserved only at second hand and in isolated fragments. Our most trustworthy information is in the form of notices of facts and events in the works of historians: Herodotus, Thucydides, Xenophon, Polybius, Plutarch, and the surviving fragments of the works of, for instance, Ephorus and Theopompus. We can place less confidence in the surviving analytical accounts of Spartan institutions that are presented in Xenophon's *Lakedaimonión Politeia*, Aristotle's *Politics*, the sixth book of Polybius' work, and Plutarch's *Lycurgus*; for it has been noted already[3] that, from the beginning of the fourth century B.C. onwards, works of this type are suspect. Under the pretext of giving an objective account of Spartan institutions, there was a standing temptation to misuse this *genre* of literature as an instrument of controversy and propaganda.

The key point in the 'Lycurgan' constitution was that it vested the ultimate sovereignty over the Spartan state in the Spartiate damos, i.e. in the politeuma constituted by the Spartiate 'homoioi' ('peers'). The qualification for becoming an 'homoios' was to be co-opted as a member of one of the 'syssitia' (military messes), which were the smallest permanent units in the Spartiate military organization in all the phases through which this passed from the inaugural date of the 'Lycurgan' constitution onwards.[4] The qualification for continuing to be an 'homoios' was to make, without fail, the contribution to the mess's supplies that was

---

[1] The texts of the rhetra and of the final clause, which is alleged to have been a later addition, are given by Plutarch, *Lycurgus*, chap. 6. They are discussed in the present Part in chap. 3, Annex IV.

[2] See p. 227, n. 5.

[3] See pp. 156–7.

[4] See pp. 303, 319, 320, 322–3, 369 and 383.

required of every member, and to perform, without fail, an 'homoios's' exacting military duties. These military duties of the 'homoios' carried with them the political right of taking part in the proceedings of the public assembly of the damos acting in its political capacity.

This damos of Spartiate 'homoioi' was a genuine damos,[1] not an aristocracy,[2] in the sense that, when first established, it probably included a majority of the Spartiate citizen-body (though it never included all Spartiatai, and the ratio of 'homoioi' ('peers') to 'hypomeiones' ('inferiors') gradually diminished as the social effects of the 'Lycurgan' regime worked themselves out in the course of time). It was also a damos that was in a position to perform its political functions, since, unlike the demos in Greek city-states in which there was an enfranchised rural population, the Spartiate damos was permanently cantoned in Sparta town, in which the public assemblies were held, and in the neighbouring town of Amyklai. At the same time, the Spartiate damos was peculiar in more than one respect.

It was peculiar in including only a fraction of the total adult male population of the Spartan city-state territory (leaving out of account the territories of Sparta's perioecic satellite city-states). The damos of Spartiate 'homoioi' not only excluded a section of the Spartiatai themselves, consisting of the 'hypomeiones'; it also excluded all the helots, who were the rural inhabitants of the greater part of the Spartan territory and who constituted the great majority of its total population.[3]

The Spartiate damos was also peculiar in consisting entirely of hoplites. In the Athenian demos, even at the peak of Athens's material prosperity on the eve of the Atheno-Peloponnesian War of 431–404 B.C., the hoplites amounted to no more than a minority of the total enfranchised citizen-body; but then in Attica at that date the ratio of enfranchised citizens to the total adult male population was much higher than it was in Spartan territory, even when full allowance has been made for the exceptionally

---

[1] Niese, 'Zur Verfassungsgeschichte Lakedaimons', pp. 58–84, on pp. 72 and 84, maintains that the Spartan damos was actually the oldest democracy in the Hellenic World. However, Aristotle observes, in *Politics*, Book IV, chap. 10 (12), § 10 (1297b), that 'constitutions of the type that we now call πολιτείας [i.e. moderate oligarchies] used, in the past, to be called democracies'. He observes ibid. in Book V, chap. 7 (8), § 4 (1308a) that ἔστι γὰρ ὥσπερ δῆμος ἤδη οἱ ὅμοιοι (διὸ καὶ ἐν τούτοις ἐγγίγνονται δημαγωγοὶ πολλάκις); Isocrates, *Panathenaïcus*, 178, reports that the Spartans maintain that they have established equality before the law (ἰσονομίαν) and democracy 'in their own community' (i.e. among the Spartiate homoioi), in contrast to the regime that they have imposed on the rest of the population of their dominions.

[2] Ehrenberg, 'Spartiaten und Lakedaimonier', p. 34.

[3] Isocrates, *Panathenaïcus*, 178, already cited, represents the Spartiatai as priding themselves on 'having established, among themselves, equality of rights (ἰσονομίαν), and democracy to a degree that is calculated to maintain concord among them in perpetuity. But they admit that they have turned their demos into perioikoi and have reduced them to the same state of spiritual servitude as the slaves' (τῶν οἰκετῶν, i.e. the helots).

high number of unenfranchised slaves, freedmen, and resident aliens (metoikoi) in Attica in that age.

The third peculiarity of the Spartiate hoplite damos was that these hoplites were not of the ordinary kind. Instead of having to earn their living in some gainful civilian occupation, they were positively debarred from engaging in remunerative work.[1] They were full-time professional soldiers maintained by contributions in kind from native rural slaves.[2] An 'homoios'—so long as he retained his status by paying his contribution to the supplies of his mess[3]—was required to spend the whole of his working time on training for war when not engaged in it.[4] When his unit, and his age-class within his unit, was not on campaign, he was obliged to remain in a permanent state of mobilization—in Sparta town or at Amyklai if he were a member of the Amyclaean oba.[5] Sparta was a military camp.[6] 'Sparta resembled a military camp in the literal sense that all the fraternity-houses of the syskeniai [syssitia] were located on Hyakinthia Street.'[7]

The democratization of Spartan political life through the introduction of the 'Lycurgan' constitution was not limited to the enfranchisement of the damos. The distribution of public land in kleroi[8] to non-nobles in

---

[1] Herodotus, Book II, chap. 167; Isocrates, *Busiris*, 18; Xenophon, *Lak. Pol.*, chap. 7, § 2; Nikolaos of Damascus, fragm. 114, §§ 1 and 7 (Müller, *F.H.G.*, vol. iii, p. 458). Plutarch, *Lycurgus*, chap. 24, commends 'Lycurgus' for providing the homoioi with an abundance of leisure by placing an absolute veto on their having anything to do with vulgar trades (τέχνης . . . ἅψασθαι βαναυσοῦ). Cp. *Inst. Lac.*, § 40.

[2] Aristotle, *Politics*, Book II, chap. 6 (9), §§ 2–4 (1269a-b), criticizes this method of maintaining a leisured class.

[3] For this condition, see further, p. 303. If a member of a mess defaulted on his dues, he lost his membership of the mess, and with it his status of being an homoios and his citizenship in the sense of his voice in the assembly of the damos. This is clearly stated by Aristotle in two passages of his *Politics*, Book II, chap. 6 (9), § 21, (1271a), and chap. 7 (10), § 4 (1272a). Xenophon's statement, in his *Lak. Pol.*, chap. 10, § 7, that 'Lycurgus' 'took no account . . . of pecuniary weakness (οὐδὲν ὑπελογίσατο . . . χρημάτων ἀσθένειαν)' does not necessarily contradict Aristotle. It may mean no more than that it was possible for a poor man to be an homoios; and this is certainly true, for the mess-dues were not large.

[4] εἰ δέ τις ἀποδειλιάσειε τοῦ τὰ νόμιμα διαπονεῖσθαι, τοῦτον ἐκεῖνος [i.e. ὁ Λυκοῦργος] ἀπέδειξε μὴ νομίζεσθαι ἔτι τῶν ὁμοίων εἶναι (Xenophon, *Lak. Pol.*, chap. 10, § 7; see also Roussel, op. cit., pp. 52–3).

[5] S. Witkowski, 'Die spartanische Heeresgliederung und der Ursprung des Ephorats', in *Eos*, 35. Band (1934), pp. 73–86, on pp. 79–80; Niese, 'Zur Verfassungsgeschichte Lakedaimons', p. 74. 'The concentration of the whole citizen-body in Sparta City—a kind of synoecism—is the key to the Spartan constitution' (Niese, ibid., p. 78). The ephorate, the democracy, the agoge, all depended on this (ibid., pp. 80–2).

[6] Isocrates, *Archidamus*, 81. See also Ehrenberg, *Neugründer des Staates*, p. 26.

[7] M. P. Nilsson, 'Die Grundlagen des spartanischen Lebens', in *Klio*, 12. Band (1912), p. 324.

[8] The distribution of kleroi is dated, as here, after the Second Spartano-Messenian War by Roussel, op. cit., pp. 42–3, and by Kiechle, *Lakonien und Sparta*, pp. 193 and 214–15. It is mentioned by Polybius, Book VI, chaps. 45, § 3, and 48, § 3 (following Ephorus?), and by Plutarch, *Lycurgus*, chap. 8, where it is ascribed to 'Lycurgus', but it is not mentioned by Herodotus, Thucydides, or Xenophon (see Meier, op. cit., pp. 71–2, and Meyer,

large numbers[1] turned these endowed non-nobles into the equivalent of nobles in effect, and, conversely, the assignment of kleroi to former nobles, as well as to former commoners, reduced the ex-nobles, in effect, to an equality with the endowed and enfranchised ex-commoners. The fusion of ex-nobles and ex-commoners[2] into a single politeuma was commemorated in their new common title. In virtue of their all being klerosholders, they were now all 'homoioi' ('peers').[3] The distribution of kleroi had not produced equality of property in land, as some of our authorities allege.[4] Ex-nobles who had now become 'peers' had not ceased to be richer than their ex-commoner fellow peers, for these had no source of income beyond their kleros, whereas the ex-nobles had

Forschungen, vol. i, p. 260). Moreover, Isocrates, *Panathenaïcus*, 259, says that there was not ever a γῆς ἀναδασμός at Sparta (Meyer, *Forschungen*, p. 260, n. 2).

George Grote, loc. cit, pp. 164–81, holds that the attribution, to 'Lycurgus', of a division of the Spartan city-state territory into 9,000 kleroi and of the perioecic city-state territories into 30,000 kleroi is an invention designed to lend the prestige of 'Lycurgus's' authority to the historical division of the same two areas into 4,500 and 15,000 kleroi, respectively, by King Agis IV. Grote suggests that this invention may have been the work of Sphairos, the philosopher who was Kleomenes III's adviser. Grote's view is adopted by Kessler, op. cit., p. 39, and Neumann, loc. cit., p. 5. Neumann, however, also notes, ibid., p. 7, that Polybius' statement (Book VI, chap. 45, § 3, and chap. 48, § 3) that there had been a γῆς ἀναδασμός at Sparta is derived, according to Polybius himself, from Ephorus, Xenophon, Callisthenes, and Plato—i.e. from sources that antedate the reigns of Agis IV and Kleomenes III.

Grote's conjecture is convincing. To arrive at the fictitious figures for the number of the kleroi alleged to have been distributed by 'Lycurgus', the historical figures of Agis IV's distribution will have been doubled (Michell, op. cit., p. 225), in consideration of the fact that Sparta's dominions had been approximately twice as extensive as they were in Agis IV's day before the loss of Messenia (though the date conventionally assigned to 'Lycurgus' was about 150 years earlier than the date of Sparta's acquisition of Messenia in the First Spartano-Messenian War). Grote's conjecture would account for 'Lycurgus's' being alleged to have distributed the perioecic states' territories, as well as Sparta's territory, into kleroi; for the perioecic territories were, in truth, carved up into kleroi by Agis IV, but this certainly for the first time in Lacedaemonian history.

However, Plutarch's figure of 9,000 'Lycurgan' kleroi in Spartan territory, besides being exactly double the number actually carved out of this territory by Agis IV, is also close to Herodotus' figure of about 8,000 for the male population of Sparta in 480 B.C. (Book VII, chap. 234), as well as to Aristotle's figure of a past maximum of 10,000 Spartiatai (*Politics*, Book II, chap. 6, § 12 (1270a)).

In any case, whatever the true figure may have been, a distribution of kleroi must have been made at the time when the 'homoioi' were created. The name 'homoioi' implies a category of citizens in which commoners had been put on a par with aristocrats; and, if the commoners, at any rate, among the 'homoioi' had not been endowed with kleroi, it would have been impossible for them to have given their whole time to military service and none of it to earning their livings.

[1] The number of the kleroi is discussed further in chap. 5.
[2] See Roussel, op. cit., pp. 43 and 52.
[3] See Chrimes, *Ancient Sparta*, pp. 245–6; Roussel, op. cit., pp. 41–2; Kiechle, *Lakonien und Sparta*, p. 255.
[4] e.g. Plutarch, *Lycurgus*, chap. 8; *Apophth. Lac.*, Lykourgos, 2; Polybius, Book VI, chaps. 45, §§ 3–4, and 48, § 3; Justin, Book III, chap. 3, § 3. Kiechle points out (*Lakonien und Sparta*, p. 190) that large estates survived the 'Lycurgan' reforms, and (p. 187) that inequality of wealth at Sparta is attested from the seventh to the third century B.C. Cp. Andrewes, *The Greek Tyrants*, p. 67.

received kleroi without forfeiting their ancestral freeholds[1] in the original nucleus of Sparta's city-state territory that was not inhabited and culti-vated by conquered and enslaved helots.

All the same, the ex-commoner's kleros sufficed, at least in the early days of the 'Lycurgan' regime, to enable him to lead the same life as the ex-noble within the limits imposed by their common full-time profes-sional military career; and, though the ex-nobles retained their former private property, there is no evidence that they retained any of their former political privileges.[2] The three hundred 'cavalrymen' (hippeis) presumably had once been a mounted corps of nobles, one hundred from each of the three Dorian phylai in which the Spartiate nobles will have grouped themselves[3] at the time when, like the Argives and some of the other North-West-Greek-speaking Peloponnesian peoples, they had adopted this articulation of the city-state from the Doris in south-western Anatolia.[4] By the fifth century B.C. the hippeis had become a select body of junior hoplite infantrymen recruited from the ranks of the 'homoioi' as a whole. The gerousia, again, will originally have been a council representing the noble families *vis-à-vis* the kings.[5] By the fifth century B.C. the gerousia had become, in respect of twenty-eight out of the thirty seats in it, an elected body, with a life-long tenure,[6] for which any 'homoios', over the age of sixty, seems to have been eligible.[7]

While the nobles had been merged in the damos of the 'homoioi', the kings had been merged in the gerousia.[8] In so far as the kings' civil authority inside the frontiers of Sparta's dominions was concerned, in contrast to their military authority, outside the frontiers, on campaign, the kings had now been reduced to being mere members of the gerousia whose position differed from that of their twenty-eight colleagues only in being theirs *ex officio* and not in virtue of election. The kings' powers in the gerousia seem to have been no greater than those of the elected non-royal members, yet it was only in their capacity as gerontes that the kings retained civil powers of any substance. The only other functions of civil administration that they retained were a responsibility for the upkeep of roads and a control over adoptions and over the disposal of the

---

[1] H. W. Stubbs, 'Spartan Austerity', in the *Classical Quarterly*, vol. xliv (1950), pp. 32–7, on p. 34; Jannet, op. cit., pp. 54–8.

[2] The term 'homoioi' testifies that there had previously been inequality, but that this had now been overcome, at least superficially (see Andrewes, *The Greek Tyrants*, p. 73).

[3] See also p. 264.

[4] See Part I, chap. 3, p. 44.

[5] Jones, *Sparta*, p. 170.

[6] Aristotle, *Politics*, Book II, chap. 6(9), § 17 (1270b).

[7] The question whether or not any vestiges of aristocratic privilege survived under the 'Lycurgan' regime is discussed in chap. 3, Annex III.

[8] Kiechle, *Lakonien und Sparta*, p. 145.

hands of heiresses (epikleroi).[1] These last two functions, however, were more important than they might appear to be at first sight.[2]

Evidently one of the objectives of the authors of the 'Lycurgan' constitution was to change Sparta's domestic balance of power in a way that would put an end to the domestic dissension (stasis) from which Sparta had been suffering ever since the incorporation of the Taÿgetan Minyai in the Spartan body politic and the subsequent expansion of Sparta's dominions through a series of conquests. This dissension had come to a head for the first time after the end of the First Spartano-Messenian War; and, though, on that occasion, Sparta had successfully avoided falling into civil war, she had achieved this merely by providing an outlet for land-hungry Spartiatai through emigration; the demands of the land-hungry majority that had stayed at home had remained unsatisfied. When the consequently continuing dissension came to a head again after the end of the first, or possibly the second, Messenian revolt, the reformers did, on this occasion, at last give the land-hungry and hitherto politically unenfranchised majority of the Spartiatai substantial satisfaction.

Some of the most productive parts of the conquered territory in the lower basin of the Eurotas and in the Stenyklaros plain were now distributed to Spartiatai—commoners as well as aristocrats[3]—in allotments, and henceforth the allotment-holder drew a contribution (apophora), with a maximum upper limit, from the enslaved native peasants (helots) who were the inhabitants and the cultivators of the allotment assigned to him. This γῆς ἀναδασμός was at the expense of the ex-nobles and the kings, if we are right in guessing that, hitherto, this so far privileged minority of the Spartiate community had kept for themselves the lion's share of the product of the helots' labour which had been won for Sparta by the common effort of the whole Spartiate people in arms. However, the lands producing the income that the privileged minority was now being required to surrender had been public, not private, property; the minority's monopoly of the income from it had not been based on any legal title; the minority, as well as the majority, was now given its proportionate share in the allotments (kleroi) into which a part of this public land was being divided up; at the same time, the minority was being allowed to retain its freehold property in Sparta's nuclear territory;[4] and the kings were being allowed to retain the temene that they had acquired in the territories of Sparta's perioecic satellite states.[5]

Thus, in Sparta's dominions, over which Sparta had recovered and

[1] Herodotus, Book VI, chap. 57.
[2] See chap. 4, section (ii), pp. 307-8.
[3] Michell, op. cit., p. 223.
[4] See Forrest, *A History*, p. 51.
[5] See p. 206, with n. 1.

confirmed her hold by eventually winning the Second Spartano-Messenian War, it proved feasible to heal the internal dissension within the Spartiate citizen-body by giving substantial economic satisfaction to the majority without causing economic detriment to the minority to an extent that would have deterred the minority from reconciling itself to the new settlement.[1] This was feasible because it could be done, and was done, at the expense of the helots. Consequently, the 'Lycurgan' settlement did achieve its objective of producing domestic harmony within the Spartiate body politic; and therefore the 'Lycurgan' regime proved stable, so long as the new politeuma of full-time professional hoplite 'homoioi' remained capable of holding the helots down.

In Attica a similar attempt at healing domestic dissension by giving satisfaction to the 'have-nots' without unduly penalizing the 'haves' was made by Solon in 590 B.C. Solon may have been inspired by the precedent of the 'Lycurgan' settlement at Sparta;[2] but Solon's problem was more difficult to solve, at least in the short run, than the Spartan reformers' was. Athens did not have helots at whose expense satisfaction could be given to all parties in the citizen-body. In Attica, as in most other Hellenic states, substantial satisfaction could not be given to the 'have-nots' without penalizing the 'haves'. Accordingly, in Attica, Solon's moderate reform, which spared the property of the 'haves', failed to avert revolution. More drastic economic and social changes were carried out in Attica under the subsequent despotic regime of the Peisistratidai; and the fall of the Peisistratid dictatorship (tyrannis) was followed by the successive democratic reforms of Kleisthenes and Ephialtes. Sparta was able to avoid dictatorship at this stage because the democratization of her constitution in the 'Lycurgan' reforms had gone far enough to satisfy a majority of the former 'have-nots' in the Spartan citizen-body; but, for Sparta, the price of avoiding dictatorship was to leave herself exposed to a perpetual threat of helot insurrections; and, even at this high price, Sparta did not escape dictatorship for ever. Between 227 B.C. and 195 B.C., Sparta had, in the end, to go through the drastic economic and social changes, carried out by a dictatorial regime, which other Hellenic states had gone through before the end of the sixth century B.C.

[1] 'Sparta had invented new machinery of government which enabled her to incorporate the hoplites without revolution, and . . . her campaign against the tyrants was also a campaign in favour of her own political solution' (A. Andrewes, *Probouleusis: Sparta's Contribution to the Technique of Government* (Oxford, 1954, Clarendon Press), p. 16). Jones, likewise, sees in the 'Lycurgan' constitution, embodied (partially) in the 'rhetra' cited by Plutarch, *Lycurgus*, chap. 6, an eventual settlement, by compromise, of a long-drawn-out struggle between the crown and the gerousia on the one side and the damos on the other. See Jones, *Sparta*, p. 28, and 'The Lycurgan Rhetra' in *Ancient Society and Institutions*, pp. 165–75, on p. 170.

[2] This is suggested by Andrewes in *Probouleusis*, p. 21.

All the same, Sparta's 'Lycurgan' constitution was a great political achievement. For, though its beneficiaries were only a small minority of the total population of the Spartan territory, the 'Lycurgan' constitution was a forerunner, and was perhaps also actually the model, of the type of constitution that afterwards became standard in the Hellenic World as a whole—and this in 'democracies' and 'oligarchies' alike—when the Hellenic city-states emerged from the previous bouts of dictatorship through which the most mature of them had passed.

In both 'democratic' and 'oligarchic' constitutions of the post-tyrannis age in the Hellenic World, the two essential elements were a sovereign assembly (with a wider or a narrower franchise, as the case might be) and a relatively small council which had the monopoly of presenting bills (in the English constitutional meaning of the word) for the assembly to consider.[1] Andrewes holds that the earliest trace of this system of constitutional government is to be found in the 'Lycurgan' rhetra.[2] The technical term for the council's work of preparing business for presentation to the assembly was 'probouleusis', and Andrewes's thesis is that 'the probouleutic system was invented at Sparta in the course of the seventh century B.C. as a means of satisfying the political aspirations of the hoplite army'.[3] The gerousia now became the 'probouleutic' council for the Spartan damos,[4] besides retaining, or obtaining, jurisdiction in important cases.[5]

If it is true, as it seems to be, that the Spartiate damos was the earliest of all demoi in the Hellenic World to win constitutional powers, it would not be surprising if these powers were less ample than those eventually secured by the Athenian demos in 461 B.C. In a fully developed Hellenic democracy the assembly was empowered to discuss and, if it chose, to amend, the 'bills' that the council presented to it; and, in the assembly's debates, private members, as well as public officers and representatives of the council, were empowered to speak about 'bills' presented by the authorities, even if they were not empowered to present private bills of their own. In the Spartan assembly the right to present bills seems originally to have been confined to the gerousia;[6] and, though eventually the ephors, too, acquired the prerogative of presenting a 'bill', they were never able to by-pass the gerousia. They had to submit their 'bills' to the

---

[1] Andrewes, *Probouleusis*, pp. 3–4. [2] Ibid., p. 4.
[3] Ibid., p. 4. Andrewes, ibid., p. 15, cites Aristotle, *Politics*, Book IV, chap. 10 (13), §§ 8–11 (1297a–b), for the political consequences of the military institution of the hoplite phalanx.

[4] τοὺς γέροντας, οἷς τὸ κράτος ἦν ἐν τῷ προβουλεύειν (Plutarch, *Agis*, chap. 11). See also Kiechle, *Lakonien und Sparta*, p. 145; Michell, *Sparta*, pp. 136 and 138.

[5] Aristotle, *Politics*, Book II, chap. 6 (9), § 17 (1270b).

[6] For an acute and convincing discussion of the gerousia's and the damos' respective powers in the conduct of the proceedings of the Assembly of the damos, see Forrest, *A History*, pp. 47–50.

gerousia in the first instance, and they could not lay their 'bills' before the assembly unless and until the 'bills' had been adopted previously by the gerousia, deciding by a majority vote.[1]

According to the 'Lycurgan' rhetra, the assembly seems to have been empowered to criticize 'bills'—perhaps even to make counter-proposals—and in any case to have had the last word. However, the last clause of the rhetra (whether this was an addition or was an integral part of the original instrument) appears to have empowered the gerousia to annul, or at any rate to ignore, a counter-proposal of the assembly's if the gerousia disapproved of it—though there is no evidence that, in this situation, the gerousia was empowered to go to the length of ratifying its own original draft of the 'bill' that the assembly had amended or rejected.[2]

According to Aristotle,[3] the powers attributed in the rhetra to the Spartan assembly were possessed by the Carthaginian assembly, but not by the Spartan.[4] Aristotle seems to imply, in this passage, that the Spartan assembly's say was limited, like a present-day computer's, to a choice, without previous debate, between the two alternative responses 'yes' and 'no' to the gerousia's proposals. This statement of Aristotle's, however, seems, if correctly interpreted, to be at variance with the surviving historical evidence. Three meetings of the Spartan assembly are noticed by Thucydides, and eight by Xenophon. The dates of these eleven meetings range from 432 B.C. to 371 B.C. Andrewes points out[5] that most of them were of major importance, and that there are several cases 'in which it is clear that there was considerable debate in the assembly'. Jones agrees[6] with Andrewes that 'the meagre reports on popular assemblies at Sparta show that there was debate'; but he holds[7] that there is no evidence that any of the participants in debates were ordinary 'homoioi', not members of the gerousia or ephors. So Jones dissents from Andrewes's conclusion[8] that 'the narrative is . . . in irremediable conflict with Aristotle'. Jones holds[9] that, on the contrary, 'Aristotle appears to be right in implying that the assembly could only

---

[1] The ephor Lysander's 'bill', embodying King Agis IV's programme of reform, was killed when it was rejected in the gerousia by a majority of one vote (Plutarch, *Agis*, chap. 11). However, it is pointed out by Andrewes, 'The Government of Classical Sparta', p. 5, that Xenophon does not mention any probouleutic discussions by the gerousia and, on p. 4, that Thucydides does not mention the gerousia in any context. 'In the historical record' the gerousia 'is conspicuous by its absence' (Jones, *Sparta*, p. 18).

[2] The clause runs: αἰ δὲ σκολιὰν ὁ δᾶμος ἔροιτο, τοὺς πρεσβυγενέας καὶ ἀρχαγέτας ἀποστατῆρας ἦμεν (Plutarch, *Lycurgus*, chap. 6).

[3] *Politics*, Book II, chap. 8 (11), § 3 (1273a).

[4] See Wade-Gery, *Essays in Greek History*, pp. 51–3.

[5] In loc. cit., p. 6.

[6] In 'The Lycurgan Rhetra', pp. 165–75, on pp. 166–7.   [7] Ibid.

[8] In 'The Government of Classical Sparta', p. 6.

[9] In loc. cit., p. 6, and also on p. 22.

vote "yes" or "no", and that there was no power of amendment by private citizens'.

In the crucial proceedings of the Spartan assembly in 432 B.C., as recounted by Thucydides[1]—proceedings which ended in the assembly's voting, by a large majority, that Lakedaimon was in a state of war with Athens—the assembly was addressed in turn by a Corinthian deputation, representing Sparta's Peloponnesian allies, by an Athenian embassy, by King Arkhidamos, and by one of the ephors of the year, Sthenelaïdas. This ephor also took the vote, and, after the assembly had voted, in its customary way, by acclamation, Sthenelaïdas made the members divide in order to make it clear, beyond question, which way the vote had gone. On this occasion, at any rate, the assembly was allowed to take a free decision on a vital issue, though its private members may not have been allowed to take part in the foregoing debate.

Thus the direct powers of the Spartan assembly, though they may have been relatively small, were genuine as far as they went; and the assembly also made itself felt, and this perhaps more potently, in an indirect way. The assembly filled, by election, the vacancies in the gerousia caused by death, and it also now elected the annual board of five ephors, who had originally been the kings' appointees. The method of electing both gerontes and ephors was 'childish', according to Aristotle.[2] For the election of the ephors, we do not know what the method was. For the election of the gerontes, the candidates had to appear, in turn, before the assembly; the assembly expressed its wishes by shouting; and a panel of reputedly honest men, shut up, within earshot, in a windowless room, had to declare which of the successive shouts had, in their estimation, been the loudest. If an estimate thus arrived at was not infallible, it was at any rate unprejudiced, since the listeners had not been able to see which candidate had evoked which of the shouts that they had been hearing.[3]

This method of election was childish indeed; but the indirect power that it conferred on the assembly was great. In filling vacancies in the gerousia, the assembly's choice was limited to candidates over sixty years of age who had special qualifications.[4] On the other hand, the ephors were 'taken from the whole demos';[5] and the ephorate was 'sovereign in the matters that were of the highest importance'.[6] As Aristotle puts it, 'the ephorate was the equivalent of a dictatorship ($\iota\sigma\sigma\tau\acute{\upsilon}\rho\alpha\nu\nu\sigma\nu$)',[7]

---

[1] Book I, chaps. 67–88.
[2] *Politics*, Book II, chap. 6 (9), § 18 (1271a), for the gerontes; ibid., § 16 (1270b), for the ephors.
[3] Plutarch, *Lycurgus*, chap. 26.   [4] See chap. 3, Annex III.
[5] Aristotle, *Politics*, Book II, chap. 6 (9), § 14 and §§15–16 (1270b).
[6] Aristotle, ibid., § 14 (1270b).
[7] Aristotle, ibid. Cp. Plato, *Laws*, 712 D. In the same passage, Aristotle comments that

and was, in fact, a substitute for one.¹ One of the ephors gave his name, like the arkhon eponymos at Athens, to his and his colleagues' year of office.²

The ephorate was not only an instrument through which the Spartan damos exercised a formidable indirect power; it was also the linch-pin of Sparta's 'Lycurgan' constitution.³

The ephorate is the institution that holds the Spartan constitution together. The demos keeps quiet because it has access to an office which is the greatest of all; and this is politically expedient, whether it has happened by design or merely by chance. It is expedient because the necessary condition for the survival of a constitution is that its existence and perpetuation should be willed spontaneously (αὐτά) by all sections of the community. At Sparta the kings are loyal to the constitution because of their prerogatives under it; the gentle-folk (οἱ δὲ καλοὶ κἀγαθοί) are loyal to it on account of the gerousia, an office that is the reward of merit; while the demos is loyal to the constitution on account of the ephorate, an office for which every member of the demos is eligible.⁴

In the course of time the ephors had managed to concentrate in their own hands a formidable array of powers.⁵ Though they are not men-

the inordinateness of the ephorate's powers had converted the regime at Sparta from an aristocracy into a democracy. Plutarch (or his source), in *Lycurgus*, chap. 29, draws the inverse conclusion from the same premisses. 'The institution of the ephorate did not bring with it, for the Spartan people, a relaxation of the regime; on the contrary, it accentuated the regime's rigour. Ostensibly it had been a move in the demos' favour; actually its effect was to make the regime more oppressively aristocratic.'

¹ Niese, 'Zur Verfassungsgeschichte Lakedaimons', p. 82.
² Pausanias, Book III, chap. 11, § 2. Thucydides, Book II, chap. 2, names the eponymous Spartan ephor of the year among his references for dating the outbreak of the Atheno-Peloponnesian War in 431 B.C.
³ See den Boer, op. cit., pp. 197–212.
⁴ συνέχει μὲν γὰρ τὴν πολιτείαν τὸ ἀρχεῖον τοῦτο. ἡσυχάζει γὰρ ὁ δῆμος διὰ τὸ μετέχειν τῆς μεγίστης ἀρχῆς, ὥστ', εἴτε διὰ τὸν νομοθέτην εἴτε διὰ τύχην τοῦτο συμπέπτωκεν, συμφερόντως ἔχει τοῖς πράγμασιν· δεῖ γὰρ τὴν πολιτείαν τὴν μέλλουσαν σώζεσθαι πάντα βούλεσθαι τὰ μέρη τῆς πόλεως εἶναι καὶ διαμένειν αὐτά· οἱ μὲν οὖν βασιλεῖς διὰ τὴν αὐτῶν τιμὴν οὕτως ἔχουσιν, οἱ δὲ καλοὶ κἀγαθοὶ διὰ τὴν γερουσίαν—ἆθλον γὰρ ἡ ἀρχὴ αὕτη τῆς ἀρετῆς ἐστιν—ὁ δὲ δῆμος διὰ τὴν ἐφορείαν—καθίσταται γὰρ ἐξ ἁπάντων(Aristotle, Politics, Book II, chap. 6 (9) § 15 (1270b)).
⁵ Both the potency of the ephorate at Sparta and the prestige of Sparta in the North-West-Greek-speaking city-states of the Hellenic World are reflected in the adoption of the title 'ephor' (see Stern, op. cit., pp. 14–15), not only by Sparta's daughter city-state Tarentum and by Tarentum's daughter the Italiot Herakleia, but also by Thera and her daughter Cyrene. Thera claimed—almost certainly without warrant (see pp. 174–5)—that she, like Tarentum, was a Spartan colony, and in her case the use of the title 'ephor' was no doubt a device for making her claim look plausible. On the other hand it is astonishing that Messene (see Busolt and Swoboda, op. cit., p. 633, n. 2) and some of the Eleutherolaconian states (ibid., p. 734, with n. 7) should also have borrowed this title from Sparta when their achievement of independence had made them free to give their public officers whatever name might take their fancy. 'Ephor' is the last name that they might have been expected to choose, considering that Sparta's ex-helots the Messenians hated Sparta with good reason, and that her ex-perioikoi the Eleutherolakones had no reason to love her. In the modern Western World the equivalent of Messene's adoption of the title 'ephor' would have been the adoption of the term 'viceroy', instead of 'president', by Eire, as the title for the head of a state that

tioned in the rhetra, they seem to have captured from the gerousia the power of taking the initiative in the assembly.[1] Indeed, they seem to have captured the power of taking the initiative in the gerousia's own 'probouleutic' activities,[2] though they were not members of the gerousia and therefore presumably had no constitutional right to take any part in the gerousia's proceedings. Like the gerousia, the ephors had important judicial functions, and, since at Sparta there were no written laws, the ephors were free to make their judgements at their own arbitrary personal discretion ($αὐτογνώμονας$).[3] The ephors were virtually in a position to hold to account the incumbents of all other public offices.[4] Without even having to wait for these other officers' terms of office to expire, the ephors could depose them, imprison them, and threaten them with the death-penalty.[5] The ephors could also fine anyone whom they chose, and could exact payment of the fine on the spot.[6]

(iii) *The Contest for Power between the Ephorate and the Dual Monarchy from the Inauguration of the Lycurgan Constitution to 227 B.C.*

Andrewes holds that 'the struggle between monarchy and ephorate is not a general key to Spartan history';[7] and both he[8] and Jones[9] point out that there was neither invariable unanimity among ephors in office nor persistent continuity in the policy of a board whose membership changed from year to year. No doubt this is true as regards all points

had won its independence as painfully and tardily as Messene had won hers. Of course, the adoption of the Spartan title 'ephor' by foreign states did not involve the conferment on these non-Spartan ephors of the powers that the Spartan ephors eventually acquired. The democratic-minded but un-austere Tarentines, for example, would never have been willing to saddle themselves with public officers wielding the Spartan ephors' arbitrary and almost tyrannical powers.

[1] Dum, op. cit., pp. 111 and 115; Ehrenberg, 'Der Gesetzgeber von Sparta', in '$Ἐπιτύμ-βιον$ *Heinrich Swoboda dargebracht* (Reichenberg, 1927, Stiepel), p. 25; Jones, *Sparta*, pp. 22 and 25; Niese, 'Zur Verfassungsgeschichte Lakedaimons', p. 63. Niese holds, ibid., p. 64, that, for important decisions, the ephors had to obtain the gerousia's concurrence. Jones—holding, as he does hold (*Sparta*, p. 25), that the ephors had established their right to introduce a motion in the assembly, and to put it to the vote, without the gerousia's previous consent—sees in this the explanation of the possibility, provided for in the third sentence of the 'rhetra' cited by Plutarch, *Lycurgus*, chap. 6, that the damos might take a 'crooked line'. 'In the rider, [i.e. the third sentence of the rhetra] the possibility of legislation initiated by some other authority than the council [i.e. the gerousia] is tacitly admitted' (Jones, 'The Lycurgan Rhetra', p. 171).

[2] Roussel, op. cit., p. 68; Jones, *Sparta*, pp. 22–3, citing occasions in 477 B.C. and in 242 B.C. In 'The Lycurgan Rhetra', p. 168, Jones notes that, according to our surviving information, it is never kings or gerontes, but always ephors, who convene the assembly, preside over it, and present motions to it. Jones conjectures (p. 169) that this monopoly of initiative in the assembly which the ephors acquired was a constitutional convention that had no juridical basis. [3] Aristotle, ibid., § 16 (1270b).

[4] Ibid., § 18 (1271a).

[5] Xenophon, *Lak. Pol.*, chap. 8, § 4. [6] Ibid.

[7] 'The Government of Classical Sparta', p. 10.

[8] Ibid., p. 8. [9] *Sparta*, p. 30.

of policy except one. This exceptional point is the policy of maintaining and increasing the ephorate's power, and, on this point, successive annual boards of ephors were unanimous, persistent, and on the whole successful until at last, in 227 B.C., the ephorate was crushed by King Kleomenes III.

In this pursuit of power the ephorate seems to have met with serious opposition from the monarchy alone among the other public authorities. There is no record of a clash between the ephors and the assembly.[1] The gerousia seems usually to have allowed itself to be out-manœuvred and by-passed by the ephorate without putting up an effective resistance. The ephorate's only formidable opponents in its progressive extension of its powers were kings.[2] The crown's resistance did delay the ephorate's progress towards becoming the dictatorship that Aristotle accuses it of having become in fact; and, though one bold king after another challenged the ephorate and suffered defeat, it was a king—Kleomenes III—who overthrew the ephorate in the end. Andrewes maintains that strong-willed kings could bring the board of ephors to heel, and he cites the cases of Kleomenes I, during the middle period of his reign, and Agesilaos.[3] Yet, in the head-on collision between Kleomenes I and the ephorate, the ephorate was eventually victorious; and, if Agesilaos managed to get his way, he seems to have achieved this by deliberately avoiding collisions with the ephorate. His trump card was tact.

It is true that the kings were officially sovereign on campaign. The ephors' powers did not legally extend beyond the Lacedaemonian state's frontiers; and, though a pair of ephors accompanied a king on campaign, they had no authority to interfere with the king's military dispositions or with the political decisions in the international sphere that it sometimes fell to a king to take as a corollary of his military command.[4] However, a king, like any other Spartiate, was subject to prosecution and trial in the ephors' court on account of his past acts, including acts performed while he had been abroad and had therefore, at the time, been outside the ephors' jurisdiction.[5] Moreover, by the date of publication of Xenophon's *Lakedaimoniôn Politeia*, the ephorate had wrested out of the crown's hands the prerogative of ordering mobilization and deciding,

---

[1] Andrewes, 'The Government of Classical Sparta', p. 14.

[2] According to Stern, op. cit., p. 47, the key to the origin and development of the ephorate is to be found in its relations to the crown in the period of Spartan history for which we have an authentic record.

[3] Andrewes, loc. cit., pp. 8–10.

[4] Xenophon, *Lak. Pol.*, chap. 13, § 5.

[5] For instance, in 494 B.C. King Kleomenes I was prosecuted in the ephors' court on the charge that he had been bribed to refrain from occupying the city of Argos after his crushing victory over the Argives in the field at Sepeia (Herodotus, Book VI, chap. 82). On this occasion, Kleomenes was acquitted. Thereafter, King Leotykhidas, the regent Pausanias, and Kings Pleistoanax and Pausanias were all both prosecuted and convicted.

on each occasion, how many age-classes were to be called up;[1] and it seems to have made this encroachment during the reign of King Kleomenes I.[2]

We do not know how much of the royal power was delegated to the ephors originally when the ephorate was first instituted to 'oversee' the administration of public affairs on the kings' behalf.[3] We do not know, either, when it was that the prerogative of appointing the ephors was transferred from the kings to the damos. We may guess that the damos' prerogative of electing the ephors and the gerontes dates from the inauguration of the 'Lycurgan' constitution and was an integral part of it; but this is no more than a guess, for the text of the rhetra, as we have it, contains no provision to this effect and, indeed, makes no mention at all of the ephorate. We may guess with greater assurance that, whether the damos acquired the prerogative of electing the ephors as part of the provisions of the 'Lycurgan' constitution or on some later occasion, the transfer of this prerogative to the damos from the kings will have been the crucial change that made the ephorate's fortune and started it on the road which led eventually to the ephorate's making itself the almost absolute master of the Spartan Government.[4]

Two points, in the relations between the ephorate and the dual crown, which Xenophon mentions in his *Lakedaimoniōn Politeia*,[5] may date from the moment, whenever it was, at which the ephors ceased to be the crown's deputies and became, instead, the damos' representatives.

Everyone rises from his seat at the king's approach, with the exception of the ephors when they are seated on their chairs of state. The ephors and the kings exchange oaths once a month—the ephors swearing on the state's behalf, and the king on his own. The king swears that he will exercise his sovereignty in accordance with the established laws of the state; the state swears that, so long as the king abides by his oath, it will maintain his sovereignty unshaken.

Both the point of etiquette and the reciprocity of the oaths signified that the dual monarchy and the damos, as represented by the board of ephors, were on a parity with each other.[6] It is conceivable that, at the stage when the ephors were the crown's deputies, they already took

---

[1] Xenophon, *Lak. Pol.*, chap. 11, § 2 (see p. 247).

[2] See pp. 246–7.

[3] See pp. 218–20.

[4] The development of the ephors' power was gradual (Michell, op. cit., p. 123; Norvin, in *Classica et Mediaevalia*, vol. iii, p. 117). Attempts to trace the course of the ephorate's progressive increase in power are made—as far as the scantiness of our information allows—by Dickins, loc. cit., pp. 1–42; A. Solari, *Ricerche Spartane* (Livorno, 1907, Giusti); Dum, op. cit. Cp. Jannet, op. cit., p. 120.

[5] Chap. 15, §§ 6–7. Cp. Plutarch, *Apophthegmata Laconica*, Anaxilas.

[6] Stern, in loc. cit., pp. 48 and 57, holds that the oath must date from a time when the king's power was still substantial.

a periodical oath to uphold the crown's prerogatives.[1] The innovation will have been the crown's oath to respect the laws of the state.

In the progressive extension of the ephors' powers, three landmarks can be descried.

Asteropos[2] was the first holder of the office to key up its powers, according to the speech, indicting the ephorate for its progressive infringement of the 'Lycurgan' constitution, which is put into the mouth of King Kleomenes III by Plutarch's source.[3] If Asteropos was the first ephor to enlarge the ephorate's powers, he must have held office earlier than Khilon, whose date is about half way through the sixth century B.C.

The second landmark is the ephors' institution of the practice of star-gazing, once in every eight years, at the oracular shrine of the goddess Ino-Pasiphaë[4] between the perioecic cities Thalamai and Oitylos. Cavaignac has pointed out[5] that this practice cannot have been introduced until the eight-years' calendar cycle had been adopted in the Hellenic World, i.e. not until after the beginning of the sixth century B.C. If, on this occasion, the ephors observed a shooting-star (and who could prove that they had not?), they assumed the right to put the kings on trial and to suspend them from office pending the receipt of an exculpatory oracle from Delphi or Olympia. In thus associating their office with an oracle,[6] the ephors were putting themselves on a par with the two royal houses in the religious sphere,[7] for one of the kings' assets was that, through their appointees and representatives, the Pythioi,[8] they were the intermediaries between Sparta and the god at Delphi.[9]

[1] Stern, in loc. cit., p. 49, holds that the institution of the oath must have been part of the settlement of a stasis between the damos and the crown. The ephors were overseers of the oath (not of the obai) (ibid., pp. 57 and 58).

[2] If the meaning of this name is 'star-gazer', not 'starry-eyed', it is possible that 'Asteropos' is not an historical figure but is a personification of the board of ephors' star-gazing rite, noticed below.

[3] Plutarch, *Cleomenes*, chap. 10. Cp. Plutarch, *Apophthegmata Laconica*, Anaxilas.

[4] See Wide, op. cit., pp. 227–31 and 241–50.

[5] In op. cit., p. 31.

[6] For the oracle of Ino-Pasiphaë at Thalamai, see Plutarch, *Agis*, chaps. 9 and 11; *Cleomenes*, chap. 7; Pausanias, Book III, chap. 26, § 1; Apollonius Dyscolus, *Historia Miraculorum*, 49; Cicero, *De Divinatione*, Book 1, 43, 96; Tertullian, *De Anima*, chap. 46.

[7] Dickins, loc. cit., p. 21; Michell, op. cit., p. 109.

[8] Herodotus, Book VI, chap. 57; Xen., *Lak. Pol.*, chap. 15, § 5.

[9] See Busolt and Swoboda, op. cit., p. 674. The Spartan royal houses' relation to the god at Delphi, like the Carolingian dynasty's relation to the apostle at Rome, was advantageous to both parties. It is therefore likely to have been one of the targets of the ephors' attack in their struggle with the crown for control over the Spartan government. This may be the explanation of Herodotus' statement (Book I, chap. 65) that 'some people say that, besides [tentatively pronouncing that "Lycurgus" was probably a god rather than a human being], the Pythia briefed him on the regime that is in force at Sparta to-day (φράσαι αὐτῷ ... τὸν νῦν κατεστεῶτα κόσμον Σπαρτιήτῃσι). The Lacedaemonians themselves, however, say that "Lycurgus" ... brought these institutions to Sparta from Crete.' If the 'some people' were the Spartan royal houses, 'the Lacedaemonians' will have been the ephors, representing the Spartan damos. The ephors will have been reluctant to admit that the 'Lycurgan' constitu-

The third landmark is the ephorate of Khilon, about half-way through the sixth century B.C.[1] The mark that Khilon made is commemorated by a herôon which was still standing in Pausanias' day.[2] Dickins holds[3] that Khilon keyed up the powers of the ephorate to a further degree: 'the Lycurgan agoge known to Aristotle, Xenophon, and Plutarch was primarily due to Khilon, however old the underlying ideas may have been'.[4] Dickins also guesses[5] that Khilon was responsible for Sparta's sudden change-over, *circa* 550 B.C., from a policy of conquests and annexations to a policy of alliances.[6]

The most vigorous opposition to the ephorate's progressive encroachments on the traditional powers of other Spartan public authorities came from the crown, as might be expected. The conflict between crown and ephors was a factor in Spartan politics—not only domestic politics, but foreign policy as well[7]—since at least as early as the reign of King Anaxandridas (*regnabat circa* 550–520 B.C.). The conflict continued, with the crown progressively losing ground to the ephorate on the whole, till 227 B.C.,[8] when the fortunes of the two offices were abruptly reversed by King Kleomenes III's success in dealing the ephorate a blow from which it never managed to recover.

A weakness of the Spartan monarchy, which the ephors knew how to exploit, was its duality. The two royal houses' only chance of holding their own against the ephorate, when this had become the damos' instrument instead of being the crown's, was to present a united front,

tion, which was the springboard from which the ephorate had soared into power, derived its validity from the fiat of a god who was the patron of the Spartan royal houses. If it was admitted that it was Apollo who had given Sparta her original constitution, this admission might open the way for the god to modify the constitution in favour of the Spartan crown at his royal protégés' instance. Tyrtaios seems to have been a partisan of the Spartan crown, and, though Tyrtaios does not mention 'Lycurgus' in any surviving fragment of his poetry, he does bring the 'Lycurgan' constitution to Sparta from Delphi, in the first of the three couplets quoted by Plutarch, *Lycurgus*, chap. 6.

In the domestic struggle at Sparta over the crown's relations with Delphi, the crown was sometimes indiscreet in letting itself be caught in the act of bribing the Delphic ecclesiastical authorities, or, alternatively, the ephors were sometimes astute in managing to convict the crown on this charge. King Kleomenes I (Herodotus, Book VI, chap. 66) and King Pausanias (Thucydides, Book V, chaps. 16–17) both laboured under this accusation.

[1] Khilon was a contemporary of the Athenian despot Peisistratos' father (Herodotus, Book I, chap. 59). Khilon's daughter married King Damaratos, and King Leotykhidas had been an unsuccessful suitor for her hand (Herodotus, Book VI, chap. 65). Huxley, op. cit., p. 69, and Kiechle, *Lakonien und Sparta*, p. 243, date Khilon's ephorate 556/5 B.C., following Diogenes Laertius, Book I, chaps. 68–73.
[2] Pausanias, Book III, chap. 16, § 4.
[3] In loc. cit., p. 25. Cp. Ehrenberg, *Neugründer des Staates*, pp. 46–9.
[4] Dickins, loc. cit., p. 26.
[5] Ibid., pp. 16–17.
[6] See pp. 182, 259–60, and 285.
[7] The effect of this conflict on Sparta's foreign policy during the century and a half *circa* 550–400 B.C. is pointed out by Dickins, loc. cit., p. 1.
[8] See Dum, op. cit., pp. 61, 62, 74.

and, on occasions on which the kings did this, they may sometimes have succeeded in holding the ephors in check.[1] More often, however, the reigning representatives of the two royal houses continued to fall out with each other, and this gave the ephors their opening for extending their power.[2] In contrast to the normal disunity of the pair of kings, the board of ephors had the reputation of never allowing a rift to appear among its members.[3] Even so, the issue of their conflict with the crown hung in the balance so long as the Agiad King Kleomenes I remained alive. Kleomenes I was energetic and resourceful; and, after he had engineered the deposition and subsequent exile of his independent-minded Eurypontid colleague Damaratos and had secured his replacement by the docile Leotykhidas,[4] Kleomenes was in a position to combat the ephors on equal terms. It was a piece of good fortune for the ephorate if Kleomenes I did, in truth, go out of his mind and commit suicide in

[1] In King Agis IV's time (*regnabat circa* 244–240 B.C.) it is said to have been contended by the reform party at Sparta that, when the kings were unanimous, the ephors had no constitutional right to oppose their will. 'The ephorate's power springs from dissension between the kings . . . when the kings are unanimous, their authority cannot legally be overridden, and opposition to them on the ephors' part becomes unconstitutional' (ἀμφοῖν δὲ ταὐτὰ βουλευομένων ἄλυτον εἶναι τὴν ἐξουσίαν, καὶ παρανόμως μαχεῖσθαι πρὸς βασιλεῖς [τοὺς ἐφόρους]) (Plutarch, *Agis*, chap. 12)).

Dum holds (op. cit., pp. 62–4) that it was, in truth, a definite rule of Spartan constitutional law that the validity of the royal prerogatives was conditional on the kings' acting unanimously and was voided if and when they were in disagreement with each other. Dum's view is rejected by Stern, op. cit., p. 38; yet there is some warrant for Dum's view in a series of passages in Herodotus' work. In 507 B.C., when King Kleomenes I's colleague and co-commander, King Damaratos, refused to take any further part in Kleomenes' campaign against Athens, the contingents of Sparta's allies felt themselves to be released from their military obligations (Herodotus, Book V, chap. 75). When Kleomenes I, by himself, went to Aegina with the intention of arresting the Aeginetans who had been responsible for Aegina's giving tokens of submission to Xerxes' envoys, the Aeginetans, on advice from Kleomenes' colleague Damaratos, refused to deliver the hostages whom Kleomenes was demanding, on the ground that Kleomenes had no constitutional authority to act in the Spartan Government's name, considering that his colleague had not accompanied him (Herodotus, Book VI, chap. 50). Kleomenes retorted by getting Damaratos replaced by Leotykhidas and then returning to Aegina with Leotykhidas in tow. The Aeginetans now allowed the pair of Spartan kings to select ten Aeginetan hostages and to hand these over to the Athenians (Herodotus, Book VI, chap. 73). After Kleomenes' death, Leotykhidas was indicted by the Aeginetans before a Spartan court and was ordered by the court to go, in person, to Athens, in order to obtain the release of the Aeginetan hostages whom Leotykhidas and Kleomenes had handed over to the Athenians. The Athenians now refused to surrender the hostages on the same ground on which the Aeginetans had refused to deliver them at the first time of asking. They declined to recognize the constitutional authority of a single Spartan king, acting without his colleague.

[2] See Dum, op. cit., pp. 65–6; Solari, op. cit., p. 157.

[3] See the testimonial to the solidarity of the ephorate which is put into Critias' mouth by Xenophon, *Hellenica*, Book II, chap. 3, § 34. However, in 403 B.C. King Pausanias did persuade three of the ephors to send him with a further body of troops to Athens to frustrate Lysander (Xenophon, *Hellenica*, Book II, chap. 4, §§ 28–9). Three was enough, since the decisions of the board of ephors were taken by a majority vote (Busolt and Swoboda, op. cit., p. 687).

[4] Herodotus, Book VI, chaps. 61–72.

prison, as was alleged; but the official account of the circumstances of Kleomenes' death[1] leaves the ephorate under suspicion of having got rid of Kleomenes by foul play.[2] Even after Kleomenes' death, the ephors found him posthumously still so formidable that they sought deliberately to play down his importance by taking the line—in flagrant contradiction with the well-known facts—that this redoubtable king's reign had been brief.[3]

After Kleomenes I's death the balance was tipped decisively in favour of the ephorate by the fates that overtook a number of members of the two royal houses. In 480 B.C. Kleomenes I's respectable and gallant half-brother Leonidas was sent, perhaps deliberately, to his death at Thermopylae. In 478 or 469 B.C. Leotykhidas was convicted of having taken bribes and had to go into exile.[4] *Circa* 470 B.C. the ill-behaved regent Pausanias came to a bad end.[5] In 446 B.C. Pausanias' son King Pleistoanax was convicted of having taken bribes and had to go into exile in 445 B.C.;[6] and in 395 B.C. Pleistoanax's son King Pausanias was prosecuted and was condemned to death on charges of misconduct while on campaign, and he escaped death only by fleeing the country.[7] Dum observes[8] that 'almost all the kings who reigned in the fifth century B.C. were tried and convicted'. The Agiad Leonidas and the Eurypontid Arkhidamos were the only exceptions. After Pausanias, no other king was deposed and condemned to death till Agis IV, who met his death *circa* 240 B.C.; but by 395 B.C. the series of depositions and convictions had done its work.

An effect of royal deaths and depositions that gave the ephorate a still further advantage over the crown in and after the fifth century B.C. was that a number of kings succeeded to the throne while they were still minors:[9] e.g. Pleistarkhos son of Leonidas (*regnabat* 480–458/7 B.C.), Pleistoanax son of the regent Pausanias (*regnabat* 458/7–445 B.C. and 426–408 B.C.), Pausanias son of Pleistoanax (*regnabat* 445–426 B.C. and 408–395 B.C.), Agesipolis son of Pausanias (*regnabat* 395–380/79 B.C.).

By Anaxandridas' day the kings were already so much at the mercy of the ephors that these, in co-operation with the gerontes, were able to

---

[1] Ibid., chap. 75.

[2] See T. Lenschau, 'König Kleomenes I von Sparta', in *Klio*, 31. Band (N.F. 13. Band) (1939), pp. 412–29, on p. 429.

[3] Herodotus, Book V, chap. 48. Kleomenes I actually reigned *circa* 520–488 B.C. For the length of Kleomenes' reign, see Lenschau in loc. cit. and Jones, *Sparta*, p. 1.

[4] Herodotus, Book VI, chap. 72. 469 B.C. is Beloch's dating (*Griechische Geschichte*, Zweite Band, Erste Abteilung (Strassburg, 1914, Trübner), p. 142).

[5] Thucydides, Book I, chaps. 94–5 and 128–34.

[6] Thucydides, Book V, chap. 17.

[7] Xenophon, *Hellenica*, Book III, chap. 5, § 25.

[8] In op. cit., p. 84. See the list of cases in Busolt and Swoboda, op. cit., p. 677, n. 5.

[9] See Dum, op. cit., p. 85.

compel Anaxandridas, by threats, to take a second wife in order to secure an heir for the Agiad house, since Anaxandridas' first wife had hitherto been childless. The furthest that Anaxandridas could go in resisting the ephors' pressure was to become a bigamist, instead of divorcing his first wife, as the ephors had originally demanded.[1] The ephors caught a tartar; for the second wife whom they had forced upon King Anaxandridas was the mother of King Kleomenes I (*regnabat circa* 520–488 B.C.); and Kleomenes I gave the ephors more trouble than any subsequent king of either house before Kleomenes I's kinsman and namesake Kleomenes III (*regnabat* 237–222 B.C.).

Kleomenes I, during his long and chequered career, had managed to keep the conduct of Sparta's foreign policy in his own hands. By the year 479 B.C., however, the ephors were, in effect, the Spartan Government. The Athenian, Plataean, and Megarian envoys who came to Sparta at this crucial moment addressed themselves to the ephors[2] as a matter of course; and in 422–1 B.C. at least one of the ephors, as well as the two kings, signed, on Sparta's behalf, the peace-treaty that ended the Archidamian War.[3]

The most significant of the ephorate's encroachments on the royal prerogative were those that they made in the military sphere; for the 'Lycurgan' constitution, which had reduced the royal prerogative to insignificance in civil affairs, seems to have left the military side of it still intact.

According to Herodotus,[4] one of the prerogatives of a Spartan king was 'to make war on any country that he chose', and, if any Spartiate sought to obstruct a king's exercise of this prerogative, the obstructor incurred a religious sanction. King Kleomenes I assumed this prerogative in 507 B.C. On this occasion he mobilized the Lacedaemonian army, including his colleague Damaratos, and called up the contingents of Sparta's Peloponnesian allies, without divulging his objective. When, however, the troops found themselves at Eleusis, confronting the Athenian army, the Corinthian contingent, the Spartan King Damaratos, and then the rest of the allies all struck, one after the other; and this brought Kleomenes' campaign to a stop.[5]

Presumably Kleomenes had been acting within his traditional rights in 507 B.C. In 508 B.C., too, he had invaded Attica on his own initiative, but this previous expedition of his had also ended in a fiasco;[6] and it looks as if Kleomenes was trying to push the traditional royal prerogative farther than it could carry in the political circumstances of the day. By

[1] Herodotus, Book V, chaps. 39–41.
[2] Herodotus, Book IX, chap. 7.
[3] Thucydides, Book V, chaps. 19 and 24.
[4] Book VI, chap. 56.
[5] Herodotus, Book V, chaps. 74–5.
[6] See Herodotus, Book V, chaps. 70–2.

this time 'the Lacedaemonians'—represented, no doubt, by the ephors—had already established a precedent, against the royal prerogative, by taking into their own hands the decision to make war on a foreign state. When they had decided to overthrow the Peisistratidai by force of arms, they had first sent an expeditionary force to Attica in 511 B.C. under the command of a private citizen, Ankhimolios, and then, when this force had been cut to pieces, they had sent a stronger force in 510 B.C. and had appointed King Kleomenes to the command of it.[1] Thus Kleomenes had first served as the ephors' appointee in command of a military expedition that had been dispatched by the ephors on their initiative, not on his, before he assumed the royal prerogative of mobilizing the Lacedaemonian army, on his own initiative, for an objective of his own choosing. Kleomenes was trying to use the royal prerogative to the full after it had already begun to become something of an anachronism; and, since his two expeditions on his own initiative in 508 and 507 B.C. were failures, while his previous expedition as the ephors' appointee had been a success, the effect of these two attempts of Kleomenes' to reinstate the royal prerogative was to cause a further encroachment on it.

The break-up of Kleomenes' expeditionary force in 507 B.C., as a result of his colleague Damaratos' parting company with him, led to the enactment, at Sparta, of a law providing that, for the future, no Spartan expeditionary force should march under the joint command of both kings.[2] This provision implied that, for the future, the ephors were always going to decide which of the kings should be given the command on each occasion; and this implied, in turn, that, henceforth, the ephors, not the kings, should always decide, as they had decided in 511 and 510 B.C., when a military expedition should be undertaken and what this expedition's objective should be.[3] In 479 B.C. it was the ephors who did decide to send an expedition to liberate Attica from Persian occupation, and it was they who appointed the regent Pausanias to command it.[4] This now became the regular practice. The technical term for the issue of a mobilization order by the ephors was 'to declare a state of defence' (φρουρὰν φαίνειν),[5] a euphemism for launching an offensive operation. In ordering mobilization the ephors announced which of the forty age-classes that were subject to military service were to report for duty on each occasion.[6]

---

[1] Herodotus, Book V, chaps. 63–4.

[2] Ibid., chap. 75.

[3] τῶν ἐφόρων ποτὲ εἰπόντων· βάδιζε, τοὺς ἡβῶντας ἔχων, ἐπὶ τὴν τούτου πατρίδα· ἡγήσεται δέ σοι αὐτὸς οὗτος εἰς τὴν ἀκρόπολιν . . . (Plutarch, *Apophthegmata Laconica*, Agis II, 1).

[4] Herodotus, Book IX, chaps. 9–10.

[5] Xenophon, *Hellenica*, Book II, chap. 4, § 29; Book III, chap. 2, § 20, *et alibi*.

[6] Xenophon, *Lak. Pol.*, chap. 11, § 2. Cf. Plutarch, *Apophthegmata Laconica*, Agis II, 1. Niese, 'Zur Verfassungsgeschichte Lakedaimons', p. 64, holds that the ephors did not acquire the prerogative of declaring war till after the Atheno-Peloponnesian war of 431–404 B.C.

One of the traditional prerogatives of the Spartan double crown was the unfettered exercise of military command in the field, outside the frontiers of Sparta's dominions. This prerogative had been left intact in the 'Lycurgan' reform, which had reduced the crown's civil powers at home almost to vanishing point.[1] In the campaign of 418 B.C. King Agis II was still exercising this prerogative in full.[2] At the date when Xenophon was writing his *Lakedaimoniôn Politeia*, a Spartan king on campaign was accompanied by two ephors. Xenophon assures his readers that these ephors-in-attendance 'do not interfere in the conduct of the military operations, but merely promote general discipline by keeping an eye on everybody's behaviour'.[3] This may have been true, but, as has already been noted, it will also have been true that, after the army had returned to Sparta, the pair of accompanying ephors will have been well posted for laying information against the king, promoting a prosecution, and serving as formidable witnesses for it.

In any case, the ten counsellors (ξύμβουλοι) that were imposed, for the future, on King Agis III by a law passed at Sparta in 418–17 B.C. were certainly intended to interfere with Agis' conduct of operations; for the law was an expression of the Government's dissatisfaction with Agis' past performance. The law debarred Agis from leading an expeditionary force beyond the frontiers without taking these ten watchdogs with him.[4] This law was without precedent,[4] and Agis seems to have succeeded in getting himself released from it. At any rate, he exercised wide powers, diplomatic as well as military, at his own discretion during the Decelean War. But the precedent set in 418/17 B.C. to the detriment of King Agis II was revived in 397/6 B.C. to the detriment of King Agesilaos II. When Agesilaos was sent to take command of the Lacedaemonian forces in western Anatolia in the winter of 398/7 B.C., he was accompanied by a delegation of thirty Spartiate watchdogs;[5] and so was Agesipolis when, in 382 B.C., he was appointed to the command of an expeditionary force against the colonial Chalcidians.[6]

In recalling Agesilaos in 394 B.C.,[7] and in instructing him, thereafter, to invade Boeotia,[8] the ephors were taking the last step in usurping the kings' original prerogative of having a free hand in the field. In 371 B.C. King Kleombrotos, who was in command of a Lacedaemonian force stationed in Phokis, asked 'the home government' (τὰ οἴκοι τέλη) for

---

[1] See pp. 232–3.
[2] Thucydides, Book V, chap. 66, § 3.
[3] πολυπραγμονοῦσι μὲν οὐδέν, ἢν μὴ ὁ βασιλεὺς προσκαλῇ· ὁρῶντες δ' ὅτι ποιεῖ ἕκαστος, πάντας σωφρονίζουσιν, ὡς τὸ εἰκός (chap. 13, § 5).
[4] Thucydides, Book V, chap. 63.
[5] Xenophon, *Hellenica*, Book III, chap. 4, § 2.
[6] Ibid., Book V, chap. 3, § 8.
[7] Diodorus, Book XIV, chap. 83, § 1; Plutarch, *Agesilaus*, chap. 15.
[8] Plutarch, ibid., chap. 17; *Apophthegmata Laconica*, Agesilaos, 47.

instructions. He was instructed to attack Thebes,[1] and, in consequence, he ended at Leuktra.

Kleomenes III abolished the ephorate in 227 B.C.[2] It was presumably re-established by Antigonos Doson when he restored the 'Lycurgan' constitution at Sparta in 222 B.C. after his victory at Sellasia and Kleomenes III's flight.[3] At any rate, there were ephors at Sparta again in 220/19 B.C. In this year a pro-Macedonian board of ephors was murdered and a pro-Aetolian board gave the Spartan crown to a non-Heraklid aspirant, Lycurgus.[4] The ephors of Lycurgus' faction were murdered in 218 B.C. in an abortive *Putsch* which had been designed to re-establish the revolutionary regime of 227 B.C.[5] Lycurgus himself, however, escaped from Laconia,[5] and lived to be recalled and reinstated in 217 B.C. by another board of ephors.[6]

After this, we lose sight of the ephorate till, on the evidence of inscriptions, we find it functioning in the Age of the Principate. If it was in existence during the reign of Nabis (*dominabatur* 206–192 B.C.), it would have been as much as the ephors' lives were worth for them to try to assert themselves against that resolute despot. In any case, the ephorate seems unlikely to have survived the abolition of the 'Lycurgan' regime by the Achaean Confederation in 188 B.C.[7] Sparta was an unwilling member of the Achaean Confederation from 192 B.C. until she was released in 146 B.C. by the dissolution of the Confederation by the Romans. The revival of the ephorate in the Age of the Principate, which is attested by inscriptional evidence, was part of the archaizing movement that was in fashion during that age, in Sparta as in other ancient and famous Hellenic states. It seems unlikely, however, that the resuscitated ephorate will have reacquired its historic powers, since it now had to co-exist with the board of patronomoi, which had been instituted by Kleomenes III as a substitute for the public authorities, other than the crown, that had been paramount under the 'Lycurgan' regime.[8]

---

[1] Xenophon, *Hellenica*, Book VI, chap. 4, §§ 2–3.
[2] Plutarch, *Cleomenes*, chap. 8.
[3] Ibid., chap. 30.
[4] Polybius, Book IV, chaps. 34–5.
[5] Ibid., chap. 81.
[6] Polybius, Book V, chap. 91.
[7] Plutarch, *Philopoemen*, chap. 16.
[8] Pausanias, Book II, chap. 9, § 1.

The Dating of the Adoption, in the Hellenic World in General and at Sparta in Particular, of the Various Components of the Hoplite Equipment, and the Dating of the Adoption of Phalanx-Tactics

THE phalanx was a close-order formation of soldiers equipped in elaborate and costly metallic defensive armour, and armed offensively with stabbing spears for fighting at close quarters. Without the equipment there could have been no phalanx-tactics. It would have been suicidal to attempt to fight in close order at close quarters without wearing protective armour. On the other hand, any of the components of the phalangite's equipment, both defensive and offensive, could be used with advantage, either singly or in combination, in the open-order long-range kind of fighting that had been normal in the Hellenic World before the phalanx formation was substituted for it.

The phalanx-tactics, which were not a necessary consequence of the hoplite equipment, may not have been an Hellenic invention;[1] but it is certain that Greek hoplites in phalanx-formation, and also non-Greek troops (e.g. Carian, Etruscan, Roman, Latin) that had adopted this element in the Hellenic way of life, proved decisively superior to opponents who were not equipped and drilled as hoplite phalangites throughout at least three centuries running from the Athenians' victory over Persian archers at Marathon in 490 B.C. to the Macedonians' defeat by Roman javelin-and-sword troops at Kynoskephalai in 197 B.C. By that time the Macedonians had carried the hoplite equipment and the phalanx-tactics *ad extremum*, and finally *ad absurdum*, by liberating the soldier's left hand from the task of holding his shield and thus enabling him to use a two-handed pike, of ever-increasing length, instead of a one-handed stabbing spear.[2] However, this innovation, which was introduced in the fourth century B.C., made no essential change in the equipment and tactics that were already going concerns in the southern states of the Hellenic World by the opening of the fifth century B.C.

When were the various components of the hoplite equipment adopted in the Hellenic World (or readopted, after having fallen out of use at the end of the Mycenaean Age)? And when were the phalanx-tactics introduced there? Our sources of information are of three kinds, two of them archaeological and the third literary. There are surviving pieces

[1] The Greeks may have been anticipated by the Sumerians in the third millenium B.C. and by the Egyptians in the Age of the New Empire.
[2] See Plutarch, *Cleomenes*, chap. 11.

of Greek and Etruscan armour and weapons. There are surviving contemporary pictures of armed men and of battles, mostly in paintings on vases. There are also surviving fragments of the works of eighth-century-B.C. and seventh-century-B.C. Greek poets—e.g. Kallinos of Ephesos, Arkhilokhos of Paros, Tyrtaios of Sparta[1]—in which armour, weapons, and tactics are described. The pioneer work on this material, which, in the aggregate, is abundant, has been done by Miss H. L. Lorimer.[2] A. M. Snodgrass has built on Miss Lorimer's work; but he has also extended it by work of his own, and, on some important points, on which he dissents from Miss Lorimer's conclusions, his findings are convincing.[3]

The questions at issue turn on a series of different ways of handling the shield; for, in the history of Hellenic warfare in all the successive periods here under consideration, the shield was the key arm. The shield was the 'hoplon' that gave the hoplite his designation.[4] The traditional way of handling a shield was to wield it in the left hand by a single handle, placed near the middle of the inner side of the shield (whatever the shield's shape might be). When the shield became heavy for handling in this way—as it did when it came to be plated with metal—the first expedient for coping with its increased weight (an expedient used, in the past, for handling the Mycenaean body-length shields of the sixteenth and fifteenth centuries B.C.)[5] was to support part of the weight on a strap (telamon) passing over the shoulder. In the eighth century B.C. Assyrian soldiers who were equipped with metal-plated round shields wielded them by using a telamon as well as the central handle.[6] The Greeks seem to have been the inventors of a more efficient way of bearing the increased weight.[7] They fitted the inner face of the round shield with a metal band (porpax) laid across the shield's diameter and gripping the left forearm, and with a handle (antilabê) placed on the inner edge of the concave part of the shield in a position in which it could be gripped in the left hand when the left forearm had been passed through the porpax.[8] This

---

[1] Tyrtaios was certainly a Spartan by adoption if he was not a Spartan by birth, as he probably was.

[2] H. L. Lorimer, 'The Hoplite Phalanx', in the *Annual of the British School at Athens*, vol. 42 (1947), pp. 76–138.

[3] A. M. Snodgrass, *Early Greek Armour and Weapons* (Edinburgh, 1964, University Press); idem, 'The Hoplite Reform and History', in the *Journal of Hellenic Studies*, vol. lxxxv (1965), pp. 110–22. Jones, *Sparta*, p. 33, accepts Snodgrass's findings, but, rather inconsequently, refuses to accept the chronological implications of these.

[4] Lorimer, loc. cit., p. 76, with n. 2.

[5] Ibid., p. 122.

[6] Snodgrass, *Early Greek Armour*, p. 38, and 'The Hoplite Reform and History', p. 111.

[7] Snodgrass, *Early Greek Armour*, p. 201. Cp. p. 66.

[8] Lorimer, loc. cit., p. 76; Snodgrass, *Early Greek Armour*, p. 61. The hoplite shield had an evenly convex shape and a sharply set-off rim (Snodgrass, loc. cit.). Surviving specimens show that the rim and the porpax were of bronze and that the shield itself was of wood, bronze-plated (op. cit., pp. 63 and 64). The surviving specimens are remarkably uniform

device made it possible to bear the weight of the heavier round shield without the aid of the clumsy telamon.[1] The subsequent change of handling from porpax-and-antilabê to okhanê,[2] whatever this new device may have been, liberated the Macedonian-style phalangite's left hand for helping to hold a two-handed pike in place of the previous single-handed stabbing-spear.

The key point in Miss Lorimer's thesis is that 'the single-grip shield was easily manœuvrable, and it could be used to cover any part of the owner's person. The hoplite shield gave complete protection only to the left side of the trunk.'[3] It was, indeed, a well-known phenomenon that, in the age of phalanx-tactics, each of two opposing phalanx-formations tended to edge towards the right as they approached each other, because the outermost man on the right, in either phalanx, instinctively sought to carry the unprotected right side of his trunk beyond the reach of the spear of his 'opposite number', the left-hand-most man on the opposite side, whose right side was protected by the projecting left-hand segment of the shield of the man on his immediate right.[4]

Miss Lorimer holds, further, that 'with the hoplite shield a single (thrusting) spear is inevitable',[5] because a left arm and hand that were locked in a porpax and in an antilabê could not, at the same time, hold an extra spear for throwing. Her conclusion[5] is that the hoplite equipment consists of a complex of inter-related components no one of which appears on any monument earlier than the seventh century B.C. The pieces of hoplite defensive armour are a plate metal corslet, a metal helmet (almost invariably of the Corinthian type, which covered the cheeks, nose, and neck), and greaves. In Miss Lorimer's view[6] the hoplite equipment and tactics are all of a piece and cannot have been introduced piecemeal.

The joint evidence of literature and archaeology supports the conclusion that the porpax shield, which implies hoplite tactics, was adopted by Corinth

(ibid., p. 64; cp. Lorimer in loc. cit., p. 76, n. 3). When once adopted, this make of shield became standard in the Hellenic World for the next 300 years (Snodgrass, op. cit., p. 64) or 350 years (p. 68).

[1] The device 'enabled the strength and size of the large Assyrian round shield to be maintained without a telamon, and without imposing an unbearable strain on the warrior' (Snodgrass, *Early Greek Armour*, p. 201).

[2] See Plutarch, *Cleomenes*, loc. cit.   [3] Lorimer in loc. cit., p. 76–7.

[4] Thucydides, Book V, chap. 71, § 1. Accordingly, what a phalangite did with his shield was not his own concern alone. The security of the whole phalanx would be threatened if any phalangite were to drop his shield and so deprive his neighbour's right side of its due protection. 'When someone asked [the Spartan King] Damaratos why it was Spartan practice to dishonour soldiers who threw away their shields, but not those who threw away their helmets and corslets, "the reason is", Damaratos answered, "because we wear our helmets and corslets for our own sakes, but carry our shields for the sake of the formation (τῆς κοινῆς τάξεως ἕνεκα)" ' (Plutarch, *Apophthegmata Laconica*, Damaratos, 2).

[5] Loc cit., p. 79.   [6] Ibid., pp. 107–8.

and Athens very early in the seventh century, by Sparta within its first quarter, by Crete and probably Boeotia at or about the same time; probably also in the Aegean islands, at all events in Paros, Chios, and Euboea, though not, apparently, at once, or at least not universally, by the Greeks of the Anatolian coast.[1]

In dissent from Miss Lorimer, Snodgrass holds that the adoption, in the Hellenic World, of the various components of the hoplite panoply and the adoption of phalanx-tactics were not simultaneous with each other. His dates for the adoption of the pieces of equipment are earlier than Miss Lorimer's, but his date for the adoption of hoplite-tactics is later than hers.

Snodgrass takes note of the sudden spurt of technological progress in the Hellenic World towards the end of the eighth century B.C., after centuries of stagnation.[2] Single components of the hoplite equipment appear as early as 750 B.C.[3] Snodgrass's date for the invention of the hoplite shield is 740–700 B.C.[4] Geometric vases begin to show what looks like the hoplite shield from *circa* 750 B.C. onwards.[5] 'The hoplite shield was certainly in use in Greece by the beginning of the seventh century, and probably during the late eighth.'[6]

Snodgrass does not believe that the carrying of more than one spear is evidence that the soldier's shield is of the pre-hoplite, single-grip type.[7] On the evidence of the pictures, throwing-spears survived into the hoplite age—and, indeed, into the phalanx age, since, in the picture on the Chigi vase, the two men who are still arming appear each to have more spears than one.[8] Soldiers are depicted carrying two or more spears in other pictures, too, dating from the seventh century B.C.[9] Indeed, in Proto-Corinthian and Proto-Attic battle-scenes, two or more spears are more frequent than single spears in the proportion of two to one.[10] 'It seems an inescapable conclusion that the early hoplite often, though not invariably, went into battle carrying two or more spears, and it is very probable that one, at least, of these was habitually thrown.'[11]

A complete metal breast-and-back has been found at Argos in a burial dating from the Late Geometric Age.[12] If the metal corslet, seen

---

[1] Ibid., p. 127. [2] *Early Greek Armour*, p. 35.
[3] 'The Hoplite Reform and History', p. 110.
[4] *Early Greek Armour*, pp. 57 and 65–6.
[5] Ibid., pp. 196–7. The porpax was in use already in the Late (before the latest) Geometric Age. Porpax does not imply phalanx ('The Hoplite Reform and History', pp. 111–12). Miss Lorimer concedes (loc. cit., p. 81) that the representation of hoplites begins about fifty years earlier than the date of the Chigi vase, which is the earliest unquestionable representation of the phalanx.
[6] Snodgrass, *Early Greek Armour*, p. 67. [7] Ibid., p. 49.
[8] Ibid., p. 138. [9] Ibid., p. 198.
[10] Ibid., pp. 198–9. [11] Ibid., p. 138. Cp. p. 139.
[12] Ibid., pp. 72–3; 'The Hoplite Reform and History', p. 112; Huxley, op. cit., p. 30.

by Pausanias and said to have belonged to Timomakhos, the Aigeid conqueror of Amyklai,[1] was genuine, its date must have been not later than the fifth decade of the eighth century B.C. 'The essential components of the hoplite's armament (the greave excepted) are . . . all known to the Aegean World before 700 B.C., and their association together is first portrayed about twenty-five years later;[2] while another full generation elapses before we have any archaeological evidence for the adoption of "hoplite" tactics.'[3]

No unity of purpose is discernible behind the development of the various items.[4] It is only to be expected that the invention of the materials for hoplite warfare should have preceded the invention of this form of warfare itself.[5] 'The arms' are likely to have been 'in use for some time before a marked change in tactics occurred'.[6] Snodgrass holds that the piecemeal adoption of the various pieces of arms and armour that were eventually combined in the hoplite panoply took about one hundred years, *circa* 750–650 B.C.[7] 'The Argos find shows that the plate-corslet was not inseparable from the hoplite shield and Corinthian helmet.'[8] It may have been reintroduced into Greece before the rest of the hoplite equipment.[9] With a few possible exceptions, 'bell-corslet and hoplite shield are never once definitely shown together on the same warrior until late in the seventh century'.[10]

'It seems that the close association of each of these items with the others, and with a set form of tactics, was not confirmed until the seventh century was well advanced; their united appearance on the Berlin aryballos and the Chigi vase (though, even here, there are discordant elements) may be the earliest evidence for what fifth-century Greece understood by hoplite warfare.'[11] 'Hoplite tactics are unknown to Geometric art.'[12] Porpax and antilabê do not necessarily imply phalanx-formation. There are representations of hoplite-shield-carriers fighting individually.[13] The Aegina stand, which dates from the second quarter of the seventh century B.C., is the earliest work of art that possibly represents the phalanx. The Berlin aryballos (*circa* 650 B.C.) is the first

---

[1] See the present Part, p. 176, and Snodgrass, 'The Hoplite Reform and History', p. 111, n. 2.

[2] See Snodgrass, ibid., p. 110; Lorimer in loc. cit., p. 80.

[3] *Early Greek Armour*, p. 90. Cp. 'The Hoplite Reform and History', p. 10.

[4] *Early Greek Armour*, p. 90.

[5] Ibid., p. 195.

[6] Ibid., p. 196. The same view is taken by Kiechle, *Lakonien und Sparta*, pp. 267 and 268.

[7] Snodgrass in op. cit., p. 202.　　　　　　　[8] Ibid., p. 83.　　　　　　　[9] Ibid.

[10] Ibid., p. 84. 'On the other hand, the hoplite shield and metal corslet are almost never shown without a metallic helmet' (ibid.).

[11] Ibid., p. 186. Cp. Kiechle, *Lakonien und Sparta*, p. 270.

[12] Snodgrass, *Early Greek Armour*, p. 83.

[13] Ibid., p. 197. Cp. p. 201. See also Lorimer in loc. cit., p. 81, already cited on p. 253, n. 5.

unquestionable representation of it.[1] Miss Lorimer's dating of the Chigi vase[2] is the same as Snodgrass's dating of the Berlin aryballos. The lead figurines found at the shrine of Artemis Orthia at Sparta and at the Menelaïon at Therapne 'have almost without exception hoplite equipment, as far as it can be checked'.[3] Snodgrass here goes as far as Miss Lorimer. He takes these Spartan figurines as being evidence, not merely for hoplite equipment, but for a hoplite phalanx.[4] Snodgrass notes, however, that the starting-date of this series of figurines is now thought to be not earlier than 650 B.C.,[5] whereas Miss Lorimer follows a previous dating of the first phase of the series ('Lead 1') *circa* 700–635 B.C. Snodgrass[6] agrees with Miss Lorimer[7] that the Carian and Ionian 'bronze men' whose services were hired by King Psammetikhos I *circa* 663 B.C. were hoplites; but for Snodgrass this is, of course, not evidence that they fought in phalanx-formation.

The literary evidence is not as clear as the archaeological evidence is. Material objects, and, *a fortiori*, portrayals of them, do not, in all cases, explain themselves unambiguously. *A fortiori*, again, this is true of verbal descriptions of material objects. Moreover, the three poets mainly in question here—namely Kallinos, Arkhilokhos, and Tyrtaios—lived in an age of literary reminiscence and technological transition. The three were approximately contemporary with each other. Kallinos lived at the time of the Cimmerians' invasion of western Anatolia, between 670 and 650 B.C. Arkhilokhos lived *circa* 680–640 B.C. according to Jacoby. Tyrtaios lived at the time of 'the Second Spartano-Messenian War' (the first Messenian revolt), which was contemporaneous with the Cimmerians' invasion of western Anatolia. All wrote in a sub-Homeric dialect; reminiscences of Homeric phrases were among the tricks of their trade; and these might be highly anachronistic,[8] while, in so far as the three poets are giving an authentic description of contemporary armour, weapons, and tactics, this is likely, considering the date, to present a picture that is not homogeneous. That is true of Kallinos; it may be true of Arkhilokhos; and it is certainly true of Tyrtaios, whose evidence is the most pertinent for ascertaining the date at which the hoplite equipment and the phalanx-tactics were adopted by the Spartans.

In Kallinos' picture, both the Ephesians[9] and their opponents[10] fight

---

[1] Snodgrass in *Early Greek Armour*, pp. 197–8.
[2] In loc. cit., p. 81. Cp. pp. 82 and 84.
[3] Lorimer in loc. cit., p. 92.
[4] 'The Hoplite Reform and History', p. 116: 'These cheap, mass-produced dedications, a sign of a unified and self-conscious hoplite class'.
[5] 'The Hoplite Reform and History', p. 116; *Early Greek Armour*, p. 181.
[6] *Early Greek Armour*, pp. 185 and 203.
[7] In loc. cit., p. 120.
[8] e.g. ἀσπίδος ὀμφαλοέσσης in Tyrtaios, 10 (Bergk–Hiller–Crusius) = 9 (12) (Diehl), l. 25.
[9] Kallinos, 1, l. 5.   [10] Ibid., l. 14.

with throwing-spears. At the same time, Kallinos exhorts his fellow countrymen to close with the enemy in single combat, poising a stabbing spear and hugging a hoplite shield.[1]

Arkhilokhos forebodes[2] that, when war breaks out in Euboea, it will be fought with swords, not with bows or slings. In this context, Arkhilokhos does not mention the hoplite's shield and stabbing spear. But Arkhilokhos himself, on Thasos, is equipped with a single stabbing spear that is inseparable from him,[3] and with a shield which must be of the heavy hoplite type, since he has to throw it away in order to escape with his life when he takes to flight.[4]

Some of Tyrtaios' exhortations to his fellow countrymen are, like Kallinos', calls to close with the enemy, hand to hand,[5] among the front-line fighters.[6] In one case, the soldier is exhorted to engage in single combat.[7] But the men are also urged to hold together,[8] and in two passages they are urged to form a phalanx.[9] These men are equipped as hoplites. They carry the hoplite shield[10] and wear the hoplite's metal helmet[11] and also his metal corslet (an inference from the expectation that the groin, which was left uncovered by the corslet, will be the spot where the soldier will receive his death-wound).[12] The soldier's weapon is alternatively either a stabbing spear or a sword.[13] These hoplites, however, are not under discipline. To stand one's ground[14] and to fight in formation is the ideal; but the expectation is that the younger men will skulk[15] and will be put to shame by the older men getting themselves killed as gallant front-fighters.[16] These hoplites' formation is loose enough for the light-armed ($\gamma\upsilon\mu\nu\hat{\eta}\tau\epsilon\varsigma$)[17] to be able to shelter behind the hoplites'

---

[1] Kallinos, 1, ll. 9–11: $\dot{a}\lambda\lambda\dot{a}$ $\tau\iota\varsigma$ $\dot{\iota}\theta\dot{\upsilon}\varsigma$ $\dot{\iota}\tau\omega$ | $\check{\epsilon}\gamma\chi\upsilon\varsigma$ $\dot{a}\nu\alpha\sigma\chi\dot{\omega}\mu\epsilon\nu\upsilon\varsigma$ $\kappa\alpha\dot{\iota}$ $\dot{\upsilon}\pi$ $\dot{a}\sigma\pi\dot{\iota}\delta\upsilon\varsigma$ $\check{a}\lambda\kappa\iota\mu\upsilon\nu$ $\check{\eta}\tau\upsilon\rho$ | $\check{\epsilon}\lambda\sigma\alpha\varsigma$.
[2] Arkhilokhos, 3. [3] Arkhilokhos, 2. [4] Arkhilokhos, 5.
[5] Tyrtaios, $\check{\epsilon}\varsigma$ τ $\alpha\dot{\upsilon}\tau\upsilon\sigma\chi\epsilon\delta\dot{\iota}\eta\nu$ (9 (Bergk–Hiller–Crusius)=8 (11) (Diehl), l. 12); $\alpha\dot{\upsilon}\tau\upsilon\sigma\chi\epsilon\delta\dot{\upsilon}\nu$ (ibid., l. 29); $\dot{\epsilon}\gamma\gamma\dot{\upsilon}\theta\epsilon\nu$ $\dot{\iota}\sigma\tau\dot{a}\mu\epsilon\nu\upsilon\varsigma$ (10 (B.–H.–C.) = 9 (12) (D.), l. 12).
[6] $\dot{\epsilon}\nu$ $\pi\rho\upsilon\mu\dot{a}\chi\upsilon\iota\sigma\iota$ (Tyrtaios, 8 (B.–H.–C.) = 6. 7 (1) (D.), ll. 1 and 30; 10 (B.–H.–C.) = 9 (12) (D.), ll. 16 and 23)); $\mu\epsilon\tau\dot{a}$ $\pi\rho\upsilon\mu\dot{a}\chi\upsilon\iota\sigma\iota$ (8 (B.–H.–C.) = 6. 7 (1) (D.), l. 21); $\dot{\epsilon}\varsigma$ $\pi\rho\upsilon\mu\dot{a}\chi\upsilon\upsilon\varsigma$ (9 (B.–H.–C.) = 8 (11) (D.), l. 4).
[7] $\dot{\iota}\theta\dot{\upsilon}\varsigma$ δ' $\dot{\epsilon}\varsigma$ $\pi\rho\upsilon\mu\dot{a}\chi\upsilon\upsilon\varsigma$ (9 (B.–H.–C.) = 8 (11) (D.), l. 4; cp. Kallinos, 1, ll. 9–11).
[8] $\pi\alpha\rho$' $\dot{a}\lambda\lambda\dot{\eta}\lambda\upsilon\iota\sigma\iota$ $\mu\dot{\epsilon}\nu\upsilon\nu\tau\epsilon\varsigma$ (8 (B.–H.–C.) = 6. 7 (1) (D.), l. 15; 9 (B.–H.–C.) = 8 (11) (D.)) ; $\theta\alpha\rho\sigma\dot{\upsilon}\nu\eta$ δ' $\check{\epsilon}\pi\epsilon\sigma\iota\nu$ $\tau\dot{\upsilon}\nu$ $\pi\lambda\eta\sigma\dot{\iota}\upsilon\nu$ $\check{a}\nu\delta\rho\alpha$ $\pi\alpha\rho\epsilon\sigma\tau\dot{\omega}\varsigma$ (10 (B.–H.–C.) = 9 (12) (D.), l. 19).
[9] 1 (D.), ll. 50–61; 9(B.–H.–C.) = 8 (11) (D.), ll. 31–3. These two passages may be prophetic, but they read more like reminiscences of *Iliad*, XVI. 214–17. The enemy's $\phi\dot{a}\lambda\alpha\gamma\gamma\epsilon\varsigma$ are mentioned in 10 (B.–H.–C.) = 9 (12) (D.), l. 21.
[10] 1 (D.), ll. 50 and 58; 9 (B.–H.–C.) = 8 (11) (D.), ll. 4, 23–4, 28, 35.
[11] 1 (D.), l. 63.   [12] 8 (B.–H.–C.) = 6. 7 (1) (D.), l. 25.
[13] 1 (D.), ll. 52 and 56; 9 (B.–H.–C.) = 8 (11) (D.), ll. 25, 28, 29–30, 34.
[14] 8 (B.–H.–C.) = 6. 7 (1) (D.), ll. 31–2; 9 (B.–H.–C.) = 8 (11) (D.), ll. 21–2.
[15] $\mu\eta\delta\dot{\epsilon}$ $\phi\upsilon\gamma\hat{\eta}\varsigma$ $\alpha\dot{\iota}\sigma\chi\rho\hat{\eta}\varsigma$ $\check{a}\rho\chi\epsilon\tau\epsilon$ $\mu\eta\delta\dot{\epsilon}$ $\phi\dot{\upsilon}\beta\upsilon\upsilon$ (8 (B.–H.–C.) = 6. 7 (1) (D.), l. 16); $\mu\eta\delta$' $\dot{\epsilon}\kappa\tau\dot{\upsilon}\varsigma$ $\beta\epsilon\lambda\dot{\epsilon}\omega\nu$ $\dot{\iota}\sigma\tau\dot{a}\tau\omega$ $\dot{a}\sigma\pi\dot{\iota}\delta$' $\check{\epsilon}\chi\omega\nu$ (9 (B.–H.–C.) = 8 (11) (D.), l. 28). Cp. 1 (D.), l. 49.
[16] 8 (B.–H.–C.) = 6. 7 (1) (D.), ll. 15–30.
[17] 9 (B.–H.–C.) = 8 (11) (D.), l. 35. Cp. 1 (D.), ll. 45 and 62. Kiechle, *Lakonien und Sparta*, pp. 192–3, is surely right in holding that Tyrtaios' 'gymnetes' were Spartiatai, not helots.

(πανόπλοισιν) shields,[1] as they did in the Roman phalanx after this had been diluted by the conscription of the poorly armed classes IV–V.[2]

If we did not happen to have been informed of the identity of these warriors who are so reluctant to be heroes, we should never have guessed that they are Spartans. This would have been the last possibility that would have occurred to us, because posterity's image of a Spartan soldier has been created by the conduct of Leonidas' Spartan soldiers in 480 B.C., not Tyrtaios' six or seven generations earlier. There is something ludicrous about the poet's forlorn attempts to breathe at least a modicum of martial spirit into the undisciplined cowards who are the military material on which he has to work. But, if Tyrtaios' war-songs make us smile, we may be sure that they will have made Leonidas and his Spartiate contemporaries wince. Tyrtaios' Spartans were ancestors of whom Leonidas' three hundred could not be proud. We know what happened to the one man out of the three hundred who was so foolhardy as to return home alive from Thermopylae because he had been incapacitated by ophthalmia. Life was made such a torment for him that he preferred to die a hero's death at Plataea next year; and, even then, his implacable countrymen gave him no credit for having retrieved his disgrace.[3]

It would have been impracticable to penalize Tyrtaios' malingering soldiers as a later generation at Sparta penalized Aristodamos 'the coward' (ὁ τρέσας). In 'the Second Spartano-Messenian War', Spartan soldiers who did not disgrace themselves were evidently exceptional. How could the rabble of commoner Spartiates have been expected to behave like heroes in the political, social, and economic circumstances of the Sparta of Tyrtaios' day? Why should they have risked their lives in trying to reconquer Sparta's lost dominion in Messenia? The original conquest, in the First Spartano-Messenian War, could not have been achieved without their participation; yet, on that occasion, after the victory had been won, the aristocratic minority of the Spartiate citizen-body had succeeded in resisting the majority's reasonable demand for a fair share in the land that had been won by a common effort. If Messenia were now to be reconquered, the minority might be expected to try, once again, to cheat the majority of its just reward. The loss of the 50 per cent quota of the Messenians' produce[4] was the Spartan aristocracy's loss, not the Spartan damos'. So why should the damos burn its fingers in order to pull the aristocracy's chestnuts out of the fire? Tyrtaios'

---

[1] 9 (B.–H.–C.) = 8 (11) (D.), ll. 35–8.
[2] For the inconsistencies in Tyrtaios' descriptions of tactics, see Lenschau, 'Die Entstehung des spartanischen Staates', pp. 272–3.
[3] Herodotus, Book VII, chaps. 229–31; Book IX, chap. 71.
[4] Tyrtaios, 6 (B.–H.–C.) = 6. 7 (5) (D.).

lurid picture of the horrors of the life of a penniless refugee[1] will have
fallen flat. The picture may have been drawn from the life. It may
have been a true portrayal of the plight of expatriated Messenians. But
how could the majority of the Spartan soldiers be worse off than they
were already? They were beggars at home. Why risk their lives just to
escape from becoming beggars abroad instead?

When, nevertheless, the Second Spartano-Messenian War, like its
predecessor, had eventually ended in a barely won Spartan victory,
there must have been some 'Lycurgus' at Sparta who was a great enough
statesman to be able to induce the Spartan aristocracy to face the hard
facts and to resign themselves to the unpalatable but now unavoidable
remedy. The Spartan army's resounding defeat by the Argives at
Hysiai in 669 B.C., followed by its poor performance in the consequent
Second Spartano-Messenian War, had made it clear that Sparta now
had a choice between a thorough-going military reform—which would
mean a social and a political reform as well—and a second collapse of her
precarious dominion over the southern two-fifths of the Peloponnese.
Possibly the second collapse did overtake Sparta before the Spartan
aristocracy gave in. A second Messenian revolt—the revolt led by Aristomenes—may have given the Spartan reform movement its final impulse.[2]

Already the first revolt had demonstrated that Sparta could not hold
her painfully recaptured conquests with an army in which the individual
hoplite was free to skulk in the rear if he did not choose to risk his life
as a front-fighter. In this undisciplined army the phalanx was a mere
temporary formation in which a bunch of hoplites might—or might not—
momentarily combine on their own initiative on the spur of the moment;
and, even then, the formation was so loose that there was room for the
light-armed majority of the levy to scurry in and out between the hoplites'
loose ranks and files. If Sparta was to continue to rule—or, indeed, to
survive—she must now build a disciplined hoplite phalanx out of her
mixed rabble of 'jay-walking' individual hoplites and miserably ill-
equipped light-armed skirmishers.

This transformation of the Spartan army was achieved as a result of
the 'Lycurgan' reforms.[3] The distribution of the conquered and reconquered lands into kleroi now provided the kleros-holder with the
economic means of devoting the whole of his working time to training
and serving as a hoplite phalangite. The concession to the damos of the
ultimate sovereignty in the Spartan state was a recognition, in the
political sphere, of the new model army's indispensability—and, though

[1] Tyrtaios, 8 (Bergk–Hiller–Crusius) = 6. 7 (1) (Diehl), ll. 1–4.
[2] See p. 226.
[3] The military reform is dated soon after Tyrtaios' time by Witkowski, loc. cit., p. 74.
Jones, too (*Sparta*, p. 38), guesses that 'discipline was tightened and made obligatory on all
after the Second Messenian War'.

the concession made in the rhetra was minimal, and was perhaps partly revoked in the additional last clause,[1] the transfer to the damos, from the crown, of the prerogative of appointing the board of ephors made the damos, by proxy, not simply a constitutional sovereign but a despot.

The economic and political reforms could be introduced in a single act. On the other hand, the full-time professional hoplite phalanx, for which these were the necessary foundations, could not be built in a day. The callow phalanx of 'homoioi' did not distinguish itself in its first ventures in the field. In a series of aggressive wars waged in the course of the first half of the sixth century B.C., Sparta failed to conquer and annex the Tegeatis, as she had conquered and annexed Messenia, five or six generations earlier, in the First Spartano-Messenian War. Tegea managed to fend off Sparta's repeated assaults, though she was no match for Sparta in man-power. Perhaps Tegea, like Argos, had anticipated Sparta in adopting phalanx-tactics, and was more than a match for Sparta at this date in expertness in this new-fangled military technique. The Spartan new model army justified its existence—and so justified the radical reforms that had brought it into existence—only when it inflicted on the Argives at Thyrea, *circa* 544 B.C., as signal a defeat as the one that the Argives had inflicted on the Spartans at Hysiai in 669 B.C.; and the date of this decisive Spartan victory at Thyrea was perhaps as much as a hundred years later, and was certainly more than fifty years later, than the date of the 'Lycurgan' reforms that had been Sparta's response to the lessons of Hysiai and of 'the Second Spartano-Messenian War' and perhaps of Aristomenes' revolt as well. No doubt, it cannot have taken a century, or even half a century, for the Spartiate 'homoioi' to become adepts in the phalanx drill. They had had no other work to occupy their time since the date when they had been endowed with their kleroi. Drill, however, would have been of little avail without *moral*; and, for building up a martial tradition, a full century may have been required.[2]

At this point in Sparta's history, about halfway through the sixth century B.C., the ephor Khilon (if the credit is truly his) proved himself as great a statesman as the anonymous author of the 'Lycurgan' reforms a century or half a century earlier. Khilon was not blinded, by the dazzling victory over Argos, to the significance of Sparta's failure to subdue Tegea. He saw that, even now that Sparta's new model army

---

[1] See chap. 3, Annex IV.

[2] Xenophon, *Lak. Pol.*, chap. 9, §§ 1–2, puts his finger on this point. 'One of the remarkable achievements of "Lycurgus" ', he writes, 'is that he has made it preferable, in Sparta, to die a noble death rather than remain alive in disgrace'. Xenophon adds the interesting observation that 'as a matter of fact, investigation reveals that there are actually fewer deaths in battle among the Spartans than in armies which give way to their fear and prefer to leave the field; so that, in reality, courage turns out to be a more effective survival-factor than cowardice'.

had proved itself, by its victory over Argos, to be the best army in the Hellenic World of the day, Sparta's military effort was already over-extended. Even with the increased military strength that Sparta had acquired through her revolutionary military reforms, she would find herself engaged, up to the hilt, in continuing to hold down her helots. The preservation, within her own dominions, of the ascendancy of the 'homoioi' would be incompatible with any further territorial expansion. Accordingly, whether or not under Khilon's inspiration, Sparta now abruptly abandoned her traditional policy of conquest and annexation for a new policy of alliances with Tegea and with other Peloponnesian states in which, with or without Sparta's assistance, a moderate oligar-chical regime had replaced a revolutionary despotism.[1]

If the findings of this Annex are correct, they date the 'Lycurgan' reforms at Sparta either shortly after the mid-point of the seventh century B.C. or even as late as that century's closing years, and not at any of the prehistoric dates that have to be adopted if 'Lycurgus' is taken to have been an historical human personality, not a timeless god. These prehistoric dates, and, with them, the historicity of 'Lycurgus', are ruled out by our knowledge of the approximate date at which the hoplite phalanx made its first appearance in the Hellenic World. The archaeo-logical and the literary evidence indicates consistently that the date of this was not earlier than the mid-point of the seventh century B.C.; and the establishment of a hoplite phalanx at Sparta is implicit in the 'Lycurgan' reforms.

PART III, CHAPTER 3, ANNEX II

The Local Obai and the Dorian Phylai at Sparta[2]

THERE is evidence that the Spartan citizen-body was sub-divided on two different systems, and that, for a time, these two systems were both in existence simultaneously. One system was based on locality;[3] the other was the set of three Dorian tribes. The set of sub-divisions based on locality was both the older-established at Sparta and the longer-lived there. In fact, this organization by locality was in existence at Sparta from the beginning to the end of her history.

The local sub-divisions were sub-divisions of Sparta City itself, not of the Spartan city-state territory and, *a fortiori*, not of Sparta's total Peloponnesian dominions, which included the territories of the perioecic dependencies.[4] This is expressly stated in the cases of Messoa and

---

[1] See pp. 182, 243, and 285.
[2] See Ehrenberg, s.v. obai, in P.–W., 34. Halbband (1937), cols. 1693–1704.
[3] See Ehrenberg, 'obai', cols. 1693, 1694, 1699.
[4] Wade-Gery, *Essays in Greek History*, p. 79.

Limnai.[1] It must therefore be true of Pitane and Kynosoura as well, since these were the other two local components of the nuclear City of Sparta—Messoa being associated, apparently, with Pitane, and Limnai with Kynosoura.[2] Amyklai—which was, of course, likewise a locality, not a region, and was only about three miles away from Sparta City— was almost certainly,[3] though not beyond question,[4] given the same status as the original four localities after the incorporation of Amyklai in the Spartan state, at a date perhaps shortly before the mid-point of the eighth century B.C. Inscriptions dating from the Age of the Principate testify that, by then, there was a sixth local sub-division, the Neopolitai,[5] which was on a par with the Limnatai, Kynosoureis, and Pitanatai, since in this age these four local sub-divisions competed with each other in contests between their respective 'sphaireis'.[6] There is no record of either the Messoatai or the Amyklaioi taking part in these contests, and the Amyklaioi did not take part in the ritual at the altar of Artemis Orthia either, though the Messoatai did.[7] Inscriptions[8] show that, in the period beginning in 146 B.C., Amyklai was still a corporate personality. There is no sure case of the name Messoa occurring on an inscription;[9] so we may infer that, by this time, Messoa had been absorbed into the Neopolitai.

We may guess that the Neopolitai had been added, as a sixth local

[1] Strabo, *Geographica*, Book VIII, chap. 5, § 3 (C. 364).
[2] See pp. 171–2. The annual ritual of flogging boys at the altar of Artemis Orthia, which was in Limnai (Pausanias, Book III, chap. 16, § 7), was said (ibid., §§ 9–11) to have arisen out of a fight at this altar between the Limnatai and Kynosoureis on the one side and the Messoatai and Pitanatai on the other.
[3] Pareti, *Storia di Sparta Arcaïca*, Parte I, pp. 179–81; Michell, op. cit., p. 99; Ehrenberg, 'Spartiaten und Lakedaimonier', pp. 28–9; Dickins, loc. cit, p. 7; Niese, 'Neue Beiträge zur Geschichte und Landeskunde Lakedaimons: Die Lakedäimonischen Periöken', p. 129.
[4] See Wade-Gery, *Essays in Greek History*, p. 76, n. 3. Busolt and Swoboda, op. cit., p. 645, n. 3, guess that Amyklai did not become an oba until Kleomenes III's revolution in 227 B.C.
[5] Ehrenberg. 'Spartiaten und Lakedaimonier', p. 29; idem, 'obai', col. 1696.
[6] These may have been either ball-players or boxers, since 'sphaira' means 'boxing-glove' as well as 'ball' (see Chrimes, *Ancient Sparta*, pp. 132–3). In Miss Chrimes's view, 'it seems safe to conclude', from the Spartan inscriptions of the Age of the Principate, 'that the phylai of the Roman period at Sparta were four in number, and that they were wholly athletic organizations, unconnected with the citizen-body except in so far as the state directly controlled the activities of the epheboi'. The inscriptional evidence does indicate that only four phylai (i.e. obai) took part in the 'sphaireis' competitions. It also proves, however, that Amyklai, which did not take part in these, was nevertheless still an oba in the second or last century B.C. (see Ehrenberg, 'obai', col. 1696). There is no evidence at all that the obai had ceased to be units of public administration. This function is not incompatible with the institution of athletic competitions between four of them. Amyklai had extensive local autonomy within the Spartan body politic at the date of *I.G.*, vol. v, fasc. 1, No. 26 (see Ehrenberg, 'obai', cols. 1696–7). This is not, of course, evidence for the local constitution of Amyklai, or of any of the other obai, in earlier periods (see ibid.).
[7] Pausanias, Book III, chap. 16, § 9.
[8] e.g. *I.G.*, vol. v, fasc. 1, Nos. 26, 27, 515; *C.I.G.* 1338; Dittenberger, *Sylloge*, 2nd ed., vol. ii, pp. 52–3, No. 451.   [9] Chrimes, *Ancient Sparta*, p. 163, with n. 4.

sub-division of the Spartan citizen-body, to the previously existing five by King Kleomenes III,[1] when, in 227 B.C., he had supplemented the existing Spartan citizen-body with 'the most eligible of the perioikoi', in order to fill his cadre of 4,000 Spartan hoplites.[2] Since the 4,000 all received kleroi carved out of Sparta's own city-state territory, these perioikoi who were now drafted into the new Spartan politeuma of 4,000 neo-homoioi must have migrated from their home-towns to Sparta; and Neopolis will have been the new local sub-division that was created to accommodate them there.

Thus the number of the local sub-divisions will have been four until the incorporation of Amyklai, five from then until 227 B.C.,[3] and six from 227 B.C. until Messoa dropped out. The new board of annual public officers called patronomoi, which Kleomenes III created to eclipse the gerousia[4] (and, no doubt, to eclipse the board of ephors as well), consisted of six members,[5] whereas the ephorate, which had probably been created after the incorporation of Amyklai,[6] consisted of five members.[7]

This system of local sub-divisions was a permanent feature of Spartan life and political organization,[8] though, as has been noted, only three out of the six of them were in existence from first to last. At different

---

[1] See Pareti, *Storia di Sparta Arcaïca*, Parte I, p. 175; eundem, 'Le tribù personali e le tribù locali a Sparta', p. 468, n. 2, and pp. 469 and 470.

[2] ἀναπληρώσας δὲ τὸ πολίτευμα τοῖς χαριεστάτοις τῶν περιοίκων, ὁπλίτας τετρακισχιλίους ἐποίησε (Plutarch, *Cleomenes*, chap. 11).

[3] This number is accepted by Lenschau, 'Die Entstehung des spartanischen Staates', p. 280. The number has been challenged (see p. 154, n. 1) by Beattie in loc. cit., pp. 46–8, on the strength of an inscription, found at Amyklai (*C.I.G.*, vol. i (p. 34), No. 15; *S.G.D.* i (iii) 2, No. 4412; *I.G.*, vol. v, fasc. 1, p. 151, No. 722). This inscription contains the words πεδ' ὅϝᾶς Ἀρκάλōν (Beattie, ibid., p. 41); and, since the names of five obai, before the creation of the Neopolitai, are known already, Beattie argues (p. 49) that the obai were more than five in number, that they were small, perhaps outlying, districts, that there may have been thirty of them (ibid.), and that, in the 'Lycurgan' rhetra, the obai may be sub-divisions of the phylai, not a separate set of units (p. 48).

The inscription is slightly suspect, since it is held to date from the early fifth or even from the late sixth century B.C. (p. 58), i.e. to be 400 years older than all but one other known inscription in Laconia. Moreover, the original stone has been lost. However, if we accept it as being an authentic document of that early date, ὅϝᾱ Ἀρκάλōν can be explained, consistently with the rest of our information, as being an alternative name for the ὤβα of the Amyklaioi that set up the inscription of a much later date that has been cited on p. 261, n. 8. As Beattie himself points out (p. 49), the Arkaloi are the people of Argalos, the mythical son and successor of the mythical eponym of Amyklai, Amyklas (Pausanias, Book III, chap. 1, § 3). Beattie's conclusions are rejected by Jones, *Sparta*, p. 172. Forrest, *A History*, pp. 42–3, takes them more seriously.

[4] Pausanias, Book II, chap. 9, § 1.   [5] Pareti, 'Le tribù personali e le tribù locali a Sparta', p. 468.   [6] See pp. 218–20, and Pareti, ibid., p. 469, n. 1.

[7] The number of the nomophylakes and of the bidiaioi, too, was five (Pareti, ibid., p. 468). The number of the bidiaioi was eventually increased to six (Pareti, ibid., p. 468, n. 2). Cp. eundem, *Storia di Sparta Arcaïca*, Parte I, pp. 175–6.

[8] The relation between the five obai that were in existence from *circa* 755 B.C. to 227 B.C. and the five lokhoi into which the phalanx of Spartiate homoioi appears to have been divided

times, and by different people, the Spartan sub-divisions of this class were called by different names. Herodotus calls them demoi,[1] perhaps on the analogy of the demes of Attica. Pausanias calls Amyklai a kome;[2] and probably most non-Spartan Greeks would have thought of all the Spartan local sub-divisions as being κῶμαι which at Sparta, as elsewhere, had combined to form a city-state but which, at Sparta, had never coalesced with each other completely. The Spartans themselves used neither of these words.[3] In the 'sphaireis' inscriptions of the Age of the Principate the four competing local communities call themselves phylai,[4] but in recording their victories they call their defeated competitors obai. Thus, in this context and age, phylai and obai were synonyms for the four local sub-divisions that took part in the 'sphaireis' competition; and it looks as if, of the two names, 'obai' must be the authentic and original one;[5] for 'oba' is a relatively rare and peculiar word, whereas, by this date, 'phyle' had become the common Greek name for any main sub-division, whether based on locality or on heredity, in the administrative structure of a city-state.[6] Moreover, the local community at Amyklai, which, in the period beginning in 146 B.C., was presumably still on a par with the local communities in Sparta town, uses the term oba to describe itself.[7]

If obai was the original name for the Spartan local sub-divisions, these sub-divisions must be what are meant by the obai into which the 'Lycurgan' rhetra directs that the Spartan citizen-body is to be divided.[8] If so, the phylai into which it is also to be divided cannot have been synonymous with the obai at the date at which the rhetra was drafted[9]—a date which, in all probability, was between the mid point and the close of the seventh century B.C. The phylai of the rhetra will have been the three Dorian[10] phylai. It has been suggested in another context[11] that the three

in 479 B.C. (see Wade-Gery in *The Cambridge Ancient History*, vol. iii (1925), p. 562) is discussed in chap. 5, section (ii), on pp. 371-2.

[1] Ἀρχίη ... αὐτὸς ἐν Πιτάνῃ συνεγενόμην· δήμου γὰρ τούτου ἦν (Book III, chap. 55).

[2] Book III, chap. 19, § 6 (see also Ehrenberg, 'obai', col. 1699).

[3] Pareti, 'Le tribù personali e le tribù locali a Sparta', p. 463.

[4] Pitane and Kynosoura are also called phylai by Hesychius, and Messoa is called a phyle by Stephanus of Byzantium.

[5] Hesychius: ὠβάτας· τοὺς φυλέτας· ὠβαὶ (ὦβοι) τόποι μεγαλομερεῖς· ὡς τὰς κώμας· ὠγὴ κώμη· οὐαὶ φυλαί, Κύπριοι. See also Ehrenberg, 'obai', col. 1693; eundem, 'Spartiaten und Lakedaimonier', p. 26; Den Boer, op. cit., p. 172.

[6] This point is made by Ehrenberg, 'obai', col. 1694.

[7] See p. 261, n. 8. 'I believe the institution of the obes to have aimed at a union of all free citizens, both the genuine Spartans and the inhabitants of Amyclae who were so closely associated with Sparta, and later those of Neopolis' (Den Boer, op. cit., p. 173).

[8] Pareti, *Storia di Sparta Arcaïca*, Parte I, p. 173; Wade-Gery, *Essays in Greek History*, p. 71; Berve, op. cit., p. 22; Hammond, 'The Lycurgean Reform at Sparta', p. 59; Huxley, op. cit., p. 116, n. 239; Roussel, op. cit., p. 30; M. Treu, 'Der Schlusssatz der Grossen Rhetra', in *Hermes*, 76. Band (1941), pp. 22-42, on p. 39.

[9] Ehrenberg, 'obai', col. 1693; Norvin, in *Classica et Mediaevalia*, vol. iii, pp. 67-8.

[10] Pareti, 'Le tribù personali e le tribù locali a Sparta', pp. 464-5; Chrimes, *Ancient Sparta*,

Dorian phylai originated in the Asian Doris, and that they were adopted in some of the nearest of the North-West-Greek-speaking city-states in the Peloponnese during the period—perhaps beginning in the latter part of the eighth century B.C.—when Asian Greek influence, artistic and literary, as well as political, was radiating actively into European Greece.

By the Age of the Principate, when the Spartan obai had taken to calling themselves 'phylai', the Dorian set of three phylai will have long since fallen into oblivion at Sparta. The draftsman of the 'Lycurgan' rhetra had taken care to preserve the Dorian phylai at Sparta side by side with the local obai.[1] This will have been part of the policy, embodied in the 'Lycurgan' settlement, of satisfying the commoners without alienating the aristocrats; for the three Dorian phylai will have been a key part of the structure of the aristocratic regime at Sparta which the 'Lycurgan' reforms were now superseding. At the same time, these reforms will have taken the first step towards putting the set of Dorian phylai out of currency if we are right in holding[2] that, in the 'Lycurgan' new model army, the hoplite phalanx was organized in five obal units in place of the three phylai that had been the units in which the aristocratic houses and their dependents had gone into battle.

The existence of the three Dorian phylai at Sparta—in one phase, at least, of Spartan history—has been certain since the discovery, in 1918, of a papyrus containing a previously unknown fragment of Tyrtaios' poetry[3] in which the members of the three tribes are mentioned as going into action separately from each other.[4] The obvious interpretation of this passage is that the Spartan army was still divided into the three Dorian phylai at the time of 'the Second Spartano-Messenian War';[5] and

p. 165; Wade-Gery, *Essays in Greek History*, p. 71; Jones, *Sparta*, p. 31; Michell, op. cit., p. 101. Ehrenberg agrees in 'Der Gesetzgeber von Sparta', p. 20, but dissents in 'Spartiaten und Lakedaimonier', p. 31, n. 1, and in *Neugründer des Staates*, p. 34.

[11] See Part I, chap. 3, p. 44.

[1] φυλὰς φυλάξαντα (? a pun on φυλή and φυλάσσειν) καὶ ὠβὰς ὠβάξαντα. See Wade-Gery, *Essays in Greek History*, pp. 70–1.

[2] See chap. 5.   [3] Fragm. 1 in Diehl's *Anthologia Lyrica*.

[4] χωρὶς Πάμφυλοί τε καὶ Ὑλλεῖς ἠ[δὲ Δυμῆνες].

[5] Hammond, 'The Lycurgean Reform at Sparta', p. 50, suggests that what Tyrtaios may have been saying in this fragment is that the formations in which our (pre-'Lycurgan') ancestors fought were the three Dorian phylai, but that our own present-day formations are different. Forrest seems inclined to adopt Hammond's interpretation (*A History*, pp. 56–7). Hammond cannot admit that Tyrtaios is saying that the Spartan army was still divided into the three Dorian phylai in his own day, because Hammond is arguing in this article that the conventional Greek dating of 'Lycurgus' in the ninth century B.C. is historically correct, and is also arguing, on the strength of the aorist participles φυλάξαντα and ὠβάξαντα in the 'Lycurgan' rhetra, that the phylai and obai that are to be organized are new units—i.e. that the phylai of the rhetra are not the Dorian phylai (p. 43, with n. 6). These assumptions are not necessary if we date the 'Lycurgan' reforms, and, with them, the 'Lycurgan' rhetra, after the end of 'the Second Spartano-Messenian War'. Kiechle, *Lakonien und Sparta*, pp. 149–50, seems likely to be right in holding that both the phylai and the obai of the rhetra were existing institutions, which the rhetra simply confirmed. It seems unnecessary to assume, as Forrest

the obvious interpretation of the 'Lycurgan' rhetra is that, in the reforms which followed that war, the three Dorian tribes were maintained,[1] in name at least, though their practical importance may have been diminished henceforward by the adoption of the five obai, in place of the three phylai, as the units for the organization of the new Spartan hoplite phalanx.[2]

Even before the presence of the three Dorian phylai at Sparta had been proved for certain by the discovery of the Tyrtaean papyrus, it had been virtually proved by Pareti's acumen in assembling and interpreting evidence that was previously known.[3] There is also indirect evidence for the presence of the three Dorian phylai at Sparta in the shape of Spartan public bodies in which the number of the members was a multiple of three:[4] for instance, the thirty members of the gerousia and the three hundred hippeis, who must have been authentic cavalry before they were transformed, under the 'Lycurgan' regime, into an élite of the youngest age-group of the hoplite phalanx of the homoioi.[5] Other traces, at Sparta, of the presence of the three Dorian phylai may be the organization of the Karneia festival there,[6] in which the participants were grouped in multiples of three,[7] and possibly, though not probably, the enigmatic 'triekades', which 'Lycurgus' is credited by Herodotus[8] with having founded, together with most other Spartan institutions except the monarchy.

assumes in *A History*, pp. 43–5, that 'Lycurgus' co-ordinated the obai and the phylai with each other.

[1] Wade-Gery, *Essays in Greek History*, p. 71; Berve, op. cit., p. 22; Pareti, *Storia di Sparta Arcaïca*, Parte I, p. 173; Kiechle, *Lakonien und Sparta*, p. 149, hold that the phylai of the rhetra are the Dorian phylai.

[2] See Wade-Gery in *The Cambridge Ancient History*, vol. iii (1925), p. 560.

[3] See Pareti, 'Le tribù personali . . .', pp. 471–3. He cites Schol. Pind. *Pyth.* I, l. 12: Παμφυλὶς καὶ Δυμανὶς φυλαὶ ἐν Λακεδαίμονι, and Schol. Aristoph., *Plutus*, l. 385: φυλαὶ ἐν Λακεδαίμονι Παμφυλεῖς καὶ Δυμανεῖς καὶ Δωριεῖς. Hesychius: Δύμη· ἐν Σπάρτῃ φυλὴ καὶ τόπος, is evidence, not that there was a local oba called Dyme at Sparta, but that the Dorian phyle Dymanes was present there (see Pareti in loc. cit., pp. 465–6; Ehrenberg, 'obai', col. 1695). Busolt and Swoboda, op. cit., p. 645, guess that Dyme was the fifth of the original obai; but on p. 645, n. 3, they note that there is no mention of a Dyme in surviving Spartan inscriptions. F. D. Harvey, however, has suggested that there may be literary evidence for there having been an oba called Dyma at Sparta ('Oxyrhyncus Papyrus 2390 and Early Spartan History', in the *Journal of Hellenic Studies*, vol. lxxxvii (1967), pp. 62–73). In l. 25 of a fragment of a commentary on a poem of Alkman's in which the four letters Δυμα occur twice, in each case with a lacuna immediately following, Harvey conjectures Δύμα[s] in the first case and Δύμα[ινα] in the second. Harvey's reconstruction of this fragment is acute, but it is, of course, no more than guesswork.   [4] See Jannet, op. cit., p. 12.

[5] Xenophon, *Lak. Pol.*, chap. 4. See also the present work and Part, chap. 3, section (ii), p. 232; chap. 4, section (iii), p. 326; and chap. 5, pp. 399 and 401–2.

[6] The Karneia were introduced into Sparta in Ol. 26, 1 (i.e. 676 B.C.) according to Sosibius apud Athenaeum, Book XIV 635 e–f. See also p. 290, n. 5.

[7] Twenty-seven phratriai grouped in nine skiades. See Demetrius of Scepsis' account in Athenaeus, Book IV, 141 e–f.

[8] Book I, chap. 65. Pareti suggests, 'Le tribù personali . . .', p. 473, that each Dorian

Qualifications for Election to the Spartan Gerousia after the 'Lycurgan' Reform

ONE feature of the Lycurgan reform was an attenuation of the previously extreme differences in power and wealth between different classes in the Spartan community. The dual monarchy, for instance, was now merged in the gerousia as far as its civil powers were concerned. The civil prerogatives now still left to the crown as such, beyond the kings' powers as *ex officio* gerontes, were unimportant.[1] Simultaneously the aristocracy[2] was merged in the damos for military purposes. Instead of continuing to serve either as cavalry or as 'jay-walking' hoplites, the aristocrats were now incorporated in the new model hoplite phalanx of the 'homoioi',[3] side by side, and on a par, with the commoners who had been given the means of likewise becoming full-time professional hoplite phalangites through being endowed with kleroi carved out of the state lands whose produce the aristocrats were now no longer able to monopolize. The corps of three hundred hippeis, which must originally have been the aristocrats' preserve, had now been transformed into a *corps d'élite* of hoplite homoioi, picked from the youngest of the age-classes of military age[4] by a method of selection that was intensely competitive.[5]

At the same time, the levelling process had not been complete. The aristocrats had received their kleroi of former state land without being deprived of their ancestral freehold estates in Sparta's non-helot nuclear territory. The kings had lost most of their special civil prerogatives, but their military prerogatives had been left to them intact. So much seems to be clear, but it is not so clear whether or not the aristocrats retained any special privileges or advantages, not shared by the rest of the homoioi, for standing as candidates for election to the gerousia.

Before the 'Lycurgan' reform the gerousia had, we may guess,[6] represented the aristocratic houses. We may also guess that, whether or

phyle was divided into three 'triekades'. A different explanation of the 'triekades' is suggested in the present Part, chap. 5, on p. 383.

---

[1] See pp. 232–3.
[2] The existence of an hereditary aristocracy at Sparta is assumed by Busolt and Swoboda, op. cit., p. 612; by Jones, *Sparta*, p. 170; and by Forrest, *A History*, pp. 29 and 63. Ehrenberg, 'Der Damos im archaïschen Sparta', pp. 298–9, finds that there is no evidence for there ever having been an aristocracy at Sparta. Cp. Berve, op. cit., *passim*.
[3] By contrast, in the Cretan city-states, the hippeis still possessed horses, and bred them, in Ephorus' day (Strabo, *Geographica*, Book X, chap. 4, § 18 (C. 481–2)).
[4] See Xenophon, *Lak. Pol.*, chap. 4.
[5] See the anecdote about the rejected candidate Paidaretos in Plutarch, *Lycurgus*, chap. 25; *Apophthegmata Laconica*, Paidaretos, 3.
[6] This is Jones's guess in *Sparta*, p. 170, and Forrest's in *A History*, p. 63.

not the members had nominally been appointed by the crown, in practice
the places had been filled by the aristocratic houses' representatives as
of right. Two out of the thirty places in the gerousia had now been assigned to the kings *ex officio*, and the remaining twenty-eight had been
made elective[1]—the electorate, for this purpose, being the damos—
though, once elected, a geron held office for the rest of his life.[2] Election
to the gerousia was a coveted honour,[3] and the electorate was canvassed
by the candidates.[4] One requisite qualification for standing for election
to the gerousia is known for certain. The candidate must have completed his sixtieth year[5] (i.e. must have reached the age at which he
became exempt from military service). Were any other qualifications
required besides this? Aristotle's references to the elections to the gerousia
suggest that there were, though his statements are not explicit.[6]

Aristotle draws a contrast between the elections to the gerousia and the
elections to the ephorate. For the ephorate, any homoios was eligible,[7]
with the consequence that men who were extremely poor were often
elected.[8] By contrast, the gerousia was the preserve of the καλοὶ κἀγαθοί.[9]
This term, like the English word 'gentleman',[10] is equivocal. It may mean
what it purports to mean, namely 'men of good breeding and good
character'; alternatively, it may bear the conventional meaning of men
who have inherited a position of social privilege through the accident
of birth, without implying that they are also living up to the literal
meaning of the label that their class has assumed. Aristotle appears to
be using the word in the literal sense when he says that election to
the gerousia is 'the prize of virtue';[11] Xenophon is certainly using the
word literally apropos of the election of gerontes at Sparta;[12] but the

---

[1] See Forrest, *A History*, pp. 46 and 51. Aristotle calls the method of electing the gerontes
'childish' (*Politics*, Book II, chap. 6 (9), § 18 (1271a, l. 10)), and so indeed it is, as Plutarch
describes it (*Lycurgus*, chap. 26). On the other hand, Isocrates, *Panathenaïcus*, 154, says that the
election of the Spartan gerontes is taken as seriously (μετὰ τοσαύτης σπουδῆς) as the election
of the Athenian Areopagitai.

[2] Aristotle, *Politics*, Book II, chap. 6 (9), § 17 (1271a), criticizes the grant of life-tenure for
an office, involving the most important judicial functions, for which candidates were not
eligible till they had reached an age at which they might become senile any day. Xenophon,
Lak. Pol., chap. 10, §§ 1–3, suggests that the keenness of the competition for election to the
gerousia, and the importance of the gerontes' judicial functions, were prophylactics against
senility. Aristotle's view is the more convincing of the two.

[3] Aristotle, *Politics*, Book II, chap. 6 (9), § 15 (1270b), and §§ 18–19 (1272a).

[4] Ibid., § 18.   [5] Plutarch, *Lycurgus*, 26.

[6] Niese, 'Zur Verfassungsgeschichte Lakedaimons', p. 64, holds that there were, in truth,
other required qualifications, but that we have no information about them.

[7] *Politics*, Book II, chap. 6 (9), § 14 (1270b, ll. 8–9); § 15 (1270b, ll. 19–20 and 25–6).

[8] Ibid., § 14 (1270b, ll. 9–10).

[9] Ibid., § 15 (1270b, l. 24).

[10] Busolt and Swoboda, op. cit., p. 662, n. 4.

[11] *Politics*, Book II, chap. 6 (9), § 15 (1270b, l. 24). Cp. Polybius, Book VI, chap. 10, § 9:
κατ᾽ ἐκλογὴν ἀριστίνδην κεκριμένοι; Plutarch, *Lycurgus*, chap. 26, τὸν ἄριστον ἀρετῇ κριθέντα.

[12] Xenophon, *Lak. Pol.*, chap. 10, §§ 1–3.

conventional meaning, signifying members—not necessarily virtuous—of a privileged class, is indicated by Aristotle's observation[1] that men who have been elected to the gerousia are notorious for taking bribes and granting favours in a big way at the expense of the public interest. Corrupt 'gentlemen' can be 'gentlemen' only by birth, not by merit; and, in another place,[2] Aristotle does imply that the gerontes were in fact elected out of a limited panel. One of the points, he tells us, that were made by people who maintained that Sparta was a democracy was that, of the two most important public offices, 'one was elected by the damos, while, for the other, the damos itself was eligible (the members of the damos elect the gerontes and are themselves eligible for the ephorate)'. Finally he notes[3] that at Elis, under a former oligarchic regime, membership of the gerousia had been restricted to a small clique; that the method of electing the gerontes had been δυναστευτική; and that the method at Sparta was similar. In this passage the exact meaning of Aristotle's word δυναστευτική is not transparent; but δυναστευτική is contrasted with πολιτική in his description of the 'remedy' for the inordinately oligarchical constitutions of the Cretan states,[4] where the kosmoi (the Cretan counterparts of the Spartan ephors) were elected from a restricted circle of privileged families, and where the gerousia was recruited from retired kosmoi. In this passage πολιτική clearly means 'constitutional', and δυναστευτική stands for the lawless overriding of the constitution by main force. Aristotle's conclusion is ἔχει τι πολιτείας ἡ τάξις, ἀλλ' οὐ πολιτεία ἐστὶν ἀλλὰ δυναστεία μᾶλλον.

The information that Aristotle has given us is inconclusive.[5] Evidently the qualifications for candidature, and the electors' choice among the qualified candidates, were manipulated in a way that made the 'Lycurgan', like the pre-'Lycurgan', gerousia a preserve for a limited section of the Spartiate citizen-body.[6] Perhaps the difference was that the *de facto* limitation was now covert,[7] instead of being openly avowed, and that the limiting qualification was now wealth instead of birth.[8] Im-

---

[1] *Politics*, Book II, chap. 6 (9), § 18 (1271a, ll. 3–5).

[2] Book IV, chap. 7, § 5 (1294b).   [3] Book V, chap. 5, § 8 (1306a).

[4] Book II, chap. 7 (10), §§ 6–7 (1272a–b).

[5] This is particularly baffling for present-day historians if Forrest, *A History*, p. 63, is right in holding that 'the composition of the Gerousia was the issue that lay at the heart of the trouble' which led to the 'Lycurgan' reform.

[6] Dum, op. cit., pp. 79, 97, 103.

[7] Jones, *Sparta*, p. 17, takes the view that, under the 'Lycurgan' constitution, there were no juridically required qualifications, either of noble birth or of wealth, for making an homoios who had turned sixty eligible for membership of the gerousia.

[8] Busolt and Swoboda, op. cit., p. 662, n. 4, hold that the 'Lycurgan' gerousia was not confined to nobles. Jannet, op. cit., p. 23, holds that the gerontes were always chosen from among the nobles only. Forrest, *A History*, pp. 46, 51, 63, 113, seems to take the same view as Jannet, but on p. 63 he suggests that, after the 'Lycurgan' reform, wealth became, *de facto*, an open sesame for election to the gerousia.

mediately after the inauguration of the 'Lycurgan' constitution, the rich would be identical with the ex-aristocrats; but, as time passed and property changed hands, wealth and aristocratic descent would tend to coincide with each other less and less closely.

We may conclude that, in theory, the 'Lycurgan' constitution abolished aristocratic privilege in all fields;[1] that, in the military field, the *Gleichschaltung* of the aristocrats in the new class of homoioi was a reality; but that, in the gerousia, the aristocracy retained its pre-'Lycurgan' monopoly *de facto*,[2] though, as time went on, the criterion for eligibility for membership in the gerousia tended to become wealth rather than birth.

Under the 'Lycurgan' constitution, Sparta was governed by the ephors with the gerontes' concurrence. If the ephors represented the poor majority of the homoioi, and the gerontes the rich minority, the government will have been carried on by compromises between wealth and numbers; and, since these were the two great powers in the Spartiate citizen-body under the 'Lycurgan' regime, the co-operation between ephors and gerontes will have been one of the factors that made for the domestic political stability for which 'Lycurgan' Sparta was celebrated.

PART III, CHAPTER 3, ANNEX IV

The Rhetra in Plutarch's Lycurgus, *Chapter 6*[3]

Διὸς Συλλανίου καὶ Ἀθανᾶς Συλλανίας ἱερὸν ἱδρυσάμενον, φυλὰς φυλάξαντα καὶ ὤβας ὠβάξαντα, τριάκοντα γερουσίαν σὺν ἀρχαγέταις καταστήσαντα, ὥρας ἐξ ὥρας ἀπελλάζειν μεταξὺ Βαβύκας τε καὶ Κνακιῶνος, οὕτως εἰσφέρειν καὶ ἀφίστασθαι· †γαμωδανγοριανημην† καὶ κράτος. Αἱ δὲ σκολίαν ὁ δᾶμος ?†ἔροιτο,?† τοὺς πρεσβυγενέας καὶ ἀρχαγέτας ἀποστατῆρας ἦμεν.

EVERYTHING relating to this text has been a subject of dispute. It is not unanimously agreed that it is a genuine document. Eduard Meyer, who

[1] Eduard Meyer, op. cit., p. 255, n. 2; Michell, op. cit., pp. 43–4; Roussel, op. cit., p. 67; Ehrenberg, 'Spartiaten und Lakedaimonier', pp. 38–9; Treu, loc. cit., p. 39; Wüst, loc. cit., p. 62.

[2] See Kiechle, *Lakonien und Sparta*, pp. 2 and 176; Wade-Gery, in *The Cambridge Ancient History*, vol. iii, p. 560, n. 1; Berve, op. cit., p. 36.

[3] There is a lucid and exhaustive discussion of the rhetra in Wade-Gery's *Essays in Greek History*, pp. 37–85. In this paper, all the important questions arising out of this text are taken up; the alternative possible answers to each question are presented; and, in each case, the pros and cons are set out. Subsequent students of Spartan affairs may or may not agree with all of Wade-Gery's conclusions, but their own conclusions will not be authoritative if they have not been made in the light of the materials for making them that Wade-Gery's paper offers. See also Forrest, *A History*, pp. 40–60, with his translation of the text on p. 41; Den Boer, op. cit., pp. 153–96; Treu, loc. cit.; Jones, 'The Lycurgan Rhetra', in *Ancient Society and Institutions*, pp. 165–75; A. G. Tsopanakis, *La Rhètre de Lycurgue: L'Annexe-Tyrtée* (Thessaloníki, 1954, parartema 6 to *Helliniká*); A. von Blumental, 'Zur "lykurgischen" Rhetra', in *Hermes*,

holds,[1] as Wade-Gery[2] and Miss Jeffery[3] hold, that Plutarch's source for
it was Aristotle, also holds that it was a forgery that had been put into
circulation not more than about fifty years before the time at which
Aristotle was accepting it as being genuine.[4] In Meyer's view, it was a
product of the controversial literature about the merits or demerits of the
Spartan constitution that was evoked by Sparta's victory over Athens
in 404 B.C. and by the Spartan King Pausanias' exile in 395 B.C. Scholars
who accept Plutarch's document as being genuine (and these are the
majority) regard it as comprising part, at least, of the 'Lycurgan' constitution; and their datings therefore differ as widely as their datings of
'Lycurgus' himself or of the anonymous historical statesman whose work
goes by 'Lycurgus's' name. The range of the variant datings of 'Lycurgus'
extends over at least 400 years, running from the tenth to the sixth
century B.C. It has been suggested in a previous annex[5] that the only
trustworthy evidence for dating the rhetra is internal evidence, and that
this points to a date after the mid-point of the seventh century B.C.,
since, according to the rhetra, the damos of hoplite phalangites already
possesses the ultimate sovereign authority in the Spartan state.[6]

There is also disagreement about what the word 'rhetra' means in this
context. The literal meaning of the word is 'a solemn pronouncement'
or perhaps, more precisely, 'a form of words to which a number of people
agree' or 'are asked to agree'.[7] At Sparta the word 'rhetra' certainly had

---

77. Band (1942), pp. 212–15; D. Butler, 'Competence of the Demos in the Spartan Rhetra',
in *Historia*, 11. Band (1962), pp. 385–96.
Anyone who tries to interpret the rhetra has to propose an emendation of the corrupt
passage γαμωδανγοριανημην in the second sentence. Most of the emendations hitherto proposed include words that, if correctly thus restored, are ἅπαξ λεγόμενα in the extant remains
of Greek literature and inscriptions. In Tsopanakis's, Blumental's, and Butler's emendations
there is in each case one restored word that, etymologically, seems far-fetched. Fortunately
the last two words of the, save for these, corrupt sentence—namely καὶ κράτος—are clear,
and it also seems certain that the first letter in the corrupt passage should be emended from
γ to δ and that the first four letters of the passage will have been δαμω. This might be either
the dative singular of δᾶμος or the first two syllables of the genitive plural of a word δαμώδης,
meaning 'member of the damos'. The existence of this term might be inferred from the term
νεοδαμώδεις, which was coined during the war of 431–404 B.C. as a label for helots who had
been released from serfdom as a reward for their having volunteered to perform military
service as hoplites. However, the genitive plural of δαμώδεις would be δαμωδέων, not the
first-declension form δαμωδᾶν. In any case, the corrupt passage must have begun with either
the word δάμῳ, or some derivative of it; and we can conclude, with some assurance, that,
whatever the correct version of the corrupt passage may be, Plutarch's interpretation of
the second sentence of the rhetra—ἐπικρῖναι κύριος ἦν ὁ δῆμος—is approximately right.

[1] Op. cit., p. 262.   [2] *Essays in Greek History*, pp. 66–7 *et alibi*.
[3] L. H. Jeffery in *Historia*, 10. Band (1961), p. 147.
[4] Eduard Meyer, op. cit., p. 267, followed by Neumann, loc. cit., p. 67, and by Kessler,
op. cit., pp. 33–4.
[5] Chap. 3, Annex I.
[6] 'The rhetra was an act of the Spartan ekklesia; it was enacted during the crisis which
succeeded the Messenian Revolt' (Wade-Gery, *Essays in Greek History*, p. 59).
[7] Ibid., p. 64.

the precise official meaning of a 'bill' presented to the damos by the gerousia, whether on the gerousia's own initiative or on an ephor's initiative. It also meant the law into which a 'bill' was converted if and when the assembly adopted it. The word is used to mean 'bill' or 'law' in Plutarch's *Agis* throughout,[1] and there is also inscriptional evidence for this usage.[2] 'Rhetra' is also used to mean a solemn treaty or agreement.[3] Plutarch, probably following Aristotle on this point too, holds that the 'Lycurgan' rhetrai (he cites three minor rhetrai besides the constitutional one) are legislative acts embodying oracles.[4]

This last-mentioned interpretation of the meaning of 'rhetra' is inconsistent with the meaning given to the word by Plutarch himself in his *Agis*. At the same time it is an alternative meaning that could also be borne by the word. The reason why Aristotle (if he is Plutarch's source here) took 'rhetra' to mean 'oracle' in this connection is because the contents of the constitutional rhetra, as paraphrased in three elegiac couplets quoted by Plutarch[5] and attributed by him to Tyrtaios,[6] are said, in the first of these couplets, to have been prescribed in oracles that had been brought back from Delphi[7] to Sparta (presumably by Pythioi representing one or both of the Spartan kings). Tyrtaios (if these couplets are truly his) does not, however, give the name 'rhetra' to the prescriptions that he is paraphrasing. He calls them 'oracles of the god and potent words'.[8] He does introduce the word 'rhetrai' in the last of the six lines, using it in the official Spartan sense of 'bills' or 'enactments'.[9] We may conclude that this, and not either 'oracle' or 'treaty', is the meaning of the word 'rhetra' as applied to the document reproduced by Plutarch.[10] This conclusion is borne out by the form of the document. It is in prose, whereas Delphic oracles were usually handed out in hexameter verse.

If Plutarch's constitutional rhetra is an enactment of the assembly of the Spartan damos, two points made by Wade-Gery must be right.

---

[1] See Wade-Gery, ibid., pp. 64–5.
[2] *I.G.*, vol. v, fasc. 1, No. 20, ll. 2–3, and No. 1498.
[3] Wade-Gery, ibid., pp. 63–4; Huxley, op. cit., p. 46.
[4] Μαντείαν ἐκ Δελφῶν ... ἣν ῥήτραν καλοῦσιν (Plutarch, *Lycurgus*, chap. 6); τὰ μὲν οὖν τοιαῦτα νομοθετήματα ῥήτρας ὠνόμασεν [ὁ Λυκοῦργος], ὡς παρὰ τοῦ θεοῦ νομιζόμενα καὶ χρησμοὺς ὄντα (chap. 13).
[5] Plutarch, *Lycurgus*, chap. 6.
[6] Eduard Meyer, in loc. cit., holds, of course, that these couplets are forgeries, like the text of the rhetra that they paraphrase. A longer version of the Tyrtaean couplets, quoted from Diodorus in the *Excerpta de Sententiis*, looks like a 'doctored' edition of the original (see Wade-Gery, *Essays in Greek History*, pp. 57–9 and 68–9); but this does not impugn the genuineness of Plutarch's version.
[7] See Wade-Gery, ibid., pp. 59–60 and 67.
[8] Μαντείας τε θεοῦ καὶ τελεέντ' ἔπεα (2 (Bergk–Hiller–Crusius) = 3b (4) (Diehl), l. 2).
[9] Wade-Gery, ibid., p. 62.
[10] See ibid., p. 37.

In the first place the subject of the infinitive verb ἀπελλάζειν and the series of preceding aorist participles in the third person singular is not an unnamed legislator, presumed to be 'Lycurgus'; the subject is the Spartan damos.[1] In the second place this rhetra is not an enactment of the 'Lycurgan' constitution as a whole. It is an enactment providing for one particular article of the constitution, namely 'the process of legislation'.[2] The assembly meets. The gerousia[3] then submits 'bills' which the assembly is empowered to criticize and perhaps to amend. The damos has the last word, but the gerousia is empowered to annul, or at least ignore, a counter-proposal of the assembly's of which the gerousia disapproves.[4] The acts, referred to in the participial clauses preceding the infinitive verb ἀπελλάζειν, are the subjects of earlier enactments by the damos which these clauses recapitulate;[5] and the recapitulation is not only summary; it is also incomplete. There is no mention here of the creation of the damos of the homoioi itself through the endowment of its members with kleroi carved out of state lands. There is no mention, either, of the transfer to the damos, from the crown, of the prerogative of appointing the annual board of ephors.[6] Yet the distribution of kleroi must have been an integral part of the constitutional reform, since, without kleroi, there could be no homoioi and no damos. The transfer of the appointment of the ephors to the damos may have been made at the same time, though it is also possible that it may have been made later. Presumably these two measures, both of which were of major importance, were enacted in separate rhetrai.

According to Plutarch[7] the original text of the rhetra dealing with the process of legislation ended with the end of the second sentence, in which it is enacted that the damos shall have the last word (κράτος). The third sentence, in which the extent of the damos' powers is diminished in the gerousia's favour, was, Plutarch says, a later addition. It is as evidence for this that Plutarch cites the three couplets that he attributes to Tyrtaios. However, as Wade-Gery points out,[8] the so-called addendum is referred to only in one word—εὐθείαις—in the second line of Tyrtaios' third couplet; all the rest of the second and third couplets is a paraphrase

---

[1] Wade-Gery, ibid,, pp. 43–4. For a discussion of the meaning of ἀπελλάζειν (? to meet at the celebration of a rite or ceremony called 'Apellai'), see ibid., pp. 44–7. 'There is no good evidence for supposing that 'apella' is Spartan for 'ekklesia' (ibid., p. 44). Cp. Forrest, *A History*, pp. 41 and 47.

[2] Wade-Gery, ibid., pp. 69–70. Cp. Tsopanakis, op. cit., p. 17. Wade-Gery guesses, ibid., p. 79, that the occasion on which this rhetra was introduced was the establishment of a new model army based on the organization of the Spartan damos by locality, in the obai.

[3] The gerousia ('the thirty', τούτους, for the MSS.' οὕτως) is the subject of εἰσφέρειν τε καὶ ἀφίστασθαι.

[4] See p. 236.
[5] Wade-Gery, ibid., pp. 69–70.
[6] See p. 227, n. 5.
[7] *Lycurgus*, chap. 6.
[8] *Essays in Greek History*, pp. 37, 54–5, and 67–8.

of the first two sentences; and there is therefore no evidence in this passage of Tyrtaios' poem *Eunomia*[1] that the third sentence was not part of the original text of the rhetra.[2]

If the text of the rhetra was derived by Plutarch from Aristotle, the Tyrtaean couplets and the belief that the third sentence of the rhetra was a later addition will presumably also have been derived from Aristotle. So, too, will Plutarch's statement[3] that the third sentence was added by Kings Polydoros and Theopompos, and that they persuaded the Spartan citizen-body to accept it by representing it, as 'Lycurgus' had represented the original text, as being an injunction from Delphi.

The attribution of the additional sentence to this pair of kings pre-supposes, of course, that the date of the original text of the 'Lycurgan' rhetra was at least as early as the First Olympiad (776 B.C.), which was Aristotle's dating of 'Lycurgus's' *floruit*. In the present work the original text of the rhetra has been dated after the middle of the seventh century B.C., on the strength of the evidence for the date of the introduction of hoplite phalanx-tactics in the Hellenic World.[4] If this dating is right, the date of the original text—and, *a fortiori*, the date of a subsequent addition (if the last sentence is in truth an addition)—must be between 100 and 150 years later than Polydoros' and Theopompos' generation.

Why did Aristotle, or his source, pick out these two kings as likely authors of the additional sentence? We may guess that he picked them out because they were the earliest two kings that were fully historical characters.[5] A seal and a house that purported to be Polydoros',[6] and a tomb that purported to be Theopompos',[7] were on view at Sparta at the date of Pausanias' visit. There were also traditions, whether authentic or fictitious, about some of Polydoros' and Theopompos' acts of

---

[1] The expanded version of the Tyrtaean couplets in Diodorus, Book VII, fragm. 12, § 6, is suspect.

[2] Jones, 'The Lycurgan Rhetra', in *Ancient Society and Institutions*, pp. 165–75, on p. 170, agrees with Wade-Gery that, *pace Plutarchi*, the third sentence of the rhetra is part of the original document, not a subsequently added rider. Forrest, *A History*, p. 47, points out that, if the last clause of the rhetra is a later addition, the word ἀποστατῆρας in this clause must be used in a different sense from the kindred word ἀφίστασθαι in the original text.

[3] In *Lycurgus*, chap. 6.

[4] See chap. 3, Annex I.

[5] See Eduard Meyer, op. cit., p. 206, and the present work, p. 222, with n. 3. Forrest, in 'The Dating of the Lycurgan Reforms', p. 160, argues that the missing subject of the verb ἔνεικαν in Tyrtaios (fragm. 2 (Bergk–Hiller–Crusius), = 3b (Diehl)) is the names 'Theopompos' and 'Polydoros'. On the strength of this hypothesis, Forrest (ibid., pp. 165–6) reconstructs Aristotle's train of reasoning as follows: 'For Aristotle, the *diskos* placed Lykourgos and his legislation in the neighbourhood of 776; the *rhetra* provided the substance of the legislation; but a poem of Tyrtaios seemed to give the credit for something very like this legislation to the kings Theopompos and Polydoros. Aristotle solved the contradiction by separating the rider from the *rhetra* (with or without further justification) and by limiting the reference of Tyrtaios to the rider.'

[6] Pausanias, Book III, chap. 11, § 10, cited on pp. 220–1.   [7] Ibid., chap. 16, § 6.

state, other than their alleged addition to the rhetra. But these other acts ascribed to each of them would make it unlikely, even if it had been chronologically possible, that they also cajoled the Spartan damos into surrendering some of the powers that it had previously won for itself.

This act, if genuine, was reactionary, whereas all other acts ascribed to Polydoros and Theopompos are liberal.[1] Theopompos is credited with having instituted the ephorate and with having been aware that, in doing this, he was diminishing the powers of the crown.[2] Polydoros is credited with having distributed 3,000 or 4,500 kleroi.[3] Among the successors of Theopompos in the Eurypontid line, names containing the word 'damos' or the word 'laos' are frequent.[4] Theopompos named his son Arkhidamos;[5] Arkhidamos named his Zeuxidamos; Zeuxidamos named his Anaxidamos. The name Arkhidamos recurs four times after its first occurrence, and, if we include in our count some recorded members of the house who were not kings, there were two Eurypontids called Leotykhidas and two called Agesilaos, besides an Anaxilaos, while the second Leotykhidas' distant cousin and rival was called Damaratos. This series of names in the Eurypontid house must have been intended to signify that, at any rate from Theopompos' reign onwards, the Eurypontidai were the damos' partisans. These facts would make it seem improbable that Theopompos and Polydoros would have promoted a reactionary piece of legislation, even if it had been chronologically possible for an addition to the 'Lycurgus' rhetra to have been made in their time.

PART III, CHAPTER 3, ANNEX V

Lycurgus, Man or God?[6]

AT the beginning of his *Lycurgus*, Plutarch presents an array of reasons for scepticism about the historicity of 'Lycurgus' that, cumulatively, is

---

[1] See Forrest in 'The Dating of the Lycurgan Reforms', pp. 170–1, and Jacoby, *F.G.H.*, Dritter Teil; Kommentar zu NR 297–607 (1955), pp. 660–1, No. 596 (15).

[2] Plutarch, *Lycurgus*, chap. 7.   [3] See p. 221.

[4] See the genealogies in Herodotus, Book VIII, chap. 131, and in Pausanias, Book III, chap. 7, §§ 5–11. Cp. Lenschau, 'Die Entstehung des spartanischen Staates', p. 284. Ehrenberg, 'Der Damos im archaïschen Sparta', pp. 291–2, finds evidence, in Spartan personal names, that at Sparta the damos was honoured already before the end of the eighth century B.C.

[5] In Pausanias' version of the genealogy, which omits Herodotus' Anaxandrides.

[6] See Eduard Meyer, op. cit., pp. 269–83: 'Die Ausbildung der Lykurgoslegende'. Huxley, in *Early Sparta*, published seventy years later (1962), was still maintaining (p. 42) that 'it is possible to assert at once that Lykourgos was not a god'. In 1963, Forrest was still believing in 'Lycurgus's' historicity ('The Dating of the Lycurgan Reforms', pp. 170 and 174–5). In 1968 he was conceding that 'Lycurgus' is 'possibly even a mythical figure' (*A History*, p. 40), but was still writing 'on the assumption that Lykourgos was a man' (ibid., p. 60).

overwhelming. Logically, Plutarch ought to have wound up his attempt
at a biography of 'Lycurgus's' at the end of this introductory passage by
pronouncing that there is no evidence that 'Lycurgus' was an historical
character, and that therefore there is nothing of any historical value
that can be said about him.

The sceptical introductory passage runs as follows:

It is quite impossible to make any statement about Lycurgus the law-giver
that is uncontroversial. There are wide divergencies in the accounts of his
genealogy, his travels, his death, and, last but not least, his legislative and
constitution-building activities, while the greatest disagreement of all is over
his date. Some authorities hold that Lycurgus was a contemporary of Iphitos',
and that he co-operated with Iphitos in drawing up the rules for the Olympic
truce. The philosopher Aristotle is a representative of this school. As evidence,
Aristotle cites the discus at Olympia on which Lycurgus' name is inscribed
in a good state of preservation. On the other hand, the chronologists—for
instance, Eratosthenes and Apollodoros—who reckon by the successive reigns
of the Spartan kings, date Lycurgus a very considerable number of years
earlier than the First Olympiad. Timaeus suspects that there were really two
Lycurguses at Sparta; that they were not contemporary with each other; and
that the acts of both of them have been attributed to one of the two because
of his celebrity. Timaeus thinks that the earlier Lycurgus was approximately
contemporary with Homer; and some authorities say that Lycurgus and
Homer met each other personally.[1] Xenophon gives an indication of the
earliness of Lycurgus' date when he says that he was a contemporary of the
Herakleidai.[2] Of course, the very latest of the kings at Sparta were also
Herakleidai by descent; but Xenophon seems, in this passage, to be intending
to refer to the first of the Herakleidai, who were the immediate successors of
Herakles himself.

This passage is damning;[3] yet Plutarch goes straight on to announce
that, in spite of the fact that the history of Lycurgus has manifestly lost
its bearings, 'we shall attempt to produce a narrative of Lycurgus' life
by following those sources that are the least self-contradictory and that
cite the best-known authorities'. The biography that follows is, of course,
worthless as such, though it contains valuable information about Spartan
institutions, as well as about the political constitution of which 'Lycurgus'
was reputed to be the author.

The one thing that we know for certain about 'Lycurgus'[4] is that, at
Sparta in the second century of the Christian Era, there was a shrine

---

[1] This story is reported by Ephorus apud Strabonem, *Geographica*, Book X, chap. 4, § 19
(C. 482).—A. J. T.

[2] Xenophon, *Lak. Pol.*, chap. 10, § 8.

[3] See Eduard Meyer, op. cit., p. 213, second paragraph.

[4] See ibid., p. 279; Neumann, loc. cit., p. 60; Norvin in *Classica et Mediaevalia*, vol. iii,
fasc. 1, p. 102.

dedicated to him, which Pausanias saw,[1] and there was an annual sacrifice in his honour.[2] 'Lycurgus's' shrine at Sparta was a temple ($\iota\epsilon\rho\acute{o}\nu$),[3] not an herôon;[4] and this means that, as Plutarch and Pausanias expressly state,[5] Lycurgus was worshipped at Sparta as a god, not as a human being who had been canonized posthumously[6]—like, for example, the sixth-century-B.C. ephor Khilon, an historical Spartan statesman whose herôon at Sparta was another of the sights that Pausanias saw there.[7] This impressively concordant literary testimony is corroborated by inscriptional evidence, which tells us that there was a public officer at Sparta bearing the title 'superintendent of the god Lycurgus'.[8]

The worship of 'Lycurgus' at Sparta as a god from at least Herodotus' day down to Pausanias' tallies with the text of an oracle from Delphi about 'Lycurgus' which had come to the notice of Herodotus[9] more than half a millennium before Pausanias' time. In this oracle, the Pythia tentatively expresses the opinion that 'Lycurgus' is a god, not a man.[10] This oracle seems likely to be genuine, because it is irrelevant to the context in which Herodotus cites it, and is therefore unlikely to have been fabricated, *ad hoc*, by Herodotus or his informants.

In this passage, Herodotus has just announced that he is going to explain how Sparta became a law-abiding community after having been about the most disorderly community in the entire Hellenic World. 'A distinguished Spartan named Lycurgus', he begins, 'came to Delphi, to the oracle, and'—we should expect Herodotus to have continued—'the Pythia gave him an oracle, briefing him on a new constitution for Sparta.' We should have expected this to be the sequel, because Plutarch says[11] that 'Lycurgus' brought his constitutional rhetra to Sparta from Delphi, and Tyrtaios, in the first of three elegiac couplets of his which Plutarch quotes,[12] says likewise that the provisions of the rhetra—which Tyrtaios paraphrases in the two following couplets—were brought back to Sparta from Delphi[13] by someone (Tyrtaios does not here say by whom, and he does not mention 'Lycurgus' in any of the surviving fragments of his poetry). This is what we should have expected; but, as Herodotus tells

---

[1] Herodotus, Book I, chap. 66; Strabo, *Geographica*, Book VIII, chap. 5 (C. 366); Aristotle, fragm. 534; Plutarch, *Lycurgus*, chap. 31; Pausanias, Book III, chap. 16, § 6. Strabo, Plutarch, and Pausanias are evidently drawing on a common source, which, according to Plutarch, is Aristotle.

[2] Strabo in loc. cit.

[3] Herodotus, Strabo, Plutarch, and Pausanias, locc. citt.

[4] Norvin, loc. cit., pp. 91–2.   [5] In locc. citt.

[6] On the other hand, Nikolaos of Damascus, fragm. 57 (in Müller, *F.H.G.*, vol. iii, p. 390), does say, apropos of the Spartans' cult of Lycurgus: $\beta\omega\mu\grave{o}\nu$ $\iota\delta\rho\upsilon\sigma\acute{a}\mu\epsilon\nu\sigma\iota$ $\theta\acute{\upsilon}\sigma\upsilon\sigma\iota$ $\acute{\omega}s$ $\mathring{\eta}\rho\omega\iota$ $\mathring{a}\nu\grave{a}$ $\pi\mathring{a}\nu$ $\check{\epsilon}\tau os$.

[7] Book III, chap. 16, § 4.

[8] $\grave{\epsilon}\pi\iota\mu\epsilon\lambda\eta\tau\grave{\eta}s$ $\theta\epsilon o\hat{\upsilon}$ $\Lambda\upsilon\kappa o\acute{\upsilon}\rho\gamma o\upsilon$ (*C.I.G.*, vol. i, p. 656, No. 1341).

[9] See Herodotus, Book I, chap. 65.   [10] See p. 242, n. 9.

[11] *Lycurgus*, chap. 6.   [12] Ibid.   [13] See p. 242, n. 9, and p. 271.

the story, 'Lycurgus' did not have time to open his mouth on the subject of constitutional reform at Sparta before the Pythia emitted the oracle about his being a god, not a mere mortal. It is only after he has quoted this, here irrelevant,[1] oracle that Herodotus goes on to add that 'some people say that, besides delivering the [irrelevant] oracle just quoted, the Pythia also briefed "Lycurgus" on the regime that is now in force at Sparta'.[2]

It seems to be a reasonable inference that Herodotus or his informants had been looking (perhaps in the royal archives at Sparta) for the hexameter text of an oracle in which this constitutional briefing had been given to 'Lycurgus' by the Pythia; that they had failed to find this pertinent text; and that Herodotus had therefore reproduced the only oracle about Lycurgus on which he had been able to lay hands, irrelevant though this oracle was to Herodotus' subject.[3]

The internal evidence of the oracle that Herodotus has quoted suggests that it is the Pythia's answer to an inquiry from Sparta that was not—or, at least, not directly—concerned with constitutional reform. It looks as if the Spartan Government had decided to establish, at Sparta, a shrine and festival for 'Lycurgus', but had been pulled up short by finding themselves in doubt as to whether the shrine ought to be a god's temple or a canonized mortal man's herôon. The kind of ritual that was to be instituted would depend on which kind of shrine 'Lycurgus's' was to be. To resolve this doubt, the Spartan Government had put in an inquiry at Delphi;[4] the Pythia's answer had, as so often, been ambiguous; but, since, on the whole, she had inclined to classify 'Lycurgus' as a god, the Spartan Government had decided that this hesitant answer of hers was sufficient to warrant them in treating 'Lycurgus' as a god.

There was, in truth, no room for 'Lycurgus' as a man at any point in Sparta's history during the period that came within the range of authentic historical knowledge. 'Lycurgus' must have been an eminent man if he qualified for being canonized even as a hero; so, if he was to be taken as having been an historical human character, his date must have been earlier than the beginning of authentically recorded Spartan history—i.e. earlier

---

[1] See Eduard Meyer, op. cit., p. 224; Andrewes, 'Eunomia', p. 92.

[2] See p. 242, n. 9.

[3] Diodorus, Book VII, fragm. 12, § 1, makes this oracle relevant to the 'Lycurgan' legislation by adding a spurious couplet.

[4] Andrewes's verdict on the oracle quoted by Herodotus is that, 'if it is genuine, it is the answer to a question put by others' (not by 'Lycurgus' himself, to whom the oracle is addressed).

'The question it asks is one which would have to be settled, for quite practical ritual reasons, before the worship of Lycurgus was established. . . . It follows that, at the time when this cult was established, the Spartans were wholly uncertain about the standing of Lycurgus' (*Probouleusis*, p. 17, n. 1; cp. eundem, *The Greek Tyrants*, p. 76; Roussel, *Sparte*, p. 41; Ehrenberg, *Neugründer des Staates*, p. 13).

than the reigns of Polydoros and Theopompos. A large enough place
could be found for even the most eminent of men in a period of Spartan
history in which most of the pages of the record were blank. Aristotle's
dating of 'Lycurgus' by the Olympic discus[1] fulfilled this condition. It
put 'Lycurgus's' *floruit* about one-third of a century before the beginning
of the First Spartano-Messenian War. Earlier dates ought to have provided 'Lycurgus' with still more ample room; and all other dates proposed for 'Lycurgus' were earlier than Aristotle's.[2] Thucydides dated the
inauguration of the law-abiding regime at Sparta nearly half a century
before the First Olympiad; the conventional date for 'Lycurgus' was
more than a century earlier than Aristotle's.[3]

Here, however, the attempt to insert an historical 'Lycurgus' into
Spartan history ran up against a difficulty. Though the authentic record
of Spartan history before the generation of Polydoros and Theopompos
was tenuous, there were already in existence genealogies of the two royal
houses which carried the two lines of kings back, in an unbroken series,
to Herakles; and 'Lycurgus's' name did not appear in either series.[4] The
earlier names in these two series were, no doubt, fictitious. They had,
however, come to be generally accepted as being genuine, and this
meant that, however important 'Lycurgus's' part in Sparta's history might
be held to be, there was no longer any room for him, even in the prehistoric age, as the king which he evidently ought to have been.

If 'Lycurgus' was not a king himself, he must at least have been a king's
uncrowned son; and, if, while not being a king, he was a law-giver and
the maker of a constitution, he could have done his legislative and con-
stitution-making work only during the minority of a king who was his
nephew and his ward. Which of the prehistoric kings had been 'Lycurgus's'
father, and which had been his ward? Since the two royal houses were
on a par with each other and were, at the same time, rivals, neither
house could afford to forgo the claim to 'Lycurgus' for itself. According
to Herodotus,[5] 'Lycurgus' had been the uncle and guardian of the Agiad
king Leobotas, and had therefore been the grandson of the Agiad house's
eponym, Agis I. According to most other authorities, 'Lycurgus's' nephew
and ward had been the Eurypontid king Kharilaos; but, in this Eurypontid version of the story, there were variants. The usual story was
that 'Lycurgus' was the son of King Eunomos (a name whose meaning

---

[1] See pp. 214, 221–2, and 279.

[2] Hammond, 'The Lycurgean Reform at Sparta', p. 62; Chrimes, *Ancient Sparta*, p. 328.

[3] See ibid., p. 328. This dating seems to have been fixed by Ephorus (see Strabo,
Geographica, Book X, chap. 4, § 18 (C. 481)). According to Den Boer, op. cit., p. 5, the
chronologists Eratosthenes and Apollodorus dated 'Lycurgus' by the first year of the reign
of the Eurypontid king Kharilaos, which, for Apollodorus, was 885/4 B.C. Ephorus' date
for 'Lycurgus' was 869 B.C. originally, 885/4 B.C. later (ibid., p. 31).

[4] Andrewes, *The Greek Tyrants*, p. 76.

[5] Book I, chap. 65.

is too suitable to be credible), and that Eunomos was Eurypon's grandson;[1] but Simonides made 'Lycurgus' Eunomos' brother, not his son, and thus made Eurypon 'Lycurgus's' grandfather.[2] Hellanikos, however, made no mention of 'Lykourgos' and attributed the Spartan constitution to Eurysthenes and Prokles, the respective fictitious progenitors of the eponyms Agis and Eurypon.[3] Pindar attributed the constitution to Aigimios.[4]

These discrepancies surely signify that, as Meyer maintains, there was no genuine historical tradition either about the genesis of Sparta's 'Lycurgan' constitution or about the personality of its maker.[5] There was no tomb at Sparta that was said to be Lycurgus'; there was only the temple in which he was worshipped as a god. According to one story, he died in Crete, and, in deference to his wishes, his corpse was cremated and the ashes were scattered over the sea. According to another story, his ashes were brought back to Sparta and were buried there, but the tomb was destroyed by a thunderbolt.[6] There was no Spartan family that claimed to be descended from 'Lycurgus', but there was said to have been a society of devotees of his, who, for ages, kept up the practice of meeting regularly to do him honour,[7] In short, the historical human being named 'Lycurgus', if he ever existed, is 'spurlos versenkt'. If 'Lycurgus' was an historical human being, and an eminent one whose memory was cherished, this complete lack of any relics of him is very strange; on the other hand, if he was a god, it is what we should expect.

'Il faut se résigner . . . à ne voir en Lycurgue qu'un nom et qu'un symbole.'[8] It is true that Aristotle believed that, in the inscription on the Olympian discus, he had found incontrovertible evidence, not only for the historicity of the Spartan 'Lycurgus', but for his date.[9] Aristotle is correct in identifying the Spartan 'Lycurgus' with the 'Lycurgus' whose name was inscribed on the discus.[10]

But this 'Lycurgus', too, is not an historical character. He is just as

---

[1] Λυκοῦργον δ' ὁμολογεῖσθαι παρὰ πάντων ἔκτον ἀπὸ Προκλέους γεγονέναι (Ephorus in Strabo, *Geographica*, Book X, chap. 4, § 18 (C. 481)). It was perhaps Ephorus who first gave currency to the Eurypontids' claim to 'Lycurgus'. Cp. Aristotle, *Politics*, Book II, chap. 7 (10), § 1 (1271b).

[2] See Plutarch, *Lycurgus*, chap. 1. According to Eduard Meyer, op. cit., p. 275, 'Lycurgus' became a Eurypontid in the fourth century B.C.

[3] Strabo in loc. cit. Strabo notes that Ephorus had combated Hellanikos' story and had vindicated 'Lycurgus's' claim to be the author of the Spartan constitution.

[4] Pindar, *Pyth.* I, l. 124.

[5] Eduard Meyer, op. cit., pp. 270, 277, 278. Cp. Chrimes, *Ancient Sparta*, pp. 319–20; Andrewes, *Probouleusis*, p. 16.

[6] Plutarch, *Lycurgus*, chap. 31.   [7] Ibid.

[8] Roussel, op. cit., p. 39. Cp. Meier, op. cit., p. 84.

[9] See pp. 214 and 221–2. On both points, Aristotle is followed by Den Boer, in op. cit., p. 154.

[10] Chrimes, *Ancient Sparta*, pp. 325–7, holds that the discus inscription was forged by the Eleans in the first decade of the fourth century B.C. Cp. Meier, op. cit., p. 89.

unhistorical as is Iphitos the founder of the [Olympic] festival, with whom [the 'Lycurgus' of the discus] collaborates in drawing up the rules for the Olympic truce. Both are, in origin, simply two well-known epic heroes. Iphitos is the son of Eurytos of Oikhalia, who is transplanted to Messenia in many sagas that are found already in Homer.[1] 'Lycurgus' is the Arcadian hero whose deeds are recounted by Nestor.[2] 'Lycurgus' [also] makes his appearance as son of the Arcadian Aleos and as king of Lepreon in Triphylia.[3] Another 'Lycurgus' is king of Nemea, and the Seven, on their expedition against Thebes, establish the Nemean festival in honour of his son Opheltas Arkhemoros.[4] Ultimately, this Peloponnesian 'Lycurgus' cannot be dissociated from Dionysus' opponent, the wild king of the Edonoi,[5] whom Zeus strikes blind[6] to punish him.[7]

Meyer[8] follows Wilamowitz in interpreting 'Lyko-orgos' as meaning 'Wolfsmuth', and he identifies this ubiquitous figure with the Arcadian wolf-god Zeus Lykaios and with the Arcadian light-god Lykaon, who was the reputed founder of the cult of Zeus Lykaios and of the festival that was associated with it—a parallel to the association of 'Lycurgus' with the festivals at Olympia and Nemea. Meyer sees in the cult of Lycurgus, as in the cults of Helen, the Dioscuri, Menelaos, and Agamemnon, a pre-Völkerwanderung stratum of Laconian religion that had survived the Völkerwanderung and had eventually been taken over by the descendants of the North-West-Greek-speaking intruders.[9]

Meyer's explanation of the Lycurgus-cult at Sparta is convincing— the more so considering that 'Lycurgus' is not the only depotentiated god who has been inserted into the history of Sparta as a fictitious human being. Phalanthos, the reputed ringleader of the conspiracy of the Partheniai and subsequent founder of the Spartan colony at Tarentum, also appears as a god as in Arcadia.[10]

---

[1] *Odyssey*, XXI. 13–41; *Iliad*, II. 596. (See also the present work, Part I, chap. 3, p. 26.)— A. J. T.   [2] *Iliad*, VII. 142–50.—A. J. T.

[3] Pausanias, Book V, chap. 5, § 5 (ἐν τῇ πόλει [Λεπρέῳ] Λευκαίου Διὸς ναὸν καὶ Λυκούργου τάφον τοῦ Ἀλέου); Book VIII, chap. 4, §§ 8 and 10.—A. J. T.

[4] Argumentum Pind. *Nem.*; Pausanias, Book II, chap. 15, § 3. At Nemea there were tombs of both Opheltas and his father 'Lycurgus' (Pausanias, loc. cit.).—A. J. T.

[5] Like Meyer, Wide, in op. cit., pp. 57, 93–4, 283, traces the Spartan Lycurgus' origin back to the Thracian Lycurgus.—A. J. T.

[6] *Iliad*, VI. 130–40. Cp. Pausanias, Book I, chap. 20, § 3.—A. J. T.

[7] Eduard Meyer, op. cit., p. 281. Meyer might have added that one of the scenes carved by Bathykles the Magnesian on the throne of the Amyclaean Apollo, which Pausanias saw, was a fight between Adrastos and Tydeus on the one side and Amphiaraos and Lycurgus son of Pronax on the other (Pausanias, Book III, chap. 18, § 12).

[8] Op. cit., pp. 281–2.

[9] Cp. Wide, op. cit., *passim*, especially p. 388; Chrimes, *Ancient Sparta*, pp. 248–71. According to Pausanias, Book III, chap. 13, § 3, the cult of Karneios at Sparta was pre-Völkerwanderung.

[10] Here he was reputed to be the grandson of Stymphalos. He was the eponym of a deserted site on a mountain called Phalanthon, on the last stage of the road from Megalopolis to

The Spartan rationalizers who brought the gods Lycurgus and Phalanthos down to Earth were precocious forerunners of Euhemeros. There is no record of their names, and it is possible that they deliberately contrived this anonymity by substituting a god for themselves as the fictitious author of their own acts.[1] If this is the truth, we can make a guess at the motive for this mystification. Both the emigration to Tarentum of the foiled Spartan conspirators after the First Spartano-Messenian War and the enactment of the 'Lycurgan' constitution after 'the Second War' (i.e. the first of the Messenian revolts) were delicate and difficult political compromises which fulfilled their purpose of averting civil war at two times of acute domestic political tension at Sparta. The contemporary human authors of these two compromises will have been, inevitably, controversial figures; and the stability of the political settlements that they had achieved might have been imperilled if these historic, but invidious, acts of state had been labelled with their true authors' controversial names. If either of the two successive attempts at a settlement of Sparta's domestic conflict was to have a chance of success, it would have to win 'bi-partisan' support; and this would be least difficult to secure if, in each case, the settlement were to be placed under the aegis of a figure that was both neutral and imposing. A figure that fulfilled both these conditions could be found in a god who had been metamorphosized, for this purpose, into a fictitious human being. As ex-gods, Phalanthos and Lycurgus were 'above the battle' between the human contending factions into which the Spartan body politic had split; and, though it is difficult to transform a god into a human being without de-potentiating him in the act, he will still retain enough of the aura of his divinity to give his human avatar a superhuman prestige which will fortify the human acts of state that have now been fictitiously attributed to him.

In the case of 'Lycurgus', we can also make a guess at the date at which this adroit politico-religious manœuvre was carried out.

We have noted that the Spartan myth-makers were unable to find for their fictitious human 'Lycurgus' a place in the list of Spartan kings of either house.[2] This means that the date at which 'Lycurgus' was credited with having been the human author of the seventh-century-B.C. Spartan constitution and of the accompanying Spartan way of life must have been

---

Methydrion (Pausanias, Book VIII, chap. 35, § 9). Wide, in op. cit., pp. 87–8, identifies the Spartan Phalanthos with Hyakinthos and with Apollo Delphidios.

[1] If 'Lycurgus' is not an historical character, the 'Lycurgan' constitution must have been the work of anonymous statesmen who were authentic human beings (see Stern, op. cit., pp. 52–3). 'The lawgiver "Lycurgus" is a creation of the genuine lawgiver of 550 [sic] B.C.; but it was only in one of the following generations that "Lycurgus" was made the creator of the entire [Spartan] kosmos' (Ehrenberg, *Neugründer des Staates*, p. 49).

[2] See pp. 278–9.

later than the date at which the eponyms of the two Spartan royal houses had been declared to be Herakleidai and had been provided with the requisite series of royal ancestors stretching right back to Herakles himself. In another context[1] it has been noticed that the earliest surviving association of Heraklid kings with inhabitants of a region called Doris who are organized in three sub-divisions is to be found in the Homeric Catalogue of the contingents in Agamemnon's expeditionary force;[2] and in that context it has been suggested that the Asian Doris, in which these features appear in the Homeric Catalogue, was the region from which the Heraklid royal genealogy, the name 'Dorieis', and the articulation of the citizen-body of a city-state into the three Dorian tribes were all derived by a number of North-West-Greek-speaking states in the southern and north-eastern Peloponnese, from Sparta to Argos and Sikyon inclusive. If it is a warrantable guess that these political institutions and pretensions in some of the North-West-Greek-speaking states in the Peloponnese were seedlings that had been transplanted from the Asian part of the Hellenic World, they are likely to have been part of the wave of 'Orientalizing' influences—political, literary, and artistic—that began to break upon the eastern coasts of continental European Greece at about the beginning of the seventh century B.C.—originating partly in Asian Greece and in Crete themselves and partly in non-Greek regions of Asia, farther to the east.

If so, the conversion of the pre-Völkerwanderung Peloponnesian god Lycurgus into the fictitious human author of the Spartan constitution that came to be placed under his auspices cannot have been contrived until after a Heraklid origin had been claimed for the two Spartan royal houses, and until the myth-makers at Sparta had also had time to put this claim into concrete shape by inventing fictitious Heraklid ancestors, right back to Herakles himself, for the Spartan royal houses' eponyms Agis and Eurypon. In one of Tyrtaios' war-songs,[3] written perhaps not long before the mid point of the seventh century B.C., the poet seems to be making Herakles the ancestor of the whole Spartiate citizen-body.[4] In his *Eunomia*,[5] which will have been written after the close of the Second Spartano-Messenian War, he adopts the opinion—which became the established convention—that the only Spartans who were Herakleidai were the members of the two royal houses, and that the rest of the Spartiate citizen-body was descended from Dorians of the Doris in central Greece who had migrated to the Peloponnese under Heraklid leadership.

[1] In Part I, chap. 1, pp. 8–9, and chap. 3, pp. 44–5.
[2] *Iliad*, II. 653–80.
[3] Tyrtaios, 9 (7) (Bergk–Hiller–Crusius) = 8 (11) (Diehl), l. 1.
[4] Ἀλλ' Ἡρακλῆος γὰρ ἀνικήτου γένος ἐστέ.
[5] Tyrtaios 1 (1) (Bergk–Hiller–Crusius) = 2 (2) (Diehl). Cp. Pindar, *Pyth.* I, ll. 119–29.

What is significant for our present inquiry is that Tyrtaios, the date of whose *floruit* was probably in the middle decades of the seventh century B.C., has accepted the Spartan royal houses' claim to be Herakleidai but is silent (at least in the surviving fragments) about 'Lycurgus', who, if he was an authentic historical figure, must have been Tyrtaios' contemporary, and must also have been the most conspicuous and the most controversial of all Spartan *soi-disant* Herakleidai up to date if this Lycurgus was, in truth, the human author of the constitution that was eventually adopted at Sparta after the close of the Second Spartano-Messenian War. If this line of reasoning is convincing, the date of the conversion of the god Lycurgus into a mortal man will have been post-Tyrtaean but pre-Herodotean.[1] In Herodotus' retrospective sketch of Sparta's history,[2] 'Lycurgus' already appears as the human author of almost every Spartan institution.[3] We may guess that the actual date at which the god Lycurgus was conscripted to play this dominant human role will have been nearer to Tyrtaios' generation than to Herodotus'. Tyrtaios may have lived to see the 'Lycurgan' constitution enacted; and, if it was the policy of the genuine human author or authors of this constitution to repudiate paternity, he or they cannot have delayed long in providing a fictitious human parent for an historic act of state.

[1] Andrewes, 'Eunomia', p. 99, makes the point that, if Tyrtaios had mentioned 'Lycurgus' anywhere in his poetry, the passage would have been preserved, because it would have been quoted by our later Greek authorities. 'On the other hand, by Herodotus's time, the legend was universal. We must look for its birth between the time of Tyrtaios and the fifth century, and the natural assumption is that it was begotten by the anonymous reformers of *circa* 600 B.C.'

[2] Book I, chaps. 65–6.

[3] Including the τριηκάδες, which were probably part of the six-morai organization of the Lacedaemonian army (see the present Part, chap. 5, section (iii), p. 383), and which, if so, will have been created in Herodotus' own lifetime. Xenophon, *Lak. Pol.*, chap. 11, §4, ascribes to 'Lycurgus' the creation of the whole six-morai organization.

4. *The Social Effects of the So-called 'Lycurgan' Reform*

(i) *Symptoms of Strain*

WHEN, at Sparta, the 'Lycurgan' settlement had been agreed between the crown, the aristocracy, and the commoners, it must at first have looked, to all parties in the Spartiate politeuma, as if satisfactory and durable solutions had now been found for the problems that, since the end of the First Spartano-Messenian War, had been confronting the Spartan state and had been creating dissension between the several factions in the Spartan citizen-body. The conversion of a majority of the Spartiate commoners into full-time professional hoplite phalangites had now at last equipped the state with a military machine that must have seemed adequate for the task of permanently holding down the enslaved rural populations of the lower Eurotas basin and the Stenyklaros plain. If the Messenian helots were ever to revolt again, Sparta could now look forward, with greater confidence, to being able to quell the revolt, this time without again coming within an ace of collapse—the nightmare that had stared Sparta in the face during her inglorious 'Second War' with her Messenian victims, and perhaps also during a second Messenian revolt in which the beau role had been played by the insurgents' leader Aristomenes. As for the Spartiate commoners who had now been put on a par with the aristocrats by being drafted into the new hoplite phalanx as homoioi, they had won at last that equality with the aristocrats in the sharing-out of the conquered lands which they had been demanding for perhaps as much as a century. The state's need for a hoplite phalanx had made it necessary to endow landless commoners with the means for devoting their full working time to this new professional career. The required endowment had been provided by distributing, to commoners and aristocrats alike, as much of the conquered lands as was being kept under helot cultivation. In obtaining their kleroi, the commoners were achieving their hearts' desire. It did not become apparent immediately that they were not going to live happily ever after.

The immediate political effect of the 'Lycurgan' reform was to avert civil war and revolution within the Spartiate citizen-body. Non-Spartan Greek observers in the fifth and fourth centuries B.C. noted that, under the 'Lycurgan' regime, Sparta had become one of the most law-abiding and stable communities in the Hellenic World after having previously been one of the most disorderly.[1] By 'taking the damos into partner-

[1] See p. 213, with nn. 2 and 3.

ship'[1] with the aristocracy and the crown, Sparta had saved herself from falling under the rule of revolutionary despots—the misfortune which had overtaken the circum-Isthmian states of continental European Greece in the same and the following chapter of the Hellenic World's political history. More than that, Sparta's 'Lycurgan' political constitution had proved, in the next chapter after that, to have been 'the wave of the future'.[2]

When, in the circum-Isthmian states, the despotic regimes had been overthrown—in some cases with Sparta's aid[3] and in others perhaps thanks to her example—the new political constitutions that had been adopted in the liberated states had been framed on the Spartan pattern. This was not only true of the moderate oligarchies that had been established in Corinth, Sikyon, Epidauros, and Megara; it was also true of the democracy that had been established at Athens in 508 B.C. by Kleisthenes and had been carried to further lengths in 461 B.C. by Ephialtes and Pericles. The structure of all these new constitutions was 'Lycurgan', though there were different gradations in the percentage of the citizen-body, and, *a fortiori*, in the percentage of the total population, that was fully enfranchised in each case.

For about four centuries, experience seemed to be proving that Sparta's 'Lycurgan' constitution was a political masterpiece. Yet, in the end, it turned out that, at Sparta, the revolutionary despotic regime that the 'Lycurgan' constitution had forestalled in the seventh century B.C. had merely been postponed, but had not been permanently averted. Kleomenes III's *coup d'état* in 227 B.C. was a belated instance of the revolution that the circum-Isthmian states had undergone 400 or 350 years earlier. This ultimate breakdown of the constitutional settlement that had seemed to be the most conspicuously successful feature of the 'Lycurgan' regime was evidence that, after all, this regime had not fully solved Sparta's pre-'Lycurgan' problems.[4]

Meanwhile, it had become apparent—and this long before Sparta's revolutionary year 227 B.C.—that Sparta, the state which, in the seventh century B.C., had been a pioneer in the political field, had fallen out of step with the rest of the Hellenic World by dropping behind other Hellenic communities in every field of activity, even including the field of military technique. Sparta's abnormality was unmistakable by the time when she emerged from the crisis into which she had been plunged by the earthquake of *circa* 466 or 464 B.C. and the consequent Messenian

[1] τὸν δῆμον προσεταιρίζεται (Herodotus, Book V, chap. 66, apropos of Kleisthenes).
[2] See Andrewes, *Probouleusis*.
[3] See pp. 182, 243, and 260.
[4] 'The problems that faced third-century Sparta, poverty and inequality, were basically the same as those that he ['Lycurgus'] had solved' (Forrest, *A History*, p. 147).

revolt.[1] This abnormality must have been developing gradually in the course of the preceding century or century and a half.[2]

There was not, of course, anything abnormal about Spartan human nature. It is true that modern psychologists have been discovering that the fundamental uniformity of human nature in all human beings is differentiated, on the surface, into several different psychological types; but the representatives of these differing types are not segregated from each other in separate communities or in separate localities; they are distributed equally, on the average, among all samples of mankind in all places and all ages. The differences—and these are striking—between different peoples are the product, not of any immutable differences in local human nature, but of constantly changing differences in mutable manners and customs. 'Les mœurs du Spartiate classique ... sont surtout le résultat d'une transformation sociale qui fut grosse de conséquences.'[3] As Strabo has put the point,[4] 'it is not anything in their respective natures that makes the Athenians take an interest in the things of the mind, in contrast to the Lacedaemonians and to the Thebans, who live still closer to the Athenians than the Lacedaemonians live. The difference is really a matter of habit.' The Spartan agoge cannot be accounted for in terms of geography.[5]

In the community of Spartiate homoioi which had been called into existence by the 'Lycurgan' reform, normal human nature was 'conditioned' progressively by successive responses to the successive challenges presented to Sparta by subsequent experiences. Some of these responses were spontaneous and unconscious; others were conscious and deliberate; and, of the deliberate decisions, some were taken by the 'homoioi' as private persons, to serve what they believed to be their own private interests, while others were taken by the Spartan Government to serve what it believed to be the public interest of the Spartan state. A tug-o'-war between public and private interests at Sparta gradually produced the peculiar Spartan spirit in which the way of life was reflected. The pressures that, at Sparta, were stamping human nature with this peculiar imprint became more and more severe as Sparta's situation, within her own dominions and abroad, became more and more difficult. But even the utmost turn of the screw could not change human nature. All that it could do was to repress nature; and, if and when the pressure was removed or was even just relaxed, the rebound of human nature was correspondingly violent.

---

[1] This was a Messenian national revolt; for the Messenian perioecic states Thouria and Aithaia took part in it (Thucydides, Book I, chap. 101), while the helot population of the lower Eurotas basin seems to have kept quiet.

[2] Forrest, too, takes this view (*A History*, p. 135).

[3] Roussel, op. cit., p. 43.

[4] In *Geographica*, Book II, chap. 3, § 7 (C. 103).   [5] Roussel, op. cit., p. 13.

In post-earthquake Sparta—and this is the earliest phase of Spartan history of which we have accounts by contemporary observers—the Government was acutely aware of the peculiarity, artificiality, and fragility of the Spartan agoge. It revealed its awareness of this by the measures that it took to reduce to a minimum the Spartiate community's intercourse with the rest of the Hellenic World. By this time it had been made illegal for a Spartan citizen to travel abroad without the Spartan Government's permission.[1] (On military service, of course, he would be going abroad under orders and in the ranks.) It was not made illegal for foreigners to visit Lacedaemonian territory,[2] but the Spartan Government held itself free to expel any foreign visitors at any moment.[3] These isolationist administrative measures of the Spartan Government's were reinforced by an automatic insulator which may not have been devised originally to serve this purpose, but which was carefully preserved after experience had shown that this was promoting the insulation which had now become the Spartan Government's objective. This automatic insulator was the Spartan form of monetary currency, which had become peculiar because it had remained old-fashioned.

Before the influx into Sparta of foreign silver and gold coin, as a result of Sparta's victory over Athens in 404 B.C.,[4] the Spartan currency had retained a form that had been common to the currencies of all Hellenic states originally. In the common Greek vocabulary, the name for the smallest coin was 'obolos', meaning 'spit', and the name for the next larger denomination was 'drakhme', meaning 'as large a clutch of spits as a human hand could grasp'. These words, like the Latin word 'pecunia', tell us that in the Hellenic World, as, later on, in Italy, the earliest monetary currency was in the form of a commodity that was in constant demand and supply. The pre-coinage iron 'spit' form of currency was perhaps introduced into continental European Greece by King Pheidon of Argos, in whose reign the Argives may have won the victory over the Spartans at Hysiai which is dated 669 B.C.;[5] and a handful of spits, possibly dedicated by Pheidon himself, has been found at the Argive

---

[1] Xenophon, *Lak. Pol.*, chap. 14, §4; Plutarch, *Lycurgus*, chap. 27; *Instituta Laconica*, § 19; Aristotle, fragm. 543 Rose, in Harpocration's comment on Isocrates, *Busiris*, 225; Isocrates, *Busiris*, 18 and 225; Nikolaos of Damascus, fragm. 114, § 5 (Müller, *F.H.G.*, vol. iii, p. 458). This rule applied to Spartiate μάχιμοι according to Isocrates, to Spartiatai according to Nikolaos of Damascus, to οἱ πολῖται according to Xenophon, to all Lakedaimonioi according to Aristotle.

[2] *Pace Nicolai Damasceni*, fragm. cit., § 5.

[3] Plutarch, *Inst. Lac.*, § 20; *Lycurgus*, chap. 27. These Spartan ξενηλασίαι were very unpopular in the rest of the Hellenic World.

[4] Plutarch, *Lycurgus*, chap. 30.

[5] See Andrewes, 'The Corinthian Actaeon and Pheidon of Argos', in *The Classical Quarterly*, vol. xliii (1949), pp. 70–8, on p. 77. Pausanias, Book II, chap. 24, § 7, records the Battle of Hysiai, but he does not mention Pheidon either in this or in any other passage of his work (Andrewes, 'Ephorus I and the Kings of Argos', p. 41).

Heraion.[1] Thus, when Sparta introduced an iron 'spit' currency in her own dominions, she was keeping abreast of the times. This happened to be a particularly convenient form of currency for Sparta, because Laconia was rich in deposits of iron-ore.

However, already by the time of the inauguration of Sparta's 'Lycurgan' regime, the iron 'spit' currency was beginning to be replaced in western Anatolia by silver and gold coins of the modern kind. These were much easier to handle than the iron 'spit' currency had been, and their standard was guaranteed by the 'image and superscription' of the issuing authority. This new form of currency rapidly superseded the previous 'spit' form in most of the states of the Hellenic World. Yet, rapid though the spread of coinage was, it did not reach Sparta's borders in time to gain an entry, as the 'spit' currency had done, before Spartan life had begun to become petrified. Sparta persisted in using her 'spit' currency, regardless of the convenience of the innovation that was being adopted in the world around her.

This conservatism was probably due, to begin with, to mere inattention and inertia. The practical effect was, inevitably, to make it difficult for Spartans to travel abroad with a currency that was bulky, heavy, and unconvertible; and visits to Sparta also now became unattractive for foreign poets and artists, since the only remuneration that they could now hope for would be either in unconvertible currency or in kind.[2] Non-human imports fell off for the same reason.[3] When the Spartan public authorities became aware of this insulating effect of their automatic monetary conservatism, they will have realized that it was promoting the isolationism that had now become their policy. They are said then to have improved on nature by treating their iron currency 'spits' chemically in a way that rendered the metal useless even for industrial purposes.[4]

---

[1] According to Ephorus apud Strabonem, Book VIII, chap. 3, § 33 (C. 358), the currency introduced by Pheidon was not the iron spit kind but was real coinage, minted for Pheidon on the island of Aigina. This can hardly be the truth unless Pheidon's true date was not *circa* 669 B.C. but was *circa* 600 B.C.—as it may have been if Pheidon's grandson Meltas' support of the Arcadians was against Sparta in one of the Spartano-Tegeatan wars, (see p. 182, n. 7), and must have been if Herodotus is correct in including Pheidon's son Leokedes among the suitors of Kleisthenes of Sikyon's daughter Agariste. In that case the dedication of the iron spits at the Heraion may have commemorated, not their introduction, but their withdrawal.

[2] Plutarch, *Apophth. Lac.*, Lykourgos, 3. Cp. Chrimes, *Ancient Sparta*, p. 308.

[3] See Andrewes, *The Greek Tyrants*, p. 70.

[4] Plutarch, *Lycurgus*, chap. 9; *Lysander*, chap. 17; Xenophon, *Lak. Pol.*, chap. 7, § 5. Sparta did not start coining in the precious metals till the third century B.C. (Huxley, op. cit., p. 134, n. 424). The Spartan mint was established in 280 B.C. by King Areus II. He coined Alexander-tetradrachms of Athenian standard, with his own name on them. In 228 B.C. Kleomenes III coined silver tetradrachms of a Seleucid model. In this he was followed by Nabis (Michell, op. cit., p. 302; see also Forrest, *A History*, p. 642).

This combination of insulating factors was potent.[1] When, however, Spartans did manage to go abroad as their own masters, it was notorious that their conduct abroad was apt to present a lurid contrast to their conduct at home. A sensational example of this was the misconduct of the regent Pausanias when he was given his opportunity by the Greek victory at Plataea in 479 B.C. His sudden liberation from the bonds of the 'Lycurgan' discipline demoralized him to a degree at which he rushed first into disgrace and finally into destruction. Pausanias' unedifying career abroad was a portent of what was going to happen on a greater scale during and after the Atheno-Peloponnesian War of 431–404 B.C. 'Naturam expellas furca, tamen usque recurret.'[2] In a non-Spartan social and moral environment, Spartan behaviour became the antithesis of what was 'Spartan' in the peculiar post-'Lycurgan' connotation that the word 'Spartan' had acquired by this date.[3]

In going to this opposite extreme, the post-'Lycurgan' Spartan abroad was not, of course, returning to normality; he was merely reacting abnormally to the abnormal pressure of contemporary Spartan life at home. On the other hand, pre-'Lycurgan' Sparta had led the normal life of one of the more precocious Hellenic communities of that age.[4] Tarentum—the Spartan colony in Calabria that had been founded *circa* 706 B.C.—was a living museum, in Sparta's post-'Lycurgan' age, of what pre-'Lycurgan' Sparta had been like. Though Tarentum was of Spartan origin, there was nothing in Tarentine life that was 'Spartan' in the post-'Lycurgan' sense. Tarentum was a community of fishermen, mariners, traders, and artisans, not of professional soldiers, and Tarentine life was not at all austere. No doubt Tarentum, as well as Sparta, developed in a characteristic way of her own after the daughter and the mother community had separated; Tarentine life was dominated and moulded by the sea, from which Sparta remained remote; but, if Sparta had been 'Spartan' already at the pre-'Lycurgan' date at which Tarentum was founded, some traces, at least, of 'Spartanism' would surely have survived in Tarentine life.

This Tarentine negative piece of evidence agrees with our positive evidence, literary and archaeological, to suggest that, during the period, *circa* 750–650 B.C. or 750–600 B.C., immediately preceding the 'Lycurgan' reform, Sparta was living under the aristocratic regime that was prevalent in the Hellenic World of that age. Like most other regimes, this one had both bad and good features. Its worst feature was the gross inequality in the distribution of power and wealth as between a dominant

---

[1] Michell, op. cit., pp. 26–7, plays down the insulating effect of Sparta's iron currency.
[2] Horace, *Epistulae*, Book I, Ep. 10, l. 24.
[3] This point is made by Polybius, Book VI, chaps. 48, § 6, and 49, §§ 7–10.
[4] See Roussel, op. cit., pp. 8, 27, 32.

minority of aristocrats and an unenfranchised and unendowed majority of commoners. In many, perhaps most, Hellenic city-states this inequality provoked dissension; and at Sparta, as has been noted, the dissension became particularly acute because of the unusually large amount of state land that Sparta had acquired by conquest in the course of the half-century that had begun with the annexation of Amyklai, Pharis, and Geronthrai and had ended with the conquest of Messenia in the First Spartano-Messenian War. One good feature of the aristocratic regime, to set against its social injustice, was the favourable opening that aristocratic patronage gave to the arts. In this phase of Sparta's history there is no trace of asceticism.[1]

If the establishment of the 'Lycurgan' regime at Sparta is to be dated in the third or fourth quarter of the seventh century B.C., our archaeological and literary evidence[2] tells us that this political, military, and social transformation of Sparta did not have any immediate damping effect on the vitality of Sparta's cultural life.[3] The most trustworthy archaeological clock is the sequence of pottery types, and at Sparta this indicates that the visual arts flourished there from before 700 B.C. until *circa* 550 B.C.[4] Our literary record tells the same tale. In the seventh century, Sparta was visited by some of the leading non-Spartan Greek poets, musicians, and artists of the day;[5] and, what is more, she produced native poets and artists of her own.[6] One of these, Gitiadas, made the bronze decorations of the temple of Athana of the Brazen House at Sparta, and also made the bronze statue of the goddess herself;[7] and he took his share in making the works of art that adorned the temple of Apollo–Hyakinthos at Amyklai,[8] though here a foreigner, Bathykles of Magnesia-on-Maeander, was commissioned to decorate Apollo's throne,[9] and Theodoros of Samos to build the Skias.[10] Gitiadas was a poet, besides being an artificer.[11] As for the poets Alkman and Tyrtaios, they too were probably Spartans born; and, if they were not, they both certainly became Spartans by adoption. Yet, whether they were Spartans by

---

[1] Ehrenberg, *Neugründer des Staates*, p. 10. Cp. Dickins, loc. cit., p. 1.

[2] Works of art and poetry are our only contemporary evidence (Ehrenberg, *Neugründer des Staates*, p. 11).

[3] See Roussel, op. cit., p. 75.

[4] See Huxley, op. cit., p. 61; Roussel, op. cit., p. 74; Michell, op. cit., p. 14; Andrewes, *The Greek Tyrants*, p. 69; Forrest, *A History*, pp. 57 and 72–3.

[5] According to Sosibius, the Karneia festival at Sparta was founded in the 26th Olympiad (i.e. *circa* 676 B.C.) (see p. 265, n. 6). According to Hellanikos, Terpander was the victor at the first celebration (Athenaeus, Book XIV, 635 e–f).

[6] See the remarkable list of these in Michell, op. cit., p. 13.

[7] Pausanias, Book III, chap. 17, §§ 2–3.

[8] Ibid., chap. 18, § 8.

[9] Ibid., chap. 18, § 9, and chap. 19, § 5.

[10] Roussel, op. cit., p. 75.

[11] Pausanias, Book III, chap. 17, § 2.

adoption or by birth, they each wrote in the dialect and in the style that were in vogue throughout the Hellenic World in their generation for the respective genres of poetry that each of them had made his own.[1]

The decay of the arts at Sparta seems to have been gradual.[2] The zenith of both the art of sculpture and the art of vase-painting seems to have been reached after the beginning of the sixth century B.C. At this date, Spartan pottery was being exported all round the shores of the Mediterranean.[3] The pottery-sequence tells us that, at Sparta, the art of vase-painting began to decline *circa* 550 B.C.,[4] but this happens to be a case in which the fortunes of pottery are not the trustworthy index that they usually are of the fortunes of the visual arts in general.[5] As for music, we need not believe the story of Terpander's being punished by the ephors, and having his instrument confiscated by them, because he had added one extra string, or the companion story of Phrynis and Timotheos each having his two extra strings cut by an ephor when he was performing at Sparta at the Karneia festival.[6] The retrospective invention of these no doubt fictitious incidents merely indicates that, at the time when

---

[1] Andrewes, *The Greek Tyrants*, pp. 69–70, points out that Alkman's poetry testifies to the normality of the Sparta of his day.

[2] Norvin, loc. cit., pp. 289–90; Kiechle, *Lakonien und Sparta*, p. 243.

[3] Roussel, op. cit., pp. 75–6. Cp. Michell, op. cit., p. 27; Andrewes, *The Greek Tyrants*, p. 69.

[4] Dickins, loc. cit., p. 18; Lenschau, 'Die Entstehung des Spartanischen Staates', p. 269. According to Hammond, 'The Lycurgean Reform at Sparta', p. 63, 'Spartan art does not decline rapidly till after 500 B.C.'

[5] The date, about halfway through the sixth century B.C., at which the art of vase-painting began to decline at Sparta coincides with the date at which, at Athens, the same art began to forge ahead. If Sparta had been the only place in the Hellenic World at which this art had begun to fall off at this time, it might have been supposed that the simultaneous advance of the art at Athens had been at least partly stimulated by the opportunity presented by a vacuum, and that this vacuum, created by the recession of the art of vase-painting at Sparta, had been a consequence of the onset, at Sparta, of the cultural climate of austerity that was certainly characteristic of Spartan life after the earthquake of *circa* 466 or 464 B.C. This explanation of the decline of the art at Sparta is ruled out, however, by the fact that, during the same decade, the decay of the vase-painting industry went to more extreme lengths at Corinth (see Chrimes, *Ancient Sparta*, p. 308; Huxley, *Early Sparta*, p. 73; R. M. Cook, 'Spartan History and Archaeology', in *The Classical Quarterly*, vol. lvi (N.S., vol. xii) (1962), pp. 156–8, on p. 156). Previously this industry had been even more flourishing at Corinth than it had been at Sparta; and Corinthian life did not become austere at any stage of Corinthian history. The decay of the industry at Corinth, as well as at Sparta, in or about the fifth decade of the sixth century B.C., is proof that the industry at Athens was not called into existence to fill a vacuum. Evidently Athens captured the Mediterranean market for painted pottery from both Corinth and Sparta, in competition with these two older seats of the industry, by surpassing them both, at this date, in the standard of her product. In Laconia the visual arts in general continued, into the fifth century B.C., to maintain themselves at the average standard of the Hellenic World as a whole (Cook in loc. cit., p. 157). 'There need not be any relationship between Laconian art and Spartan austerity' (Cook, in loc. cit., p. 156). In Laconia 'the practice of the arts was left to the perioeci '(ibid.). Cp. Forrest, *A History*, pp. 57 and 72–3.

[6] Plutarch, *Inst. Lac.*, § 17, *Agis*, chap. 10.

these stories became current, the Spartan Government, though possibly not the Spartan people, had become hostile to foreign musicians, especially when they brought technical innovations with them. The date of even the oldest of these stories might be later than the date of the great earthquake at Sparta *circa* 466 or 464 B.C. At any rate, contemporary evidence for the almost pathological Spartan conservative-mindedness and xenophobia that became notorious does not go back farther in time than that.

It is certain that the Spartans continued to cultivate, not only military music, which was a practical aid to keeping the phalanx in formation,[1] but also peace-time community singing and dancing[2] at religious festivals. The festival of Artemis Orthia[3] was Sparta's own; the Hyakinthia festival[4] had been annexed by her with Amyklai, where it was celebrated; the Karneia festival had presumably been imported from the Asian Doris,[5] together with the Dorian phylai and the Heraklid genealogy of the royal houses; the Gymnopaidiai festival, which had been founded in the fourth decade of the seventh century B.C., was embellished,[6] long before the time when vase-painting began to decline in Laconia, to commemorate Sparta's decisive victory over Argos at Thyrea. At this festival, Thaletas' and Alkman's poems were sung by the dancers.[7] At Sparta the major annual festivals were taken almost as much in earnest as war was— and this even in the Post-'Lycurgan' Age, when war had become Sparta's national industry. Indeed, the celebration of a festival was sometimes given precedence over military considerations, even when the military situation was critical. In 480 B.C. the celebration of the Karneia detained the Spartan army (so it was said)[8] from following up Leonidas and his three hundred in full force, in time to save them from being overwhelmed. It was not till that year's Karneia were over, and the Olympia too, that the Peloponnesian forces assembled to fortify and hold the entrance into the Peloponnese from the Isthmus of Corinth.[9] Next year the Spartans dallied over the celebration of the Hyakinthia till they had

---

[1] Plutarch, *Inst. Lac.*, § 16; *Apophth. Lac.*, Agesilaos, 26; and the Chigi vase.

[2] Plutarch, *Lycurgus*, chap. 21; *Inst. Lac.*, §§ 14–15.

[3] See Wide, op. cit., pp. 112–16.

[4] For Hyakinthos, see ibid., pp. 285–93.

[5] See Wide, op. cit., pp. 73–87. Outside Laconia, there were cults of Karneios in Messenia at Pharai and in the Karnasian grove, and also at Argos, Sikyon, Megara, Thera, Kyrene, Kos, Knidos. One of the months was named 'Karneios' in the calendars of Byzantium, Rhodes, Kalymnos, Nisyros, Syracuse, Tauromenion, Gela, Akragas. There was a Karneia festival at Thourioi. On the other hand, not all the European Greek communities that had taken to calling themselves 'Dorian' had adopted the cult of Karneios. This had not been adopted at Corinth, Phlious, Aigina, Epidauros, Hermione, Troizen, nor anywhere in Crete (ibid., p. 86).

[6] See p. 184, n. 2.

[7] Wade-Gery, 'A Note on the Origin of the Spartan Gymnopaidiai', p. 80.

[8] Herodotus, Book VII, chap. 206.   [9] Herodotus, Book VIII, chap. 72.

come within an ace of driving the Athenians, in despair, into negotiating with Mardonios.[1] 'The Amyklaioi always went home for the Hyakinthia festival, to chant the paean at it, whether they were on active service or were away on other business at the time.'[2] Accordingly, Agesilaos gave leave of absence to all the Amyklaioi in his army in the middle of the campaign of 390 B.C. The mora that had been detailed to escort the home-going Amyklaioi beyond the range of enemy action was on its way back to Lekhaion when it was caught and mauled by Iphikrates' peltasts.[3]

This abiding Spartan devotion to Sparta's national festivals[4] was a saving grace; but even this was marred by the touch of eccentricity and vein of rigidity which had been becoming characteristic of Spartan life in all its aspects.[5] At about the year 550 B.C., Spartans dropped out of the competitions at Olympia for about three-quarters of a century, after having taken part since *circa* 720 B.C.[6]—and this with outstanding distinction. In the years 720–576 B.C., forty-six Olympian victors out of a total of eighty-one had been Spartans; in the years 548–400, only twelve out of 200 were Spartans.[7] The general deterioration of the quality of Spartan art after the close of the sixth century B.C. was a symptom of the increasing strain from which Sparta was suffering under the 'Lycurgan' regime; and it is significant that the mid sixth century B.C. was about the date at which Sparta went over from a programme of conquest to a policy of alliances—a new policy which she continued to follow, notwithstanding her signal victory over Argos at Thyrea *circa* 544 B.C.[8] This volte-face is evidence that, already by that date, the strain on Sparta had become severe enough not merely to be felt consciously by the Spartan Government and damos but actually to move them to take a major new departure in their foreign policy. What were the causes of this evidently unforeseen long-term untoward effect of the 'Lycurgan' reforms?[9]

[1] Herodotus, Book IX, chaps. 6 and 11.
[2] Xenophon, *Hellenica*, Book IV, chap. 5, § 11.
[3] Ibid., §§ 12–17.
[4] It was not a festival, but a superstition, that inhibited the Spartans, in 490 B.C., from arriving in Attica in time to take part in the Battle of Marathon, according to Herodotus, Book VI, chaps. 106–7 and 121. According to Plato, the cause of the Spartans' tardiness on this occasion was a Messenian revolt (see p. 186, n. 2).
[5] See Kiechle, *Lakonien und Sparta*, pp. 2 and 247; Ehrenberg, *Neugründer des Staates*, p. 10.
[6] Chrimes, *Ancient Sparta*, p. 311; Roussel, *Sparte*, p. 79.
[7] Ehrenberg, *Neugründer des Staates*, p. 10. According to Lenschau, 'Die Entstehung des spartanischen Staates', p. 270, the figures are: forty Spartan victors, 615–580 B.C.; 580–316 B.C. only two, or possibly five (excluding victors in the chariot races). In the fifth century B.C. there were festivals, including athletic competitions, at the perioecic city Thouria and on Sparta's own territory at Helos, on the evidence of Damonon's inscription.
[8] See p. 182.
[9] Grote, op. cit. (Everyman's Library edition), vol. iii, p. 116, attributes the eventual peculiarity of Sparta to the effects of the 'Lycurgan' constitution.

(ii) *Causes of the Strain*

Under the 'Lycurgan' regime, Sparta found herself having to respond to an increasing pressure with a decreasing fund of military man-power. It was proving more and more difficult for her to make both ends meet. Her response was to key up the tension of the 'Lycurgan' agoge—the Spartiate homoioi's way of life. Perhaps this was the only recourse that Sparta had left open to herself in the self-made trap in which she was now caught.

The Spartans had decided their own destiny for themselves when, in the course of their conquests, they had abandoned their initial liberality towards the vanquished. Apparently they had incorporated the conquered Amyklaioi in the Spartan body politic; but undoubtedly they had enslaved the conquered populations of the lower Eurotas basin and the Stenyklaros plain; and this harsh and heartless violation of a fundamental human right brought its nemesis in and after 'the Second Spartano-Messenian War'.

In the long view of the gods the [resubjugated] Messenian insurgents had secured their revenge on Sparta, in the sense in which Hannibal was to have his revenge on Rome. The Second Messeno–Spartan War changed the whole rhythm of Spartan life and deflected the whole course of Spartan history. It was one of those wars in which the iron enters into the survivors' souls. It was so terrible an experience that it left Spartan life fast bound in misery and iron, and it 'side-tracked' Spartan evolution into a blind alley. And, since the Spartans were never able to forget what they had gone through, they were never able to relax, and therefore never able to extricate themselves from the impasse of their post-war reaction. . . .

The Spartans, having conquered Messenia in the First War in order to live unto themselves, are constrained, in the Second War and ever after, to give up their lives to the task of keeping Messenia. They live as the obedient humble servants of their own dominion over Messenia from this time forth for evermore.[1]

The Spartans reckoned, no doubt, that the full-time professional hoplite phalanx of the homoioi was a just sufficiently potent military instrument for holding the helots down—unreconciled to their servitude though the helots were—so long as Sparta had only her helots to deal with. The Spartans' nightmare—which was to become an accomplished fact in 370 B.C.—was that some hostile foreign power might come to the helots' rescue, and that it might then prove to be beyond even the new model Spartan army's strength to cope with a combination between the domestic and the foreign enemy in a war that would have been carried into Sparta's home territory. The earliest and nearest menacing foreign

[1] A. J. Toynbee, *A Study of History*, vol. iii, pp. 53–4. Norvin, in loc. cit., vol. ii, p. 273, points out that Sparta expanded at her neighbours' expense in the Peloponnese when other Greek states were expanding overseas. Tarentum was Sparta's only overseas colony.

power was Argos, and Sparta was successful in exorcizing her Argive peril. Argos had missed the opportunity of crushing Sparta that had been offered to Argos during 'the Second Spartano-Messenian War', and again during the second Messenian revolt, led by Aristomenes, if in truth there was this second revolt at the close of the seventh century B.C. After Sparta's decisive victory over Argos at Thyrea *circa* 544 B.C., Sparta was able to isolate her; and her crushing victory over Argos in 494 B.C. at Sepeia eliminated Argos from the international arena for the span of a generation. Yet, before Sparta had given Argos this temporary quietus, Sparta, in her turn, had missed her opportunity of scotching Athens; and Athens, though more distant from Sparta than Argos was, proved to be a vastly more dynamic adversary. When, in 425 B.C., Athens did eventually join hands at Pylos with Sparta's Messenian helots, Sparta became eager to escape from the war with Athens to which she had committed herself reluctantly six years earlier.

From about halfway through the sixth century B.C. onwards, Sparta sought to conjure away the peril of a combination between the helots and a hostile foreign power by surrounding the two-fifths of the Peloponnese that she had brought under her own dominion with an insulating cordon of Peloponnesian allies. This policy was rational, and Sparta pursued it successfully until her failure, in the years 511–507 B.C., to draw Athens into her net. Meanwhile, and still more sedulously after this serious political reverse, Sparta sought to avoid being drawn into military adventures.

The greatest irony in Sparta's situation was the fact that, when she had sacrificed everything that made life worth living to the single object of forging an irresistible military instrument, she found that she dared not make use of her dearly-bought power because her social equilibrium under the 'Lycurgan' system was so exact, and her social tension so high, that the slightest disturbance of the *status quo* might have disastrous repercussions; and this disaster might be brought on by a victory that would increase the permanent demands on Sparta's man-power almost as readily as by a defeat that would open the way for an invasion of Sparta's home-territories. In the event, the total victory of 404 B.C. and the consequent total defeat of the year 371 B.C. duly brought upon the Spartans the disaster which they had never ceased to dread since they had succeeded in making themselves into the most formidable military power in their world.

Yet Spartan statesmanship managed to postpone the evil day for nearly two centuries, dating from the completion of the 'Lycurgan' reforms, by declining to accept for Sparta the greatness which circumstances incessantly sought to thrust upon her. In this frame of mind the Spartans evaded, time and again, the challenge to assume the leadership of Hellas which the Achaemenian peril presented to them.[1]

---

[1] Toynbee, op. cit., vol. iii, p. 70. Cp. Forrest, *A History*, p. 81.

In the pursuit of this unheroic policy, Sparta was first embarrassed and eventually frustrated by the rise and expansion of the Persian Empire and by Athens' seizure of the opportunity which this threat to the Hellenic World offered to some Hellenic state for playing the beau role of protagonist in a Panhellenic resistance movement. Sparta's diplomatic insulation of Argos *circa* 550 B.C., at the price of coming to terms with Tegea, had been, from the Spartan point of view, a prudent act of renunciation; but in foreign eyes it had made Sparta the leading power in the Hellenic World.[1] On this account, King Croesus of Lydia asked Sparta to enter into an alliance with him on the eve of the Lydo-Persian War of 547 B.C., and this flattering proposal was accepted by the Spartan Government.[2] But Sparta took no military action to save Lydia from being conquered and annexed by the Persian empire-builder Cyrus; and, when, after the fall of Sardis, Cyrus went on to subjugate the continental Asian Greek states that had previously been subject to Lydia, and when these, in their turn, appealed to Sparta for military aid, Sparta rejected their plea and merely sent to Cyrus a diplomatic mission with the message that Sparta 'would not stand idly by if he should presume to maltreat any of the states of the Hellenic World'. Cyrus treated this message with contempt, and Sparta let him complete the subjugation of the continental Asian Greek states without intervening on their behalf.[3] Consistently, the Spartans

forbore to send help to the Asian Greek insurgents [against Persian rule] in 499 B.C.; they arrived too late to fight at Marathon in 490 B.C.; and, after covering themselves with glory, under protest, at Thermopylae and Plataea, they abdicated from the high command of the forces of liberation in 479–478 B.C. Rather than incur the risks which greatness involved for Sparta, they deliberately left their own repudiated greatness lying derelict for Athens to appropriate; and yet, even at this bitter price, they were ultimately unable to elude their tragic destiny. For the Spartans' great refusal to accept the challenge of 499–479 B.C. did not, and could not, purchase for Sparta more than a brief immunity from her peculiar dilemma. In preferring, to the risks of acceptance, the lesser immediate evil of giving the Athenians their opportunity, the Spartans were opening the door for the menace to Hellenic liberties to recur in the shape of an Athenian peril; and this time the Spartans found themselves confronted with a challenge which it was impossible for them to ignore. In the opinion of Thucydides,[4] 'the fundamental . . . cause of the Atheno-Peloponnesian War was the fear inspired in the Lacedaemonians by the rise of Athens to greatness; and this fear compelled them to take up arms'—under threat of seeing the 'sanitary cordon' of their Peloponnesian alliance dissolve and their Athenian enemy from beyond the Isthmus join hands, to their undoing, with their Messenian enemy within their gates.

[1] See p. 183, n. 2.
[3] Herodotus, Book I, chaps. 152–3.
[2] Herodotus, Book I, chap. 69.
[4] Thucydides, Book I, chap. 23.

In 432 B.C. Corinthian diplomacy succeeded in compelling Spartan states-manship to assume the leadership of Hellas at last; and, in the Great War of 431–404 B.C., the Spartan military machine—now tested, for the first time, to the uttermost—performed all that its makers had intended, and all that Sparta's neighbours hoped or feared. . . . When this first stage in the self-inflicted attrition of the Hellenic Society came to an end in the year 404 B.C., it was Athens and not Sparta that lay prostrate. Yet the Spartan King Arkhi-damos's prophecy—uttered at the moment when the die was cast—that 'this day' would prove to 'be the beginning of great evils for Hellas'[1] came true in respect of the victors no less than the vanquished; for the greatness which Sparta now tardily and involuntarily retrieved from her prostrated rival proved to be a veritable Shirt of Nessus.[2]

The epitaph of the 'Lycurgan' system has been written by Aristotle in the form of a general proposition.[3]

Peoples ought not to train themselves in the art of war with an eye to sub-jugating neighbours who do not deserve to be subjugated. . . . The paramount aim of any social system should be to frame military institutions, like all other institutions, with an eye to the circumstances of peace-time, when the soldier is off duty; and this proposition is borne out by the facts of experience. Mili-taristic states are apt to survive only so long as they remain at war, while they go to ruin as soon as they have finished making their conquests. Peace causes their metal to lose its temper; and the fault lies with a social system which does not teach its soldiers what to make of their lives when they are off duty.

This verdict is applied by Aristotle to Sparta explicitly in another passage.[4]

The whole regime is directed towards securing a high standard in one department only, namely the military field. This is, of course, the key to victory; so the Spartans did well while they were at war, but came to grief when they had acquired an empire. This was because they did not know what to make of peace-time. They had made their training for war paramount over training for anything else.

In 404 B.C.,

a people trained consummately but exclusively for warlike contact with its neighbours found itself suddenly compelled, by the outcome of one particular war, to enter into non-military relations for which they were not only un-prepared but were positively unfitted by their peculiar institutions and habits and êthos. These peculiarities which the Spartans . . . had developed in order to grapple with a previous problem, and which had given them superhuman strength within the limits of the narrow environment within which their lines had previously been cast, now took their revenge upon this peculiar people

---

[1] Thucydides, Book II, chap. 13.
[2] Toynbee, op. cit., vol. iii, pp. 70–2.
[3] Aristotle, *Politics*, Book VII, chap. 12 (13), §§ 14–15 (1333b–1334a).
[4] Ibid., Book II, chap. 6 (9), § 22 (1271b).

by making them inhumanly or infra-humanly incompetent to live in the wider world into which the fortunes of war had eventually carried them. The very exactness of their adaptation to their previous environment made any re-adaptation to a new environment so difficult for them as to be virtually impossible; and the very qualities which had been the secret of their success in the one situation became their worst enemies when they found themselves in the other. . . . The Spartans came to grief when, in consequence of a military victory, they had to take upon their own shoulders the imperial responsibilities of Athens instead of merely holding the naval and military power of Athens at bay.[1]

The apparently total victory of Sparta over Athens in 404 B.C. did, in fact, upset Sparta's 'Lycurgan' way of life in two ways.

On the one hand, it put an end to Sparta's previous automatic monetary insulation from the outer world by deluging her with a flood of gold and silver coin. The post-war invasion of Sparta by 'the owls of Athena', which by this time had become the international currency of the entire Mediterranean World, was more damaging than the invasion of Sparta's coasts by Athenian landing-parties during the foregoing hostilities. The invading Athenian marines had subverted the helots; the invading Athenian 'owls' subverted the Spartan homoioi themselves; and the arrival of these migratory birds created still greater consternation among the Spartan authorities than the importation of musical instruments with excessive numbers of strings.[2] The authorities now ruled that, at Sparta, the holding of gold and silver coin should be legal for the Spartan state,[3] but that it should be a state monopoly and should be illegal for private citizens,[4] and, in at least one conspicuous case, they made an example of a citizen who had violated this law. Gylippos, the Spartiate who had done perhaps as much as any other single man to bring Athens to the ground in the war of 431–404 B.C. by foiling the Athenian attempt to conquer Sicily, was forced to go into exile after the restoration of peace when his servant laid information that there was 'a bevy of owls in the tilery'.[5] But these measures were ineffective. The Government failed to save Sparta from being exposed belatedly, and therefore disastrously, to the subversive social effects of a money economy from which her citizens had so long been artificially sheltered. 'The date at which Lakedaimon was first attacked by social disease and corruption practically

[1] Toynbee, op. cit., vol. iii, p. 72.

[2] See p. 291.

[3] Polybius, Book VI, chap. 49, §§ 7–10, and chap. 50, §§ 3–4, points out that an agricultural economy and an iron currency that had no exchange value ceased to provide an adequate economic and financial basis for the Spartan state's foreign policy when Sparta's range of action came to extend beyond the bounds of the Peloponnese.

[4] Xenophon, *Lak. Pol.*, chap. 7, § 6; Plutarch, *Lysander*, chap. 17; *Apophth. Lac.*, Lysandros, 15.

[5] Plutarch, *Lysander*, chap. 16.

coincides with the moment at which she overthrew the Athenian Empire and gorged herself with the precious metals.'[1]

The introduction of a money economy was subversive because it brought in its train an overt revolution in the Spartan attitude towards the transfer of private property from one hand to another.[2] The concentration of property in fewer and fewer hands, which had been taking place gradually since, and in consequence of, the inauguration of the 'Lycurgan' regime, now gathered speed in going to inordinate lengths.

The importation of the precious metals into Sparta after the Spartan victory in 404 B.C. was accompanied by an exportation from Sparta of Spartiate homoioi; and this other consequence of victory was disastrous for Sparta in more obvious ways. Now that Sparta had inherited from Athens a domination over the whole Hellenic World, she found herself compelled to second her homoioi from military service, from which they could not safely be spared, to non-military duties with which they could not safely be entrusted. At Leuktra in 371 B.C. there were only 'about seven hundred' Spartiatai in the Lacedaemonian line of battle;[3] and, though this drop in numbers was, in part, a reflection of the gradual decline in the total numerical strength of the homoioi since the inauguration of the 'Lycurgan' regime, we may guess that it was due, to a greater extent, to the reduction, since the Decelean War, in the number of homoioi that could still be retained for the performance of military service. Since then, an increasing number of the homoioi had been eagerly[4] serving abroad in civilian capacities, and this had been a misfortune for Sparta herself as well as for the ex-subjects of Athens who had now come under Spartan rule.

In the exchange of Athenian itinerant commissioners for Spartan resident 'harmostai', these subject Greeks' chastisement had been 'escalated' from whips to scorpions. The euphemistic term 'harmostai' ('adjusters') could not conceal the truth that a Spartiate who had been 'conditioned', from childhood, to make a good phalangite—and even a good enomotarkhes, pentekoster, lokhagos, or polemarkhos—made an intolerable governor for a non-Spartan Greek community. The homoios abroad was neither fish, flesh, nor fowl. He ceased to be 'Spartan' as soon as he was released from the convergent pressures of custom, public opinion, and governmental tyranny to which he had been subject at home; but the effects of the previous conditioning that had failed to keep the homoios still 'Spartan' abroad also inhibited him, abroad, from becoming 'Hellenic' in the contemporary connotation of the word in the world outside Sparta's frontiers.

[1] Plutarch, *Agis*, chap. 5.   [2] See the present Part, chap. 4, Annex II.
[3] Xenophon, *Hellenica*, Book VI, chap. 4, § 15. See also the present Part, chap. 5, Annex IV.
[4] Xenophon, *Lak. Pol.*, chap. 14, §§ 2 and 4.

Besides having, from the time of the Decelean War onwards, to second an increasing number of homoioi to unfamiliar jobs in which they were apt to bring discredit on themselves and on their country, the Spartan Government was now also having to provide for its growing demands on the homoioi out of a pool that had been gradually dwindling in size since the date at which the 'Lycurgan' regime had been inaugurated. The numbers of the homoioi continued to diminish. Like the increasing peculiarity of the Spartan way of life, this was a development that no one at Sparta can have intended or foreseen at the time when the 'Lycurgan' regime was introduced there. Manifestly this decline in numbers was inimical to the public interest. How, then, is it to be accounted for? The cause of the constant diminution of the numbers of the homoioi is to be found in the terms of the 'Lycurgan' settlement itself. The conditions on which the kleroi had been granted to their holders can be seen, in retrospect, to have been improvident. It can also be seen, in a longer retrospect, that these improvident terms had been a consequence of the Spartan commoners' reaction to their previous struggle with the aristocrats for the possession of Sparta's helot-cultivated conquered lands.

The 'Lycurgan' agoge at Sparta had some features in common with the contemporary regime in the city-states in Crete. Some of these common features were conspicuous and important enough to have led to the conjecture that the 'Lycurgan' regime at Sparta was a copy of a Cretan prototype.[1] There was, however, at least one significant difference between the two systems. In the Cretan states, as in Sparta's dominions before the close of the eighth century B.C., there were lands cultivated by conquered native rural slaves for the benefit of a dominant community. Again, in the dominant community in Crete and in Sparta alike, there were men's messes, originally known as 'andreia' at Sparta as well as in Crete.[2] The provision for these messes was, however, not the same in the two cases. In a Cretan city-state the state itself retained in its own hands enough of the dominant community's slave-cultivated lands to provide for the messes at the public expense. By contrast, at Sparta, under the 'Lycurgan' settlement, all the helot-cultivated public land was, so far as we know, distributed in irrevocable kleroi to Spartan private citizens. At any rate, the Spartan public treasury was notoriously penurious;[3] and, in consonance with this, the provision for a Spartan mess was the responsibility, not of the Spartan state, but of the individual members of the mess,[4] drawing on the produce of their kleroi.

Why, in the 'Lycurgan' settlement, had the Spartan state parted, as

---

[1] See chap. 4, Annex I.
[2] See ibid.
[3] Thucydides, Book I, chap. 81; Aristotle, *Politics*, Book II, chap. 6 (9), § 23 (1271b).
[4] Ibid., § 21 (1271a); chap. 7 (10), § 4 (1272a).

it appears to have done, with all Sparta's helot-cultivated lands? And why, when it distributed all these lands to individual Spartiatai as kleroi, had the state not retained an ultimate right over this public property?[1] The kleroi could have been granted to their holders on a life-tenure and then, on the death of each successive holder, a kleros could have been allocated by the state to whatever applicant for it might have seemed most eligible in the public interest.

Some 2,000 years after the probable date of the 'Lycurgan' settlement at Sparta, Sparta's two-fifths of the Peloponnese, together with vast further territories, extending south-eastwards into Syria and north-westwards into the middle basin of the Danube, were carved up into the equivalent of Spartan kleroi by the builders of the Ottoman Empire; and in this case the government that allocated the allotments did, for several centuries on end, assert its eminent domain over these allotments effectively by resuming possession at the death of each grantee and then reallocating the fief to whomsoever it pleased. It was not till well on in the seventeenth century, when the Ottoman regime had begun to decay, that an Ottoman timariot or zā'im could begin to reckon on his probably being able to hand on his fief to one of his sons.

Why had the Spartan Government failed to retain for itself a corresponding control?[2] The question arises because it was in the Spartan

---

[1] On this point, see Grote, op. cit., Part II, chap. 6, pp. 174–81. Grote here argues convincingly that the Spartan state did not retain for itself any control over the holding of land, with a view to preventing an increase in the inequality of the size of estates, and that the homoioi, for their part, did not co-operate voluntarily for this purpose. Roussel, op. cit., pp. 54–5, takes the same view as Grote. Roussel, on p. 122, holds that the Spartan state did not forbid kleros-holders either to split up their kleroi or to acquire more kleroi than one. See also Michell, op. cit., pp. 208–9; Meier, op. cit., p. 39, p. 40, n. 3, pp. 41, 54, 67. At Sparta 'there were no provisions giving the state a right of eminent domain over the soil, no governmental measures for keeping the number of kleroi constant, and, in general, no regulations for the avoidance of changes of ownership' (Meier, op. cit., p. 78; cp. p. 82).

[2] There is one passage in Plutarch's *Lycurgus*, chap. 16, which implies that the Spartan Government, like the Ottoman Government, did resume possession of kleroi, vacated by the kleros-holder's death, in order to reallocate them. According to this passage, if a new-born male child had been passed as being physically fit by the seniors among the members of its father's phyle, these not only gave him licence to survive but 'assigned to him one of the 9,000 kleroi'. This statement is suspect because it is in contradiction with all our other information. As far as we know, a kleros, once allocated, could be acquired at Sparta originally only by inheritance from a previous holder. After the enactment of the rhetra of Epitadeus (see chap. 4, Annex II), a kleros could be acquired alternatively by gift or by bequest made by the present holder.

Even if the state had had kleroi at its disposal, it is most unlikely that it would have allocated one of them to a new-born infant merely on the strength of this infant's having been passed as being physically fit. The function of a kleros was to provide for the maintenance of an homoios, but, in order to become an homoios, a Spartiate had to satisfy two conditions. First, he must have passed, with credit, through all the stages of the Spartan system of education from the beginning of his eighth year to the end of his twentieth year. In the second place, he must be co-opted into a mess by a unanimous vote of the existing members. It is incredible that the Spartan state should have been either able or willing to earmark a kleros—

Government's interest, just as much as it was in the Ottoman Government's interest, that its kleroi should be made to maintain the maximum number of soldiers of the highest quality; and this important public interest could not be secured if a kleros, once allocated to its original recipient, was allowed by the state to be bequeathed by this first holder to his heirs as if it had been his freehold property.

One reason for the difference between Spartan and Ottoman policy on this point was, no doubt, a technical one. It would be impossible for a government to call in and reallocate vacant kleroi unless it had a large enough and expert enough corps of professional civil servants to see to this; and neither Sparta nor any other Hellenic state before the foundation of the Ptolemaic Monarchy possessed this requisite administrative equipment. On the other hand, the Ottoman Imperial Government did command the services of a numerous and literate body of administrators. However, even if the Spartan Government had possessed the administrative facilities for keeping control over its kleroi on the relatively petty scale of the Lacedaemonian body politic, it seems improbable that a settlement on this basis could have been agreed in the political circumstances of the time at which the 'Lycurgan' regime was inaugurated.

The Spartiate commoners who were being converted into homoioi had, by this time, been cheated of their share in the conquered lands for so long that they had become suspicious. By this time, they will have been insistent that the kleroi should be allotted to them outright on the sole condition that the kleros-holder should be under an obligation to perform full-time military service. If it had been stipulated that the commoner recipient's kleros should escheat to the state at his death, he would have suspected this stipulation of being a trick to enable the state to hand his kleros back again to the aristocrats. *A fortiori*, the commoner recipients of kleroi would have been suspicious of dishonest intentions on the aristocracy's part if it had been proposed at Sparta that enough of the disputed state lands should remain in the state's possession to allow of the provision for the messes being made by the state. The commoner would have suspected that the product of undistributed state lands would actually be used, not for provisioning the messes, but for subsidizing the aristocracy, as in the past. The commoners will have wanted the maximum number of kleroi to be distributed, and this with the minimum number of restrictions on the kleros-holder's rights over his kleros.

On these points the commoner recipients of kleroi seem to have had

not to speak of keeping it vacant—for twenty years on the chance that the infant to whom they were allocating it would eventually succeed in becoming an homoios.

We may conclude that Plutarch's statement, in the passage here in question, is incorrect. The most that the elders can have had it in their power to do for an infant whom they had reprieved from infanticide will have been to certify that he was physically eligible for holding a kleros, supposing that he were to inherit one at some future date.

their way. It was, however, a necessary corollary of a settlement on these lines that the provision for the messes should be made, not by the state, as in Crete, but by the messmates themselves out of the produce of their respective kleroi.[1] No other source remained from which the messes could be provided for now that the state had divested itself of all its helot-cultivated lands in favour of the individual kleros-holders. Moreover, the obligation that was thus inevitably imposed on the individual member of a mess had to be strictly enforced; for, if the members were to fail to produce their quota of the necessary provision, the mess would cease to function, and Sparta could not afford to see this happen. She could not, because the mess, which had originated as a private club, had become a public institution as well under the 'Lycurgan' regime. At Sparta under the 'Lycurgan' regime the messes (andreia, phiditia, philitia, syskeniai, syssitia)[2] had been brought under the control of the polemarchs, who were the highest military public officers under the crown; and they had been made to serve as the basic permanent units in the organization of the new model army: the hoplite phalanx of homoioi.[3] Thus the maintenance of all the messes had become a military necessity; the survival of a mess could not be allowed to be placed in jeopardy by a member's defaulting on his obligations; and consequently the penalty for defaulting had to be severe. A defaulting member forfeited his membership[4] to make way for the co-option of a new member who seemed more likely to prove solvent. The ex-messmate, in losing his place in his mess, also lost his status as an homoios and, with it, his voice in the assembly of the damos.

The size of a Spartan homoios' kleros must have been large compared to the average size of a hoplite's estate in any other Greek community. In other Greek states a hoplite had to earn his living in agriculture, trade, or industry.[5] A Spartan homoios' kleros was expected to support one hoplite as a full-time professional soldier. We may guess, however, that the contributions (ἀποφοραί) due to a kleros-holder from the helot cultivators of his kleros could not provide for the requirements of more than a single rentier who had to pay his dues to his mess besides maintaining

---

[1] The Ottoman janissaries, too, financed their messes—in this case, out of the pay that they received from the state (B. Ramberti, *The Second Book of the Affairs of the Turks* (1534), translated from the Italian by A. H. Lybyer, in *The Government of the Ottoman Empire in the Time of Suleiman the Magnificent* (Cambridge, Mass., 1913, Harvard University Press), p. 249.

[2] Alkman, quoted by Strabo, *Geographica*, Book X, chap. 4, § 18 (C. 482), calls them andreia, which was the term used in Crete. Xenophon uses the terms syskeniai and syskenoi, and also philitia. Hesychius glosses ὑσκανία as being equivalent to ὑσσίτιον.

[3] See Norvin, *Classica et Mediaevalia*, vol. iii, fasc. 1, p. 80, and the present work, pp. 228, 319–20, 322–3, 369 and 383.

[4] See p. 230.

[5] See the anecdote cited on pp. 160–1 from Plutarch, *Agesilaos*, chap. 26, and *Apophth. Lac.*, Agesilaos, 72.

a wife and children; and the Spartan kleros-holder had not any means
of augmenting his income if he was not one of those fortunate few homoioi
of aristocratic origin who possessed freehold estates in addition to their
kleroi. Though the Spartan state seems at least tacitly to have renounced
its right to resume possession of the kleroi when once these had been
distributed, it had imposed on the kleros-holder some conditions which,
in combination, were economically onerous for him. The state had fixed
a ceiling for a helot's contribution to the holder of the kleros in which
the helot's plot of land was included;[1] the kleros-holder was debarred
from augmenting his income by exacting more from his helots than that;
and he was also debarred from augmenting it by engaging, for his own
part, in a gainful occupation.[2]

These vetos were reasonable from the state's point of view. The state's
whole purpose in distributing the kleroi had been to secure the services
of so many full-time professional soldiers. If it had allowed the homoioi
to draw their incomes from their kleroi and to engage in gainful occupa-
tions as well, the state would have been surrendering a necessary safe-
guard of the kleros-holder's military efficiency. This point is illustrated
by the history of the Ottoman Empire's professional soldiers and administrators. In the Ottoman Pādishāh's slave-household, which was the
Ottoman counterpart, not of the Spartan heloteia, but of the damos
of Spartiate homoioi, the mastering of a manual trade was an obligatory
part of the educational curriculum; and this was incumbent even on
a future pādishāh, since he, too, was a member of the slave-household in
virtue of his being the son of a slave-mother. Hence, when, in the days of
the Ottoman Empire's decline, the depreciation of the currency reduced
the value of the janissaries' official salaries, they supplemented their
salaries by earnings from their trades. This saved the janissaries from
falling into economic distress, but it also eventually converted them from
full-time soldiers into full-time tradesmen. The Spartiate homoios was
precluded from keeping the wolf from the door in the janissary's un-
soldierly way.

As for the ceiling that had been placed on the helots' contribution
to the kleros-holder, the Spartan Government was as provident in fixing
this as the Ottoman Government was in similarly protecting its ra'īyeh
against undue exactions on the part of the timariots and zā'ims. Both
governments realized that their armies were perched on the contributing
peasantry's shoulders, and that, if they allowed the soldier to make life
impossible for the peasant, the military machine would collapse.

Thus there was good reason, from the Spartan Government's point of
view, for its vetos on the kleros-holder's either rack-renting his helots or

---

[1] See pp. 202–3 and 230.
[2] Xenophon, *Lak. Pol.*, chap. 7, § 2; Plutarch, *Lycurgus*, chap. 24.

supplementing his fixed income from his kleros by making earnings on the side. At the same time, this rigid limitation of the kleros-holder's income worked together with the rigid insistence on the payment of mess-dues to place him in a quandary; for, though his income from his kleros might have been nicely calculated to suffice for his own needs, he could not foresee whether it would run to enabling all his descendants, too, to become solvent members of messes—which was the qualifying condition for their becoming homoioi in their turn. 'The existence of this rate-paying qualification is the capital fact in the history of the Spartan constitution—especially when we couple with it the other fact, that no Spartan acquired anything by any kind of industry.'[1]

As far as the next generation was concerned, solvency would be assured if the present holder of the kleros had only one son, or if all his sons except one were to pre-decease him through dying of disease or being killed in war. Suppose, on the other hand, that the present holder were to leave behind him several surviving sons, and suppose that some, at least, of these were to leave several surviving sons in their turn; then, sooner or later, a point would be reached at which the produce of the family kleros would not suffice to enable all adult and fully qualified male members of the family to become, and to remain, homoioi by each paying an homoios' dues to a mess. In that case, some of the present holder's descendants would be reduced—not by personal demerit, but simply by irremediable poverty—to having to spend their lives as hypomeiones. This was an unenviable status, and the possibility that some of a kleros-holding homoios' descendants might be condemned to this through no fault of their own would cause a kleros-holder anxiety if he were not one of the lucky few who owned freehold property in addition to their kleroi.[2]

This anxiety would be a standing inducement to a commoner kleros-holder (and the commoners must have been in a great majority) to take two precautions that were both contrary to the public interest. The kleros-holder would be tempted to limit the number of his children;[3] and he would be on the look-out for chances of augmenting his kleros by acquiring other kleroi (or fractions of kleroi) or by acquiring freeholds.

Various Spartan practices that would have the effect of keeping down the size of families are, in fact, on record. One such practice that had nothing to be said against it was the postponement, at Sparta, of marriage —and this for both sexes—to a considerably older age, on the average, than was customary in other Greek communities.[4] Another restrictive

---

[1] Grote, loc. cit., p. 165, n. 2.
[2] This point is made by Forrest, *A History*, p. 136.
[3] This point is made by Jones, *Sparta*, p. 136, and by Forrest, *A History*, p. 136.
[4] Xenophon, *Lak. Pol.*, chap. 1, § 6; Plutarch, *Lycurgus*, chap. 15; idem, *Apophth. Lac.*, Lykourgos, 16.

device was polyandry. According to Timaeus, as reported by Polybius,[1] there were cases at Sparta in which three or four or more brothers would all marry the same wife—an arrangement that would limit the number of children begotten by several fathers to the number that one mother could bear in the course of her child-bearing years.[2] Another reported custom was for a husband to invite an eligible man who was not his brother to share his wife with him. This practice of wife-sharing with a non-relative seems to have taken three alternative forms. The wife's children by the outsider might count as, and be brought up as, the children of her legal husband;[3] or the wife might maintain two separate establishments: one with the legal husband and the other with the outsider;[4] or she might be handed over by her husband to the outsider completely.[5] Under any of these arrangements the effect on numbers would be the same as when the wife-sharers were brothers. The effect would be to limit the number of children begotten by more than one man to the number that one woman could bear.[6]

Another practice that made indirectly for a restriction of the number of births was paederasty, since this practice offered satisfaction to the male sexual appetite in a form of sexual intercourse that was infertile. Evidently paederasty was rife at Sparta[7]—though this practice was not peculiar to Sparta but was current throughout the Hellenic World. Xenophon[8] avers that, at Sparta, paederasty was an exclusively spiritual relation, with no physical side to it; but this is hard to believe.[9]

The state tried to combat restrictive family planning by legislation in favour of fathers of large families. A father of three children was exempt from military service; a father of four was exempt from taxation as well.[10] Conversely, a man who went to the length of remaining a bachelor exposed himself to the more powerful sanction of hostile public opinion. In private life he would be treated with studied disrespect by his juniors;

---

[1] Polybius, Book XII, chap. 63, § 8.

[2] However, in loc. cit., the reason for this custom is said to have been the scarcity of women as a result of the earthquake of *circa* 466 or 464 B.C. The wish to restrict the number of children is not mentioned in this context.

[3] Xenophon, *Lak. Pol.*, chap. 1, § 7; Plutarch, *Lycurgus*, chap. 15.

[4] Xenophon, *Lak. Pol.*, chap. 1, §§ 8 and 9; Plutarch in loc. cit.

[5] Polybius in loc. cit.

[6] L. Ziehen, 'Das spartanische Bevölkerungsproblem', in *Hermes*, 68. Band (1933), p. 237, guesses that the Spartiate women, for their part, refused to bear the maximum number of children.

[7] Plutarch, *Lycurgus*, chap. 17.

[8] In *Lak. Pol.*, chap. 2, § 13.

[9] Plutarch, too, in *Inst. Lac.* 7, denies that there was a physical side to this relation. In *Lycurgus* he does not deny it expressly, but indicates that it had a spiritual aspect. A boy's lover was held responsible for the boy's behaviour (*Lycurgus*, chap. 18). See also Roussel, op. cit., pp. 46–7; Berve, op. cit., p. 47.

[10] Aristotle, *Politics*, Book II, chap. 6 (9), § 13 (1270b).

and all bachelors are said to have been subjected annually to a public ordeal in which they were made objects of ridicule and obloquy.[1] These counter-measures are indications that the restrictive practices were recognized to be having the effect of reducing the number of the homoioi to a dangerous extent.

Besides trying to keep down the number of his children, the Spartan homoios tried to increase the amount of his property. This had been made difficult for him by law as well as by custom. It was illegal to sell a family's original kleros; it was deemed dishonourable to give away or to bequeath to someone other than one's legal heirs any land of either category until gifts and bequests to non-kinsmen were legitimized by the enactment of Epitadeus' rhetra.[2] Presumably it had been expected, at the time of the 'Lycurgan' settlement, that law and custom, between them, would militate effectively against any tendency for property to become concentrated in a diminishing number of hands. However, human ingenuity is apt to find a way of circumventing both law and custom when there is a powerful motive for doing so; the status-preservation motive for accumulating property was very powerful in 'Lycurgan' Sparta; and we may guess that the enactment of Epitadeus' rhetra merely legalized a practice that was actually current already.

Besides gift and bequest, illicit or legalized, there were at least three other ways in which property could be transferred from one family to another.

One way was adoption. If an homoios had no son, or no surviving son, of his own, he might adopt a male member of another family in order to save his own family from extinction. In this situation his private interest would coincide with the state's interest. Presumably, a boy, eiren, or grown man who was willing, or whose father was willing for him, to be adopted into another family would be one who had no prospect of inheriting from his own father enough property to enable him to pay dues to a mess. An homoios who did have surviving sons of his own would be unlikely to adopt a member of some other family unless he was rich enough to feel sure of being able to endow his adopted son, as well as his own son or sons, with at least the minimum amount of property that a member of a mess needed to have. In this case again the adoptive father's private interest and the state's interest would coincide. The state would be acquiring an additional recruit for its hoplite phalanx; the adoptive father would be acquiring an additional voice for his family in the assembly of the damos of homoioi.

A second way in which property could be transferred from one family to another was through the marriage of an epikleros: a woman who was

---

[1] Plutarch, *Lycurgus*, chap. 15; *Apophth. Lac.*, Lykourgos, 14.
[2] See chap. 4, Annex II.

her father's heir because she had no brothers, or none surviving.[1] At Sparta, no doubt, as at Athens and in other Hellenic communities, the nearest collateral male relative had a first claim to the heiress's hand. But, if there were no surviving unmarried male relatives, however distantly related, her father could betroth her to anyone whom he might choose; and in Aristotle's day he might perhaps pass over a living relative who had a valid claim in favour of a more advantageous marriage with a member of some other family.[2] Wealth has a tendency to marry wealth, and this leads to the concentration of property in the hands of a minority.[3]

A third means of transferring property from one family to another was the giving of dowries. According to Aristotle,[4] Spartan dowries were big. According to Plutarch, Justin, and Aelian,[5] dowries were not given at Sparta. Perhaps dowries were one of the forms of gift that were legitimized by the enactment of Epitadeus' rhetra.

Under the 'Lycurgan' constitution, two of the three surviving prerogatives of the kings in the civil sphere were to act as registrars of adoptions and to choose husbands for heiresses whose fathers have not done this for them.[6] If, in this second field of jurisdiction, the kings used their discretion in order to serve the public interest, they will have betrothed uncommitted heiresses to indigent but worthy hypomeiones who needed only an endowment to convert them into good homoioi. It is perhaps more likely that the kings played politics by betrothing the heiress to some influential rich man who was on the look-out for opportunities of adding field to field.[7]

An homoios must have been perpetually anxious to make sure that neither he nor any of his male descendants should be reduced by poverty to the unhappy status of hypomeiones; and this must be part of the explanation of the cupidity that was a notorious Spartan vice. The dictum χρήματ' ἀνήρ was attributed to a Spartiate named Aristodamos by the Lesbian poet Alkaios;[8] and at Sparta this cynical equation was justified

---

[1] Epikleroi were numerous at Sparta in Aristotle's day (*Politics*, Book II, chap. 6 (9), § 11 (1270a)). Presumably an epikleros could inherit her father's kleros, as well as any private freehold real estate that he might have possessed.

[2] Aristotle, *Politics*, Book II, chap. 6 (9), § 11 (1270a).

[3] This point is made by Forrest, *A History*, p. 137.   [4] Aristotle in loc. cit.

[5] Plutarch, *Apophth. Lac.*, Lykourgos, 15; Justin, Book III, chap. 3, § 8; Aelian, *V.H.*, Book VI, chap. 6.

[6] Herodotus, Book VI, chap. 57.

[7] Grote, loc. cit., p. 181, n. 1, considers that the kings did not have any power to influence either the disposal of heiresses or the choice of adoptive sons. Roussel, op. cit., p. 122, takes the same view. By Aristotle's time, the prerogative of choosing a husband for an heiress whose father had neglected to choose one for her before his death had passed from the king to the person whom the father, in his will, had designated as his heir (*Politics*, Book II, chap. 6 (9), § 11 (1270a)).

[8] Alkaios, 101 (49), in Diehl, *Anthologia Lyrica Graeca*, 2nd ed., fasc. 3, pp. 139–40.

by the hard fact that, without property, a Spartan citizen could not become or remain an homoios, because he could not become or remain a member of a mess. The nemesis of this cupidity was proclaimed in the, no doubt, retrospective oracle (said to have been given to 'Lycurgus'): 'Cupidity will be Sparta's ruin; she is proof against everything but that (ἁ φιλοχρηματία Σπάρταν ὀλεῖ, ἄλλο δὲ οὐδέν).'[1] Aristotle stigmatizes both the ephors[2] and the gerontes[3] for their proneness to turn their power to account for making private profits for themselves. The homoioi were reluctant taxpayers,[4] and, 'since most of the land is their property, they connive at each other's tax-evasions.[5] Consequently, their public finances are in a bad way; the treasury is empty; and the "Lycurgan" legislation has had the untoward effect of beggaring the state by making the private citizens avaricious.'[6] 'Conditioned to repress fear, the Spartan compensated by indulging greed; bribery, not cowardice, was his fatal weakness.'[7]

The stimulation of private cupidity among the Spartiate homoioi was an ironical outcome for a regime that had been designed to make the homoioi uneconomic-minded, in order that they should dedicate themselves exclusively and whole-heartedly to their military career. Sparta had not only forborne to equip herself with a gold or silver coinage; she had made a minimal use even of her antiquated currency of iron 'spits'. Most economic transactions continued to be conducted in kind. The helot paid in kind his contribution to the homoios who was his master;[8] and, out of this, the homoios paid in kind his dues to his mess, except for a tiny payment in (presumably iron) money.[9] But this archaic economy did not produce its intended effect of acting as a prophylactic against greed. The homoios had been condemned by the terms of the 'Lycurgan' settlement to live, ever after, under constant economic pressure; his inevitable reaction was an urge to insure his solvency by accumulating property; and property did not need to be converted into gold and silver coin[10] in order to excite his cupidity.

[1] Diodorus, Book VII, fragm. 12, § 5. According to Plutarch, *Inst. Lac.* 41, this oracle had been delivered to Kings Alkamenes and Theopompos.
[2] Aristotle, *Politics*, Book II, chap. 6 (9), § 14 (1270b).
[3] Ibid., § 18 (1271a).
[4] Thucydides, Book I, chap. 80; Aristotle, *Politics*, Book II, chap. 6 (9), § 23 (1271b).
[5] Aristotle, ibid.   [6] Ibid.
[7] T. W. Africa, *Phylarchus and the Spartan Revolution* (Berkeley and Los Angeles, 1961, University of California Press), p. vii.
[8] Plutarch, *Lycurgus*, chap. 8.
[9] Ibid., chap. 12. See also Dicaearchus in Athenaeus, Book IV, 141 c (Müller, *F.H.G.*, vol. ii, p. 242).
[10] According to Xenophon, *Lak. Pol.*, chap. 7, § 6, domiciliary visits were made to find out if any Spartan was in possession of gold or silver, and the penalty for possessing it was a fine. There had been an influx of the precious metals into Sparta after 404 B.C. (Plato (?), *Alcibiades*, 1, 122 C–123 A), and it had been ruled that the state might possess them, but not

This preoccupation with the acquisition of property produced an ever more extreme inequality in the distribution of property among the homoioi,[1] not to speak of their poverty-stricken fellow Spartiatai the hypomeiones. Wealthy Spartans are mentioned by Herodotus[2] and by Xenophon.[3] Some Spartans now prided themselves on possessing gold.[4] They made a conspicuous display by breeding horses.[5] There were Spartan winners of the four-horse-chariot race at Olympia throughout the fifth and fourth centuries B.C.[6] In 370 B.C. the Arcadian contingent in the enemy forces that were invading Laconia found the rich Spartiates' country-houses very well worth looting.[7] By Aristotle's time, 'the inequality in the distribution of property is one of the reprehensible features of Spartan life. Some Spartans are excessively wealthy; others are excessively poor. Consequently, the country has fallen into the hands of a small minority.'[8]

By Aristotle's time, Spartans outside this privileged minority were having to turn to and cultivate their lands with their own hands.[9] Apparently, by the date of King Agis IV's accession, *circa* 244 B.C., only about 100 out of the 700 Spartiate homoioi of the day possessed any land to speak of.[10] 'Le jeu de l'égoïsme familiale . . . a récrée une aristocratie fondée sur la fortune.'[11]

private citizens (see p. 298, with n. 4). Lysander is said to have deposited a golden model of a trireme and some money, on his own account, in the Treasury of Brasidas and the Acanthians at Delphi (Plutarch, *Lysander*, chap. 18). However, Lysander died a poor man (ibid., chap. 30). Rich Spartans are said to have deposited money in Arcadia (Poseidonius in Athenaeus, Book VI, 233 f).

The passage in the *Alcibiades* runs as follows: 'In the whole of the rest of the Hellenic World there is not as much gold and silver as there is in Lakedaimon alone. For many generations by now, the precious metals have been flowing into Sparta from the whole Hellenic World, and often from the non-Hellenes as well. None of this flows out again to any quarter. . . . So it is a fact of certain knowledge that the Lacedaemonians are the richest of all the Hellenes in gold and silver; and, among them, the king is the richest man of all.'

[1] See Eduard Meyer, op. cit., p. 257.

[2] Herodotus, Book VI, chap. 61.

[3] Xenophon, *Hellenica*, Book VI, chap. 4, § 11; *Lak. Pol.*, chap. 5, § 3.

[4] Xenophon, *Lak. Pol.*, chap. 14, § 3.

[5] Xenophon, *Hellenica*, loc. cit.; Plutarch, *Apophth. Lac.*, Agesilaos, 49; Pausanias, Book III, chap. 8, § 1, and chap. 15, § 1.

[6] Kiechle, *Lakonien und Sparta*, p. 190. By far the oldest, certainly authentic, surviving Laconian inscription—the boastful one dedicated to Athana Khalkioikos at Sparta by Damonon about half-way through the fifth century B.C. (see p. 154)—is a record of victories in four-horse-chariot races and horse-races. However, Damonon's and his son's numerous successes seem all to have been gained, not at the international festival at Olympia, but at local festivals within Sparta's own dominions (e.g. at Helos and Thouria and in the Maleatis), where the competition will have been much less severe.

[7] Xenophon, *Hellenica*, Book VI, chap. 5, § 30.

[8] *Politics*, Book VI, chap. 6 (9), § 10 (1270a). On this, see Roussel, *Sparte*, p. 55.

[9] Aristotle, *Politics*, Book II, chap. 2 (5), § 11 (1264a).

[10] Plutarch, *Agis*, chap. 5. Plutarch's words are: ἀπελείφθησαν οὖν ἑπτακοσίων οὐ πλείονες Σπαρτιᾶται, καὶ τούτων ἴσως ἑκατὸν ἦσαν οἱ γῆν κεκτημένοι καὶ κλῆρον· ὁ δ' ἄλλος ὄχλος ἄπορος

[*Notes 10 and 11 continued opposite.*

This extreme economic inequality as between the rich minority and the poor majority of the homoioi must have been made all the more exasperating for the majority by their common label—'the peers'—and by the hypocritical show of egalitarianism that was the rich minority's facile tribute to the 'Lycurgan' ideal of austerity.[1] According to Aristotle:

καὶ ἄτιμος ἐν τῇ πόλει παρεκάθητο. The equivalent of these Greek words in English is: 'Not more than 700 Spartiatai were left, and of these, those who possessed any real estate and a kleros amounted to perhaps 100. The residual populace consisted of unenfranchised paupers, domiciled in the city but superfluous.'

The natural interpretation of these words is that at Sparta in 244/3 B.C. there were 700 Spartiatai in all, of whom about 100 were homoioi (i.e. kleros-holders who might possess some freehold real estate as well), while the remaining 600 were hypomeiones. This may indeed have been what Plutarch believed that his source Phylarchus meant to say. It may even have been what Phylarchus himself did mean to say. But it can hardly be a correct representation of the situation at Sparta in 244/3 B.C.

Phylarchus' figures, interpreted according to the natural meaning of Phylarchus' words, are incredible for two reasons. The first of these is an *a priori* one. Let us make the maximum allowance for the steady decline in the numbers of the homoioi through the play of the economic and social forces examined in the present section. Even so, it is incredible that the numbers could have fallen to 100 from nearly 1,000 in 127 years—and the adult, homoioi were still nearly 1,000 strong in 371 B.C. (Aristotle, *Politics*, Book II, chap. 6 (9) § 11 (1270a)) and over 3,500 strong after the earthquake of *circa* 466 or 464 B.C., if the post-earthquake number of homoioi of military age (over twenty and under sixty) was then still about 3,200 (see p. 386). The second reason for scepticism is cogent. In 244/3 B.C. the gerousia, twenty-eight of whose members were elected out of homoioi over sixty years old, was not only still in existence; it asserted itself more vigorously than on any known previous occasion (Plutarch, *Agis*, chaps. 9 and 11). But twenty-eight men over sixty could not have been supplied out of a total of only about 100 men over twenty. This telling point has been made by Busolt and Swoboda, op. cit., p. 726, n. 1, and by A. Fuks, 'The Spartan Citizen Body in Mid-Third Century B.C. and its Enlargement Proposed by Agis IV', in *Athenaeum*, vol. 1 (N.S., vol. xl) (1962), pp. 244–63, on pp. 245–6.

In the light of these two considerations, we have to interpret Plutarch's words as meaning that not only his 100 property-owners but all his 700 Spartiatai were homoioi; that his 600 landless homoioi (a contradiction in terms) were a different category from his 'residual populace'; and that this residue, not the 600, represents the hypomeiones Spartiatai of the day (see Fuks in loc. cit., pp. 246, 248, 249, 254, 256). The 100 who were rich in 244/3 B.C. (Plutarch, *Agis*, chap. 5) will then correspond to the fourteen men killed and the eighty exiled by Kleomenes in 227 B.C. (Plutarch, *Cleomenes*, chaps. 8 and 10). Forrest, *A History*, p. 144, assumes that this is the correct interpretation.   [11] Roussel, op. cit., p. 124.

---

[1] The achievement of genuine equality (ἰσότης) was the objective of Kings Agis IV (*regnabat circa* 244–240 B.C.) and Kleomenes III (*regnabat* 237–222 B.C.) according to Fuks, 'Agis, Cleomenes, and Equality', in *Classical Philology*, vol. lvii, No. 3 (July 1962), pp. 161–6. One facet of the equality at which these two reformer-kings were aiming was common subjection to the agoge (the 'Lycurgan' discipline); another facet was uniformity in diaita (the 'Lycurgan' way of life and standard of living); a third was the redistribution of the land into equal allotments (p. 161). The two kings' measures included 'a complete redistribution of the Spartan land, coupled with a comprehensive filling-up of the citizen-body' (p. 162). Kleomenes reserved eighty plots of land for his temporarily exiled opponents (p. 162). These eighty whom he had exiled, together with the fourteen whom he had killed, accounted for the whole of the rich minority of the homoioi, who had numbered 100 at the beginning of Agis' reign (p. 164). Agis' and Kleomenes' policy of equalization applied to movable property as well as to real estate (Plutarch, *Agis*, chap. 9). The policy also applied to the land (and presumably also the movable property) of the perioecic communities, as well as to Sparta's own χώρα πολιτική (pp. 162–3).

Many people argue that Sparta is a democracy, because the regime has a number of democratic-looking traits. There is the educational system, to start with. The children of the rich are brought up like the children of the poor, and the kind of education that they are given is within the reach of the poor as well. At the following age, and again when they reach maturity, it is the same. It is not apparent who is rich and who is poor. The food is the same for all in the syssitia, and the rich dress in a way that any poor man could afford.[1]

Thucydides[2] had noted already that 'the Lacedaemonians were the first to wear simple clothes in the modern fashion, and it was at Sparta that, in general, the rich put themselves more or less on a level with the poor in their way of life'.

This equality in simplicity was the rule for Spartan funeral rites as well.[3]

Besides flattering the poorer homoioi by this visual show of conformism, the richer homoioi appeased them by giving them sops—and this in the literal sense. At the messes the minimum 'Spartan' fare was provided out of the dues that were paid at a flat rate by rich and poor messmates alike. But the richer members occasionally supplemented these commons with meat from a sacrifice or with game from a hunt,[4] or even with such a luxury as bread.[5] Xenophon points out sanctimoniously[6] that the Spartan cult of austerity kept these supplements to the commons within such modest limits that the habit of making them was no incentive to acquisitiveness. It is, indeed, true that the rich homoioi acquitted themselves of their hospitality to their poorer messmates at a trifling cost to themselves.[7] But Xenophon's question is a rhetorical one when he asks

[1] Aristotle, *Politics*, Book IV, chap. 7 (9), § 5 (1294b).
[2] Book I, chap. 6.
[3] 'There was a veto on engraving on the tombstone the name of the deceased, except in the case of a man who had died in battle and a woman who was a priestess' (Plutarch, *Lycurgus*, chap. 27). Mourning and wailing were forbidden too (*Inst. Lac.*, § 18). These sumptuary rules for the funerals of Spartan citizens did not apply to the kings. At their funerals (though not during their lifetimes) the kings were treated as ἥρωες (Xenophon, *Lak. Pol.*, chap. 15, § 9; cp. Herodotus, Book VI, chap. 58; Pausanias, Book IV, chap. 14, §§ 4–5; Aelian, *V.H.*, Book VI, chap. 1). When King Agis II died in 400 B.C., ἔτυχε σεμνοτέρας ἢ κατὰ ἄνθρωπον ταφῆς (Xenophon, *Hellenica*, Book III, chap. 3, § 1).
[4] The richer homoioi artfully provided their poorer messmates with facilities in the hunting-field which enabled these paupers to cherish the illusion that they, too, were *grands seigneurs*. A poor homoios who went hunting in the countryside was at liberty to borrow his richer messmates' slaves, hounds, and horses, and even to help himself from the larders of the rich men's country-houses (Xenophon, *Lak. Pol.*, chap. 6, §§ 3–4; Plutarch, *Inst. Lac.*, § 23). Thus the poor homoioi were enabled to enjoy the amenities of sport at a cost to the rich which was inconsiderable, and which, no doubt, repaid itself, in the rich homoioi's calculations, inasmuch as it might be expected to have some effect in reconciling the beneficiaries to the gross inequalities in the homoioi's private fortunes.
[5] Xenophon, *Lak. Pol.*, chap. 5, § 3; Plutarch, *Lycurgus*, chap. 12.
[6] Xenophon, *Lak. Pol.*, chap. 7, § 4.
[7] In private, the rich themselves may have fared more sumptuously when they contrived

what motive there could be at Sparta for desiring to be rich, considering that there were no opportunities for spending on food, clothes, or luxuries.[1] Xenophon must have been as well aware as, in a later generation, Aristotle was that wealth was coveted eagerly at Sparta nevertheless. He must have been equally well aware of the motives. The negative motive was the fear of being deprived, by poverty, of the status of being homoioi; the positive motive was a thirst for the social and political influence that wealth carried with it at Sparta, as elsewhere.

Thus, from the moment when the 'Lycurgan' regime was inaugurated, the rule that a Spartiate could not become or remain an homoios if he were unable to pay dues to a mess set up a tug-o'-war between the interest of the individual homoios and the interest of the Spartan state.[2] The state's interest was that the number of the homoioi should be maintained at the maximum figure that the number of the kleroi could support.[3] The interest of the individual homoios was that he and his descendants should retain their status.

The individual homoios sought to make sure of this by restricting the number of his children and by increasing the amount of his property if he could. To restrict the size of his family was within every homoios' power. On the other hand, the struggle to secure for himself the largest possible share of the limited total fund of agricultural land in Sparta's city-state territory was highly competitive; and, since the gift for acquiring wealth is unevenly distributed in any human community, the effect of the competition at Sparta was, as we have seen, to concentrate property, both freeholds and kleroi, in fewer and fewer hands. The combined effect of the two tendencies, interacting with each other, was to drive the numerical strength of the homoioi downwards in a vicious descending spiral. A minority acquired more property than was needed for the maintenance of their status; their enrichment of themselves was at the cost of impoverishing the majority; and this impoverishment confronted the majority, in ever sharper terms, with the choice between sinking to the status of hypomeiones and keeping the number of their children down to a minimum. An homoios' loss of his status did not diminish the size of the total population of Sparta's dominions;[4] the restriction of the number of an homoios' children did diminish this; and both alternatives diminished the numerical strength of the homoioi themselves.

to take a meal at home. At any rate, Alkman says of himself: οὔτι γὰρ ἦυ τετυγμένον ἔσθει, | ἀλλὰ τὰ κοινὰ γὰρ, ὥσπερ ὁ δᾶμος, | ζατεύει (fragm. 17 (23) (Bergk–Hiller–Crusius)).

[1] Xenophon, *Lak. Pol.*, chap. 7, § 3.
[2] See Roussel, op. cit., p. 55.
[3] Aristotle, *Politics*, Book II, chap. 6 (9), § 12 (1270a).
[4] When Xenophon, *Lak. Pol.*, chap. 1, § 1, wrote ἡ Σπάρτη τῶν ὀλιγανθρωποτάτων πόλεων οὖσα, he was thinking in terms of the numbers, not of Lakones or of Spartiatai, but of homoioi (see Busolt and Swoboda, op. cit., p. 718, n. 1; Fuks, 'The Spartan Citizen Body in Mid-Third Century B.C. and its Enlargement Proposed by Agis IV', pp. 250, 252, 262.

According to Aristotle, the number of homoioi in 371 B.C.—the date of Sparta's catastrophe at Leuktra—was less than 1,000,[1] as contrasted with a pristine figure of 10,000; and there were only 700 homoioi at the date of King Agis IV's accession *circa* 244 B.C.[2] 'Sparta's bane was paucity of numbers; she crumpled up under a single blow.'[3] Though 'Lycurgan' Sparta was an authoritarian state, the 'Lycurgan' regime had left to the individual homoios enough freedom of initiative to enable him to make his private interests prevail. The rich did have one private interest that operated, to some slight extent, for the replenishment of the reservoir of homoioi which the cupidity of the rich and the restrictive practices of the poor were depleting. An homoios who was rich enough to be relieved of all anxiety about the maintenance of his and his descendants' status might feel moved to invest his surplus wealth in acquiring the status of homoioi for clients of his who would then become his political supporters in the damos. A rich homoios sometimes made provision for a promising boy, who started as an outsider, to go through the Spartan educational curriculum and, if he made good, to go on to being co-opted into a mess.[4] In the balance-sheet of the numbers of the homoioi, the occasional enfranchisement of adopted ex-outsiders were entries on the credit side; but the effect in offsetting the constant losses was inconsiderable.

Though the forces making for a reduction of the number of the homoioi must have been at work from the start, the earliest indication that this untoward effect of the 'Lycurgan' regime was making itself felt is the abandonment by Sparta, *circa* 550 B.C., of her previous policy of conquest. We have no explicit information that the demographic factor was one of the considerations that led to this important change of policy at this date; it is only a guess; yet the guess seems a reasonable one. However, paucity of numbers does not seem yet to have been felt acutely at Sparta in 480 B.C. Herodotus' estimate of the number of adult male homoioi at that date is 'about 8,000';[5] and the Spartan Government did not hesitate, in this year, to send three hundred of them to almost certain death. On the other hand, in 425 B.C., the loss, on Sphakteria, of 112 men killed and 308 captured was taken tragically at Sparta. Evidently,

---

[1] Aristotle, *Politics*, Book II, chap. 6, § 11 (1270a). Though the subject of this sentence of Aristotle's is not explicit, he must be thinking here in terms of homoioi only, not of Spartiatai including hypomeiones, since he is contrasting his figure of 'less than 1,000' with his estimate of 1,500 cavalry and 30,000 hoplites as being the number of soldiers that the Spartan dominions, before the loss of Messenia, had been capable of maintaining.

[2] Plutarch, *Agis*, chap. 5, as interpreted on p. 310, n. 10.

[3] μίαν γὰρ πληγὴν οὐχ ὑπήνεγκεν ἡ πόλις, ἀλλ᾿ ἀπώλετο, διὰ τὴν ὀλιγανθρωπίαν (Aristotle, *Politics*, Book II, chap. 6, § 11 (1270a)).

[4] For these adopted boys, see chap. 4, Annex III.

[5] Herodotus, Book VII, chap. 234. Herodotus' ἄνδρες must be homoioi, since he makes Damaratos say that they are the peers of Leonidas' three hundred.

at some date between 480 B.C. and 425 B.C., the problem of diminishing numbers had become, for Sparta, a major anxiety.[1]

We may guess that the critical event had been the earthquake of *circa* 466 or 464 B.C. Among modern scholars there have been widely divergent estimates of the earthquake's adverse effect, both immediate and ultimate, on the numbers of the homoioi.[2] Yet, even if we were to accept the most moderate of these estimates, it would not follow that the demographic effects of the earthquake were not grave; for, by this time, Sparta may well have been already in the situation on which Aristotle has put his finger in noting her inability to recover from the blow dealt her in 371 B.C.[3] The vicious spiral of diminishing numbers may already have reached a point at which Sparta had no margin of homoian man-power to spare; and, in that situation, even small losses might have devastating effects.

This decline in the numbers of the homoioi, who were Sparta's politeuma, was the more serious for Sparta because, like so many other features of Spartan life under the 'Lycurgan' regime, it was peculiar to Sparta herself. In the Hellenic World as a whole, a comparable decline in numbers did not set in till the second century B.C.; and, in this point, the vast majority of the population of Sparta's own dominions, who were not homoioi, kept in step with the rest of the Hellenic World. There is no evidence that the Spartiate hypomeiones or the helots or the perioikoi declined in numbers *pari passu* with the homoioi. So far from that, every insolvent homoios who sank to becoming an hypomeion augmented the hypomeiones' numerical strength.[4] In the reorganization of the Lacedaemonian army at some date between 479 B.C. and 425 B.C.[5] the perioikoi appear to have been drawn upon in the ratio of six perioikoi to every four homoian Spartiatai. As for the helots, they continued to be so numerous that the Spartan Government was able to raise any number of helot volunteers at any moment. It drew largely on this source of military man-power between the years 424 and 370/69 B.C.[6] In 370/69 B.C. 6,000 helots responded to a call for volunteers, and 6,000 again in 223/2 B.C.[7] Seven hundred of the 4,000 hoplitai[8] whom Kleomenes III endowed in 227 B.C. with kleroi carved out of Sparta's city-state territory will have

---

[1] This point is made by Huxley, op. cit., p. 147, n. 667; Meier, op. cit., pp. 12 and 77; Ziehen, loc. cit., pp. 218–37, on p. 225.

[3] See the passage quoted on p. 313, with n. 3. [2] See chap. 4, Annex IV.

[4] See Kromayer, 'Studien über Wehrkraft und Wehrverfassung der griechischen Staaten', Zweiter Teil, pp. 199 and 200.

[5] See chap. 5, sections (iii) and (iv). [6] See pp. 200–1, with p. 201, n. 4.

[7] See p. 203.

[8] Plutarch, *Cleomenes*, chap. 11. Presumably Kleomenes' hoplitai will have been men who were not over military age, i.e. not older than sixty. They may have all been men who were still of an age to be mobilizable for active service, i.e. not older than fifty-five. At Sparta, after the catastrophic reduction in the number of the homoioi as a result of the earthquake

been the 100 rich and the 600 poor homoioi;[1] the other 3,300 will have been Spartiate hypomeiones and perioikoi. As a result of the successive enfranchisements of helots and perioikoi by Kleomenes III and Nabis, Sparta's citizen army was more numerous in those two reigns than it had ever been before.[2]

These figures bear out Aristotle's estimate[3] that the country under Sparta's rule[4] could have maintained a force of 1,500 cavalry and 30,000 hoplites. At any time from the date or dates, in the seventh century B.C., of the resubjugation of Messenia onwards, Sparta commanded the manpower for raising an army of this size. It would have been a large enough and strong enough army to annihilate Argos, crush Athens, dominate the entire Hellenic World, and overrun the Persian Empire besides. It could, however, have been raised only on a condition which the homoioi were unwilling to accept. 'The reason why the Spartans never mobilized more than about 6,000 men for a single campaign is to be found simply and solely in the political and social structure of their state.'[5] The necessary condition was that in the Spartan dominions, as in Attica, the whole of the autochthonous population[6] should be enfranchised. The price would have been the surrender of the homoioi's onerous position of privilege. Rather than make this patriotic sacrifice in good time, the homoioi preferred to let Sparta's power gradually decline and eventually collapse.

of *circa* 466 or 464 B.C. (see **chap. 4**, Annex IV), it seems probable that the upper limit of the active-service age had been raised from forty-five to fifty-five (see pp. 351–2 and 377). If one or other of these interpretations of the word 'hoplitai' is correct, the total number of the kleroi into which Sparta's own city-state territory (ἡ πολιτικὴ χώρα) was carved up by Kleomenes in 227 B.C. may have been, not 4,000, but the 4,500 that had been provided for in the abortive rhetra that had been proposed, at Agis' instance, by the ephor Lysander in 244/3 B.C. (Plutarch, *Agis*, chap. 8). This is suggested by Fuks, 'Agis, Cleomenes, and Equality', p. 166, n. 17.

The rhetra had provided that the 15,000 kleroi into which the territories of the perioecic states were to be carved up were to be allotted τοῖς ὅπλα φέρειν δυναμένοις, and the same qualification would presumably have applied to recipients of the 4,500 kleroi that were to be allotted to Spartiatai, either Spartiate-born or naturalized. The technical meaning of this phrase is not 'men physically fit for military service'; it is 'men endowed with sufficient property to qualify for serving as hoplites while they are of an age to perform military service'. This qualification will have been acquired by any man who was endowed with a kleros.

The eighty kleroi reserved by Kleomenes for the opponents of his whom he had driven into exile (Plutarch, *Cleomenes*, chaps. 10 and 11) will have been taken from among the 4,000 'active-service-age' kleroi or the 500 'post-active-service-age' kleroi according to the age of each particular exile in 227 B.C.

---

[1] See p. 310, with n. 10.
[2] See chap. 5, section (v), and cp. K. J. Beloch, 'Griechische Aufgebote', II, in *Klio*, 6. Band (1906), pp. 34–78, on p. 74.
[3] Aristotle, *Politics*, Book II, chap. 6 (9), § 11 (1270a).
[4] Sparta's dominions, before she lost Messenia, were about three times the size of Attica (Roussel, op. cit., p. 14); and Attica was one of the larger city-state territories of the Hellenic World.   [5] Beloch, 'Griechische Aufgebote', II, p. 73.
[6] Autochthonous in the sense of not including immigrants, slave or free, or their descendants, whether slaves or freedmen or free-born.

(iii) *The Attempt to Make Both Ends Meet by Keying up the Agoge*

Our earliest surviving account of the 'Lycurgan' agoge is Xenophon's in his *Lakedaimoniôn Politeia*.[1] This was written perhaps as much as 250 years, and certainly not less than 200 years, after the date of the inauguration of the 'Lycurgan' regime, and at least seventy years after the earthquake of *circa* 466 or 464 B.C. at Sparta. By this time, Sparta will already have been feeling severely the tension between the increasing demands on the homoioi and their diminishing numbers, and the attempt to make both ends meet may already have produced changes in the original 'Lycurgan' dispensation. We have no information about this, but we may guess that, even if the 'Lycurgan' institutions themselves had been left intact, the demands made in virtue of them will have been keyed up by this date; so we cannot tell how far Xenophon's account tallies with the original structure and operation of the regime. Moreover, Xenophon's pamphlet is a flagrant piece of pro-Spartan propaganda, except for chapter 14, which strikes a discordant note. Xenophon has selected—and evidently to some extent also twisted—the information that he gives, in order to make it serve his eulogistic purpose. His statements therefore have to be taken critically and cautiously, except in so far as they are unfavourable to Sparta. As for Plutarch, he was writing his *Lycurgus* four and a half or five centuries after the date, in the course of the fourth century B.C., at which the conventional picture of Sparta which he reproduces had taken shape. His sources are of different dates and different degrees of authoritativeness. A present-day student of Spartan affairs cannot refrain from drawing on Plutarch's *Lycurgus* and *Instituta Laconica* for information that Plutarch alone offers; but, just because, on so many points, Plutarch is our sole source, we have no means of checking what he tells us.

A male Spartiate who succeeded in becoming an homoios by being co-opted into a mess after having passed through the Spartan educational system with credit[2] had to spend fifty-three years of his life—from the beginning of his eighth year[3] to the end of his sixtieth, if he lived that long—at the disposal of the Spartan state; and, though, after reaching the age of sixty, he was nominally his own master again, for the first time since he had reached the age of seven, it was expected of him that, in his

---

[1] The question whether this is a genuine work of Xenophon's has been discussed on p. 156, n. 2.

[2] This was the only avenue to membership of a mess and enrolment in the ranks of the homoioi (Plutarch, *Inst. Lac.*, § 21; Xenophon, *Lak. Pol.*, chap. 3, § 3; Sosibius apud Athenaeum, Book XV, 674 a–b (fragm. 4 in Müller, *F.H.G.*, vol. ii, p. 626); Teles (a contemporary of Phylarchus) apud Stobaeum, Book XL, chap. 8 (τὸν δὲ μὴ ἐμμείναντα, κᾶν ἐξ αὐτῶν τῶν βασιλέων, εἰς τοὺς εἴλωτας ἀποστέλλουσι, καὶ τῆς πολιτείας ὁ τοιοῦτος οὐ μετέχει)). 'The qualifying conditions for acquiring Spartan citizenship were agoge and kleros, *not* to be of pure Spartan race, born in lawful wedlock' (Ehrenberg, 'Spartiaten und Lakedaimonier', p. 63). [3] Plutarch, *Lycurgus*, chap. 17.

sixties, he would continue to keep himself fit physically by spending his time on hunting.[1]

Spartiatai who were undergoing the Spartan education as boys or adolescents (eirenes), or who were performing their forty years of military service[2] as adults, were elaborately graded and grouped. The fifty-three years from the eighth to the sixtieth inclusive were divided into three consecutive series of age-classes—one series for each of the three ages of life. Within each of the three series, boys, adolescents, or adults respectively were grouped in a number of chronologically parallel associations, each of which included representatives of all the age-classes in that series, whichever of the three series it might be.

The three consecutive series of age-classes appear to have been classified as follows:

8th year	ῥωβίδας		
9th ,,	προκομιζόμενος	(? error for προμικιζόμενος)	
10th ,,	μικιζόμενος	(μικιχιζόμενος in inscriptions)	Boys[3]
11th ,,	πρόπαις	(πρατοπάμπαις in inscriptions)	
12th ,,	παῖς	(ἀτροπάμπαις in inscriptions)	
13th ,,	μελλείρην		

14th–20th year   Εἴρενες = *Adolescents*[4]

21st–60th ,,   οἱ ἐν ἡλικίᾳ, οἱ ἔμφρουροι=*Adults* still of military age[5]

---

[1] Xenophon, *Lak. Pol.*, chap. 4, § 7.

[2] Xenophon, *Hellenica*, Book V, chap. 4, § 13. Cp. Book VI, chap. 4, § 17.

[3] Following a gloss on the word εἴρην in Herodotus, Book IX, chap. 85, as interpreted by M. P. Nilsson, 'Die Grundlagen des spartanischen Lebens', in *Klio*, 12. Band (1912), pp. 309–10; Busolt and Swoboda, op. cit., p. 696, n. 3; A. Billheimer, 'Age-Classes in Spartan Education', in *Transactions and Proceedings of the American Philological Association*, vol. lxxviii (1947), pp. 99–104. This gloss runs: παρὰ τοῖς Λακεδαιμονίοις ἐν τῷ πρώτῳ ἐνιαυτῷ ὁ παῖς ῥωβίδας καλεῖται, τῷ δευτέρῳ προκομιζόμενος, τῷ τρίτῳ μικιζόμενος, τῷ τετάρτῳ πρόπαις, τῷ πέμπτῳ παῖς, τῷ ἕκτῳ μελλείρην, ἐφηβεύει δὲ παρ' αὐτοῖς ὁ παῖς ἀπὸ ἐτῶν ιδ' μέχρι καὶ κ'. A gloss on Strabo's *Geographica* makes this series of age-classes begin at the opening of a boy's fifteenth year, not his eighth, and makes them all into sub-stages of the epheboi-stage, not assigning any of them to the paides-stage. This gloss on Strabo is less convincing than the gloss on Herodotus. The gloss on Strabo leaves the paides-stage blank, and ascribes to the epheboi-stage labels which sound too childish to have been applied to adolescents.

[4] Billheimer, in loc. cit., p. 102 (cp. vol. lxxvii (1946), p. 217), points out that Plutarch, *Lycurgus*, chap. 17, says, in agreement with the gloss on Herodotus, εἴρενας δὲ καλοῦσι τοὺς ἔτος ἤδη δεύτερον ἐκ παίδων γεγονότας, μελλείρενας δὲ τῶν παίδων τοὺς πρεσβυτάτους. On the strength of these words of Plutarch's, Nilsson, in loc. cit., makes the unconvincing guess that a Spartiate boy had a vacation during his fourteenth year. Xenophon, *Lak. Pol.*, chap. 2, § 2, distinguishes παῖδας from ἡβώντων. Billheimer concludes, convincingly, that Xenophon's ἡβῶντες are identical with the adolescent-class that the Spartans themselves labelled εἴρενες, and the Athenians ἔφηβοι, and that a Spartiate boy entered the adolescent group of age-classes on his thirteenth birthday.

Plutarch must be in error in saying, in loc. cit., that the εἴρην who was placed in command of an agelê of paides was turned twenty. The same error is made by Photius, κατὰ πρωτείρας· πρωτείραι οἱ περὶ εἴκοσιν ἔτη παρὰ Λακεδαιμονίοις. (Cp. Hesychius, κατὰ πρωτείρας· ἡλικίας ὄνομα οἱ πρωτείρ⟨εν⟩ες παρὰ Λακεδαιμονίοις.) If the gloss on Herodotus is right, the πρωτείρενες

[*Notes 4 and 5 continued opposite.*

The age-groups needed to be distinguished from each other because they were saddled with different burdens, of different weights; but the principal associations in which boys, adolescents, and men were enrolled for the performance of their public duties were so organized that each association included representatives of all the age-groups that were comprised in whichever of the three series of age-groups it might be. For instance, each of the messes (ἀνδρεῖα, φιδίτια, συσκηνίαι, συσσίτια),[1] which were the basic permanent units in which the homoioi were grouped, appears to have contained representatives of each of the eight sets of five-year-classes among which the men of military age were distributed.[2] The agelai ('droves'), in which the boys were enrolled, were organized on the same pattern. Each agelê—and each of the ilai ('squadrons') into

or πρωτεῖραι ought to be the youths who are in their fourteenth year, not youths above twenty years old. Herodotus will have been committing a still grosser error if he has made eirenes of Amompharetos, who was in command of the Pitanatas lokhos at Plataea in 479 B.C., and of the three other homoioi who were buried with Amompharetos in the same grave, separate from the common grave of the other fallen homoioi (Book IX, chaps. 53–7, 85). Perhaps, however, the error is, not Herodotus'. The MSS. read ἱρέας ('priests'). εἴρενας is Valckenaer's emendation (see Den Boer, op. cit., pp. 288–98). ἥρωας (i.e. canonized dead mortals) is my guess.

If the eirenes had been, not adolescents, but adults turned twenty, they would not have been at the paidonomos' disposal for being placed in charge of agelai of boys. This task required constant and unremitting attention, and therefore it could have been entrusted only to someone who could be sure of being in continuous residence at Sparta. This would have to be either an adolescent under twenty or else an old man over sixty. Men in the intervening forty year-classes might be alerted at any moment to go on campaign beyond the frontier. Adult age (ἥβη) was attained at the completion of an adolescent's twentieth year (Billheimer, 1946, pp. 216–17, citing inscriptional evidence which confirms the gloss on Herodotus). Forrest, *A History*, p. 52, is surely mistaken in identifying the εἴρενας with τὰ δέκα ἀφ' ἥβης.

⁵ Busolt and Swoboda, op. cit., p. 696, n. 3. The men of military age (οἱ ἔμφρουροι: Xenophon, *Lak. Pol.*, chap. 5, § 7) were grouped in eight sets of age-classes, each set comprising five year-classes. The youngest two five-year groups (τὰ δέκα ἀφ' ἥβης) might be ordered to make sorties from the ranks of the phalanx (Xenophon, *Agesilaus*, chap. 1, § 31; *Hellenica*, Book III, chap. 4, § 23). In the engagement at Corinth in 390 B.C., first τὰ δέκα ἀφ' ἥβης, and then τὰ πεντεκαίδεκα, were ordered to charge (ibid., Book IV, chap. 5, §§ 14 and 16). Cp. Thucydides, Book IV, chap. 125, where τοὺς νεωτάτους must signify τὰ δέκα ἀφ' ἥβης. See Billheimer, in *Transactions of the American Philological Association*, vol. lxxvii (1946), pp. 214–20.

In and after the Atheno-Peloponnesian War of 431–404 B.C., the first seven out of the eight sets of five year-classes seem to have been called up, as a rule, for active service in the field (e.g. in 425 B.C., to confront the Athenian landing-party at Pylos (Thucydides, Book IV, chap. 8) and in 371 B.C., in the force that ended at Leuktra (Xenophon, *Hellenica*, Book VI, chap. 4, § 17). The oldest set (men in their fifty-sixth to their sixtieth year) were called up only in extreme emergencies, e.g. after the disaster at Leuktra in 371 B.C. (Xenophon, *Hellenica*, Book VI, chap. 4, § 17). On the other hand, in the emergency of 479 B.C., only τὰ εἴκοσι πέντε ἀφ' ἥβης seem to have been called up (see Wade-Gery, *Essays in Greek History*, p. 82). This was perhaps the normal extent of mobilization before the earthquake of circa 466 or 464 B.C.

---

¹ See pp. 228, 303, 320, 321, 322–3, 369, and 383.
² '"Lycurgus" mingled old and young, so that the young should be thoroughly educated by their elders' experience. The Spartan custom was for any citizen's creditable achievements to be topics of conversation in the philitia' (Xenophon, *Lak. Pol.*, chap. 5, § 5). For the eight military age-class groups, see the present Part, chap. 5, section (i), pp. 369–71.

which the agelai were brigaded—included groups of boys of each of the ages from the eighth year to the thirteenth year inclusive. At the same time, each agelê was also sub-divided, by age-classes, into bouai ('herds'), each of which consisted exclusively of boys of one particular age-class.[1] This cross-division and sub-division of the boys' organization took account of the facts of human nature. Between the ages of seven and twelve, human beings change, both physically and psychically, more rapidly and radically than they change between the ages of twenty and fifty-nine.

Nilsson has pointed out[2] that there are correspondences between Spartan institutions and primitive peoples' institutions, and that these correspondences are too numerous for it to be credible that they are just accidental. At Sparta, however, these primitive institutions had been deliberately and skilfully adapted to serve a new purpose—namely, the Spartan state's purpose of maintaining the homoioi's ascendancy over hypomeiones, helots, and perioikoi—and, in Nilsson's view,[3] this looks as if it had been the conscious and purposeful work of some single organizing mind[4]—or meeting of minds that saw eye to eye.

In this adaptation, one cannot refuse to discern something which is more than the mere result of an automatic development. The methodical and purposeful way in which everything has been made to lead towards one single goal forces us to see here the intervention of a consciously shaping hand. . . . The existence of one man, or of several men working in the same direction, who have remodelled the primitive institutions into the *agoge* and the *kosmos*, is a necessary hypothesis.[5]

If the 'Lycurgan' syssitia, agelai, bouai, and other sets of associations were, in truth, pre-'Lycurgan' institutions that had been taken over by the 'Lycurgan' Spartan state, this would account for the division of the control over them, in the Post-'Lycurgan' Age, between the public authorities and the members of the associations themselves. For example, in the Post-'Lycurgan' Age the syssitia had come to be military formations.[6] They had come, in fact, to be the basic permanent units out of which the Spartan wing of the Lacedaemonian army was built up.[7]

[1] Nilsson, loc. cit., pp. 312–14. According to Nilsson, p. 313, there is inscriptional evidence that the members of a boua were all in the same age-group. See also Busolt and Swoboda, op. cit., p. 496, n. 1.

[2] Nilsson, loc. cit., p. 308.

[3] Ibid., p. 340.

[4] According to the conventional account, this mind was 'Lycurgus's', and 'Lycurgus' had borrowed his institutions from Crete. For the relation between Cretan and 'Lycurgan' Spartan institutions, see chap. 4, Annex I.

[5] Nilsson, loc. cit. Cp. Roussel, op. cit., pp. 39, 44, 46; Ehrenberg, 'Spartiaten und Lakedaimonier', pp. 34 and 39; eundem, *Neugründer des Staates*, pp. 9 and 52.

[6] Herodotus, Book I, chap. 65; Polyaenus, Book II, chap. 3, § 11: Λακεδαιμόνιοι . . . κατὰ λόχους καὶ μόρας καὶ ἐνωμότια καὶ συσσίτια στρατοπεδεύοντες (cited by Nilsson in loc. cit., p. 316).

[7] See p. 319, n. 1.

Accordingly, in the Post-Lycurgan Age, the syssitia were under the authority of the polemarchs.[1] At the same time, the choice of new recruits for a syssition—a crucial decision on which the quality of the phalanx of homoioi ultimately depended—had been left in the hands of the existing members of each syssition, and a single adverse vote was enough to exclude a candidate.[2] Each syssition also had an officer entitled the 'carver' ($\kappa\rho\epsilon\omega\delta\alpha\iota\tau\eta s$),[3] and, so far as we know, this officer was elected by the members, not appointed by the state. The aspect of the syssition in which it was, primarily, a private club was impressed upon each newly admitted member when he was admonished that all talk within the doors of the club-house was strictly confidential.[4] The sanction for the syssition's autonomy was economic. Its commons were provided by the members, not by the state,[5] and this economic self-sufficiency was a bulwark against the imposition of complete state control.[6]

Naturally there was no corresponding autonomy for the associations of eirenes and boys. The eirenes were supervised by a board of public officers styled bidiaioi (inspectors),[7] the boys by the paidonomos,[8] assisted by a police-force of eirenes.[9] The office of paidonomos was recognized as being one of capital importance, and anyone who had acquitted himself well in it had a prospect of rising thereafter to the highest offices in the state.[10] The paidonomos appointed, from among the eirenes, the commanders of the agelai,[11] and presumably the ilarkhai[12] and the bouagoi as well. The rations received by the boys were issued to them by the commanders of the agelai, so presumably they were provided by the state. They were purposely inadequate,[13] the purpose being to force the boys into the 'educative' exercise (educative for future foraging on campaign) of making up the deficiency by stealing—under pain, if caught, of being punished mercilessly, not for their criminality, but for their inefficiency.[14]

---

[1] See the anecdote recounted by Plutarch, *Lycurgus*, chap. 12.

[2] Plutarch, *Lycurgus*, chap. 12. There was, however, the limiting condition mentioned on p. 317, n. 2.

[3] Plutarch, *Lysander*, chap. 23; idem, *Quaestiones Conviviales*, Book II, chap. 10, § 2; Pollux, Book VI, chap. 34. Cp. the soup-maker (chorbaji), who was the spokesman of each mess of the Ottoman Janissary Corps. Each Janissary mess had its own steward and cook (Ramberti in Lybyer, op. cit., p. 249).

[4] Plutarch, *Lycurgus*, chap. 12; *Inst. Lac.*, § 1.

[5] See chap. 4, section (ii), *passim*.

[6] For the syssitia, see, in general, Xenophon, *Lak. Pol.*, chap. 5, §§ 1–7; Plutarch, *Lycurgus*, chaps. 10 and 12.

[7] Pausanias, Book III, chap. 11, § 2.

[8] Xenophon, *Lak. Pol.*, chap. 2, § 2; Plutarch, *Lycurgus*, chap. 17.

[9] Xenophon, *Lak. Pol.*, chap. 2, § 2. [10] Ibid.

[11] Plutarch, *Lycurgus*, chap. 17.

[12] For these, see Xenophon, *Lak. Pol.*, chap. 2, § 11.

[13] Ibid., chap. 2, § 5.

[14] Ibid., chap. 2, §§ 5–9; Plutarch, *Lycurgus*, chaps. 16–17.

Thus, in the structure of post-'Lycurgan' Spartan society, there was a working compromise between the powers assumed by the state over associations that had originally been private and the rights of corporate self-government which the members of these associations still retained. On the other hand there was an unresolved tension between the claims of masculine club and barrack life and the conflicting claims of home and family life on the allegiance and the affections of the homoios. As has been noted already,[1] the homoios was expected to marry, and, if he remained a bachelor, he was made to suffer for it. Yet, if and when he did marry, he remained the prisoner of his syssition till he had turned thirty. During the first ten years of adult life, his visits to his wife had to be rare and furtive.[2] He was not even allowed, during those years, to do the family shopping in the market. His relatives or his lover officiously undertook this for him.[3] Indeed, even when he had become a senior in his turn, and even if he were a king just home from a ten-years-long tour of duty abroad on active service, his messmates might see fit to remind him that the syssition's claim on him overrode his wife's, and the syssition's disciplinary action might be supported by the authority of the state. A member of a syssition

was allowed to dine at home if he came back late from sacrificing or hunting; no other excuse was admitted. They went to great lengths in the rigidity with which they maintained this obligation to dine together. There is the case of King Agis [II]. He had just come home from the campaign on which he had beaten Athens to her knees. He wanted to have dinner with his wife; so he sent [to his syssition] for his portions. The polemarchs refused to send them. Agis was so angry that, the next morning, he refused to perform a sacrifice which it was his duty to perform. The authorities then fined him.[4]

There was an important military reason for insisting that the homoios' attachment to his syssition should take precedence over his attachment to his home. The syssitia were, as has been noted,[5] the basic units out of which the Spartiate wing of the Lacedaemonian army was built up. Under the 'Lycurgan' regime this army was organized as a hoplite phalanx. The efficiency of the phalanx as a fighting-machine depended on the solidarity of the phalangitai with each other in the psychological as well as in the physical sense. Their paramount loyalty must be given to their comradeship with each other; and the corporate life of the members of a syssition was a device for creating this feeling of solidarity and for maintaining it. The numerical strength of a syssition was kept

---

[1] See pp. 306–7.
[2] Xenophon, *Lak. Pol.*, chap. 1, § 5; Plutarch, *Lycurgus*, chap. 15; *Apophth. Lac.*, Lykourgos, 17.
[3] Plutarch, *Lycurgus*, chap. 25.
[4] Ibid., chap. 12; *Apophth. Lac.*, Lykourgos, 6.
[5] See pp. 228, 303, 319, and 320. See further, pp. 369 and 383.

small enough to allow of all the members being on terms of intimacy with each other. The eventual figure was 'about fifteen'.[1] It had perhaps been about twenty—i.e. one half of the complement of an enomotia containing one representative of each of the forty year-classes subject to military service—before the organization of the Lacedaemonian army was changed from a set of five pairs of lokhoi to a set of six morai.[2] The psychological value of the comradeship fostered by the syssitia explains why this form of corporate life was maintained so zealously by the Spartan military authorities, as well as by the members of the syssitia themselves.

'In general, ["Lycurgus"] trained his citizens neither to wish for private life nor to know how to lead it. He trained them to be, like bees, inseparable (συμφυεῖς) from the commonweal and to bunch together in a swarm round the queen.' The effect was that an homoios' male 'classmate and friend counted for much more in his life than his wife did. His feeling for the honour of his class was very sharply accentuated; his feeling for the honour of his family was considerably blunted, to say the least.'[3]

The common life of the syssition, which captivated the homoios from the age of twenty onwards for the rest of his life, was part of the life-long education to which the Spartiate was subjected. One of the principal uses that the 'Lycurgan' reformers made of the primitive institutions that they took over and adapted for their own purposes was to make the whole of a boy's, youth's, and man's progression through the series of age-classes into a perpetual educative process.[4] 'Educating', however, is perhaps too good a word to describe what was done to the Spartiate from the age of seven onwards. To call the process one of 'conditioning', in the present-day psychologist's meaning of this word, would be nearer the mark. Like the 'Osmanlis two thousand years later, the Spartans had condemned themselves to the penal servitude of holding down by force a harshly treated subject population that was many times more numerous than the dominant minority was. Like the 'Osmanlis, the Spartans sought to solve their problem by creating a corps of full-time professional

---

[1] Plutarch, *Lycurgus*, chap. 12, and *Apophth. Lac.*, Lykourgos, 3. Lysander's rhetra, embodying King Agis IV's programme of reforms, perhaps reinstituted the syssitia in about this same strength, if A. Bielchowsky, *De Spartanorum Syssitiis* (Breslau, 1869) is right in emending the last sentence of Plutarch, *Agis*, chap. 8, from σύνταξιν δὲ τούτων εἰς πεντεκαίδεκα γενέσθαι φιδίτια κατὰ τετρακοσίους καὶ διακοσίους to σύνταξιν δὲ τούτων εἰς τριακόσια γενέσθαι φιδίτια κατὰ πεντεκαίδεκα (see Kessler, *Plutarchs Leben des Lykurgus*, p. 52, n. 3).

[2] See chap. 5, section (iii). The numerical strength of a mess in the Ottoman Janissary Corps was about ten (Ramberti in Lybyer, op. cit., p. 249).

[3] Nilsson, in loc. cit., p. 333.

[4] Ibid., p. 323. ἡ δὲ παιδεία μέχρι τῶν ἐνηλίκων διέτεινεν (Plutarch, *Lycurgus*, chap. 24). τὸ γὰρ ὅλον καὶ πᾶν τῆς νομοθεσίας ἔργον εἰς τὴν παιδείαν ἀνῆψε [Lycurgus] (ibid., chap. 13).

guardians of their oppressive regime; and, like the 'Osmanlis again, the Spartans found that, if the guardians were to be made fit for performing their unnatural function of maintaining an unnatural state of affairs, violence must be done to the human nature of the guardians, as well as to that of their victims.

In the Spartan system, as in the Ottoman, the outstanding feature—the feature which accounts for the system's astonishing efficiency and for its fatal rigidity and for its consequent breakdown—was its 'grand disregard for human nature';[1] and, when we compare the two systems from this standpoint, we find that, while in some respects the 'Lycurgan' *agoge* set human nature at defiance rather less truculently than the Ottoman slave-household, in other ways it challenged it still more provocatively.[2]

The Spartan agoge did not go so far as the regime of the Ottoman Pādishāh's slave-household in ignoring the customary claims of birth and heredity. A Spartiate homoios could inherit property and could pass it on to his heirs, whereas an Ottoman *qul* (imperial slave) started his career propertyless, and any property that he might have acquired in the course of his official career escheated to the Pādishāh automatically at the *qul*'s death. Also, the Spartiate who became an homoios—unlike the Ottoman *qul* who became an administrator or a soldier—began and ended his career as a free man. This was, at least, his juridical status. However, as Herodotus makes the deposed and exiled Spartan king Damaratos say to the Persian emperor Xerxes, 'free though the Spartans are, they are not free altogether. They too serve a master in the shape of law, whom they dread far more intensely than Your Majesty's servants dread Your Majesty'.[3]

Thus the Spartiate homoios, though free in law, was a slave psychologically; and there were some homoioi—namely mothakes[4] born of helot mothers—who, like the Ottoman *ajemoghlanlar* ('alien boys'), were slaves in the juridical sense.

Moreover, there were points in which the god 'Lycurgus' went still farther in defying human nature—or what was held to be human nature—than the sultan Murād I.

The Spartans took the children from their homes and put them into the educational mill at the age of seven, the 'Osmanlis not until the age of twelve and upwards. . . . The Spartans not only anticipated the 'Osmanlis in conscripting and training girls as well as boys, but they went far further towards an identical treatment of both sexes.[5] For Spartan girls, as well as for Spartan boys, conscription was universal; and the Spartan girls were not trained in

---

[1] See Lybyer, op. cit., especially pp. 36, 45–6, 57–8.
[2] Toynbee, *A Study of History*, vol. iii, p. 56.
[3] Herodotus, Book VII, chap. 104.
[4] For the mothakes, see chap. 4, Annex III.
[5] See chap. 4, Annex V.

special female accomplishments, nor kept in seclusion from the men, like the girls in the female section of the Ottoman Pādishāh's slave-household. Spartan girls, like Spartan boys, were trained on a competitive system in athletics; and girls, like boys, competed naked in public before a male audience.[1]

The Spartan system does not bear comparison with the Ottoman. It was cruder, more brutal, less intellectual, and less intelligent. The Ottoman system's major aim was to produce skilled administrators; its production of disciplined soldiers was a by-product of this. The Spartan system aimed at producing soldiers exclusively; and its trainees proved to be entirely unfitted for serving as administrators when, during and after the Decelean War, the Spartan Government had to second homoioi to the unaccustomed task of serving as harmosts.[2] In the Ottoman curriculum, boys who qualified for being passed into the stream of candidates for administrative posts were given a first-rate literary education; facilities for learning to read and write were given, in their last probationary stage, to the less able boys who were destined to be made into soldiers; the same facilities continued to be at their disposal after they had been enrolled in a janissary company (*orta*);[3] and all trainees, including a boy who might eventually become the Pādishāh, were taught some manual trade.[4] Spartan boys were taught the rudiments of reading and writing,[5] but that was as far as their intellectual education went. Above all, the Spartan system was more cruel and was less intelligent in the sense of being less intelligently designed for accomplishing its purpose. There was nothing in the Ottoman system that corresponded, even remotely, to the deliberate Spartan policy of keeping the boys inadequately clothed, with the intention of hardening their physique,[6] and inadequately fed, with the intention of teaching them to steal.[7] Nor was there anything corresponding to the organized fights between opposing gangs which, at Sparta, were so favourite a method of 'conditioning' not only the youths (eirenes) but also the adults in the age-classes from twenty to thirty (τὰ δέκα ἀφ' ἥβης).

At Sparta there were two annual gang-fights for the eirenes and one for the youngest age-classes of the men of military age. The eirenes of

---

[1] Toynbee, op. cit., vol. iii, p. 59. The girls competed naked according to Plutarch, *Lycurgus*, chap. 14; *Apophth. Lac.*, Lykourgos, 13. According to another account, they wore slit skirts.

[2] See p. 299. Cp. p. 289.

[3] See I. M. d'Ohsson, *Tableau Général de l'Empire Ottoman*, vol. vii (Paris, 1824), p. 327.

[4] See p. 304.

[5] Plutarch, *Lycurgus*, chap. 16; *Inst. Lac.*, § 4. According to Isocrates, *Panathenaïcus*, 209, they were not taught even that much.

[6] Xenophon, *Lak. Pol.*, chap. 2, § 4; Plutarch, *Lycurgus*, chap. 16. There was an 'escalation' of austerity at the age of twelve (Plutarch, ibid.). Cp. *Inst. Lac.*, § 6.

[7] Plutarch, *Lycurgus*, chaps. 17 and 18; *Inst. Lac.*, §§ 12–13; Xenophon, *Lak. Pol.*, chap. 2, §§ 5–9.

the obai of Pitane and Messoa fought the eirenes of the obai of Limnai and Kynosoura at the altar of Artemis Orthia in Limnai—the attacking party's objective being to steal cheese-offerings from Orthia's altar at the risk of life and limb.[1] This battle was eventually transformed into a North-American-Indian-like competition in the endurance of physical pain. The competing eirenes submitted themselves to be flogged at Orthia's altar; and Plutarch—who lived in an archaizing age in which resuscitated rites were carried to extremes—had seen, with his own eyes, youths dying under this ordeal.[2] The second annual gang-fight for the eirenes was in an arena called the Platanistas, which was surrounded by a wet ditch, with access by a bridge at each end. This fight—which was confined to eirenes of the oldest year-classes in this series[3]—was savage: 'they box, kick, bite, and gouge out eyes'.[4] The annual gang-fight for the young men of military age was incidental to the selection, out of the youngest adult age-classes, of the 300 hippeis (alias κόροι)[5] by three hippagretai who were appointed by the ephors. To be made a hippeus was an eagerly coveted honour; the competition was passionate; and, after the selection had been made, the unsuccessful competitors boxed with those who had been selected whenever and wherever any representatives of the two factions encountered each other—the object of the unsuccessful competitors being to demonstrate that they were in truth the better men, in spite of their having been passed over.[6]

These Spartan training-practices of fighting and stealing were unintelligent, besides being barbarous, because the qualities that they fostered were pugnacity and dishonesty, whereas the sovereign qualities required for making a good hoplite phalangite were loyalty and discipline. They were, in fact, the same qualities as those required for making a good musketeer in the Janissaries' 'thin blue line'. The Ottoman method of training was far better calculated than the Spartan to produce the identical result at which both systems were aiming. Their common objective was discipline, and this was the distinctive quality of the Janissaries, which struck sixteenth-century and seventeenth-century Western observers forcibly because of its contrast with the êthos of contemporary Western troops.[7] Janissaries at that date made the same kind of impres-

---

[1] Xenophon, *Lak. Pol.*, chap. 2, § 9.
[2] Pausanias, Book III, chap. 16, §§ 9–11; Plutarch, *Lycurgus*, chap. 18; *Inst. Lac.*, § 39; Xenophon, *Lak. Pol.*, chap. 2, § 9.   [3] Pausanias, Book III, chap. 14, § 6.
[4] Ibid., chap. 14, §§ 6–10, and chap. 20, § 2.
[5] Busolt and Swoboda, op. cit., p. 706. See also the present work, pp. 232 and 265.
[6] Xenophon, *Lak. Pol.*, chap. 4, §§ 1–6.
[7] See, for example, the Habsburg ambassador O. G. Busbecq's account of his impressions of Sultan Suleiman's camp at Amasīyeh in A.D. 1555 (*O. Gislenii Busbequii Omnia quae Extant* (Leyden, 1633, Elzevir), pp. 99–102; English translation by E. S. Forster in *The Turkish Letters of Ogier Ghiselin de Busbecq* (Oxford, 1927, Clarendon Press), pp. 59–62; cp. Sir Paul Rycaut, *The Present State of the Ottoman Empire* (London, 1668, Starkey and Brome), p. 205).

sion on Western observers as Roman Catholic Christian monks.[1] If one of their highly skilled trainers had come across an account of the Spartan method of training, he would, no doubt, have been disgusted at its brutality; but, even more, he would have been contemptuous of its ineptness as a means for attaining its purpose.

Notwithstanding the superiority of the Ottoman system—and its superiority is conspicuous—the two fundamental assumptions underlying the two systems were the same. The first assumption was that nature can be overcome by nurture in the training of human beings, as it can be, indisputably, in the training of domesticated animals and birds.[2] The second assumption was that, in the case of human beings, the most effective stimulus for overcoming nature is ambition, given scope by competition.

One effective and comparatively attractive way in which the 'conditioning' of Spartan boys and youths was achieved was through a constant and intensive social intercourse between them and the grown men. Since the homoioi were debarred from earning their living, they had an abundance of leisure[3] after they had performed their stints of drilling on the parade-ground; and they spent a large part of this ample spare time of theirs on assisting in the training of the rising generation. This was a public concern in which they took the keenest interest. They would watch the boys playing and training, would take a personal part in the proceedings, and would get to know each boy individually.[4] Reciprocally, the boys were allowed and encouraged to sit in when the men were dining in their club-houses, to give the boys an opportunity of educating themselves by listening to the conversation and watching what went on.[5]

The upbringing of the boys and the eirenes was recognized as being

---

[1] Xenophon, *Lak. Pol.*, chap. 3, §§ 4–5, avers that the Spartan training turned the Spartan boys, likewise, into models of modesty and decorum.

[2] 'We Westerners obtain many sorts of pleasure and service from a well-broken-in horse, dog, and hawk, while the Turks obtain from a man whose character has been cultivated by education (*ex homine bonis moribus informato*) the vastly greater return that is afforded by the vast superiority and pre-eminence of human nature over the rest of the animal kingdom' (Busbecq, 'Exclamatio, sive de Re Militari contra Turcam Instituenda Consilium', in op. cit., p. 439).

According to Plutarch, *Apophth. Lac.*, Lykourgos, 1, 'Lycurgus' gave a demonstration, by training dogs, that education counts for more than race. He trained two puppies of the same litter, one to be a lap-dog and the other to be a hound; or he trained two dogs of different breeds, a lap-dog to behave like a hound, and a hound to behave like a lap-dog. According to the story, this was 'Lycurgus's' way of moving the Spartans to see that it was not enough for them to say 'We have Herakles to our father'. They must do what Herakles himself did; they must train. The story is fictitious, but the effect of the 'Lycurgan' system of training is unquestionable.

'Ce qui caractérisait la caste dominante dans l'État lacedémonien, ce n'était pas l'origine ou la descendance mais l'éducation uniforme qu'elle avait reçue' (Roussel, op. cit., p. 21).

[3] Plutarch, *Lycurgus*, chaps. 24 and 25; *Inst. Lac.*, § 40.

[4] Plutarch, *Lycurgus*, chaps. 16, 17, 18.

[5] Xenophon, *Lak. Pol.*, chap. 3, § 5; Plutarch, *Lycurgus*, chap. 12.

a collective responsibility of all the homoioi. Any homoios would feel it to be his duty to correct and punish any boy, and, in the performance of this duty, he would be backed up by the boy's own father and by the public authorities.[1] This informal collective intervention of the homoioi in the 'conditioning' process was double-edged. On the one hand, they egged the boys on to be pugnacious and competitive.[2] On the other hand, there were situations in which their intervention was humane. For instance, they would inspect the way in which the eiren who was the leader of an agelê dealt out punishments to the boys under his command, and, when the boys were no longer present, they would hold an inquest on the eiren's use or abuse of his powers.[3] Again, when the hippeis and their rejected competitors were fighting in the streets, 'any [senior homoios] who happened to be on the spot had authority to part the combatants. If any of the brawlers disobeyed this order, the paidonomos would prosecute him in the ephors' court, and the ephors would impose a heavy fine on him. They were determined to establish the principle that temper should never be allowed to prevail over obedience to the law'.[4]

The most unattractive, though perhaps also the most effective, of all the ways in which a male Spartan, of all ages, was kept up to the mark was through the enormous pressure of public opinion. A Spartan who offended against Spartan standards of conduct—especially if the offence of which he had been convicted was cowardice—would have his life made intolerable for him. He would be boycotted, insulted, and humiliated at every turn.[5] The classical victim of this odious Spartan practice was 'Runaway Aristodamos', who had been the only one of Leonidas' three hundred—or, according to another account, one of two— to return from Thermopylae to Sparta alive.[6] Aristodamos was one of two men who had been invalided to the rear because they had been incapacitated by ophthalmia. Aristodamos' fellow invalid had made his helot batman guide him back to Thermopylae, and had duly got himself killed there. When Aristodamos reappeared in Sparta instead of having done likewise, he was treated there in the way that Xenophon describes with approval. In consequence, Aristodamos, in his turn, got himself killed at his next opportunity, which was next year, at the Battle of Plataea. Before falling, he had performed prodigies of valour; but his countrymen remained implacable. They refused to award him posthumous honours, on the ground that there was no merit in his heroism because life had lost its value for him. This treatment of Aristodamos was

---

[1] Xenophon, *Lak. Pol.*, chap. 2, § 10; chap. 6, §§ 1–2; Plutarch, *Lycurgus*, chap. 17.
[2] Plutarch, *Lycurgus*, chap. 16.
[3] Ibid., chap. 18.
[4] Xenophon, *Lak. Pol.*, chap. 4, § 6.   [5] Ibid., chap. 9.
[6] For the story of Aristodamos, see Herodotus, Book VII, chaps. 229–31, and Book IX, chap. 71.

bad enough, but it was outdone by the treatment of another survivor from Thermopylae—if this second story, for which Herodotus does not go bail, is true. 'There is also said to have been another survivor of the three hundred named Pantitas, who had been sent with dispatches to Thessaly and who returned to Sparta, was treated with contumely, and committed suicide.'[1]

To drive into suicide a soldier who had survived as a consequence of his having carried out orders was an atrocity in which cruelty was aggravated by irrationality.

At Sparta, public opinion was a more potent 'conditioning' force than the ephors' arbitrary power. Yet there was another force that was more potent still, and this was the effectively 'conditioned' homoios' own inexorable conscience.

PART III, CHAPTER 4, ANNEX I

The Relation of Sparta's 'Lycurgan' Regime to the Institutions of the Cretan City-States[2]

ACCORDING to Herodotus,[3] 'some people say that . . . the Pythia briefed "Lycurgus" on the regime that is in force in Sparta to-day. The Lacedaemonians themselves, however, say that "Lycurgus" . . . brought these institutions to Sparta from Crete.'

At the previous point in this chapter at which this passage has been quoted, it has been suggested that Herodotus' 'some people' may be the Spartan royal houses. Under the 'Lycurgan' regime, one of the principal surviving political assets of the Spartan crown was that it continued to be the channel of official communications between Sparta and Delphi. If 'Lycurgus' himself was of royal blood, and if the 'Lycurgan' regime had been spelled out to him by the Pythia, the Spartan crown could claim to have been the principal human agency in the inauguration of the 'Lycurgan' regime, and consequently might also claim to have the last word in the interpretation of the rhetra or rhetrai in which the 'Lycurgan' constitution was embodied. For this reason the pretension that 'Lycurgus' had been briefed by the Pythia would be unacceptable to the ephors as trustees for the sovereignty that the 'Lycurgan' constitution had vested in the damos of the homoioi. In the conventional account of the origins of the 'Lycurgan' regime which crystallized in the fourth century B.C., these two older accounts of it were reconciled by the hypothesis that 'Lycurgus' got his ideas in Crete but persuaded Delphi to endorse them

---

[1] Herodotus, Book VII, chap. 232.
[2] See Chrimes, *Ancient Sparta*, pp. 205–47.
[3] Book I, chap. 65, quoted already on p. 242, n. 9.

as a preliminary to persuading his countrymen to adopt them.[1] As Herodotus presents the case, however, the two accounts are mutually exclusive. If we are right in seeing in them the two rival accounts given by the two powers—the crown and the ephorate—which, after the establishment of the 'Lycurgan' constitution, were competing for supremacy at Sparta, it will follow that each account was inspired by a political motive, and this will make us sceptical about the veracity of either of them. We are not bound to accept the thesis that the 'Lycurgan' regime was imported to Sparta from abroad, whether from Delphi or from Crete or from both. The primitive social institutions[2] and the new constitutional ideas[3] that the 'Lycurgan' regime at Sparta had incorporated may both have been indigenous. The stories about their having originated either at Delphi or in Crete may have been mere fables deliberately fabricated for political purposes.

The story of a Delphic origin of the 'Lycurgan' regime is explained satisfactorily by the two Spartan royal houses' connection with Delphi. But, if the story of a Cretan origin is the ephorate's counterblast to this, why should the ephorate have chosen Crete, in particular, to be the foreign source, other than Delphi, from which the 'Lycurgan' constitution had been derived? The answer is that there were a number of striking similarities (besides some important differences) between Cretan institutions and Sparta's 'Lycurgan' institutions; and that both sets of institutions were peculiar. There was nothing like them anywhere else in the Hellenic World; and it was therefore natural to infer that one of these two similar, and similarly peculiar, sets of institutions had been derived from the other.[4]

There is, of course, the possible alternative explanation that both the Cretan and the 'Lycurgan' Spartan institutions were derived, independently of each other, from a common cultural heritage. Both the members of the Cretan 'ascendancy' and the Spartans were speakers of the North-West-Greek dialect. Might not the common elements in their institutions have been brought in by their respective ancestors in the course of the post-Mycenaean Völkerwanderung? Some, at least, of the institutions common to Sparta and Crete have a primitive appearance. It might seem reasonable to attribute them to the North-West-Greek-speaking migrants, who were a primitive people by comparison with the peoples of the Mycenaean World which they had invaded. This hypothesis may look plausible at first sight, but there is an objection to it that seems

---

[1] See, for example, Plutarch, *Lycurgus*, chaps. 4–6.

[2] See Nilsson, 'Die Grundlagen des spartanischen Lebens', *passim*.

[3] See Andrewes, *Probouleusis*.

[4] Forrest, *A History*, pp. 53 and 65, holds that the similarity between the Spartan and Cretan social systems was an inheritance from a common past, but he concedes on p. 65 that the political similarities 'could have been the result of some early borrowing'.

decisive. There is no substantial evidence for the survival of even vestiges of corresponding institutions in any other North-West-Greek-speaking communities of the post-Völkerwanderung Hellenic World—either in the south-eastern vanguard of the migration, which had come to call itself 'Dorian', or in the north-western rearguard, which had not adopted the label 'Dorian' though it spoke the self-styled 'Dorians'' dialect.

Moreover, Aristotle—or Ephorus,[1] followed by Aristotle—declares that the peculiar institution of the North-West-Greek-speaking 'ascendancy' in Crete, to which Sparta's 'Lycurgan' institutions bore a resemblance, had not been brought into Crete by these invaders, but had been taken over by them from the conquered population of the island.[2] This population had now been reduced to the status of being rural slaves ('perioikoi' in the institutional vocabulary of post-Völkerwanderung Crete).[3] But these rural slaves were still living under the laws which their conquerors had borrowed from them, and the originator of these laws was reputed to be Minos, the eponym of the Mnoïa, which was the conquerors' collective name for their publicly owned rural slaves.[4] If the post-Völkerwanderung institutions of the North-West-Greek-speaking conquerors of Crete were, in truth, the institutions of the pre-Völkerwanderung population of Crete, then it is not surprising that they should be strikingly different from the institutions of the continental Hellenic World, both European and Asian, and in these circumstances it seems credible, and indeed probable, that Sparta—the one continental Greek state whose institutions resembled the Cretan—should have borrowed these 'Lycurgan' institutions from Crete on the occasion of the establishment of the 'Lycurgan' regime.

Both Ephorus and Aristotle held that Sparta's 'Lycurgan' institutions were of Cretan origin. According to Polybius,[5] Ephorus went so far as to describe the two sets of institutions in identical words, except for the proper names. This must be an exaggeration, since Polybius himself cites Ephorus, together with Xenophon, Callisthenes, and Plato, as admitting at least two exceptions to these authorities' common thesis that the two sets of institutions were similar or even identical. They admitted that the veto on the possession of money at Sparta and the equality in the size of her citizens' holdings of land[6] were something peculiar to Sparta.[7]

---

[1] A précis of the main points in Ephorus' account of Cretan institutions is given by Strabo in *Geographica*, Book X, chap. 4, §§ 16–22 (C. 480–4).

[2] κατέλαβον δὲ οἱ πρὸς τὴν ἀποικίαν ἐλθόντες τὴν τάξιν τῶν νόμων ὑπάρχουσαν ἐν τοῖς τότε κατοικοῦσιν. δι' ὃ νῦν οἱ περίοικοι τὸν αὐτὸν τρόπον χρῶνται αὐτοῖς, ὡς κατασκευάσαντος Μίνω πρώτου τὴν τάξιν τῶν νόμων (Aristotle, *Politics*, Book II, chap. 7 (10), § 1 (1271b)).

[3] Aristotle in loc. cit., § 3. See also Busolt and Swoboda, op. cit., p. 739, n. 1.

[4] See p. 334.   [5] Book VI, chap. 46, § 10.

[6] If these authorities did hold that the land in Sparta's city-state territory was all equally distributed, they were in error. See pp. 231–2.

[7] Polybius, Book VI, chap. 43, §§ 3–4; chap. 48, § 3.

In Crete there was no veto on the possession of money, and the holdings of land were not equal in size.[1] All the same, Ephorus, like Aristotle, was impressed by the points of resemblance between the two sets of institutions, and they both held that the Spartan set was derived from the Cretan one.

In comparing the two sets of institutions, both Ephorus and Aristotle draw, from the internal evidence, a telling argument in support of their common thesis. As Ephorus puts it, these institutions had been invented by the Cretans but had been refined by the Spartans.[2] Similarly, Aristotle notes that most of the Cretan institutions are less competently finished off.[3] 'It is said—and this seems probable—that most of the Spartan institutions are copies of the Cretan; and it is true that ancient institutions are generally less well articulated than more modern institutions are.' There is little force in Aristotle's second argument, which is that 'Lycurgus' went to the Cretan city-state Lyttos and studied Cretan institutions there because Lyttos was a Spartan colony. After Sparta had become powerful and famous, a number of North-West-Greek-speaking communities to the south-east of her, including the islands of Melos and Thera, claimed to be Spartan colonies; but Sparta cannot have planted colonies overseas before she had acquired a seaboard, i.e. not before the second half of the eighth century B.C. Tarentum was Sparta's first and last genuine colony, so far as we know.

Aristotle's and Ephorus' arguments in favour of a Cretan origin of Sparta's 'Lycurgan' institutions can be reinforced by two others. The Spartan makers of the 'Lycurgan' constitution had to improvise a social and military organization for the hundreds of Spartiate nobles and thousands of Spartiate commoners who were now being endowed with kleroi in order to enable them to serve as full-time professional hoplite phalangites, permanently mobilized for military duty. The nobles and their retainers were already organized in the three phylai that appear to have been taken over from the Asian Doris.[4] But this simple political structure was inadequate for organizing such large numbers. An alternative basis for organizing the new damos of homoioi was the existing set of five local obai; and the obai seem actually to have been utilized for this purpose, if we are right in holding[5] that the five obai were the respective bases of the five lokhoi of the original 'Lycurgan' military organization. However, this fivefold indigenous Spartan political structure, like the threefold imported Dorian political structure, was too

---

[1] Polybius, Book VI, chap. 46, §§ 1–3.

[2] ηὑρῆσθαι μὲν ὑπ' ἐκείνων, ἠκριβωκέναι δὲ τοὺς Σπαρτιάτας (Ephorus apud Strabonem, in loc. cit., § 17).

[3] τὸ δὲ πλεῖον [ἔχει] ἧττον γλαφυρῶς (Aristotle in loc. cit., § 1).

[4] See Part I, chap. 3, p. 44, and Part III, chap. 3, Annex II.

[5] See the present Part, chap. 5, section (ii).

simple for meeting the 'Lycurgan' reformers' purpose. For the men of military age, the reformers needed a large number of associations that would be on a small enough scale to allow of there being an intimate personal relation between the members of each of them.[1] For 'conditioning' the boys and youths to become good recruits for the professional hoplite phalanx upon reaching military age, the reformers also needed a corresponding number of other associations on a corresponding scale. The constitution-makers had to find, somewhere, the prototypes for these new Spartan institutions that they were having to create. It is possible that they found these prototypes already existing at Sparta itself in the form of loosely organized private clubs. Such clubs, however, both for adults and for children and adolescents, were, as we know, a feature of the Cretan 'ascendancy's' life;[2] and, when the same institutions appear at Sparta, they appear there under their Cretan names. The men's messes at Sparta were originally called by the Cretan name 'andreia' before they came to be called 'philitia' or 'phiditia' or 'syssitia' or 'syskeniai'.[3] The boys' troops continued to be called at Sparta by the Cretan name 'agelai'.

If these names of two of the key institutions of 'Lycurgan' Sparta point to a Cretan provenance, so does the testimony of archaeology. Our archaeological evidence tells us that, in the Archaic Age of Hellenic history, a wind of cultural change was blowing into European Greece from Crete and from Asian Greece and from older seats of civilization on the far side of them. 'Daedalic' Crete wafted into continental European Greece artistic motifs, works of art, and artists, and also religious rites and adepts in these. It would not be surprising if the continental European Greek state that lay nearest to Crete drew upon Crete, in the seventh century B.C., for political institutions as well.

Such evidence as we have makes it possible and even probable, though, evidently, by no means certain, that some, at least, of the 'Lycurgan' Spartan institutions were adaptations of Cretan institutions. The Spartan andreia (philitia, phiditia, syssitia, syskeniai) and agelai are cases in point. In each of these and other Cretan-like Spartan institutions, there were

---

[1] See pp. 322–3.

[2] See Dosiadas' account of the andreia in the Cretan city-state Lyttos, quoted by Athenaeus, Book IV, 143 a–d. ἕκαστος [of the rural public serfs] τῶν γινομένων καρπῶν ἀναφέρει τὴν δεκάτην εἰς τὴν ἑταιρείαν καὶ τὰς τῆς πόλεως προσόδους, ἃς διανέμουσιν οἱ προεστηκότες τῆς πόλεως εἰς τοὺς ἑκάστων οἴκους [the houses of each of the citizens of Lyttos]. τῶν δὲ δούλων ἕκαστος Αἰγιναῖον φέρει στατῆρα κατὰ κεφαλήν. In Cretan terminology a hetaireia was a citizens' club and an andreion was a club-house in which all the hetaireiai composing the citizen-body of a Cretan city-state lived together (Busolt and Swoboda, op. cit., pp. 746, 754, 755–6, with p. 756, n. 1). Both these Cretan terms are represented by the Spartan terms andreion, philition, phidition, syskenia, syssition.

[3] Ephorus apud Strabonem in loc. cit., § 18; Aristotle in loc. cit., § 3; cf. Plutarch, Lycurgus, chap. 12.

differences, as well as resemblances, between the Spartan institution and its possible Cretan prototype; but these differences do not necessarily point to a difference of origin; they may have been alterations of a Cretan prototype that had been made deliberately to suit local Spartan circumstances.

The most crucial difference has been noticed already in a previous context.[1] In Sparta's city-state territory, all the helot-cultivated land seems to have been distributed by the state irrevocably to individual Spartiate homoioi, and therefore the provision for the syssitia had to be found from dues paid by the members themselves out of the contributions received by them from the helots attached to their respective kleroi. By contrast, in Crete, the native rural slaves, for whom the generic name here was perioikoi, were divided into two categories: the mnoïa, who were slaves of the state, and the aphamiotai (*alias* klarotai), who were slaves of private citizens.[2] Thanks to this provident conservation, in the hands of the Cretan states, of part of the lands that had originally come into the states' possession by conquest,

the syssitia are better organized in the Cretan states than they are at Sparta. At Sparta each [messmate] individually pays in his dues, and, if he defaults, he then, by law, [automatically] forfeits his citizenship. . . . In Crete the organization of the syssitia is more socialistic ($\kappa o\iota\nu o\tau\acute{\epsilon}\rho\omega s$). Out of all the crops and livestock from the state [domains] and from the tribute paid by the rural [state] slaves ($o\acute{\iota}\ \pi\epsilon\rho\acute{\iota}o\iota\kappa o\iota$), one fixed quota is allocated to cults and public works, and another to the syssitia. By this arrangement everyone [i.e. every member of the ascendancy] is fed at the public expense—women, children, and men alike'.[3]

In the Cretan states the children attended the syssitia in order to get their own meals there and to wait upon the adults as well as upon each other.[4] At Sparta, the boys frequented the syssitia as part of their education,[5] but the membership of the syssitia was confined to males of military age—as it must have been in Crete too, originally, to judge by the name andreia.[6]

As for the boys' agelai, they are explicitly recorded to have been maintained at the state's expense in Crete,[7] as they appear to have been at Sparta too.[8] At Sparta the state also controlled the administration of the

---

[1] On p. 300.

[2] Sosicrates, cited by Athenaeus, Book VI, 263 e–f.

[3] Aristotle, *Politics*, Book II, chap. 7 (10), § 4 (1272a). Chrimes, *Ancient Sparta*, pp. 230–5, holds that this passage is derived, probably via Ephorus, from the passage of Dosiadas' *Cretica* preserved by Athenaeus, Book IV, 143 a-d and cited already on p. 333, n. 2.

[4] Ephorus apud Strabonem, in loc. cit., § 18.

[5] See p. 327.

[6] Miss Chrimes holds, in the teeth of Aristotle's explicit statement to the contrary, that the Cretan andreia were always confined to men (*Ancient Sparta*, pp. 234–6).

[7] Ephorus apud Strabonem, in loc. cit., § 20. 　　　　　[8] See p. 321.

agelai. The ilarkhai, agelarkhai, and bouagoi were appointed by a public officer, the paidonomos.[1] In the Cretan states, a paidonomos was attached to each andreion;[2] but these Cretan paidonomoi had charge of the little boys only; the bigger boys were grouped in agelai; and the organization of these Cretan agelai seems to have been left entirely to private enterprise. 'The agelai are organized by the boys from the most distinguished and powerful families. Each of these organizers enlists as many followers as he can. As a rule, each agelê is commanded by the boy-organizer's father. He has authority to take the boys out hunting and on cross-country runs, and to punish them for breaches of discipline.'[3] In Crete, as at Sparta, there were organized fights. At Sparta, as we have seen,[4] these seem to have been confined to eirenes and to the youngest age-classes of men of military age. In Crete, there were fights for the bigger boys,[5] and some of these with iron weapons, and not just with fists; and there were even fights for the little boys—the boys of one syssition against those of another, and the boys of one and the same syssition against each other.[6]

In spite of Aristotle's explicit statement[7] that the Cretan 'ascendancy's' institutions had been borrowed from their conquered and enslaved Minoan subjects, it seems probable that at any rate the andreia, the agelai, and the brutal 'conditioning' of the boys were not parts of the set of institutions that had been borrowed by the Cretan 'ascendancy' from the Minoans, but were new institutions that had been created by and for the 'ascendancy' itself, after the conquest, as instruments for holding the conquered Minoans down. If this is the truth, it would mean that at least these particular institutions of the Cretan 'ascendancy' were peculiar in the post-Völkerwanderung Hellenic World, not because they had been borrowed from the Minoans, but because they had been created by the 'ascendancy' itself to meet a peculiar situation. It would then be natural that the Spartan 'ascendancy' should have subsequently borrowed these institutions from the Cretan 'ascendancy' when, as a result of the Spartan conquests in the eighth century B.C., the Spartans had saddled themselves, as the Cretan 'ascendancy' had by its conquests in the twelfth century B.C.,

---

[1] See p. 321.

[2] Ephorus apud Strabonem, in loc. cit., § 20.

[3] Ephorus, ibid.

[4] On pp. 325–6.

[5] Miss Chrimes, *Ancient Sparta*, p. 219, with n. 2, holds that Ephorus' 'bigger boys', in this Cretan context, were youths of the age of the Spartan eirenes (i.e. were epheboi). Her evidence is Hesychius' entry: ἀπάγελος· ὁ μηδέπω συναγελαζόμενος παῖς· ὁ μέχρι ἐτῶν ἑπτακαίδεκα· Κρῆτες. But surely Hesychius' interpretation of the word ἀπάγελος must be wrong. The word must mean, not someone who has not yet been enrolled in an agelê, but someone who has ceased to be enrolled in one. If so, the agelai will have been in Crete, as they were at Sparta, troops of boys who were not yet of the eiren or ephebos age.

[6] Ephorus, ibid.

[7] See p. 331, with n. 2.

with the formidable problem of trying to hold down permanently a conquered population that was many times more numerous than the conquerors themselves.

Some of the Spartan political institutions under the 'Lycurgan' regime were more modern than the corresponding Cretan institutions, while others were more archaic. At Sparta, the kingship survived, and this with a life-long tenure of the office, whereas in Crete the kingship was extinct.[1] On the other hand, the powers of the Spartan damos seem to have been greater than those of the Cretan public assemblies. At these, 'all [adult male citizens] are free to attend, but the assembly's sole pre-rogative is to endorse the decisions of the gerontes and the kosmoi'.[2] If the makers of Sparta's 'Lycurgan' constitution did remodel the Spartan gerousia and ephorate on a Cretan pattern, they failed to eliminate the faults of their Cretan prototypes. In Crete, as at Sparta, the gerontes were elected for life;[3] they were anhypeuthynoi (not subject to audit); and the kosmoi (the Cretan counterparts of the Spartan ephors) acted according to their own will and pleasure, since, in Crete too, there was not any written law to which they had to conform.[4] Only ex-kosmoi were eligible for the Cretan gerousia, and candidates had to have good per-sonal qualifications as well.[5] Only the members of certain (noble) families were eligible for the Cretan boards of kosmoi.[6] Yet, in spite of this limita-tion, persons of inferior character managed to get themselves elected kosmoi, as they got themselves elected ephors at Sparta,[7] and the poor quality of the Cretan kosmoi must have affected the quality of the Cretan gerousiai.

If the 'Lycurgan' constitution-makers at Sparta did get some of their new ideas from Crete, their adaptations of the borrowed Cretan institu-tions not only made these more efficient for achieving their oppressive purposes; the Spartans also transformed the spirit of the borrowed Cretan institutions by infusing into them a grim single-mindedness that was foreign to the Cretan 'ascendancy's' fantastically undisciplined êthos. The Spartans subordinated everything else in life to their paramount purpose of holding the helots down, and the whole 'Lycurgan' regime was designed systematically to produce this result. Yet, as Aristotle notices, the helots kept on revolting at every opportunity, whereas the Cretan 'ascendancy' never had any trouble with its perioikoi, though it

---

[1] Aristotle, *Politics*, Book II, chap. 7 (10), § 3 (1272a); Polybius, Book VI, chap. 45, § 5.
[2] Aristotle in loc. cit., § 4.
[3] Polybius, Book VI, chap. 45, § 5, and chap. 46, § 4, seems to be under the mistaken impression that the Cretan gerontes, unlike the Spartan, were elected, not for life, but only for annual terms of office.
[4] Aristotle, in loc. cit., § 6.
[5] Ephorus apud Strabonem in loc. cit., § 22: Aristotle in loc. cit., § 5.
[6] Aristotle in loc. cit., § 5.
[7] Aristotle, ibid.

indulged recklessly in civil wars,[1] as well as in wars between one Cretan city-state and another. Aristotle[2] attributes the Cretan 'ascendancy's' immunity from rural slave-revolts to Crete's geographical isolation. The Cretan rural slaves, he implies, did not have, within reach, any potential foreign ally from whom they could hope for effective aid. Crete was an island; and, though it was divided among a number of separate sovereign city-states that frequently went to war with each other, there was a 'gentlemen's agreement' between the representatives of the 'ascendancy' in each of the Cretan states that they would not give support to an enemy state's agricultural slaves if these revolted. An alternative explanation of the Cretan perioikoi's quiescence is that they may have been better treated than Sparta's Laconian and Messenian helots were.[3] At any rate, they did not seize the opportunities that their masters offered them for shaking off their yoke. The political life of the 'ascendancy' in the Cretan city-states was perpetually dissolving into sheer anarchy.[4] Powerful men defied the jurisdiction of the courts; the only remedy for misbehaviour on the part of the kosmoi was to throw them out by force; sometimes this was done by some of their colleagues, sometimes by private enterprise; each Cretan politeuma was divided into factions whose strife frequently degenerated into civil war.[5] If the Spartiate homoioi had indulged in this extravagant licence, their domination over the helots would have been short-lived. The Spartan 'ascendancy's' discipline may seem more admirable than the Cretan 'ascendancy's' turbulence; but the impunity with which the Cretan 'ascendancy' was able to play the fool testifies indirectly to the comparative humaneness of their treatment of their victims, and this testimony makes the Cretan regime, on balance, the less repulsive of the two.

PART III, CHAPTER 4, ANNEX II

Epitadeus' Rhetra

ACCORDING to Aristotle, 'Lycurgus' 'placed a moral embargo on the buying or selling of existing [holdings of property in land].... But he gave licence, to anyone who chose, to give away land or to bequeath it, and this inevitably produced the same effect [as if land had been allowed to come into the market]'.[6] In reproducing this passage of Aristotle's

---

[1] Aristotle, loc. cit., § 8 (1272b).
[2] Ibid. and in chap. 6 (9), § 3.
[3] See Lotze, Μεταξὺ Ἐλευθέρων καὶ Δούλων, p. 25.
[4] Aristotle, loc. cit., § 7 (1272b).   [5] Ibid.
[6] ὠνεῖσθαι μὲν γάρ ἢ πωλεῖν τὴν ὑπάρχουσαν ἐποίησεν οὐ καλόν ... διδόναι δὲ καὶ καταλείπειν ἐξουσίαν ἔδωκε τοῖς βουλομένοις· καίτοι ταὐτὸ συμβαίνειν ἀναγκαῖον ἐκείνως τε καὶ οὕτως (Aristotle, *Politics*, Book II, chap. 6 (9), § 10 (1270a).

work, Heracleides Ponticus adds, explicitly apropos of Sparta, a further proviso which Aristotle mentions only in general terms, and this in a different context. 'The buying and selling of the original portion is positively illegal.'[1] 'The original portion' means, on the face of it, the kleros that had been granted to the ancestor of a present-day homoios at the time of the inauguration of the 'Lycurgan' regime. This original portion is assumed to have been kept, as a rule, in the family's possession ever since, by being handed on from father to son.

If this were all the information on this point that had come down to us, we should conclude that the licence to give away land of all categories, or alternatively to bequeath it, had been an integral part of the original 'Lycurgan' constitution. However, Plutarch informs us[2] that, when 'Lycurgus' had distributed the kleroi, his intention had been that each kleros should be handed down from father to son, and that the purpose, behind this intention, had been to keep the number of families with the status of homoioi up to its original strength. According to Plutarch, this intention, and the underlying purpose, had been fulfilled, more or less, until an ephor named Epitadeus persuaded the Spartan damos to adopt a rhetra, drafted by him, making it legal for an homoios to give away his estate and his kleros to anyone whom he chose, either by gift *inter vivos* or by a provision in his will.[3] It was the enactment of this rhetra that made the concentration of property at Sparta in a small number of hands go with a run. From that time onwards, 'the powerful people added to their own property unrestrainedly by ejecting other people from the heritages that were theirs by right, with the result that wealth came rapidly to be concentrated in a few hands at the cost of impoverishing the citizen-body as a whole'.[4]

It will be seen that the licence to give away property, including (according to Plutarch's source) a family's ancestral kleros, or alternatively to bequeath it by will—a licence which Aristotle and Heracleides take to have been one of the original provisions of the 'Lycurgan' constitution— is said by Plutarch's source to have been the work, not of 'Lycurgus', but of an ephor named Epitadeus who lived at a date that Plutarch's

---

[1] τῆς δὲ ἀρχαίας μοίρας οὐδὲ ἔξεστιν (Heracleides Ponticus in Müller, *F.H.G.*, vol. ii, p. 211, No. 7). Cp. Plutarch, *Inst. Lac.*, § 22: a foreigner who had passed through the Spartan educational system with credit κατὰ τὸ βούλημα τοῦ Λυκούργου μετεῖχε τῆς ἀρχῆθεν διατεταγμένης μοίρας· πωλεῖν δ' οὐκ ἔξεστιν. The corresponding passage in Aristotle's *Politics* runs: ἦν δὲ τό γε ἀρχαῖον ἐν πολλαῖς πόλεσι νενομοθετημένον μηδὲ πωλεῖν ἐξεῖναι τοὺς πρώτους κλήρους (Book VI, chap. 2 (9), § 5 (1319a). Cp. ibid., Book II, chap. 4 (7), § 4 (1266b): ἐν Λοκροῖς νόμος ἐστὶ μὴ πωλεῖν, ἐὰν μὴ φανερὰν ἀτυχίαν δείξῃ συμβεβηκυῖαν, ἔτι δὲ τοὺς παλαιοὺς κλήρους διασώζειν.

[2] Plutarch, *Agis*, chap. 5.

[3] ῥήτραν ἔγραψεν ἐξεῖναι τὸν οἶκον αὐτοῦ καὶ τὸν κλῆρον ᾧ τις ἐθέλοι καὶ ζῶντα δοῦναι καὶ καταλιπεῖν διατιθέμενον (Plutarch in loc. cit.).

[4] Plutarch, ibid.

source places very much later than the date of the 'Lycurgan' constitution itself.[1]

Which is right? Aristotle-cum-Heracleide or Plutarch's source? Aristotle's attribution of this provision to 'Lycurgus' himself carries little weight, because, by Aristotle's day, it had become common form to ascribe the creation of every Spartan institution to Lycurgus. Already, Herodotus ascribes to him the creation of the socio-military units called the triakades, as well as the creation of the syssitia and the enomotiai,[2] though, as is argued in the next chapter of the present Part,[3] the triakades were probably an innovation that had been introduced in Herodotus' own lifetime. In the light of this, Aristotle's dating does not weigh heavily against Plutarch's. We can believe in the historicity of the ephor Epitadeus[4] and his rhetra without being committed thereby to believing that Epitadeus' motive for presenting his rhetra to the Spartan assembly was a personal grudge of his against his own son.[5]

Plutarch's source dates the enactment of Epitadeus' rhetra much later than the inauguration of the 'Lycurgan' constitution, but he does not specify Epitadeus' date more closely than that; and, in representing Epitadeus as having been actuated by purely personal motives, he leaves us in the dark about the historic occasion that prompted the enactment at Sparta of such a momentous piece of new legislation. We know the date of one Spartiate homoios who bore the name Epitadas (and 'Epitadas' and 'Epitadeus' must surely be the same name). This Epitadas, son of Molobros, was killed in action in 425 B.C. as commandant of the Lacedaemonian force that had been stationed on the island of Sphakteria.[6] The vagueness of the dating of the ephor Epitadeus by Plutarch's source would equally well allow of our identifying him with Thucydides' Epitadas son of Molobros himself or with this Epitadas' grandfather or with his grandson. An Epitadas of any of these three generations would have been living in a time of economic and social crisis at Sparta that might have given occasion for new legislation relaxing previous restrictions on the transfer of property. Epitadas son of Molobros' grandfather would have lived through the crisis at Sparta which had followed the earthquake of *circa* 466 or 464 B.C.; Epitadas the son of Molobros himself would have lived through the crisis brought on by the outbreak of the Archidamian War in 431 B.C.; and this Epitadas' grandson would have

---

[1] Chrimes, *Ancient Sparta*, p. 350, n. 2, guesses that Plutarch and Aristotle had a common source in Ephorus.

[2] Herodotus, Book I, chap. 65.

[3] In chap. 5, section (iii), on p. 383.

[4] Forrest, who believes in the historicity of 'Lycurgus', is sceptical (*A History*, p. 137) about the historicity of Epitadeus.

[5] As it is said to have been by Plutarch in loc. cit.

[6] See Thucydides, Book IV, chaps. 8, 31, 33, 38, 39.

lived through the crisis precipitated by Sparta's military disaster at Leuktra in 371 B.C. and by her consequent loss of Messenia next year. An early dating seems to be indicated by Aristotle's evident unawareness that the licence to give away or bequeath land was not part of the original 'Lycurgan' dispensation; and we know, from the Spartans' reaction to their losses at Sphakteria in 425 B.C.,[1] that, by that date, they were already seriously concerned about the decline in the numerical strength of the homoioi—a decline that had been due, at least partly, to an increase in the inequality of the distribution of property among the homoioi.[2] However, our sources give the general impression—it is nothing more definite —that the maldistribution of property at Sparta, and the concomitant decline in the numbers of the homoioi, did not get completely out of hand till after Sparta's victory in 404 B.C., and this would point to the ephor who was the author of the rhetra being the grandson of the Epitadas who met his death in 425 B.C.

Our surviving information does not enable us to decide between these three alternative possible datings of Epitadeus' rhetra. We can only guess at the date by guessing at the motives—that is to say, by guessing at the intentions and expectations in the minds of the ephor who drafted this rhetra and of the members of the damos who enacted it.

No one at Sparta can have expected that, if gifts and bequests of Spartiate land were made legal, landowners would give or bequeath land for love. Obviously, if they were going deliberately to alienate land from their own family, they would be doing this only for a consideration which, to their minds, was adequate. Gifts and bequests of land would be made only in exchange for some valuable commodity of another kind; and, in 'Lycurgan' Sparta, there were only three valuable commodities in which an homoios could deal. It was illegal for him to acquire the precious metals, and there was little opening now left for him to invest in industry. Sparta's export of painted pottery had come to an end in the course of the sixth century B.C., and, since then, industrial production within the frontiers of Sparta's dominions must have dwindled to the minimum that was required for supplying elementary domestic needs. Nor would it have been attractive for an homoios to accumulate a heap of local iron currency-spits. This Spartan currency had no foreign-exchange value; even in domestic transactions, it probably played only a small part by comparison with exchange in kind; and it was useless even for serving as scrap-iron as a result of the chemical treatment that had been given to it on purpose to make it unutilizable. The three commodities that did have a value in 'Lycurgan' Sparta were land, subsidies from the proceeds of someone else's land, and social and political influence. The removal of the embargo on giving away or bequeathing land would have had no

---

[1] See p. 314. [2] See p. 313.

point if it was not practicable, in return, to obtain either subsidies or influence. Subsidies would be the poor man's *quid pro quo* for giving away his land; influence would be the rich man's corresponding consideration.

In the section of the present chapter to which this annex attaches, it has been suggested that, under the 'Lycurgan' regime, the first concern of every Spartiate homoios was to make it as sure as possible that he and his male descendants would be able to continue to pay membership-dues to a syssition, since a member who defaulted on these lost not only his membership in his syssition but also his status as an homoios, including the right to a voice in the assembly of the damos. The best insurance against this extreme calamity would be to accumulate more and more land to supplement one's ancestor's original kleros and his original free-hold if he had been a member of the small aristocratic minority of Spartiatai that had been landowners already in the age before the distribution of the 'Lycurgan' kleroi. But suppose that an homoios found himself among the majority that had failed to insure their, and their descendants', status in this substantial way. Suppose that, among his recent forebears, there had been a succession of large families of male children, and that these had not been prematurely killed off by disease or by war, but had lived to beget large families of male children in their turn. By this time the number of heirs to a share in the family's original kleros might have passed the limit at which the produce of the kleros would provide syssition-dues for them all. Was there any device by which each of them could still make his inadequate fraction of a kleros provide him with the means of paying his syssition-dues all the same? Perhaps he could arrange for this by doing a deal with some other homoios who was rich enough in land already to have a surplus beyond the utmost that would be required in order to insure his, and his descendants', status.

The poor homoios might make a gift or bequest of his surviving parcel of land to the rich homoios in exchange for an undertaking, on the rich recipient's part, that he would guarantee the syssition-dues of the donor and perhaps of some of his descendants as well. In the western provinces of the Roman Empire in the fifth century of the Christian Era, a small landowner did sometimes give his property to a big landowner in exchange for receiving the big landowner's protection; and the big landowner, for his part, also found this transaction advantageous. Besides bringing him a small addition to his property, it brought him an additional client, and every additional client brought him additional influence. Big and small landowners may have thought and acted in a similar way in Sparta under the 'Lycurgan' regime as soon as the enactment of Epitadeus' rhetra gave them leave.

When the licence given by Epitadeus' rhetra was used to transfer land from the hands of the poor into those of the rich, the rhetra would be producing effects that would be favourable to the long-term interests of the rich homoioi and to the short-term interests of the poor homoioi, but that would be unfavourable to the long-term interests of the Spartan state. On the other hand, it would be to the state's advantage if the licence were used to transfer land from the hands of the rich into the hands of the poor; and it was conceivable that a rich homoios, who owned more land than he needed for insuring his own, and his descendants', status, might convert some of his surplus land into influence by giving it away to a poor homoios in exchange for the poor man's social and political support. Influence might count for little or nothing in the elections to the ephorate. We do not know how these elections were conducted, but we do know that poor and obscure homoioi, who presumably had no influence, did get elected to the ephorate nevertheless.[1] On the other hand, influence seems likely to have counted for much in the elections to the gerousia, in which the competition between candidates was intense and their electioneering activities were assiduous.[2] Accordingly, for a rich man who could afford the luxury, influence was a commodity that might be valuable enough to induce him to purchase it at the price of parting with surplus land.

It seems evident that the licence given by the enactment of Epitadeus' rhetra might cut both ways. It might work against the concentration of land in fewer hands by allowing big landowners to part with surplus land in order to increase their fund of influence. Conversely, it might work in favour of the concentration of landholdings by allowing poor men to part with inadequate holdings to big landowners in exchange for having their syssition-dues underwritten by the rich recipients. The Spartan Government may have presented the rhetra to the Spartan damos in the hope that its effect might be to arrest the progress of the concentration of landholdings; the homoioi may have enacted the rhetra in the hope that it was going to serve their divers interests. The poor homoioi may have seen in it a prospect of getting their syssition-dues underwritten by rich homoioi; the rich homoioi may have seen in it a prospect of enlarging their holdings of real estate and/or of increasing their influence. The eventual effect of the enactment was to promote the long-term interests of the rich homoioi at the expense of both the short-term interests of the poor homoioi and the long-term interests of the Spartan state; and, in the end, this was disastrous for all Spartan interests alike.

As regards the still unanswered question of the date of the enactment, it seems most likely that the rhetra was enacted at a date when the decline in the numbers of the homoioi had already gone to alarming lengths,

---

[1] Aristotle, *Politics*, Book II, chap. 6 (9), § 14 (1270b); chap. 7 (10), § 5 (1272a).
[2] Ibid., chap. 6 (9), §§ 18–19 (1271a).

and that the rhetra was drafted by a representative of the Government, bona fide, as a measure for arresting this decline, though, in the event, the enactment had just the opposite effect. This seems, on the whole, to point to a date later than 371 B.C. If so, the draftsman of this rhetra seems likely to have been a grandson of the Epitadas who lost his life on Sphakteria in 425 B.C.

PART III, CHAPTER 4, ANNEX III

The Institution of Homoioi by Adoption
(Σύντροφοι, Τρόφιμοι, Μόθακες)

I N the immediately preceding annex it' has been suggested that social and political influence was a valuable commodity for any Spartan homoios who could afford to purchase it. One way in which he could secure a future client among the homoioi would be to adopt a promising boy from a poverty-stricken homoian family or from the hypomeiones class, finance his ascent up the Spartan educational ladder, and then, if and when this adoptive son of his qualified for admission into a syssition and was duly co-opted into one, to give him at least a big enough share in the produce of his adoptive family's property to cover his syssition-dues. Of course, the legal act of adoption would commit the adoptive father to an indissoluble relation with his adoptive son. Short of making this far-reaching commitment, a rich homoios could secure a future client by adopting a poor homoios' son or a hypomeion Spartiate's son, not juridically, but informally, as his protégé and pensioner, and, on this informal alternative basis, he would be free to take under his wing a non-homoios who was not a Spartiate of either homoios or hypomeion status. He might choose a helot who might or might not be his own bastard son. He might also choose a free-born foreigner.[1] So long as this protégé passed through the Spartan educational system with credit, was co-opted into a syssition,[2] and did not default on the payment of his

---

[1] At Sparta the naturalization of a foreigner was rare according to Herodotus, Book IX, chap. 35; but the case here in question is that of a foreigner who had not climbed the Spartan educational ladder. According to Teles (a contemporary of Phylarchus) apud Stobaeum, Book XL, chap. 8, Λακεδαιμόνιοι . . . τὸν μὲν μετασχόντα τῆς ἀγωγῆς καὶ ἐμμείναντα, κἂν ξένος κἂν ἐξ εἵλωτος, ὁμοίως τοῖς ἀρίστοις τιμῶσι.

[2] Wüst, 'Laconica' II: Κάσεν—Μόθακες—'Υπομείονες, pp. 61–2, holds that, though a protégé could obtain admission into a syssition, his status as a messmate was slightly inferior to that of members who had made their own way without the aid of a patron. Wüst guesses that the hypomeiones were messmates of this 'slightly inferior' status. He rejects the prevalent view (accepted in the present book) that the hypomeiones were Spartiatai who had either never been co-opted into a syssition or had dropped out because of their having failed to pay their dues.

syssition-dues, he could become and remain an homoios,[1] even though he were of non-Spartiate birth on one side or even on both sides.[2]

The existence of this institution at Sparta in the Age of the Principate is attested by a wealth of inscriptional evidence. In this age, the protégé boy was called a 'kasen', which seems to mean a 'brother'—in the informal sense of foster-brother, not in the legal sense of an adoptive brother. A 'kasen' was the foster-brother of the son of the patron by whom the 'kasen's' education was being financed simultaneously with the education of the patron's son himself.[3] We do not know whether the 'kasen' system of the Age of the Principate was a direct continuation of the 'protégé' system that was in existence in Xenophon's time, or whether it was an archaistic revival of this. On either hypothesis it would be rash[4] to seek to supplement our scanty evidence for the fourth-century-B.C. 'protégé' system by taking our more abundant evidence for the 'kasen' system as being applicable to this earlier system—similar though the two systems evidently were to each other in a general way.

The 'protégé' system was perhaps the sole way in which the private interests of the homoioi—in this case, the interest of the rich homoioi in acquiring, not land, but clients—worked towards making good some of the wastage in the numbers of the homoioi. An homoios who was too poor to be able to pay syssition-dues for his son as well as for himself, or who, himself, had sunk to the status of being an hypomeion through having defaulted on the payment of his syssition-dues, might still hope that at least one of his sons might rise to be an homoios through being taken up by a rich homoios as his protégé. This intake into the pool of the homoioi will have been all to the good from the Spartan state's point of view; but its volume must have been much smaller than the volume of the wastage, considering that the decline in the numerical strength of the homoioi seems to have set in soon after the inauguration of the 'Lycurgan' constitution, and to have continued throughout the next 400 years, until it was abruptly reversed in 227 B.C. by King Kleomenes III's revolution.

Our extant evidence for the 'protégé' system that was in existence in

[1] According to Plutarch, *Inst. Lac.*, § 22, some authorities said that the achievement of passing through the Spartan educational system with credit entitled a foreigner to become a holder τῆς ἀρχῆθεν διατεταγμένης μοίρας. Perhaps it did, but it did not provide him automatically with one of the original kleroi. This would have to be given to him by some homoios who was the present possessor of it; and there was little chance of an homoios' being willing to part with so substantial an asset. The foreigner who had successfully climbed the Spartan educational ladder would have a better chance of persuading the homoios who had been his patron up to this point to guarantee his foreign protégé's syssition-dues if a syssition were prepared to co-opt the foreigner on the assurance that he was going to be solvent.

[2] See Ehrenberg, 'Spartiaten und Lakedaimonier, p. 63, quoted on p. 317, n. 2.

[3] See Chrimes, *Ancient Sparta*, pp. 84–117, with Appendix IV, pp. 442–62.

[4] As is prudently held by D. Lotze, 'Mothakes', in *Historia*, 11. Band (1962), pp. 427–35, on p. 427.

the fourth century B.C. is inadequate.[1] All the same, it is a surprising fact that there is no explicit mention in it of protégés who were the sons of Spartiatai (either poor homoioi or hypomeiones), though it would seem probable that this was both the most numerous and the most important of the several categories of protégés. We hear of protégés who were bastard sons of Spartiate homoioi by helot women[2] (μόθακες may have been the technical term for these);[3] we hear of others who were

[1] Such evidence as has survived is reviewed by Ehrenberg in P.–W., 31. Halbband (1933), cols. 382–4, s.vv. μόθακες and μόθωνες, and by Lotze in loc. cit.

[2] The νόθοι τῶν Σπαρτιατῶν of Xenophon, *Hellenica*, Book V, chap. 3, § 9.

[3] The following glosses on the words μόθακες and μόθωνες have been assembled by Lotze in 'Mothakes', pp. 427–8: Harpocration, s.v. μόθων· . . . μόθωνας δὲ καλοῦσι Λάκωνες τοὺς παρατρεφομένους τοῖς ἐλευθέροις παῖδας; scholion on Aristophanes' *Pluto*, l. 279: Λάκωνες τοὺς παρατρεφομένους τοῖς ἐλευθέροις παῖδας μόθωνας καλοῦσι; scholion on Aristophanes' *Knights*, l. 634: μόθωνας γὰρ ἐκάλουν οἱ Λάκωνες τοὺς παρεπομένους τοῖς ἐλευθέροις; Hesychius, s.v. μοθῶνες· οἱ ἅμα τρεφόμενοι τοῖς υἱοῖς δοῦλοι; Hesychius, s.v. μόθωνες· τοὺς παρατρεφομένους τοὺς λεγομένους παιδίσκους· Λάκωνες; *Etymologicum Magnum*, s.v. μόθων· οὕτω καλοῦσι Λακεδαιμόνιοι τὸν οἰκογενῆ δοῦλον, ὃν οἱ Ἀθηναῖοι οἰκότριβά φασι. Lotze points out that the first five of these six glosses are obviously derived from a common source; that the interpretation 'house-born slaves' (the Latin *verna*), which is given by the *Etymologicum Magnum* alone, is obviously incorrect; that the μοθᾶνες are labelled 'slaves' by Hesychius alone, s.v.; and that in Aelian, *V.H.*, Book XII, chap. 43, the crucial descriptive word has dropped out of the text, and that the restoration δούλοις here is merely a conjecture of Casaubon's. This passage of Aelian's work runs: ὄνομα δὲ ἦν ἄρα τοῦτο [i.e. μόθακες] τοῖς τῶν εὐπόρων ⟨ ⟩, οὓς συνέπεμπον αὐτοῖς οἱ πατέρες συναγωνιουμένους ἐν τοῖς γυμνασίοις, ὁ δὲ συγχωρήσας τοῦτο Λυκοῦργος τοῖς ἐμμείνασι τῇ τῶν παίδων ἀγωγῇ πολιτείας Λακωνικῆς μεταλαγχάνει. Lotze, in 'Mothakes', p. 430, draws the conclusion that the term μόθακες may have covered protégés who were free-born (i.e. who were Spartiatai hypomeiones), as well as the helot-born sons of helot mothers, whether by Spartiate or by helot sires. However, of the five glosses on the term μόθακες–μόθωνες–μοθᾶνες that have a common source, one does describe them as δοῦλοι outright, another calls them παιδίσκοι, and the remaining three brand them as servile implicitly by contrasting them with οἱ ἐλεύθεροι.

On the other hand, Lotze's interpretation of the term 'mothax' to include hypomeiones Spartiate freemen, as well as helots, is supported by the immediately preceding sentence in Aelian's work: Καλλικρατίδας γε μὴν καὶ Γύλιππος καὶ Λύσανδρος ἐν Λακεδαίμονι μόθακες ἐκαλοῦντο, and also by Phylarchus apud Athenaeum, Book VI, 271 f: τούτων [i.e. τῶν μοθάκων] ἕνα φασὶ γενέσθαι καὶ Λύσανδρον . . . πολίτην γενόμενον διὰ ἀνδραγαθίαν. Plutarch, *Lysander*, chap. 2, says that Lysander's father was a Heraklid, though not a member of either of the royal houses, and this would rule out the possibility of his having been a helot. He must have been a Spartiate, but he may have been an impoverished homoios or an hypomeion; for Plutarch goes on to say that Lysander himself was brought up in poverty. If the family was poor but aristocratic, it seems likely that Lysander's education will have been financed, and his syssition-dues have been subsequently guaranteed, by a wealthy patron outside his own family (see Lotze, 'Mothakes', p. 434). Isocrates, *Panegyricus*, 111, stigmatizes Lysander as having been a helot (ἠροῦντο δὲ τῶν εἱλώτων ἑνὶ δουλεύειν). If, correctly or incorrectly, Lysander was said by some people to have been a mothax, Isocrates, correctly or incorrectly, must have believed that the term 'mothax' implied helot blood. However, Lysander's father's poverty makes it improbable that Lysander's mother was a helot. A poverty-stricken Spartiate would be unlikely to have burdened himself with a bastard son. As for Xenophon's observation that τοὺς μὲν εἵλωτας ἁρμοστὰς ἀξιοῦσι καθιστάναι (*Hellenica*, Book III, chap. 5, § 12), Lotze, in loc. cit., pp. 432–3, points out that these helots may have been neodamodeis, but are more likely to have been mothakes of helot origin.

As for the δύο τῶν συντρόφων τοῦ Κλεομένους οὓς μόθακας καλοῦσιν (Plutarch, *Cleomenes*, chap. 8), Lotze, in loc. cit., p. 431, points out that King Kleomenes III cannot have had any

foreigners;[1] we do not hear, for certain, of those who were Spartiate by birth.[2] The most convincing explanation of this omission is to be found in the trickiness of Spartan technical terms. Students of Spartan affairs might overlook the existence of the hypomeiones through wrongly assuming that the term 'homoioi' was co-extensive with the term 'Spartiatai', as undoubtedly they sometimes overlooked the existence of the perioikoi through wrongly assuming that the term 'Spartiatai' was co-extensive with the term 'Lakedaimonioi'.[3] They might also forget that the son of an homoios did not himself become an homoios by right of birth. He had to qualify; and one of the conditions for qualifying was financial. The means must be forthcoming for providing, first for his education, and then for the regular payment of his syssition-dues.

PART III, CHAPTER 4, ANNEX IV

The Earthquake of circa *466 or 464* B.C. *at Sparta City*

MODERN students of Spartan history have differed in their estimates of the order of magnitude of the casualties inflicted on the Spartan citizen-body by the earthquake that devastated Sparta city *circa* 466 or 464 B.C.[4]

σύντροφοι in the technical sense, since heirs to the Spartan throne were exempt from having to climb the 'Lycurgan' educational ladder (Plutarch, *Agesilaus*, chap. 1; *Agis*, chap. 4).

[1] Xenophon's ξένοι τῶν τροφίμων καλουμένων (*Hellenica*, Book V, chap. iii, § 9). Xenophon himself was advised by Agesilaos to enter his own sons for admission to the Spartan educational ladder (Plutarch, *Agesilaus*, chap. 20; *Apophth. Lac.*, Agesilaos, 40). Cp. Phylarchus apud Athenaeum, Book VI, 271 e–f: οἱ μόθακες ἐλεύθεροι μέν, οὐ μὴν Λακεδαιμόνιοί γε, μετέχουσιν δὲ τῆς παιδείας. In this sentence, however, Phylarchus may be incorrect in his usage both of the term μόθακες (see p. 345, n. 3) and of the term Λακεδαιμόνιοι (see the present page, n. 2).

[2] Sosibius' οἱ ἐκ τῆς χώρας παῖδες, whom he contrasts with οἱ ἐκ τῆς ἀγωγῆς (Athenaeus, Book XV, 674a–b), might be the legitimate sons of poor homoioi or of hypomeiones, but they might alternatively be the bastard sons of homoioi by helot women. The legitimate sons of poor homoioi or of hypomeiones seem to be the class that Phylarchus, in loc. cit., is describing under the possibly inaccurate label 'mothakes': εἰσὶ δ' οἱ μόθακες σύντροφοι τῶν Λακεδαιμονίων· ἕκαστος γὰρ τῶν πολιτικῶν παίδων ὡς ἂν καὶ (or κατὰ) τὰ ἴδια ἐκποιῶσιν οἱ μὲν ἕνα, οἱ δὲ δύο, τινὲς δὲ πλείους ποιοῦνται συντρόφους αὐτῶν. Since the sentence εἰσὶν οὖν οἱ μόθακες ἐλεύθεροι μέν, οὐ μὴν Λακεδαιμόνιοί γε, quoted above in n. 1, follows on here, Phylarchus must be intending to refer to the same category in both sentences. If so, Lotze, in loc. cit., p. 429, will be right in holding that Phylarchus is using the word Λακεδαιμόνιοι, incorrectly, to stand for Σπαρτιᾶται (Lotze himself here means Σπαρτιᾶται ὅμοιοι). Then by οὐ μὴν Λακεδαιμόνιοί γε Phylarchus will be meaning, not ξένοι, but Σπαρτιᾶται ὑπομείονες (Lotze, loc. cit., p. 430). If this rendering of Phylarchus' meaning is right, the institution here described by Phylarchus is closely akin both to the 'kasen' system, for which we have abundant evidence in Spartan inscriptions of the Age of the Principate, and to the organization of the agelai in Crete as described by Ephorus (see pp. 334–5).

[3] See pp. 159–61.

[4] The earthquake is usually dated 464 B.C. on account of the estimated date of the revolt of Thasos against Athens. The earthquake overtook Sparta at the moment when the Spartans were on the point of responding to an appeal from the Thasians to intervene by military action on their behalf, and this appeal was not made until the Thasians had been defeated at sea and in the field and were under siege. Meanwhile the Athenians had suffered, after

Some scholars have held that the consequent reduction—immediate and long-term—of the Spartiate population had a major effect on Sparta's subsequent policy and fortunes.[1] Other scholars have played down the earthquake's effects[2]—some of them to the extent of virtually writing them off. The meagreness of our information makes it impossible to reach any sure conclusion about either the statistical facts themselves or their demographic, social, political, and military consequences. There can, however, be no doubt that, in contemporary Greek estimation, the earthquake was, for Sparta, a supreme disaster.

Sparta's enemies and rivals indicated their estimate of the disaster by their acts. The Messenians immediately revolted—and not only the Messenian helots, but also two perioecic Messenian communities, Thouria and Aithaia.[3] The insurgents held out on Mount Ithome for four years at least, and perhaps more probably for ten.[4] The Athenians'

their victory at sea over the Thasians, a disastrous defeat on land, at Drabeskos, at the hands of the Edonoi and the other local Thracian peoples, in the course of an attempt to establish an Athenian colony at 'Nine Ways', on the site of the future Amphipolis. (This Athenian disaster presumably encouraged the Spartans to respond favourably, as they did, to the now besieged Thasians' appeal to them.) These events are recorded by Thucydides in Book I, chaps. 100–1. In Book IV, chap. 102, apropos of the capture of Amphipolis by Brasidas in 424 B.C., Thucydides notes that Amphipolis has been founded by the Athenians successfully in the twenty-ninth year after their abortive attempt to found a colony on the same site ('Nine Ways') at the time of the revolt of Thasos. The date of the successful foundation of Amphipolis is known to have been 437/6 B.C.; and, in terms of the usual Greek method of inclusive reckoning, the twenty-ninth year before this year would be 465/4 B.C. Since the Spartans' decision to intervene militarily on the Thasians' behalf was taken after the Athenians' disaster at Drabeskos, and since the earthquake at Sparta was subsequent to the Spartans' decision to intervene, the date of the earthquake will have been 464 B.C. according to the information provided by Thucydides (see Beloch, *Griechische Geschichte*, 2nd ed., Zweiter Band, Zweite Abteilung, pp. 193–5, § 74).

The year of the earthquake is, however, also said to have been the fourth year of the Eurypontid King Arkhidamos II's reign (Plutarch, *Cimon*, chap. 16). Arkhidamos II reigned for forty-two years according to Diodorus, Book XI, chap. 48, § 2, and Book XII, chap. 35, § 4. Arkhidamos was still alive in the summer of 428 B.C. (Thucydides, Book III, chap. 1, § 1), but his son Agis II had already succeeded him by the summer of 426 B.C. (ibid., chap. 89, § 1). Therefore Arkhidamos II must have died in either 428/7 B.C. or 427/6 B.C., and consequently must have come to the throne in either 470/69 B.C., or 469/8 B.C. (see Beloch, *Griechische Geschichte*, 2nd ed., Erster Band, Zweite Abteilung, p. 184). This would date the earthquake in either 467/6 B.C. or 466/5 B.C.

[1] Ziehen, loc. cit.; Roussel, op. cit., p. 101; Dickins, loc. cit., p. 35; Michell, op. cit., p. 238.

[2] e.g., E. M. Walker in *The Cambridge Ancient History*, vol. v (1927), p. 69. Forrest, *A History*, holds that it was disastrous, even allowing for exaggeration in the reports of the loss of life and of the material damage (p. 101). He rightly maintains (p. 135) that it would not have had long-term effects if the numbers of the homoioi had not already been declining as a result of the operation of secular social causes.

[3] Thucydides, Book I, chap. 101.

[4] In Thucydides, Book I, chap. 103, δεκάτῳ ἔτει is the reading of the MSS. and the same figure—ten—is given by Diodorus, Book XI, chap. 64; δ' [i.e. τετάρτῳ] ἔτει is Krüger's emendation. Pseudo-Xenophon, *Ath. Pol.*, chap. 11, dates the Spartans' resubjugation of the Messenians as having preceded the hostilities in 457 B.C. between them and the Athenians. If we date the earthquake in 466 B.C., not in 464 B.C., pseudo-Xenophon's version of the order

estimate was evidently the same as the Messenians'. They threw down
the gauntlet to Sparta in a series of provocative acts—evidently discount-
ing Sparta's ability to retaliate. First, perhaps in 461 B.C., Athens broke
with Sparta and made an alliance with Sparta's ancient Peloponnesian
rival and implacable enemy Argos; then she provided an asylum for the
expatriate insurgent Messenians and took into her own alliance a seceding
ally of Sparta's, Megara; then, perhaps in 459 B.C., she committed herself to an unlimited naval and military liability in Egypt by going to the
help of Egyptian insurgents against the Persian Empire; after that, in
457 B.C., she attacked Sparta's allies Aigina, Epidauros, and Corinth.
Athens would not have ventured to go to war with the Peloponnesian
League and the Persian Empire simultaneously if she had not reckoned
that Sparta, the military dynamo of the Peloponnesian League, was at
least temporarily *hors de combat*.

The event proved that both the Messenians and the Athenians had
over-estimated the extent to which the earthquake had crippled Sparta
militarily. The Spartans did succeed in resubjugating Messenia, and they
did then take military action against Athens—first in 457 B.C. and again
in 446 B.C. On the former of these two occasions, Sparta's action was
ineffective; on the second occasion it was not pressed home. All the same,
Sparta was militarily strong enough in 445 B.C. to compel Athens, in the
peace-settlement of that year, to renounce her ambition to extend her
empire permanently over continental central Greece, where, for a few
years, the Megarians had been Athens' allies and the Boeotians (except
for the Thebans) had been her subjects, together with the Phocians and
the Opuntian Locrians. Sparta thus just succeeded in foiling Athens'
attempt to make herself a land power as well as a maritime power. All the
same, the nearness of Athens' approach to a decisive victory in her
audacious war on two fronts gives the measure of the degree and the
duration of Sparta's paralysis owing to the earthquake of *circa* 466 or
464 B.C.

Can we get any closer to grips than this with the statistics of Sparta's
earthquake casualties? There are two extant accounts of the earthquake
that give some details, one in Plutarch's *Cimon*[1] and the other in Diodorus'
Library of Universal History.[2] According to Diodorus, 'the earthquake
shocks were continuous over a long period of time, during which the
houses were falling and the city was being brought to the ground.
Many human bodies were caught and killed by the collapse of walls, and

of events gives us no reason for changing δεκάτῳ in the text of Thucydides to δ'. However,
it is possible that pseudo-Xenophon's version of the order of events may be wrong, for
Athens' attack, in 457 B.C., on Sparta's allies Aigina, Epidauros, and Corinth would have
been very rash if Athens had not then still calculated—miscalculated, as it turned out—
that Sparta was not yet capable of intervening.

[1] Chap. 16.   [2] Book XI, chap. 63.

the earthquake also ruined a considerable amount of the movable property in the houses.' In this passage, Diodorus estimates the total number of deaths at 20,000. According to Plutarch,

the whole of the city itself was wrecked. Only five houses survived; all the rest were thrown down by the earthquake. In the middle of the stoa the eirenes (τῶν ἐφήβων) and the men of the youngest age-classes subject to military service (τῶν νεανίσκων) were doing physical exercises together when, so it is said, a hare made its appearance outside. Without waiting even to wipe off the oil from their bodies, the young men rushed out to chase the animal for fun [and so escaped death]; the eirenes remained behind; the gymnasium fell in upon them and there was not a single survivor.

What are we to make of the figures that these two passages give us?[1] If 20,000 people did lose their lives, what percentage of the total population of the city was this? And what were the numbers of the eirenes (ἔφηβοι) who perished *en masse*?

For estimating the total population of Sparta City *circa* 466 or 464 B.C., the only figure that we have to go upon is the statement, put by Herodotus into the ex-king Damaratos' mouth, that in 480 B.C. the total number of the Spartiate homoioi was about 8,000.[2] There is no reason to think that, between 480 B.C. and 466 or 464 B.C., the number of the homoioi had diminished appreciably; but, if we take the figure 8,000 as representing the approximate numerical strength of the homoioi in 466 or 464 B.C. as well as in 480 B.C., we have to allow for the hypomeiones too in order to arrive at the total number of adult male Spartiatai; and on this we have no information at all. We can merely guess that, in 466 or 464 B.C., the number of the hypomeiones will still have been small. The creation of this depressed class of Spartiatai had, it is true, been one of the effects of the establishment of the 'Lycurgan' regime; it had been an effect of the rule that an homoios forfeited his status if he failed to pay his syssition-dues; but this effect had been unintentional, not deliberate, and in the earlier days of the regime it must have been making itself felt only gradually.[3] If it is true that the original number of the homoioi had been 9,000[4] and that the number had sunk to 8,000 by 480 B.C., we may perhaps infer that, by then, the number of the hypomeiones had risen, correspondingly, to 1,000. If we apply our figures for 480 B.C. to the years 466 or 464 B.C., and if we reckon that the total adult male Spartiate population will have been about one-quarter of the total Spartiate population of all ages and both sexes, we arrive at a figure of

---

[1] Jones, *Sparta*, pp. 60–1, holds that the casualties were heavy and that the consequences of them were serious. Busolt and Swoboda, op. cit., p. 719, point out that the loss of life in the earthquake had been preceded by casualties in wars with the Arcadians and the Argives and was followed by casualties in the war with the insurgent helots.

[2] Herodotus, Book VIII, chap. 234, quoted already on p. 314.

[3] See p. 228.   [4] See p. 230, n. 8. The evidence on this point is suspect.

about 36,000 for the total Spartiate population, including hypomeiones as well as homoioi, and women and children as well as men.

The whole Spartiate community was permanently domiciled in Sparta City itself,[1] and it must have constituted most of the city's population. For reasons of security, the Government must have been unwilling to see helots, or even perioikoi, take up their permanent residence in the City in more than minimum numbers; but the wives of the homoioi will, no doubt, have had helot female domestic servants (since they themselves are known to have felt domestic work to be beneath them);[2] and there may also have been resident perioecic, as well as hypomeionic Spartiate, artisans. If we allow a total figure of 4,000 for these non-Spartiate residents in Sparta City in 466 or 464 B.C. we shall probably be on the safe side. Reckoning, then, the total population of the City at this date at a maximum of 40,000, we find that the 20,000 deaths in the earthquake signify that at least half the population of the City was wiped out.

The heaviest casualties of all must have been among the Spartiate women and girls in the families of the homoioi and among the male children below the age of seven;[3] for these, unlike the males of all ages from the beginning of the eighth year onwards, spent most of their time in their homes, and it is said that only five houses were left standing. The homoioi themselves will have escaped comparatively lightly. The 'neaniskoi', who were presumably the homoioi of the youngest year-classes,[4] had escaped death by a lucky accident. As for the rest, we know that they had an abundance of leisure, and that they liked to spend it in passing the time of day in public, hobnobbing with each other and with the eirenes and the boys from the age of seven upwards.[5] This was the favourite occupation not only of the Spartiate homoioi but of all adult male Greeks who had been brought up in the city-state way of life. For instance, when the Emperor Darius I's homesick Crotoniate Greek personal physician Demokedes found himself at home again in his native

---

[1] Lotze, Μεταξὺ Ἐλευθέρων καὶ Δούλων, pp. 37–8, points out that the Spartiate women, as well as the men, lived for most of the time in the City, and that this is implied in the institution of compulsory physical training for girls.

[2] See chap. 4, Annex V, p. 363.

[3] This point is made by Ziehen, loc. cit., pp. 232–3. Ziehen holds (ibid., p. 235) that, after the earthquake, women had a scarcity value at Sparta, and that this was one of the reasons for the liberal treatment of women there. He also holds (ibid., pp. 234–5) that the famine of Spartiate man-power after the earthquake accounts for the liberal treatment of the homoioi's bastard sons by helot women (μόθακες). The scarcity of Spartiate women after the earthquake may have been one of the reasons for the institution of polyandry at Sparta (see pp. 305–6).

[4] We do not know how many year-classes the term 'neaniskos' covers. If the total number of the homoioi at this time was still about 8,000, the average numerical strength of each of the forty year-classes will have been something less than 200 (the 8,000 will have included the time-expired homoioi who were over sixty). The gymnasium can hardly have held more than two year-classes of neaniskoi simultaneously with the seven year-classes of the eirenes.

[5] See pp. 327–8.

Kroton as a result of his own wily machinations, the first thing that he did, according to the story as told by Herodotus, was to pass the time of day in the agora there.[1] The homoioi could afford to spend more of their time on lounging than any other Greek male community of the same size; on the day of the earthquake they were, no doubt, engaged in their usual occupation; their casualties will have been relatively light; and, when the young King Arkhidamos, who was not among the casualties, had the presence of mind to sound the trumpet-call for parading under arms, the homoioi were able to fall in in formidable enough numbers to dash the hopes of the helots who, at the news of the earthquake, had marched on Sparta, from the nearest helot-inhabited districts of Sparta's city-state territory, with the intention of finishing off the god Poseidon's good work.[2] What conclusions does our information enable us to draw with regard to the earthquake's demographic effects on the numbers of the homoioi?

The most serious effect of all will have been the long-term effect of the heavy female casualties. The immediate diminution in the number of births in homoian families will have been drastic, and it will have continued to make itself felt for the next third of a century, i.e. until the date at which girl-babies who perished in 466 or 464 B.C. would have passed the child-bearing age if they had survived. This reduction in the number of the Spartiate women of the child-bearing year-classes will have set up a chain-reaction which will have taken several generations to work itself out, since the diminution in the total number of births in one generation will have produced a diminution in the number of child-bearing women in the next generation. A virtually permanent drastic reduction in the number of the homoioi must have been the consequence of the heavy female Spartiate casualties in 466 or 464 B.C.[3]

The next most serious effect will have been the wiping out of the seven year-classes that in 466 or 464 B.C. were in the eiren stage, i.e. the youths of the fourteenth to the twentieth year of age inclusive. If all these seven year-classes really were wiped out, the effect on the numbers of the homoioi will have begun to make itself felt in 465 or 463 B.C.; it will have reached its maximum in 459 or 457 B.C.; and it will have remained at its maximum till 430 or 428 B.C., since the end of either the one or the other of those two years would have been the date at which the oldest of the seven annihilated year-classes would, had it survived, have passed the age of fifty-five, i.e. the age to which the liability to active service, as distinguished from garrison duty at home, appears to have been raised, after the earthquake, from forty-five as one of the expedients for off-setting the

---

[1] εὑρόντες δέ μιν ἀγοράζοντα (Herodotus, Book III, chap. 137).
[2] Plutarch, *Cimon*, chap. 16. See pp. 194–5.
[3] See the present Part, chap. 5, sections (iii) and (iv).

losses that the earthquake had caused.[1] Throughout the thirty years 459 or 457 B.C. to 430 or 428 B.C. inclusive, the Spartan army—with as many as seven year-classes missing—will have been short of even its post-earthquake standard active-service strength by 20 per cent, and short of its standard post-earthquake total strength by 17·5 per cent; and it is only after the end of the year 430 or 428 B.C. that the effect of the wiping out of the eirenes in 466 or 464 B.C. will have started to diminish again with every additional year.

The casualties in 466 or 464 B.C. among male children below the age of seven will have weakened the Spartan army almost equally severely at a later date. This second set of male earthquake casualties will have begun to make itself felt in the army in 452 or 450 B.C.; this effect will have reached its peak in 445 or 443 B.C.; it will have remained at its peak till 416 or 414 B.C.

The strength of the active-service year-classes—that is to say, the classes including men from their twenty-first year to their fifty-fifth year inclusive—will have been affected by both sets of male Spartiate earthquake-casualties simultaneously from the year 452 or 450 B.C. onwards, and the effects of the two sets will have been at their peak simultaneously from 445 or 443 B.C. to 430 or 428 B.C. inclusive.

These facts and figures are illuminating.[2] They tell us why, from about 461 B.C. onwards, Athens ventured to go to ever greater lengths in giving Sparta provocation. They also tell us one of the reasons why Sparta gave Athens peace on easy terms in 445 B.C.;[3] why she did not intervene against Athens when Samos and Byzantium revolted from Athens in 440 B.C.; and why, in 432 B.C., she was no longer absolutely unwilling to go to war with Athens again, but was still nevertheless very reluctant to do so, whereas Pericles was advising his countrymen that, if they had to have a 'show-down' with Sparta, it would be better to have it now without delay.

PART III, CHAPTER 4, ANNEX V

The Position of Women at Sparta

LET us imagine that a present-day Western or Westernized woman could travel, in H. G. Wells's 'time-machine', against the current of the time-

---

[1] See Wade-Gery, *Essays in Greek History*, pp. 74 and 83, and the present book, p. 377.

[2] It will be noticed that the facts and figures do not lose their force if the datings of the effects of the earthquake on Spartan military man-power are raised by two years, as they all have to be if the earthquake is dated, not in 464 B.C., but in 466 B.C., as it must be dated if we are to give credit to Plutarch's statement (see p. 346, n. 4) that the year of the earthquake was the fourth year of King Arkhidamos II's reign.

[3] Forrest, *A History*, p. 107, finds this puzzling. His puzzle is solved, I think, by a consideration of the earthquake's continuing demographic consequences.

stream, back into the next to last and then into the last millennium B.C. Let us imagine her selecting dates within this span of two millennia for visiting some of the communities then in existence in the Mediterranean basin, in order to observe how the representatives of her own sex were faring in these different times and places. We will make her visit Knossos and Mycenae in the sixteenth or fifteenth century B.C.; Athens, Sparta, and Macedon in the Archaic Age of the Hellenic city-state culture and again in the fifth century B.C., and finally Alexandria, Antioch, and Pergamon, as well as Athens and Sparta, in the third century B.C. What would be this time-machine-traveller's findings? In which of these various times and places would she find the status and êthos of the women most like her own, and in which of them would she find them least like hers?

We are assuming that our imaginary observer is an 'emancipated' woman in the present-day sense. She has free and intimate social relations with men, on a footing of equality, and this outside as well as inside her own family circle. She thinks of this relation of equality between the sexes as being 'modern', and she deprecates, as being 'oriental', a relation in which the women are subordinated, secluded, and confined to the sphere of domestic life. In which of the 'ancient' Mediterranean communities that our present-day observer is deemed to be visiting is she going to find the women most familiarly 'modern', and in which is she going to find them most distastefully 'oriental'?

In the royal palaces at Knossos and Mycenae in the sixteenth or fifteenth century B.C., our present-day visitor will meet women whose êthos and outlook are like enough to her own to enable her to put herself *en rapport* with them. If she goes out into the countryside, she will realize that these 'emancipated' court ladies are rare birds, but she will remind herself that her own modern Western forerunners were likewise rare birds in seventeenth-century and eighteenth-century France. When our time-machine-traveller moves on into the post-Völkerwanderung Hellenic World, and breaks her journey, this time, at Athens and Sparta and Macedon in the Archaic Age, she will be conscious at once that the Völkerwanderung has produced a far-reaching social and cultural change. The Minoan–Mycenaean sophistication is now a thing of the past, but the free and equal relation between the sexes has survived; indeed, the social circle in which this freedom and equality prevail is perhaps now a wider one than before. When she revisits these same three Hellenic communities in the fifth century B.C., she finds Macedon unchanged; Macedon is still living in the Archaic Age, and Macedonian women still retain their free and equal status. The present-day woman will receive her first shock—and it will be a great one—when she arrives at fifth-century-B.C. Athens.

In the Athens of this age, the men are in clover. Slaves have the bearing of freemen,[1] and proletarian freemen have the self-confidence of aristocrats. All fifth-century-B.C. Athenian men have, in fact, raised themselves to a psychological equality with the Archaic Hellenic lords and the Mycenaean and Minoan princes. In their ascent, however, they have left the Athenian women behind them—or, rather, they have kicked them downstairs in the process of climbing upstairs themselves. The fifth-century-B.C. Athenian woman, and her fourth-century-B.C. grand-daughter no less, is a creature who has been oppressed and effaced. Our visitor is in Pericles' audience when he makes his speech in honour of the Athenian men who have been killed in action in the first year of the Atheno-Peloponnesian War that has broken out in 431 B.C. While Pericles is talking about these fallen Athenian soldiers, he is impressive; when he goes on to talk about Athens herself, he becomes sublime; but, for the present-day Western woman who is listening in, the grand effect is brusquely undone by the unprovoked yet apparently deliberate brutality of the concluding remarks with which this fifth-century-B.C. Athenian male speaker disposes of the Athenian women.

I suppose I must also say something about what can be demanded of the women, with reference to the war-widows. I can say all that I have to say in quite a few words of admonition. It will do you widows great credit if you do not fall below the level to which you are limited by your sex. The greatest credit will go to the woman who is least talked about, for either good or evil, by the men.[2]

For a present-day woman's ears, these words are not only shocking; they are, above all, surprising. In Pericles and his generation of male Athenians, she has met the first sophisticated people that have appeared in the Aegean World since the fall of Mycenae. But the sophistication of these Athenian men turns out to have short and sharp limits. What could be more insensitive, what could be more obtuse, than the words about women, and to women, that Pericles has just been uttering without appearing to realize how devastatingly these words reflect upon the speaker himself and upon his beloved Athens?

The present-day woman visitor does not feel the atmosphere of Periclean Athens congenial, but curiosity leads her to stay on till she finds herself attending, in 411 B.C., the first performance of Aristophanes' *Lysistrata*. The poet's female Athenian dramatis personae serve their creator's turn well enough. He has created them as his instruments for showing up the folly and perversity of the Athenian men; he has not been concerned to make them true to life, and indeed they bear no resemblance to the

---

[1] Pseudo-Xenophon, *Ath. Pol.*, chap. 1, § 10.
[2] Thucydides, Book II, chap. 45, § 2.

real Athenian women of the day, so far as the alien spectator can see. But now Aristophanes has brought on a woman who is not an Athenian but a Spartan; and here, at last, the spectator has the impression of being in the presence of a 'modern' woman again. Is Aristophanes' characterization of Lampito just another flight of his exuberant fancy, or are fifth-century-B.C. Spartan women truly like that? Our visitor's curiosity now shifts from Athens to Sparta. She is curious enough to go and see for herself; and at Sparta she finds, to her amazement and delight, that Aristophanes' portrait of a Spartan woman is substantially true to life.[1] Here at Sparta the visitor is at last meeting fifth-century-B.C. Greek women with whom she once more feels at home.

Of course, if she were a man and a slave, she would rather be an Athenian industrial entrepreneur's slave-partner than be a Spartan homoios' helot. But, since she happens to be a woman, she would certainly choose to be a Spartan woman if she were condemned to be a woman in one or other of the states of the fifth-century-B.C. Hellenic World. After regretfully taking leave of the women friends that she has made at Sparta, she gives Athens a last chance. She looks in on the Athenian exile Xenophon at the farm that the Spartan Government has given him at Skillous in Triphylia. Xenophon plumes himself on being a Laconizer; so he, if any male Athenian, may be expected to have acquired the liberal attitude towards women that is characteristic of male Spartans. But at Skillous the visitor runs into the bigoted Attic atmosphere again. Xenophon reads her a lecture on the theme that 'a woman's place is in the home'.[2]

Our observer's final visit is to the Hellenic World in the third century B.C. This post-Alexandrine Hellenic World is as different from Pericles' world as the pre-Alexandrine Hellenic World was from King Minos' world. In third-century-B.C. Alexandria, Antioch, or Pergamon the twentieth-century Western woman feels so much at home that she can hardly believe that she is not still in her own native world and age. Even at Athens the position of women has now been improved—though perhaps not as much as it ought to have been—by the general change of the Hellenic social climate in the female sex's favour. And what about Sparta? At Sparta there has been no change in the position of women, because here no change was called for. Through all the political and military vicissitudes of Sparta's history the position of Spartan women has been consistently good.

This is a twentieth-century Western verdict on the position of women at Sparta, but our imaginary observer from our world would have had a cold reception from Aristotle if she had been rash enough to report her impressions to him. In Aristotle's sustained attack on the 'Lycurgan'

[1] See Huxley, op. cit., p. 62.   [2] Xenophon, *Oeconomicus, passim.*

regime[1] his opening broadside—after one range-finding shot against helotage—is directed, not against the homoioi themselves, but against their women-folk.[2]

The failure [at Sparta] to keep the women in order (ἡ περὶ τὰς γυναῖκας ἄνεσις)[3] is detrimental both to the objective of the regime and to the welfare of the state. A household consists of a man and a woman and, analogously, one has to think of a state as being a community that is divided, in approximately equal numbers, between the male and the female section of the population. Accordingly, in regimes in which the women's role is unsatisfactory (φαύλως ἔχει τὸ περὶ τὰς γυναῖκας), one has to recognize that one half of the community is unregulated (ἀνομοθέτητον).[4] That is what has happened at Sparta. The legislator's intention was to make the whole community hardy (καρτερικήν). In his legislation for the men, this intention of his is obvious, but he has entirely neglected to deal with the women. The Spartan women live profligately—there is no form of profligacy in which they do not indulge—and they live luxuriously too.[5] Consequently it is inevitable that, in a community of this kind, wealth should be prized—and this especially if the men happen to be subject to 'the monstrous regiment of women' (ἄλλως τε κἂν τύχωσι γυναικοκρατούμενοι), which is usually the situation in militaristic and warlike tribes, with the exception of the Celts and other peoples that have given overt approval to homosexual relations between males. The inventor of the myth of Ares' union with Aphrodite was a good sociologist. All militaristic peoples turn out to have a compulsive passion for sexual relations either with other males or with women; so it is not surprising to find the Laconians addicted to this, or to observe that, when Sparta was a great power, the management of Spartan affairs was largely in the women's hands. It makes no difference whether the women exercise their rule directly or whether they exercise it indirectly by ruling the [male] rulers. It comes to the same thing.

Aggressiveness (θρασύτητος) has nothing at all to be said for it in daily life; if it has any value, it is for war; but [these aggressive] Spartan women were as detrimental as they could be in war as well [as in peace]. They showed their true colours on the occasion of the Theban invasion. They were good for nothing—just like the women in other countries—and they gave more trouble than the enemy gave.

There is no mystery about the reason why the Laconians failed, from the start, to keep their women in order. They were away from home on campaign for long periods [at a time], waging war against the Argives and then against the Arcadians and the Messenians; and, when they had a breathing-space, they offered themselves to the legislator pre-conditioned (προωδοπεποιημένους) by their military life (a way of life that has many good points). But the Spartan women! Well, it is said that 'Lycurgus' attempted to make the women

---

[1] Aristotle, *Politics*, Book II, chap. 6 (9) (1269a–1271b).

[2] Ibid., §§ 5–9 and § 11. There is a counterpart of this passage, which may be an actual reminiscence of it, in Plutarch, *Agis*, chap. 7.

[3] The same word ἄνεσις is used by Plato too, in *Laws*, Book I, 637 C, to describe the laxity of women's sexual conduct at Sparta and also at Tarentum.—A.J.T.

[4] Cp. Plato, *Laws*, Book VII, 806 C.—A.J.T.   [5] Cp. Plato, ibid.—A.J.T.

amenable to his legislation, but gave up the attempt in the face of their resistance.[1] These are the causes of what has happened [at Sparta], including, manifestly, this particular miscarriage. However, the question with which I am concerned is not who is or is not to blame, but whether the results are good or bad; and, as has been suggested already, the unsatisfactoriness of the position of women at Sparta appears not only to be a blemish on the regime itself, but also to have been a contributory cause of Spartan cupidity.... Nearly two-fifths of the whole country is now in the women's hands, owing to the numbers of the heiresses and the magnitude of the dowries. It would have been better to rule that there should be no dowry, or, short of that, only a small or a moderate one. As for the disposal of an heiress, in the present state of the law her father is at liberty to give her to anyone that he chooses, and, if the father dies without having provided for this in his will, the person whom he has designated as his heir inherits the right to give the heiress to anyone that he likes.[2]

What are we to make of this tirade of Aristotle's? It is clear that we have to discount it to some extent on at least two grounds. In the first place, it is evident that Aristotle has a personal animus against the Spartans in general and against the Spartan women in particular. We do not know the cause of this, but the fact is conspicuous. In the second place, Aristotle was writing this passage in the social climate of pre-Alexandrine Athens, if not actually at Athens itself, and it has been noted that in pre-Alexandrine Athens the position of women was worse than it was in any other city-state in the pre-Alexandrine Hellenic World—bad though it was in all pre-Alexandrine Hellenic city-states with the notable exception of Sparta. Outside Sparta, Periclean Athens' deliberate depreciation of women set the tone for the rest of the Hellenic World till the new turn given to the course of Hellenic history by Philip and Alexander of Macedon substituted the liberal Macedonian tradition on this point for the illiberal Athenian tradition as the norm for the status of women in the Post-Alexandrine Age.

Attic or Atticizing Greek sociologists seem to have assumed, as a matter of course, that, in any community in which the women were socially 'emancipated' in the present-day Western sense, this convicted them of being also sexually promiscuous. This was the Greeks' assumption about the Etruscan women;[3] it was the non-Spartan Greeks' assumption about the Spartan women too. These were accused of having sunk to being women of easy virtue.[4] There was the equivocal claim that

---

[1] This assertion of Aristotle's is contested by Plutarch, *Lysander*, chap. 14, but is supported by Plato, *Laws*, Book VII, 806 c.—A.J.T.

[2] On this last point, see pp. 307–8.—A.J.T.

[3] See, for example, Theopompos apud Athenaeum, Book XII, 517 d–518 b (Jacoby, Zweiter Teil, B, pp. 577–8, Theopompos 204 (222). See also Athenaeus, Book IV, 153 d.

[4] τῆς ὕστερον λεγομένης γενέσθαι περὶ τὰς γυναῖκας εὐχερίας (Plutarch, *Lycurgus*, chap. 15); *Apophth. Lac.*, Lykourgos, 20.

adultery was an impossibility at Sparta.[1] On the face of it, this meant that the sexual probity of Spartan wives was invincible; but it could also be interpreted as meaning that at Sparta the code of sexual morals was so lax that there was no degree of sexual licence that would brand a married woman as an adulteress.[2] Then there was the Spartan practice of polyandry,[3] and the Spartan instances of the antithetical practice of bigamy and trigamy, exemplified in the marital history of two Spartan kings, the Agiad bigamist Anaxandridas[4] and the Eurypontid trigamist Ariston.[5] Herodotus is fair-minded. He notes that bigamy was 'un-Spartan'.[6] All the same, the smear stuck. Spartan women were under fire. Among other accusations, they were said to emulate the male Spartans' paederasty by practising Lesbianism.[7] The asseveration that in both cases the relation was a purely spiritual one left Spartan reputations still exposed to innuendos.

This denigration of the Spartan and the Etruscan women's sexual conduct by non-Spartan Greeks may or may not have been partially founded on fact, but in either case it reflects more pointedly on the status of women in the denigrators' own communities. The only 'emancipated' women that a pre-Alexandrine Athenian male will ever have encountered in Attica will have been hetairai—from Pericles' Milesian consort Aspasia downwards. When the male Athenian met women outside Attica who were as highly cultivated as Aspasia was, his native experience condemned him to conclude that their sexual life must be as irregular as hers. If we could call up Pericles out of the past, put him on board our Wellsian time-machine, and convey him to the twentieth-century United States, Pericles would undoubtedly report back home to Athens that, in this shocking new world, 80 per cent of the girls were loose-livers. How will the fifth-century-B.C. Athenian visitor have managed to make such a comprehensive investigation into the intimacies of private life in an exotic society? Why, it will have been very simple. Pericles will simply have noted the percentage of the juvenile female population that was admittedly receiving a higher education. ὁπόσαι 'co-eds', τόσαι harlots. His statistical procedure will have been as simple as that. We may guess that the non-Spartan Greek observers of Spartan life in the Pre-Alexandrine Age went just as wildly wide of the mark as this in their assessment of the sexual morals of their female Spartan contemporaries.

These considerations may incline a present-day Western student of

---

[1] See the story recounted by Plutarch, ibid.
[2] This is Nilsson's interpretation in loc. cit., pp. 326–7.
[3] See pp. 305–6.
[4] Herodotus, Book V, chaps. 39–41.
[5] Herodotus, Book VI, chaps. 61–3.
[6] οὐδαμῶς Σπαρτιητικά (Book V, chap. 40).
[7] Plutarch, *Lycurgus*, chap. 18.

Spartan affairs to discount heavily Aristotle's allegation that his female Spartan contemporaries were profligate sexually,[1] as well as in other ways. This is, however, only one of the charges in Aristotle's comprehensive indictment. He also accuses contemporary Spartan women of aggressiveness (θρασύτης); of cowardice when their pose of superhuman heroism was eventually put to a practical test; of recalcitrance to the 'Lycurgan' discipline to which their menfolk had meekly submitted; and of the possession and misuse of an inordinate share of the community's wealth. These charges, too, are serious, and, between them, they cover most sides of human life. Have we any independent evidence by which we can test them?

Three independent sources are Plutarch's *Lakainôn Apophthegmata*, his *Agis* and *Cleomenes*, and Stobaeus' scrapbook;[2] yet these works, like Aristotle's *Politics*, have to be discounted to some extent. The sayings attributed to Spartan women probably exaggerate the degree to which they managed to rise above—or sink below—normal human feelings. The character-sketches of the women who are the true heroes of Plutarch's *Agis* and *Cleomenes* possibly exaggerate their virtues, for Plutarch's source here is Phylarchus, and though Phylarchus was a good historian he was also a sentimentalist and a romanticist.

Many of the sayings with which the Spartan women are credited are so felicitously Laconic that their authenticity is suspect. Take, for instance, the Spartan mother's alleged admonition to her son when he is leaving for the front. 'My child, come back either with it or on it',[3] says the mother, pointing to the young man's shield. There will have been Spartan mothers who will have wished that they had thought of saying that; but it is hardly credible that anything so epigrammatically grim can have been an impromptu 'happy' thought. The most felicitous—which, in this context, means the most repellent—of the sayings attributed to Spartan women 'smell of the lamp', and we may write them off as having been *ben trovati, non veri*. No doubt, this implies that there was an original stock of authentic grim sayings by Spartan women that stimulated ingenious Athenian male minds to invent a host of fictitious variations that took the shine out of the genuine prototypes.

This point is illustrated by the flood of spurious 'Spoonerisms' with which the English-speaking World has been inundated in our time. They are evidence that Warden Spooner of New College was an historical character and that, in the course of his life, he did commit a few spontaneous 'Spoonerisms' himself. They are not evidence that Warden

---

[1] However, one authoritative present-day Western scholar, Nilsson, takes Aristotle's view. 'Das Jünglingshaus und die freie Liebe gehören zusammen' (loc. cit., p. 332; cp. p. 335). At Sparta, Nilsson sums up, 'die Ehe war geboten, die eheliche Treue nicht' (ibid., p. 335).

[2] Stobaeus, Book LXXVIII, chap. 83.

[3] Τέκνον, ἢ τὰν ἢ ἐπὶ τᾶς. This is impossible to translate into equally laconic English.

Spooner is the author of the whole corpus of 'Spoonerisms', and some of the finest of them are undoubtedly brilliant fakes. This point is an important one; for Plutarch's *Lakainôn Apophthegmata* has done even more than Aristotle's *Politics* to give the Spartan women a bad name. Profligacy, luxuriousness, and even cowardice are human enough weaknesses to be pardonable. But there is nothing to be said for the virago who implacably demands of her husband, sons, and brothers an unflinching response to a challenge from which the nagging woman herself is exempt thanks to the accident of her sex.

As for Phylarchus, whose work is reproduced in Plutarch's *Agis* and *Cleomenes*, his treatment of his subject is frankly dramatic.[1] His theme is 'how Lakedaimon, in her death agony, demonstrated that Virtue is proof against outrageous Fortune's assaults'. Lakedaimon demonstrated this 'by staging a drama with a female cast that competes worthily with the drama played by her men'.[2] Phylarchus recapitulates and endorses Aristotle's general indictment against the Spartan women[3] as a foil to set off the virtues of his Spartan heroines. These are Arkhidamia, Agis IV's grandmother; Agesistrata, his mother; Agiatis, his wife, who, after Agis had been put to death, was compelled to marry Kleomenes III and then inspired this second husband of hers to embrace her first husband's ideas and to carry out his unfulfilled mission;[4] Khilonis, who rallied first to her father Leonidas and then to her husband Kleombrotos when each of them, in turn, fell into serious political adversity;[5] Kleomenes' mother Kratesikleia; and Panteus' unnamed wife, who has run away from home to rejoin her husband in exile at Alexandria, and who comforts Kratesikleia when the two women, with Kleomenes' children, are on their way to be put to death.[6] The pictures of these Spartan women that Phylarchus has painted for us are perhaps idealized. Panteus' anonymous wife may even be a mythical figure.[7] But the other five women are unquestionably historical characters. 'Women are far more prominent in Phylarchus' work than they were in the world in which it was composed;[8] ... he ... drew the queens of Sparta a little larger than life[9] ... [Yet,] as a contemporary, Phylarchus would be handicapped in composing a

---

[1] However, Phylarchus' romanticism can be, and has been, exaggerated—as, for instance, by E. Bux, in 'Zwei sozialistische Novellen bei Plutarch' (*Klio*, 19. Band (1925), pp. 413–31), —according to Africa, op. cit., pp. 47–8. Phylarchus' 'account of third-century Sparta remains the focal point of any study of the subject' (Africa, ibid., p. 48).

[2] ἡ μὲν οὖν Λακεδαίμων ἐφαμίλλως ἀγωνισαμένη τῷ γυναικείῳ δράματι πρὸς τὸ ἀνδρεῖον, ἐν τοῖς ἐσχάτοις καιροῖς ἀπέδειξε τὴν ἀρετὴν ὑβρισθῆναι μὴ δυναμένην ὑπο τῆς τύχης (Plutarch, *Cleomenes*, chap. 39).

[3] Plutarch, *Agis*, chap. 7, cited on p. 356, n. 2.

[4] Plutarch, *Cleomenes*, chaps. 1 and 22.

[5] *Agis*, chap. 17.

[6] *Cleomenes*, chap. 38.

[7] See Toynbee, *A Study of History*, vol. vi (1939), pp. 460–4.

[8] Africa, op. cit., p. 43.

[9] Ibid., p. 46.

plot that diverged from the actual sequence of events, [though] this re-
straint would not apply to details or interpretation.'[1] Subject to these
reservations, Phylarchus' five royal heroines are the five Spartan women
about whom we are best informed, out of all the Spartan women of whom
some record has survived; and, when we have discounted Phylarchus'
heightening of the colours, these five characters shine bright enough, in
action, to refute Aristotle's charges.

These high-born Spartiate women were not aggressive ($\theta\rho\alpha\sigma\epsilon\hat{\iota}\alpha\iota$).
There is no record of their goading their menfolk to their deaths, or of
their bullying them into carrying out political programmes that are not
the men's own. Agiatis won Kleomenes for Agis' policy, not by mastering
his will, but by winning his love.[2] Agis' mother Agesistrata did not put
Agis' revolutionary ideas into his head; she was not his instigator; she
was his convert.[3] Archidamia,[4] Agesistrata,[5] and Agiatis[6] are explicitly
said to have been rich,[7] and we may assume that Kratesikleia was rich
too. We hear nothing, however, of their having been luxurious, and they
were certainly not avaricious. Agis' womenfolk voluntarily surrendered
their wealth out of loyalty to Agis and because they believed sincerely
in his idealistic mission to regenerate Sparta.[8] Above all, these women
were not cowards. It was not Agiatis' or Khilonis' fate to meet the executioner, but Arkhidamia, Agesistrata, and Kratesikleia all went to their
deaths with the traditional fortitude and dignity of a Leonidas at Thermopylae.[9] Kratesikleia had already shown her mettle in the alacrity with
which she had volunteered to leave Sparta for Alexandria in order to
put herself in King Ptolemy III Euergetes' hands as a hostage on her son
Kleomenes III's behalf.[10]

If these five Spartan women were peculiar, their peculiarity lay in their
rising above the average standard of conduct of the Hellenic women of
their day; and this moral superiority of theirs is indeed what we should
have expected *a priori*; for the 'Lycurgan' regime at Sparta was as
stimulating for the women as it was depressing for the men.

At first thoughts, this judgement may seem surprising; for life at
Sparta was not peculiar in one point that was decidedly unfavourable
to the position of women in the Hellenic World as a whole. An Hellenic
city-state was a men's club, to which the clubmen's womenfolk were not
admitted. The men spent the minimum amount of their time at home

[1] Ibid., p. 48. [2] *Cleomenes*, chap. 1.
[3] *Agis*, chaps. 6–7. [4] Ibid., chap. 4.
[5] Ibid. and chaps. 6–7. [6] *Cleomenes*, chap. 1,
[7] 'Probably Phylarchus exaggerated the feminine factor in Spartan economic life, but he
did not invent it or copy it from Aristotle. He was writing contemporary history' (Africa,
op. cit., p. 64).
[8] *Agis*, chap. 9. [9] Ibid., chap. 20; *Cleomenes*, chap. 38.
[10] *Cleomenes*, chap. 22.

and the maximum amount of it in each other's company in the agora, the palaestra, and the gymnasium. They were gregarious, not domesticated; and the measure of their elimination of the women from their gregarious masculine social life was the rifeness among them of paederasty.[1] In this point, Sparta, not Athens, was Hellados Hellas. Sparta was a male club to an extreme degree. The homoios' spiritual home was his syssition; and paederasty played a more prominent part in the life of the Spartiate homoioi than in that of any other Hellenic male community except, perhaps, the 'hieros lokhos' at Thebes—the military machine that eventually dealt the Spartan phalanx its knock-out blow. In this apparently hyper-Attic masculine atmosphere, how did the Spartan women manage to fare better than their sisters in other Hellenic city-states?

The answer is that, in this peculiar community, the women had some peculiar assets. One of these was a legacy from pre-'Lycurgan' Sparta; others were incidental effects of the 'Lycurgan' regime.

The legacy from pre-'Lycurgan' Sparta was 'Lycurgan' Sparta's abiding devotion to community singing and dancing.[2] In these social activities the girls' and women's role was as prominent as the boys' and men's. The female as well as the male performances were important public occasions, and this was a social setting in which men and women could meet in a natural way on equal terms.[3] Our earliest picture of Spartan girls is in Alkman's ode written for the girls' chorus in honour of Artemis Orthia. The poet's relation to the girls is 'modern' in the present-day Western sense; and Alkman was writing after—though perhaps not very long after—the establishment of the 'Lycurgan' regime; for, in other places, he speaks of dining in an andreion.[4]

An incidental positive effect of the 'Lycurgan' regime on the position of women at Sparta was a result of the 'Lycurgan' cult of physical fitness as a means to victory in phalanx-warfare. At 'Lycurgan' Sparta, there was compulsory physical training, not only for boys, youths, and men, but also for girls,[5] on the theory that physically healthy mothers would be likely to bear physically healthy children.[6] Like the community singing and dancing, this community physical training brought the two sexes

---

[1] 'Die Kehrseite des erschwerten Umganges zwischen Mann und Frau ist die Päderastie' (Nilsson, loc. cit., p. 233). 'The bond between [male] contemporaries and friends was stronger than the bond between husband and wife. The males had been living together since they had reached the age of seven. In such circumstances homosexual relations develop almost as a matter of course' (Busolt and Swoboda, op. cit., p. 700).

[2] See pp. 292–3.

[3] See Plutarch, *Lycurgus*, chap. 14; *Inst. Lac.*, § 34: κόραις καὶ κόροις κοινὰ τὰ ἱερα.

[4] Alkman, fragm. 17 (23) (Bergk–Hiller–Crusius), quoted on p. 312, n. 7, and fragm. 32 (37).

[5] Nilsson, loc. cit., pp. 324–5, conjectures that the girls were organized in gangs corresponding to the boys' gangs.   [6] Xenophon, *Lak. Pol.*, chap. 1, § 4.

together in a natural way on equal terms;[1] and the girls had all the advantage of this practice without the concomitant drawbacks that it entailed for the boys.[2] The girls' competitions took civilized forms— running races, wrestling, and throwing the discus and the javelin;[3] the girls were not hounded into brutal fights with each other; and, unlike their unfortunate brothers, the girls were not condemned for life to the parade-ground and the barrack-room.[4] This early training of a mildly masculine kind did, however, have a lasting effect on the girls' attitude to life. It made them unwilling to immerse themselves in the housework within which Xenophon seeks to confine the Attic housewife's horizon. The Spartan housewife resisted any pressure upon her to become 'thoroughly domesticated';[5] and there were several peculiar features of Spartan life which worked together to enable her to resist domestication victoriously.

The most important of these advantageous features was the custom, at 'Lycurgan' Sparta, of postponing marriage to a relatively late age. In another context[6] it has been suggested that this custom was established, not for the wife's benefit, but for the husband's. Marrying late was one of the expedients by which a Spartiate homoios sought to keep the number of his sons within limits that would allow of syssition-dues for all of them being provided from the produce of the family property. The wife, however, was a still greater gainer from late marriage than her husband or her sons. There is nothing so effective as child-marriage for reducing a wife and mother to being a slave; and a Spartiate homoios' wife was saved from this fate by the homoios' anxiety to make sure that he and his male descendants should not be reduced to the status of being hypomeiones. The Spartiate girl was not required to marry till she was of an age at which she would be mature enough to be able to hold her own;[7] and here, as Aristotle has pointed out,[8] 'Lycurgus' had unintentionally played into her hands. The regime, which had given the wife

---

[1] Plutarch, *Lycurgus*, chap. 14.
[2] See Toynbee, *A Study of History*, vol. iii, p. 75, with n. 4.
[3] Plutarch, loc. cit.
[4] Plato, *Laws*, Book VII, 806 A–B.
[5] Xenophon, *Lak. Pol.*, chap. i, §§ 3–4; Plato in loc. cit.; Cicero, *Quaestiones Tusculanae*, Book II, 15, § 38: 'Itaque illi, qui Graeciae formam rerumpublicarum dederunt, corpora iuvenum firmari labore voluerunt. Quod Spartiatae etiam in feminas transtulerunt, quae ceteris in urbibus mollissimo cultu parietum umbris occulantur. Ibi autem voluerunt

> nihil horum simile esse apud Lacaenas virgines,
> quibu' magi' palaestra, Eurotas, sol, pulvis, labos,
> militia studio est quam fertilitas barbara.'

[6] See p. 305.
[7] 'When someone asked a Spartan woman whether she had had relations with a man, she said: "It was not that way round; it was the man who had relations with me"' (Plutarch, *Lakainôn Apophthegmata*).
[8] In the third paragraph of the passage cited on pp. 356–7.

a stimulating musical and physical education, had sentenced her husband to penal servitude for life. From his twenty-first to his thirtieth year inclusive, he was the prisoner of his mess for about twenty-three hours out of the twenty-four. During those ten years of his life, he could pay no more than hurried furtive visits to the house and wife that were nominally his. So the house became his wife's house in fact;[1] and, when, after he had turned thirty, his syssition slightly relaxed its grip on him, it was too late for him, in the home, to reverse the *fait accompli*. By this time, the wife's paramountcy in the home will have become impregnable; if Ziehen is right, it was the wife, not the husband, who decided how many children she should bear;[2] Xenophon himself could not now have succeeded in domesticating her.

The earthquake of *circa* 466 or 464 B.C. may have given a further impetus to a tendency which the 'Lycurgan' reform had initiated. After the earthquake, women will have had a scarcity value at Sparta.[3] Last but not least, the power that wealth gives tended, in 'Lycurgan' Sparta, to accumulate in female hands. Aristotle's emphatic statement to this effect is amply corroborated by other testimony. It may be debated whether this was a good or a bad thing in itself, and whether, even if it was not intrinsically a bad thing, the rich Spartan women did or did not misuse their wealth. What is indisputable is that this mounting wealth progressively strengthened the Spartan women's hand.

How did the Spartan women become property-owners at all, not to speak of their acquiring property on the grand scale? Of course, after the enactment of Epitadeus' rhetra, a father would be at liberty to bequeath all his property to his daughter or daughters if he chose. But the most likely date of this enactment is after the Battle of Leuktra,[4] and, before that, King Agesilaos' sister Kyniska was already a rich enough woman to be able to compete at Olympia in the chariot-race.[5] Kyniska's position may have been exceptional. She was commemorated at Sparta in an herôon near the Platanistas.[6] As a member of one of the two royal houses, she may have been entitled to a share in the produce of the royal demesne in the territories of Sparta's perioecic states. It is also possible that, in Spartan law, an epikleros' fortune and a wife's dowry were the woman's property, not only in name, but in the practical sense of being under her control and at her disposal. We have no information about this, but we do know that women constituted a big minority of the small minority of Spartiatai in whose hands the wealth of Sparta came to be concentrated.

[1] See Busolt and Swoboda, op. cit., pp. 701-2.
[2] See p. 306, n. 6. [3] See p. 350, n. 3.
[4] See pp. 339-40 and 343.
[5] Plutarch, *Apophth. Lac.*, Agesilaos, 49, cited on p. 310, n. 5.
[6] Pausanias, Book III, chap. 8, § 1, and chap. 15, § 1.

5. Changes in the Strength and in the Organization of the Lacedaemonian Army after the Establishment of the 'Lycurgan' Regime at Sparta[1]

(i) The Permanent Basic Organization

(a) The Brigading of the Perioikoi with the Spartiatai

IT has been noted in previous chapters that the 'Lycurgan' reform was a greater success on the political side than it was on the economic and social sides. It did succeed in staving off a political revolution at Sparta for a span of perhaps more than four centuries ending in the year 227 B.C. By contrast, in the economic and social fields, the 'Lycurgan' regime, so far from preventing undesired and undesirable developments, actually set and kept these in motion. Under the 'Lycurgan' regime the numerical strength of the Spartiate homoioi declined; and, among those Spartiatai who still managed to attain and retain the status of being homoioi, property in land, which was the economic basis of the homoian status, tended to accumulate in a smaller and smaller number of hands. These untoward economic and social changes at Sparta were bound eventually to be reflected in changes in the numbers and organization of the Spartiate component of the Lacedaemonian army; and any change in this component was bound to bring with it changes in the army as a whole, including the other component of it, which was provided by the perioikoi.

The term 'Lakedaimonioi' was misleading—and, no doubt, intentionally misleading[2]—when it was used by the Spartans as the official name for their state and government. The government was in the hands of the Spartiate homoioi alone, and the rest of the population of Sparta's dominions had no say in it, though the hypomeiones Spartiatai, helots, and perioikoi together far outnumbered the homoioi. For the army, on the other hand, 'the Lacedaemonians' was an accurate name;[3] for, in the army, the perioecic Lacedaemonians were supplying 50 per cent of the phalangites in 479 B.C. and 60 per cent of them by 425 B.C., and were normally serving in the field, side by side with the Spartiate homoioi, down to 222 B.C., which is the latest year for which we have a record of the Lacedaemonian army's composition. On

---

[1] Forrest's views on this subject are discussed in the supplementary note at the end of the present Part of the present work (pp. 416–17).

[2] See pp. 159–61.

[3] Herodotus, Book IX, chap. 29, distinguishes the Σπαρτιατικὴ τάξις from the λοιποὶ Λακεδαιμόνιοι.

many occasions falling within the span of 258 years including 479 B.C. and 222 B.C., the presence of perioikoi in the Lacedaemonian army is expressly recorded or is implied; and, except in cases in which it is expressly noted that the homoioi were operating without being accompanied by a corresponding contingent of perioikoi, it may be assumed that, where the perioikoi are ignored in the surviving record of Lacedaemonian military history, this points, not to their absence, but to an oversight or an error on the historian's part.

The Spartans drew upon their Lacedaemonian perioikoi and their other Peloponnesian allies for military man-power, as the Romans drew upon the Latins and their other Italian allies; and there is a parallel between the problems and the policy of the two paramount powers. Like Rome, Sparta would have been unable to sustain the role of being a great power if she had not had a reservoir of ally man-power to draw upon in addition to her own citizen-body. Sparta's perioecic military man-power, like Rome's ally military man-power, was more abundant than her own citizen man-power was, and this fact raised a question of policy.

Throughout the successive changes in the organization and composition of the Lacedaemonian army from 479 B.C. down to 222 B.C., the demand upon the perioikoi for military man-power was lighter, in proportion to the numbers of the perioecic population of the hoplite class, than the demand on the Spartiate homoioi was in proportion to homoian numerical strength. Since the Spartan Government had the right and the power to call up perioecic troops in any numbers that it might choose, it was under a temptation to draw upon them up to the maximum. This would have enabled the Spartan Government either to abate the demand on its own citizens or alternatively to increase the Lacedaemonian army's total strength. On the other hand, political prudence counselled the Spartan Government, as it counselled the Roman Government, not to mobilize its non-citizen troops in very much greater numbers than its citizen troops, even if this self-denying ordinance involved, as it did involve, keeping the actual size of the army considerably below its potential size, and also involved denying to the citizen-body any relief from its disproportionately heavy load.

In 479 B.C. the Spartiate homoioi and the perioikoi were mobilized in equal numbers, but not in equal proportions to their respective total strengths. The Spartiate component was mobilized in full force up to, and inclusive of, the men who were in their forty-fifth year,[1] while the perioecic contingent is expressly stated to have been a *corps d'élite*.[2] In 425 B.C. we find the perioikoi being drawn upon in the proportion of six perioikoi to every four Spartiate homoioi, in place of the former parity

---

[1] See the present Part, chap. 5, section (ii), p. 372.
[2] λογάδες (Herodotus, Book IX, chap. 11).

of absolute, as distinct from relative, numbers. By this stage, the normal scale of mobilization for active service had probably been raised, in the Spartiate contingent, by ten year-classes, to include the men who were in their fifty-fifth year.[1] But we may guess that, even now that the perioikoi were being required to supply 60 per cent of the total Lacedaemonian field force, they were still able to raise the requisite number of men without having to go beyond the men who were in their forty-fifth year.

At first thoughts the constant relative abundance of perioecic military man-power may seem to present a surprising contrast to the relative scarcity of homoian Spartiate military man-power. The perioecic part of Sparta's Peloponnesian dominions probably amounted to less than half of the whole, and it was certainly less fertile, on the average,[2] than the part which belonged directly to the city-state of Sparta: the so-called πολιτικὴ χώρα.[3] The total population of Sparta's own city-state territory was, no doubt, considerably larger than the aggregate population of the territories of the perioecic city-states. But the great majority of the inhabitants of Sparta's city-state territory were helots, not Spartiatai; and, even among the Spartiate minority, only those Spartiatai who could afford to pay mess-dues were eligible for service in the Spartiate component of the Lacedaemonian army. The homoioi, who constituted this component, were inevitably few in numbers in proportion to the amount of agricultural land that was required for supporting them, because they were full-time professional soldiers living off the labour of agricultural slaves. On the other hand, the perioecic hoplites, like most other Hellenic hoplites, were men who were earning their own living. As soldiers, they were, no doubt, no match for their homoian Spartiate comrades in arms; in compensation, they were more numerous. An area that was both smaller and poorer could maintain ordinary hoplites in larger numbers than the maximum number of full-time professionals that could be maintained by Sparta's large and fertile πολιτικὴ χώρα.[4]

---

[1] See the present Part, chap. 5, section (iii), pp. 377 and 379.
[2] See pp. 210–11.　　　　　　　　　　　　　　　　　　　　　　[3] See p. 189.
[4] The relative sizes of the respective total populations of Sparta's πολιτικὴ χώρα and the territories of her perioecic states come to light in Herodotus' figures for the total numbers of the Lacedaemonian troops—including light-armed as well as hoplites—that were mobilized for the campaign of 479 B.C. According to Herodotus, Book IX, chaps. 28–9, the πολιτικὴ χώρα provided 40,000 men in all (35,000 light-armed helots besides the 5,000 homoian Spartiate hoplites), and the perioecic territories only 10,000 men in all (5,000 light-armed perioikoi in addition to 5,000 perioecic hoplites). Even when we have allowed for the fact that the 5,000 perioecic hoplites mobilized on this occasion did not represent the total perioecic hoplite strength, we shall conclude that in 479 B.C. the population of the perioecic territory must have been very considerably smaller than the population of the Spartan πολιτικὴ χώρα.

The light-armed troops were combatants (Herodotus, ibid.), and the helots suffered casualties (ibid., chap. 85). However, light-armed troops were of little importance in Hellenic warfare during the quarter of a millennium that began with the introduction of phalanx-fighting *circa* 650 B.C. and ended, soon after the opening of the fourth century B.C.,

Moreover, the perioikoi were not living under the 'Lycurgan' regime, and therefore they were not subject to the economic pressure, built into this regime, that drove the homoioi into limiting the size of their families and into competing with each other *à outrance* for possession of the Spartan city-state territory's agricultural land. Nor, so far as we know, was any perioecic city hit, as Sparta was, by the earthquake of *circa* 466 or 464 B.C. Though the range of this earthquake was not confined to Sparta City,[1] there was no other comparable concentration of population anywhere else in either Laconia or Messenia at that date. The perioikoi were widely dispersed among a large number of small communities, and consequently their earthquake casualties, if they suffered any at all, will have been much lighter than the Spartiates' casualties were. Hence, after the earthquake, the difference, as between perioikoi and Spartiatai, in the severity of the degree of the incidence of the demand for soldiers will have become even greater than it had been previously.

These facts had two consequences. In the first place, the reservoir of perioecic military man-power was never drawn upon up to its full capacity[2]—not even at times when Sparta was hard put to it to find the troops that she needed. Consequently the strength of the Lacedaemonian army was never determined by the size of the population of Sparta's dominions[3] until after the revolution of 227 B.C. Kleomenes III and Nabis were the first rulers of Sparta who raised the Lacedaemonian army to anything approaching the potential strength that had always been latent in the size of the total population of the country under Sparta's rule. From the date of the 'Lycurgan' reform down to 227 B.C. the limiting factor in determining the Lacedaemonian army's strength had been the strength of the Spartiate component of the army at each successive phase of Lacedaemonian history. Before 227 B.C. the Spartan Government did not ever dare to mobilize the perioikoi, or to emancipate and enlist the helots, in numbers that would have swamped the Spartiate component.

(b) *The Enomotia*

Another permanent basic feature of the 'Lycurgan' Lacedaemonian army, besides the brigading of the perioikoi with the Spartiatai, was the enomotia, which was the smallest tactical unit in the army's organization.

---

with the invention, by the Athenian professional soldier Iphikrates, of effective light-armed troops in the new shape of peltasts.

[1] See Plutarch, *Cimon*, chap. 16.

[2] See E. Cavaignac, 'La Population du Péloponnèse aux ve et ive siècles', in *Klio*, 12. Band (1912), pp. 261–80, on p. 266.

[3] See Aristotle, *Politics*, Book II, chap. 6, § 11 (1270a).

Each single enomotia was a permanent[1] association, as its name implies.[2] The name means an *Eidgenossenschaft*, a band of sworn brothers. The enomotia was also permanent in the further sense of being a permanent historical institution. In the course of the 'Lycurgan' Lacedaemonian army's history there were changes in the total number of enomotiai and in the structure of the hierarchy of the larger commands in which the enomotiai were grouped; but, as far as we know, the army was always composed of enomotiai throughout its successive metamorphoses, and the perioecic, as well as the homoian Spartiate, component of the army must have been organized in enomotiai. We can infer this from the fact that the two components operated as a single phalanx; for this would not have been possible if the basic tactical unit had not been uniform.[3] It will have been uniform in the technical senses of having a standard numerical strength, a standard composition in terms of its component year-classes, and a standard order of battle.[4] Subject to this technical uniformity, the social and political structure of an homoian Spartiate enomotia and a perioecic enomotia will not have been the same. An homoian enomotia was composed of a pair of syssitia.[5] The perioecic communities had no syssitia, since they had no helots, no kleroi, no 'Lycurgan' regime, and no permanent mobilization of their hoplites as full-time professional soldiers. Some of the perioecic city-states were so small and so poor that they may have had to club together to raise even a single enomotia of hoplites between them. Others will have been required by the Spartan military authorities to raise one complete enomotia each, and others, again, several enomotiai. The social constitution of a perioecic enomotia—though not its numerical strength or its composition in terms of year-classes—will have been each perioecic state's own affair.

Our surviving evidence tells us that every one of the forty year-classes that were subject to military service was represented in every enomotia,[6] and also that each year-class was represented in it by one man only[7]— or, perhaps it would be more accurate to say, each of the eight groups of

---

[1] Chrimes, *Ancient Sparta*, p. 389; Roussel, op. cit., p. 83.

[2] *Pace* Cavaignac, who holds, in *Sparte*, p. 26, that the enomotiai were improvised *ad hoc* at each mobilization.

[3] 'Tout se réglait sur la nécessité de l'homogénéité de la phalange' (Cavaignac in 'La Population du Péloponnèse . . .', p. 267).

[4] 'La constitution de la file est seule importante, et elle est restée la même d'un bout à l'autre de l'histoire de Sparte' (Cavaignac, ibid., p. 266).

[5] See pp. 228, 303, 319, 320, and 322, and also chap. 5, section (iii), p. 383.

[6] See Chrimes, *Ancient Sparta*, p. 388; Forrest, *A History*, p. 45; and G. Busolt, 'Spartas Heer und Leuktra', in *Hermes*, 40. Band (1905), pp. 387–449, on p. 415. Busolt points out, ibid., p. 416, that at Mantinea in 418 B.C. all the enomotiai were in the Lacedaemonian battle line, though the oldest and youngest year-classes, amounting to one-sixth of the whole army, had previously been sent home.

[7] Chrimes, *Ancient Sparta*, pp. 388–9.

five year-classes was represented by five men only.[1] On either way of reckoning, the total strength of an enomotia will have been forty men.

We know that all eight of the groups of five year-classes were represented in each enomotia because we know that the Lacedaemonian troops marched in column of enomotiai (the leading enomotia in the column was called the agema)[2] and that they deployed for battle (καθίσ-ταντaι) into line of enomotiai. The enomotia in line might form in single file or in three files or in six files,[3] i.e. with a front of one man only or of three men or of six. The formation could be varied easily and rapidly at the enomotarkhes' word of command.[4] At the battle of Mantinea in 418 B.C. the enomotiai were formed with a front of four men.[5] Now one of the manœuvres of the Lacedaemonian phalanx was for the commanding officer to order a sortie of a certain number of the youngest groups of year-classes. The number was usually τὰ δέκα ἀφ' ἥβης, but, in a critical situation, as at Lekhaion in 390 B.C., it might be as many as τὰ πεντεκαίδεκα.[6] This manœuvre would not have been possible to carry out if these youngest groups of year-classes had not been posted in the front ranks all along the line; and, since the line was a line of enomotiai, we can infer that each of the eight groups of year-classes was represented in each enomotia.

There is also evidence that, in each enomotia, there was not more than one representative of each of the forty year-classes, or, in more accurate words, there were not more than five representatives of each of the eight groups of five year-classes each. In the campaign of 371 B.C., for instance, 'the first thirty-five years [out of the forty] were mobilized',[7] and, at the battle of Leuktra in this campaign, the Lacedaemonian enomotiai formed with a front of three men each, which gave the Lacedaemonian phalanx an average depth of not more than twelve on this occasion.[8] Thus the average strength of an enomotia in this campaign was not more than thirty-six, i.e. it was virtually equal to the number of the year-classes that had been mobilized. In the campaign of 418 B.C. the Lacedaemonians, for the first time in their history, marched out πανδημεί[9]—that is to say, the mobilization extended, on this occasion, to all the forty year-classes; but, after the army had crossed the frontier, one sixth of it, consisting of

---

[1] See Chrimes, *Ancient Sparta*, p. 390, and the present work, p. 319, with n. 2, for the forty year-classes subject to military service—namely the twenty-first year of life to the sixtieth inclusive—and for the eight age-groups consisting of five year-classes each.

[2] Xenophon, *Lak. Pol.*, chap. 13, § 6.

[3] Ibid., chap. 11, § 4.   [4] Ibid., § 6.

[5] Thucydides, Book V, chap. 68, § 3.

[6] See p. 318, n. 5, for these and other examples.

[7] Xenophon, *Hellenica*, Book VI, chap. 4, § 17.

[8] Ibid., § 12.

[9] Thucydides, Book V, chap. 64. All forty year-classes were mobilized again in 371 B.C. after the disaster at Leuktra (Xenophon, *Hellenica*, Book VI, chap. 4, § 17).

the oldest and the youngest year-classes, was sent home[1] to do garrison duty there; and at the subsequent battle of Mantinea the oldest of the men who had not been sent home were kept out of the line and were posted in the rear.[2] We know that in this battle the average strength of an enomotia was thirty-two men (a front of four and a depth of eight).[3] We may infer that the number of year-classes that had been sent back home from the frontier was seven (the integral number that is nearest to being one-sixth of forty). These seven will have been the four oldest year-classes and the three youngest. This left the men in their fifty-sixth year still with the colours; but, since this was one of the five year-classes that were usually exempted from active service, as being no longer physically fit for phalanx-fighting, this year-class was not sent into action when it came to the point. On this reckoning, all the forty year-classes are accounted for on the assumption that there was one, but not more than one, representative of each of them in every enomotia.

(ii) *The Ten-Lokhoi Hoplite Army*

According to Aristotle,[4] Sparta's army, at some stage in its history, was organized in five lokhoi. One of these was named the Messoatas or Messoages lokhos; the names of the other four were Ἐδωλός (or Αἰδώλιος), Σίνις, Ἄριμας (or Σαρίνας), Πλοάς.[5] Since the Messoatas lokhos manifestly derived its name from the oba Messoa, and since the number of the lokhoi was the same as the number of the obai, namely five, it seems reasonable to infer that each of the other four lokhoi, too, was recruited from one of the obai,[6] in spite of their bearing 'fancy' names. The name 'Ploas', for instance, looks like a nickname for the lokhos of the oba Limnai. If each of the five lokhoi was in truth recruited from one of the five obai, but this without bearing the name of its oba, except in the single case of the Messoates lokhos, that would account for Herodotus'

---

[1] Thucydides, Book V, chap. 64.   [2] Ibid., chap. 72.
[3] Ibid., chap. 68, § 8.   [4] Fragm. 541, Rose.
[5] These five names, with the readings Μεσσοάγης and Ἄριμας, are given in a scholion on Aristophanes, *Lysistrata*, l. 453, where the scholiast is correcting Aristophanes' implicit assumption that there were only four Lacedaemonian lokhoi. The same correction of Aristophanes' implicit figure (four) is made by Hesychius, s.v. λόχοι· Λακεδαιμονίων φησὶν Ἀριστοφάνης τέτταρας· πέντε γάρ εἰσιν, ὡς φησὶν Ἀριστοτέλης. A scholion on Thucydides, Book IV, chap. 8, gives the same five names, with the readings Μεσσοάτης, Σαρίνας, and Αἰδώλιος. This last name is also given by Hesychius, s.v. Ἐδωλός· λόχος Λακεδαιμονίων οὕτως ἐκαλεῖτο. These passages are all printed in Rose, loc. cit.
[6] This is Neumann's opinion in loc. cit., p. 42; Andrewes's opinion in *The Greek Tyrants*, p. 71; and also Kiechle's opinion in *Lakonien und Sparta*, p. 147, n. 4. On the other hand, Ehrenberg, in P.-W., 34. Halbband (1937), cols. 1693–1704, s.v. obai, notes, in cols. 1701–2, that there is no evidence that the five lokhoi were based on the five obai. Ehrenberg holds that it is only a coincidence that the number of the lokhoi and the number of the obai were the same. Cp. eundem, 'Der Gesetzgeber von Sparta', pp. 25–6; Den Boer, op. cit., p. 172; Witkowski in loc. cit., pp. 77–8; Cavaignac in loc. cit., pp. 266–7.

references to a Pitanatas lokhos[1] and for Thucydides' comment[2] that 'there never was such a thing as a Pitanatas lokhos at Sparta', as some people mistakenly suppose. Herodotus would be giving a common-sense explanatory paraphrase of an esoteric technical term; Thucydides' criticism would be formally correct but would be captious and academic.

If, in truth, there were in the Lacedaemonian army, at some stage, five lokhoi corresponding to Sparta's five local obai (four in Sparta City itself, and the fifth at Amyklai),[3] these five lokhoi will, of course, have comprised only the homoian Spartiate enomotiai. There will have been another set of five lokhoi comprising an equal number of perioecic enomotiai. It looks as if this was the organization of the Lacedaemonian army in 479 B.C.[4] In that year, 5,000 homoian hoplites and 5,000 perioecic hoplites were mobilized.[5] Neither levy was up to full strength. The 5,000 perioecic hoplites were a *corps d'élite* (λογάδες);[6] the 5,000 homoioi were only about five-eighths of Sparta's total strength, at this date, in men of military age.[7] This indicates that only the twenty-five youngest of the forty year-classes of military age were called out on this occasion, i.e. the men in their twenty-first year to those in their forty-fifth year inclusive;[8] and, if no more than that number were called out in so serious a crisis, this would imply that, at this stage of Lacedaemonian history, the fifteen year-classes, running from the men in their forty-sixth year to those in their sixtieth year inclusive, were never called up for active service in the field.[9] This is, indeed, what we should expect, considering the nature of phalanx-fighting. Only men in their physical acme—men who had already turned twenty but had not yet turned forty-five—could be expected to be able to stand the strain.[10]

The Lacedaemonian army, as it was in 479 B.C., will have consisted of 400 enomotiai, 200 of them homoian Spartiate and 200 perioecic. There will have been forty enomotiai in each of the ten lokhoi, and it seems probable that, in the army of 479 B.C., as in the army of 418 B.C.

[1] Herodotus, Book IX, chap. 53. [2] Thucydides, Book I, chap. 20.
[3] See p. 262, n. 8. [4] See Neumann in loc. cit., p. 43.
[5] Herodotus, Book IX, chaps. 10–11. [6] Ibid.

[7] Herodotus, Book VII, chap. 234. Cavaignac, *Sparte*, p. 58, holds that the figure 5,000 represents total strength, not strength in the field. But he is ignoring Herodotus' statement, in loc. cit., that Sparta's total man-power was 8,000 at this date.

[8] See Wade-Gery, *Essays in Greek History*, p. 73. Cp. Chrimes, *Ancient Sparta*, p. 351.

[9] See Wade-Gery, *Essays in Greek History*, pp. 82–3.

[10] Wade-Gery, in loc. cit., points out that, in the Roman army too, active service ended at the end of the soldier's forty-fifth or forty-sixth year. On the other hand, within the period within which we have trustworthy information about the Roman army's organization, military service began at the beginning of the eighteenth year, or perhaps even the seventeenth. But this was at a stage in the Roman army's history at which its transformation from a phalanx army into a maniple army had been completed. The physical strain of manipular fighting was not so great, and the Roman soldier's equipment at this stage was less heavy than the hoplite's. A youth under twenty could hardly have stood the strain of phalanx-fighting in a hoplite's panoply.

and after, of which we have descriptions from Thucydides[1] and Xeno-phon,[2] there will have been, in between the enomotia and the lokhos, a middle term called the pentekostys. If this word, in its technical usage in the Lacedaemonian military terminology, means, not a body of fifty men, but a fiftieth part of some larger command, there will have been four enomotiai in each pentekostys in 479 B.C., as there were in the dif-ferently organized army of 418 B.C., supposing that in 479 B.C. the pentekostys was a fiftieth part of *each* of the two wings of the army; and there will then have been ten pentekostyes in each lokhos. Alternatively, the pentekostys may have been one-fiftieth part of the *whole* army; and, in that case, there will have been, in 479 B.C., eight enomotiai in each pentekostys, and five pentekostyes in each lokhos.[3]

There is no reason to suppose that the organization of the Lacedae-monian army, as it was in 479 B.C., was not the original 'Lycurgan' organization that had been introduced, about a century and a half earlier, at the time of the establishment of the regime itself.[4] Though we have found reason for guessing that the numerical strength of the homoioi had been declining gradually, ever since the regime had been inaugurated —and this is a consequence of certain tendencies that had been uninten-tionally built into the structure of the regime—the decline will not have gone far enough, before the earthquake of *circa* 466 or 464 B.C.,[5] to make it imperative, at any earlier time, to reorganize the army as it did have to be reorganized when the problem of military man-power had been brought to a head by the casualties that the earthquake inflicted.

(iii) *The Six-Morai Hoplite Army*

After 479 B.C. the next date for which we have any information about the organization of the Lacedaemonian army is 425 B.C. The information given us by Herodotus[6] about the organization and strength of the Lacedaemonian expeditionary force that served in the Plataea campaign of 479 B.C. indicates that the Lacedaemonian hoplite army of that date was the ten-lokhoi one. The information given us by Thucydides[7] about the Lacedaemonian military reaction to the Athenians' occupation of

---

[1] Thucydides, Book V, chap. 68.

[2] Xenophon, *Lak. Pol.*, chaps. 11–13, and *Hellenica, passim.*

[3] For the pentekostys see further, chap. 5, Annex I.

[4] The organization of the Spartiate wing of the Lacedaemonian army in five lokhoi based on Sparta's five local obai is unlikely to have been older than the 'Lycurgan' reform; for, though the obai were older than Sparta itself, the three Dorian phylai were, according to Tyrtaios, the basis of the pre-'Lycurgan' army's organization (see p. 264). In the 'Lycurgan' constitution the phylai, as well as the obai, were retained, but there is no indication that they ever played any part in the organization of the new army of homoioi.

[5] See p. 315 and chap. 4, Annex IV.

[6] In Book IX, chaps. 10–11 and 28–9.

[7] In Book IV, chap. 8.

Pylos in 425 B.C. indicates that, by this date, the Lacedaemonian hoplite army was already organized in six morai,[1] each consisting of two lokhoi, though the term mora (μόρα) itself is never used by Thucydides, and the earliest-dated surviving explicit use of it is in Xenophon's *Hellenica*, apropos of operations in 403 B.C.[2]

In this new organization there were six morai of cavalry, as well as six of hoplites,[3] but it is the six hoplite morai[4] that are our main concern. In the Lacedaemonian army under the 'Lycurgan' regime, in which the pre-'Lycurgan' corps of 300 hippeis had been converted into a *corps d'élite* of junior hoplites, there seems to have been no cavalry arm at all before 424 B.C., when the occupation of Kythera by the Athenians, following upon their occupation of Pylos, moved the Spartan Government to take the unprecedented step of improvising a corps of 400 cavalry to cope with Athenian raids on Lacedaemonian territory.[5] Xenophon estimates the Lacedaemonian army's cavalry strength as being one-tenth of its hoplite strength in 394 B.C.[6] In 390 B.C. the hipparmostes commanding the cavalry mora at Lekhaion was under the command of the polemarch commanding the hoplite mora at the same place.[7] In 371 B.C.

the Lacedaemonian cavalry was wretched. The richest [of the homoioi] bred horses; and then, when a mobilization-order was issued, the man detailed for this service would present himself and would take delivery of his horse and of whatever arms might be given to him, and would go on campaign without previous training (ἐκ τοῦ παραχρῆμα). These mounted men were the least fit physically and the lowest in *moral* of the [Lacedaemonian] troops.[8]

The Lacedaemonian hoplite army of six morai ran to twelve lokhoi, which means that each mora was a brigade consisting of a pair of lokhoi.[9]

---

[1] Cavaignac, in loc. cit., p. 269, holds that the organization of the Lacedaemonian army, as described by Thucydides apropos of the battle of Mantinea in 418 B.C., is identical with its organization as described by Xenophon.

[2] Xenophon, *Hellenica*, Book II, chap. 4, § 31.

[3] Xenophon, *Lak. Pol.*, chap. 11, § 4.

[4] Aristotle, *Lak. Pol.*, apud Harpocrationem, s.v. μορῶν· φησὶ δὲ ὡς εἰσὶ μόραι ἕξ (in some MSS. πέντε) ὠνομασμέναι. Cp. Xenophon, *Hellenica*, Book VI, chap. 4, § 17: ταῖν ὑπολοίποιν μοραῖν, after the four morai that had constituted Kleombrotos' expeditionary force in central Greece (Book VI, chap. 1, § 1) had been cut to pieces at Leuktra. Diodorus, Book XV, chap. 32, talks of τῶν Λακεδαιμονίων αἱ πέντε μόραι when he is speaking of an expeditionary force under Agesilaos' command, because he has it in mind that one mora was sent to Thespiai in the winter of 378/7 B.C. after the death of Phoibidas. The date of the campaign of Agesilaos which Diodorus is here recording was, in truth, not after the dispatch of this mora to Thespiai, but before it. Diodorus is mistaken here in his chronology, but he is not mistaken in reckoning the number of Lacedaemonian morai to have been six in all.

[5] Thucydides, Book IV, chap. 55, §§ 2–3. This passage must have been overlooked by Michell when he was writing n. 6 on p. 259 of his *Sparta*.

[6] *Hellenica*, Book IV, chap. 2, § 16.

[7] Ibid., chap. 5, §§ 11–12.

[8] *Hellenica*, Book VI, chap. 4, § 11.

[9] See Beloch, 'Griechische Aufgebote', II, p. 58; Busolt in loc. cit., p. 420.

In his *Hellenica*, Xenophon is constantly mentioning morai; he mentions lokhoi in three passages only;[1] but, in the last two of these passages, he states explicitly that, in the Lacedaemonian army, there were twelve lokhoi in all.[2]

The reason why, in these passages, Xenophon writes in terms of lokhoi and not in terms of morai is clear in each case. In the first case, Xenophon is recounting how King Arkhidamos III, before an engagement, walked along the front of the Lacedaemonian army, drawn up in line of battle, addressing the troops.[3] Presumably he paused to address each lokhos in turn, because his voice would not carry farther than the front and depth of one lokhos at a time. In each of the two other cases the Lacedaemonian forces that Xenophon is describing consisted, not of one or more integral morai, but of a mora and a half[4]—a force that it was simplest for Xenophon to describe as being 'three lokhoi out of the twelve'.[5] Thus the use of the term 'lokhoi' in these three passages is not an indication of a new reorganization of the Lacedaemonian army in which the morai had been abolished and the lokhoi had once again become the largest commands. Busolt holds[6] that, after the Spartiate homoioi's loss of their kleroi in Messenia in 370 B.C., as a result of the Lacedaemonian disaster at Leuktra in 371 B.C., the Lacedaemonian army was reorganized and the number of lokhoi in it was halved. In Busolt's view, the twelve lokhoi represent this post-mora organization, not the mora organization. The same view is taken by Kromayer.[7] On the other hand, Beloch[8] holds that the six-morai organization was not abolished after the battle of Leuktra.

One point in favour of Busolt's view is that Xenophon[9] makes the mora consist of four lokhoi, which would give a total of twenty-four lokhoi under the mora-system, not twelve. A second point is that the date of Xenophon's last mention of morai is immediately after the date of the battle of Leuktra; the date of his first mention of lokhoi is 365 B.C., and the dates of his mentions of 'the twelve lokhoi' are 364 B.C. and 362 B.C. Thus his uses of the terms 'morai' and 'lokhoi' do not overlap chronologically.

The first of these two points is discussed in another place.[10] In regard

[1] Book VII, chap. 1, § 30; chap. 4, § 20; chap. 5, § 10.

[2] τῶν δώδεκα λόχων (VII. 4, 20); τῶν λόχων δώδεκα ὄντων (VII. 5, 10).

[3] πρὸ τῶν λόχων παριόντα τοιάδε παρακελεύσασθαι (Xenophon, *Hellenica*, Book VII, chap. 1, § 30).

[4] This point is made by Beloch, 'Griechische Aufgebote', II, p. 58.

[5] καὶ ἐκ τούτου δὴ Ἀρχίδαμος στρατεύεται μετὰ τῶν πολιτῶν, καὶ καταλαμβάνει Κρῶμνον. καταλιπὼν δ' ἐν αὐτῷ τῶν δώδεκα λόχων τρεῖς (VII. 4, 20); τῶν λόχων, δώδεκα ὄντων, οἱ τρεῖς (VII. 5, 10). However, Xenophon does employ the expression 'half a mora' in *Hellenica*, Book IV, chap. 3, § 15.

[6] Busolt, 'Spartas Heer und Leuktra', p. 426.

[7] 'Studien über Wehrkraft und Wehrverfassung der griechischen Staaten', 2. Teil, p. 187.

[8] 'Griechische Aufgebote', II, p. 59.   [9] *Lak. Pol.*, chap. 11, § 4.

[10] In the present Part, chap. 5, Annex II.

to the second point, it has been noticed above that there were good reasons for writing in terms of 'lokhoi', not of 'morai', in each of the three cases in which Xenophon does use the term 'lokhoi'.

Moreover, a halving of the number of Lacedaemonian lokhoi in consequence of the loss of Messenia would have been tantamount to a public recognition that this loss was an accomplished fact; and it is most unlikely that this admission will have been made, even implicitly, by such a proud, tenacious, and conservative people as the Spartans were.[1] Indeed it is recorded by Xenophon[2] that, in 365 B.C., the Spartans told their allies that they were free to make peace if they liked, but 'that they themselves were going to go on fighting, come what might. They had inherited Messenia from their forefathers and they would never submit to being deprived of it.' For the same reason, Sparta stood out of the general peace that was concluded after the battle of Mantinea in 362 B.C.[3]

No doubt, after Sparta's loss of Messenia in 370 B.C., there would have been a catastrophic fall in the number of homoioi if the authorities had continued to insist on a strict observance of the rule that an homoios who defaulted on his mess-dues must forfeit his place in the mess and in the assembly and—in the phalanx. But after the catastrophe at Leuktra, Sparta could not any longer afford militarily to discharge phalangites for mere economic reasons. We may guess that the old rule was not abrogated but was ignored. In the circumstances, rich homoioi whose estates lay mostly to the east of the Taÿgetos range could hardly have refused to provide, out of their produce, the contributions due to their mess from their less fortunate messmates who had been mainly or entirely dependent on the produce of kleroi in Messenia.

As for the perioecic component of the Lacedaemonian army, its strength will not have been impaired seriously by the re-establishment of an independent Messenia in 370 B.C. Whereas Sparta herself will have lost, in 370 B.C., the whole of her own city-state territory in Messenia, the only perioecic communities that were incorporated in Messenia at this date were, so far as we can guess, Aulon, Aithaia, and Thouria.[4]

We have evidence that the twelve lokhoi (and therefore, presumably, the six morai too) were in existence already in 425 B.C., twenty-two years before the earliest date at which, for the first time, we hear of morai being the Lacedaemonian army's major units.

---

[1] This point is made by Beloch in 'Griechische Aufgebote', II, pp. 66 and 67.

[2] *Hellenica*, Book VII, chap. 4, § 9.

[3] συνθέμενοι δὲ [οἱ Ἕλληνες] κοινὴν εἰρήνην καὶ συμμαχίαν, κατέταττον ἐν τῇ συμμαχίᾳ καὶ τοὺς Μεσσηνίους. οἱ δὲ Λακεδαιμόνιοι διὰ τὴν πρὸς τούτους ἀκατάλλακτον ἀλλοτριότητα τῶν σπονδῶν οὐ προσείλοντο κοινωνεῖν, καὶ μόνοι τῶν Ἑλλήνων ὑπῆρχον ἔκσπονδοι (Diodorus, Book XV, chap. 89).

[4] On this, see the present Part, chap. 6, and Kromayer, 'Studien über Wehrkraft und Wehrverfassung der griechischen Staaten', 2. Teil, p. 188, with nn. 1 and 2.

After the occupation of Pylos by the Athenians in 425 B.C., and after the subsequent withdrawal of the Peloponnesian force that had invaded Attica in the spring of that year, the Spartiatai and the perioecic contingents from the nearest perioecic states[1] marched straight for Pylos, and the rest of the Lacedaemonian army followed more slowly.[2] After the whole Lacedaemonian land-army had been concentrated in the neighbourhood of Pylos,[3] the Lacedaemonian high command threw on to the island of Sphakteria a force of hoplites 'taken by lot from all the lokhoi'.[4] This garrison was relieved from time to time, and the last batch of troops on duty there, who were caught there by the Athenian fleet, was 420 men strong.[5]

It seems improbable that the lots for serving on this duty were drawn between individual soldiers. This would have taken a long time, and it would have produced an incoherent squad of men who had never fought side by side before. It seems much more likely that the lots were drawn between the smallest permanent units in each lokhos—that is to say, between the enomotiai.[6] During the period covered by Xenophon's *Hellenica*, namely 411–362 B.C., the number of homoian Spartiate year-classes usually called up for active service seems to have been thirty-five out of the forty,[7] as contrasted with the twenty-five that appear to have been mobilized in 479 B.C.;[8] and, though our explicit evidence for this is only of this later date, it seems reasonable to guess that the raising of the maximum age for active service for the homoioi from the forty-fifth year of life to the fifty-fifth had been one of the Spartan Government's expedients for offsetting, to some extent, the loss of man-power caused by the earthquake of *circa* 466 or 464 B.C.[9] We may guess, that is, that this was already the standard degree of mobilization for active service in 425 B.C. If so, the strength of an enomotia in the Lacedaemonian field army in that year will have been thirty-five, and, if a detachment consisting of one enomotia from each lokhos amounted to 420 men, the total number of lokhoi in the whole Lacedaemonian army in that year will have been twelve.

If the number of lokhoi in the Lacedaemonian six-morai hoplite army was twelve, what were the numbers of the pentekostyes and the enomotiai in a lokhos? If we can ascertain the number of the enomotiai, we can calculate the six-morai hoplite army's numerical strength, since we know

---

[1] This phrase is ambiguous. It might mean either 'nearest to Pylos' or 'nearest to Sparta'.
[2] Thucydides, Book IV, chap. 8, § 1.
[3] Ibid., chap. 8, § 2.
[4] ἀποκληρώσαντες ἀπὸ πάντων τῶν λόχων (ibid., § 9).   [5] Ibid.
[6] This is Busolt's view ('Spartas Heer und Leuktra', p. 413).
[7] See, for instance, *Hellenica*, Book VI, chap. 4, § 17.
[8] See p. 372.
[9] See Wade-Gery, *Essays in Greek History*, pp. 74 and 83, cited on p. 352, n. 1.

that the full complement of an enomotia was constant at forty (i.e. at five representatives of each of the eight age-groups into which the forty year-classes of military age were divided).

There are two extant accounts of the structure of the post-earthquake Lacedaemonian hoplite army. The first of these is given by Thucydides,[1] the second by Xenophon.[2] Both accounts put the total number of enomotiai in the whole of the Spartiate–perioecic citizen army[3] at ninety-six. This agreement on a point of fundamental importance might seem, prima facie, to indicate that the figure is correct. However, the two accounts arrive at this identical figure by quite different counts of the units higher than the enomotiai, and each of these counts is unsatisfactory.

The count of four lokhoi to the mora in the text of Xenophon's *Lakedaimonión Politeia*, as this has come down to us, is incompatible with the evidence, in Xenophon's *Hellenica*, that the number of lokhoi in a mora was, not four, but two. Thucydides' count of four enomotiai to the pentekostys and four pentekostyes to the lokhos is unexceptionable (though not confirmed by any independent testimony) as far as it goes. But Thucydides is ignorant of—or ignores—the existence of the mora, and he uses the term 'lokhoi' for the seven major units in the Lacedaemonian army at Mantinea in 418 B.C., though it is evident that these seven units were, in truth, morai, i.e. brigades of two lokhoi each.

Thucydides' and Xenophon's accounts both bristle with difficulties that are discussed in greater detail elsewhere in this chapter.[4] The insuperable difficulty is one that is common to both authors. If, as they both give us to understand, the total number of enomotiai in the post-earthquake Lacedaemonian army was only ninety-six, the total strength of the army—including all forty year-classes of both homoian Spartiatai and perioikoi—will have been only 3,840, and this figure is incredibly small for two reasons. In the first place, so great a drop as this from the corresponding figure of 16,000 men for the ten-lokhoi hoplite army of 479 B.C. is not credible, even if we estimate at the highest possible figure the destruction of homoian Spartiate man-power that had been caused by the earthquake of *circa* 466 or 464 B.C. Moreover, if Lacedaemonian citizen hoplite man-power had dwindled to this figure after the earthquake, Sparta must inevitably have ceased to be a great power. Her Peloponnesian allies would have fallen away from her, and Athens would have become the undisputed mistress of continental European Greece as well as of the Aegean. Sparta was able to prevent this from happen-

---

[1] In Book V, chaps. 64–8.

[2] In his *Lak. Pol.*, chap. 11, § 4.

[3] i.e. the Λακεδαιμόνιοι αὐτοί of Thucydides, Book V, chap. 67, § 1, and the πολιτικαί μόραι of Xenophon in loc. cit. For Xenophon's usage of the terms πολῖται and πολιτικός apropos of the Lacedaemonian army, see the present Part, chap. 5, Annex II, pp. 392–3.

[4] In chap. 5, Annexes II and III respectively.

ing; and, though, no doubt, she saved her historic position only at the cost of putting a great strain on the surviving homoioi, no amount of exertion could have achieved this if, by this time, Sparta had had at her command no more than 3,840 citizen Lacedaemonian hoplites (i.e. homoian Spartiate hoplites and perioecic hoplites added together).

It therefore seems best to accept Thucydides' count of sixteen enomotiai to the lokhos, and Xenophon's count—in his *Hellenica*, as opposed to his *Lakedaimoniôn Politeia*—of two lokhoi to the mora. This gives us a total of 192 enomotiai[1] and 7,680 citizen Lacedaemonian hoplites (1,280 in each of the six morai), supplemented, during and after the Atheno-Peloponnesian War of 431–404 B.C., by emancipated helot hoplites such as the Brasideioi and neodamodeis who, at Mantinea in 418 B.C., seem to have constituted a seventh mora between them.[2] Our figure for the number of citizen hoplites in the six-morai army is exactly double Thucydides' and Xenophon's figure;[3] yet even this is less than half the corresponding figure, 16,000, that is indicated for the year 479 B.C. by Herodotus' data. This comparison is in terms of the whole gamut of forty year-classes. The comparison in terms of the usual extent of mobilization for active service is less unfavourable if we hold that, before the earthquake, the normal limiting age for active service was forty-five, and that, after the earthquake, this was raised, for homoian Spartiatai, to fifty-five.[4] On this reckoning, the post-earthquake Lacedaemonian six-morai field army would have a standard strength of 6,720, as compared with a standard strength of 10,000 for the pre-earthquake ten-lokhoi field army; and the standard strength, in the field, of a single mora would be 1,120. In other words, the field army's strength will have declined to hardly more than two-thirds of what it had been previously.

The figure 6,720 for the six-morai army's strength in the field tallies with figures given by Xenophon in his *Hellenica*. At the Nemea River in 394 B.C. 'the concentration of Lacedaemonian hoplites approximated to a strength of 6,000 men'.[5] Only five morai were present, since one mora was in garrison at Orkhomenos at the time.[6] (Presumably it had been left there by King Pausanias in 395 B.C.) If the mobilization of the five morai had extended to men in their fifty-fifth year, the total field strength of these five morai would have been 5,600 men; and, if we add 300 for the hippeis, who formed a special bodyguard for the king, outside the morai,[7] the exact total number of Lacedaemonian hoplites present

---

[1] See Wade-Gery, *Essays in Greek History*, p. 83.
[2] See chap. 5, Annex III.
[3] Jones, *Sparta*, pp. 61–2, holds that Thucydides' and Xenophon's figure is only half the true figure.
[4] See p. 337, with n. 9.
[5] συνελέγησαν ὁπλῖται Λακεδαιμονίων ἐς ἑξακισχιλίους (Book IV, chap. 2, § 16).
[6] Ibid., chap. 3, § 15.   [7] See the present Part, chap. 5, Annex IV, p. 401.

will have been 5,900.[1] However, it is perhaps more likely that Xenophon was leaving the 300 hippeis out of account and was reckoning the strength of a mora, mobilized up to and including its thirty-fifth year-class, at the round number of 1,200; for he puts the strength of the mora that was cut to pieces by Iphikrates' peltasts in 390 B.C. at 'about 600',[2] and there is reason for thinking that this mora, which had been in garrison at Lekhaion for at least a year, was at half strength—that is to say, was represented only by the single lokhos that contained the mora's homoian Spartiate component.[3]

According to Plutarch,[4] different authorities gave different figures for the strength of a Lacedaemonian mora. Ephorus put its strength at 500,[5] Kallisthenes put it at 700, while others, including Polybius, put it at 900. We need not infer that the strength of the mora really varied at different dates. The discrepancies in the different estimates can be accounted for partly by variations in the number of year-classes mobilized for active service and partly by the fact that a mora, while normally at two-lokhoi strength, was occasionally only at one-lokhos strength.[6]

[1] It has been suggested that a large part of the 6,000 Lacedaemonian hoplites at the Nemea River were neodamodeis (for this category of emancipated helots, see pp. 200–1, with notes). We have no complete register of the numbers of the neodamodeis that were enlisted from time to time (the extant information is presented by Ehrenberg in P.–W., 16. Band (1935), cols. 2397–8). But our information, as far as it goes, suggests that in 394 B.C. there were few, if any, of them at the Spartan Government's disposal in continental European Greece.

The Spartan Government had posted a garrison of neodamodeis at Lepreon in Triphylia in 421 B.C. (Thucydides, Book V, chap. 34, § 4; cp. chap. 49, § 1), where they had been reinforced by the Brasideioi repatriated from the north coast of the Aegean (ibid., chap. 34, § 1). At Mantinea in 418 B.C. Brasideioi and neodamodeis had been present at an aggregate strength of one lokhos according to Thucydides (ibid., chap. 68, § 3), but probably at the strength of a mora (i.e. two lokhoi) in reality (see chap. 5, Annex III). In the spring of 413 B.C. a *corps d'élite* of about 600 neodamodeis and helots had been sent to Sicily (Thucydides, Book VII, chap. 19, § 3; chap. 58, § 3); and in 412 B.C. a force of about 300 neodamodeis had been sent to King Agis II at Decelea (Book VIII, chap. 5, § 1). In 409 B.C. there were a few neodamodeis in the garrison under Klearkhos' command at Byzantium (Xenophon, *Hellenica*, Book I, chap. 3, § 15). In the summer of 400 B.C. about 1,000 neodamodeis had been sent with Thibron to Asia (Xenophon, *Hellenica*, Book III, chap. 1, § 4; cp. Diodorus, Book XIV, chap. 36), and about 2,000 more were sent there with Agesilaos in the winter of 397/6 B.C. (Xenophon, ibid., chap. 4, § 2; Xenophon, *Agesilaus*, chap. 1; Plutarch, *Agesilaus*, chap. 6; also Xenophon, *Hellenica*, Book III, chap. 4, § 20). At the time of the battle of the Nemea River, these 3,000 were all either in garrison in Asia (Xenophon, *Hellenica*, Book IV, chap. 2, § 5) or were marching on Boeotia in Agesilaos' returning army (ibid., chap. 3, § 15). It seems improbable that in this year 394 B.C. the Spartan Government will have had any neodamodeis in reserve to send to the Nemea River.

[2] *Hellenica*, Book IV, chap. 5, § 12.
[3] See the present Part, chap. 5, Annex II, pp. 394–5.
[4] *Pelopidas*, chap. 17.
[5] This figure of Ephorus' is also given by Diodorus, Book XV, chap. 32.
[6] For example, 900 men might represent the strength of a two-lokhos mora mobilized up to its thirtieth year-class inclusive; 700 might represent its strength mobilized up to its twenty-fifth year-class inclusive; 500 might represent a mora at one-lokhos strength mobilized up to its thirty-fifth year-class inclusive.

In the five homoian Spartiate lokhoi of the previous ten-lokhoi Lace-daemonian army, the syssitia, which were the basic units of the army's Spartiate wing, will presumably have been grouped in five sets of forty syssitia each, corresponding to the five obai, and a Spartiate will have been eligible for admission only into one of the syssitia belonging to the oba that was the man's own legal domicile. In the Spartiate wing of the six-morai army, this topographical basis of organization had evidently been discarded.[1] In 390 B.C. the homoioi whose domicile was Amyklai were to be found in all the units of the army;[2] and the men who lost their lives in the mora that was cut to pieces by Iphikrates' peltasts on this occasion had sons, fathers, and brothers in other units.[3]

This abolition of the topographical basis of organization in the Spartiate wing of the army was a common-sense organizational reform, since the five obai represented, not different districts of Sparta's city-state territory, but only wards of the metropolitan area; and, since the homoioi were all permanently cantoned, at close quarters with each other,[4] in this area, it made no practical difference whether a soldier's legal domicile was this ward or that one. The breaking-down, for military purposes, of the divisions between the wards will have simplified the process of assigning candidates for admission to syssitia. Any candidate could now be co-opted into any syssition that happened to have a vacancy at the moment. This change had completed Sparta's synoecism. Sparta had now become a unitary state, and her citizen-body had been consolidated into one single homogeneous community.

The six-morai Lacedaemonian hoplite army, and the six morai of cavalry likewise, included the perioikoi as well as the homoian Spartiatai. 'The morai-organization includes all the Lacedaemonians.'[5] King Kleombrotos' four morai that fought at Leuktra in 371 B.C. included Lacedaemonians who were not Spartiatai.[6] Agesilaos' army in 370 B.C. included non-Spartiate Lacedaemonians who are expressly recorded to have been perioikoi,[7] and so did the three lokhoi of Lacedaemonian hoplites that were overrun by the Arcadians at Kromnos in 364 B.C.,[8]

---

[1] Wade-Gery, *Essays in Greek History*, p. 73. Cavaignac, *Sparte*, p. 31, dates this change in the early sixth century B.C., but the indications are that the five-lokhoi organization of the Spartiate wing of the Lacedaemonian army—an organization in which, presumably, each of the five lokhoi was raised from one of the five obai—was still in existence in 479 B.C. See the present work, pp. 371–3; Wade-Gery, *Essays in Greek History*, p. 77.

[2] τοὺς ἐκ πάσης τῆς στρατιᾶς Ἀμυκλαίους κατέλιπε μὲν Ἀγησίλαος ἐν Λεχαίῳ (Xenophon, *Hellenica*, Book IV, chap. 5, § 11).

[3] Ibid., § 10.

[4] Amyklai was only one hour's walk from the four obai that constituted Sparta City (see Ehrenberg in P.–W., 34. Halbband (1937), col. 1696).

[5] διῄρηνται εἰς τὰς μόρας Λακεδαιμόνιοι πάντες (Aristotle, *Lak. Pol.*, apud Harpocrationem, s.v. μορῶν).

[6] Xenophon, *Hellenica*, Book VI, chap. 4, § 16, read together with chap. 1, § 1.

[7] Ibid., Book VI, chap. 5, § 21.   [8] Ibid., Book VII, chap. 4, § 27.

as well as the Lacedaemonian cavalry unit that was mauled by the Theban cavalry in 375 B.C.[1]

Can we ascertain the ratio between perioikoi and Spartiatai in the six-morai Lacedaemonian army? In the previous ten-lokhoi army they had served in equal numbers; but there is evidence that, in the six-morai army, the ratio of Spartiatai to perioikoi was no longer 5:5 but was now 4:6.[2]

Out of the 420 Lacedaemonian hoplites who had been cut off on the island of Sphakteria in 425 B.C., 128 were killed and the 292 survivors capitulated and were conveyed to Athens. The surrender made a great impression on the Hellenic public because it was a sensational departure from traditional Lacedaemonian practice.[3] Non-Lacedaemonians could account for it only by supposing that the majority of the Spartiatai in the Lacedaemonian force on Sphakteria had been among the men who had fallen, and that the remnant had been unable to prevent the perioikoi from laying down their arms. If the captors had tried to discover, by individual interrogation of the prisoners, which of these were perioikoi and which of them were Spartiatai, they might have drawn blank, since Lacedaemonian soldiers were well trained in secretiveness. But one prisoner was asked the deliberately wounding question: 'Your comrades who fell—were they men of honour (καλοὶ κἀγαθοί)?' And this insinuation stung the prisoner into blurting out: 'It would be a fine arrow that could pick the best men.' From this it was inferred that the losses had fallen on Spartiatai and perioikoi with impartial severity; and this indication gave the Athenian Government a clue for calculating approximately the number of Spartiatai that it now had in its hands.

The proportion between Spartiatai and perioikoi among the prisoners would be about the same as the proportion between the two categories of Lacedaemonian troops in the Sphakteria force while the force had been still intact. The force had been composed of equal drafts from all the lokhoi of the Lacedaemonian hoplite army. Therefore the proportion between Spartiatai and perioikoi in the Sphakteria force must have been the same as the standard proportion in the regular tactical organization of the Lacedaemonian army as a whole. Evidently this standard proportion was a matter of common knowledge; for the prisoner's unguarded answer enabled the Athenian Government to estimate that the number of Spartiatai among their 292 prisoners was 'about 120'.[4] If the Athenian intelligence officers were reckoning with the round number of about 300 prisoners, it becomes evident that they were assuming that, in a fair

---

[1] Xenophon, *Hellenica*, Book V, chap. 4, § 39.

[2] See Busolt, in loc. cit., p. 421, for the diminution in the ratio of Spartiatai in the six-morai army as compared with the previous five-lokhoi army.

[3] Thucydides, Book IV, chap. 40.

[4] Ibid., chap. 38, § 5, read together with chap. 40.

sample of the Lacedaemonian army of the day, four men out of every ten would be Spartiatai, while the remaining six would be perioikoi.[1]

If this was in truth the proportion between the two categories in the Lacedaemonian six-morai army, this means that there will have been perioikoi in both of the two lokhoi of which each mora was composed.[2] One lokhos will have been wholly perioecic; in the sister lokhos, one-fifth of the personnel will also have been perioecic, and the whole of the homoian Spartiate component will have provided only four-fifths of the 'Spartiate' lokhos' strength. In each enomotia in the 'Spartiate' lokhoi, there will now have been only thirty-two Spartiatai, and the enomotia's full strength of forty men will have been made up by a complement of eight perioikoi.

This conclusion from data given by Thucydides is borne out by data given, independently, by Herodotus and by Plutarch's sources. Herodotus' list of the military institutions established by 'Lycurgus' is 'enomotiai and triakades and syssitia'.[3] This classification of the Spartiate syssitia as being military institutions is confirmed by Polyaenus,[4] and also by the information, given by Plutarch, that the syssitia were under the authority of the polemarchs,[5] and that the average number of the members of a syssition was about fifteen.[6] Putting these pieces of information together, we may infer that, in the six-morai organization, the triakas was the Spartiate component of each enomotia in the 'Spartiate' lokhos of each mora, and that a triakas was composed of two syssitia.[7] We may guess that the exact standard strength of a triakas will have been thirty-two men, i.e. four-fifths of the total standard strength, including all forty year-classes, of an enomotia in a 'Spartiate' lokhos.

Under this dispensation, each of the two component syssitia would have to recruit only two new members in every five years. The fifth member of each of the eight five-year age-groups in the 'Spartiate' enomotia to which these two syssitia belonged would be a perioikos. He would be a full permanent member of the enomotia, though presumably he would not be admitted to membership of either of the two Spartiate syssitia that, together, constituted this enomotia's Spartiate triakas. It looks as if these perioecic members of Spartiate enomotiai were the perioikoi

---

[1] This point is made by Busolt in 'Spartas Heer und Leuktra', pp. 407–9. Cp. Roussel, op. cit., p. 83; Michell, op. cit., p. 238.

[2] See Berve, op. cit., p. 95; Wade-Gery, *Essays in Greek History*, p. 83.

[3] μετὰ δὲ, τὰ ἐς πόλεμον ἔχοντα, ἐνωμοτίας καὶ τριηκάδας καὶ συσσίτια, ... ἔστησε Λυκοῦργος (Herodotus, Book I, chap. 65). See p. 283, with n. 3.

[4] See p. 320, n. 6.

[5] Plutarch, *Lycurgus*, chap. 12, and *Apophth. Lac.*, Lykourgos, 6, cited on pp. 321 and 322. See also pp. 228, 303, 319, and 369.

[6] συνήρχοντο δὲ ἀνὰ πεντεκαίδεκα καὶ βραχεῖ τούτων ἐλάττους ἢ πλείους (Plutarch, *Lycurgus*, chap. 12; cp. *Apophth. Lac.*, Lykourgos, 4).

[7] Michell, too, infers this (op. cit., p. 237).

whom Isocrates had in mind particularly when he wrote[1] that, 'in campaigns under the [Spartan] King's command, [the Spartans] incorporate individual perioikoi in their own formations, and they post some of these in the front line'.[2]

The presence of eight perioikoi in every enomotia of the 'Spartiate' lokhos of a Lacedaemonian mora thus seems to be indicated by the evidence. But this interpretation of the evidence leaves one difficult question unanswered. How did the perioecic members of a 'Spartiate' enomotia obtain the long and strenuous training which a Spartiate boy and youth had to pass through with credit in order to become eligible for admission to a syssition? And who financed the permanent cantonment of these Spartanly-trained perioikoi at Sparta as full-time professional soldiers? Perioecic members of 'Spartiate' enomotiai must have been as severely trained as their Spartiate comrades in arms before reaching military age, and, during their subsequent forty years of military service, they must have been permanently stationed at either Sparta or Amyklai in order to take part in their enomotia's daily drill and to be ready to march with the rest of the enomotia the moment that a mobilization-order was issued. Both Thucydides[3] and Xenophon[4] lay stress on the intricacy and the effectiveness of the Spartan chain of command and of the tactical evolutions that this chain of command made not only possible but easy. The homoian Spartiate wing of the Lacedaemonian army was as well drilled as the sixteenth-century Ottoman Janissary Corps and as the standing armies of the eighteenth-century Western World; and this professional efficiency was recognized as being one of the secrets of the Lacedaemonian army's success. Drill, however, requires constant practice, and the 'Spartiate' formations of the Lacedaemonian army would have forfeited their special excellence if one man in every five had been an amateur, and if this amateur had been domiciled normally, not in Sparta, but in his native perioecic city, which might be as much as fifty miles away.

How, then, were these perioecic members of 'Spartiate' enomotiai financed? We are without information on this pertinent point. We know that the Spartan Government itself had no public funds. It was incapable of financing even its own homoioi out of public revenues. It would have been within the Spartan Government's power to impose on the perioecic states a charge that it was unable to meet out of its own resources. But the perioecic states were poor, not only in public revenue, but in national

---

[1] In *Panathenaïcus*, 180.

[2] ἔν τε γὰρ ταῖς στρατείαις αἷς ἡγεῖται βασιλεύς, κατ' ἄνδρα συμπαρατάττεσθαι σφίσιν αὐτοῖς, ἐνίους δὲ καὶ τῆς πρώτης τάττειν. The perioecic members of a 'Spartiate' enomotia who were posted in the front line will have been those in the youngest two five-year age-groups, τὰ δέκα ἀφ' ἥβης.

[3] Book V, chap. 66, § 3.

[4] *Lak. Pol.*, chap. 11, §§ 4–10.

wealth. Their territories were mostly mountainous and barren, compared with Sparta's. To maintain 768 of their citizens as full-time professional soldiers at Sparta would have been so crushing a burden for them that it is not credible that the paramount power should have saddled them with it. Therefore the most likely answer to our question—though this answer is no more than a guess—is that the training and subsequent maintenance of perioecic members of the 'Spartiate' enomotiai in the six-morai Lacedaemonian army were financed, on the adoptive system,[1] by that minority of the Spartiate homoioi in whose hands a larger and larger quota of Sparta's own national wealth was coming to be concentrated. These were the only parties, private or public, in any part of Sparta's dominions who could have afforded to undertake this financial commitment.

No doubt there will have been no legal compulsion on the rich homoioi to shoulder this burden. Like their Athenian 'opposite numbers' who undertook 'leitourgiai', they will have been deemed to have been acting voluntarily, out of pure public spirit. The sanction that made their 'voluntary' action virtually compulsory in practice will have been the pressure of public opinion. At Sparta this pressure could be formidable, as we know it to have been when it was applied to homoioi who had been stigmatized as cowards,[2] or even when it was applied to bachelors.[3] If similar pressure was applied to rich homoioi in order to induce them to perform a necessary public service, it will have been justified. The Spartiate community will simply have been constraining an inordinately rich minority of its members to give back to the community as a whole part of the wealth that this minority had managed to acquire at its fellow citizens' expense.

(iv) *The Occasion of the Transition to the Six-Morai System from the Ten-Lokhoi System*

We can only guess at the method by which Sparta financed the dilution of the 'Spartiate' wing of the Lacedaemonian army with perioikoi in the ratio of one perioikos to every four homoioi. On the other hand, the purpose of this innovation is revealed by the figures. These indicate that Sparta was increasing her post-earthquake effectives by 20 per cent—from an establishment of ten lokhoi to one of twelve[4]—at a financial cost, perhaps, to the rich minority of the homoioi, but without any increase—indeed, so far from that, with a slight reduction—in the demand that was being made on homoian military man-power.

It seems reasonable to assume that the structure and the numerical

---

[1] See the present Part, chap. 4, Annex III.   [2] See pp. 328–9.
[3] See pp. 306–7.   [4] See Kromayer in loc. cit., p. 189, n. 4.

strength of the lokhos in the six-morai army had been taken over, unchanged, from the ten-lokhoi army in the latest phase (i.e. the post-earthquake phase) of this army before the six-morai army was substituted for it. If we accept Thucydides' testimony,[1] this lokhos consisted of sixteen enomotiai, and its full strength, at forty men in each enomotia, was therefore 640 men. It also seems reasonable to assume that the reduction of the number of homoian Spartiatai in a Spartiate enomotia from forty to thirty-two was made simultaneously, as part of the new organization. At only thirty-two Spartiatai to a 'Spartiate' enomotia in the six-morai organization, the total number of Spartiatai required for manning the six 'Spartiate' lokhoi in this new organization would be 3,072. On the other hand, at the previous figure of forty Spartiatai to a Spartiate enomotia in the immediately preceding (i.e. post-earthquake) ten-lokhoi organization, the total number of Spartiatai required for manning the five Spartiate lokhoi in this organization would have been 3,200.

It looks as if, after the earthquake, the demand on surviving homoian Spartiate man-power[2] had been extended, to the furthest possible limit, by raising the age of exemption from active service in the field from forty-five to fifty-five, while simultaneously the total strength of the Lacedaemonian army, including the age-classes that were exempted from service in the field, had dropped from the figure of 16,000, at which it had stood in 479 B.C., to no more than 6,400—a drop which represents a suppression of 240 enomotiai out of the 400 comprised in the army as a whole in 479 B.C.[3] This figure will have been manifestly too small to enable Sparta to sustain her historic role in the Hellenic World; and accordingly the Spartan Government will have decided to increase the total number of its effectives, which will have been reduced so drastically through loss of Spartiate lives in the earthquake, by relaxing its previous rule that the perioikoi must not be drawn upon for military service in greater numbers than the homoioi and by diluting the 'Spartiate' enomotiai with a quota of perioecic members. To change the ratio from the previous 5:5 to 4:6 and to dilute the Spartiate enomotiai will have been accepted as being the lesser evil, when the alternative was seen to be a risk that Sparta might be unable to continue to play the part of a great power.[4]

[1] In Book V, chap. 68, § 3 (see p. 398).

[2] The effect of the earthquake in reducing Spartiate military man-power is stressed by Cavaignac, 'La Population du Péloponnèse', p. 272.　　　　　　　　　　　[3] See p. 372.

[4] Jones, *Sparta*, pp. 61 and 137, holds that the Lacedaemonian army was reorganized after the earthquake. Busolt and Swoboda, op. cit., p. 712, hold that there was a reorganization between 479 B.C. and 431 B.C. and that, in this reorganization, perioikoi were incorporated with Spartiatai in the same units, but they do not identify this new organization with the morai-organization. They date the introduction of the morai-organization after 418 B.C. (p. 710).

If, after the reduction of homoian Spartiate man-power in the earth-quake, the Spartan Government did, in the first instance, abide by the traditional rule of parity between homoian Spartiatai and perioikoi in the Lacedaemonian phalanx, it will have soon become obvious that the consequences of this rigidity were unacceptable. The crux lay in the fact that the number of the homoian Spartiate hoplites determined the numerical strength of the Lacedaemonian hoplite army as a whole. If the number of the homoioi had, in truth, now fallen from 8,000 to 3,200, and if this remnant was now being burdened with ten additional years of active service, the previous inequality between the relative demands on homoian Spartiate and on perioecic military man-power was being accentuated to an unbearable degree. The surviving 3,200 homoioi were now having a heavier demand made on them than had been made on their forebears. At the same time, as a consequence of the reduction in the homoian Spartiatai's numbers, the parity rule was having the effect of lightening the already lighter demand on the perioikoi. These had suffered only slight losses, if any, in the earthquake; yet, under the parity rule, they were now being required to provide, for field service, a *corps d'élite* of only 2,800 hoplites, instead of the previous figure of 5,000.

Thus the purpose of the change-over from the ten-lokhoi organization to the six-morai organization will have been twofold. While one motive will have been to increase the total strength of the Lacedaemonian hoplite phalanx from the low figure to which it had dropped as a result of the earthquake, a second motive will have been to make the balance of sacrifice rather less unfavourable to the Spartiate component of the army by drawing more freely on the reservoir of perioecic military man-power, even though this involved changing the traditional ratio of 5:5 to a new ratio of six perioikoi to every four Spartiatai.

The additional burden thus imposed on the perioikoi will not have been excessive. In the six-morai hoplite phalanx, the perioikoi will have provided 4,608 men out of the total of 7,680—that is to say, the 3,840 men for their own six lokhoi, together with a supplement of 768 men for the six 'Spartiate' lokhoi. Thus the reorganization will have increased the post-earthquake demand on the perioikoi by 1,408 men, while reducing the post-earthquake demand on the Spartiatai by 128 men. At the same time, even this increased figure was little more than half the amount of the pre-earthquake demand on the perioikoi, which had been 8,000 men; and in 382 B.C. the mora-system still bore so lightly on the perioikoi that 'numerous perioecic volunteers of good social standing' accompanied King Agesipolis on his campaign against the colonial Chalcidians.[1] Even at the earlier figure of 8,000, the perioikoi will have been able to provide their 5,000 for active service without having to

---

[1] Xenophon, *Hellenica*, Book V, chap. 3, § 9.

call up men over the age of forty-five. Under the six-morai system, they will have been able to do this still more easily in raising their own lokhoi, though the 768 perioikoi who were now supplementing the 'Spartiate' lokhoi as full-time professional soldiers will, presumably, have had to go on active service up to the age of fifty-five, like their homoian Spartiate comrades in arms.

(v) *King Kleomenes III's Army*[1]

The primary purpose of the revolution at Sparta which King Agis IV planned and which King Kleomenes III carried out was not philanthropic; it was military.[2] For these two Herakleidai at Sparta, as for the two Gracchi at Rome a century later, the purpose of redistributing the ownership of land was to endow soldiers. Agis and Kleomenes aimed at raising the number of the homoian Spartiatai, which had stood at only about 700 when Agis came to the throne,[3] to as high a figure as could be attained now that Sparta possessed only her Laconian city-state territory, after having lost, in 370 B.C., the Messenian territory that had also been at the disposal of the seventh-century-B.C. 'Lycurgan' reformers for providing their homoioi with kleroi.

The revolutionary Spartan kings' purpose was not just to endow ordinary amateur hoplites who would have to earn their own living; it was to re-create a force of full-time professional soldiers on the original 'Lycurgan' model.[4] This objective limited the size of the standing army that they could endow out of the resources at their disposal. Agis had hoped to be able to provide 4,500 kleroi on the 'Lycurgan' scale for Spartiatai.[5] Kleomenes found himself able to provide kleroi for 4,000 Spartiate hoplites.[6] Since there were only about 100 wealthy homoian Spartiatai before Kleomenes' reform,[7] and only about 600 impoverished homoioi,[8] Kleomenes filled the remaining 3,300 (or 3,800) vacancies by enfranchising and endowing hypomeiones Spartiatai and by naturalizing and endowing perioikoi.[9]

[1] See J. Kromayer, *Antike Schlachtfelde in Griechenland*, 1. Band (Berlin, 1903, Weidmann), pp. 226–7.

[2] See Jones, *Sparta*, p. 158. Jones points out on p. 161 that Nabis, too, 'was no socialist, but a Spartan patriot'.

[3] Plutarch, *Agis*, chap. 5, as interpreted on p. 310, n. 10.

[4] 'The Spartan revolution came from above' (Africa, op. cit., p. 25). 'The aims of Agis and Cleomenes were military, not humanitarian. Like the Gracchi, the kings sought to resurrect an army of land-holding soldiers from the dry bones of pauperized citizens' (ibid.). Cleomenes 'saw the cause of reform chiefly as a useful instrument of policy' (ibid., p. 58). 'Cleomenes effected economic reforms chiefly to further his imperial ambitions' (ibid., p. 14; cp. pp. 27 and 55).

[5] Plutarch, *Agis*, chap. 8.

[6] Plutarch, *Cleomenes*, chap. 11. It is possible that Kleomenes provided 4,500 kleroi for adult Spartiatai, including those above the age for active military service (see p. 315, n. 8).

[7] Plutarch, *Agis*, chap. 5.   [8] Ibid.   [9] Plutarch, *Cleomenes*, chap. 11, chap. 23.

It will be seen that Agis and Kleomenes did nothing to ameliorate the position of the helots,[1] and were, indeed, precluded from doing anything for the helots by the nature of their own objective. Helot-cultivated kleroi were the indispensable economic basis for the maintenance of full-time professional hoplites, such as the Spartiate homoioi were.[2] It was not till he found himself at war with Macedon as well as the Achaean Confederation, and, even then, not till Orkhomenos, Mantinea, and Tegea had fallen, that Kleomenes allowed 6,000 helots to purchase their freedom and enrolled 2,000 of these emancipated helots in his phalanx.[3]

In 222 B.C. at Sellasia, Kleomenes was able to muster about 20,000 men in all.[4] His army was composed of four categories of troops: Spartiatai,[5] perioikoi, mercenaries, and allies.[6] The Spartiatai were 6,000 strong,[7] including the 2,000 neodamodeis as well as the 4,000 kleros-holders. If Kleomenes had re-established the ratio of perioikoi to homoian Spartiatai that had prevailed in the six-morai Lacedaemonian army, his 4,000 kleros-holders will have been matched by 6,000 perioikoi. His mercenaries and his light-armed troops amounted, together, to about 5,000 men.[8] The light-armed, as well as the 2,000 additional members of the phalanx, were presumably emancipated Laconian helots; and the number of the mercenaries will probably have been considerably less than 3,000; for 3,000 was the number of Antigonos Doson's mercenary infantry;[9] and Macedon's financial resources for hiring mercenaries were much greater than Sparta's at this date—poor though Macedon was by comparison with the Seleucid and Ptolemaic monarchies. It is recorded[10] that Kleomenes was hard put to it to find the pay for his mercenaries, as well as the rations for his national troops. The mercenaries may well have been no more than one thousand strong, and the national light-armed troops may have been as much as 4,000 strong—i.e. they may have comprised all those 4,000 of the newly emancipated helots who had not been enrolled in the phalanx. These figures leave over a figure of 3,000 for the troops provided by Sparta's allies. This would be a surprisingly large number in this desperate last phase of the war; and that suggests that our estimate of 6,000 for the strength of the perioecic hoplites may have been too low.

---

[1] See p. 203. [2] See Africa, op. cit., p. 65.

[3] These neodamodeis, like Kleomenes' 4,000 homoioi, were equipped in the Macedonian fashion (Plutarch, *Cleomenes*, chaps. 11 and 23).

[4] Polybius, Book II, chap. 65, § 7, followed by Plutarch, *Cleomenes*, chap. 27.

[5] Both Polybius, ibid., § 9, and Plutarch, op. cit., chap. 28, call these 'Lakedaimonioi', but they mean 'Spartiatai', since Polybius distinguishes them from the perioikoi.

[6] Polybius, ibid.

[7] Plutarch, *Cleomenes*, chap. 28.

[8] Polybius, Book II, chap. 69, § 3.

[9] Ibid., chap. 65, § 2.

[10] By Plutarch, *Cleomenes*, chap. 27.

In any case, at a minimum, Kleomenes probably put into the field, in 222 B.C., 16,000 native Laconian troops,[1] 12,000 of whom were hoplites. This was the largest army that Sparta had raised for active service since 479 B.C. It is true that, in that year, the total Lacedaemonian field-army of native troops had amounted to 50,000, if we can believe Herodotus' statement that, in that campaign, each homoian Spartiate hoplite was accompanied by seven light-armed helots, and each perioecic hoplite by one light-armed perioikos. In 222 B.C. Kleomenes had a maximum of 4,000 native light-armed troops; on the other hand, he may have had 12,000 or even 14,000 native hoplites, as against Pausanias' 10,000.

It was left to Nabis to liberate for military use almost the whole of Sparta's potential military man-power. Nabis appears to have enfranchised the helots *en masse*,[2] and Sparta's military strength, in absolute numbers, had never been greater than it was in Nabis' day—not even during the three and a half centuries, or thereabouts, during which Sparta had possessed Messenia as well as Laconia. At the beginning of the campaign of 195 B.C., Nabis had a field-army of 15,000 men, which consisted of 10,000 native Laconians, including emancipated helots (castellanis agrestibus), 2,000 ally Cretans, and 3,000 mercenaries.[3] This army was afterwards reinforced by the whole of his garrison at Gythion and by 3,000 men (1,000 mercenaries and 2,000 Argives) from his garrison at Argos.[4] After these 3,000 had returned from Argos to Laconia, there were still Lacedaemonian garrisons left in Argos and in other places in the Argeia.[5] It will be seen that Nabis' total forces in 195 B.C. were of approximately the same strength as Kleomenes III's in 222 B.C., namely about 20,000 men, including mercenaries and allies as well as native Laconians. In order to bring Nabis to terms in 195 B.C., T. Quinctius Flamininus brought to bear against him all Rome's allies in Greece except the Aetolians, as well as the Roman consular army with which Flamininus had broken the power of Macedon in 197 B.C. Even then, Flamininus found it prudent to be content with peace-terms that fell short of unconditional surrender on Nabis' part. Flamininus did, however, detach from Sparta all her remaining perioecic states, together with Sparta's own port and naval arsenal at Gythion; and these territorial losses dealt a blow to Sparta's military power from which it never recovered.

[1] Fourteen thousand is Kromayer's estimate in 'Studien über Wehrkraft und Wehrverfassung der griechischen Staaten', 2. Teil, p. 199, and Beloch's estimate in 'Griechische Aufgebote', II, p. 74.

[2] See p. 203.

[3] Livy, Book XXXIV, chap. 27, § 2.

[4] Ibid., chap. 29, §§ 13–14.

[5] Ibid., chap. 33, § 3, and chap. 35, § 3.

The Pentekostys

THE meaning of the word 'pentekostys' is obscure in its technical usage in the Lacedaemonian military terminology. It is equally admissible, linguistically, to make it mean 'a body of fifty men' and to make it mean 'a fiftieth part' of some larger command. The similarly formed word 'trittys' is normally used to mean 'a third part' (as in the administrative terminology of Kleisthenes' constitution for Athens), but it is also sometimes used to mean 'a set of three'. In the constitutional terminology of the Ionian city-states, 'hekatostys' is made to mean a (notional) 'hundred' or 'centuria', and 'khiliastys' to mean a (notional) 'thousand'.[1] The title of the officer commanding a pentekostys is usually spelled 'pentekonter' in the manuscripts, but sometimes it is spelled 'pentekoster'. In this less usual form, it plainly means 'commander of a pentekostys', but it does not tell us what 'pentekostys' means. In the form 'pentekonter', it could mean either 'commander of fifty men' or 'one of a set of fifty commanders'. The pentekostys of 418 B.C. was not a body of fifty men, since it was a group of four enomotiai,[2] and the strength of an enomotia varied, according to the number of age-classes called up, from forty to twenty-five (in the Lacedaemonian line of battle at Mantinea in 418 B.C. the average strength was thirty-two).[3] Thus in the Lacedaemonian army of this date the pentekostys was 100 men strong even on a minimum mobilization of the youngest twenty-five year-classes only, and it was 160 men strong at its full strength. However, this is not evidence that the pentekostys was not originally a body of fifty men. The Roman centuria was certainly a body of 100 men originally; yet, at the earliest date at which we have explicit information about it, it was only sixty strong.

However, it seems, on the whole, more probable that, in Lacedaemonian military parlance, 'pentekostys' means a fiftieth part,[4] and the structure of the six-morai army suggests that the command of which the pentekostys was one-fiftieth was the Lacedaemonian army as a whole, rather than one of the army's two wings. In the six-morai army of which we catch our first sight in 425 B.C., there were forty-eight pentekostyes—four in each of the twelve lokhoi. As Wade-Gery points out,[5] 'this is as near to 50 as a multiple of 6 can be'. We may guess that, in the antecedent ten-lokhoi army, there were exactly fifty pentekostyes; and, since this army was originally 16,000 strong, the pre-earthquake strength of

[1] See Wade-Gery, *Essays in Greek History*, pp. 82 and 84.
[2] Thucydides, Book V, chap. 68, § 3.   [3] Ibid.
[4] See Michell, op. cit., p. 240.   [5] In *Essays in Greek History*, p. 82.

each of its pentekostyes will have been 320 men, and there will have been five pentekostyes in each lokhos, and eight enomotiai in each pentekostys. Alternatively, as has been noted already,[1] the ten-lokhoi army's pentekostys may have been one-fiftieth, not of the whole army, but of each of its two wings; and this alternative, too, has some support in the structure of the six-morai army; for in that case the ten-lokhoi army's pentekostys, like its successor the six-morai army's pentekostys, will have been, at full strength, a body of 160 men divided into four enomotiai. In that case, however, the total number of pentekostyes in the ten-lokhoi army will have been 100, in contrast to the six-morai army's total of only forty-eight.

PART III, CHAPTER 5, ANNEX II

The Structure of the Mora according to Xenophon in his Lakedaemoniôn Politeia, *chapter 11, § 4*

THIS passage—which evidently refers to the six hoplite morai only—runs as follows in the text as this has come down to us: ἑκάστη δὲ τῶν πολιτικῶν τούτων μορῶν ἔχει πολέμαρχον ἕνα, λοχαγοὺς τέτταρας, πεντηκοντῆρας ὀκτώ, ἐνωμοτάρχας ἑκκαίδεκα: 'each of these citizen morai has one polemarch, four lokhagoi, eight pentekonteres, sixteen enomotarkhai'.

We have first to try to ascertain what is Xenophon's usage of the word πολιτικός here. Polybius[2] uses it in the term πολιτικὴ χώρα to denote Sparta's own city-state territory, in contrast to other parts of Sparta's dominions that were perioecic territory.[3] On the other hand, Xenophon himself, in his *Hellenica*,[4] uses the word πολῖται to describe a Lacedaemonian force that included perioikoi as well as Spartiatai. Presumably, therefore, the term οἱ πολιτικοί in another passage of the *Hellenica*[5] likewise includes perioikoi. Here Xenophon seems to be distinguishing Sparta's national troops from her allies' troops and from the mercenaries that had been sent to her help by Dionysius I. In this usage, οἱ πολῖται or πολιτικοί would be equivalent to Thucydides' Λακεδαιμόνιοι αὐτοί in his description of the Lacedaemonian order of battle at Mantinea.[6] The term would include all citizens of either Sparta or any perioecic state, but would exclude emancipated helots such as the Brasideioi and neodamodeis who, in 418 B.C., were in the line side by side with the homoian Spartiatai and

[1] On p. 373.   [2] Book VI, chap. 45, § 3.
[3] See pp. 159 and 189.
[4] In Book IV, chap. 4, § 19; Book V, chap. 3, § 25, and chap. 4, § 41, the πολῖται are contrasted with the σύμμαχοι, and they must therefore be intended to include the perioikoi, since these certainly did not rank as σύμμαχοι. In Book VII, chap. 4, § 20, read together with § 27, the πολῖται turn out to include some perioikoi explicitly.
[5] Book VII, chap. 1, § 28.   [6] In Book V, chap. 67, § 1.

the perioikoi.[1] It looks, therefore, as if, in the *Lakedaimoniôn Politeia*, Xenophon will have been using the term πολιτικαὶ μόραι, as he certainly does use the terms πολῖται and οἱ πολιτικοί in the *Hellenica*, to mean a force composed of both Spartiatai and perioikoi, but of these two categories only. In writing τῶν πολιτικῶν τούτων μορῶν, he is distinguishing these Spartiate-perioecic morai from units of mora strength which were composed of other elements, e.g. the formation of Brasideioi together with neodamodeis that was in the line at Mantinea in 418 B.C.

The crux of the passage lies in the structure that is here attributed to the mora by Xenophon—or by some careless transcriber or officious emender of Xenophon's authentic text. As the text now reads, it states that there were four lokhoi in each mora, i.e. that in the six-morai army there were twenty-four lokhoi in all. This conflicts with Xenophon's own evidence in the *Hellenica*—evidence which is confirmed by Thucydides— pointing to the total number of lokhoi in the six-morai army being, not twenty-four, but twelve.[2] The next figure—eight pentekostyes in the mora—is convincing, since this gives the six-morai army forty-eight pentekostyes, and, as Wade-Gery has pointed out,[3] 'this is as near to 50 as a multiple of 6 can be'. The last figure in this passage—sixteen enomotiai in the mora—is as great a stumbling-block as the statement that there were four lokhoi in the mora. While four lokhoi is twice as many as there really were, sixteen enomotiai is only half as many as there really were.[4] Thucydides states[5] that in 418 B.C. there were sixteen enomotiai in the lokhoi, not in the mora, and there is no reason to think that he is in error in giving this figure, though he does err in this passage in being ignorant of—or ignoring—the existence of the mora and in consequently assuming that in 418 B.C. the lokhos, not the mora, was the largest of the units into which the Lacedaemonian army was articulated, and that at Mantinea in 418 B.C. there were only six lokhoi of 'the Lacedaemonians themselves', not twelve.[6] Moreover, Xenophon's and Thucydides' identical count of ninety-six enomotiai in the whole Lacedaemonian army gives a total strength of only 3,840 men, and this is an incredibly low figure.[7]

We therefore seem to be driven into having to reject two out of the four figures in this passage of Xenophon's *Lakedaimoniôn Politeia*. At the same time, it is hardly credible that the wrong figures—if they are wrong —were written into the original text by Xenophon himself. Xenophon surely could not have been guilty of making such gross errors on points of such capital importance in a field with which he was so well acquainted.

[1] This is Busolt's interpretation of Thucydides' word αὐτοί ('Spartas Heer und Leuktra', p. 380). The same view is taken by Kromayer, 'Wehrkraft und Wehrverfassung der griechischen Staaten', 2. Teil, p. 192.

[2] See pp. 374–6.

[3] See p. 391.

[4] See pp. 378–9 and chap. 5, Annex III.

[5] In Book V, chap. 68, § 3.

[6] See chap. 5, Annex III.

[7] See p. 379.

This seems the more improbable when we recall that the suspect figure, here given, for the number of lokhoi in a mora is in contradiction with Xenophon's own figure for this in his *Hellenica*, where, as we have seen,[1] the number of lokhoi in a mora is implied to be, not four, but two. It therefore looks as if the wrong figures in the passage in the *Lakedaimonión Politeia* must be due to the subsequent corruption or emendation of Xenophon's original text.

What can have led to this? One possible source of confusion, and of consequent error, may have been the ambiguity of the terms πολῖται and πολιτικός as employed in Lacedaemonian technical terminology. We have seen that, while Polybius uses the term πολιτικός to mean 'Spartiate' to the exclusion of 'perioecic', Xenophon uses the same term to mean 'Spartiate and perioecic combined'. We may also note that, while it was normal for the perioecic component of the Lacedaemonian army to be mobilized for active service simultaneously with, and together with, the homoian Spartiate component, there were two kinds of occasion on which the Spartiate component might be in the field without its complement of perioikoi.

This might happen when there was need for speed. The Spartiate homoioi, being permanently mobilized at Sparta and Amyklai, from which all routes leading northward radiated, could reach and cross the frontier more quickly than the perioikoi, most (though not all) of whom lived at points farther from the frontier, and all of whom had to be called away from their civilian daily work in field, workshop, and counting-house before they could assemble under arms and march off. In 479 B.C. the 5,000 Spartiatai had already crossed the frontier before the 5,000 perioikoi had been able to get on the move.[2] In 395 B.C. likewise, King Pausanias crossed the frontier with the homoioi alone, and had reached Tegea before he paused to wait for the perioikoi to catch him up.[3] From Tegea, without waiting any longer,[4] he marched on Boeotia.

The other kind of situation in which the homoian Spartiate contingent of the Lacedaemonian army might be in the field without its complement of perioikoi was a war which lasted for more than a single campaigning season and thus required the continuous absence from home of some, at least, of the troops for a longer period. In these circumstances the Spartan high command would have to let the perioikoi go home at the close of the first campaigning season, because the perioikoi, like Sparta's non-Lacedaemonian allies, had to earn their own living by cultivating their fields. By contrast, the homoioi could be kept in the field for an indefinite length of time, because, wherever they themselves might happen to be,

---

[1] On pp. 374–5.   [2] Herodotus, Book IX, chaps. 10–11.
[3] Xenophon, *Hellenica*, Book III, chap. 5, §§ 6–7.
[4] οἱ Λακεδαιμόνιοι οὐκέτι ἔμελλον (ibid., § 17).

their estates were being cultivated for them by their helots and there was therefore no economic difficulty about their remaining abroad. There was no psychological difficulty either; for the hardship of being separated from their families would be offset, for the homoioi, by the fact that, on active service, drill was lighter, discipline milder, and food more appetizing than in barracks at Sparta.[1] Their master's absence on campaign merely imposed on the helots the additional fatigue duty of delivering the produce required for covering his mess-dues at, say, the Isthmus of Corinth, after they had delivered the bulk of their contribution, as usual, to their master's wife in Sparta City or in Amyklai. This was the situation in 390 B.C.; for, by that date, part, at least, of the Lacedaemonian force at Lekhaion had been there since 391 B.C., and perhaps continuously since 392 B.C.[2]

Now, when a mora was on campaign at its normal strength of two lokhoi—one wholly perioecic and the other mainly homoian Spartiate—the chain of command was one polemarch, commanding the whole mora,[3] and, under him, two lokhagoi, one for each of the mora's two lokhoi.[4] When, however, the lokhos that was composed mainly of homoian Spartiatai was by itself, the polemarch who was the mora-commander remained in command of the mora that was now represented by one lokhos only of its two lokhoi, and in these circumstances the polemarch dispensed with the services of a lokhagos. He was able to act as his own lokhagos, since he now had only one lokhos under his command. This abbreviated chain of command was the chain in King Pausanias' force in 395 B.C. and in King Agesilaos' force in 390 B.C. On each occasion, Xenophon records[5] that the king convened a council-of-war consisting of his polemarchs and pentekonters, without any mention of lokhagoi.[6] On both occasions, we have found reason to believe that the Lacedaemonian force in the field consisted only of the lokhoi containing the homoian Spartiate component of the morai.

[1] Plutarch, *Lycurgus*, chap. 22.

[2] The mora that was in garrison at Lekhaion in the spring of 390 B.C. (Xenophon, *Hellenica*, Book IV, chap. 5, § 11) was the one that had been operating from Lekhaion in 391 B.C. (ibid., chap. 4, § 17). It may, indeed, have been the mora—Praxitas' mora—that had captured Lekhaion in 392 B.C. (ibid., chap. 4, §§ 7–13). This is not certain, since, at the close of the campaign of 392 B.C., Praxitas is recorded to have dismissed his army and himself to have gone home to Sparta (ibid., chap. 4, § 13). But it is also recorded that he left garrisons at Sidous, Krommyon, and Epieikeia (ibid.) and also at Lekhaion (§ 17), and the garrison at Lekhaion was a mora (§ 17); so it looks as if Praxitas had left the Spartiate component of his mora behind.

[3] See Xenophon, *Lak. Pol.*, chap. 13, § 6: ἔστ' ἄν γένηται ἐν μέσῳ δυοῖν μόραιν καὶ δυοῖν πολεμάρχοιν; Thucydides, Book V, chap. 71, § 3. However, Busolt, in loc. cit., pp. 418–19, holds that the polemarchs did not have commands but were staff-officers. But he admits, ibid., p. 425, that the polemarchs were mora commanders at the battle of Leuktra.

[4] For the chain of command, see p. 398.

[5] *Hellenica*, Book III, chap. 5, § 22; Book IV, chap. 5, § 7.

[6] This is pointed out by Beloch in 'Griechische Aufgebote', II, p. 59.

Thus the chain of command would be different in two different situations. In the normal situation, in which the mora was two lokhoi strong, the chain would be one polemarch, two lokhagoi, eight pentekonteres, thirty-two enomotarkhai.[1] On the other hand, in the exceptional situation in which the mora was represented by one only of its two lokhoi, the chain would be one polemarch, four pentekonteres, sixteen enomotarkhai. Since Xenophon is describing the structure of a πολιτικὴ μόρα— i.e. one which, in his usage of the term, included perioikoi as well as Spartiatai, and which was therefore of two-lokhoi strength—we may infer that, in his own original text, he gave the full chain of command, and gave it correctly. If the present text represents a corruption or emendation of Xenophon's text, this may have been the work of an editor who was informed of both the full and the abbreviated chain of command, and who jumped to the mistaken conclusion that they were variant accounts of the same chain and that they must therefore be harmonized with each other. This hypothetical editor will then have substituted the abbreviated chain's ἐνωμοτάρχας ἑκκαίδεκα for the full chain's ἐνωμοτάρχας δύο καὶ τριάκοντα, which was, we may guess, the figure that he found in Xenophon's original text. This conjecture does not explain how an original λοχαγοὺς δύο came to be changed into λοχαγοὺς τέτταρας. Here we may suspect a textual corruption. An original δύο may have been mistaken for δ′, which is the Greek sign for the numeral 4. However, the reading τέτταρας is supported by the quotation of the passage in Stobaeus' work.[2]

PART III, CHAPTER 5, ANNEX III

The Organization and Strength of the Lacedaemonian Army at Mantinea in 418 B.C.

OUR sole authority here is Thucydides.[3] We can, however, control his statements and estimates to some extent, partly from the internal evidence, and partly from information in other places—including other passages of Thucydides' own work[4]—about the names, numbers, and strengths of the units of which the Lacedaemonian army was constituted in this phase of its history. This information, taken together with Thucydides' account of the campaign of 418 B.C., suggests that either the perioecic wing of the Lacedaemonian army did not take part in this campaign[5]

---

[1] Thucydides, Book V, chap. 66, §§ 3–4, gives the full hierarchy of command, but does not state the number of the officers of each rank.

[2] Stobaeus, Book XLIV, chap. 36.

[3] Book V, chaps. 64–72.   [4] e.g. Book IV, chap. 8, § 9.

[5] This is Kromayer's view in loc. cit., pp. 190–2.

or, alternatively, that Thucydides has estimated the aggregate number of the Spartiate and perioecic troops in the Lacedaemonian line of battle at Mantinea at only half the true figure. This second alternative is made probable[1] by the unlikelihood that the perioikoi will have been absent.

This is unlikely for several reasons. In the first place, Thucydides himself says that 'the Lacedaemonians themselves and the helots marched in full force; the operation was swift, and there had never been any previous one to match it'.[2] The expression 'in force' ($\pi\alpha\nu\delta\eta\mu\epsilon\acute{\iota}$) may refer in part to the fact that all forty year-classes of military age were called up on this occasion; yet this expression could hardly have been used if, on this occasion, one half of the army, which would normally have been mobilized, was left at home for some unexplained reason. Moreover, in Spartan military parlance, 'the Lacedaemonians' is the technical term for 'the combined forces of the homoian Spartiatai and the perioikoi'.[3] In the second place, it seems unlikely that, if only the Spartiate wing of the Lacedaemonian army had been mobilized, the Spartan command would have felt that it could afford to send back from the frontier the oldest and the youngest year-classes, amounting, together, to about one-sixth of the whole force,[4] for garrison duty at home. Indeed, if the whole perioecic wing had been left at home, it would have amply sufficed to hold in awe those of the helots who had not been mobilized. The arrival of the perioecic wing of the army, at the heels of the Spartiate wing, was probably the event that led the Spartan command to send home the oldest and the youngest year-classes. In the third place, it is inconceivable that the Spartan Government should have left one half of its own Lacedaemonian army unmobilized when it was calling up, not only its Arcadian allies the Tegeatai, Heraieis, and Mainalioi,[5] but also such distant allies as the Corinthians, Boeotians, Phocians, and Locrians. In the fourth place, it cannot be supposed that the perioikoi, though called up, were unable to reach the front in time to take part in the action at Mantinea. Sparta's distant northern allies did fail to arrive in time. They not only had far to go; they would also have had to force a passage across enemy territory.[6] On the other hand, Sparta's Arcadian allies all arrived in time,[7] though Heraia was on the opposite edge of Arcadia from Mantinea; and so did the Brasideioi and neodamodeis,[8] who had to march from their station at Lepreon, in southern Triphylia.

---

[1] See Beloch, 'Griechische Aufgebote', II, p. 68.

[2] $\dot{\epsilon}\nu\tau\alpha\hat{\upsilon}\theta\alpha$ $\delta\dot{\eta}$ $\beta o\dot{\eta}\theta\epsilon\iota\alpha$ $\tau\hat{\omega}\nu$ $\Lambda\alpha\kappa\epsilon\delta\alpha\iota\mu o\nu\acute{\iota}\omega\nu$ $\gamma\acute{\iota}\gamma\nu\epsilon\tau\alpha\iota$, $\alpha\dot{\upsilon}\tau\hat{\omega}\nu$ $\tau\epsilon$ $\kappa\alpha\grave{\iota}$ $\tau\hat{\omega}\nu$ $E\grave{\iota}\lambda\acute{\omega}\tau\omega\nu$, $\pi\alpha\nu\delta\eta\mu\epsilon\grave{\iota}$ $\dot{o}\xi\epsilon\hat{\iota}\alpha$ $\kappa\alpha\grave{\iota}$ $o\hat{\iota}\alpha$ $o\check{\upsilon}\pi\omega$ $\pi\rho\acute{o}\tau\epsilon\rho o\nu$ (Thucydides, Book V, chap. 64, § 2).

[3] See pp. 365–6.

[4] Perhaps these were the four oldest year-classes and the three youngest (see pp. 370–1).

[5] Thucydides, Book V, chap. 64, § 1, and chap. 67, § 1.

[6] Book V, chap. 64, § 4.

[7] Book V, chap. 64, § 5, and chap. 67, § 2.

[8] Book V, chap. 67, § 1.

We cannot escape the conclusion that the perioikoi were present in the Lacedaemonian line of battle at Mantinea, and that Thucydides has overlooked their presence, and has failed to take their numbers into account, in his estimate of the total strength of the Lacedaemonian army in this engagement.

The authentic information possessed by Thucydides was that, in the Lacedaemonian line of battle, there were seven corps of the largest size,[1] not counting the Skiritai;[2] that the chain of command ran from polemarchs through lokhagoi and pentekonteres to enomotarkhai;[3] that the two of the seven corps which were stationed on the extreme right wing of the Lacedaemonian line[4]—separated from the rest of the Lacedaemonian formations by an intervening wedge of ally Arcadians (Tegeatai, Mainalioi, Heraieis)[5]—were each commanded by a polemarch;[6] that six of the Lacedaemonian corps—i.e. these two, together with four in the centre of the line—were formations of 'the Lacedaemonians themselves' (Λακεδαιμόνιοι αὐτοί), i.e. the fully enfranchised citizens of both Sparta and the perioecic states,[7] in contrast to the seventh corps, which was stationed between the centre and the Skiritai (who were on the extreme left wing) and which consisted of the Brasideioi together with the neodamodeis;[8] that a Lacedaemonian lokhos comprised four pentekostyes, each of which comprised four enomotiai;[9] and that, in the Lacedaemonian line of battle on this occasion, each enomotia was drawn up with a front of four men abreast.[10]

---

[1] Book V, chap. 68, § 3. 'The veterans of Brasidas, along with the neodamodeis, cannot possibly fail of inclusion in the given total of seven Lakedaimonian battalions. . . . The specific exclusion of the Skiritai, and of the Skiritai alone . . . guarantees that all other 'Lakedaimonian' elements are included in the aforesaid total of seven Lakedaimonian battalions in the field' (W. J. Woodhouse, *King Agis of Sparta and his Campaign in Arcadia in 418 B.C.* (Oxford, 1933, Clarendon Press), p. 139; cp. pp. 140–1).

[2] Thucydides, Book V, chap. 68, § 3. The Skiritai had the privilege of forming the vanguard of the Lacedaemonian army when it was on the march in column of route (Xenophon, *Lak. Pol.*, chap. 13, § 6) and of forming the extreme left wing when the army was in line of battle (Thucydides, Book V, chap. 67, § 1). According to Thucydides, ibid., chap. 68, § 3, the Skiritai were 600 strong in the line of battle at Mantinea in 418 B.C., and this figure is confirmed by Diodorus, Book XV, chap. 32, who—perhaps drawing on Ephorus—speaks of 'the Skirites lokhos'. 'The Skirites lokhos in the Spartan [meaning 'Lacedaemonian'] army is not drawn up with the rest of the troops. It has a special formation of its own, and is posted next to the kings. It comes to the rescue of whatever parts of the line are being hard pressed at the moment. Since it is a *corps d'élite*, it plays a decisive part in engagements.' For the topography of the Skiritis, see pp. 208–9.

[3] Thucydides, Book V, chap. 66, § 3. Cp. Xenophon, *Lak. Pol.*, chap. 13, § 4: πάρεισι δὲ . . . πολέμαρχοι, λοχαγοί, πεντηκοντῆρες.

[4] These two lokhoi must be included in Thucydides' total of seven (Woodhouse, op. cit., pp. 141–2).   [5] Thucydides, Book V, chap. 67, § 1.

[6] Ibid., chap. 71, § 3.   [7] See Busolt, 'Spartas Heer und Leuktra', p. 388.

[8] Thucydides, Book V, chap. 67, § 1. Cp. Woodhouse, op. cit., p. 140.

[9] Thucydides, Book V, chap. 68, § 3.

[10] Ibid. Thucydides goes on to say that the depth of the enomotiai was not uniform, and no doubt it was not, since not all the enomotiai in the line will have been exactly thirty-two

There is no reason to think that any of this information is incorrect. Thucydides' error is his identification of the Lacedaemonian corps of major size, commanded by a polemarch, with the Lacedaemonian lokhos, whereas we know that a polemarch's command was a mora, and that the mora consisted, not of a single lokhos, but of a pair of them, except on unusual occasions, of which this was not one, on which the mora was represented by its Spartiate lokhos alone.[1]

As a result of having fallen into this fundamental error, Thucydides reckons the number of enomotiai in the line to have been only 112, when in reality it will have been 224; and, since the front of each enomotia was four men broad, he reckons the total breadth of the front of the whole Lacedaemonian line—excluding the Skiritai (and, of course, excluding the Arcadian allies too)—to have been only 448 men, when in reality it will have been 896 men. Thucydides does not venture to estimate the strength of the seven Lacedaemonian major corps. The only two units whose strengths he gives are the 600 Skiritai[2] and the 300 hippeis[3] (i.e. the *corps d'élite* of young homoian Spartiate hoplites who constituted the King's bodyguard). Since, however, Thucydides knew, or inferred, that the average depth of an enomotia in the Lacedaemonian line was eight men, he implies that the total strength of the seven Lacedaemonian major corps in the line of battle was about 3,584, when in reality, with thirty-two year-classes in the line, it will have been about 7,168.[4]

strong (representing thirty-two year-classes; see p. 371). Thucydides goes on to say that each lokhagos was given discretion to draw up the enomotiai under his command at whatever depth he chose. This must be wrong, since he was under orders to draw them up with a front of four men abreast, and the depth of each enomotia will have been determined by that. The reason why the average depth of the enomotiai on this occasion was eight men was because the front of each enomotia was four men broad and because thirty-two year-classes were in the line.

[1] The same conclusion has been reached independently by Woodhouse in op. cit., p. 139, n. 9. Apropos of the unit that Thucydides calls a 'lokhos', Woodhouse, too, holds that 'its proper designation was "mora" ("brigade"). The mora embraced two linked battalions ("lokhoi"). Since he perversely chose to use the familiar Attic term "lokhos" in speaking of this highest multiple of the enomotia, Thucydides entangled himself in his own terminology and unwittingly dropped one grade in the Lacedaemonian military hierarchy of enomotia (platoon), pentekostys (company), lokhos (battalion), and mora (brigade); with the result that the estimate to which his words have led his interpreters is just half the true figure for the brigade, as fully manned upon a πανδημεί mobilization. Thucydides entirely forgot, if indeed he ever knew, that one complete lokhos in each mora was provided by perioikoi. 'Though the conclusion thus summarily here stated was reached by me many years previously, by a process apparently quite different from his, it agrees, I find, essentially with that of Mr. Toynbee.'

Woodhouse's reference here is to A. J. Toynbee, 'The Growth of Sparta', in *The Journal of Hellenic Studies*, vol. xxxiii, Part 2 (1913), pp. 246–75. Compare section VIII of this paper, 'First Mantinea', ibid., pp. 269–71, with Woodhouse, op. cit., Excursus B, 'The Numbers Engaged', on his pp. 131–46.   [2] Thucydides, Book V, chap. 68, § 2.

[3] Ibid., chap. 72, § 4. The hippeis, as well as the Skiritai, were outside the seven formations that Thucydides calls 'lokhoi' (see Busolt in loc. cit., p. 415; Kromayer in loc. cit., p. 193, n. 3).

[4] In addition to these troops that were put into the line of battle, there were, to the rear

This conclusion is supported by two considerations. Firstly, the Brasi-deioi must have constituted a lokhos by themselves; for their original strength had been 700,[1] and there is no indication that their losses in the north had been exceptionally heavy. Therefore the corps in which the Brasideioi were brigaded with neodamodeis must have been larger than a lokhos, i.e. it must have been a two-lokhoi mora. Secondly, the battle was notable for the size of the forces engaged,[2] and, of the two armies, the Lacedaemonian 'looked as if it were the larger'.[3]

The great bulk of the Lacedaemonian army consisted of Lacedae-monian troops. Of the ally contingents in the Lacedaemonian line of battle, we can perhaps set off the Tegeatai[4] against the Mantineis'[5] on the opposite side, and the Heraieis and Mainalioi[6] against the Mantineis' Arcadian allies.[7] If so, the Lacedaemonian formations must have seemed to outnumber the rest of the opposing army. The figures given by Thucy-dides show that this remainder was more than 7,000 men strong.[8] If the aggregate strength of the Lacedaemonian formations in the Lace-daemonian line of battle was 8,068,[9] the Lacedaemonians and their allies would not merely have looked numerically stronger than their opponents; they would actually have been numerically stronger. On the other hand, if the aggregate strength of the Lacedaemonian forma-tions had been only 4,484, as Thucydides leads us to suppose,[10] the Lacedaemonians and their allies would have been so decisively inferior in numbers that the numerical disparity could not have been camouflaged even by the most ingenious tactical disposition of the Lacedaemonian forces, and the Lacedaemonians would hardly have been able to win the victory that they did win in this hard-fought battle.

These considerations seem to confirm the conclusion that Thucydides'

of the line, the oldest of the hoplites who had not been sent home from the frontier (Book V, chap. 72, § 3)—i.e. probably the men who were in their fifty-sixth year of life. There were also the helots, who, being light-armed, unlike the ex-helot Brasideioi and neodamodeis, had no part to play in a pitched battle between hoplite phalanxes.

[1] Thucydides, Book IV, chap. 80, § 3.

[2] Thucydides, Book V, chap. 74, § 1. Beloch, 'Griechische Aufgebote', II, p. 68, points out that at Delion in 424 B.C. there had been 7,000 hoplites on each side (Thucydides, Book IV, chaps. 93–4).

[3] Book V, chap. 68, § 1. [4] Book V, chap. 67, § 1.

[5] Ibid., § 2. [6] Ibid., § 1.

[7] Ibid., § 2. These had not included the Parrhasioi since the Parrhasioi had been liberated from Mantinean rule by Sparta in 421 B.C. (Thucydides, Book V, chap. 33). The Mantineis may have captured the hegemony over south-west Arcadia from the Tegeatai in 424 B.C. (see Book IV, chap. 134).

[8] It consisted of one Argive *corps d'élite* of 1,000 men (Book V, chap. 67, § 2); five lokhoi of ordinary Argive hoplites (ibid. and chap. 72, § 4); Argos' perioikoi the Kleonaioi and Orneatai (Book V, chap. 67, § 2 and chap. 72, § 4: strength not stated), and the Athenian contingent of 1,000 hoplites. Presumably the ordinary Argive lokhoi were each of the same strength (1,000 each) as the *corps d'élite*.

[9] i.e. 7,168 in the seven morai, together with 600 Skiritai and 300 hippeis.

[10] i.e. 3,584+600+300.

estimate of the size of the seven major Lacedaemonian corps that took part in this battle is only half the true figure.

The Organization and Strength of the Lacedaemonian Army at Leuktra in 371 B.C.

T H E Lacedaemonian component of King Kleombrotos' army at Leuktra in 371 B.C. consisted of four morai,[1] which did not include the *corps d'élite* of 300 hippeis who were the King's bodyguard. These morai had been mobilized up to the normal strength, for active service, of thirty-five ἔτη ἀφ' ἥβης.[2] The aggregate strength of the four morai in this battle was therefore 4,480. Out of the total number of Lacedaemonians present, about 700 were Spartiatai.[3] The total number of Lacedaemonians killed was about 1,000;[4] of these, about 400 were estimated to have been Spartiatai.[5]

Why were the Spartiatai's losses so disproportionately heavy? They lost more than half their number, whereas the Lacedaemonians as a whole lost less than a quarter of theirs. The explanation must be that the Spartiatai were not distributed evenly along the whole Lacedaemonian line. Out of the 700 of them, 300, namely the hippeis, were concentrated round the King on the right flank.[6] These 300 bore the brunt of the fighting; for the Theban 300—the 'Hieros Lokhos', led by Pelopidas and massed in column of assault—made a dead set at the point in the Lacedaemonian line at which King Kleombrotos was stationed.[7] Kleombrotos fell almost immediately; but it was not till he had been carried to the rear, and till the troops covering him had suffered the severest losses, that the hard-pressed Lacedaemonian right wing began to fall back.[8] This makes it probable that the 300 Spartiate hippeis were almost annihilated. On this assumption, the number of Spartiatai serving in the morai who were killed turns out to have been only about 100, when the approximately 300 deaths among the hippeis are subtracted from the total of about 400 Spartiate deaths. If we subtract the strength of the 300 hippeis from the total Spartiate strength of 700,

---

[1] Xenophon, *Hellenica*, Book VI, chap. 1, § 1.
[2] Ibid., chap. 4, § 17.
[3] Ibid., chap. 4, § 15.
[4] ἐγγὺς χιλίους, Xenophon, ibid.; πλείους ἢ χίλιοι, Pausanias, Book IX, chap. 13, § 12.
[5] Xenophon in loc. cit., § 15.
[6] See Busolt in loc. cit., p. 422.
[7] Plutarch, *Pelopidas*, chap. 23, read together with chap. 20. See also Busolt in loc. cit., pp. 437 and 448-9.
[8] Xenophon, *Hellenica*, Book VI, chap. 4, §§ 13-14.

we are left with 400 as the number of the Spartiatai serving in the morai at the start of the battle.

The 100 deaths among the Spartiatai serving in the morai amount to 10 per cent of the total number of Lacedaemonian deaths. The number of the Spartiatai serving in the morai, if it was 400, was approximately 10 per cent of the total number of the Lacedaemonians serving in the morai. Perhaps we can infer, from a comparison of these two sets of almost identical percentages, that the ratio of Spartiatai in the morai was known to have been one in every ten hoplites, and that this ratio was taken as a basis for arriving at the number of the Spartiatai among the 1,000 Lacedaemonian dead, on the two assumptions that all the 300 Spartiatai in the corps of hippeis lost their lives, but that, in the morai, the losses had fallen on Spartiatai and on non-Spartiate Lacedaemonians impartially, i.e. in approximate proportion to the numbers in each category that were present at the start of the battle. The number of Spartiatai who had been killed must have been arrived at by some such calculation;[1] for, though the Thebans remained in possession of the field and were therefore able to count the total number of Lacedaemonian corpses, they would have been unable to distinguish between Spartiate and non-Spartiate corpses, and the number of the Lacedaemonian dead that were Spartiatai had to be estimated indirectly, since this figure would never have been divulged by the Spartan high command.[2]

If only one hoplite in every ten in Kleombrotos' four morai was a Spartiate, this means that, by 371 B.C., only one man in every five was a Spartiate in the so-called 'Spartiate' lokhos of each mora, as compared with the ratio of four Spartiatai in every five which appears to have been the standard ratio in 425 B.C.[3]

This further drop in the number of homoian Spartiatai in the Lacedaemonian phalanx is as sensational as the previous drop which had been caused by the destruction of life at Sparta in the earthquake of *circa* 466 or 464 B.C.[4] But there is no reason to suppose that this second drop was due, as the first drop had been, to a proportionate decline in the number of the homoioi. The change that accounts for the second drop is not a demographic change; it is a political one.

Sparta's victory in the Atheno-Peloponnesian War of 431–404 B.C. had brought with it changes in Sparta's position in the Hellenic World and

---

[1] If the calculation has been reconstructed correctly here, there will have been one error in it. The calculator will have overlooked the point that the 1,000 Lacedaemonian dead included the 300 hippeis, and that the number of Lacedaemonian deaths in the morai was therefore only 700. If about 10 per cent of these Lacedaemonian dead in the morai were Spartiatai, the absolute number of these will have been, not 100, but seventy, and the total number of Spartiate dead will have been 370 out of 1,000, not 400 out of 1,000.

[2] See chap. 1, p. 153, n. 4.

[3] See pp. 382–3.

[4] See the present Part, chap. 4, Annex IV, and pp. 386–7.

consequent changes in her policy towards her allies. Sparta's system of alliances, like Athens' system in the preceding century, had turned into an empire that had to be held by force now that it was no longer being held together voluntarily by common interests and by mutual good will. It is true that, before 371 B.C., the area of Sparta's post-war empire had contracted as a result of the King's Peace of 387 B.C. and the organization of a new maritime league under Athenian leadership. However, what remained of Sparta's empire in continental European Greece had still to be garrisoned and administered; and, while Sparta's garrisons might be supplied by her neodamodeis, her harmosts had to be homoian Spartiatai.[1] In short, there were now political calls on the homoioi that took precedence over the military service in the ranks of the hoplite phalanx which had been the homoioi's original *raison d'être*.

In 394 B.C., at the battle of the Nemea River, Sparta had still been able to put four Spartiatai into the morai for every six perioikoi.[2] Now that she had reduced the ratio to only a single Spartiate for every nine non-homoian Lacedaemonians, she could not challenge with impunity such redoubtable hoplites as the Theban, led by such brilliant tacticians as Epameinondas and Pelopidas. At Leuktra in 371 B.C. the *moral* of the three hundred Spartiate hippeis was as high as the *moral* of Leonidas' three hundred Spartiatai had been in 480 B.C. On the other hand, the *moral* of the diluted morai was low. When the left wing saw the right wing being driven off the field, it retreated without waiting to be assaulted in its turn,[3] and the polemarchs did not venture to order either the ally or the Lacedaemonian troops to go into action again.[4]

What were the sources of military man-power for the non-Spartiate complement of the 'Spartiate' lokhoi of the morai of 371 B.C.? We have found indications that, in 425 B.C., one man in every five in a 'Spartiate' lokhos was a non-Spartiate, and that this non-Spartiate was a perioikos.[5] As late as 382 B.C. the Spartan demand on perioecic man-power was light enough to allow of there being perioecic volunteers in addition to the perioecic conscripts.[6] If, however, we are right in thinking that, by 371 B.C., the ratio of non-Spartiates in a 'Spartiate' lokhos had been raised from one man to four men in every five, it is hardly credible that the reservoir of perioecic man-power could have run to supplying four-fifths of the men in every 'Spartiate' lokhos, while continuing to supply the whole personnel of the perioecic lokhoi. It seems more probable that at least two of the three additional non-Spartiates in every five men in a 'Spartiate' lokhos will have been raised from among the neodamodeis.

---

[1] See Busolt in loc. cit., pp. 430 and 431.   [2] See pp. 379–80.
[3] Xenophon, *Hellenica*, Book VI, chap. 4, § 14.
[4] Ibid., § 15.   [5] See pp. 382–3.
[6] See p. 387.

Sparta could afford to pay for neodamodeis in larger numbers, now that she was exacting tribute from her 'allies'.

There was, however, still a political limitation on the number of the helots whom she could venture to emancipate and to arm; and service in the line, in addition to garrison service, will have taxed the man-power of Sparta's neodamodeis, as well as the man-power of her perioikoi, to the limit. In 382 B.C. there had been neodamodeis, as well as Skiritai and other perioikoi, in the force of 2,000 hoplites that had been sent, under Eudamidas' command, against the colonial Chalcidians;[1] but it is evident that in 371 B.C. Sparta had no reserves of neodamodeis that were still uncommitted. She was reduced to calling up the two surviving morai in full strength, i.e. including the oldest five year-classes of military age[2] in the case of the homoioi, at any rate. The last that we hear of the neodamodeis is that there were some of them in the garrison, 400 strong in all, which was annihilated in 370 B.C. at Oion in the Skiritis.[3]

---

[1] Xenophon, *Hellenica*, Book V, chap. 2, § 24.
[2] Ibid., Book VI, chap. 4, § 17.
[3] Ibid., chap. 5, §§ 24–6.

6. Changes of Sovereignty and Frontiers in Sparta's Former Dominions, 370 B.C.—A.D. 78

S PARTA seems to have acquired her dominions in the southern Peloponnese, to the west of Mount Parnon, in the course of less than half a century.[1] The outside dates for her territorial expansion which began with the conquest of Amyklai, Pharis, and Geronthrai and ended with the conquest of Messenia are *circa* 760–710 B.C. After her conquest of Argos' dominions east of Mount Parnon, from the island of Kythera and Cape Malea through Kynouria to the Thyreatis inclusive, Sparta's frontiers remained unchanged for about 173 years. Changes began again after Sparta's disaster at Leuktra in 371 B.C. Sparta was then mulcted of territory in four successive stages: in 370 B.C. by Epameinondas; in 338 B.C. by King Philip II of Macedon; in 222 B.C. by King Antigonos Doson of Macedon; and in 195 B.C. by the Roman proconsul T. Quinctius Flamininus. After that, there was a slight turn of the tide in Sparta's favour. She benefited from the dissolution of the Achaean Confederation in 146 B.C., and again from the short-lived favour that her leading citizen C. Iulius Eurykles found with Augustus on account of services rendered at the time of the battle of Actium.[2] Conversely, Sparta may have been affected adversely by Eurykles' subsequent disgrace; and in A.D. 25 the Roman Imperial Government gave an award in Messenia's favour in a dispute between Messenia and Sparta over the possession of the temple of Artemis Limnatis in the Dentheliatis[3]—the bone of contention that had been the cause of the outbreak of the First Spartano-Messenian War, more than seven and a half centuries earlier. The frontier between Sparta and Messenia was delimited and demarcated definitively by the Roman Imperial Government in A.D. 78.[4] So far as we know, there was no further change in this frontier till all frontiers in continental European Greece were obliterated by the Slav Völkerwanderung in the sixth and seventh centuries of the Christian Era.

When, in 370 B.C., Epameinondas liberated the Messenians and synoecized the resuscitated Messenian state round a new city laid out at the foot of Mount Ithome, he detached from Sparta, and incorporated in the independent state, all Sparta's former city-state territory in Messenia. He must also have detached from Sparta, and have incorporated

[1] Jones, *Sparta*, p. 11, holds that this is too short a reckoning.
[2] See Chrimes, *Ancient Sparta*, p. 172.
[3] Tacitus, *Annals*, Book IV, chap. 43.
[4] See Chrimes, *Ancient Sparta*, pp. 60–7.

in the state of Messenia, the two perioecic city-states Thouria and Aithaia, as well as the outlying perioecic city-state Aulon, at the extreme north-west corner of Sparta's former dominions. After the earthquake of *circa* 466 or 464 B.C., Thouria and Aithaia had revealed their Messenian national feeling by revolting from Sparta in company with the Messenian helots.[1] They, too, after their resubjugation, had presumably still continued to long for independence. Moreover, without them, the revived Messenian state would hardly have been viable. Sparta's dominions would still have extended to within a few miles of the new city of Messene; the new capital would have been cut off from its nearest access to the sea; and Messenia would have had to restart life without possession of the Makaria plain, which, together with the adjoining Stenyklaros plain, was the most fertile part of the country.

On the other hand, Asine and Methone, at the two tips of the south-western prong of the Peloponnese, retained their existing status of being two of Sparta's perioecic city-states,[2] though, henceforth, their communications with Sparta overland were cut by the interposition of an independent Messenia. These were two communities of refugees from the Argeia to whom Sparta, after the First Spartano-Messenian War, had given new homes in this corner of the Messenian territory that she had conquered.[3] It was natural that they should have continued to be loyal to Sparta. They were subsequently detached from Sparta, possibly in 338 B.C. by Philip II[4] and, at the latest, in 195 B.C.—the date at which Sparta was deprived of all her hitherto remaining perioecic states, together with Gythion, and was thus cut off from all access to the sea. Thereafter, both states became members of the Achaean Confederation individually, without having been incorporated in Messenia.

In 369 B.C.[5] Epameinondas followed up the synoecism of Messene by synoecizing the numerous little cantons of south-western Arcadia in the new city-state of Megalopolis; and this was a second blow for Sparta. It was, indeed, little less serious for her than the loss of Messenia was. Hitherto, south-western Arcadia had been kept disunited and weak by a tacit conspiracy between Sparta, Tegea, and Mantinea; and the rivalry between these two east-Arcadian city-states for the hegemony over south-western Arcadia[6] had played into Sparta's hands. South-western

---

[1] Thucydides, Book I, chap. 101.

[2] Pausanias, Book IV, chap. 27, § 8; Pseudo-Scylax, § 17.

[3] See p. 181, with nn. 2, 3, and 4.

[4] See Ernst Meyer, s.v. 'Methone', in P.–W., 15. Band (1932), cols. 1382–4, in col. 1384, citing Polybius, Book IX, chap. 28, § 7; Oberhummer, s.v. 'Asine', in P.–W., 2. Band (1896), col. 1582, citing Polybius, Book XVIII, chap. 42, § 7.

[5] This, or 370 B.C., seems to have been the date given by the Marmor Parium. Beloch prefers the date 368/7, which is Diodorus' in Book XV, chap. 73 (see Beloch, *Griechische Geschichte*, 2. Auflage, 3. Band, 1. Abteilung (1922), p. 186, n. 2).

[6] See, for example, Thucydides, Book V, chap. 33.

Arcadia had served Sparta as an ever-open avenue for offensive military operations beyond Sparta's own frontiers. The synoecism of the south-west Arcadian cantons in Megalopolis blocked this avenue—and blocked it permanently.

It is true that Megalopolis quickly failed to sustain the ambitious role, for which it had been cast originally, of serving as the federal capital for a united Arcadia. The momentarily aroused Arcadian national con-sciousness[1] quickly subsided, and the Arcadian states soon fell apart from each other;[2] but the new Arcadian city-state Megalopolis did not dis-integrate. Once founded, it continued to be one of the most powerful city-states, not only in Arcadia, but in the Peloponnese as a whole; and Megalopolis had been planted on Sparta's door-step. From the founda-tion-date of Megalopolis onwards the feud between Sparta and Megalo-polis was, if possible, more bitter than the feud between Sparta and Messenia. The frontier forts on the Spartan–Megalopolitan border round the watershed between the Eurotas basin and the Alpheios basin were constantly changing hands. The accession of Megalopolis to the Achaean Confederation in 235 B.C. created an irreconcilable conflict of interests between Sparta and the Confederation as a whole. This conflict was exacerbated by the prominence of the part in the Achaean Confedera-tion's politics that was played, from that date onwards, by Megalo-politan statesmen—above all, by Philopoimen. The inextinguishable feud between Megalopolis and Sparta was the ultimate cause of the Achaean Confederation's catastrophic end in 146 B.C.

After these losses of territory in 370–369 or 370–367 B.C. at the hands of Thebes and her allies, Sparta suffered a second set of losses in 338 B.C. at the hands of King Philip II of Macedon. Philip's decisive victory over Thebes and Athens at Chaeronea did not move Sparta to come to terms with him. He invaded Laconia, but he did not take the City of Sparta itself, and Sparta was the only continental European Greek state that held aloof from the newly founded Confederation of Corinth. Philip took his revenge on Sparta by paring down her dominions on all sides for the benefit of her neighbours.[3]

Messenia received the Dentheliatis—the highland district, containing

[1] In 370 B.C. even the Skiritai, who had played so distinguished a role in Lacedaemonian military history, appear to have remembered that they were Arcadians and to have seceded from Sparta; and the Arcadians even succeeded in occupying Sellasia and Pellana (for Pellana, see Diodorus, Book XV, chap. 67). However, Karyai was resubjugated by Sparta in 368 B.C. (see Xenophon, *Hellenica*, Book VII, chap. 1, § 28; Plutarch, *Agesilaus*, chap. 33; Diodorus, Book XV, chap. 72). In 365 B.C. Sparta reconquered Sellasia (Xenophon, *Hel-lenica*, Book VII, chap. 4, § 12). By 362 B.C. she had reconquered Pellana as well (ibid., chap. 5, § 9).

[2] See Jones, *Sparta*, pp. 131–2.

[3] Polybius, Book IX, chap. 28, § 7, and chap. 33, §§ 8–12; Book XVIII, chap. 14, §§ 6–7. See also Beloch, *Griechische Geschichte*, vol. cit., p. 575, n. 1.

the temple of Artemis Limnatis, on the west side of the Taÿgetos range, astride the road between Sparta and Pharai.[1] Messenia could hardly have received the Dentheliatis without receiving Pharai as well, since Pharai lay on the only road between the Dentheliatis and the main body of Messenia. Actually, Philip seems to have transferred from Sparta's sovereignty to Messenia's, not only the Dentheliatis and Pharai, but also Sparta's perioecic states between Taÿgetos and the eastern shore of the Messenian Gulf as far south as Leuktra inclusive, up to the mouth of the southern Pamisos River,[2] with the off-lying islet Pephnos,[3] but not including Thalamai. Megalopolis received the Belbinatis,[4] and therefore presumably also any parts of the Aigytis and the Maleatis that she had not received already at the time when she was synoecized. Tegea probably received the Karyatis.[5] Argos, which had come out empty-handed in 370/69 B.C., now received back, from Philip, part of her former Cynurian dependencies,[6] which she had lost to Sparta more than two centuries earlier. The territory transferred on this occasion seems not to have extended as far south as Zarax, since Zarax was attacked and destroyed by the émigré Spartan prince Kleonymos, who was serving in Pyrrhus' army when Pyrrhus invaded Laconia in 273 B.C.[7] At this date, therefore, Zarax must have belonged, not to Argos, but to Sparta.

In 222 B.C., at Sellasia, Sparta suffered the third of her major military disasters to date (the first of these had been her defeat by the Argives at Hysiai *circa* 669 B.C., and the second her defeat by the Thebans at Leuktra in 371 B.C.). In 222 B.C. Sparta City was occupied by a victorious enemy army—for the first time, so far as we know, since the post-Mycenaean Völkerwanderung. The victor, King Antigonos Doson of Macedon, seems to have confirmed the transfers of territory that had been made by his predecessor King Philip II, or to have renewed those transfers in so far as they had been reversed by King Kleomenes III of Sparta.[8] Doson's adjudication of the Dentheliatis to Messenia is explicitly

---

[1] See Tacitus, *Annals*, Book IV, chap. 43.

[2] The southern Pamisos seems to have been made the frontier between Sparta's dominions and Messenia by King Philip II of Macedon (Strabo, *Geographica*, Book VIII, chap. 4, § 6 (C. 361)). The Pamisos that was the boundary between Laconia and Messenia according to Euripides, as cited by Strabo, *Geographica*, Book VIII, chap. 5, § 6 (C. 366), is more likely to have been the great Pamisos than this little river of the same name. Euripides will have been counting the perioecic states in south-eastern Messenia as being part of Laconia. At the time when Euripides was writing, the whole of Messenia was, of course, under Spartan rule.

[3] Pausanias, Book III, chap. 26, § 3.

[4] Livy, Book XXXVIII, chap. 34.

[5] This is an inference from Stephanus of Byzantium's citation of Theopompos' *Philippica*, s.v. Karyai.

[6] See Pausanias, Book II, chap. 20, § 1.

[7] See Plutarch, *Pyrrhus*, chap. 26.

[8] See Chrimes, *Ancient Sparta*, pp. 21–2.

recorded.[1] Moreover, Argos, at any rate, seems to have received additional Lacedaemonian territory from Doson; for Lycurgus, who obtained the Spartan crown in 220/19 B.C., then conquered, from Argos, Leukai, to the west of Zarax, which must have been Sparta's in 273 B.C. if Zarax was hers at that date. In the same campaign, King Lycurgus also reconquered from Argos Kyphanta, Polikhna, and Prasiai, which may have been transferred from Sparta to Argos either by Doson in 222 B.C. or by Philip II in 338 B.C. On the same occasion, Lycurgus attacked Zarax,[2] and Glyшpeis too, but failed to take them.[3]

Sparta's military power, which had been broken by Doson in 222 B.C. after it had been revived by Kleomenes III, was revived again by Nabis— only to be broken again, and this time beyond all possibility of recovery, by Flamininus in 195 B.C. In the peace-settlement of that year, Flamininus cut Sparta off from all access to the sea by depriving her, not only of all her remaining perioecic states, but also of her port at Gythion, in her own city-state territory.[4] On this occasion Kynouria, from Zarax to Prasiai inclusive, may have been handed back to Argos, since Prasiai was in Argos' possession, and Epidauros Limera was the most northerly Laconian state along this coast, at the date of Strabo's source, Artemidoros,[5] who was writing towards the end of the second century B.C.[6] The rest of the ex-perioecic states (i.e. those not given to Argos), together with Gythion, were placed under the Achaean Confederation's protection.[7] The κοινὸν τῶν Λακεδαιμονίων, the existence of which is attested by inscriptions dating from before the reign of Augustus,[8] may have constituted the τάξιν τινὰ πολιτείας that the liberated Laconian states received when they went over to the Roman side at a time when Sparta was under the rule of a tyrant who, presumably, was Nabis.[9]

[1] By Tacitus, in loc. cit.

[2] Presumably Zarax had been given to Argos in 222 B.C. by Antigonos Doson.

[3] See Polybius, Book IV, chap. 36.

[4] For the previous status of Gythion, see pp. 192–3. Gythion will have lain in the helot-inhabited part of Sparta's city-state territory; and the detaching of Gythion from Sparta in 195 B.C. may be the event referred to in the inclusion of the words καὶ οἱ εἴλωτες in a passage of Strabo's *Geographica* (Book VIII, chap. 5, § 5 (C. 366)) which seems to refer to the settlement made in 195 B.C.: συνέβη δὲ καὶ τοὺς Ἐλευθερολάκωνας λαβεῖν τινα τάξιν πολιτείας ἐπειδὴ Ῥωμαίοις προσέθεντο πρῶτοι οἱ περίοικοι τυραννουμένης τῆς Σπάρτης, οἵ τε ἄλλοι καὶ οἱ εἴλωτες. The passage is slipshod; for the helots were not perioikoi, and the κοινὸν τῶν Ἐλευθερολακώνων is shown, by inscriptional evidence, not to have been pre-Augustan. The association in which the former perioecic states of Sparta were grouped in 195 B.C. was the κοινὸν τῶν Λακεδαιμονίων (see pp. 409–10).

[5] See Strabo, *Geographica*, Book VIII, chap. 6, § 1 (C. 368).

[6] See Chrimes, *Ancient Sparta*, pp. 435–6, with p. 436, n. 1.

[7] For the peace-settlement of 195 B.C., see Livy, Book XXXIV, chaps. 35–6; Book XXXV, chap. 12, § 7; Book XXXV, chap. 13, § 2; Book XXXVIII, chaps. 30–1.

[8] Chrimes, *Ancient Sparta*, p. 435.

[9] See Strabo, *Geographica*, Book VIII, chap. 5, § 5 (C. 366), quoted above in n. 4. If this passage does refer to the settlement of 195 B.C., Strabo's use of the term Ἐλευθερολάκωνες

During the half-century 195–146 B.C., Sparta was at the lowest ebb of her fortunes. In 192 B.C. she was bullied into becoming a state-member of the Achaean Confederation;[1] in 188 B.C. the 'Lycurgan' regime was forcibly abrogated at Sparta by Philopoimen.[2] Sparta's situation did not begin to improve again till after 146 B.C.,[3] when the dissolution of the Achaean Confederation by Rome had turned both Sparta herself and the Laconian states that had been under Achaean protection into direct dependencies of Rome. On this occasion, Sparta failed to recover the Dentheliatis from Messenia,[4] but she may have recovered the Belbinatis and the Aigytis from Megalopolis,[5] and she may also have been admitted to membership in the κοινὸν τῶν Λακεδαιμονίων[6]—not as hegemon, though inevitably as *prima inter pares*. There is inscriptional evidence[7] that Sparta became a member of the κοινόν at some stage,[8] and this cannot have happened so long as the Achaean Confederation was in existence.[9]

This κοινὸν τῶν Λακεδαιμονίων which, from 146 B.C. onwards,[10] probably included Sparta as well as the ex-perioecic cities that had been liberated in 195 B.C., appears to have been dissolved by Augustus and to have been replaced by two separate political units: a city-state of Sparta, standing by itself, and a κοινὸν τῶν Ἐλευθερολακώνων, which was no longer associated with Sparta.[11] There are inscriptions, dating from the Age of

here is an error, since the Eleutherolaconian League seems to have been a creation of Augustus'. The year 195 B.C. is the date of the creation of the κοινὸν τῶν Λακεδαιμονίων in the opinion of A. Gitti, 'I perieci di Sparta e le origini del *KOINON TΩN ΛAKEΔAIMONIΩN*', in *Rendiconti della R. Accademia dei Lincei*, Classe di Scienze Morali, Storiche, e Filologiche, serie sesta, vol. xv (1939), pp. 189–203, on pp. 191 and 198–9.

[1] Livy, Book XXXV, chap. 37, § 1; Plutarch, *Philopoemen*, chap. 15; Pausanias, Book VIII, chap. 51, § 1.

[2] Polybius, Book XXII, chaps. 3, 7, 10, 11, 12; Book XXIII, chap. 4; Livy, Book XXXVIII, chap. 34; Book XXXIX, chaps. 33 and 37; Plutarch, *Philopoemen*, chap. 16.

[3] Livy, Book XLV, chap. 28, is not evidence that the 'Lycurgan' agoge had been re-established already by 167 B.C.

[4] See Tacitus, loc. cit. Messenia's title to possess the Dentheliatis was upheld by L. Mummius.

[5] Chrimes, *Ancient Sparta*, p. 67, on the strength of Polybius, Book XVI, chap. 17, § 4.

[6] See Cavaignac, *Sparte*, p. 218.

[7] From the temple of Apollo Hyperteleatas at Asopos.

[8] Chrimes, *Ancient Sparta*, pp. 436–7.

[9] There are coins, bearing the monograms of both the Achaean Confederation and the Lacedaemonians, which must have been struck within the half-century during which the κοινὸν τῶν Λακεδαιμονίων was an Achaean protectorate (see Chrimes, *Ancient Sparta*, pp. 438–9). In Miss Chrimes's view, these coins indicate that Sparta was a member of the κοινόν at this stage, and that she was admitted to it after her incorporation in the Achaean Confederation. This dating seems most improbable. A reunion of Sparta's ex-perioecic states with Sparta would have been obnoxious to the Achaean Confederation, as well as to the liberated Laconian states themselves. The Achaean Federal Government's policy was to give direct membership in the Confederation to the greatest possible number of constituent states of the smallest possible size (see Plutarch, *Philopoemen*, chap. 13; *Comparison between Philopoemen and Flamininus*, chap. 1). The reunion cannot have taken place till after the Achaean Confederation had been dissolved.

[10] See Gitti in loc. cit., p. 200.　　　　　　　　[11] Pausanias, Book III, chap. 21, § 6.

the Principate, which refer to the κοινὸν τῶν 'Ελευθερολακώνων, but the inscriptions referring to the κοινὸν τῶν Λακεδαιμονίων seem all to be pre-Augustan.[1] Augustus, however, did not simply divide the former κοινὸν τῶν Λακεδαιμονίων, as it stood, into two separate entities. He seems, at the same time, to have made a complicated redistribution of territory between Sparta, the new κοινὸν τῶν 'Ελευθερολακώνων, Argos, and Messenia.

According to Pausanias,[2] the κοινὸν τῶν 'Ελευθερολακώνων consisted, in his day, of the following eighteen states: Gythion,[3] Teuthrone, Las, Pyrrikhos, Kainepolis, Oitylos, Leuktra, Thalamai, Alagonia,[4] Gerenia,[5] Asopos, Akriai, Boiai, Zarax, Epidauros Limera, Prasiai,[6] Geronthrai, Marios. Zarax, Marios, and Prasiai must have been transferred to the Eleutherolaconian koinon from Argos, to whom these three Cynurian states had belonged in Artemidoros' day.[7] Leuktra, Alagonia, and Gerenia must have been transferred to the koinon from Messenia, to whom they had been transferred from Sparta by Philip II of Macedon.[8] This may have been in compensation for the reunion of six of the original twenty-four Eleutherolaconian states[9] with Sparta.[10] Three of these six were Kardamyle,[11] on the eastern shore of the Messenian Gulf, and the two states on the island of Kythera.[12]

[1] Chrimes, op. cit., p. 435.   [2] Book III, chap. 21, § 7.

[3] See *I.G.*, vol. v, fasc. 1. No. 1160, p. 217, [Σεβασ]τοῦ Καίσαρος [υἱὸν] ἡ πόλις ἀποκατα-στήσαντα μετὰ τοῦ πατ[ρὸς] τὴν ἀρχαίαν ἐλευθερίαν. Chrimes, op. cit., p. 440, points out that the association of Tiberius with Augustus in this inscription suggests that the κοινὸν τῶν 'Ελευθερολακώνων was created at a late date in Augustus' reign. See, however, p. 412, n. 3.

[4] See also Pausanias, Book *III*, chap. 26, § 11.

[5] See also ibid., chap. 26, §§ 8–11.   [6] See also ibid., chap. 24, § 3.

[7] See p. 409.   [8] See p. 408.

[9] According to Strabo, Book VIII, chap. 4, § 11 (C. 362), the number of the cities in Laconia, excluding Sparta (i.e. the number of the ex-perioecic city-states) had dropped to about thirty from a former inclusive total of 100. One hundred was a conventional figure, but eighty are entered in Stephanus of Byzantium's gazetteer (see p. 205, n. 2). This drop in the number of states does not necessarily indicate a decline in population or even a diminu-tion in the number of inhabited towns and villages in the ex-perioecic territories. According to Isocrates, *Panathenaïcus*, 270, cited already on p. 204, n. 2, it had been Sparta's policy to keep her perioikoi divided up politically into the smallest possible units in the largest possible numbers. If so, many of these ex-perioecic states—e.g. Glympeis, Kyphanta, Polikhna— may not have proved viable as sovereign independent states. It is therefore possible, and indeed likely, that the liberation of Sparta's remaining perioecic states in 195 B.C. was followed by numerous acts of synoecism, which will have decreased the number of these states while increasing their average size. As has been noticed already on pp. 204-6, Sparta's perioikoi, unlike the Spartans, were normal Hellenes throughout their history; and, in the Hellenic World as a whole, with the exception of the Spartan homoioi and the Macedonian peasantry, the population explosion that had begun in the eighth century B.C. does not seem to have given way to the perceptible beginnings of a shrinkage in numbers till about halfway through the second century B.C.

[11] Pausanias, Book *III*, chap. 21, § 7.

[13] Ibid., chap. 26, § 7.

[12] Strabo, *Geographica*, Book VIII, chap. 5, § 1 (C. 363); Dio Cassius, Book LIV, chap. 7, § 2, *sub anno* 733 A.U.C. (21 B.C.).

Augustus' redistribution of territory in the southern Peloponnese bore hardly on Messenia. Besides being required to cede Leuktra, Alagonia, and Gerenia to the koinon of the Eleutherolakones, Messenia was also required by Augustus to cede Thouria[1] and Pharai[2] to Sparta. Thus Sparta, which had been a land-locked state since 195 B.C., now received from Augustus two frontages on the coast, one at Messenia's expense and the other (Kardamyle) at the Eleutherolakones' expense. Both these frontages were, however, on the far side of the Taÿgetos Range from Sparta, and it is noticeable that Augustus refrained from restoring to Sparta the historic Spartan port of Gythion, which offered the nearest and most convenient access to the sea for Sparta and which also lay in what had once been part of Sparta's own city-state territory. Presumably, by this date, Gythion was too important a state, and its separate civic sense had become too highly developed, for it to be feasible to deprive Gythion of the autonomy that it had been enjoying since 195 B.C.[3]

Augustus' transfer of Thouriai and Pharai from Messenia to Sparta seems to have been rescinded before Pausanias' day, since, in his day, Messenia had a common frontier with the Eleutherolakones in the Khoirios Wood, which must have stood on the banks of the Khoiros River, between Gerenia and Abia. The retrocession of Thouria and Pharai by Sparta to Messenia may have been the event that reopened the controversy over the title to possession of the Denlheliatis which was decided in Messenia's favour in A.D. 25.[4] It has been noted already[5] that the award of the Dentheliatis to Messenia by Kings Philip II and Antigonos Doson of Macedon must have carried with it the award of Pharai as well, since the Dentheliatis would have been inaccessible from Messenia if Pharai had remained in Sparta's hands. Conversely, when Augustus retransferred Pharai to Sparta, he must have retransferred to her the Dentheliatis too; and, when Pharai was handed back to Messenia again, Sparta may have tried still to retain the Dentheliatis. We have inscriptional evidence for the survey and delimitation, in A.D. 78, of the frontier between Messenia and Sparta from the temple of Artemis Limnatis, in the Dentheliatis, northwards.[6] Surviving boundary-stones

[1] Pausanias, Book IV, chap. 31, § 1.

[2] Ibid., chap. 30, § 2.

[3] A possible interpretation of *I.G.*, vol. v, fasc. 1, No. 1160, cited on p. 411, n. 3, is that Augustus had originally reunited Gythion with Sparta, but that this had been resented so strongly by the Gytheatai that eventually, at Tiberius' instance, Augustus had made Gythion a member of the κοινὸν τῶν Ἐλευθερολακώνων, thus restoring to Gythion the liberty that she had enjoyed, after 195 B.C., as a member of the κοινὸν τῶν Λακεδαιμονίων. If this interpretation of the inscription is the right one, the inscription will have been later than the original creation of the κοινὸν τῶν Ἐλευθερολακώνων, and will have been contemporaneous with the transfer, in compensation, of six Eleutherolaconian states to Sparta.

[4] See Tacitus, loc. cit.   [5] On pp. 407–8.

[6] See *I.G.*, vol. v, fasc. 1, No. 1431 (pp. 283–4), and the discussion in Chrimes, *Ancient Sparta*, pp. 61–7.

show that this frontier ran approximately parallel to the Taÿgetos Range, but to the west of the Range's crest.

There is inscriptional evidence[1] that Thalamai, on the little Pamisos River, belonged to Sparta in the reign of the Emperor Hadrian. Perhaps Thalamai had been transferred to Sparta from the Eleutherolakones as a partial compensation for Sparta's retrocession of Pharai and Thouria to Messenia. Thalamai must have belonged to Sparta in Pausanias' day, since Pausanias was travelling and writing during the reigns of Antoninus Pius and Marcus Aurelius. This suggests that Pausanias' list of eighteen Eleutherolaconian cities—a list which includes Thalamai—represents, not the membership of the koinon in Pausanias' own time, but its membership as this had stood when Augustus' redistribution of territory in the southern Peloponnese had been completed.

Supplementary Note on W. G. Forrest, A History of Sparta, 950–192 B.C. (*London, 1968, Hutchinson*)

NOWADAYS research is so active that a book may begin to fall behind the times during the interval between the latest date at which the script can still be revised and the date of publication. The present book had just not reached this point of no return when Forrest's book was published; so I have been able to take account of this book in the text and footnotes of my Part III, but not as full account there as is required; and I have therefore also added the present supplementary note.

Forrest's work is important, and this not only because of the judiciousness of its appraisement of our fragmentary, ambiguous, and inconclusive evidence, but also because of the sensitiveness with which the author feels his way into the state of mind of people whose outlook and conduct were not the same as ours. On points on which I find that my own view is the same, or nearly the same, as Forrest's, I now feel more confident that my judgement may have been right. On points on which I find that we differ, I feel more diffident. All students of Spartan history and institutions are groping in the dark. One of Forrest's many virtues is his recognition of this baffling truth. He seldom claims that his findings are certainties.

Forrest's book is, as its title indicates, mainly an historical narrative, whereas mine is mainly a study of institutions and manners and customs. Forrest has dealt with the 'Lycurgan' reform at Sparta and with the population question in excursuses. These two excursuses, together with

---

[1] *I.G.*, vol. v, fasc. 1, Nos. 1314 and 1315 (pp. 244–5).

his chapters 1–3 and 15, are the parts of his book that have the closest bearing on mine. The following notes deal with two topics, particularly relevant to the subject of my book, on which I have not been able to make adequate references to Forrest's view in the text and footnotes of my Part III.

(i) *The Date of the 'Lycurgan' Reform*

Forrest holds, as I hold, that none of the various traditional dates can be right (pp. 55 and 58), and that 700 B.C. is the *terminus post quem* (pp. 55–6 and 58). His arguments are cogent. A written rhetra cannot have been earlier than the Greeks' adoption and adaptation of the Phoenician alphabet *circa* 750 B.C. The Delphic Oracle did not win international recognition before *circa* 725 B.C. He also holds that the reform cannot be dated more exactly than within the half-century round 650 B.C. (p. 58). But, within these chronological limits, he favours a date before, not after, Sparta's crushing defeat by Argos at Hysiai in 669 B.C. and the subsequent, and probably consequent, first revolt of the Messenian helots, commonly known as the Second Spartano-Messenian War. He conjectures (p. 58) that the actual date of the 'Lycurgan' reform may have been 676 B.C., which is the date of a reorganization of the *Karneia* festival. He suggests that the festival may have been reorganized to celebrate and commemorate the reform.

Whether the 'Lycurgan' reform was earlier than or later than the Second Spartano-Messenian War is the most important question on which Forrest and I differ. I have the following comments to make.

(*a*) Forrest (pp. 59–60) rightly thinks it incredible that 'Lycurgus' could be the shadowy figure that he is if he was a real person whose lifetime fell late enough in the seventh century B.C. to make him a contemporary of Periander and Solon. I should say that 'Lycurgus's' shadowiness would be almost equally incredible if he was a real person who made history in 676 B.C. Forrest's judgement has been affected here by his acceptance of the legend, as I hold it to be, that 'Lycurgus' was a human being and not a god. The 'shadowiness' of 'Lycurgus' is, in my judgement, presumptive evidence, not that the date of the 'Lycurgan' reform cannot have been as late as the generation of Periander, but that 'Lycurgus' is not an authentic person.

(*b*) Forrest (p. 59) holds that a later date than his for the 'Lycurgan' reform is incompatible with the tradition that Kings 'Theopompos and Polydoros played an important part in Sparta's political development'. But they may have played their part during the political crisis at Sparta that was the sequel to the First Spartano-Messenian War. Forrest suggests (p. 66) that Polydoros co-operated with 'Lycurgus'. I have suggested (in the present work, pp. 220–1) that Polydoros was a contemporary of, and was in sympathy with, the fomenters of the abortive revolution at Sparta, after the First Spartano-Messenian War, that was averted by the plantation of a colony of the Spartan malcontents at Tarentum *circa* 708–706 B.C.

(*c*) Forrest has to explain why the 'Lycurgan' reform (he considers it radical enough to be called, as he does call it, a revolution) should have 'come at the end of a period of success, before Sparta's defeat by Argos at Hysiai in 669 and the Messenian revolt'. He observes that 'successful revolutions are made by men whose real power is increasing but [who] are being barred from the recognition to which they feel entitled'. But his dating of the reform compels him to guess that the barrier which the 'Lycurgan' reform removed 'will probably be no more than the persistent resistance of the established order to ever-mounting demands for change'. It seems to me to be more likely that the 'establishment's' resistance was broken by their disconcerting experience under the double ordeal of the Argive victory and the Messenian revolt.

Sparta had come within an ace of failing to subdue the revolt, and the reasons were clear. The traditional Greek conduct of war by a handful of well-armed aristocratic champions accompanied by an ill-armed rabble of commoners had proved to be out of date now that the age of phalanx-fighting had dawned. The well-armed champions, fighting individually, had been too few and too disorderly to be able to win, and the rabble had been not only ill armed but reluctant. They had had no stomach for risking their lives in order to reconquer land in which they had been given no share. The aristocrats had now realized that, if Sparta did not equip herself with a phalanx, she would go under; that, if she was to have a phalanx, the hitherto militarily ineffective mass of the Spartan people must be converted into phalanx-hoplites; that this could be done only by giving them the means and the incentive; and that this requirement, in turn, called for economic and political sacrifices on the aristocrats' part. They would have to make the commoners their peers by redividing up the reconquered Messenian land into the maximum number of allotments of a minimum size—the size that would provide, from the surplus product of its helot cultivators, just enough income to set the Spartiate rentier free to spend his whole working time on military training—and they would have to give these commoner hoplites, who would now be well endowed, well armed, and well trained, a genuine voice in the conduct of Sparta's public affairs.

The 'Lycurgan' reform of the Spartan economy, social structure, military organization, and political constitution will, in fact, have been the Spartan aristocrats' reaction to their realization that this was now the necessary condition for Sparta's survival and for theirs as well—and the Spartan aristocrats had much to lose. Even after they had shared out

the helot-inhabited lands equally with the Spartan commoners and
had given these a voice—indeed, perhaps professedly the last word—
in the taking of political decisions, the aristocrats were still privileged
politically (they probably continued to dominate the gerousia) and they
were also still privileged economically. Besides retaining kleroi in the
helot-inhabited lands, they still had their ancestral freehold estates in the
Vale of Sparta itself (Forrest, p. 51).

This case for holding that the 'Lycurgan' reform was a response to
the lesson of military defeat seems to me to be a strong one, and I do not
think that it is invalidated by Forrest's contention (p. 59), with which I
agree, that, at the start, the psychological effect of the reform, for the
commoners who had been promoted to the status of 'homoioi', was
exhilarating, not depressing. It was necessary to raise the *moral* of the
men whose military performance in the Messenian revolt had been so
poor, if these men, or their descendants, were to be transformed into
phalanx-hoplites whose *moral* could rise to the standard exemplified by
King Leonidas I's three hundred.

(*d*) My belief that the date of the 'Lycurgan' reform is later, not
earlier, than the Battle of Hysiai and the subsequent Messenian revolt is
partly based on my interpretation of Tyrtaios' account of the style of
fighting during the Messenian revolt and on my acceptance of Snodgrass's revision of Miss Lorimer's dating of the introduction of phalanx-
tactics in the Hellenic World. Forrest holds (p. 62) that 'in recent years
the political consequences of the adoption in Greece of hoplite battle
tactics may have been exaggerated, as has the suddenness of the adoption
itself'. In my judgement, Forrest is here under-estimating the cogency of
the evidence that Miss Lorimer and Snodgrass have presented.

(ii) *The Reorganization of the Lacedaemonian Army between the Years 479 and
390 B.C.*

Forrest (p. 134) agrees that, between these two dates, the organization
of the Lacedaemonian army was changed from one in which a Spartiate
homoios served in a unit correlated with his own oba to one in which
a member of any oba might be assigned to any unit. Forrest also (p. 133)
entertains the idea that this change in the military organization of the
Spartiate homoioi may have been associated with an abandonment of the
previous system under which Spartiatai and perioikoi had served in
separate units. They may now, he here agrees, have been brigaded
together in new units, the morai, in which the Spartiate complement
was smaller than the perioecic complement. He also agrees that this
conjecture is supported by the figures given by Thucydides for the Lacedaemonian force posted on Sphakteria in 425 B.C. and for the ratio of
Spartiatai to perioikoi among the survivors of this force who surrendered.

He agrees too (pp. 132–4) that Thucydides and Xenophon have under-estimated the strength of the Lacedaemonian armies that went into action in their day; they have overlooked the presence of perioikoi, as well as Spartiatai, in the Lacedaemonian army's ranks. In all these points I believe that Forrest is right. However, on p. 134, he tentatively concludes that in 418 B.C. the Spartiatai and the forgotten perioikoi were still fighting in separate units, and that the figure 700 for the number of Spartiatai present at Leuktra in 371 B.C. is a mistake for 1,700, whether the mistake was made by Xenophon himself or by some transcriber of the text of this passage of the *Hellenica*. I do not think that Forrest's emendation is warranted. The figure 700 that has come down to us is credible at a date at which many Spartiatai were serving in a civilian capacity as harmosts, or on the staffs of harmosts, in the states then under Sparta's domination (see the present work, p. 299).

PART IV

THREE LIVES

---

1. *The Role of Individuals in Human Affairs*

In human affairs the role of individuals is problematical. Individuals are the only realities. They alone do things and have things done to them. When we say that a government or a nation or a church or a company takes action or has experiences, we are talking the language of mythology. Institutions are not persons; they are networks of relations between persons; and, when we speak of them as if they were persons, we are not being true to life. It is true, however, that a particular individual is not always irreplaceable. His role is not always one that he alone can play. It is notorious that a discovery is sometimes made, or that a movement is sometimes started, by two or more individuals acting simultaneously yet independently of each other. In the nineteenth-century Western World, Charles Darwin and Russell Wallace arrived simultaneously at a non-supernatural explanation of the origin of species. In seventh-century Arabia, Muhammad and Maslamah simultaneously denounced polytheism and idolatry and preached monotheism. The explanation of these apparently accidental coincidences is, of course, that the intellectual or spiritual pioneers in question were independent of each other without being independent of the intellectual or spiritual milieu of the time and place that were their common setting; and this common setting made the particular individual expendable, however eminent and however dynamic he might be. If Darwin or Muhammad had failed to fulfil his mission—if his life had been cut short by a premature death or if he had lost his wits or his nerve—Russell Wallace and Maslamah would still have been there, and each of them would then have performed approximately the same service for his fellow human beings. Cases such as these raise the question whether there have ever been any counter-cases in which the sequel to some eminent individual's premature death has demonstrated that this individual was irreplaceable. This would be demonstrated if, in the sequel, no other individual arose to carry on to completion the work on which the dead man had been engaged at the time when his life was cut short.

A test case presents itself in the history of the west end of the Old-World Oikoumene during the hundred years ending in the second decade of the third century B.C.—a decade which, as things turned out, actually saw the close, in the year 281 B.C., of a forty-two-years-long struggle among the successors of Alexander the Great over the territorial spoils of the Persian Empire that Alexander had overthrown. Within the fifteen or sixteen years 338/7–323 B.C., three individuals, each of whom was of outstanding political potency in this part of the World, had their lives cut short suddenly and unexpectedly, one after the other, while each of them was still in mid career. In 338 or 337 B.C. the Persian Emperor Artaxerxes III Ochus was murdered by poisoning at an age that is not noted in our surviving records, but that was certainly far short of what would have been the end of his active life if he had lived to die a natural death. Philip II, the King of Macedon, was assassinated in 336 B.C. at the age of about forty-six. Philip's son Alexander the Great was carried off in 323 B.C. by a sudden fatal illness before he had reached the age of thirty-three. Would history have taken a markedly different course from the course that it did take, supposing that one or two or all three of these 'makers of history' had lived out his or their full natural term of life?

In estimating what this full term might have been, we have to make arbitrary assumptions. Let us assume that the length of Ochus' reign, if Ochus had died in his bed, would have been equal to the average length of the reigns of those of his predecessors, from Cyrus the Great onwards, who did die in their beds. There were four of these—Darius I, Artaxerxes I, Darius II, Artaxerxes II—and the average length of these four reigns is thirty-five years. Give a reign of this length to Ochus, and he dies in his bed in 325 B.C., instead of dying by poison in 338 or 337 B.C. Give Philip the age, at death, that was attained by his contemporary and right-hand man Antipater. It is reported that Antipater lived to be over eighty years old. Give Philip that age, and he will have died a natural death not earlier than 302 B.C., instead of being assassinated in 336 B.C. As for Alexander the Great, his life was cut short at an unusually early age, while a number of the Macedonian officers of his generation lived to a ripe old age—including some of those among them—e.g. Antigonus, Lysimachus, and Seleucus—who eventually met with violent ends. Let us give Alexander the average of the lifetimes of two who died peacefully, the prudent Ptolemy I, who lived to be eighty-four, and the reckless and dissolute Demetrius Poliorcetes, who managed to live to be fifty-four. This will make Alexander die at sixty-nine in 287 B.C., instead of dying, as he actually did, at thirty-three in 323 B.C.

Though these figures are arbitrary, they depart less widely from

Ochus', Philip's, and Alexander's reasonable expectations of life than the historical figures do. Let us imagine that our arbitrary figures are historical, and let us make imaginary reconstructions of the course that history might have taken if those three relatively short-lived titans had, in fact, lived on to the dates which we have found to be reasonable dates on the supposition that they had all died natural deaths.

2. *If Ochus and Philip had Lived on*

PHILIP II of Macedon had a dual personality. In his public life he was invariably self-controlled and calculating; in his private life he had fits of being undisciplined and impulsive. He enjoyed getting drunk and running after women, but he had never let this personal self-indulgence interfere with the pursuit of his military and political aims so long as he had not yet made himself master of the city-states of continental European Greece. He achieved this objective in 338 B.C., when, at Chaeronea, he utterly defeated the combined forces of Thebes and Athens. This resounding military victory enabled Philip to associate with himself all the continental European Greek states, except Sparta, in his well-built Confederation of Corinth. Meanwhile, he had been letting himself relax. At Chaeronea, on the night after the battle, he had celebrated his victory in drunken revelry. This was customary among Philip's own Macedonians, but it cheapened him in the eyes of the Macedonians' more highly cultivated fellow Greeks who, by this date, had been living for centuries under the city-state dispensation. This damage to his personal reputation could hardly be afforded by a King of Macedon who had now become the hegemon of the Hellenes. However, Philip was in a holiday mood; and, on his return to Macedon in 337 B.C., he committed a more serious personal indiscretion.

In the past, Philip had kept a series of mistresses, and this had outraged his wife, Queen Olympias. She was a proud and self-willed woman, and she was a king's daughter and a king's sister, besides being a king's wife. Her brother was Alexander, the reigning king of Epirus and her husband's ally. However, Olympias had ignored Philip's mistresses, and had taken more than her full revenge for Philip's unfaithfulness to her by making life a misery for him whenever he had tried to share his private life with her. He had not tried often, for Olympias' company did not offer him rest and change from the anxieties and exertions of his strenuous public career. Philip now went a long step farther than ever before. He let his fancy fall upon a girl whom, if he took her, he must take as his wedded wife, since her family was too distinguished to allow of her mating with Philip on any less honourable terms than that. Young Cleopatra was the niece of Attalus, a Macedonian grandee who held a high rank in the king's service. Philip now married Cleopatra, and brought on himself the family quarrel that was the inevitable consequence of this provocative act. The insulted Olympias left Macedon for her brother King Alexander's court in her native Epirus. Philip's outrageous behaviour to her might have been condoned by Macedonian public opinion (of which a king of Macedon had to take account). After all, Olympias was a foreigner, and, besides, the Macedonian aristocracy's standards of marital fidelity were not strict. What was more serious for Philip was the alienation of his and Olympias' son Prince Alexander, the heir to Philip's throne.

Philip admired and loved his son. Alexander was attached to his mother. He was also attached to his rightful heritage, and this was now in jeopardy. Philip was still young enough for a son of his by Cleopatra to come of age before Philip's death. What if Cleopatra and her ambitious uncle were to persuade Philip to transfer the succession from Olympias' to Cleopatra's child? Alexander had double cause for being indignant; and he advertised his feelings, as Olympias advertised hers, by leaving Macedon. Officially he went off on a punitive expedition against one of the unneighbourly Illyrian peoples beyond Macedon's northern border. But was he really going to chastise these Illyrians, or was he intending to recruit them for a campaign to oust his father from the throne to which Alexander's eventual succession had now become uncertain? Philip immediately realized that he had gone too far; and, since his public ambitions meant far more to him than his private escapades, he did his utmost to repair the damage that he had done to his own political interests.

There was nothing that Philip could do now about Olympias; but, to appease his brother-in-law King Alexander, he offered him the hand of his own and Olympias' daughter and King Alexander's niece, Cleopatra. This other Cleopatra was the child of a king who was now the second most powerful sovereign at the west end of the Old World, next to the reigning Persian Emperor, Artaxerxes III Ochus. Philip was the greatest man who had yet been produced by Europe in the judgement of the eminent historian Theopompus of Chios. For a king of Epirus, it was an honour to marry a daughter of Philip's, and this a legitimate daughter, not a bastard. Alexander swallowed Philip's bait; and Philip also succeeded in the more difficult task of appeasing the other Alexander, his own son. Prince Alexander responded to his father's appeal by returning to Macedon, and this in peace and not at the head of an invading Illyrian war-band. After his return, he was still sulky, and no wonder. With his mother in voluntary exile, and with a young woman of his own age enthroned in her stead, he now found his position at his father's court awkward and disagreeable. However, he had refrained from taking up arms against Philip, and Philip, on his side, in appealing to Alexander to return, had implicitly reconfirmed Alexander's succession to the throne of Macedon.

Philip now felt that he had his hands free again to take the next step in the execution of his far-reaching military and political plans. The establishment of his ascendancy over the city-states of continental European Greece, which had been accomplished in the preceding year, had not been the consummation of his ambitions. It had been a step towards embarking on a far more ambitious enterprise than any on which he had ever ventured before. Philip was planning now to weld the Confederation of Corinth and the Kingdom of Macedon together by leading them on a joint war of revenge for injuries received a century and a half ago: the temporary subjugation of Macedon during the years 492–479 B.C. and the unsuccessful invasion of Macedon's southern Greek neighbours in 480–479 B.C. In the autumn of 337 B.C. Philip launched this joint military undertaking by sending a Macedonian expeditionary force, under Attalus' command, to invade the Persian dominions on the Asian side of the Hellespont.

In making this move, Philip was challenging a formidable power. No doubt the Persian Empire had been visibly in decline ever since Xerxes' ignominious military failure. The superiority of Greek arms over the gigantic empire's total forces had been demonstrated dramatically when, in 401 B.C., 10,000 Greek mercenaries, hired by the Persian prince Cyrus, the pretender to his brother the Emperor Artaxerxes II's crown, had marched into Babylonia, the Persian Empire's central economic power-house, and had then made their way home via the Black Sea after their employer Cyrus had been killed in the battle that they had won for him at Cunaxa. Yet, in spite of this proven military inefficiency, the Persian Empire had more than once shown a surprising capacity for recuperating during Artaxerxes II's forty-four-years-long reign. In 386 B.C., for instance, Artaxerxes had successfully re-established his Empire's sovereignty over the continental Asian Greek city-states along the eastern shore of the Aegean, which had been lost to the Empire since 479 B.C. It was true that Artaxerxes had won this success mainly thanks to the chronic fratricidal warfare between the city-states of continental European Greece; and these, with the single exception of Sparta, had now been united at last under the hegemony of Macedon. However, after 386 B.C., Artaxerxes II had succeeded in putting down a concerted revolt on the part of the governors of a number of the Empire's western provinces, and this in spite of the support that the rebel governors had received from Egypt, which had seceded from the Persian Empire in 404 B.C. It was true that Artaxerxes owed his victory over the satraps to his employment of Greek mercenaries; but, for the Persian Empire, this was not necessarily a bad omen. There was still a powerful force of Greek mercenaries in Persian service, and this force was likely to be augmented by citizens of the states members of the Confederation of Corinth who had not reconciled themselves to the imposition of Macedon's hegemony on the city-states of continental European Greece.

Moreover, since 359 B.C., the lackadaisical Artaxerxes II had been replaced by a son of his, Artaxerxes III Ochus, who was made of much sterner stuff. This grim Achaemenid contemporary of Philip's would be an antagonist of Philip's own stature. While Philip had been making himself master of south-eastern Europe, Ochus had not been letting the grass grow under his feet. In 343/2 B.C., Ochus had reconquered Egypt. In 337/6 B.C., just about the time when Philip had been encountering his own domestic crisis, Ochus had discovered that his *alter ego*, the eunuch Bagoas, was plotting to poison him. Ochus had given Bagoas short shrift. Ochus had been a ready killer since his accession, when he had put his Achaemenid kinsmen to death by the dozen.[1] The Emperor was now more firmly seated on his throne than ever, and his Empire looked as if it were more solidly established than it had been at any time since 479 B.C.

Philip's plan for 336 B.C. was to enter in earnest upon a trial of strength with Ochus, but first to secure his rear by celebrating his daughter Cleopatra's marriage with his ex-brother-in-law Alexander of Epirus in grand style. During the wedding festivities a plot to assassinate Philip was detected just in time. Philip's life was saved, but his domestic crisis was re-inflamed, and this with far graver consequences than those of the preceding year.

When the foiled assassin, Pausanias, was questioned under torture, he declared that he had been acting as the agent of the ex-queen Olympias and of her son the reinstated heir apparent, Prince Alexander. In our day historians are still discussing whether Pausanias' statement was true or false. Decisive evidence is not forthcoming, and probably it never was. The allegation could well be untrue; for Pausanias had a feud of his own with Philip's new wife's uncle Attalus; and this would have provided a sufficient motive for his attempt on the life of his enemy's royal nephew-in-law. However, the question of the truth or falsity of the allegation is not material to the sequel; for Prince Alexander did not wait to have his conduct investigated. We shall never know whether he was guilty or whether, though innocent, he feared that Attalus' influence over Philip might move Philip to take Alexander's guilt for granted without proof. Prince Alexander forestalled further investigation by fleeing across the border into Epirus—and his uncle and namesake the king of Epirus fled with him, abandoning his Macedonian bride. Now that King Alexander's sister Olympias was under accusation of having plotted to have her ex-husband Philip assassinated, the king drew the same conclusion as the prince his nephew. He, too, concluded that Macedon had become too

---

[1] Q. Curtius Rufus, *Historiae Alexandri Magni*, Book X, chap. 4, § 23.

hot to hold him. The two refugees were both in a desperate mood, and Olympias knew how to work upon their feelings. Under Olympias' potent influence, the uncle and nephew hastily decided that their only practicable means of self-defence lay in taking the offensive at once. They decided to invade Macedon forthwith, with intent either to expel Philip or to kill him and, in either case, to enthrone Prince Alexander in his stead. King Alexander called up the Epirot levy. Prince Alexander went off to enlist the Illyrians with whom he had established contact in the preceding year.

In thus challenging Philip's overwhelmingly superior strength, the two Alexanders were counting on two supposed assets, neither of which materialized in the tragic event.

In the first place they hoped that the people of the Macedonian highland cantons, Parauaea, Tymphaea, Orestis, Lyncestis, and Elemiotis, which lay between Lower Macedon and Epirus, would rise to join forces with them in order to recover their lost autonomy. It was true that Philip had deprived them of an autonomy that had been their traditional prerogative, and that his reduction of them to the status of territories under the direct administration of the Macedonian crown had been resented—by the Orestae in particular. It was also true that, in some ways, the Parauaeans and Tymphaeans, at any rate, had less affinity with Macedon than they had with Epirus. However, the two Alexanders' hope of enlisting the Macedonian highlanders on their side was not fulfilled. By the time the Alexanders crossed the border, the highlanders had responded to Philip's mobilization order. Either prudence or loyalty (who knows which?) had already brought them into the ranks of the Alexanders' opponents.

The Alexanders' second hope had lain in the supposed popularity of Prince Alexander himself in Macedon. It was true that, when he had left the country in the preceding year, there had been widespread concern, and it was also true that there had been no less widespread relief when he had subsequently returned and had been reconciled with his father officially. Undoubtedly the prince's fighting qualities were highly esteemed by his fellow countrymen. Macedonians admired nothing so much as courage carried to the point of foolhardiness and then justified by strength and skill in the use of arms; and Prince Alexander had given a superb exhibition of these characteristic Macedonian military virtues in the cavalry engagement at Chaeronea. However, Prince Alexander's popularity in Macedon was subject to some serious reservations, as the event was to show. For one thing, this son of an Epirot queen was half a foreigner, and no pure-blooded Macedonian liked that. In the second place, he had become half alienated from the rustic Macedonian and Epirot Greek way of life by the sophisticated Hellenic education that his father had perversely insisted on giving him. Philip had hired a philo-sopher to be Prince Alexander's tutor, and this philosopher was a citizen of one of those colonial south-Greek city-states that had been planted along the Aegean coast of Thrace before the north-Greek Kingdom of Macedon had expanded into the adjoining hinterland. These intrusive south-Greek settlements were an eyesore to Macedonian imperialists. If Alexander's tutor Aristotle's home town had been, not Stagirus, but some city-state to the south of Tempe, the Macedonians might perhaps have disliked Aristotle rather less; but they would have disliked him in any case for his signal success in infecting his pupil the heir apparent with his own zeal for the city-state kind of Greek culture. These two blots (as they were, in Macedonian eyes) on Alexander's scutcheon were not of Prince Alexander's own making, but the prince had now committed an offence that was both deliberate and grave. Macedonian public opinion might have forgiven him for rebelling against his sire and sovereign. Cut-throat strife within the bosom of the Argead dynasty was a familiar feature of Macedonian public life. But the Macedonian prince's fellow countrymen could not forgive him for raising a band of Illyrian mer-cenaries and leading them in an invasion of Macedon. The Illyrians were barbarians and they were Macedon's hereditary national enemy. For a Macedonian to make common cause with Illyrians was high treason, and, in the heir apparent to the Macedonian throne, this crime was peculiarly heinous. It was too heinous to be redeemed by Prince Alexander's prowess as a fighting-man.

Thus the war that the two Alexanders had started had been lost by them in advance. The hostilities were brief, and the single battle in which the fighting began and ended was short, though sharp. It was fought in Elemiotis, between the Pindus Range and the Haliakmon River. The invaders found the entire man-power of Macedon arrayed against them. While Prince Alexander had been raising his Illyrians, Attalus had been ferrying his expeditionary force back from Asia to Macedon by sea. He had lost no time in commandeering the transports; his own life hung on the issue of the impending conflict on European soil. When both Attalus' troops and the highland levies had joined the Lower Macedonian levies, Philip had in hand an army that was as decisively superior to the Alexanders' army in numbers as it was in discipline, equipment, and tactics. Prince Alexander fought as furiously in Elemiotis in 336 B.C. as he had fought in Boeotia two years back. But what could a single paladin do? The Illyrian and Epirot horsemen were both few and poor in quality. Furiously though the prince fought, he was taken prisoner.

This operation cost valuable Macedonian lives, but no Macedonian subject was willing to assume the responsibility for taking the life of King Philip's son and heir. When the prince was brought, bound, into his father's presence, Philip immediately killed him with his own hand. Philip dared not leave his traitor son alive, and no other Macedonian except the traitor's sovereign and father dared to serve as executioner. In doing this gruesome deed, Philip was setting a bad example for peers of his in later ages. The consequences for the succession to the throne were ironical. Shortly before the detection of Pausanias' plot, Queen Cleopatra of Macedon had borne her first child, but it had been a girl. The only grown male heir to the throne now alive was one who was juridically the reigning monarch. This was Philip's nephew and ward Amyntas IV, who, while still a minor, had been elbowed off the throne by Philip not long after the death of Amyntas' father and Philip's elder brother and predecessor Perdiccas III. Philip had spared his nephew's life and had allowed him to attain manhood; and now Philip had taken the life of his own son. His hope must be that Cleopatra's next child would be a boy, and that Philip himself would live on long enough for this boy to have come of age before Philip's own death. Philip's heart was heavy, but his hands were free again.

What had Ochus been doing while this unexpected tragedy was being played out on the European side of the Hellespont? In sending Attalus' expeditionary force into Persian territory in the autumn of 337 B.C., Philip had shown his hand; and, when the force was hastily withdrawn, Ochus cannot have had any illusions. He will have realized that, whatever might be the outcome of the impending conflict in Europe, the impending Macedonian assault on his Empire had merely been postponed without being cancelled. Why, then, did Ochus not seize the opportunity that the outbreak of war between Philip and the Alexanders might seem to have offered him? Why did he not send a counter-expeditionary force of his own into Europe, to tip the balance against Philip in the struggle there? If Philip had been defeated by the Alexanders with Ochus' help, Philip's only recourse would have been to throw himself on Ochus' mercy and to seek asylum on Persian soil as a suppliant; and for Artaxerxes III this would have been as great a stroke of good fortune as it had been for Artaxerxes I when Themistocles had come knocking at his palace door. To grant one's arch-enemy asylum is to put salt on his tail. Yet, in 336 B.C., Ochus did not intervene in Europe; and, in refraining, he showed a good understanding of the principles of strategy.

When Cyrus the Great and Cambyses had extended the Persian dominions westward to the shores of the Black Sea and the Aegean and the eastern Mediterranean, they had been performing a logistical *tour de force*. The means of communication at man's command in this age were not good enough to allow a power whose reservoir of trustworthy manpower lay in western Iran to operate with safety anywhere to the west of the River Euphrates. This had been the lesson of the military reverses with which Darius I and Xerxes I had met when they had attempted to expand their dominions in this quarter still farther. Moreover, in their day Macedon had been puny, whereas she had grown, by now, to be a giant. With these cogent considerations in mind, Ochus resisted the temptation to hazard a European adventure. He used his reprieve, instead, to build up his defences on the west; and he was wise enough to build them in depth. He concentrated his efforts on fortifying and garrisoning the east bank of the Euphrates. A Persian army posted there would have the granary of Babylonia immediately to its rear, and the man-power reservoir of western Iran immediately behind Babylonia.

Ochus was now expecting Philip's attack to be delivered in 335 B.C.; but in this year, again, and in the following year, too, the attack did not materialize. Philip, too, understood logistics; he realized, as clearly as Ochus himself did, the difficulties with which Ochus would meet if he were to take the offensive. Philip calculated that Ochus would hold back, and he concluded that his own eastern plans could wait while he turned his arms, first, in the very opposite direction. In taking this decision, Philip was taking a calculated risk; for an invasion of Macedon overland was not the only possibility of damaging Macedon that Ochus had at his command. In this age, ships and gold were much more mobile than land-forces were, and ships and gold could make mischief in Macedon's 'soft under-belly', the southern part of continental European Greece. Though all the city-states, save one, in continental European Greece were now members of the Confederation of Corinth, many of them were disaffected towards Philip, and one of them, Sparta, had refused outright to accept Philip's hegemony. Persian gold, followed up by Persian ships, might give Philip trouble in this quarter at any time, so long as the Persian Empire possessed a seaboard somewhere on the Mediterranean or on any of its backwaters. This was a logistically feasible form of counter-offensive for Ochus; and, in fact, he had been considering it carefully. He had found, however, that he had not the time or the money for both intervening in southern Greece and fortifying the line of the Euphrates. So Ochus chose to play for safety, as Philip had expected that he would.

For the moment, therefore, Philip turned his back on Ochus in order to finish dealing with King Alexander of Epirus. The king had eluded the fate that had overtaken the prince his nephew and namesake. He had fled back from the battlefield south-westwards over Pindus, but Philip gave him no respite. He invaded, occupied, and annexed Alexander's kingdom, and drove King Alexander himself into the sea. After all, King Alexander had been guilty of gross ingratitude towards Philip, not to speak of egregious folly. He owed his throne to Philip, and a kingmaker has the power to unmake a king whom he has made. Olympias disdained to share either her brother's or her son's fate. She neither fled nor waited to be taken prisoner. She committed suicide, and so spared her ex-husband the odium of putting her to death. As for the peoples of Epirus—Thesprotians, Chaones, and King Alexander's own clansmen the Molossians—they acquiesced in the change of regime. King Alexander's ludicrous military fiasco had shattered his personal prestige at home; and the Epirot peoples had little feeling of national identity or solidarity. The Epirot nation was still in the inchoate stage of formation in which the Macedonian nation had been before Philip's accession to the Macedonian throne. Like the Macedonian highlanders, the Epirots resigned themselves to coming under the direct rule of the Macedonian crown. This crown's dominions now stretched right across northern continental European Greece from the Aegean to the Ionian Sea.

Meanwhile, King Alexander had taken ship across the Straits of Otranto. At Hydrus, Tarentum's naval station at the point of the 'heel' of Italy, he had inquired whether Tarentum would give him asylum. He received a quick refusal. Tarentum could not afford to be quixotic. She was now standing at bay against the rising Oscan powers in her hinterland. Nothing could save her now but military and political support from continental European Greece. She had appealed first to her parent-state Sparta; and Archidamus III of Sparta had fought Tarentum's battles on Italian soil for five years. In 338 B.C. he had died fighting in Italy, at about the time when Philip was invading Laconia and was punishing Sparta for her obstinate unco-operativeness by mulcting her of slices of her territory and presenting these to her more accommodating neighbours and hereditary enemies Argos, Megalopolis, and Messene. How could Tarentum now venture to offend a man who held the whole of continental Greece except Sparta in the hollow of his hand? The fugitive king of Epirus therefore sailed on up the north-east coast of peninsular Italy till he reached the Adriatic seaboard of the Samnite Confederation, and here his request for asylum was not rejected. In 336 B.C., Samnium stretched from coast to coast in southern Italy, as Macedon now did in northern Greece. Samnium had a frontage on both the Adriatic and the Tyrrhene Sea. She was the largest, most populous, and most powerful state in all Italy at this time, and she was not afraid of anybody, least of all of any Greeks. When King Alexander arrived at Bovianum in the autumn of 336 B.C., the Samnite Federal Government told him that if at some future date he were to seek to reconquer his kingdom he would be free to recruit as many Samnite volunteers as he could afford to hire.

This piece of news did not take long to reach Philip's ears. His intelligence service had always been good. Philip also learnt through the same channel that the war which was now being waged in central Italy might be decisive for the destiny of the whole Italian peninsula. The year before, Rome's former allies, the Latin and Campanian confederations, which had already been at war with Samnium, had rashly gone to war with Rome as well. Consequently Rome and Samnium had made common cause and had jointly compelled the Campanians to lay down their arms. Samnium was now leaving it to Rome to deal with the Latins, and it looked as if the Latins were going to be crushed in the coming year 335 B.C. if the Italians were left to fight out their own battles by themselves. Latium was a confederation of small city-states; Rome was a large unitary city-state; and this solid political structure gave Rome a decisive military advantage. If the Latins, as well as the Campanians, were now to be eliminated from the Italian arena, Rome and Samnium would be left face to face. Presumably they would clash; and then the prize of victory in the struggle between them would be the hegemony over all Italy and over who knows how much more of the World besides. After considering this information, Philip decided to intervene in Italy. He decided to intervene in force, and this in the next campaigning season, namely the year 335 B.C. It looked like a case of now or never. The year 334 B.C. might be too late.

In taking this decision Philip was moved by more motives than one. He wanted to dissipate the gathering clouds in the West; he wanted to put his brother-in-law and son-in-law King Alexander quite out of action; and he wanted to bind the Epirots and the Spartans to himself. Like other *Realpolitiker* in later ages, Philip reckoned that the quickest and surest way of turning the enemy of yesterday into a friend is to enlist him as an ally against a third party. Philip planned to wage his Italian war mainly with Epirot and Spartan forces; and he knew what would be the telling appeals. To the Spartans he offered a prospect of avenging King Archidamus' death, and to both the Spartans and the Epirots he promised generous allotments of expropriated Samnite and Roman land.

This promise of land to the Spartans was astute; for Sparta had been having, for the last third of a century, to contend with a land-problem that had been insoluble hitherto. The liberation of Messene from Spartan rule after the Spartan disaster at Leuctra in 371 B.C. had deprived Sparta of the land-allotments in Messenian territory which had previously made it possible for all the Spartan 'peers' to serve as full-time soldiers. Since then, Sparta had been burdened with a new proletariat of pauperized 'peers' who were now disqualified for military service because they no longer held their former Messenian allotments. These beggared Spartans had been demanding that new allotments should be provided for them by dividing up the large estates in the Eurotas valley that were owned by a small minority of the Spartan citizen-body. Philip's present offer promised to relieve the rich Spartan landowners from the menace of a γῆς ἀναδασμός at their expense by opening up for their impoverished fellow citizens the prospect of obtaining alternative new land-allotments overseas. If this prospect were to materialize, the rich minority at Sparta would retain the ownership of its lands at the military price of seeing Sparta's reservoir of soldiers, which was already in low water, now virtually run dry. This would reduce Sparta to political impotence; and that would suit Philip's book. But the rich minority could be relied upon to put its personal economic interest above the public interest if it were compelled to make the choice; and it had the power to make it, because it controlled the government. So Philip's proposals were favourably received at Sparta, as well as in Epirus, and, therewith, Philip's coming battle in Italy was already half won.

The Italian campaign of 335 B.C. was conducted by Philip on lines that he had not tried before. He mobilized all the naval contingents of the states members of the Confederation of Corinth, and this fleet was a hostage as well as a weapon. Like the Ionian Greek fleet that Darius I had once taken with him to the Danube, Philip's European Greek fleet was a material guarantee for the good behaviour of the states from which it had been levied. At the same time the fleet was a weapon for taking the Romans and the Samnites by surprise. In the spring of 335 B.C., Spartan and Epirot troops—and Macedonian troops as well—were taken on board ship and were landed at a number of points along the coasts of south-eastern Italy. There were landings at Tarentum, Thurii, Croton, Caulonia, Paestum, Neapolis, Cumae, Circeii, and Antium, as well as at Sipontum on the Adriatic side. Since Philip held the command of the sea, the Samnites were at a loss to know which of these landings were serious and which were feints. They concentrated their forces in the passes through the mountains that were Samnium's natural rampart over against Campania. They were then taken in the rear by a powerful force that had landed at Sipontum and had thrust its way into Samnium across Samnium's open frontier over against Apulia. As for Rome, the city was found undefended by the force that had landed at Antium. The Roman army was away, besieging Praeneste. Caught between the Latin levy and the Macedonian force that had occupied Rome, the Roman army was compelled to capitulate. The war was over, and the military decision was confirmed in the peace-settlement.

The Italiot Greek states now joined the Confederation of Corinth. The Calabrians, Peucetians, Apulians, Campanians, and Latins became the Confederation's and Macedon's permanent allies. The whole of the territory of the Bruttii was expropriated (more than half of it had been Italiot Greek territory as recently as twenty years ago). Half the territory of the Lucanians, and, in Samnium, the territory of the Hirpini and the

Caudini, was expropriated too. The Caudine city-states were now incorporated in the Campanian Confederation. The rest of the expropriated Oscan lands were earmarked for allotment to Spartan and Epirot colonists, while the evicted Oscan population was told to stand by for eventual deportation to an overseas destination that was not yet disclosed. Philip dealt with Rome as Epameinondas had dealt with Sparta. Epameinondas had crippled Sparta by reconstituting an independent state of Messene and by synoecizing the little cantons of south-western Arcadia into the new city-state of Megalopolis. Philip reduced Rome's territory by reconstituting both Alba Longa and Veii. The resurgent Alba Longa was incorporated in the Latin Confederation, and with it went the presidency of the festival of Iuppiter Latiaris. The resurgent Veii took its place again in the association of Etruscan city-states. The rump of the Ager Romanus, including the City of Rome itself, was handed over to a colony of Macedonian veterans. There was no need to change the city's name. In Greek, ῥώμη means 'strength', and the colonization of the site by Macedonian Greeks showed how strong the Greek World was when it was united. The Roman people was deported *en masse* to the Italian shore of the Adriatic. They were dumped in the territory of the Senonian Gauls, who were evicted to make room for them. Henceforward the expatriated Romans were to guard the north-eastern approach to peninsular Italy against the great Gallic World beyond Ariminum. These measures won for Philip the goodwill of all Italians except, of course, the Senones, the Romans, and the Oscan highlanders. The Senones had been a thorn in Italy's flesh; the Romans' and the Samnites' political ambition had been a threat to the Italian peoples' independence. The Etruscans were particularly delighted with the Romans' and the Senones' fate. The Etruscans, too, now became Philip's allies, and, therewith, the whole of peninsular Italy had been brought within Philip's sphere of influence.

Philip's new Italian allies showed their gratitude to him by sending contingents to join the army that was to invade the Persian Empire in 333 B.C. (The Italian campaign had occupied the year 335 B.C., and the following year had been spent on working out the Italian peace-settlement.) The Asian campaign of 333 B.C. was as swift and as decisive as the Italian campaign had been. Things did not go as Ochus had expected. Though Ochus had sited his main line of defence as far east as the east bank of the Euphrates, he had had no intention of surrendering his western provinces. He had reckoned that Philip would get bogged down in western Anatolia, as Agesilaus had got bogged down there, two-thirds of a century back. Ochus had also reckoned that a revolt of European Greek city-states in Philip's rear would force him to evacuate Asia in his turn. Ochus does not seem to have remembered the Ten Thousand's escapade; and Philip's thirty thousand were much more mobile than Cyrus' Ten Thousand had been. Like a whirlwind the invading army swept across Anatolia and over the Antitaurus and the Taurus. The left wing kept to the north of the central Anatolian desert and marched up the Persian Empire's Great North-West Road till they reached the west bank of the River Euphrates at Melitene. The right wing kept to the south of the desert and marched up the Little North-West Road through the Cilician Gates and the Amanus Gates till they reached the west bank of the Euphrates at Carchemish. The campaigning season was still young. What next?

At a council of war held at Hierapolis, an aggressive officer named Antigonus spoke vehemently in favour of delivering a general assault on Ochus' fortified line across the river. 'The Euphrates is the enemy's last ditch', Antigonus shouted. 'Take the Euphrates line by storm, and the whole Persian Empire will be ours up to the Oxus and the Indus.' Philip dismissed the council and continued the debate with an inner conclave consisting of Antipater, Parmenio, and Ptolemy—an officer who was as cautious an Antigonus was impulsive, though Ptolemy was Antigonus' junior by as much as twenty-three years. When these four put their heads together, they found immediately that they were all of one mind. Antigonus' proposal was unsound. Supposing that they did accept the casualties that it would cost them to break through Ochus' Euphrates line, they would be plunging into infinity and so be risking eventual disaster. Northern Syria, as well as everything north-west of it, must be held. This was unquestionable; for a power installed in northern Syria would command the interior lines. But thus far and no farther, neither eastward nor even southward.

So, once again, the fighting was over. This time both the opposing forces were still in the field; but it was not a stalemate; for, at the news that Philip had reached the Euphrates, the Egyptians had risen against the Persians and had placed on their throne a member of the Egyptian dynasty that Ochus had overthrown ten years back. Philip now sent them a small force by sea to help them to mop up the Persian garrisons. When this had been done, the Macedonian force was withdrawn at once. Philip made it clear to the Egyptians that he had no intention of trying to step into Ochus' shoes. An independent Egypt was just what would suit him; for, to the south of northern Syria, his policy was a purely negative one. His sole concern in this quarter was to see to it that the Persian Empire should not retain any seaboard on the Mediterranean and should therefore no longer have it in its power to send subversive ships and gold to Greece. The new Egyptian national government took the point of this policy of Philip's, and it showed its appreciation of it by sending supplies of cereals to the Macedonian army in north Syria.

F f

The Phoenician states, which lay between north Syria and Egypt, did not share the Egyptians' anti-Persian feelings. The Persians had always treated the Phoenician states well. They had given them not only autonomy but also miniature empires of their own in Philistia and in Coele Syria. The Phoenicians could not, of course, do anything to help Ochus now that the Macedonian army had cut Phoenicia's communications with the Euphrates line. Philip did not try to force the Phoenicians' hand, but, when they asked him to recognize their independence and to respect their territorial integrity, he readily agreed.

Ochus was a realist. He accepted facts, however unpalatable. After having recovered a lost dominion, he had lived to lose it again, and this time, probably, to lose it for ever. The loss of Egypt—the dissident province that he himself had reconquered—tormented Ochus more than the loss of Anatolia and Syria. Nevertheless, he now opened peace *pourparlers* with Philip, and an agreement was quickly reached. Philip, for his part, knew just what he wanted and what he did not want; Ochus proposed that the new frontier between the two empires should follow the line of the Euphrates to the point at which the Euphrates sheers off south-eastward toward Babylonia, and this was the frontier that Philip already had in mind. The only additional stipulation that Philip put forward was that the independence of the Phoenician and other south Syrian states and the independence of Egypt should be recognized and guaranteed by Ochus and himself in identical terms. Ochus did not demur; for, with Macedon entrenched in north Syria, the Persian Empire would have no hope of recovering any of its former territories to the south and south-west of that.

The evicted south-east Italian highlanders now learnt where their new habitat was to be. Philip planted them on the west bank of the Euphrates along the whole length of his new eastern frontier. This was a big operation, but Philip commanded the resources for carrying it out, now that, for the moment, he had no other enterprise on hand. He kept the whole of the year 332 B.C. free for this. He was able to give generous allotments of Asian land to his Oscan deportees, since much of this region had been only sparsely inhabited hitherto. However, he did not give land-allotments to all of them. While they had been waiting in concentration camps to learn what was to be their fate, Philip had had them 'screened', and he had had a secret roster made of those among them who seemed likely to prove irreconcilable. After the deportees' arrival at the Euphrates, he kept this militant minority of them under guard, while he inquired of Ochus whether Ochus would appreciate the gift of a force of first-class fighting-men who were expendable. Ochus joyfully accepted Philip's offer. The Central Asian nomads had always been a menace to the Persian Empire's north-east frontier. The founder, Cyrus the Great, had met his death in an unsuccessful attempt to push the nomads back. At the news of Ochus' reverse in the west, the nomads, like the Egyptians, had gone on the warpath. Expendable Oscan troops could be thrown into the breach and might perhaps turn the tide. The Oscan expendables were now ferried across the Euphrates, and Philip threw in with them a last-minute offer of an expendable commander for them. Whom should he send? Should he send the ex-King Alexander of Epirus? Or should he send Antigonus? Philip decided that Antigonus should be the victim. This Macedonian officer's ability was equalled by his ambition, and those two qualities, in combination, might get the better of his loyalty. The elimination of Antigonus would be an irreparable loss, but it might also be a good riddance. Ex-King Alexander, on the other hand, did not need to be liquidated. He had ceased to be a danger, for by this time he had discredited himself irretrievably. (After the rout of the Samnites at Maluentum, King Alexander had deserted from their ranks and had thrown himself at Philip's feet.) Moreover, the ex-king was Philip's ex-brother-in-law and son-in-law, and Philip was not in the habit of putting his near relatives to death except when there was no alternative, as in the case of his son Prince Alexander. For instance, he had not taken the life of his nephew King Amyntas IV. So Antigonus was Philip's choice; and Antigonus and his Oscan Myrmidons were ferried across the Euphrates together unarmed, for their new employer, Ochus, to equip them. Nothing more was ever heard of them by anyone to the west of the Euphrates; but it did transpire that, in the years immediately following the conclusion of the Perso-Macedonian peace-settlement, Ochus had succeeded in re-establishing his control over Farghāna and over Khwārizm; so presumably Antigonus and his men had been expended on that.

The intention behind Philip's gift of Antigonus and his Oscan troops to Ochus had been to keep Ochus occupied at the Persian Empire's opposite end. This diversion was required by Philip's plans, for Philip now had another job to do in the West.

At the time of Philip's Italian campaign of 335 B.C., the Siceliot Greeks' affairs were in better shape than they had been at any previous time within memory. This had been thanks to the statesmanship of the Siceliots' disinterested Corinthian saviour Timoleon, who had done so much better for them than King Archidamus III of Sparta had done for the Italiots. Timoleon had seemed to have found a cure for the Siceliot Greeks' chronic and ruinous fratricidal strife. He had devised for them a federal constitution on the Boeotian and Chalcidian pattern. Every Siceliot Greek, and every Hellenized Sicel too, now became a citizen of Syracuse while also continuing to be a citizen of his own local city-state. This constitution worked smoothly till after Timoleon's abdication, and indeed until after his death. What kept the Siceliots and the Sicels in harmony with each other was a common veneration for Timoleon's personality; but by the year 333 B.C. the Timoleontic constitution, now bereft of its maker, was beginning to show signs of strain. The Sicels, in particular, were complaining that the juridical parity with the Syracusans that the constitution had secured for them in theory was not being given to them in practice.

While Philip was still in camp on the Euphrates, he received a call from Sicily to come over and help her people to re-do what Timoleon had done; and Philip agreed on two conditions. One was that each of the Siceliot and Sicel states should severally join the Confederation of Corinth on a footing of perfect equality with every other state-member. Philip's second condition was that the combined forces of the Hellenic World should now expel the Carthaginians, once for all, from all their beach-heads at the western end of Sicily. The terms were agreed in 333 B.C. and were executed within the next two years. It took these two years for the Panhellenic army of liberation to reduce the massive Carthaginian fortresses at Heraclea Minoa and Lilybaeum. When once this military objective had been attained, peace was made as quickly and as easily as it had been made previously on the Euphrates. The peace-making was easy because Philip had a genius for setting himself limited aims and for stopping resolutely when he had attained them. Out of consideration for his allies the Etruscans, Philip did insist that the island of Corsica should now be neutralized. But he made no move to deprive Carthage of Sardinia's ores and cereals; he emphatically disclaimed all intention of trespassing on Carthage's preserves in Africa; and he turned a deaf ear when the Massaliots importuned him to expel the Carthaginians from Spain and to close the Straits of Gibraltar to Carthaginian shipping.

Philip was determined to refrain from any exploitation of his victory in Sicily that might spur the Carthaginians to launch a war of revenge. Philip wanted to be quit of further western complications; for, east of the Straits of Otranto, he had still enough work in prospect to occupy the rest of his life—and this on the assumption that, having escaped the assassin's blade in 336 B.C., he was now going to go on living to the end of his life's natural span.

Philip's first task was to organize what he held and, in particular, to consolidate his hold on what he had conquered in Asia in 333 B.C. His relation with the Confederation of Corinth presupposed that the Confederation and his Kingdom were partners of approximately equal strength. But, since 338 B.C., the balance had been inclined in the Confederation's favour by the admissions to it of the Italiot, Asian, and Siceliot Greeks and the Sicels; and the numerous and populous non-Greek and semi-Greek city-states of Italy, Caria, Lycia, and Pamphylia were also in the same relation to Macedon as the Confederation of Corinth was.

The Asian Greeks had been admitted to the Confederation *en bloc* during the first weeks of the Asian campaign. To right the balance, Philip annexed to Macedon all territory in Anatolia and in north Syria that was not already included in the domain of some autonomous Greek or non-Greek city-state; but at the same time he laid down the principle that, in Asia west of Euphrates, the royal territory was gradually to decrease and the city-state territory to increase. He actively promoted the planting of new colonial Greek city-states in three Asian areas in particular. North Syria was given the first priority in this colonization scheme; the second priority went to the hinterland of the ancient Greek city-states along the eastern shore of the Aegean; Cilicia—the half-way house between north Syria and Ionia—came third. In planting these Greek colonies, care was taken to avoid inflicting more than the inevitable minimum of hardship on the existing population. For the most part, this population was left undisturbed. There were, however, two apparently irreclaimable Anatolian peoples whose depredations on their neighbours had been tolerated by the easy-going Persian regime. These were the Pisidians on their jagged mountains and the Bithynians among their brush-clad hills. Philip was more severe. He uprooted both peoples from their Anatolian homes and transplanted them to the drier half of the territory of the Boian Gauls, between the Appennines and the River Po.

In organizing and consolidating Ciseuphratean Asia, Philip could not afford to slacken his pace; for, in Transeuphratean Asia, Ochus was organizing and consolidating too. Ochus was not too proud to learn from his victorious enemy, and Philip, in his turn, was not too proud to learn from Ochus. It had become manifest to Ochus that the major weakness in the Persian Empire's internal structure hitherto had been the size of the provinces and the consequent power of their governors. Darius had sought to reduce the governors' power by providing that the provincial secretaries and the commandants of the local fortresses should deal direct with the Imperial Government over the provincial governors' heads; but these would-be checks and balances had proved ineffective. Ochus now set about gradually substituting new city-state units of local government for the existing provinces. Babylonia had been a cluster of city-states for more than 2,500 years past. Ochus abolished the province of Babylonia forthwith and made the Babylonian city-states autonomous. He planned to extend this administrative reform to Iran and to Persian Central Asia. This was a land of oases, and an oasis offers a natural setting for a city-state.

This last chapter in killer Ochus' career was heroic, for he had to defend his own life while he was reorganizing his realm. Ochus' great reverse in 333 B.C. had given the signal for a rapid series of further attempts to take his life. He detected and forestalled each of these plots in turn. Each time, dozens of lives were taken, and no doubt many innocent people were liquidated along with the guilty. It was horrible; but something more than Ochus' personal security was at stake; he had the regeneration of his Empire to live for. In spite of his crimes, Ochus lives in his countrymen's memory as the greatest of all the emperors of the Achaemenian line. They believe that it is thanks to Artaxerxes III Ochus that the empire which Cyrus the Great founded is still a going concern today. The Persian Empire has survived, so present-day Persians hold, thanks to Ochus' wisdom and foresight in consolidating it within frontiers that are not too far-flung—the historic frontiers along the Rivers Jaxartes, Indus, and Euphrates.

The greatest of Ochus' feats was to manage to die in his bed. He died in 325 B.C., and his death released Philip from his Asian preoccupations. Not that Philip's relations with Ochus had been bad. So far from that, the two monarchs had followed up the peace-settlement of 333 B.C. by co-operating constructively. When they had jointly surveyed the northern branch of the Euphrates up to its source, they had been faced with the question of where the frontier was to run beyond this point. Provisionally they had left this question open. They had simply agreed that the Caspian Sea was to be a Persian lake and the Black Sea a Macedonian one, and that the defence of the passes through the Caucasus against raids by nomads from the steppes was to be the joint responsibility of the two powers.

What interested Philip in Ochus' reorganization of the Persian Empire's internal structure was the demonstration, in the oases of Iran, that the city-state way of life could be adopted successfully by peoples to whom this social dispensation was not native. The Macedonians, as well as the Iranians, were in this category. In their language the Macedonians were Greeks, but in their way of life they were Greeks of the Mycenaean Age rather than of the Hellenic Age, in which the master-institution of the Greek World had come to be the city-state. In consequence, the city-state Greeks looked upon the Macedonian Greeks as being semi-barbarians, while the Macedonians' attitude towards the city-state Greeks was ambivalent. The sense of superiority that the Macedonians paraded betrayed the sense of inferiority that underlay it.

Philip determined to educate his Macedonians into becoming city-state Greeks of just as high a quality as the Athenians or the Milesians. This policy of acculturation was, indeed, an indispensable accompaniment of Philip's policy of expansion in Europe. Before he had won his victory at Chaeronea and had founded the Confederation of Corinth, Philip had annexed to Macedon the adjoining Thracian peoples as far eastward as the western shore of the Black Sea and as far northward as the south bank of the Lower Danube. He now embarked on the more arduous enterprise of subjugating and assimilating the Illyrians, whose domain stretched away from Macedon's western and north-western borders into the heart of Europe. This was the quarter in which barbarism was within the closest range of Macedon's heart. Even the semi-barbarian Kingdom of Paeonia, int he upper part of the Axius basin, was attached to Macedon, so far, merely by a loose alliance. The Thracians and Illyrians could not be expected to feel any impulse to transform themselves into Macedonians unless and until the Macedonian way of life had come to be unmistakably superior to theirs, and it would not come to be that unless and until the Macedonians themselves had adopted the Hellenic city-state culture. Moreover, if south-eastern Europe, as well as Anatolia and north Syria, was to be captivated by Macedon and by Hellenism, this region too must be sown thick with Greek city-states. In Macedon's European hinterland these Greek colonies must become integral parts of Macedon itself. The Kingdom could not agree to letting itself be encircled by the Confederation of Corinth; and this would be its fate if Greek colonies on Illyrian soil were to be allowed to join the Confederation instead of their being incorporated in Macedon. At the same time, Greek colonists for Illyricum would not be forthcoming if their destiny was to be absorbed into a Macedon that would still be living under the pre-city-state dispensation. For city-state Greeks, this would be tantamount to forfeiting their birthright, and they would not be willing to do that. Since Greek colonization in Illyricum would be indispensable for the reclamation of the Illyrians that Philip had in view, the only possible solution was that Macedon herself should now become an integral part of the Hellenic city-state world.

The reclamation of Illyricum was the task to which Philip devoted himself during the twenty-three years that elapsed between Ochus' death in 325 B.C. and Philip's own death in 302 B.C. On his death-bed, Philip dictated a Laconic political testament for his successor: 'The future of the Hellenic World lies up the Danube, not down the Euphrates.'

Philip's successor was not Amyntas IV, though this nephew of Philip's was then still alive. It was Philip's son Amyntas V (called, like his cousin, after their common grandfather, King Amyntas III; the name 'Alexander' had, of course, become tabu for the Argeadai since Prince Alexander's tragic end; and, in any case, this ancient Argead family name might have lost its traditional glamour for the Argeadai now that they had become familiar with the *Iliad*, in which a Trojan Alexander is world-famous as the villain of the piece). Amyntas V's mother was Queen Cleopatra of Macedon. It was lucky for her that her second child had been a boy. This boy had been born in 334 B.C., while Philip was still away in Italy, making the peace-settlement there after the war of 335 B.C. Amyntas V at his accession was thus already thirty-two years old. So long as Amyntas IV lived, Amyntas V would be juridically a usurper, as Philip had been throughout his reign. But he, in his turn, refrained from taking the life that Philip had spared. Amyntas IV had fairly earned his exemption from being put to death; for he had accepted his destiny without making a nuisance of himself. Since he had been debarred from becoming a soldier or a statesman, he had become a scholar. When Aristotle had been serving as tutor to Amyntas IV's cousin Prince Alexander of unhappy memory, the older boy had listened in, and, after Aristotle had left Pella, he had kept in touch with Aristotle by correspondence. This had brought on him a disappointment that he had felt more keenly than his ouster from the throne. After Aristotle had opened his academy at Athens, Amyntas IV had asked Philip for his permission to become a student at the Peripatos, and Philip had refused to give it. From Philip's point of view, this refusal was not unreasonable. It was one thing to spare his royal nephew's life; it would be quite another thing to allow him to expose himself to being led by the nose by fanatically Philippophobe Athenian politicians. For Philip, this was plain prudence; for Amyntas it was hard lines.

When we survey our present-day World, do we see any of Philip's and Ochus' handiwork in it? Well, we are living in a global society in which the social cells are city-states. Though the society is global in the uniformity of its structure and of its culture, it is not united politically under a single World-Government. Politically, the World's city-states are organized in a number of regional associations, each of which is independent of the others. We pride ourselves on their being able to remain independent of each other without their ever going to war with each other, and surely we are indebted to Philip and Ochus for this. It was these two statesmen who set for their successors a standard of moderation that was so high that no statesman, since their time, has had the face to descend below it.

The city-state structure of society and the grouping of the city-states in regional associations that keep the peace with each other—these are enduring monuments of the two great men's deliberate policy. But we also have to credit them with two other salient features of present-day society which Ochus and Philip created by inadvertence. Today the whole World worships the local god of Jerusalem and the whole World uses the Aramaic language as its lingua franca. The language and the religion have conquered the World together, as we know; and this opportunity, which they have jointly seized, has been given to them by Ochus' agreement with Philip that the states of southern Syria should be independent and neutral. Shall our verdict be that, while what Philip and Ochus did deliberately is good, what they did inadvertently is still better?

3. *If Alexander the Great had Lived on*

IT was just dawn on the third morning after the night on which—not for the first time—the King had made himself ill by a characteristic disregard of the limits of what flesh and blood can stand. Perdiccas and Eumenes and Ptolemy were already in the anteroom of the garden palace[1] across the river. They had come from their quarters in the City of Babylon to get an early medical bulletin. They had entered on tiptoe, but the physicians had heard them, and one of them put his head through the curtains that separated the anteroom from the bedroom. By the look on the doctor's face, they could see at once that he was feeling some appreciable relief from the anxiety under which everyone had been labouring for the last two days and three nights.

'So the fever has abated, has it?' Perdiccas asked. 'Why no', the physician answered; 'he had constant fever all night.[2] It is the worst night that he has had since he was taken ill three nights ago. In fact, those of us who have been attending him since he came to the throne have never seen him so ill before, and that is saying much.' 'Then what are you looking so happy about?' said Perdiccas testily (everyone's nerves were taut by now). 'This is no time for mystifications. Kindly tell us the truth.' 'Why, the truth is that our patient has given us a chance—the first time in all his hair-raising medical history.' 'And what do you mean by that?' Perdiccas asked. 'I think I can guess', said Ptolemy. 'Am I right, doctor? The patient has agreed to obey your orders?' 'Well, how did you guess that? It sounds like divination; but, as I know, Ptolemy, that you are an agnostic, it must be just sheer intellectual power. You should have taken up medicine instead of soldiering. You have the brains for it. Yes, that is precisely it. Forty minutes ago, he gave in. This gruelling night has been too much, even for Alexander. By now he could hardly speak above a whisper, but he used all the voice that was left to him to say that, from now on, he is going to do whatever we tell him. And this from Alexander! And unsolicited! It is unprecedented; it is a portent; naturally it gives us hope.' 'Then what orders have you given him?' Eumenes asked. 'Well, we lost no time over that. Make hay while the sun shines. Our orders were: Till further notice from us, there are to be no more baths, no more solid meals, and, above all, no more conferences with any of you about this wretched Arabian expedition; the sailing-date is postponed indefinitely.' 'And what was his reaction?' 'He took it like a lamb,

---

[1] Arrian, *Alexandri Anabasis*, Book VII, chap. 25, § 3.　　　[2] Ibid., § 4.

and we followed up our victory in proper Alexandrine style. We wrote it all down on a loose papyrus-sheet and got his seal affixed. He couldn't lift his hand, so we had to guide his signet-ring-finger for him. He didn't resist.'

'But what about the fever?' Perdiccas asked. 'You doctors seem to have lost interest in that.' 'Oh, the fever does not worry us', the doctor explained. 'We can deal with that. After all, we are the most experienced team of doctors in the World today, I suppose. Our problem, in working to keep the King alive, has never been his illnesses; it has been himself; he must have been quite the worst patient that anyone in our profession has ever had to deal with. When he has made himself ill by defying Nature, he has invariably then made himself worse by defying his physicians too—every time till this morning. But, now, as I have said, he has given us a chance, and that is why you have found me looking happy. Here, this is for you', the doctor said, as one of his colleagues from behind the curtain passed a paper to him. 'These are the orders I was talking about; here you have them in writing, and sealed. Is the impress clear enough to be recognized as being authentic? It is? That is splendid. Well, I am shy of expressing opinions about public affairs; that is not my job; but, if I were you,' the doctor said, as he handed the amazing document to the Imperial Secretary-General, 'I should have this registered quick in your secretariat, and then get Perdiccas and Ptolemy, here, to see that the necessary action is taken. Au revoir! I must return to my patient. Wouldn't it be awful, now, if he went back on his word? However, I think he won't do that. I don't know why I think that, but, anyway, that is my expectation.'

While the three men were being ferried back across the broad river to Headquarters in the City, they were silent. Each of them was overwhelmed by a torrent of feelings and thoughts. What was most in the minds of all three was the nightmarish future from which they, and the whole World with them, had perhaps now been reprieved, if the doctors' optimism was justified. Of the three, it was Eumenes whose thoughts were ranging the widest and whose feelings were running the deepest. The other two were military men, with a limited responsibility and a limited outlook. Even Ptolemy, who had so much more than a mere soldier's wits, did not see or feel quite as much as Eumenes did. Eumenes, the Imperial Secretary-General, was a city-state Greek from Cardia, on the main water-thoroughfare of the Hellenic World, and he was now carrying the whole World's destiny and burden and anxiety on his shoulders. The Secretary-General's responsibilities had swollen to this magnitude since Alexander had become the successor of the Persian Emperors in addition to being hegemon of the Confederation of Corinth and King of Macedon. For at least the last forty-eight hours, Eumenes had been having to reckon with the possibility that, this time, Alexander might really be going to die; and Alexander was not expendable. Mankind's destiny did now hinge upon this one man's life. Man? For the last ten years, Alexander had been claiming that he was a god, and this, of course, was nonsense; it was one of those childish foibles that great men are apt to cherish. It had been serious nonsense, though, from the physicians' point of view. Alexander was truly Olympian in having a will-power of more than ordinary human strength and impetus. He would go on obstinately behaving as if he were a god when his sick body was reporting that he was only a mortal; and this made him a desperately bad patient, as the doctor had truly said. Alexander would drive straight on with his plans, as if it were really true that nothing could stop him. These two last days, for instance. On each of them he had insisted on carrying on with the series of all-day planning-conferences for the Arabian expedition. In this Babylonian hot season these successive sessions had been exhausting even for participants who were physically fit. The effect of each session in aggravating Alexander's illness had been distressingly apparent. It had been evident, from the first day, that the King was not going to be able to go on board ship and weigh anchor within the four days that he had laid down as his deadline.[1] So all this talking 'about it and about' had been so much waste of breath, besides being so much added danger for one indispensable life. Well, today's news made it look as if, after all, Alexander might not be going to die this time. But suppose that he had continued to aggravate his illness to a point of no return, how would the balance-sheet have stood for Eumenes and Perdiccas and Ptolemy, here in Babylon, and for far-off Antipater at Pella, who, between them, would then have had, *sans* Alexander, to try to keep in being the embryonic 'One World' that Alexander had brought into gestation in the womb of time.

Thank heaven, some of the most urgent and most essential action on the World-Secretariat's agenda had been taken already since Alexander's return, last year, to Susa from outer space—well, from Gedrosia. Provincial governors who had taken advantage of the King's prolonged absence to exceed and abuse their powers had been summarily chastised—some, perhaps, too summarily and too savagely; but to err on the side of harshness was to err on the right side for a would-be World-Government that was actually living in a chaotic transition between two worlds —a Persian World that was dead and an Alexandrine World that was still waiting to be born till Alexander could find the time to bring it to birth. The first step towards bringing this new World to birth had been the integration of the old imperial people with the new one, and the concomitant dilution of the army's Macedonian man-power with select

[1] Arrian, op. cit., Book VII, chap. 29, § 2.

Iranian recruits. These operations had been imperative; for the Macedonian people had conquered a far bigger empire than it was capable of governing single-handed. The Macedonians lacked the requisite numbers and also the requisite experience. A World-State that now extended from the Ionian to the Indian Sea must be based on a broader foundation than Macedon, by herself, could provide. Yes, that job had had to be done, but how near it had come to precipitating a disaster!

If the Macedonians had had the wit to take the point, they would have realized that the integration and dilution that they had resented so furiously were necessary safeguards for their own national interests. Already, Macedon had been drained of most of her men of military age by the drafts with which the original expeditionary force had been repeatedly replenished; the northern barbarians could overrun Macedon easily now; and they would invade her forthwith if they were to become aware of her present weakness. Macedon must recruit her strength now if she was to continue to play the role that Philip's genius and Alexander's genius had won for her. But these Macedonians! They were so stupid, besides being so emotional and so turbulent. They were like wayward children. You could not talk things over with them. They would not listen to reason; but they would recognize their master when they found him through being beaten by him in a trial of strength—brute strength of imperious will; and here, as so often before, Alexander had done something that he alone could have done. The troops had defied him; in three days he had brought them to heel;[1] and now the time-expired men had been paid off with extravagant generosity and had set off, without making further trouble, on their long march from Babylon to the Hellespont.[2] Well, this major item on the agenda could now be crossed off as being by this time an accomplished fact. But could it really? Suppose that the doctors' optimism was premature. Suppose that, the day after tomorrow, Alexander were to be dead. Would integration and dilution survive him? Eumenes admitted to himself that he could not guarantee that.

If he could not, then the positive side of the balance-sheet was precarious, while the negative side of it was appalling—and had been so ever since Alexander had succeeded his father thirteen years ago. This imminence of catastrophe with which Eumenes and the others had been living for these last three days—well, it was really nothing new; if they could bring themselves to face the truth, they had been living with it ever since Philip had been struck dead by Pausanias' sword. From that day to this, Alexander had been taking daily risks—risks for himself, for his kingdom, and for the World. In a monarchy, what is the reigning

[1] Arrian, op. cit., Book VII, chap. 11.
[2] Ibid., chap. 12, §§ 1-4.

monarch's first and last duty? It is to make provision for an orderly and effective succession to the throne at whatever moment death may over-take him. Of course it is that. But what had been Alexander's first act after his own accession? His first act had been to kill off every possible heir to his throne except his half-witted half-brother Philip Arrhidaïos, who was with the army here in Babylon now; and Alexander had spared Philip just because Philip was unfit. (Poor wretch; it is hard on a half-wit to have to answer to the name 'Super-Fighting-Man'.) Alexander had killed all his other bastard half-brothers and half-sisters. He had also killed his unoffending cousin King Amyntas IV, whom the man's uncle, Alexander's father Philip II, had spared. Why did Alexander need to kill Amyntas? Amyntas had never made himself a nuisance. If only they could have had Amyntas with them alive in Babylon now, instead of poor half-wit Philip Arrhidaïos! They would then have had in hand a legitimate King of Macedon—*the* legitimate King of Macedon, in fact; for both Philip II and Alexander III had been usurpers of Amyntas IV's throne. The killing of Amyntas had been a black deed, but it had been quite inhuman of Alexander to kill his own infant half-sister, baby Europa. One might perhaps pass over the killing of Europa's mother, Queen Cleopatra. When Cleopatra had consented to oust Olympias from Philip's bed, she had been asking for what had duly come to her. Olympias would have killed Cleopatra in any case. Alexander's mother was beyond even Alexander's control.

But, when Alexander had made this clean sweep, what had he done next? They had all begged him to put off the Asian campaign till he had a son to leave at home, to succeed him should he unfortunately fall in battle. Had he listened? Not he. He had marched off without waiting; at the first engagement—that battle on the Granicus—he had galloped straight into a cavalry mêlée and had very nearly got himself sabred. He had kept on taking risks like that, without ever yet providing any substitute for the heirs whom he had liquidated at the start. Again and again, he had plunged into the thick of the battle and had been the first to put his foot on the scaling-ladder at a siege; and, when he had been thirsty on the march, he had slaked his thirst with stagnant water foul enough to kill a cow. Now that he was lying at the point of death, he still had no heir except poor Arrhidaïos, though, thank goodness, Roxana was now with child, and was expecting delivery in a few weeks. If the child were a boy, Alexander would have a valid successor for the first time since his murder of his cousin Amyntas IV after his own accession. It all came of the same defects; it came of impulsiveness, in-continence, and irresponsibility. Alexander had killed Cleitus when he was in his cups. When once he had started drinking, he could not bring himself to stop. One round of drinks too much! That had been the death of Cleitus; it had been the death of Hephaestion this year;[1] and it might have been the death of Alexander this month.

Hephaestion! Eumenes could now remove his name, anyway, from the agenda. Dead men don't bait, and Eumenes had been baited by Hephaestion long enough. A Macedonian aristocrat with the mind of a cavalry officer! Hephaestion had disliked Eumenes because Eumenes was not a Macedonian himself, and because Eumenes' work for Alexander was beyond Hephaestion's comprehension. Hephaestion had presumed on being Alexander's foster-brother and boon-companion. In the public interest, Eumenes had had to put up with it. He had had to offer Hephaestion the olive-branch and to swallow a rebuff. He had had to think up extravagant ways of honouring Hephaestion's unlamented memory. Well, there are occasions when hypocrisy is the only alternative to death. If, as everyone was praying, Alexander now survived, the task of managing Alexander alone, without Hephaestion, would be child's-play.

Was Alexander another Hephaestion? Yes, he was that, since he too was a Macedonian aristocrat. But he was not just that. He was something worse, besides being, of course, also something far better. He was something worse than just the murderous drunkard who had killed Cleitus. Killing and getting killed in hot blood was a favourite Macedonian sport; but Alexander had killed in cold blood too, and, to do the Macedonians justice, it must be admitted that this was an 'un-Macedonian' activity. Alexander had killed his co-heirs in cold blood at the start. He had killed Philotas and Parmenio in cold blood later. To murder Parmenio! What ingratitude! That deed of Alexander's would be incredible if it were not a fact—a fact that could not be undone and could not be expunged from the record, either. This cold-blooded killing was in the Persian, not the Macedonian, style. It was like Ochus and other predecessors of Alexander's on the Persian imperial throne. Or, if you will, it was like Phalaris or Polycrates or the Dionysii or a dozen other non-Macedonian Greek despots.

Yes, but Alexander was 'un-Macedonian' for better as well as for worse. Besides being a killer in cold blood, Alexander was a statesman with a penetrating insight and even a philosopher with a sublime vision. A quite paradoxical compound of opposites! In that, he was like a city-state Greek. A Macedonian Alcibiades! He was as good—and as bad— as if he had been an Athenian—or a Cardian.

The ferry-boat touched the bank, and, still chased by his racing thoughts, Eumenes landed, mounted, rode to his office, and started on his daily round of receiving callers and dictating minutes and dispatches.

For the next six days, Alexander's condition was still critical; yet,

---

[1] Arrian, op. cit., Book VII, chap. 14, § 1.

from that historic morning onwards, he began to recover his strength, and, each night, the fever progressively relaxed its grip on him. What was saving his life was his decision to let himself rest—physically and, above all, mentally too. The physicians' prognosis had been correct. He did obey their orders, and this did give them their chance to bring their medical skill into play.

Meanwhile, three men—Eumenes, Perdiccas, and Ptolemy—were keeping Alexander's regime running smoothly for him. They were a well-matched team; for Perdiccas and Ptolemy were Macedonian aristocrats of an uncommon kind. Neither man was class-conscious; neither man was insolent. (This was even more creditable to Perdiccas than it was to Ptolemy; Perdiccas was not clever; Ptolemy was; Ptolemy was a Macedonian Odysseus.) These were two Macedonians with whom a city-state Greek could work; and Eumenes needed Macedonians to work with; for the common run of Macedonians, officers and privates alike, would have been loath to obey orders issued over a non-Macedonian Greek secretary's signature, even if those orders were issued in the King of Macedon's name. Orders signed by one of themselves—e.g. Perdiccas —did not arouse the Macedonians' opposition. So Eumenes left it to Perdiccas to sign the papers, while Perdiccas left it to Eumenes and Ptolemy to work out the policies and to draft the documents. Together, the three men constituted an unofficial board of regency—unofficial because, by the third morning of his illness, Alexander, after he had sealed the doctors' orders, had been too far gone to be able to perform any act of state; and, if he had not been as ill as that, he might have been unwilling to delegate any of his royal authority. What was important and significant was that this self-constituted board of regency was obeyed by Macedonian Greeks, city-state Greeks, and non-Greeks alike.

What moved the three men to work together so harmoniously and responsibly and dutifully? It was not the vision of a World-State, for which Alexander's government had now come to stand. That vision had not been theirs; it had been Alexander's and his alone. What moved them all was a personal loyalty to Alexander. (Ptolemy had made up his mind during these last three days that, if Alexander did die, he, Ptolemy, would play for his own hand. Why not? But, as long as Alexander lived, he would remain faithful to his king and commander-in-chief.) Perhaps, subconsciously, the three were moved by loyalty to something in Alexander that was greater than Alexander himself.

The unofficial regency had been governing the World for seven weeks before the doctors allowed Alexander to be out and about again. When the King came back to life and work, he neither disestablished the regency nor recognized it officially. His tacit acceptance of it amounted to recognition *de facto*, and the regency became a permanent institution.

Its constitutional relation to the crown was never defined; both parties deliberately avoided raising this delicate and otiose question. The regents' powers were dependent on their tact; and they were tactful enough to save their powers from being challenged.

The physicians now lifted their embargo on the sailing of the Arabian expedition, and they agreed that Alexander might sail with it, on condition that he undertook to spend every night on board ship. As an aid to their patient's convalescence, they would have preferred a voyage in the Black Sea or in the Adriatic to one in the Persian Gulf. In August the Persian Gulf can be hot (as I know by experience). Even so, being confined to his ship would set a limit to Alexander's physical exertions; and, if he had been told to stay behind, he might have worn himself out physically by fretting. The regents were relieved when, just before the fleet sailed with Alexander on board, Queen Roxana gave birth to a boy —the future Alexander IV; but, in 323 B.C., this new Alexander's accession was still thirty-six years off in the future.

If Alexander III had insisted on killing himself by launching the Arabian expedition at his appointed date, this characteristic exhibition of impatience and lack of self-control would have been his supreme act of folly. In itself, however, this expedition was the rational next step in Alexander's programme. Alexander had not renounced his dream of conquering the whole World. He had not reconciled himself to his defeat by his own Macedonians at the River Beas in 326 B.C. He had consoled himself for this bitter disappointment by accepting it as a tactical retreat only—the tactics of *reculer pour mieux sauter*. One day he would find troops who would be willing to follow him beyond the Beas to the ends of the Earth. But he now recognized that there was a limit to the distances that even the most agile and most long-suffering soldiers could traverse on foot. Before he could extend his present Graeco-Persian nucleus for a World-State, he must provide quicker and less arduous means of communication for this already huge nuclear area; and, at the stage at which technology stood in the Age of Civilization before the Industrial Revolution, water-transport was incomparably superior to land-transport in point of both speed and ease. Alexander must therefore develop water-transport, and his Arabian expedition had been planned as a means to this end.

When Alexander turned his attention to this solution for his logistical problem, he followed, move by move, in the wake of his Persian predecessors Darius I and Xerxes. Was it simply that an identical geopolitical situation suggested identical moves to equally imaginative and resourceful minds? Or had Alexander consulted the records of these two emperors' acts in the archives at Susa? Whatever the source of Alexander's inspiration may have been, it is a fact that he did re-inaugurate Darius' and Xerxes' maritime policy.

After Darius had reached the upper basin of the Indus overland, via Arachosia and the Paropanisadae, he had commissioned a Carian pilot, Scylax of Caryanda, to sail down the Indus, out into the Indian Ocean, and up the Red Sea, to one of Egypt's Red Sea ports. Scylax had executed this commission successfully;[1] and Darius had followed Scylax's achievement up by reopening the ship-canal from the head of the Gulf of Suez to the head of the Delta of the Nile. This combination of measures had given the Persian Empire a continuous water-route between its north-eastern extremity in Gandhara and its south-western extremity in Egypt. Alexander, when he had sailed down the Indus, had, consciously or un-knowingly, been retraversing the first stage of Scylax's voyage; and, in commissioning Nearchus to make the coastal voyage, up the Iranian side of the Persian Gulf, from the Delta of the Indus to the mouths of the Rivers Eulaeus and Tigris and Euphrates, Alexander had been taking the initial step towards the repetition of another of Darius' maritime-minded enterprises.

Darius had deported the most militant of the Median rebels of the apocalyptic year 522 B.C. to islands in the Persian Gulf;[2] and one motive for this measure had been the political one of penalizing the *déracinés* and at the same time putting it beyond their power ever to challenge his authority again; but Darius had also had the further motive of establish-ing the Iranian people's hold over the only backwater of the Ocean on which Iran had a coastline. By 323 B.C., these penal settlements of Iranians had long since evaporated in the torrid atmosphere of the Gulf. The shock of the disaster of 480–479 B.C. had broken the Persian Imperial Government's *élan* and had weakened its grip, and the *déracinés*' descen-dants had taken advantage of this slackening of governmental control. They had drifted back to the highland homes of their ancestors in western Iran without asking the Government's leave. However, in 323 B.C. the descendants of the Milesians who had been deported, in their turn, after the sack of Miletus in 494 B.C., to the gulf coast of Babylonia at the mouth of the Tigris,[3] were still *in situ*; and the survival here of these maritime-minded deportees from the Mediterranean may have given Alexander his idea of repopulating the coasts and islands of the Persian Gulf with colonists who, unlike the Iranians, were seafarers and traders. Before he had fallen ill, he had planned to induce Phoenicians to settle here;[4] and the Phoenicians' favourable response to his recruiting cam-paign was, as we know, the origin of the Phoenicians' present monopoly of the oceanic carrying-trade.

Alexander had already prepared a base of operations in Babylonia

---

[1] Herodotus, Book IV, chap. 44.   [2] Herodotus, Book VII, chap. 80.
[3] Herodotus, Book VI, chap. 20.
[4] Arrian, op. cit., Book VII, chap. 19, §§ 4–5.

for maritime activities in the Persian Gulf and beyond. He had removed obstructions to the navigation of the Tigris which the Persians had placed there to serve as defences against a possible invasion of the Empire from the Indian Ocean,[1] and on the Euphrates, at Babylon, he had dug a great harbour for sea-going ships and had equipped it with dockyards.[2] He had also sailed down the Pallacopas canal, and had planted a colony of Greek veterans at its mouth at the head of the Gulf.[3] The fleet that had been assembled at Babylon for the Arabian expedition was partly composed of Phoenician ships. These had been carried in sections over the portage between the Mediterranean and the westward elbow of the Euphrates. They had then been reassembled at Thapsacus and had sailed down-stream to Babylon from there.[4] Alexander's Arabian expedition was to follow the Arabian shore of the Persian Gulf and was then to retraverse the second and third stages of Scylax's voyage, in which Scylax had followed the coasts of Arabia all the way to Egypt through the waters of the Indian Ocean and the Red Sea.

Meanwhile, Alexander had sent three pinnaces down the Gulf to reconnoitre this sea-route to Egypt and to report back to him before he sailed himself. Before Alexander had fallen ill, all three captains had duly reported back, but not one of them had succeeded in repeating Scylax's feat. One of the three had come almost within hail of Egypt's Red Sea coast; but here, where he had been within an ace of accomplishing his mission, he, too, had turned back.[5] What Alexander had learnt from these unenterprising sea-scouts of his was the location of the two islands of Kuwayt and Bahrayn[6] and the magnitude of Arabia. He had learnt that Arabia was a peninsula on the scale of India.[7]

Before the fleet sailed from Babylon, with Egypt as its destination, a land-force had gone ahead, with instructions to march along the east coast of Arabia. This army was to keep pace with the fleet and to maintain continuous contact with it. Alexander was now repeating the disastrous mistake that he had made on his return from India to Susa; and it is strange that he should have failed to learn from so harrowing an experience. His Gedrosian escapade ought to have taught him once for all that a fleet and an army could not keep in touch with each other effectively in an area in which both the coast and the interior were desert; and the reports from the captains of his reconnaissance vessels ought to have made him realize that, by comparison with eastern Arabia, Gedrosia was an earthly paradise. After leaving the last fresh water and the last green vegetation behind at the mouth of the Pallacopas canal,

---

[1] Arrian, op. cit., Book VII, chap. 7, § 7.
[2] Ibid., chap. 19, § 4.
[3] Ibid., chap. 21.
[4] Ibid., chap. 19, §§ 3–4.
[5] Ibid., chap. 20, §§ 7–8.
[6] Ibid., chap. 20, §§ 2–6.
[7] Ibid., chap. 20, § 8.

the army immediately began to suffer privations and losses comparable to those that had been experienced on the Gedrosian trek. The army now laboured on southwards as far as the oasis of Hofūf; but its commander Seleucus had the good sense to decline to tempt providence further. After his exhausted troops had recuperated in the lovely oasis, Seleucus marched them to the coast opposite Bahrayn Island, where the fleet was waiting to re-establish contact with them, and he then persuaded Alexander to send back to Babylon for transports to carry the army by sea from that point onwards. Seleucus had saved his men and himself from going to their deaths in the Rub'-al-Khāli. They survived to provide military landing-parties at the points at which the fleet put in to shore on the remaining stages of the voyage.

The twofold delay caused by Alexander's illness and by the subsequent wait at Bahrayn had lost so much time that Nearchus proposed that the fleet should now winter at Bahrayn and should complete the voyage to Egypt in the sailing-season of the next year. On this point, Alexander refused to yield; he insisted on pressing forward to Egypt during the current navigation-season; but he did agree to make the rest of the voyage at top speed, without waiting to plant settlements on the Arabian coast or to send exploring parties into the interior. The fleet found and entered the Straits of Bāb-al-Mandab without mishap, and reached Suez, as planned, in the late autumn of 323 B.C.

Alexander's intention had been to invade the Carthaginian Empire as soon as he had established his sea-communications between India and Babylonia and Egypt; but he now found himself with arrears of work on hand that made it necessary to put off the west-Mediterranean expedition for a year.

Alexander had not been in Egypt since he had started from there, nine years back, on the crowning campaign in his war against the Persian Emperor Darius III; the Egyptian Greek Cleomenes of Naucratis, whom Alexander had left in charge of the financial administration of Egypt with wide powers, had improved the shining hour by filling his own pockets as unscrupulously as had Harpalus, Alexander's Macedonian Greek finance-officer at Babylon. But the Naucratite peculator, unlike Harpalus, did not lose his nerve at Alexander's approach. He had the effrontery, not only to stand his ground, but to ask for a bonus to reward him for the magnificence of the herôon that he had been building at Alexandria for Hephaestion on Alexander's instructions.[1] Before Alexander had had time to consider Cleomenes' bare-faced request, Eumenes had demanded from Cleomenes a statement of account, and Cleomenes' utter failure to produce a satisfactory one gave Eumenes a leverage for inducing Alexander to commission Ptolemy to inquire into Cleomenes'

[1] Arrian, op. cit., Book VII, chap. 23, §§ 7–8.

financial record. Ptolemy's report was competent and damning. He reported that Cleomenes was another Harpalus, and he followed this up by asking Alexander to give him Cleomenes' job; but Alexander knew Ptolemy's character well enough to refuse to put the natural fortress of Egypt in Ptolemy's hands. He preferred to continue to use Ptolemy's ability in a post in which Ptolemy would be out of temptation's way; so he retained him for service in the unofficial triumvirate.

As for Cleomenes, this clever rascal managed to keep, for the rest of his life, the post in which he had so outrageously abused his trust. This was a scandal, yet it was one that, on a short view, was not disadvantageous for the World-Government either politically or financially. Cleomenes, unlike Ptolemy, had no political ambitions. For Cleomenes, the amassing of wealth was an end in itself; and his financial ability was so great, and his understanding of Egypt's economy was so intelligent, that it actually paid the Treasury to turn a blind eye to his perennial defalcations. The sufferer was not the Treasury; it was the Egyptian peasantry, and, in the long run, of course, this exploitation of the Egyptian people, besides being unjust in itself, was damaging for the World-State that Alexander was striving to create. The turns that Cleomenes knew how to give to his financial screw made even the hated Persian regime seem preferable in retrospect. The Persians had humiliated the Egyptians, but they had been too lax and too incompetent to fleece them.

In failing to deal sternly with Cleomenes, Alexander was failing in his duty as the ruler of Egypt. He failed in this because his attention was being taken up with other things. His first concern was to study and revise the plan of his rising city of Alexandria-on-Nile. The Hephaestioneum is still the centre-point of the World's capital today, and this is the abiding result of a personal decision of Alexander's. Since Alexander was Pharaoh, besides being emperor of Asia and king of Macedon and hegemon of the Confederation of Corinth, the Egyptians were surprised that he did not now start to build for himself a tomb that would dwarf the Fourth Dynasty's pyramids. Was he not the ruler of an empire that outstripped the Old Kingdom of Egypt in size and population and resources? Alexander was, indeed, Pharaoh, but this had not made him Egyptian-minded. Having recently come so near to dying, he did not choose to occupy his mind with plans for a tomb for himself. A tomb is the symbol of mortality; so let the monumental tomb at Alexandria be Hephaestion's, since Hephaestion was already dead beyond recall. Hephaestion had been deified only posthumously. Alexander himself, however, had been declared to be the god Ammon's son, and this by the god himself, ten years ago. Alexander was a live god; and, in spite of the silent testimony of a long row of pharaonic tombs and pharaonic mummies, it was contrary to Hellenic reason that a living god should eventually have to taste death. For Zeus Ammon's living son to build a selpulchre for himself would be for him to deny his own immortality.

Alexander's main modification of the original plan for Alexandria was to double its size. In 331 B.C. he had planned this city to serve merely as the Egyptian terminal for the direct sea-route between Egypt and the Aegean. At that date the political destiny of the Oikoumene east of Euphrates was still undecided. Now that Alexander had become emperor of Asia, and was planning to make himself thalassocrat of the western as well as the eastern Mediterranean, Alexandria was going to have to serve as the capital of the World; and the site was providentially apt for a city that was to play this supreme role in future. Alexandria stands at the point where the Mediterranean backwater of the Atlantic Ocean and the Red Sea backwater of the Indian Ocean very nearly meet head to head. It needed no more than a Poseidonian trident-stroke to cleave the intervening neck of land; and, for Alexander, this stroke was easy; he had only to strike where Necho II and Darius had struck before. Alexander now followed Darius in rehabilitating Necho II's canal between the Gulf of Suez and the Nile.[1] He thus reopened the continuous waterway from the Indus Delta to the Nile Delta; and this turned Alexandria-on-Nile into a second Corinth, with frontages on two seas. Corinth's two seas are two inlets of the Mediterranean. Alexandria's two seas are two bays of the globe-encompassing Ocean. The city had to be on the scale of its geographical setting; and Alexandria's location is unique. This has made her the World-State's capital from Alexander's day to ours. Where else could the World's capital be placed?

The water-route that Alexander had now followed from the Beas tributary of the Indus to the Canopic mouth of the Nile was already beckoning him on through the Straits of Lilybaeum to the Pillars of Herakles. But, before he could start on his westward sweep, he had still to consolidate his hold on the sea-route that he had already explored. He had been agreeably surprised by the alacrity of the Phoenicians' response, while he had been in Babylon, to his call to them to help him in opening up the Persian Gulf. He now showed his appreciation of their unexpected co-operativeness by responding to this on his own part in a series of princely measures. First he gave orders that Tyre should be refounded and that all surviving Tyrians should be repatriated and indemnified. Next he provided that all three major Phoenician city-states—Tyre, Sidon, and Aradus—should retain all the privileges that they had enjoyed under the Persian regime. In the third place he decreed that the original Phoenician tripolis on the Syrian coast should be reproduced twice over by the planting of one new trio of Phoenician cities in the

[1] See Herodotus, Book II, chap. 158, and Book IV, chap. 42.

Persian Gulf and another in the Red Sea. The sites in the Gulf that he designated were the three islands of Kuwayt, Bahrayn, and Kishm in the narrows. His sites in the Red Sea were Aden, Tajurra Bay, and Masāwah. Alexander had chosen these sites himself, *en route* from Babylon to Suez. Each daughter Phoenician city was to have the same privileges as its parent city. Each was to have the same far-reaching autonomy, and was to be endowed with as large a territorial domain as it could utilize.

In thus introducing the Phoenicians into the Indian Ocean, Alexander was not only securing his own hold on his World-State's main waterway; he was also giving the Phoenicians compensation for his previous assault on Tyre and for his coming assault on Carthage, and at the same time he was broadening the World-State's political basis by promoting the Phoenicians to the rank of an imperial people. After his return from India, Alexander had doubled the size of his politeuma by taking the defeated Iranians into partnership with the victorious Greeks. By now he had realized that this was not enough; and, in taking the Phoenicians, too, into partnership, he was carrying out a less hazardous political operation than the previous one. The introduction of Iranian recruits into the Macedonian military formations had provoked a Macedonian mutiny which even Alexander had barely been able to quell. In now giving the Phoenicians the command of oceanic waters, he was taking a new departure which would have more momentous consequences; but sea-power was something that the Macedonian soldiery did not understand and therefore did not grudge to 'lesser breeds'.

The Phoenicians did understand sea-power and the relation of this to trade; and they therefore seized, with both hands, the opportunity that Alexander had now opened up for them. This opportunity was unprecedentedly promising, because the empire that had now been given to them for their commercial hinterland was larger than any in which they had been included before, and it was growing larger still. It looked, in fact, as if it were going to grow into a literally world-wide World-State. Tyre had resisted Alexander, and had paid heavily for her temerity; she had previously resisted Nebuchadnezzar, with the same catastrophic results for herself. Even the most commercial-minded peoples are apt to sacrifice economics to politics if an issue between them arises; and the Phoenicians had reacted like other peoples. However, experience had proved that, whenever they had been incorporated in an empire against their will, their commerce had benefited by this. In 322 B.C. they foresaw the world-wide range of Phoenician commerce which, today, is still one of the salient features of the World's economic life.

In 322 B.C. the Phoenicians immediately perceived that there were two weak points in their position, and that they must repair these if they were to harvest the commercial fortune that was being offered to them. At this date the Phoenicians were suffering, as they always had suffered, from a scarcity of man-power; and they were not in control of the overland trade-routes connecting their new entrepôts in the Red Sea and the Persian Gulf with their base of operations on the Syrian coast. They dealt with the first point by recruiting additional personnel from the kindred peoples in the interior of Syria: Idumaeans, Jews, Samaritans, Moabites, Ammonites, Damascenes, and the rest. They had always enlisted additional man-power from here when they had needed it; but this time they did this on the grand scale, and the prospects were so attractive that their recruiting-offices were besieged till the inland cantons had been almost emptied of their population. In the second place the Phoenicians bought an interest in the overland routes by negotiating agreements, for a division of profits, with the peoples who held these overland routes in their hands. The principal peoples in question were the Nabataeans, who, at Petra, commanded the trail between the Gulf of 'Aqabah and the Mediterranean; the Gerrhaeans, who held the Arabian mainland opposite Bahrayn; and the Minaeans and Sabaeans, who were in competition with each other for the command of the trail between Aden and Damascus.

This network of commercial partnerships that the Phoenicians now so wisely wove between themselves and their continental neighbours had unforeseen consequences on the linguistic and religious planes. On the linguistic plane it restored the fortunes of the Aramaic language; on the religious plane it reduced Yahweh, the 'jealous' god of the Samaritans and the Jews, to the more modest and more sociable role of being one member, among others, in an international pantheon.

The Aramaic language had been gaining ground since the progressive conquest of the Aramaeans by the Assyrians. It had not only become the lingua franca of south-western Asia; it had also begun to supplant its sister Semitic languages—Akkadian, Canaanite, and Arabic—as the vernacular language of the Semitic-speaking peoples. The Aramaic language's fortune had been made by the handiness of its alphabetic script, and this had led the Persian Imperial Government to adopt this foreign language and script as the media for its official correspondence and records. The overthrow of the Persian Empire by Alexander had been threatening to supplant Aramaic by Greek (the Greek version of the alphabet was handier still); and it was evident that, from now on, Greek would be one of the world-languages. It was, however, now also evident that Aramaic was going to retain its previous position, side by side with Greek, thanks to Alexander's policy of making the Phoenicians' commercial fortune. Within a few generations, the Phoenicians' ancestral Canaanite language had been supplanted by Aramaic or Greek, or both, everywhere except in the Phoenician colonies in the western basin of the Mediterranean.

As for the god Yahweh, his fate was settled by the voluntary mass-migration of his Palestinian worshippers to the new Phoenician colonies in the Red Sea and the Persian Gulf. The fanatical faction among his worshippers had always been a minority. These fanatics had contended, against all precedent and all probability, that this particular local god was actually the Lord of the Universe, and that all other local gods were his subordinates. Some Yahweh-maniacs had even asserted that Yahweh was the only god who really existed. These extravagances had never been acceptable to the majority of the Yahweh-worshippers. This majority had not seen why their worship of their local god should not be combined, in the usual way, with the worship of any other gods who might take their fancy. The wholesale fusion of the Samaritans and the Jews with the Phoenicians in and after 322 B.C. made the fanatics' position untenable; and this was the end of a queer episode in the history of the religion of these two little Palestinian peoples.

After having spent the year 321 B.C. in Egypt exclusively on works of peace, Alexander was becoming impatient to launch the western campaign that was to be the counterpart of his conquest of the Persian Empire. In Asia he had been the conquering Dionysus seeking the legendary Nysa and finding it in the Paropanisadae at the southern foot of the passes over the Hindu Kush. In the Mediterranean he would be the conquering Herakles seeking the Garden of the Hesperides and the oxen of Geryon. He would make the circuit of the Mediterranean, overthrowing the Carthaginian Empire on his way out and wresting the hegemony over Italy from the Samnites on his way back.[1] Actually he would be following, here again, in the wake of Persian predecessors. Cambyses had wanted to attack Carthage,[2] and Darius I had sent a naval squadron to make a reconnaissance of the Greek colonial world to the west of the Straits of Otranto.[3]

Alexander proposed now to move straight on from Alexandria with the ships and men that he had brought with him by sea from Babylon; but the triumvirate eventually convinced him of the wisdom of 'hastening slowly'. This was the hardest struggle that they had yet had with Alexander; for on this occasion the physicians could not help them. In the spring of 321 B.C. Alexander was in better health than at any time since his arrival in Carmania after the torturing march through Gedrosia in 326 B.C.

---

[1] Arrian, op. cit., Book VII, chap. 1; Q. Curtius Rufus, *Historiae Alexandri Magni*, Book X, chap. 1, §§ 17–19.
[2] Herodotus, Book III, chap. 17.
[3] Ibid., chaps. 135–8.

First of all, Alexander had to be convinced of the folly of making, for the third time, the costly mistake of moving on land and sea simultaneously along a desert coast. This had been disastrous in Gedrosia; it had been disastrous again in Arabia; and it might be doubly disastrous in Libya. On those two previous deadly desert marches Alexander had been heading for a country that was already under his rule. This time his objective would be an enemy country, the Carthaginian domain in north-west Africa; and his weary troops would have to meet unfatigued Carthaginian armies without any pause for recuperation. He had tasted the Libyan desert already, ten years back, when he had visited his 'father' Zeus Ammon in the oasis of Siwah. Surely once was enough. In the second place, how could Alexander expect Macedonian soldiers and Phoenician sailors to have any stomach for attacking Carthage? The Macedonians had seen the point of the Asian campaign. Macedon had been subjugated temporarily by Darius I; for them their attack on Darius III had been a war of revenge. By contrast, the western Mediterranean meant nothing to the Macedonians; they had not been participants in the Greek colonization movement in that quarter in the eighth, seventh, and sixth centuries B.C. They had no more inclination to march to the Garden of the Hesperides than they had had to cross the River Beas. What the Macedonian troops in Egypt wanted now was to be shipped from Alexandria straight back home. As for the Phoenician naval personnel, if Alexander were now to ask them to sail against Carthage, he would undoubtedly receive the answer that Cambyses had received from their forefathers. They would refuse to lend their skill and prowess to an attack on their colonial Phoenician kinsmen.[1] For his western campaign, Alexander must recruit men who would have their hearts in it. He must recruit, in the first instance, the western colonial Greeks, and, in the second instance, the Aegean Greeks whose colonists the western Greeks were. But before he could do that he must respond to the more and more urgent calls that the triumvirate had been receiving, for some time past, from Antipater in Macedon and Thrace and from Antigonus in Phrygia.

In Thrace the Odrysae had revolted in 326 B.C., after Zopyrion had brought upon himself on the Scythian steppes the disaster that Darius I had barely eluded there. In Macedon, Antipater, with his depleted holding-force, had been faced with the threat of a general revolt of the states members of the Confederation of Corinth when a premature report of Alexander's death had reached Athens at the time of his critical illness at Babylon. In Phrygia, Antigonus had been doing wonders, for the last twelve years, in keeping open the line of communications between Macedon and Babylonia; but for some time past Antigonus had been reporting that the resistance movement led by local Persian magnates in

[1] Herodotus, Book III, chap. 19.

Cappadocia had now attained such proportions that, at any moment, the insurgents might succeed in cutting the vital road through the Cilician Gates. 'Come over into Macedonia and help us', Antigonus and Antipater were crying in unison. Eumenes had been submitting their dispatches to Alexander; Alexander had been pigeon-holing them. If he continued to neglect the Macedonian source and centre of his world-power, his inchoate World-State might collapse. If the Odrysae were in Pella and the Peloponnesians were in Larisa, what would it profit Alexander to be at Gades?

Sulkily, Alexander surrendered to facts which even a god could not conjure away. In the spring of 321 B.C. he sailed, not for Carthage, but for the Thermaic Gulf; and he then spent this year on repeating what he had done in 335 B.C.

Alexander made his presence felt in Europe again by staging a pair of military demonstrations. First he marched north-eastward across Odrysia to the Lower Danube; then he marched southward, through Corinth, to Megalopolis. The Odrysae submitted again. The Scythians and the Spartans shook in their shoes. After that, every able-bodied man or boy who could still be found in Macedon was sent to join Antigonus. Even some of the veterans who had been brought home by Craterus and Leonnatus in 323 B.C. were re-enlisted. Antigonus, thus reinforced, was instructed to pass over to the offensive. He was to subjugate thoroughly the ex-Persian territories in north-eastern Anatolia that Alexander had left unconquered on his anabasis. Antigonus was to press on eastwards till he reached the western border of the territory under the control of Atropates, the loyal Iranian governor of Media. Antigonus now bounded forward like a hound unleashed. Before the end of the campaigning season of 321 B.C. (and the season is short in Armenia), Antigonus had completely pacified the dissident area. Alexander marked Antigonus out for some greater mission in the future. Meanwhile, Alexander had to make a new appointment to the governorship of Thrace. This had been vacant since Zopyrion had met his death on the steppes in 326 B.C., and Antipater had been serving as locum tenens; but to keep watch on two critical fronts simultaneously was too heavy a permanent load even for a soldier of Antipater's stature. Moreover, Antipater was growing old. Lysimachus applied for the vacant post, but Alexander did not appoint him to it. He was unwilling to lose Lysimachus' service on his personal staff. Instead, he appointed Craterus. Evidently the governors of Thrace and Macedon must work together like brothers if they were to make a success of their two difficult tasks; and Craterus and Antipater were known to be congenial to each other.

Alexander's administrative and military activities in 321 B.C. might have been supposed to have given him a full-time occupation during this year of his working life. Actually, he had to fit in these important public calls on him, as best he could, while he was up to the neck in family affairs. What kept Alexander awake at night this year was not Greece or Thrace or Cappadocia. It was his mother Olympias and her daughter and his sister—his full sister—Cleopatra. Now he understood the subconscious motive for his reluctance to come home from Egypt instead of pressing on to Gades. He understood why his father had perpetually been running after other women and had eventually jilted Alexander's mother, to marry Alexander's sister's namesake, Attalus' niece. Now he understood what Antipater had been having to put up with for the last thirteen years. He understood why Antipater's hair had turned grey and why his backbone had begun to sag.

Olympias' demonic personality had fascinated her son ever since he had first awoken to consciousness. As a boy, he had taken her side against his father. Surely his father's unfaithfulness to his mother was inexcusable. This bond of personal sympathy had been reinforced by one of political interest when, in 337 B.C., Philip had taken Attalus' niece to wife. This jilting of Olympias had threatened to bring the disinheriting of Alexander along with it. This threat to mother and son had been removed by Pausanias' sword-stroke; but the intimate tie between them had survived the dramatic upward turn in their common fortunes, and had even survived their continuing proximity, till they had been parted by Alexander's departure from Pella for the Hellespont in 334 B.C. After that, Alexander had been plagued by Olympias' long plaintive and vituperative letters (her target had, of course, been Antipater); but even the most vexatious correspondence can be borne when the exchange of letters takes six months. Now, however, Alexander was face to face with his mother once again. On the news that Alexander was heading for Macedon from Egypt, Olympias had flown back to Macedon from Epirus and had arrived in Pella a few days before her son. Antipater now gave Alexander an ultimatum: if Olympias was to be allowed to stay in Europe, he, Antipater, would resign. Alexander saw that Antipater meant what he was saying, and the prospect filled him with dismay. In Alexander's estimation, Antipater was the only man capable of holding the fort for him in continental European Greece while Alexander himself was away. If Antipater resigned, Alexander would have to stay in Pella permanently. He would have to delegate the conquest of the still un-conquered quarters of the World to his officers. Alexander could not abide the thought. Rather than that, he must relegate Olympias to some place from which her letters would, once again, take three months to arrive and another three months to receive their replies. But where? And how?

The answers to both these questions came to Alexander in the small hours of a wakeful night. The answers solved the Olympias problem so brilliantly that Alexander could only suppose that they had been direct communications from his father Zeus Ammon. After all, the god had some responsibility for Alexander's present plight, if it was true, as the god had asserted, that Alexander was Olympias' son by him and not by Philip. How to remove Olympias from Europe? Why, by doctors' orders, of course. Alexander had been taught this trick of the politician's trade by the triumvirate's use of it against him at Babylon in June 323 B.C. And where to send her? The answer to this second question followed from the answer to the first. The doctors must order her to reside, for the rest of her life, in some genial clime where she would be spared the rigours of an Epirot or Macedonian winter; and Alexander now remembered that he had the very place in his pocket. *En voyage* from Bahrayn to Suez he had called at the Island of Socotra and had annexed it. It was an earthly paradise, and it was still at his disposal; for, by inadvertence, he had omitted to name it in his deed of gift to the Phoenicians.

Now that Alexander had the solution, he acted swiftly. His obliging physicians made the necessary medical report next morning, and Olympias was on her way to Socotra before nightfall. She was accompanied by a small bodyguard of septuagenarian veterans who were genuinely longing to return to the tropics after having spent the last two winters at home again. A hundred septuagenarians in Socotra would hardly be able to make a world-revolution on Olympias' behalf, however stormily she might rage. So Olympias was deported to Socotra and was interned there for the rest of her long and lusty life (the tropical climate failed to make her languid). As empress of Panchaia, she could no longer hope to be regent of either Macedon or Epirus. This made her furious, but there was nothing that she could do about it now.

To dispose of Cleopatra was the less disagreeable of Alexander's two domestic tasks. Cleopatra, poor girl, was not a demon, like their mother. She was just unfortunate. First she had lost her husband King Alexander of Epirus, Olympias' brother and her and her brother's uncle. Alexander of Epirus had been killed in Italy in 331 B.C. Cleopatra had hardly had time to take over the regency of the Kingdom before her mother had arrived in Epirus (she had just left Pella in a huff) and had snatched the regency out of Cleopatra's hands. Cleopatra was still a widow, and, at her age, this was unfair to her and discreditable to her brother. Alexander could not evade his duty of finding a new husband for her. But whom? The nominee must be a suitable match for Alexander's sister, and at the same time he must be loyal to Alexander, and to Alexander's child and namesake too. Cleopatra was King Philip's only other legitimate child besides Alexander. Her hand would therefore endow her husband, whoever he might be, with a formidable claim on the succession if Alexander III were to die while the future Alexander IV was still a minor—and in 321 B.C. the child Alexander was only two years old. Finding the right husband for Cleopatra was as difficult a problem in its way as finding the right place of residence for Olympias.

Alexander's first choice was Craterus. He was well born, loyal, and intelligent. But Craterus was already married—and this at Alexander's instance—to Amastris, Darius III's niece, and he had not repudiated this Persian wife of his so far. Perso-Macedonian mixed marriages ministered to Alexander's policy of unifying mankind. He could not afford to dissolve one of these politic international marriages in order to substitute for it a marriage between Macedonian and Macedonian. Moreover, the repudiation of Amastris would be an affront to the Achaemenidae, and Alexander felt a chivalrous concern to spare the feelings of the surviving members of the fallen imperial house. Accordingly, Alexander married Cleopatra to Leonnatus. This new brother-in-law of Alexander's had his comrade Craterus' good qualities, and he was even better born. He was a descendant of the princes of Lyncestis, one of those Macedonian highland cantons that had been deprived of their autonomy by Philip. Since Antipater was now visibly aging, Alexander kept Leonnatus in reserve; and, when Antipater died in 319 B.C., he appointed Leonnatus to succeed him as his vicegerent in Macedon and southern Greece.

Antipater on his death-bed advised Alexander not to employ his (Antipater's) son Cassander. Alexander followed this advice; for he, too, had come to the conclusion that Cassander was unscrupulous and ruthless. Cassander was, however, also resentful and energetic. He retorted to being passed over by deserting. He fled to Carthage, warned the Carthaginian Government of what was coming to them, and put his sword at their service.

With all this on his hands in 321 B.C., Alexander had had to delegate to other hands the task of preparing for the attack on Carthage by making preliminary diplomatic moves in Sicily. Alexander had put this business in Ptolemy's hands, and Ptolemy had fulfilled his mission with consummate ability. Since Timoleon's retirement and early death, his admirable settlement of Siceliot Greek affairs had gone to pieces. By 321 B.C. the Greek and Sicel states in the island were, once again, at sixes and sevens with each other, and Carthage had been re-extending her influence eastwards, beyond the eastern frontier of her epikrateia in Sicily, by playing off Greek against Greek. It looked, in fact, as if Siceliot Greek history were relapsing into the cyclic rhythm that had been characteristic of it in the past. For 200 years, save for the brief Timoleontic interlude, the Greek or Hellenized two-thirds of Sicily had oscillated between anarchic bouts of local independence and despotic bouts of unity. By

321 B.C. it was looking as if the current post-Timoleontic bout of anarchy were soon going to be followed by a new bout of unity under a despot in the style of the Deinomenidae and the Dionysii. A possible candidate for the succession to Dionysius II was already being pointed out. He was a young officer in the Syracusan service named Agathocles. Ptolemy called a conference of representatives of the Siceliot and Sicel states and put two proposals to them in Alexander's name. The first was that they should enter with each other into a new Confederation of Syracuse which should have the same constitution as the Confederation of Corinth. The second proposal was that, with the Confederation of Corinth's aid and under Alexander's hegemony, they should expel Carthage from her domain in western Sicily. Both proposals were accepted; for, though the Siceliot Greeks did not relish the prospect of being incorporated in Alexander's World-State, they did not have any more attractive alternative in view. Ptolemy divined their mood and took effective measures for making sure that they should not be able to go back on their word. He posted Macedonian garrisons on Ortygia Island, on 'the reaping-hook' at Messana, and on the Athenaeum at Akragas; and he enticed Agathocles out of Sicily by taking it on himself to offer him a position on Alexander's personal staff (Alexander ratified this act of Ptolemy's promptly when he met Agathocles and took the measure of his energy and ambition).

The story of Alexander's subsequent Sicilian and African campaigns can be told briefly. He conducted them both with non-Macedonian Greek troops exclusively (he had realized in 321 B.C. that Macedon needed a rest). In the Confederation of Corinth's expeditionary force the contingents supplied by Corinth and Chalcis were given a leading role in consideration of the importance of the Corinthian and Chalcidian elements in the Greek population of Sicily. Lilybaeum was besieged and captured in 320 B.C., Carthage in 319 B.C. (Cassander died there in the last ditch). Carthage's resistance to Alexander was as heroic as her mother-city Tyre's had been in 332 B.C., and her consequent fate was the same. This was embarrassing for Alexander; for he had committed himself to giving the Phoenicians the rank of an imperial people, and he was counting on the Phoenicians' co-operation for the development of the World-State's maritime communications. Alexander therefore now took special pains to retain the Phoenicians' goodwill. After the fall of Carthage in 319 B.C., he rehabilitated the city as handsomely as he had rehabilitated Tyre in 322 B.C., but, of course, he did not re-establish the Carthaginian Empire. To replace it, he united the Phoenician colonial states round the western basin of the Mediterranean and beyond the Pillars of Herakles in a Confederation of Utica, modelled on the pattern of the Confederations of Corinth and of Syracuse; he compelled his restored

Carthage to share with some of the other colonial Phoenician cities—Utica, Hippo Diarrhytus, Acholla, Hadrumetum, Thapsus—the continental African domain that Carthage had previously monopolized; and he opened the Straits of Gibraltar for shipping of all nationalities. To ensure that henceforward the Straits should be under his own command, he planted at Gibraltar a Greek colony, manned mainly by Massaliots and Phocaeans, which he named Alexandreschata Heraclea, to match his Alexandreschata Dionysiaca on the River Jaxartes.

But was '-eschata' really the appropriate termination for either city's name? The Macedonian Dionysus-Herakles was determined not to rest from his labours till he had united the whole of the Oikoumene in the World-State that he was building up; and the ends of the Oikoumene were not within sight at either of these two Alexandrias, though these were the most distant of all the Alexandrias that their eponym had founded so far. Beyond Alexandria-on-Jaxartes there were the vast steppes; beyond Alexandria-on-the-Straits there was the vast Ocean; and, of course, beyond the never-to-be-forgotten River Beas there was the still untrodden major part of the sub-continent of India. Alexander now removed the negative prefix to Pindar's famous dictum τὸ πόρσω δ' ἄβατον, 'Ne plus ultra'. 'Plus ultra' was Alexander's counter-slogan; and he duly provided for the expansion of his World-State westwards beyond the forbidding pair of 'pillars' that had been the limit of Greek navigation for 200 years past. He entrusted the exploration of the Atlantic to Gades and Massalia; and, for the dividing line between these two maritime cities' respective spheres, he laid down the parallel of latitude that runs through the Thalweg of the Straits of Gibraltar. During the siege of Carthage, which had been long protracted, Alexander had found time to read two accounts of explorations beyond the Straits. One was the Carthaginian Hanno's narrative of his voyage along the Atlantic coast of Africa 200 years ago; the other was the narrative of the Massaliot Pytheas' recent voyage along the Atlantic coast of Europe and round some of the offshore islands. Alexander made a rendezvous with Pytheas to meet him at Gades, and this meeting bore fruit. Alexander allocated a large annual grant to both Massalia and Gades for the systematic following-up of Pytheas' and Hanno's pioneer expeditions.

The Gadeirites were quicker than the Massaliots in getting to work. Pytheas' reports of frozen seas and midnight suns and an annual six-months-long night had intimidated the minority of his countrymen who had not written him off as a romancer. Where there was twenty-four-hours-long daylight there might also be cannibal Laestrygonians; and anyway these weird north-western waters did not seem to lead to any goal that was worth reaching. The Gadeirites, on the other hand, knew just what they were about. They were going to circumnavigate Africa from west to east, and their objective would be to open up a line of regular maritime communications with their Phoenician kinsmen whom Alexander had just planted at the mouth of the Red Sea. The Gadeirites were not daunted by the knowledge that the sole previous attempt at circumnavigation in this direction had failed. Its failure had been a foregone conclusion, considering that it had not been made under Phoenician auspices. The ship and crew had been Egyptian; the commander had been a Persian, Xerxes' nephew Sataspes.[1] The Gadeirites also knew, however that Africa had been circumnavigated successfully in the opposite direction by a squadron of Phoenician ships that had been commissioned by Pharaoh Necho II as soon as the completion of his Nile–Suez canal had made it possible to sail from Phoenicia into the Red Sea. It had taken these kinsmen of the Gadeirites the best part of three years to reach the Mediterranean coast of Egypt via the Straits of Gibraltar. But eventually they had arrived; so the enterprise had been proved to be possible.[2] By the year 310 B.C. a Gadeirite ship had reached Suez via the Cape of Good Hope and had returned to Gades by the same route. From that time onwards the circum-African sea-route has been one of the World's regular shipping-lanes. From that time, too, all long-distance navigation has been in Phoenician hands.

Alexander, as has been mentioned, made an excursion through the Straits to Gades. His heart had been set on sailing upon this western reach of Ocean Stream. It had also been set on completing his circum-ambulation of the western basin of the Mediterranean. But at the Straits, as at the River Beas, Alexander's advance was brought to a halt by two gods who, between them, were stronger than Ammon's son. One of these prohibiting gods was Human Nature. At the Straits, as at the Beas, Alexander's army turned mulish and could not be prevailed upon to march farther. The other prohibiting god was Non-Human Nature. An organized army, carrying a siege-train with it, can only move on waterways or on roads. It cannot make its way through the unreclaimed wilderness. The triumvirate induced Alexander to hold a consultation with his corps of bematistae; and these expert surveyors revealed to him the disillusioning truth about his triumphal march across south-western Asia. What had made this possible, the experts now explained to Alexander, had not been his own Dionysiac *élan*; it had been the bematistae's Persian predecessors' patience and skill. For 200 years before Alexander had set foot on Persian imperial territory the Persian engineers had been building a network of magnificent roads. Alexander had profited from Persian labours that he had ignored. The Macedonian infantryman had been more clear-sighted. When he had reached the easternmost Persian road-head, he had recognized that it was time to stop—and Spain, the

[1] Herodotus, Book IV, chap. 43.   [2] Ibid., chap. 42.

bematistae pointed out, was as roadless as India beyond the Beas was. These representations finally convinced Alexander that he could not invade Italy via Spain, but must return to Greece to invade Italy via the Straits of Otranto. This is, as we know, what Alexander did in 317 B.C. But, before giving a brief account of the Italian campaign of that year, let us allow ourselves a digression into the imaginary realm of what might have been. Actually, no army has ever yet marched overland from Utica to Italy, though north-west Africa, Spain, and Gaul have all been opened up long since. But we can imagine a situation in which this adventurous march might have been made.

Let us imagine that Alexander had died at Babylon in June 323 B.C. (This first instalment of our parenthetical piece of fiction is not difficult to accept, considering that, for some days in that month, Alexander truly was at death's door.) If Alexander had died in 323 B.C., the Carthaginian Empire would certainly have remained standing, and the Samnite Confederation would probably have succeeded in making itself the mistress of peninsular Italy. It might have achieved this by joining hands with the Etruscans. The Etruscans and Samnites had a common interest: Rome was a menace to both parties; and, in concert, they could have crushed Rome like a nut caught in a pair of nut-crackers. After that, Samnium would probably have gone on to dispute with Carthage the possession of Sicily—and of Sardinia too. Oscan mercenary soldiers had been serving in Sicily since the time of Dionysius I. Their reports of an El Dorado there might have whetted the appetite of the continental Oscan power. What would have happened if Samnium and Carthage had become locked in combat? The Samnites, with their superior man-power, might easily have overrun the interior of Sicily, but they could hardly have captured the coast-towns so long as Carthage retained command of the sea. The historic expulsion of the Carthaginians from Sicily by Alexander in 320 B.C. was achieved by sea-power, as we know. Let us now suppose that unseamanlike Samnium somehow succeeded in establishing her ascendancy at sea as well as on land. I must apologize to my readers for making such an extravagant demand as this on their powers of imagination. I am asking them to entertain a belief in an imaginary achievement that is all but unimaginable; but I cannot avoid making this demand, because it is a necessary prelude to the denouement of my imaginary story.

Well then, the Samnites wrest the command of the sea from Carthage and force her to purchase peace at the price of ceding both Sardinia and Sicily. What will Carthage do next? She will be thirsting for revenge. But how is she to get at her adversary now? The sea lies between the enlarged Samnite Empire and the diminished Carthaginian Empire, and the sea has passed under Samnite command irretrievably. If Carthage is to attack Samnium under these conditions, she will have to do it overland. She will have to convey a land-army to within striking distance of the Samnite Commonwealth's soft under-belly in the north-west. If a Carthaginian expeditionary force can reach the Po Valley, the Gauls and Ligurians will rise *en masse* to join it. They will rise because they are under threat of being attacked and conquered by the Samnites and Etruscans if they remain passive. This mass of barbarian man-power, added to a highly trained professional Carthaginian force, might conceivably get the better of the united forces of Samnium and her peninsular Italian allies. Let us imagine that some Carthaginian general conceives this plan and succeeds in carrying it out. Of course this is not credible. The most brilliant strategist, combined in the same person with the most magnetic leader, would not really be able to pilot an army, encumbered with a siege-train and possibly with elephants as well, across the Pyrenees and the Rhône and the Alps and the Po and the Appennines. If we are to believe that, it will be a case of 'credo quia incredibile'. Let us return to the sober facts of history 'wie es eigentlich gewesen ist'.

Actually, as we know, neither Samnium nor our imaginary Carthaginian military genius was ever given a chance of trying to do what we have just been imagining. Alexander ruled that out by crushing Carthage in 319 B.C. and crushing Samnium in 317 B.C.

The Italian campaign, like the Sicilian campaign, was preceded by diplomatic moves; and, once again, Ptolemy conducted the negotiations on Alexander's behalf. By the year 317 B.C. it was high time for Alexander to take a hand in Italian affairs. In the winter of 318/17 B.C., Samnium was overshadowing the whole Italian peninsula. She had been overshadowing it since 320 B.C., when she had trapped a Roman army that had been rashly trying to invade Samnium through the wild and wooded Caudine section of the Appennines. The captured Roman army had had to purchase its release by concluding a humiliating peace with Samnium, and Rome had then been further embarrassed by revolts on the part of some of her own restive allies and subjects. The hegemony over the whole of peninsular Italy was now almost within the Samnites' grasp—almost, but not quite; for the very magnitude of Samnium's victory over Rome at the Caudine Forks had been moving those among the south-eastern Italian states that still retained some freedom of manœuvre to get together with each other and with Rome in the hope of salvaging the independence of each and all by concerted action. This had given the Romans an opening for embarking on a new strategy. Their previous frontal attack on Samnium had ended in disaster. Might they not be able to return to the charge with better prospects of success if they were to work their way across the peninsula to the Adriatic coast, enlisting new allies as they advanced? They could then attack Samnium via Apulia, where the ascent of the Samnite plateau is more open and is therefore easier. By 318 B.C. Rome had negotiated with the highland cantons of central Italy a right of way for Roman armies from the Tiber basin to the Adriatic through the Aternus gorge; and, when a Roman army had marched by that route in that year into the territory of the Frentani, the Frentani had seceded from the Samnite Confederation under cover of this Roman expeditionary force. In the winter of 318/17 B.C., two Apulian city-states, Teanum Apulum and Canusium, were negotiating with the Roman Government with a view to following the Frentani's example. It was at this juncture that Ptolemy appeared on the scene.

Ptolemy landed at Tarentum, and the Tarentine Government needed no prompting. Ever since Alexander's uncle and brother-in-law and namesake the late King of Epirus had met his death in Italy in 331 B.C., Tarentum had been sending message after message to Alexander of Macedon, urging him to avenge his uncle's death and to carry out his unfinished work with more powerful forces than those that Epirus had been able to put into the field. Passing through Tarentum, Ptolemy made a rapid tour of the principal states of Peucetia and Apulia, offering them alliances with Alexander against Samnium and assuring them that Alexander himself, with an overwhelmingly powerful army, would be arriving in Italy from Greece to crush Samnium in the coming campaigning season. Ptolemy devoted most of his time and effort to Canusium and Teanum Apulum. He advised their governments to think twice before committing themselves to Rome—a minor power on the far side of the Appennines—now that they were being offered the alternative choice of allying themselves with the ruler of the World-State. Ptolemy won Canusium and Teanum, and the rest of the Apulian and Peucetian states as well, for the alliance with Macedon; and, having thus achieved the first part of his mission, he travelled on, through the Aternus gorge, to Rome.

In the Roman Senate at this date, there was a considerable fund of political ability and experience. These Roman nobles were as supple in their diplomacy as they were persistent in the pursuit of their objectives. However, Ptolemy had two winning cards in his hands. He was the representative of the world-conqueror to whose quarters at distant Babylon the Roman Government had sent a propitiatory embassy in 323 B.C., and he had caught Rome at a moment when she was still under the shadow of her Caudine disaster. Probably Rome would have tried conclusions again with Samnium in any case. Her new strategy and her new south-east Italian alliances offered her at least a faint hope of reversing the Caudine military and political decision against her. But now Rome was being virtually assured of a conclusive triumph over Samnium by being offered an alliance with the ruler of the World. The doubtful question was whether an alliance between two parties that were so unequal in strength might not turn out, for Rome, to be another name for servitude; and the Roman nobility would not voluntarily acquiesce in that.

Ptolemy divined what was passing through the Roman negotiators' minds, and he set himself to allay their anxieties. His design for Rome was to persuade her to accept the role of an Italian counterpart of Alexander's Indian ally Porus; and this was a role that was compatible with Roman pride. Ptolemy explained—and he convinced the Romans of his sincerity—that Alexander wanted to have the Romans for his honoured partners, and that he had no thought of trying to reduce them to becoming his subjects. This was not just a diplomatic phrase. Ptolemy showed what he meant by putting it in concrete terms. First and foremost, he explained, he was not asking Rome to surrender any territorial or political asset that she already held. He did not challenge her recent alliance with the Frentani, or her hardly less recent alliance with Neapolis. Since this alliance, too, was an accomplished fact, it, too, would not be called in question—though he added that Alexander did not like to see Greek communities left under the hegemony of non-Greek powers (the preservation or restoration of the independence of all the Italiot Greek states except Neapolis would be the primary objective of Alexander's coming Italian campaign). Rome was to retain her existing commonwealth intact, including Neapolis. When Samnium had been overthrown by the joint efforts of Alexander and his Italian allies, Rome's share of the Samnite territorial spoils was to be the Caudine canton and the fertile upper Volturnus and Sagrus valleys, and she was to have a free hand to bring the central Italian cantons and the Sabines and the Picentes into whatever relations with herself she might be able to persuade or to compel them to accept. That would be Rome's own affair. Alexander would not interfere in that quarter, and the effect, for Rome, would be to give her access to the plains of the Po basin, with all their potential agricultural wealth. In the opposite direction, Alexander would agree to Rome's incorporating Nola and the Nucerine Pentapolis in her commonwealth if she could win them by persuasion—she must refrain from trying to win these states by force.

Ptolemy then turned to the more delicate business of setting out the limits to Rome's expansion that Alexander would be laying down. The north-eastern part—i.e. the major part—of Samnium, and the whole of Apulia, Peucetia, Calabria, Lucania, Bruttium, and Magna Graecia (always excepting Neapolis) were to be out of bounds for Rome. These south-east Italian territories were to be organized into a Confederation of Tarentum, on the pattern of the Confederations of Corinth and Syracuse and Utica. To mark the new Italiot Confederation's bounds, Alexander would be planting Greek colonies at Maluentum, at Luceria, and at some point in the upper basin of the River Aufidus in the neighbourhood of Mount Vultur.

Ptolemy then went on to raise the question of the future of the Etruscan and Umbrian city-states. Of course he did not question Rome's possession of the Ager Veientanus. This was a long-since-accomplished fact and an irreversible one. However, Ptolemy took note of the fact that, since Rome had come into collision with Samnium, she had been almost demonstratively conciliatory to those Etruscan states—and they were the majority—that had retained their independence so far. For instance, Rome had made long-term truces with Caere and Tarquinii on terms in which the independence of these two Etruscan states was expressly assured. Ptolemy complimented the Romans on their wisdom in having taken such care to avoid giving the Etruscans any incentive to ally themselves with the Samnites. This, he said, would be Alexander's policy too, and Ptolemy then announced Alexander's consequent intention of making treaties of his own with Caere and Tarquinii on terms that would be identical with those of their existing truces with Rome. Ptolemy proposed that, in regard to north-western Italy, Rome and Alexander should agree with each other on four points. They should jointly guarantee the independence and the territorial integrity of all Etruscan and Umbrian states (with the exception of Veii, of course). They should respectively hold themselves free to make alliances with any of these states, on the understanding that in every case the terms of alliance should leave the Etruscan or Umbrian contracting party independent and intact. Any such alliance that either Rome or Alexander might make should automatically also carry with it an identical alliance for Alexander or for Rome. In the fourth place, Alexander and Rome would not press any of the Etruscan and Umbrian states to go to war with Samnium. The two allies could crush Samnium without the Etruscans' help; and, if these north-west Italian states were permitted to stay neutral during the coming conflict in peninsular Italy, they would be able to perform the useful service of guarding the peninsula against any of the Gallic peoples who might be tempted to try to cross the Appennines while Rome and Alexander were engaged in Samnium.

These terms that Ptolemy set out were precise, and he indicated, in very tactful language, that the Roman Government must either accept them or reject them as they stood. There could be no negotiation with a view to modifying them. He also managed to indicate, without giving offence, that, if Rome were not merely to reject Alexander's offer but were to throw in her lot with Samnium against him, this lunatic act on Rome's part would not upset Alexander's plans. For the coming Italian campaign, Alexander had concentrated such numbers of first-rate troops that he was in a position to conquer peninsular Italy even if every non-Samnite Italian state were to fight on Samnium's side.

The Roman negotiators understood Ptolemy and liked him; and the debate in the Senate did not take long; for the Senate had already made up its mind. The public officers told Ptolemy before nightfall that Rome gladly accepted Alexander's offer as it stood.

The army that Alexander had assembled at Oricum was indeed as formidable as Ptolemy had declared it to be. It included the élite of Alexander's Macedonian and Iranian troops, as well as the whole levy of Epirus and of the Confederation of Corinth. Alexander's south-east Italian allies were assembling at Tarentum. The levy of the Confederation of Sicily was being taken by sea to reinforce the Roman armies in Campania and on the River Liris. The keenest contingent was the Epirot one. The Epirots had the death of their King Alexander to avenge. The Spartans, too, had recently lost a king in Italy; King Archidamus III had been killed there in 338/7 B.C.; but, in Italy in 317 B.C., the Spartan army was conspicuous by its absence.

Ptolemy had failed to induce the Spartans to take part in Alexander's Panhellenic campaign for making Italy safe for Hellenism. This was Ptolemy's one signal failure in the course of his long and brilliant diplomatic career. The Spartans proved quite intractable. Avenge Archidamus III's death? That could wait till they had avenged Agis III's. Come to the rescue of their daughter-city Tarentum? Once had been enough; for they had not approved of the Tarentines when they had met them. Tarentum was the spitten image of the frivolous archaic Sparta on which the soldierly modern Sparta had turned her back. Sparta did not want to be reminded of her regrettable past by being faced with the Tarentine caricature of it. The negativeness of the Spartan reaction to Ptolemy's representations was not Ptolemy's fault. If Philip had still been alive, he might perhaps have persuaded the Spartans to march on this occasion, in spite of their dislike and mistrust of him. But their dislike and mistrust of Alexander were far greater. These Spartan feelings were an obstacle that even Ptolemy could not overcome. Accordingly, in 317 B.C. the Spartan army stayed at home, as it had done more than once before at moments at which history was being made.

The Italian campaign of 317 B.C. was carried out according to plan. The peace-settlement was made on the terms that Ptolemy had negotiated. Alexander had now eaten the second half of the Hesperides' apple; but, not being a demigod of Herakles' build, he had been unable to devour the whole fruit in a single bite.

Alexander was now master of the Mediterranean basin, besides south-western Asia, but he had also learnt that these two regions, combined, were far from being the whole World. His libido now flowed back to the River Beas. His defeat there by his own Macedonians had never ceased to rankle in his mind. Now that his hands were free in other quarters, he would cross the Beas as soon as he could find troops that would march and a guide to conduct them. He now had the troops. They were the survivors of the defeated Samnites and their Lucanian and Bruttian allies. These Oscan fighting-men would have to go wherever Alexander might choose to send them; for they had lost their Italian homes. Alexander had uprooted them to make way for Greek colonists. Only Alexander could find new homes for them, and, in sending them beyond the Beas, he would be achieving two purposes. He would be sending the expatriate Oscans so far from their native Italy that they would never be able to make their way back; and he would be completing his conquest of the World (so he imagined) by annexing the remainder of the Indian sub-continent.

By the spring of the year 314 B.C. the Oscan deportees were already in position along the Beas' northern bank. They had been transported by sea from the Italian to the Phoenician ports; had marched overland to the Panjab; and had then had a year in cantonments there for recuperating and acclimatizing. The necessary guide was also on the spot by this time.

It has been mentioned that when, in the summer of 323 B.C., Alexander was lying at death's door in Babylon, a false report that he had died had travelled westward to Greece. In that quarter of the World-State, Antipater had been able to contradict the report authoritatively before any of the dissident-minded members of the Confederation of Corinth had had time to take up arms. The truth had taken longer to catch up with the falsehood in the Indus Valley; and, in the belief that Alexander was dead, a young Indian soldier of fortune named Chandragupta had made an audacious attack on the Macedonian garrison there. Chandragupta's raid had been repelled even before it had become known that Alexander had recovered, and Chandragupta had been lucky to escape back alive into a hiding-place in the Indian desert. From here he had had the effrontery to send a message to the local Macedonian authorities, offering them his services. He argued that he had demonstrated his value by having come so near to driving them out. His impudent message had been relayed to Alexander, and eventually the answer had come back that Chandragupta was to be offered employment as a secret agent for Alexander in the Kingdom of Magadha, the dominant Indian state in the Ganges Valley. Chandragupta was to be paid by results. If he were successful in preparing the ground for the conquest of Magadha, his reward would be substantial. Chandragupta had accepted these terms and had not been heard of again for the next seven years; then in 315 B.C.

he had contacted the Macedonian outposts on the Beas and had reported that the fruit was now ripe for plucking. It was not only ripe; it was rotten; for what Chandragupta had been doing during his seven years underground had been to recruit a 'fifth column' that was now ready to come into action as soon as Alexander attacked. Chandragupta had recruited it among the peoples that the Kingdom of Magadha, in the course of its expansion, had annexed but had failed to assimilate. This anti-Magadha movement was particularly lively in the little sub-Himalayan city-state of Kapilavastu. Its citizens could not forget that they were the kinsmen of Siddhartha Gautama the Buddha.

On receiving Chandragupta's report, Alexander set out for the River Beas at full speed. He rode relays of post-horses (Bucephalus had died in the Panjab in 326 B.C.). He took Seleucus with him. Seleucus had done well in Arabia, and he had shown a liking for distant commands, in spite of his chronic homesickness for his Macedonian home-town, Europus. The Magadha campaign was soon over. The march from the Beas to the Jumna was not a long one, and this was the dry season. On the Jumna, Chandragupta had prepared a flotilla of troop-transports; and when the boats, with the army on board, reached Pataliputra, the Kingdom of Magadha fell to pieces. Alexander's defeat on the Beas had now been expunged, but not Alexander's chagrin; for Pataliputra, now that he had reached it, proved to be just as far from World's end as the River Beas had been. Alexander found himself at a confluence of mighty rivers; he sailed on down to the sea through a delta that dwarfed the deltas of the Indus and the Nile. He was now gazing out at yet another reach of Ocean Stream; and here were his faithful and efficient Persian-Gulf Phoenicians waiting for him. He had ordered them to circumnavigate the Indian sub-continent while he was traversing it, and they had reached the farther side of India just before his own arrival there. Their report was that the Indian peninsula was at least as big as the Arabian peninsula. The completion of Alexander's self-imposed task of World-conquest was still eluding him.

Chandragupta now submitted that he had earned his substantial reward, and he suggested that the governorship of Magadha would be the appropriate form of it. Alexander summarily refused this large request, and appointed Seleucus instead. Chandragupta was a clever rogue, and he knew Magadha too well to be entrusted with it. Leaving Seleucus behind to secure the submission of the peninsular Indian states, Alexander took Chandragupta back with him to Alexandria and quickly sent him up the Nile, at the head of a brigade of Illyrian mercenary troops, to conquer the Kingdom of Napata and to instal himself as Alexander's viceroy there. Chandragupta not only occupied Napata; he went on up-stream to Meroe, where rich deposits of iron-ore had recently been discovered, and he then pushed on, above the sixth and highest cataract, into a region that reminded him of his native India— a green country that was visited, like India, by the monsoon. Chandragupta was now standing on the threshold of tropical Africa. The exploration of this new world kept him busy and loyal for the rest of his life. To secure his long line of communications with Egypt, Chandragupta posted half his Illyrians on the rock of Ibrim and the other half on the holy mountain Jabal Barkal. These northerners have left their mark in the blue eyes and pale skins of their present-day descendants, and in the graffiti that they have scratched on Ramses II's gigantic statues at Abu Simbel. Their Illyrian names—Monunios, Longaros, Baton, and the like—are still legible, side by side with the Greek and Carian names of Psammetichus III's soldiers.

Thanks to Chandragupta, Alexander had won the Indian campaign of 314 B.C., but it proved to be the Buddha who had won the war. In the Indus Basin the Greeks had been meeting Hindu ascetics; now in Magadha they met Buddhist monks, and they found these still more intriguing. The Hindu ascetics were exhibitionists; their self-mortifications were, and were intended to be, sensational. The Buddhists mortified themselves no more harshly than was required for the practical purpose of performing effectively the spiritual exercises that their founder had prescribed; and these exercises were not an end in themselves; their objective was Nirvana—'Extinguishedness' (what was extinguished, upon the attainment of Nirvana, was desire).

Though the Buddha had had local roots in Kapilavastu (his father had been king there), his philosophy was not just one for local use. His message was addressed to all sentient beings, and his followers' mission was to carry the message to the ends of the Earth. In Magadha in 314 B.C. the World-Religion and the World-State met each other for the first time. Since then, they have never been parted.

World-mission? Then what was the Buddhists' attitude towards the innumerable local gods whom they would find in possession of every square yard of their mission-field? Their attitude was the antithesis of the Yahweh-maniacs' attitude. The Buddhists did not denigrate the gods; still less did they deny their existence; they simply put them in their place in the queue of aspirants to Nirvana. This place was a middling one; it was behind mankind's place, but in front of the animals'. However, the Buddhists did not discourage their converts from continuing to pay respect to their ancestral gods; they were left free to do that, so long as they did not let this deflect them from the all-important quest for Nirvana.

Within the next few years, Buddhist missionaries were arriving in the West. They had travelled westwards along Phoenician sea-lanes and along Persian roads. The impression that they made here was profound; but the path from selfhood to Nirvana which the Buddha had traced for his followers was too hard for the Greeks—culpably easy-going though it might seem to the Hindus. The radicalness of Indian thought and action was beyond the Greeks' spiritual capacity; and, in the presence of this Indian virtue, the Greeks felt abashed. They were fascinated by the Buddhist ideal, but, in practice, they could not rise to it. They were extricated from this psychological impasse by two local philosophers. Epicurus and Zeno each worked out a diluted form of Buddhism for Greek consumption. Both dilutions were weak enough for Greeks to be able to swallow them; so, at the western end of the Oikoumene, these two sub-Buddhist philosophies were widely welcomed. Epicurus opened his institute in 306 B.C.; Zeno opened his in 300 B.C. They both chose Athens for the locale, and this choice gave Athens a new lease of life.

When, at Alexandria, Seleucus' laconic dispatch had been registered and interpreted, the World-conqueror believed for a moment that he had completed his life-work. The dispatch contained the single word καλλίνικα ('cheers-for-victory'), and it took Ptolemy's acumen to read the pun. Seleucus was reporting that he had attacked and conquered Kalinga, the nearest to Magadha of the peninsular Indian kingdoms, and it turned out that this initial victory had intimidated all the rest of the peninsula into submitting without resistance. In Kalinga, the resistance had been stubborn; the slaughter and devastation had been proportionably great; and the lesson had been taken to heart by Kalinga's neighbours. It did not occur to Alexander to feel remorse for the sufferings that had been inflicted on his Kalingan fellow human beings in pursuance of his personal orders. He was pre-occupied with a conflict of feelings: a sense of elation at having conquered the World and a sense of frustration at having no more worlds left to conquer; but both these emotions were put out of mind by the next piece of business on that morning's agenda.

This next business of Alexander's was to give audience to an embassy from the associated colonial Greek city-states along the Scythian shore of the Black Sea. The embassy had come to ask for men and money to help these northern outposts of the Hellenic World to keep the nomads in their hinterland at bay. The ambassadors' principals had been anxious to convince Alexander that, though remote, they were important; so they had instructed their ambassadors to tell the World-ruler about the mysterious civilized society at the far end of the long trail that ran north-eastward across the Eurasian steppe from the mouth of the River Don.[1] This Far-Eastern people was a considerable importer of Greek luxury goods, and its own works of art, which it exported in exchange,

---

[1] Herodotus, Book IV, chaps. 13 and 21–7.

were exquisite—especially the bronzes. Greeks and Far-Easterners had never yet met face to face. The trade between them was conducted by several relays of middlemen. But the Far-Easterners' products proved, beyond question, the existence of these products' makers. As the ambassadors told their tale, a new world swam into Alexander's ken. He once more had another world to conquer.

How to reach this far-eastern extremity of Asia? To follow the trade-route across the steppe would court the disaster that had overtaken Cyrus and Darius and Zopyrion, one after the other, when they had trespassed on nomads' land. In planning his venture into outer space, Alexander decided to take off, not from any of the Black Sea ports, but from the Alexandreschata on the upper Jaxartes. By the spring of 312 B.C. his preparations were complete. He had assembled a highly mobile mixed force of Iranians and colonial Greeks, all drawn from the provinces to the north-east of the Caspian Gates. What officers should he take with him? Antigonus, for one. Antigonus had shown himself to be forceful and ambitious. That dare-devil Agathocles for another. Agathocles enjoyed burning his boats. The expedition clambered over the Tien Shan, hobbled from oasis to oasis round the northern rim of the Tarim Basin, crossed the Gobi desert at its waist, and stopped to reconnoitre when it had come within ten days' march of the north-westernmost outposts of the state of Ch'in. By now it was the spring of 311 B.C.

How to take one's bearings in this hitherto unknown new world? Alexander and his companions had this problem solved for them by a stroke of luck. A mission from the League of Eastern States stumbled on their camp. This mission was not in search of Alexander. In eastern Asia, Alexander had not yet been heard of. The only Greek whose name was already known there was the semi-legendary Aristeas of Proconnesus.[1] The mission was on its way to try to persuade the Wu-sun nomads (the Greeks pronounced this people's name 'Issedones') to make common cause with the Six Eastern States against Ch'in, east Asia's march-state in 'the Land Beyond the Passes' that had become a menace to all its neighbours. The Easterners and the Greeks could communicate with each other; for, *en route*, Antigonus had picked up, and brought along with him, an Issedonian trader who had some knowledge of both Greek and Chinese. Alexander was thus able to inform himself about the East-Asian international situation.

He learnt that Ch'in, the Eastern States' and the Issedones' common enemy, was the east-Asian counterpart of his own Macedon. Like Macedon, Ch'in had been a backward semi-barbarian country as recently as three-quarters of a century ago. Ch'in and Macedon had risen in the world contemporaneously, and they had achieved this by the same

[1] Ibid., chaps. 13–15.

means. Ch'in, like Macedon, had imported instructors from kindred countries that were farther advanced than she was in civilization. Kings Hien and Hiao of Ch'in had, however, been more thorough-going than Philip and Alexander. When Philip's contemporary Hiao had come to the throne in 361 B.C., he had commissioned the sophist Shang Yang to reorganize his kingdom for him from top to bottom; and within the next twenty-three years Shang Yang had duly equipped Ch'in with a professional army and civil service and with a rationalized system of land-tenure and agriculture to provide a solid economic foundation for this expensive military and political superstructure. Thus renovated, Ch'in had carried all before it. In 333 B.C. the Six Eastern States had sought to stem the tide of Ch'in's expansion by forming their League; but in 318 B.C. Ch'in had defeated the League's united forces. In 316 B.C. she had annexed the vast and potentially rich virgin territory of Szechuan in the south-west; and only last year, while Alexander's expeditionary force had been plodding along towards Ch'in's north-west frontier, Ch'in had started to encircle Ch'u, the biggest of the Eastern Six, from the south.

What impressed the Greeks most in this exposition was the magnitude of the figures in terms of which the Chinese talked. The Greeks thought in myriads; Greek life had been on a scale that did not require a larger measure of magnitude than that. The Chinese talked all the time in millions. Everything in eastern Asia seemed to run to millions—populations, armies, acres, and whatnot. Alexander and his advisers put their heads together. If Ch'in were now to succeed in unifying this eastern end of the Oikoumene, as Macedon had just succeeded in unifying the western end of it, Ch'in's power would be overwhelming. She would have it in her power to take over Alexander's would-be World-State as and when she chose. Was it possible that Philip and Alexander had been working for the King of Ch'in, without knowing it? Zeus Ammon must have inspired those Black Sea Greeks to send their embassy to Alexandria when they did. Thanks to that, Alexander was now encamped at Ch'in's back-door in the nick of time. In the critical present circumstances an alliance between the Eastern Six and Alexander was taken as a matter of course by both parties, and a plan of campaign was quickly agreed. The Six were to reopen hostilities with Ch'in on the east, and Alexander, supported by the Issedones, was to try to take Ch'in by surprise from the west—a quarter from which Ch'in was not expecting an attack. Compared to Ch'in's man-power, Alexander's numerical strength was derisorily small, but his troops' equipment was superior, and audacity might do the rest. Alexander pledged himself to launch his attack on Ch'in's rear as soon as the ambassadors should have had time to regain the East by the circuitous route by which they had come.

The history of the east Asian campaign of 311 B.C. is common knowledge. While the Six were keeping the bulk of Ch'in's army in play at the Passes, incredible news reached Ch'in's field-headquarters. The Kingdom's capital, Hsien-Yang, had been occupied by an unknown enemy without resistance. The result was a panic; Ch'in's *moral* collapsed; her army dissolved; and her eastern and western assailants joined hands. There was unanimous agreement that the victors could not afford to let their prostrate enemy survive. They also agreed that the surest way of making it impossible for Ch'in to revive would be for Alexander to annex its territory to his World-State and to sow the country thick with Greek and Iranian colonists. At Alexander's suggestion the League of the Six Eastern States entered into permanent relations with him on the now standard pattern of his relations with the Confederation of Corinth.

By the time when Alexander reappeared above the Western World's horizon, four years had passed since he had left Alexandreschata-on-Jaxartes for an unknown destination; but, this time, Alexander's absence had not tempted any of his restive subjects and allies to try to shake off the World-State's yoke. People had learnt by this time that Alexander invariably recovered from his illnesses, however grave, and invariably returned from his expeditions, however lengthy. The World was no longer in a mood to gamble on rebelling in the hope of escaping retribution.

Alexander left Antigonus behind to govern 'the Land beyond the Passes', to plant the Greek and Iranian settlers there when these arrived, and to maintain amicable relations with the Eastern Six. This was a commission that was worthy of Antigonus' stature; but, at the very outset, he nearly paid for the recognition of his merits by losing his life. Alexander had left Agathocles behind, too, to be Antigonus' right-hand man; and, as soon as Alexander's back was turned, it occurred to Agathocles that he had only to assassinate Antigonus and step into his shoes, and he would find himself king of half the World. As this thought flashed through his mind, his sword flashed out of its scabbard; but Antigonus' son Demetrius was still quicker on the draw; so in 309 B.C. it was Agathocles, not Antigonus, who died. Antigonus died eventually in his bed, in his residency at Hsien-Yang, at the age of eighty-eight, in the year 293 B.C. His son Demetrius carried on in Alexander's name till a rescript from Alexandria informed him that he had been appointed officially to be his father's successor.

When Alexander arrived at Alexandria in the autumn of 309 B.C. his first act was to instruct the Red-Sea and the Persian-Gulf Phoenicians jointly to search for a sea-passage between the Indian Sea and the reach of Ocean Stream which washed the Six Kingdoms' eastern coasts, so the Easterners had told him. The Phoenicians had already established entrepôts on Elephanta Island and on Ceylon and at Arikamedu and on the River Hoogly. From the Hoogly they now followed the eastern shore of the Bay of Bengal. As they coasted it, the Asian Continent stretched southward and southward, never opening a sea-passage towards the east, till the explorers found themselves on the Equator and there, at last, slipped through the Straits of Malacca. The dramatic story of the discovery of this connecting link between the Indian Sea and the Eastern Sea has been told by Nearchus in the last and most enthralling of his accounts of his voyages. By the year 308 B.C. Nearchus had already retired from his professional career as a navigator. He had accompanied the Far Eastern maritime expedition as a passenger, and had had all the more time to observe and to record.

The arrival of this Phoenician squadron at the estuary of the River Yangtze produced a sensation throughout Eastern Asia; and the reports that the Phoenicians brought with them, of fertile southern lands, sparsely populated by backward peoples, stimulated the Six to organize a joint-stock company for opening up and colonizing the new world that the Phoenicians had brought to their knowledge. This was the beginning of a movement which, since then, has expanded the Chinese people's domain from the Yangtze Basin southwards to Tasmania.

The dispatch of the Phoenician expedition to Far Eastern waters in the autumn of 309 B.C. was the last of Alexander's significant acts. At this date, Alexander still had nearly twenty-two more years of life and reign ahead of him; but his last phase was a melancholy anticlimax. In 'the Land beyond the Passes' in 311 B.C., Alexander had, at last, truly achieved his objective of conquering the whole of the Oikoumene and uniting it under his rule. There was now no civilized society, anywhere on the face of the globe, that had not been included in the World-State; and, with no more worlds left to conquer, Alexander had lost his occupation.

There was, of course, a multitude of things that were still crying out to be done. World-conquest and World-unification were only the beginning of the World-Government's task. The conquered and united World had now to be organized and to be reconciled. The work did not stop. The triumvirate went on with it in Alexander's name; and, when, after his death, they retired, their successors took up the laborious task. But Alexander ceased to take a personal interest in it. The beneficent enterprise of peaceful reconstruction could not arouse in him the demonic energy that had so often been aroused in him by war. Moreover, his youthful intemperance was now taking its revenge on his physique. In 309 B.C., Alexander was only forty-seven—just one year older, that is, than his father Philip had been when, in 336 B.C., his life had been cut short. Alexander, bereft of his previous stimulus, now suddenly became lethargic. By the year 295 B.C. he was becoming feeble-minded; and, for some years before his death in 287 B.C. at the age of sixty-nine, people were saying—either compassionately or ironically according to their feelings towards him—that it might have been better for him if, at Babylon in June 323 B.C., he had brought a premature death upon himself by persisting in his characteristic habit of refusing to obey his doctors' orders.

Looking back to the year 287 B.C. with the perspective given to us by the time-span of nearly 2,300 years that separates our present age from Alexander's, we shall be inclined to comment that, if Alexander had indeed died in 323 B.C., this might have been fortunate for him but would certainly have been a disaster for the World. The unity that mankind has been enjoying from 309 B.C. till now is Alexander's gift to posterity; and to create this world-unity took Alexander all his time and strength throughout the twenty-seven years that elapsed between his accession and his return to Alexandria from the Far East.

In this essay we are concerned with Alexander's career, not with the post-Alexandrine history of the Alexandrine World in which we, in our day, still live and move and have our being. If there is to be an epilogue, it must be confined to notices of three new departures that cannot be traced back, either directly or indirectly, to Alexander's initiative or even to his influence. Each of these new departures has been the work of a man who was great enough not to be dwarfed by the world-bestriding colossus who inaugurated the present ecumenical epoch of human history. The three are Alexander IV, Hannibal Hamilcar's son, and Alexander XIII. Alexander IV was Alexander III's son and successor; Alexander XIII was one of the descendants and successors of them both; Hannibal was a colonial Phoenician whose home-town was Carthage.

When, in 287 B.C., Alexander III died at last, neither his successor nor anyone else could foresee what was going to happen. The late World-ruler had long ceased to govern. His son, who was now succeeding him, had been acting as regent for the last eight years. Yet by this time all public acts had been performed in Alexander III's name for forty-nine years, and his deeds during the first twenty-seven years of his reign had made his name one to conjure with. So what was going to happen when it was announced, not for the first time, that Alexander the Great was dead, but when, for the first time, the announcement was not going to be a false report?

During the night following the day of his father's death, the new World-ruler fortified his soul by reflecting that, at the worst, what might be going to happen tomorrow could not be anything like so disastrous as what might have happened if his father had died in 323 B.C., as he so very nearly had. In June 323 B.C., Alexander IV had been still in his gentle Iranian mother Roxana's womb, and the only living legitimate heir for Alexander III had been the unborn babe's half-uncle, poor feeble-minded Philip Arrhidaïos. In that situation, would the triumvirate —Perdiccas, Eumenes, Ptolemy—have been able to hold the World together? Even if a catastrophe could have been staved off till Roxana had given birth, an infant would have been a poor reinforcement to a half-wit. If a scramble for the territorial spoils of the prostrate Persian Empire had started then, what would have been the prospects for the infant and his mother and for his uncle? It seemed probable that one of the ferocious competitors for the spoils would have liquidated them sooner or later. Well, tomorrow could not be so bad as that. The unborn babe of 323 B.C. was now a mature man of thirty-six—three years older than his father had been in that perilous year. He had had eight years' experience of ruling the World already. He had proved his capacity, and, if his authority were to be challenged, he would be able to give a good account of himself. If the worst came to the worst, he would know how to take whatever might come to him. He would, he hoped, be able to take it with dignity and with fortitude, and with no surrender of his spiritual integrity and independence. The new World-ruler had been trained in self-command by a master. When Zeno had opened his institute at Athens in 300 B.C. the Crown Prince had become one of the institute's original fellows; and he had stayed there till he had been called to assume the regency for a father whose mind had eventually gone the same sad way as Philip Arrhidaïos' mind had.

When the news of Alexander III's death did break, the disorders that it excited were much milder than the new World-ruler and the old triumvirate had expected them to be. They had all had their eyes on three countries: Persis, Magadha, and Laconia; but neither the Spartans nor the Magadhans nor the Persians moved. In spite of their truculent response to Ptolemy in 317 B.C., the Spartans did not, after all, now try to avenge the death of their King Agis III. They never have avenged it, from that day to this. The Magadhans and the Persians had been suspect because they too had past histories that were too glorious to be easily forgotten. Their tranquillity in 287 B.C. was a tribute to their governors' success in winning hearts. Seleucus and Peucestas had each identified himself with the high-spirited ex-imperial people that had been placed in his charge. Peucestas had gone so far as to take to wearing Persian dress and to learn to speak the Medo-Persian language as idiomatically as if he had been Iranian born. In a Greek, this sensitiveness and sympathy for a non-Hellenic way of life were unusual. Most Greeks expected their non-Greek fellow human beings to come all the way to meet them by Hellenizing themselves one hundred per cent. Where did

Peucestas acquire his un-Greek liberalism? Perhaps from a non-Greek homeland. His name suggests that he may have been an immigrant to Macedon from Peucetia.

In 287 B.C. the only immediate breach of the peace occurred in an unexpected quarter. The nearest Thracians to Macedon's north-eastern border were the Maedi. Philip had subdued the Maedi in the course of his systematic incorporation of Thrace in his dominions; but, at Philip's death, the Maedi had quietly resumed their independence and had retained it, unmolested, from then till now. Alexander had overlooked the Maedi; his gaze had been fixed on far horizons; but the Maedi had not overlooked the quantities of loot that had been piling up in Pella ever since Philip had sacked Olynthus. In 287 B.C., at the news of Alexander's death, the Maedi rose, and the World-State was caught napping. Alexander had planted garrisons at Gibraltar and Jabal Barkal and Bharatpur, but he had never thought of planting one at Iamphorinna. When, in 287 B.C., the insurgent Maedi headed for Pella, there was nothing to stop the raiding party; and there was still nothing to stop it when it straggled back to its highland fastnesses laden with the spoils of the looted Macedonian looters. The incident would have been comic if it had not been so annoying. It was an outrageous affront to the World-Power; but it was not a serious menace to its survival.

The most serious menace to this in 287 B.C. had been one that Alexander IV did not hear of till twelve months later. The news of Alexander III's death had taken six months to travel to Hsien-Yang; but, the day after its arrival, the governor—Demetrius, Antigonus' son—had declared his independence and had proclaimed himself emperor of eastern Asia. Demetrius had inherited all his father's energy and ambition, but this without any ballast of stability. He had no judgement, and no hesitation in putting his ill-considered impulses into action. His present escapade was instantly fatal to him. His six years in his father's seat had been enough to demonstrate that he was unfit to rule; and his traitorous assumption of sovereign powers caused consternation. He was striking a dangerous blow at World-unity and World-peace. If he were successful, he might plunge eastern Asia back into Chan Kuo, the agony of 'the warring states'. Demetrius' official entourage—Greeks, Iranians, and Easterners—were unanimous. They court-martialled Demetrius, sentenced him to death, and executed the sentence forthwith. Alexander IV did not receive their report till six months after the event. By that time the crisis caused by Alexander III's death was already ancient history.

Alexander IV's policy was pointedly different from his father's. The contrast was not only pointed; it was deliberate; and no doubt one of the motives for this reaction of the new World-ruler's was of a personal kind. To find himself the successor of such an overwhelming figure was embarrassing for him. The dead World-ruler could not be ignored. If Alexander IV was to be something more than Alexander III's executor, he must be his critic; and Alexander IV had long been critical of his extraordinary father on grounds that had nothing to do with his own personal relation with him. Since Alexander IV had first awoken to consciousness, he had been painfully aware, in contemplating his father's complex character, of the wayward child that had never learnt to grow up. In the son's mental picture of the father's personality, this incurable childishness had eclipsed the godlike insight and genius which the triumvirs had appreciated and admired, conscious though they, too, were of their master's disconcerting weaknesses.

Alexander IV was not incapable of hero-worship, but his hero was, not the father whom he had seen, but the grandfather whom he had not seen—that is to say, his Macedonian grandfather Philip, not his Iranian grandfather Oxyartes. At his first conference with the triumvirate, his first words were: 'I shall be taking up my grandfather's work where my father left it'; and this initial declaration of policy was to govern all Alexander IV's acts of state throughout his reign.

Already, during his regency, he had had a search made, in the archives at Pella, for Philip's neglected state papers, and two of those that had been brought to his notice had struck a responsive chord in him. One of these documents was a plan for transforming the Kingdom of Macedon into an association of city-states like the Confederation of Corinth. The other was a plan for the incorporation and acculturation of the Illyrian peoples. Alexander IV made it his first business to carry out Philip II's political testament; and in this he was successful. Long before the end of his reign, he had carried Macedon's north-west frontier up to the south-west bank of the River Drave and up to the head of the Adriatic. He did not seek to conquer the Veneti. They were an old-established outpost of city-state civilization in the midst of a barbarian wilderness. Alexander IV made alliances with the Venetian city-states on the pattern of the alliances with the Umbrian and Etruscan city-states and with Rome that he had inherited from Alexander III. He also assisted the Romans, Umbrians, and Etruscans jointly to conquer and colonize the Gallic territories between the Appennines and the south bank of the River Po.

These were the only conquests that Alexander IV ever made or countenanced. Now that all peoples which had passed the threshold of civilization had been united politically in the World-State, he believed that the rest of mankind would be attracted progressively to join the civilized vanguard. He was impressed by the success of the Easterners' policy of 'peaceful penetration'. Already this policy had brought into the fold of civilization all the barbarians beyond the southern watershed of the

Yangtze Basin as far south as Canton; and the advance of civilization in this quarter was still in full swing. Alexander IV instructed Chandragupta and his son and successor Bindusara to follow this East-Asian policy in the interior of Africa.

As soon as Alexander IV had had time to find his feet, the original triumvirs retired. They were concerned to establish the principle that it was improper for public servants to cling to office till they were past work. Alexander IV appointed Demetrius' son Antigonus to replace Perdiccas, Eumenes' assistant Philetaerus to replace Eumenes, and Seleucus' son Antiochus to replace Ptolemy. The quality that Alexander IV valued particularly in Antiochus and in Antigonus was their loyalty to their fathers. Alexander IV rightly saw in this a guarantee that they would be loyal to their sovereign too. He did not hold it against Antigonus that he was Demetrius' son. Antigonus' devotion to his father was the one characteristic that he shared with Demetrius. In most respects he was more akin to Alexander IV. Like him, he was adult-minded and conscientious. It was Antigonus who coined Alexander IV's favourite motto: 'Monarchy is slavery in an honourable form.'

Ptolemy, being human, could not help being disappointed that his friend and colleague Seleucus' son, and not his own son and heir by his second marriage, had been appointed to succeed him; but he recognized the judiciousness of Alexander IV's choice. Ptolemy's younger son lacked the toughness that had been characteristic of all Philip's and Alexander's Macedonian paladins; and this toughness was still required in the second generation of the World-State's political administrators. Alexander IV gave Ptolemy's younger son a consolation prize. He invested him with full authority and with ample funds for founding, at Alexandria, an institute for research in both the sciences and the humanities. Ptolemy the Younger threw himself into this work with enthusiasm and made a brilliant success of it. We all know what the Museum has done for the advancement of learning. It has justly made Ptolemy the Younger more celebrated than his famous father. Alexander IV did nothing for Ptolemy's disinherited elder son, 'the Thunderbolt'. This man's nickname was apt. He had none of the un-Macedonian-like prudence that his half-brother had inherited from their father. 'The Thunderbolt' reminded Alexander IV of Perdiccas' account of Pausanias, Alexander IV's grandfather Philip's assassin. 'The Thunderbolt', too, was hot-tempered and embittered. When 'the Thunderbolt' volunteered for the Illyrian war, Alexander IV was relieved. When the news came that 'the Thunderbolt' had been killed in action, Alexander IV was not sorry.

Later on, Alexander IV found fruitful openings for two younger men. Pyrrhus, the unsuccessful claimant to the throne of Epirus, was a blend of Alexander III and Demetrius, exaggerated to the verge of caricature.

Alexander IV employed this fire-brand in Illyricum. Pyrrhus was a Greek whom Illyrians could understand and admire. After he had sated his appetite for war by playing an ultra-gallant part in the Illyrian campaigns, he displayed a surprising gift for winning the Illyrians over to the cause of civilization. Ashoka, Chandragupta's grandson, was the antithesis of Pyrrhus. When Alexander IV offered him the succession to his father Bindusara in Ethiopia, Ashoka declined. Ashoka did not want to spend his life on administration, and war was abhorrent to him. Like the younger Ptolemy, Ashoka had a vocation for the works of peace, but, unlike the Ptolemies and unlike his own Maurya forebears, Ashoka was, not a worldling, but an idealist. He begged Alexander to give him authority and funds for establishing a world-wide network of hospitals. These were to minister to animals as well as to human beings, and the Macedonians thought this quaint, but Alexander IV ruled that Ashoka was to have his way. The younger Ptolemy aided Ashoka by developing the medical faculty at the Museum. Ashoka's world-wide medical service was the germ of all the welfare work that, today, is the major part of the World-State's activities. Ashoka's veterinary service led, incidentally, to the astonishing subsequent improvements in the breeds of domesticated animals.

Hannibal was the most distinguished of all the subjects of Alexander VI and Alexander VII. Like his father Hamilcar, Hannibal was a born soldier, but there had been no career for a soldier at Carthage since Carthage had lost her empire, so this soldierly father and son had to find non-military outlets for their abilities. Hamilcar had persuaded the association of colonial Phoenician states in the Western Mediterranean to make him director of a joint-stock company for opening up tropical West Africa on the lines on which the Easterners had been opening up tropical East Asia. He hoped to be able to join hands, across Africa, with the pioneers who had been pushing into the interior from Ethiopia (eventually the two entering wedges of civilization did meet at Lake Chad). Hannibal worked with his father at Hamilcar's headquarters at Dakar; but Hannibal's eyes were turned seawards, not landwards. Hannibal's ambition was to demonstrate the correctness of the theory that the Earth was a globe. He would sail westwards from Dakar into the blue till he arrived at Shanghai, the easternmost of the eastern Phoenicians' entrepôts. Hannibal threw himself into the study of naval architecture and navigation. He designed a build of ship that could keep the sea for months on end without having to put in at a port. His design was a masterly combination of features in the naval architecture of the Eastern Seas, the Mediterranean, and the European littoral of the Atlantic. Hannibal did reach the opposite shore of the Atlantic and, in achieving this, he gave a new turn to the history of mankind. But the land that he found was not eastern Asia; it was Atlantis (Atlantis! Hannibal had proved that Plato's 'myth' was sober truth).

The last of our four titans is Alexander XIII. It is to him that we owe 'the annihilation of distance' by the advance of technology. We owe this to him, not as the inventor of the turbine-engine, but as its promoter. The inventor of it was, of course, Heron, and Heron was not the first or last inventor of his kind. Alexandria was a natural breeding-ground for inventors. By this time the city had become the workshop of the World, besides having become a hospitable home for the arts and sciences. Heron's particular invention had been a clever one; but Heron himself might have made nothing of it if Alexander XIII had not had the imagination to perceive the practical possibilities that it opened up; and Alexander XIII's insight had more genius in it than Heron's virtuosity had.

Like most Greek inventors, Heron was a devotee of theoretical science. The practical exploitation of his invention did not interest him. However, he had to earn his living; so he applied the principle of the turbine-engine to the construction of a number of ingenious mechanical toys of the kind that the wives of well-to-do Alexandrian Greek business men liked to buy. Alexander XIII was presented with one of these clever playthings, and the spectacle of steam-power moving metal set the World-ruler's mind working furiously. Here was the first inanimate force of Nature that had been harnessed by human ingenuity since the winds had been harnessed to propel sailing-ships more than three thousand years ago. Here was the means of knitting the World together physically. Here was something that he and his eleven predecessors had been needing ever since the World had been united politically and commercially by Alexander III. To unite the World, and to keep it united, with no more potent physical agencies than wind-power and the muscle-power of human beings and domesticated animals—that had been a marvellous feat of human energy and determination; but the results had been inadequate for meeting the requirements. If the unity of the World was ever to be consolidated, the means of communication must become much more powerful and more rapid, and here was this means, presented to him in this steam-driven toy that was demonstrating its performance before his eyes.

Alexander XIII sent for Heron and ordered him to stop misusing his invention on frivolities. Heron must now go to work, with all his might, to produce steam-driven ships and steam-driven wheeled vehicles. Alexander XIII would give Heron the tools to do the job. He would transform the Hephaestioneum into a laboratory for turning to practical account the harnessing of steam and of any other of the inanimate forces of Nature, beyond wind and steam, that Heron and his fellow mechanics might succeed in harnessing in the future. The Hephaestioneum! Alexander III's folly! For four hundred years that vast pile of useless architecture, dedicated to Alexander III's deified boon-companion, had cumbered the ground and had cost a fortune, annually, to keep in repair. Now at last a worthy use had been found for it; but first it must be re-dedicated. Instead of continuing to commemorate the pseudo-god Hephaestion, it was to be dedicated, from now on, to the fallen Olympian from whom Hephaestion had derived his name. Not the Hephaestioneum but the Hephaesteum henceforth. It was to become the temple and work-shop of Hephaestus himself.

Heron had suddenly become an important public figure, with a gigantic engineering enterprise on his hands. He was not altogether pleased with this change in his fortunes. Athene, the symbol of pure science, was the goddess to whom Heron was devoted; Hephaestus, con-summate artisan, was a vulgar god by comparison. However, Heron had been given an imperial command; he had to carry it out; and he could hardly fail, now that the whole World's technological and financial resources were at his disposal. The consumption of charcoal and metal at the Hephaesteum was enormous, but the success was rapid. The first locomotive and the first steamship were soon in being. Within a year of that, a steamship, operated by Alexandrian Greek engineers, had arrived at the estuary of the Yangtze; within two years another had arrived at the estuary of the Amazon; within three years the first of the World's railways had been built. It ran from Alexandria to Suez, side by side with the ship-canal. Within ten years the Nile–Euphrates railway had been completed. This branched off from the Alexandria–Suez railway at the head of the Nile Delta, and it struck the Euphrates at Thapsacus. The building of the section that ran through the Valley of Esdraelon must have been watched, from the southern brow of the Galilaean hill-country, by a boy whose father was a carpenter at Nazareth.

Alexander III, Alexander IV, Hannibal, and Alexander XIII: who can deny that, between them, these four men have made history? But who can guess the turn that history might have taken if Philip II King of Macedon and the Persian Emperor Artaxerxes III Ochus had not had their lives cut short? If these two previous makers of history had lived on to die eventually in their beds, our present-day World might be a quite different one from what it is in the time of the reigning (but not, of course, governing) World-ruler Alexander LXXXVI.

BIBLIOGRAPHIES

FOR PART I

ALLEN, T. W.: *The Homeric Catalogue of Ships*: Oxford, 1921, Clarendon Press.

ATKINSON, B. F. C.: *The Greek Language*: London, 1932, Faber.

BELOCH, (K.) J.: *Griechische Geschichte*, 2nd ed., 1. Band, 1. Abteilung, 1912; 1. Band, 2. Abteilung, 1913: Strassburg, Trübner.

BLUMENTAL, A. VON, 'Zur "lykurgischen" Rhetra', in *Hermes*, 77. Band (1942), pp. 212–15.

BURR, V.; Νεῶν Καταλόγος: Leipzig, 1944, Dieterich.

BUSOLT, C., and SWOBODA, H.: *Griechische Staatskunde*, 3rd ed., Zweite Hälfte: Munich, 1926, Beck.

CHADWICK, J.: 'The Greek Dialects and Greek Pre-history', in *The Language and Background of Homer*, edited by G. S. Kirk (Cambridge, 1964, Heffer), pp. 106–18.

HAMMOND, N. G. L.: *Epirus*: Oxford, 1967, Clarendon Press.

—— 'Prehistoric Epirus and the Dorian Invasion', in *The Annual of the British School at Athens*, vol. xxxii (1934), pp. 131–79.

HEURTLEY, W. A.: *Prehistoric Macedonia*: Cambridge, 1939, University Press.

JACHMANN, G.: *Der homerische Schiffskatalog und die Ilias*: Köln and Opladen, 1958, Westdeutscher Verlag.

LATTE, K.: 'Phyle', in Pauly–Wissowa, 39. Halbband (1947), col. 994.

LEAF, WALTER: *Homer and History*: London, 1915, Macmillan.

—— *Troy: A Study in Homeric Geography*: London, 1912, Macmillan.

MAY, J. M. F.: *The Coinage of Damastion and the Lesser Coinages of the Illyro-Paeonian Region*: London, 1939, Oxford University Press.

NIESE, B.: *Der homerische Schiffskatalog*: Kiel, 1873.

NILSSON, M. P.: *The Mycenaean Origin of Greek Mythology*: Cambridge, 1932, University Press.

PAGE, D. L.: *History and the Homeric Iliad*: Berkeley and Los Angeles, 1959, University of California Press.

PALMER, L. R.: *Mycenaeans and Minoans: Aegean Prehistory in the Light of the Linear B Tablets*: London, 1961, Faber.

PARETI, L.: *Storia di Sparta Arcaïca*, Parte I: Florence, 1920, Felice le Monnier.

RISCH, E.: 'Die Gliederung der griechischen Dialekte in neuer Sicht', in *The Language and Background of Homer*, edited by G. S. Kirk (Cambridge, 1964, Heffer), pp. 90–105.

SIMPSON, R. HOPE: *A Gazetteer and Atlas of Mycenaean Sites*: London, 1965, Institute of Classical Studies, Bulletin Supplement No. 16, pp. 171–7.

——'Identifying a Mycenaean Site', in *The Annual of the British School at Athens*, vol. lii (1957), pp. 231–59, and 'The Seven Cities Offered by Agamemnon to Achilles (*Iliad* IX. 149 ff., 291 ff.)', in vol. lxi (1966), pp. 113–31.

TAYLOUR, LORD WILLIAM: *The Mycenaeans*: London, 1964, Thames and Hudson.

WILLETTS, R. F.: *Ancient Crete: A Social History*: London, 1965, Routledge and Kegan Paul.

—— *Aristocratic Society in Ancient Crete*: London, 1955, Routledge and Kegan Paul.

FOR PART II

BELOCH, (K.) J.: *Griechische Geschichte*, 2nd ed., 1. Band, 1. Abteilung, 1912; 1. Band, 2. Abteilung, 1913: Strassburg, Trübner.

BON, A.: *Le Péloponnèse byzantin jusqu'en 1204*: Paris, 1957, Presses Universitaires de France.

BOUÉ, A.: *La Turquie d'Europe*: Paris, 1840, Bertrand, 4 vols.

—— *Recueil d'itinéraires dans la Turquie d'Europe*: Vienna, 1854, 2 vols.

BURY, J. B.: *A History of the East Roman Empire*: London, 1912, Macmillan.

CASSON, S.: *Macedonia, Thrace and Illyria*: London, 1926, Oxford University Press.

CONWAY, R. S.: *The Italian Dialects*: Cambridge, 1897, University Press, 2 vols.

CROSS, G. N.: *Epirus*: Cambridge, 1932, University Press.

DASCALAKIS, A.: *The Hellenism of the Ancient Macedonians*: Thessaloníki, 1965, Institute for Balkan Studies.

FRANKE, P. R.: *Alt-Epirus und das Königtum der Molosser*: Kallmunz, Opf., 1955, Lassleben.

GEYER, F.: *Makedonien bis zur Thronbesteigung Philipps II.*: Munich and Berlin, 1930, Oldenbourg.

GOLTZ, BARON W. L. C. VON DER: *Ein Ausflug nach Makedonien*: Berlin, 1894, Decker.

GRISEBACH, A.: *Reise durch Rumelien und nach Brussa, 1839*, vol. ii: Göttingen, 1841, Vandenhoeck und Ruprecht.

HAMMOND, N. G. L.: *Epirus*: Oxford, 1967, Clarendon Press.

—— 'Prehistoric Epirus and the Dorian Invasion', in *The Annual of the British School at Athens*, vol. xxxii (1934), pp. 131–79.

HOFFMANN, O.: *Die Makedonen*: Göttingen, 1906, Vandenhoeck und Ruprecht.

KRETSCHMER, P.: *Einleitung in die Geschichte der griechischen Sprache*: Göttingen, 1896, Vandenhoeck und Ruprecht.

KROMAYER, J.: *Antike Schlachtfelde in Griechenland*, 2. Band: Berlin, 1907, Weidmann.

LAWSON, J. C.; *Modern Greek Folklore and Ancient Greek Religion*, 2nd ed.: New Hyde Park, N.Y., 1964, University Books.

MAY, J. M. F.: *The Coinage of Damastion and the Lesser Coinages of the Illyro-Paeonian Region*: London, 1939, Oxford University Press.

MEYER, EDUARD: *Forschungen zur alten Geschichte*, vol. i: Halle, 1892, Niemeyer.

PARETI, L.: *Storia di Sparta Arcaïca*, Parte I: Florence, 1920, Felice le Monnier.

SANCTIS, G. DE: *Atthis*: Turin, 1912, Bocca.

THUMB, A.: *Handbuch der griechischen Dialekte*, 1. Teil, 2nd ed., ed. E. Kiechers: Heidelberg, 1932, Winter.

TOZER, H. F.: *Researches in the Highlands of Turkey*: London, 1869, J. Murray, 2 vols.

TUMA, Col. A.: *Griechenland, Makedonien und Süd-Albanien, oder die südliche Balkan-Halbinsel, militärgeographisch, statistisch und kriegshistorisch dargestellt*: Hannover, 1888, Helwing.

VASMER, M.: *Die Slawen in Griechenland*: Berlin, 1941, De Gruyter.

WACE, A. J. B., and THOMPSON, M. S.: 'A Latin Inscription from Perrhaebia', in *The Annual of the British School at Athens*, vol. xvii (1911), pp. 193–204.

WADE-GERY, H. T.: 'The Dorians', in *The Cambridge Ancient History*, vol. ii: 1924.

WALBANK, F. W.: *Philip V of Macedon*: Cambridge, 1940, University Press.

FOR PART III (MODERN WORKS)[1]

AFRICA, T. W.: *Phylarchus and the Spartan Revolution*: Berkeley and Los Angeles, 1961, University of California Press.

*ANDREÁDHIS, A. M.: Δημοσία Οἰκονομία τῶν Σπαρτιατῶν: Athens, 1915, Sakellarios.

---

[1] Books and articles marked with an asterisk have not been read by me.—A. J. T.

ANDREWES, A.: 'Ephorus I and the Kings of Argos', in *The Classical Quarterly*, vol. xlv (1951), pp. 39–45.

—— 'Eunomia', in *The Classical Quarterly*, vol. xxxi (1937), pp. 89–102.

—— *Probouleusis: Sparta's Contribution to the Technique of Government*: Oxford, 1954, Clarendon Press.

—— 'The Corinthian Actaeon and Pheidon of Argos', in *The Classical Quarterly*, vol. xliii (1949), pp. 70–8.

—— 'The Government of Classical Sparta', in *Ancient Society and Institutions: Studies Presented to Victor Ehrenberg*: Oxford, 1966, Blackwell, pp. 1–20.

—— *The Greek Tyrants*: London, 1956, Hutchinson: pp. 66–77, chap. 6: 'The Spartan Alternative to Tyranny'.

*BAZIN, H.: *La République des Lacédémoniens de Xénophon*: Paris, 1885, Leroux.

BEATTIE, A. J.: 'An Early Laconian Lex Sacra', in *The Classical Quarterly*, vol. xlv (1951), pp. 46–58.

BELOCH, (K.) J.: 'Griechische Aufgebote', II, in *Klio*, 6. Band (1906), pp. 34–78.

—— *Griechische Geschichte*, 2nd ed., 1. Band, 2. Abteilung, 1913; 2. Band, 1. Abteilung, 1914; 3. Band, 1. Abteilung, 1922: Strassburg, Trübner.

BERVE, H.: *Sparta*: Leipzig, 1937, Bibliographisches Institut.

*BIELCHOWSKY, A.: *De Spartanorum Syssitiis*: Breslau, 1869; Berlin, Calvary (dissertation).

BILLHEIMER, A.: 'Age-Classes in Spartan Education', in *Transactions and Proceedings of the American Philological Association*, vol. lxxviii (1947), pp. 99–104.

—— Tὰ Δέκα ἀφ' Ἥβης, ibid., vol. lxxvii (1946), pp. 214–20.

BLUMENTAL, A. VON: 'Zur "lykurgischen" Rhetra', in *Hermes*, 77. Band (1942), pp. 212–15.

BOER, W. DEN: *Laconian Studies*: Amsterdam, 1954, North Holland Publishing Company.

BÖLTE: 'Geronthrai', in P.–W., 13. Halbband (1910), col. 1268.

*BOURGUET, E.: *Le Dialecte laconien*: Paris, 1927, Champion.

BOWERSTOCK, G. W.: 'Eurycles of Sparta', in *The Journal of Roman Studies*, vol. li (1961), pp. 112–18.

*BUSOLT, G.: *Die Lakedaimonier und ihre Bundesgenossen*, 1. Band: Leipzig, 1878, Teubner.

—— 'Spartas Heer und Leuktra', in *Hermes*, 40. Band (1905), pp. 387–449.

—— and SWOBODA, H.: *Griechische Staatskunde*, 3rd ed., Zweite Hälfte (Munich, 1926, Beck), 'Der Staat der Lakedaimonier', pp. 633–737.

BUTLER, D.: 'The Competence of the Demos in the Spartan Rhetra', in *Historia*, 11. Band (1962), pp. 385–96.

BUX, E.: 'Zwei sozialistische Novellen bei Plutarch', in *Klio*, 19. Band (1925), pp. 413–31.

CAVAIGNAC, E.: 'La Population du Péloponnèse aux vᵉ et ivᵉ siècles', in *Klio*, 12. Band (1912), pp. 261–80.

—— *Sparte*: Paris, 1948, Fayard.

CHRIMES, K. M. T.: *Ancient Sparta: A Re-examination of the Evidence*: Manchester, 1949, University Press.

—— *The Respublica Lacedaemoniorum Ascribed to Xenophon*: Manchester, 1948, University Press.

COOK, R. M.: 'Spartan History and Archaeology', in *The Classical Quarterly*, vol. lvi (N.S. vol. xii) (1962), pp. 156–8.

*DAUBLER, TH.: *Sparta: Ein Versuch*: Leipzig, 1923.

DEN BOER: see Boer, W. Den.

DICKINS, G.: 'The Growth of Spartan Policy', in *The Journal of Hellenic Studies*, vol. xxxii (1912), pp. 1–42.

*DIESNER, H. J.: 'Sparta und das Helotenproblem', in *Die Wissenschaftliche Zeitschrift der Universität Greifswald*, geschichtliche und sprachwissenschaftliche Reihe 3 (1953/4), pp. 219 seqq.

DUM, G.: *Entstehung und Entwicklung des spartanischen Ephorats, bis zur Beseitigung desselben durch König Kleomenes III*: Innsbruck, 1878, Wagner.

EHRENBERG, V.: 'Asteropus', in *Die philologische Wochenschrift*, Jahrgang xlvii (1927), No. 1, pp. 27–9.

—— 'Der Damos im archaischen Sparta', in *Hermes*, 68. Band (1933), pp. 288–305.

—— 'Der Gesetzgeber von Sparta', in *'Επιτύμβιον Heinrich Swoboda dargebracht*: Reichenberg, 1927, Stiepel: pp. 19–28.

—— 'Mothakes' and 'Mothones', in P.–W., 31. Halbband (1933), cols. 382–4.

—— 'Nabis', in P.–W., 16. Band (1935), cols. 1471–82.

—— 'Neodamodeis', in P.–W., 16. Band (1935), cols. 2396–401.

—— *Neugründer des Staates: Ein Beitrag zur Geschichte Spartas und Athens im vi. Jahrhundert*: Munich, 1925, Beck.

—— 'Obai', in P.–W., 34. Halbband (1937), cols. 1693–704.

—— 'Spartiaten und Lakedaimonier', in *Hermes*, 59. Band (1924), pp. 23–72.

FORREST, W. G.: *A History of Sparta 950–192 B.C.*: London, 1968, Hutchinson.

—— 'The Dating of the Lycurgan Reforms in Sparta', in *The Phoenix*, vol. xvii (1963), pp. 157–79.

FUKS, A.: 'Agis, Cleomenes, and Equality', in *Classical Philology*, vol. lvii, No. 3 (July 1962), pp. 161–6.

—— 'The Spartan Citizen Body in Mid-Third Century B.C. and its Enlargement Proposed by Agis IV', in *Athenaeum*, vol. l (N.S. vol. xl) (1963), pp. 244–63.

GEYER, F.: 'Skiritis', in P.–W., 2. Reihe, 5. Halbband (1927), cols. 536–7.

GITTI, A.: 'I perieci di Sparta e le origini del *KOINON ΤΩΝ ΛΑΚΕΔΑΙΜΟΝΙΩΝ*, in *Rendiconti della Reale Accademia dei Lincei*, Classe di Scienze Morali, Storiche, e Filologiche, serie sesta, vol. xv (1939), pp. 189–203.

GROTE, GEORGE: *A History of Greece*, Part II, chap. 6: 'Laws and Discipline of Lycurgus of Sparta', in vol. iii, pp. 112–86, in Everyman's Library edition.

HADAS, M.: 'The Social Revolution in Third-Century Sparta', in *The Classical Weekly*, vol. xxvi (1932), No. 9 (whole number 700), pp. 65–8, and No. 10 (whole number 700), pp. 73–6.

HAMMOND, N. G. L.: 'The Lycurgean Reform at Sparta', in *The Journal of Hellenic Studies*, vol. lxx (1950), pp. 42–64.

HAMPL, F.: 'Die lakedaimonischen Periöken', in *Hermes*, 72. Band (1937), pp. 1–49.

HARVEY, F. D.: 'Oxyrhyncus Papyrus 2390 and Early Spartan History', in *The Journal of Hellenic Studies*, vol. lxxxvii (1967).

*HEIDENMANN, L.: *Die territoriale Entwicklung Lakedaimons und Messeniens bis auf Alexander*: Berlin, 1904, Weidmann (dissertation).

HUXLEY, G. L.: *Early Sparta*: London, 1962, Faber.

JANNET, C.: *Les Institutions sociales et le droit civil à Sparte*, 2nd ed.: Paris, 1880, Pedone–Lauriel.

JEFFERY, L. H.: 'The Pact of the First Settlers at Cyrene', in *Historia*, 10. Band (1961), pp. 139–47: on the Lycurgan Rhetra, pp. 145–7.

JONES, A. H. M.: *Sparta*: Oxford, 1967, Blackwell.

—— 'The Lycurgan Rhetra', in *Ancient Society and Institutions: Studies Presented to Victor Ehrenberg*: Oxford, 1966, Blackwell, pp. 165–75.

KAHRSTEDT, U.: 'Die spartanische Agrarwirtschaft', in *Hermes*, 54. Band (1919), pp. 279–94.

*KAHRSTEDT, U.: *Griechisches Staatsrecht,* I: *Sparta und seine Symmachie*: Göttingen, 1922, Vandenhoeck und Ruprecht.

KAZAROW, G.: 'Zur Geschichte der sozialen Revolution in Sparta', in *Klio,* 7. Band (1907), pp. 45–51.

KESSLER, E.: *Plutarchs Leben des Lykurgos*: Berlin, 1910, Weidmann.

KIECHLE, F.: *Lakonien und Sparta: Untersuchungen zur ethnischen Struktur und zur politischen Entwicklung Lakoniens und Spartas bis zum Ende der archaischen Zeit*: Munich and Berlin, 1963, Beck.

—— *Messenische Studien*: Kallmünz, Opf., 1959, Lassleben.

KRAHE, H.: *Die alten balkanillyrischen Namen*: Heidelberg, 1925, Winter.

KROMAYER, J.: *Antike Schlachtfelde in Griechenland,* 1. Band: Berlin, 1903, Weidmann.

—— 'Studien über Wehrkraft und Wehrverfassung der griechischen Staaten', 2. Teil: *Klio,* 3. Band (1903), pp. 173–212: 'Die Wehrkraft Lakoniens und seine Wehrverfassung'.

*KROYMANN, J.: *Pausanias and Rhianus* [   ] 1943 [   ].

—— *Sparta und Messenien: Untersuchungen zur Überlieferung der messenischen Kriege*: Berlin, 1937, Weidmann.

LEAHY, D. M.: 'The Spartan Defeat of Orchomenos', in *The Phoenix,* vol. xii (1958), pp. 141–65.

LENSCHAU, T.: 'Die Entstehung des spartanischen Staates', in *Klio,* 30. Band (N.F. 12. Band) (1937), pp. 269–89.

*—— 'König Kleomenes I von Sparta', in *Klio,* 31. Band (N.F. 13. Band) (1938), pp. 412–29.

LORIMER, H. L.: 'The Hoplite Phalanx', in *The Annual of the British School at Athens,* vol. xlii (1947), pp. 76–138.

LOTZE, D.: Μεταξὺ Ἐλευθέρων καὶ Δούλων: Berlin, 1959, Akademie-Verlag.

—— 'Mothakes', in *Historia,* 11. Band (1962), pp. 427–35.

*LÜDEMANN, *Sparta*: [   ] 1939 [   ].

*MANSO, J. C. F.: *Sparta: Ein Versuch zur Aufklärung der Geschichte und Verfassung dieses Staates,* Leipzig, 1800–1805 [   ], 3 vols.

MEIER, TH.: *Das Wesen der spartanischen Staatsordnung* = *Klio,* Beiheft 42 (1939); 2nd ed., Aalen, 1962, Scientia Verlag.

MEYER, EDUARD: *Forschungen zur alten Geschichte,* 1. Band: Halle, 1892, Niemeyer: 'Die Entwicklung der Überlieferung über die lykurgische Verfassung', pp. 211–86.

MEYER, ERNST: 'Methone', in P.–W., 15. Band (1932), cols. 1382–4.

—— 'Oresthasion', in P.–W., 35. Halbband (1939), cols. 1014–16.

MICHELL, H.: *Sparta*: Cambridge, 1952, University Press.

MOMIGLIANO, A.: 'Sparta e Lacedemone: una ipotesi sull'origine della diarchia spartana', in *Atene e Roma,* nuova serie, anno xiii (1932), pp. 3–11.

*MUNDT, J.: *Nabis König von Sparta (206–192 B.C.)*: Köln, 1923, Bachem.

NEUMANN, K. J.: 'Die Entstehung des spartanischen Staates in der lykurgischen Verfassung', in *Die Historische Zeitschrift,* 96. Band (N.F. 60. Band) (1906), pp. 1–80.

NIESE, B.: 'Epitadas Molobrou' and 'Epitadeus', in P.–W., 11. Halbband (1907), cols. 217–18.

—— 'Neue Beiträge zur Geschichte und Landeskunde Lakedaimons: Die lakedaimonischen Perioöken', in *Nachrichten von der Königlichen Gesellschaft der Wissenschaften zu Göttingen,* Philologisch-historische Klasse (1906), pp. 101–42.

—— 'Zur Verfassungsgeschichte Lakedaimons', in *Die historische Zeitschrift,* 62. Band (N.F. 26. Band) (1889), pp. 58–84.

NILSSON, M. P.: 'Die Grundlagen des spartanischen Lebens', in *Klio,* 12. Band (1912), pp. 308–40.

*Norton, P. C.: *Socialism at Sparta in Greek Political Experience*: Princeton, 1941.

Norvin, W.: 'Zur Geschichte der spartanischen Eunomia', in *Classica et Mediaevalia*: Copenhagen, Gyldendal: vol. ii (1939), pp. 247–93; vol. iii (1940), pp. 47–118.

Oberhummer: 'Asine, No. 2', in P.–W., 2. Band (1896), col. 1582.

Oehler, J.: 'Heloten', in P.–W., 15. Halbband (1912), cols. 203–6.

Ollier, F.: *Le Mirage spartiate: étude sur l'idéalisation de Sparte dans l'antiquité grecque de l'origine jusqu'aux Cyniques*: Paris, 1st ed., 1933, Boccard; 2nd ed., 1943, Les Belles Lettres.

—— 'Le Philosophe stoïcien Sphairos et l'œuvre réformatrice des rois de Sparte Agis IV et Cléomène III', in *La Revue des Études Grecques*, vol. 49 (1936), pp. 536–70.

—— *Xénophon, la république des Lacédémoniens*: Lyons, 1934, Bosc and Rioux (text, translation, commentary).

Pareti, L.: 'Le tribù personali e le tribù locali a Sparta', in *Rendiconti della Reale Accademia dei Lincei*, Classe di Scienze Morali, Storiche, e Filologiche, serie quinta, vol. xix (1910), pp. 457–73.

—— *Storia di Sparta Archaïca*, Parte I: Florence, 1920, Felice le Monnier.

Pauly–Wissowa, 'Sparta', in Zweite Reihe (R–Z), Dritter Band (1929), cols. 1265–1528.

Pearson, L.: 'The Pseudo-History of Messenia and its Authors', in *Historia*, 11. Band (1962), pp. 397–426.

Petit-Dutaillis, C.: *De Lacedaemoniorum Reipublicae Supremis Temporibus (222–146 B.C.)*: Paris, 1894, Noizette (thesis Facultati Litterarum).

Porter, W. H.: 'The Antecedents of the Spartan Revolution of 243 B.C.', in *Hermathena*, No. xlix (1935), pp. 1–15.

*Rignalda: *De Lacedaemoniorum Re Militari*: Leuwarden, 1893.

Roussel, P.: *Sparte*: Paris, 1939, Boccard; 2nd ed., 1960.

Shimron, B.: 'Polybius and the Reforms of Cleomenes III', in *Historia*, 13. Band (1964), pp. 147–55.

Snodgrass, A. M.: *Early Greek Armour and Weapons*: Edinburgh, 1964, University Press.

—— 'The Hoplite Reform and History', in *The Journal of Hellenic Studies*, vol. lxxxv (1965), pp. 110–22.

Solari, A.: *Ricerche Spartane*: Livorno, 1907, Giusti.

Stern, E. von: 'Zur Entstehung und ursprünglichen Bedeutung des Ephorats', in *Berliner Studien für klassische Philologie und Archeologie*, 15. Band, 2. Heft, pp. 1–62: Berlin, 1894, Calvary.

Stubbs, H. W.: 'Spartan Austerity: A Possible Explanation', in *The Classical Quarterly*, vol. xliv (1950), pp. 32–7.

Toynbee, A. J.: *A Study of History*: London, Oxford University Press: vol. iii, (1934), pp. 50–79 and 455–7.

—— 'The Growth of Sparta', in *The Journal of Hellenic Studies*, vol. xxxiii, Part 2 (1913), pp. 246–75.

Treu, M.: 'Der Schlusssatz der Grossen Rhetra', in *Hermes*, 76. Band (1941), pp. 22–42.

Tsopanakis, A. G.: *La Rhètre de Lycurgue; L'Annexe-Tyrtée*, parartema 6 to *Helleniká*: Thessaloníki, 1954.

Wade-Gery, H. T.: 'A Note on the Origin of the Spartan Gymnopaidiai', in *The Classical Quarterly*, vol. xliii (1949), pp. 79–81.

—— *Essays in Greek History*: Oxford, 1958, Blackwell, pp. 37–85: 'The Spartan Rhetra in Plutarch's Lycurgus VI.'

—— 'The Dorians', in *The Cambridge Ancient History*, vol. ii (1924), pp. 518–41.

WADE-GERY, H. T.: 'The Growth of the Dorian States', VII: 'Sparta: The Eunomia', in *The Cambridge Ancient History*, vol. iii (1925), pp. 558–65.

—— 'The Rhianus-Hypothesis', in *Ancient Society and Institutions: Studies Presented to Victor Ehrenberg*: Oxford, 1966, Blackwell, pp. 289–302.

WALBANK, F. W.: 'The Spartan Ancestral Constitution in Polybius', in *Ancient Society and Institutions: Studies Presented to Victor Ehrenberg*: Oxford, 1966, Blackwell, pp. 302–12.

WALKER, E. M., in *The Cambridge Ancient History*, vol. v (1927), p. 69.

WIDE, SAM: *Lakonische Kulte*: Leipzig, 1893, Teubner.

WILLETTS, R. F.: *Ancient Crete: A Social History*: London, 1965, Routledge and Kegan Paul.

—— *Aristocratic Society in Ancient Crete*: London, 1955, Routledge and Kegan Paul.

—— 'The Neodamodeis', in *Classical Philology*, vol. xlix (Jan.–Oct., 1959), pp. 27–32.

WITKOWSKI, S.: 'Die spartanische Heeresgliederung und der Ursprung des Ephorats', in *Eos*, 35. Band (1934), pp. 73–86.

WOODHOUSE, W. J.: *King Agis of Sparta and his Campaign in Arcadia in 418 B.C.*: Oxford, 1933, Clarendon Press.

WÜST, F. R.: 'Laconica' (I, 'Zur pseudo-xenophontischen Λακεδαιμονίων Πολιτεία'; II, 'Κάσεν—Μόθακες—Ὑπομείονες'), in *Klio*, 37. Band (1959), pp. 53–62.

ZIEHEN, L.: 'Das spartanische Bevölkerungsproblem', in *Hermes*, 68. Band (1933), pp. 218–37.

INDEXES TO MAPS, NOTES, AND ITINERARY

Index to Map 2: The Spartan Dominions in the Southern Peloponnese

Notes on Map 2: Sparta's Dominions circa 544–370 B.C.

There is relatively little doubt about the course of Sparta's northern frontier over against the territories of Argos, Tegea, the cantons of south-western Arcadia, and Triphylia. After the transfer of Kythera, Kynouria, and the Thyreatis from Argos to Sparta, the eastern end of the frontier started from a point on the west shore of the Gulf of Navplia, somewhere between Myli and the skála of Astros, where the mountains touch the coast. The valley of the Tanos River will have been on Sparta's side of the line. After crossing the northern end of Mount Parnon (Malevo), not far from the point where Sparta's, Argos', and Tegea's frontiers met,[1] the frontier will have cut across the upper valley of the Sarandopótamos at Phylake to the upper valley of the Frangóvrysi headwater of the Alpheios. Oresthasion,[2] where the Lacedaemonian army seems usually to have crossed the frontier when it was heading for the Isthmus of Corinth, must have lain somewhere at the southern edge of the little plain of Asea. (Since Lacedaemonian armies had no right of way through the Argeia, they must have reached the Isthmus via Asea, Pallantion, Mantinea, Orkhomenos, Stymphalos, Sikyon.) From Oresthasion the frontier will have followed the Frangóvrysi to its junction with the two headwaters that run northwards to the east and to the west of Leondári. Thence the frontier will have crossed the Alpheios basin, south of the site of the future city of Megalopolis and south of Lykosoura, till it struck the eastern end of the watershed between the basins of the rivers Neda and Pamisos. In the westernmost section of its course the frontier will have run along the lower course of the River Neda.

There is less certainty about the internal boundaries, on the Lacedaemonian side of this international frontier, between different categories of Lacedaemonian territory; and the boundaries shown on this map are all conjectural. These internal boundaries are: (i) those between the territories of Sparta's perioecic city-states and Sparta's own city-state territory; (ii) the boundaries between the different perioecic city-state territories; (iii) within Sparta's own city-state territory, the boundaries between the nuclear territories of the five Spartiate obai and the helot-inhabited additions to Sparta's territory; (iv) within the helot-inhabited area, the boundaries between the land that was divided up into kleroi, cultivated by helots and held by

[1] See Pausanias, Book III, chap. 10, § 6.
[2] See Herodotus, Book IX, chap. 11.

Spartiate homoioi, and the land that was used as grazing-grounds and hunting-grounds. The Thyreatis may have had a peculiar status. It may have been Spartan public land, and the native inhabitants—if they had not emigrated to the Argeia at the time of the annexation—may not have had the status of perioikoi, but at the same time they may not have been reduced to the status of helots.[1]

The traditional number of Sparta's perioecic city-states was one hundred, and Isocrates says that it was Spartan policy to keep the periokoi divided up among the largest possible number of separate states of the smallest possible average size.[2] Niese claims that, out of the reputed total number—namely, one hundred—about eighty perioecic city-states can be located with certainty, and about ten more with some probability.[3] However, some of Niese's 'certainties' seem doubtful, and three of them—Gythion, Aigiai, Krokeai—seem more likely to have lain in Sparta's own city-state territory.[4] On the present map the number of separate perioecic states shown is only fifty-three. If the Skiritis were counted not as a single state, but as five separate cantons—Karyatis, Oiatis, Belbinatis, Maleatis, Aigytis—the total number of perioecic states would be fifty-seven. The true number must have been considerably larger, though no doubt the round number of one hundred is an exaggeration. There are a number of perioecic cities whose names we know but not their locations—for instance, Aitolia, Ataia, Litaiai, and perhaps Tenos. *I.G.*, vol. v, fasc. i, p. 174, No. 931, [.... τῶν δικαστᾶν τ]ῶν ἐκ Τήνου τῶν περὶ [......], may be an indication that there was a Laconian Tenos somewhere in the neighbourhood of Zarax.

Index to Map 3: A. J. Toynbee's Journeys in the Southern Peloponnese in 1912

A	Aigina (route from)	D 1	E	Epidauros Lîmêrâ	D 3	
	Aipy	A 1		Ermióni	D 2	
	Alepokhóri	C 3		Eurotas, R.	B 2 and C 3	
	Álika	B 4				
	Alpheios, R.	A 1	G	Gharghaliáni	A 2	
	Andrítsena	A 2				
	Aphísou	B 2	I	Iron Bridge	C 3	
	Apidhiá	C 3		Ithômê, Mt.	A 2	
	Arákhova	C 2				
	Argos	C 1	K	Kalamáta	B 2	
	Ástros	C 2		Kalývia Yeoryitsiátika	B 2	
	Ástros skála	C 2		Kardhamýli	B 3	
	Áyios Andréas	A 3		Karvéli	B 2	
	Áyios Pétros	C 2		Karyoúpolis	B 3	
	Áyios Yoánnis	C 2		Karýtena	B 2	
				Katavóthra	C 3	
B	Bassai, Temple of	A 2		Káto Vezáni (Helos)	C 3	
				Kávvalos	B 3	
C	Cape Matapan (Taínaron)	B 4		Kelephína, R.	B 2	
				Khelmós, Khani of	B 2	
D	Dhimitsána	B 1		Khrýsapha	C 2	

[1] See pp. 183, n. 2.   [2] See p. 204, n. 2.
[3] B. Niese, 'Neue beiträge zur Geschichte und Landeskunde Lakedaimons: Die Lakedaimonischen Periöken', in *Nachrichten von der Königlichen Gesellschaft der Wissenschaften zu Göttingen*, Philologisch-historische Klasse (1906), pp. 101–42, on p. 126.
[4] See the present work, pp. 191–3.

Kítta B 3
Koróni (Coron) A 3
Kótronas B 3
Kréstena A 1
Krevatás, Khani of B 2
Kyparissía A 2

L
Ládha B 2
Laghía B 4
Laghíou C 3
Langháda Pass B 2
Leonídhi skála C 2
Liméni B 3
Lyghoudhísta A 2

M
Mavrommáti A 2
Mistrá B 2
Módhon A 3
Moláous C 3
Monemvasía D 3
Myloi C 1

N
Navaríno A 3
Neápolis (Boiai) D 3

O
Olympia A 1

P
Pákia C 3
Páliros B 4
Pâmîsos, R. A 2 and B 2
Pássava (Las Vetus) C 3
Pávlitsa (Phigaleia) A 2
Petalídhi A 3
Pétses D 2
Philiatrá A 2
Poros D 1
Porto Marinári B 4
Porto Quaglio B 4
Port Trakhéla B 3
Pyrgos B 3

R
Rénglia skála B 3
Rikhéa D 3

S
Samikó A 1
Sellasía B 2
Sellasía battlefield B 2
Soulimá A 2
Sparta B 2

T
Therapnê B 2
Thermísi D 2
Thyrea C 2
Trínisa C 3
Trýpi B 2
Tsepheremíni A 2
Tsímova B 3
Tsinán (Megalopolis) B 2

V
Vytína B 1

Y
Ýdhra D 2
Yeráka D 3
Yeráki C 3
Yiánnitsa B 2
Ýýthion C 3

Z
Zárax fjord D 3
Zevghalatió A 2

Map 3: Itinerary of A. J. Toynbee's Journeys in the Southern Peloponnese in 1912

Note: These journeys were made on foot, except where some other means of conveyance is mentioned.

Feb. 20: Athens–Kalamáta (by train)
21: Kalamáta–Petalídhi–Áyios Andréas–Koróni (Coron) (by steamer)
22: Koróni–Módhon–Navaríno
23: Navaríno–Lyghoudhísta–Gharghaliáni–Philiatrá
24: Philiatrá–Kyparissía; Kyparissía–Olympia (by train)

Apr. 15: Thermísi–Ermióni; Ermióni–Pétses–Leonídhi skála–Ástros skála (by steamer)
16: Ástros skála–Thyrea–Áyios Pétros–Arákhova
17: Arákhova–Kelephína valley (with the Judas trees in blossom)–Khani of Krevatás–Sellasía battlefield–Sellasía–Sparta
18 and 19: At Sparta; visit Therapnê

Apr. 20: Sparta–Khrýsapha–Yeráki
 21: Yeráki–Alepokhóri–Apidhiá–Moláous
 22: Moláous–Neápolis (Boiai)
 23: Neápolis–Monemvasía
 24: Monemvasía–Epídauros Limerá–Zárax fjord–Yeráka
 25: Yeráka–Rikhéa–Katavóthra–Pákia–Káto Vezáni (Helos)
 26: Káto Vezáni–iron bridge over R. Eurotas–Laghíou–Trínisa–Ýthion
 27: At Ýthion
 28: Ýthion–Pássava (Las Vetus)–Karyoúpolis–Tsímova–Pyrgos
 29: Pyrgos–Kítta–Álika–Porto Marinári–Porto Quaglio–Páliros–Cape Matapan (Taínaron)–Páliros
 30: Páliros–Laghía–Kótronas (by mule)
May 1: Kótronas–Kávvalos–Tsímova (by mule)
 2: Tsímova–Liméni
 3: Liméni–Port Trakhéla–Rénglia skála–Kardhamýli–Kalamáta (by steamer)
 4: Kalamáta–Athens (by train)

 10: Athens–Argos (by train)
 11: Argos–Nemea station (by train)–Nemea–Áyios Yeórgios
 12: Áyios Yeórgios–top of Mt. Phouká–Vasilikó (Sikyôn)
 13: Vasilikó–Soúli–Kleménti–Dhoúsia
 14: Dhoúsia–Stymphâlos–Gkoúra
 15: Gkoúra–Lake Pheneós–Orkhomenós–Levídhi
 16: Levídhi–Vytína–Dhimitsána
 17: At Dhimitsána
 18: Dhimitsána–Karýtena–Tsinán (Megalopolis)
 19: Tsinán–across north-eastern headwaters of R. Alpheios–across Alpheios–Eurotas watershed–Khani of Khelmós
 20: Khani of Khelmós–Kalývia Yeoryitsiátika–Sparta
21 and 22: At Sparta
 23: Sparta–Mistrá–Trýpi
 24: Trýpi–Langhádha Pass–Ládha–Karvéli–Yiánnitsa–Kalamáta
 25: Kalamáta–Tsepheremíni (by train); Tsepheremíni–Mavrommáti–top of Mt. Ithômê–Mavrommáti
 26: Mavrommáti–bridge over R. Mavrozoúmeno–Soulimá–Pávlitsa (Phigaleia)
 27: Pávlitsa–temple at Bassai–Andrítsena
 28: Andrítsena–Aipy
 29: Aipy–Samikó–Kréstena–Olympia

In August 1921, Professor H. T. Wade-Gery and I walked from Sparta via Trýpi and the Langhádha Pass to Kalamáta, took the train to Tsepheremíni for Mavrommáti, went over the top of Mt. Ithômê to Meligalá station, and took the train to Kyparissía.

Index

Abantes, in Homeric Catalogue, 51.
Abia, 27, 412.
Abu Simbel, 473.
Abydon (Amydon), 14 n., 148 n.
Abydos, 8 n.
Acanthians, 310 n.
Acarnanians, 5, 39 n., 65, 113. *See also* Akarnania.
Accaus, Accavus, as Pelignian personal name, 91.
Achaean city-states, as unimportant to Sparta, 185.
Achaean Confederation: abolishes 'Lycurgan' regime, 249; Asine and Methone as members of, 406; coins of, 410 n.; dissolution of, 158, 249, 405, 410; feud in, between Megalopolis and Sparta, 407; Sparta as member of, 410; Sparta's ex-perioecic states placed under protection of, 409; at war with Sparta, 152, 389.
Achaeans, Akhaioi; as advance guard of North-West-Greek-speakers, 35–6, 47, 52–3, 108; as Alexander I's ancestors, 72; as ancestors of all North-West-Greek-speakers, 35, 38; in Asian Greece, 41; in Asian Greek epic poetry, 41; as back-woodsmen, 24, 37–8, 52; conquest of Crete by, 120 and n.; Hellenic-Age, associated with Ionians, 41; in Hittite and Egyptian documents, 20; Italiot, language of, 20 n.; as Kleomenes I's ancestors, 72, 167; as North-West-Greek-speakers, 20, 21, 39; rearguard of, 24, 108.
  Peloponnesian, wrongly identified as pre-Völkerwanderung survivors, 31; institutions of Asian Doris borrowed by, 52; Polybius quoted on, 65. *See also* Akhaïa, Peloponnesian.
  Phthiotic, 37 n., 38; language of, 20 n.; as members of Delphi–Anthela amphictyony, 51. *See also* Akhaïa, Phthiotic.
  post-Völkerwanderung, habitats of, 20; language of, 21–2.
  pre-Völkerwanderung, language of, 21–2; national and personal names of, 23; as rulers of Mycenaean World, 23–4, 38, 52, 108.
  See also under Akhaioi.
Achaemenidae, 424, 438, 461.

Acheron River, in Epirus, also in Greek Hades, 112.
Achilles, Achilleus, 4, 6 n., 35, 73, 115; connection of name with Akheloïos and Enkhelanes, 22; domain of, in Homeric Catalogue, 9 and n., 10 and n., 36, 50; offered seven cities by Agamemnon, 25–8; ships of, in Homeric Catalogue, 11.
Acholla, 463.
Actium, battle of, 405.
Aden, 454–5.
Admetos, 9, 10.
Adrastos, 7 n., 25, 280 n.
Adriatic coast, 56, 91 n.; Corinthian colonies on, 72, 145; Enkhelanes, Hellenic-Age, living on, 22; linguistic frontier from, 55; route of Via Egnatia to, 83, 142–4.
Adriatic Sea, migrations across, 91, 100, 128, 217.
Aegean Archipelago, 16.
Aegean civilization, 18.
Aegean coast, 83; as habitat of Pieres, 67; as possible habitat of Paiones, 94; North-West-Greek-speaking migrations from, 32; rise of Hellenic civilization on, 59.
Aegean Greeks, as recruits for Alexander III, 457.
Aegean islands, 65, 175; as Greek-speaking, post-Völkerwanderung, 56, 131; hoplite equipment and phalanx-tactics in, 253–4; Ionic- and North-East-Greek-speakers in, 30; North-West-Greek-speaking communities in, 65, 98; place-names in, 13, 174.
Aegean Sea, 20, 52; Argead expansion towards, 144; migration routes to, 40; portages to, from Corinthian Gulf, 16.
Aegina, *see* Aigina.
Aegina stand, as evidence of phalanx-tactics, 254.
Aeginetan refugees, in Thyrea, 183 n.–184 n., 207 and n., 208.
Aeginetans, sea-power of, under Spartan command (494 B.C.), 184 n.
Aeneas, 37.
Aeolians, Aeolic peoples, 34, 39, 40 n., 41. *See also* Aiolis; Greek language: North-East-Greek (Aeolic) dialect, *and* Greek-speaking peoples, North-East (Aeolic).

M m